THE ULTIMATE WH[illegible] GUITAR V[illegible]

230 SONGS • GUITAR TAB

Alfred Publishing Co., Inc.
16320 Roscoe Blvd., Suite 100
P.O. Box 10003
Van Nuys, CA 91410-0003
alfred.com

ISBN-10: 0-7579-1414-4
ISBN-13: 978- 0-7579-1414-0

CONTENTS

CONTENTS

ARTIST INDEX

ARTIST INDEX

ADDICTED TO LOVE

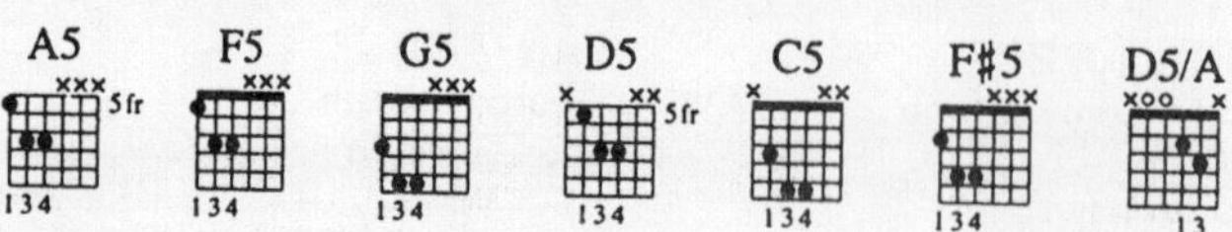

Words and Music by
ROBERT PALMER

Intro
Moderately ♩ = 112

(drums & kybd.)
Gtr. 1 (dist.)
bass enters
G5 A5 G5 A5 F5 G5 F5
mf

* Key signature denotes A Mixolydian.

G5 C5 D5 C5 D5 A5
w/ bar

F5 G5 F5 G5 C5 D5 C5 D5 A5

Verse
A5 F5 G5
* Gtr. 2 (dist.)
f

1.The lights are on but you're not home. Your mind is not your
signs, but you can't read. You're run-nin' at a dif-f'rent

Gtr. 1
w/ bar
simile on repeats
P.M.

* Play 2nd & 3rd times only.

D5
G5
own. Your heart sweats, your bod - y shakes. An - oth - er
speed. Your heart beats in dou - ble time. An - oth - er
P.M.
A5
Verse
A5
kiss is what it takes. 2. You can't sleep, you can't
kiss and you'll be mine. 4. A one track mind; you can't be
5. See Additional Lyrics
(Whoa. __)
F5 G5
C5
eat. There's no doubt __ you're in deep. __ Your throat is
saved. Ob - liv - i - on __ is all you crave. __ If there's

D5
A5
tight, you can't breathe. An - oth - er kiss is all you
some left for you, you don't mind if you
Pre-Chorus
G5 F#5
Gr. 2: w/ Fill 1, 3rd time
need.
do.
Whoa, you like to think that you're im - mune to the stuff, oh, yeah.
w/ bar
w/ bar
Fill 1
Gtr. 2
P.H.
w/ bar
+1 1/2
-2 1/2
-2 1/2
pitch: F#
D
F#

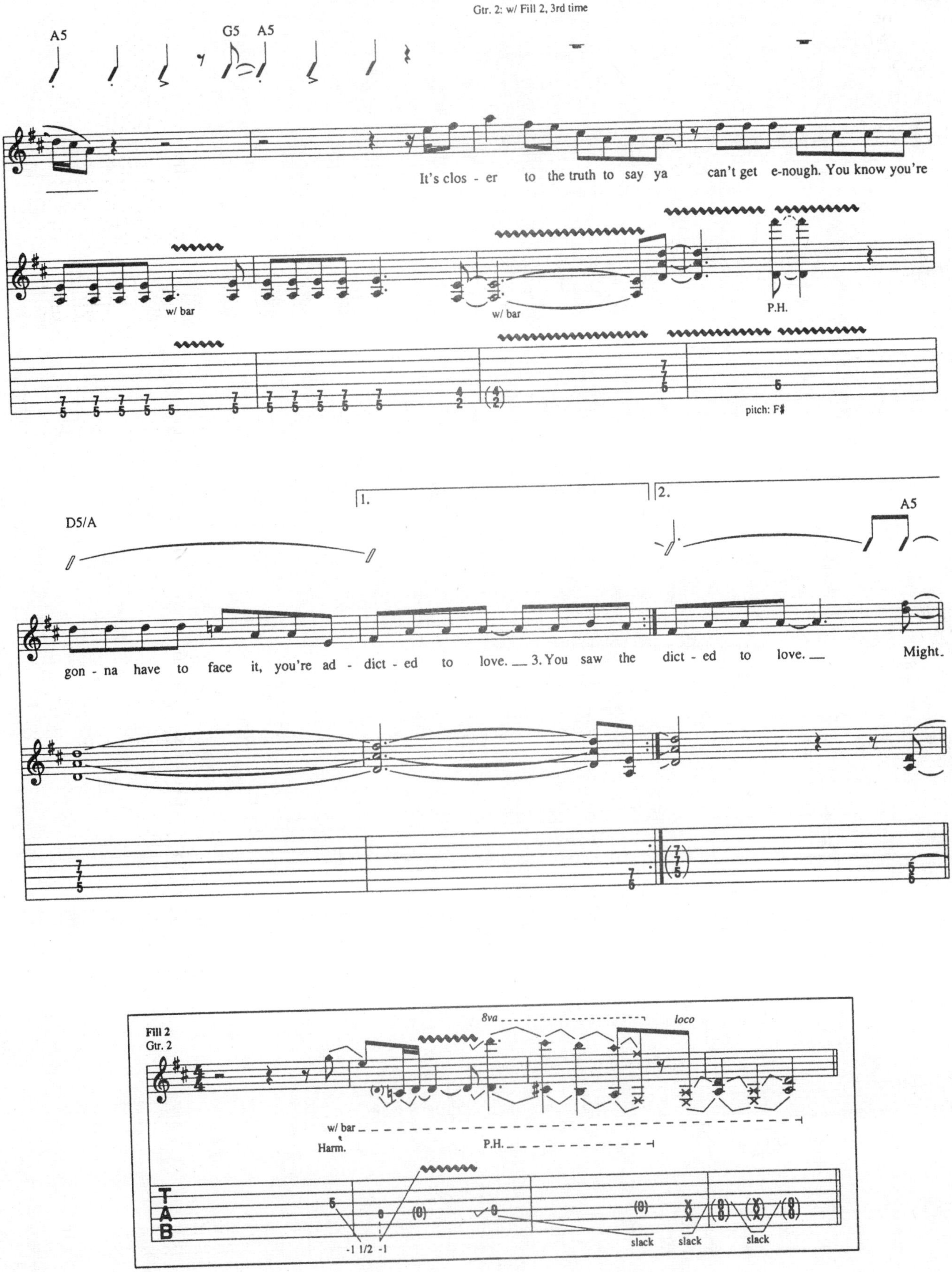

Gtr. 2: w/ Fill 2, 3rd time

A5 G5 A5

It's clos - er to the truth to say ya can't get e-nough. You know you're

w/ bar w/ bar P.H.

pitch: F♯

1. 2.

D5/A A5

gon - na have to face it, you're ad - dict - ed to love. ___ 3. You saw the dict - ed to love. ___ Might

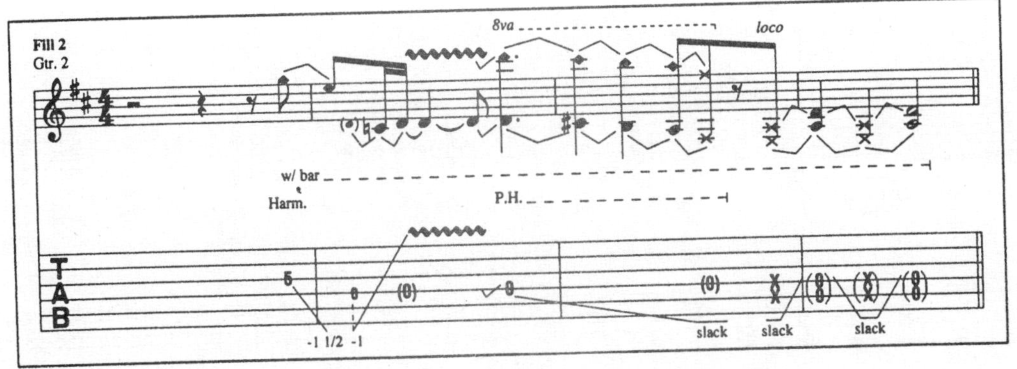

Chorus

G5
A5
G5
— as well face it, you're ad - dict - ed to love. — Might — as well face it, you're ad -
(Oo, — yeah. —)
w/ bar
C5
D5
C5
D5
A5
G5
dict - ed to love. — Might — as well face it, you're ad - dict - ed to love. — Might — as well face it, you're ad -
To Coda
A5
C
8fr
A
5fr
G
3fr
(cont. in notation)
dict - ed to love. — Might — as well face it, you're ad - dict - ed to love. —
(cont. in slash)

Gtr. 1: w/ Rhy. Fill 1
Guitar Solo
A5
Gtr. 1
w/ bar
F5
G5
F5
G5
C5
Hee,
yeah.
Gtr. 2
full
full
1/2
full
grad. bend

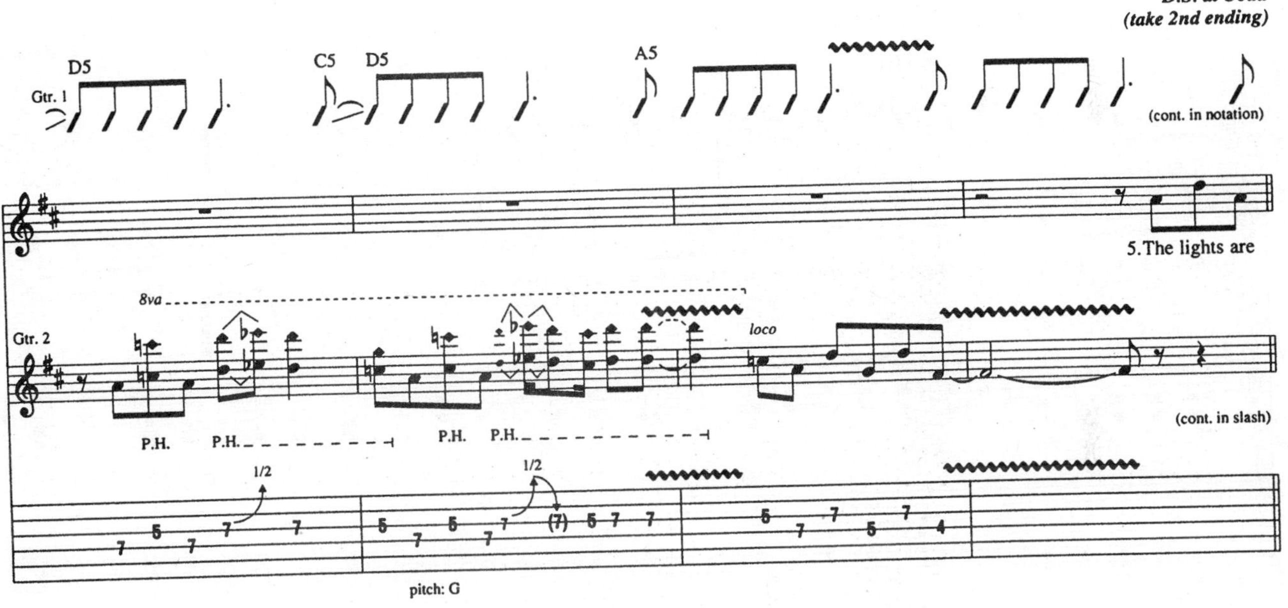

D.S. al Coda
(take 2nd ending)
D5
C5
D5
A5
Gtr. 1
(cont. in notation)
5.The lights are
8va
loco
Gtr. 2
P.H.
P.H.
P.H.
P.H.
(cont. in slash)
1/2
1/2
pitch: G

Rhy. Fill 1
Gtr. 1
8va
loco
Harm.
T
A
B

Coda

Chorus

Begin Fade

A5 G5 A5 G5

— as well face it, you're ad - dict - ed to love. — Might — as well face it, you're ad -

(Oo, — yeah. ———)

w/ bar

C5 D5 Gtr. 2: w/ Fill 3 C5 D5 A5 G5

Fade Out

dict - ed to love. — Might — as well face it, you're ad - dict - ed to love. — Might — as well face it, you're ad -

Additional Lyrics

5. The lights are on, but you're not home.
Your will is not your own.
Your heart sweats, your teeth grind.
Another kiss and you'll be mine.

AFTER MIDNIGHT

Words and Music by
JOHN J. CALE

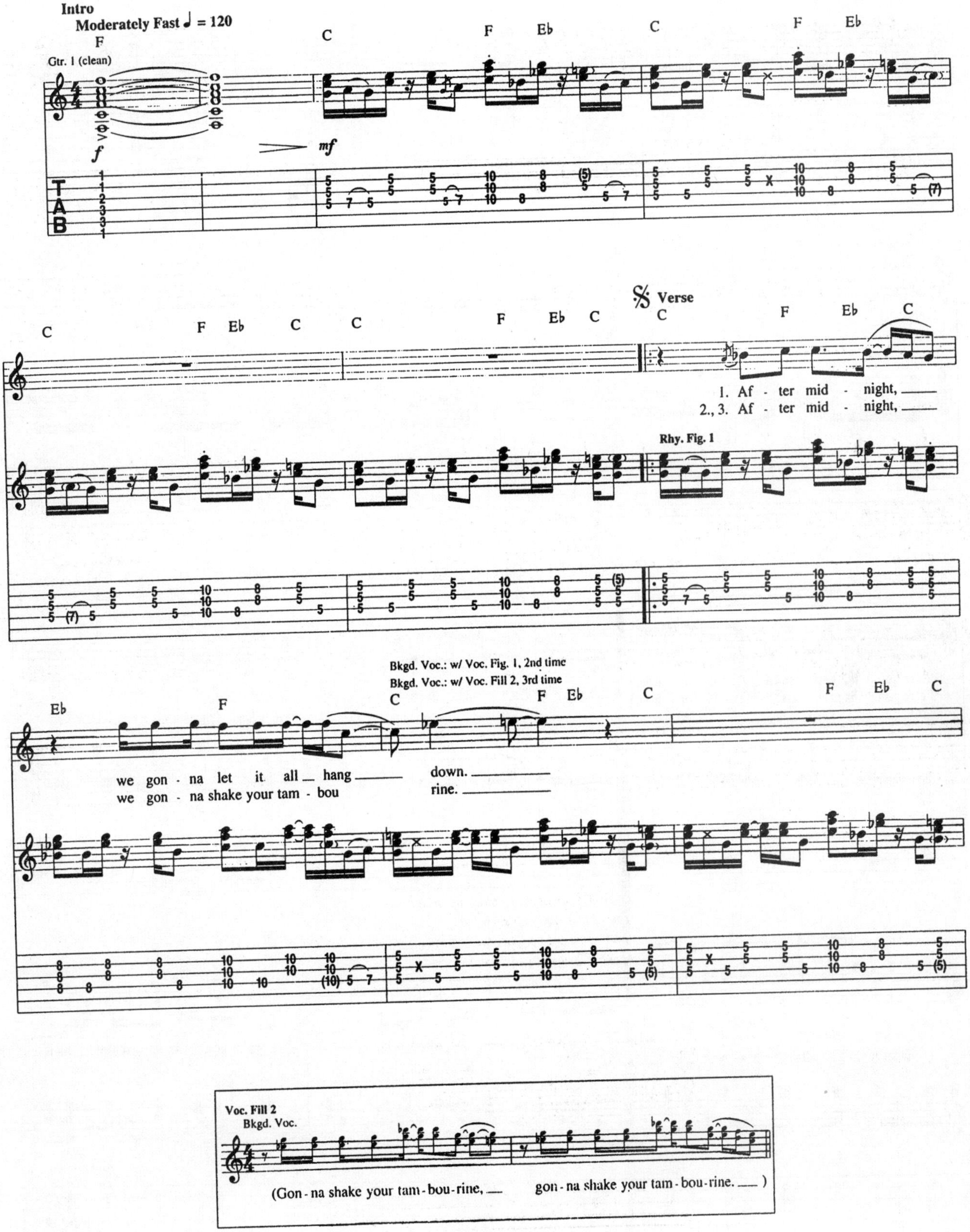

Intro
Moderately Fast ♩ = 120

F C F Eb C F Eb

Gtr. 1 (clean)

f *mf*

C F Eb C C F Eb C

𝄋 Verse

C F Eb C

1. Af - ter mid - night, ___
2., 3. Af - ter mid - night, ___

Rhy. Fig. 1

Bkgd. Voc.: w/ Voc. Fig. 1, 2nd time
Bkgd. Voc.: w/ Voc. Fill 2, 3rd time

Eb F C F Eb C F Eb C

we gon - na let it all ___ hang ___ down. ___
we gon - na shake your tam - bou rine. ___

Bkgd. Voc.: w/ Voc. Fig. 1, 2nd time
Bkgd. Voc.: w/ Voc. Fill 2, 3rd time
F Eb C Eb F C F Eb C
Af - ter mid - night, we gon - na chug - a - lug and shout.
Af - ter mid - night, 's all gon - na be peach - es and cream.
F Eb C
Gon - na stim - u - late some ac - tion.
Gon - na cause talk and sus - pi - cion.
F G
We're gon - na get some sat - is - fac - tion.
We're gon - na give an ex - hi - bi - tion.
We're gon - na find out what it is all a - bout.
(Oo.)
(What it is all a - bout,
what it is all a - bout.)
End Rhy. Fig. 1
C F Eb C Eb F
Woo! Af - ter mid - night, we're gon - na let it all hang

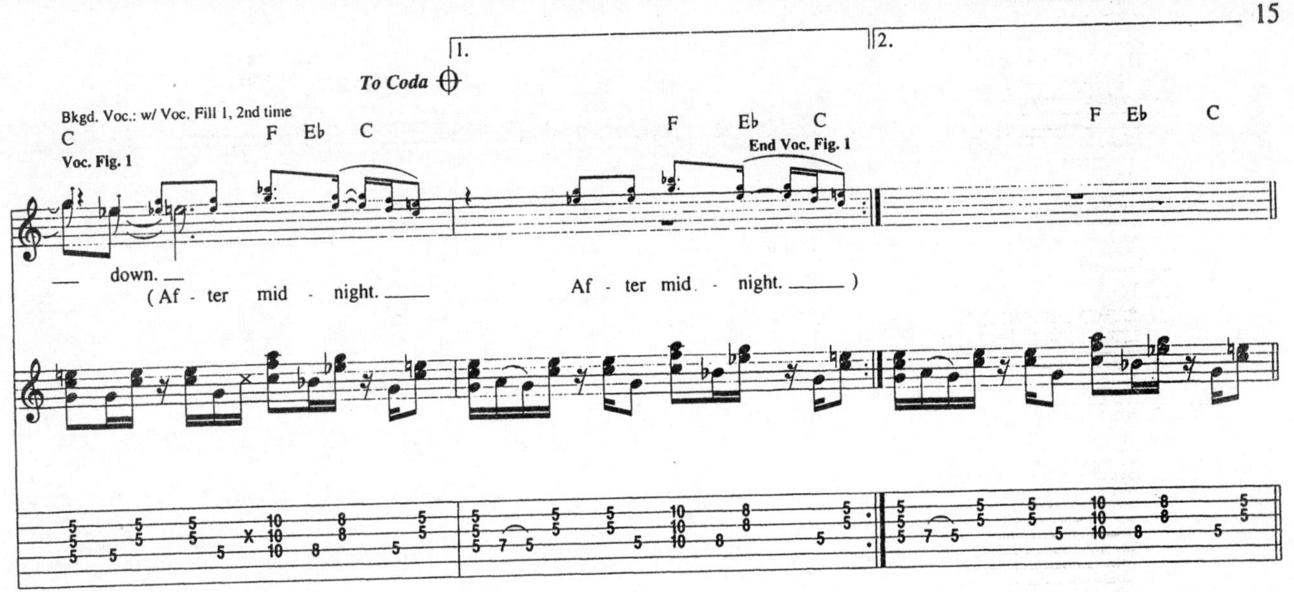

1.
2.
To Coda
Bkgd. Voc.: w/ Voc. Fill 1, 2nd time
C
F Eb C
F Eb C
End Voc. Fig. 1
F Eb C
Voc. Fig. 1
down.
(Af - ter mid - night.
Af - ter mid - night.)

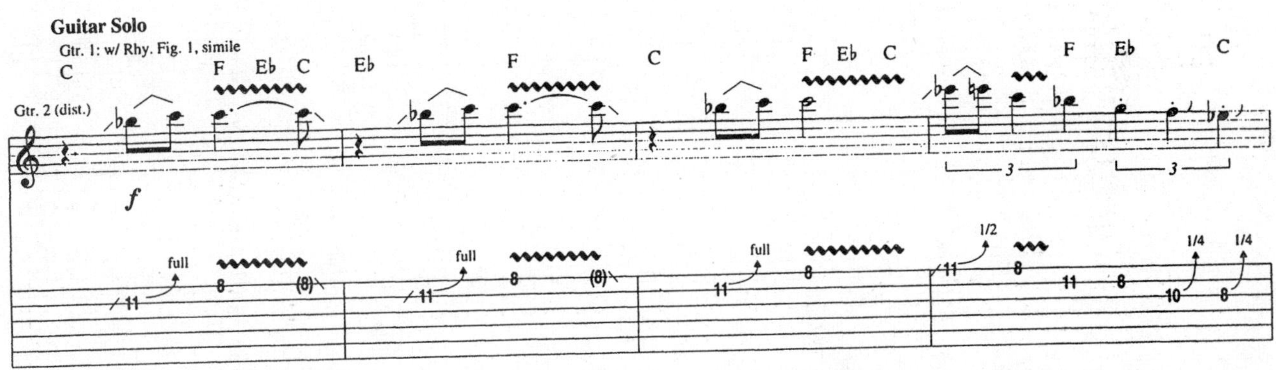

Guitar Solo
Gtr. 1: w/ Rhy. Fig. 1, simile
C
F Eb C
Eb
F
C
F Eb C
F Eb C
Gtr. 2 (dist.)
f
full
1/2
1/4

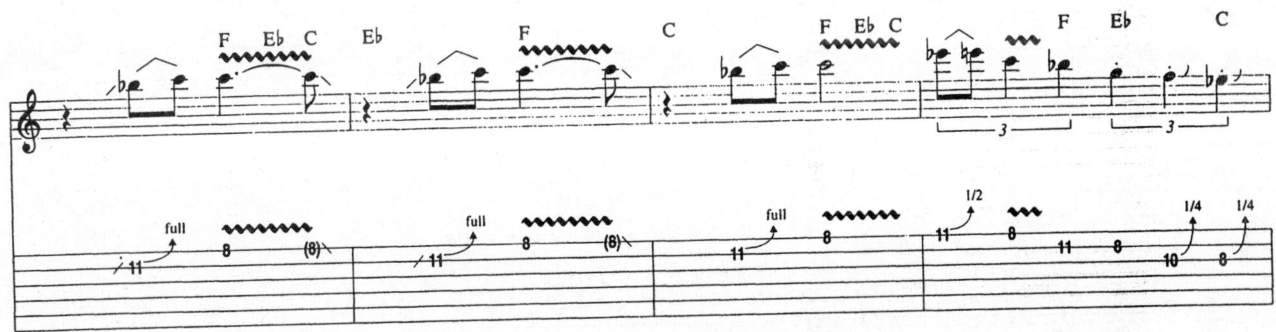

F Eb C
Eb
F
C
F Eb C
F Eb C
full
1/2
1/4

Voc. Fill 1
(Gon - na let it all _ hang down..)

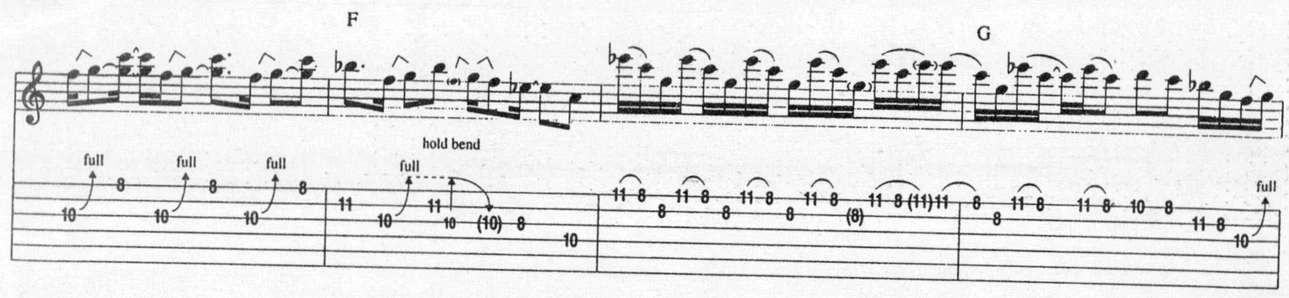
F
G
full
full
full
hold bend
full
full

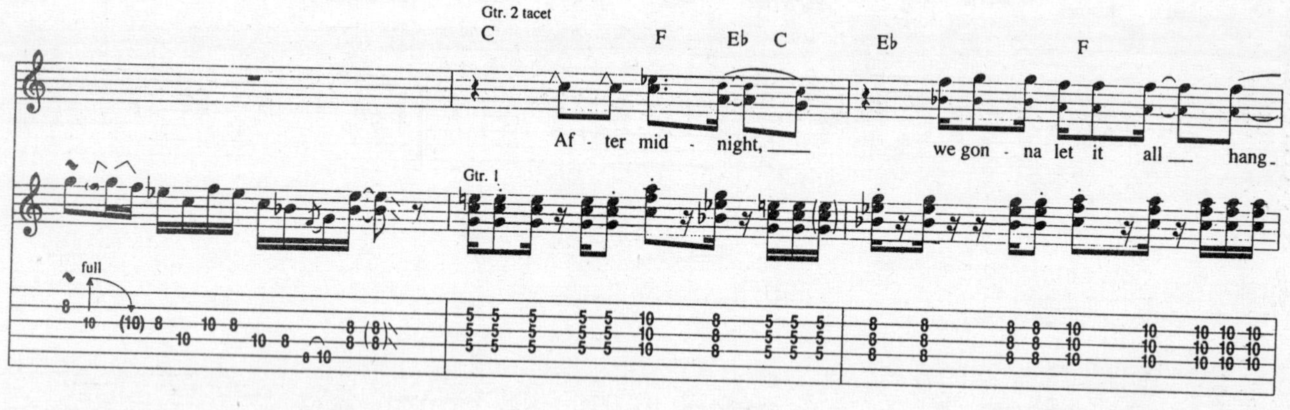
Gtr. 2 tacet
C
F
Eb
C
Eb
F
Af - ter mid - night,
we gon - na let it all hang -
full
Gtr. 1

Bkgd. Voc.: w/ Voc. Fill 1
C
F
Eb
C
F
Eb
C
D.S. al Coda
down.

Coda
Outro
Gtr. 1: w/ Rhy. Fig. 1, 1st 4 meas. simile, till fade
Voc. Fig. 2
F
Eb
C
C
F
Eb
C
Eb
F
Af - ter mid - night,
we gon - na let it all hang -
(Af - ter mid - night,)
(Oo,
oo,
oo.

Bkgd. Voc.: w/ Voc. Fig. 2, simile, till fade
C
F
Eb
C
F
Eb
C
End Voc. Fig. 2
F
Eb
C
down.
Gon-na let it all hang down.
Gon-na let it all hang down.)
Af - ter mid - night,
Gtr. 2
full
full
1/4
we gon' let it all hang down.
1/4
Begin Fade
F
Eb
C
Eb
F
C
F
Eb
C
Af - ter mid - night,
we're gon - na let it all hang down.
F
Eb
C
F
Eb
C
Eb
F
C
Fade Out
F
Eb
C
Af - ter mid - night,
we gon - na let it all hang down.
full
1/2

AIN'T THAT A SHAME

Words and Music by
ANTOINE DOMINO and
DAVE BARTHOLOMEW

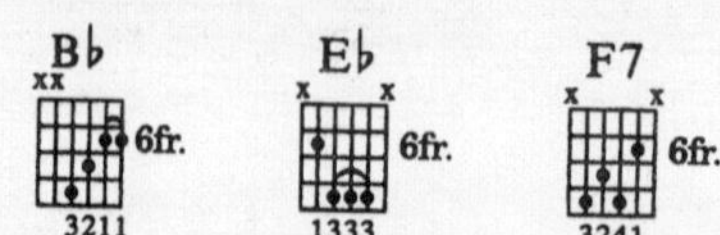

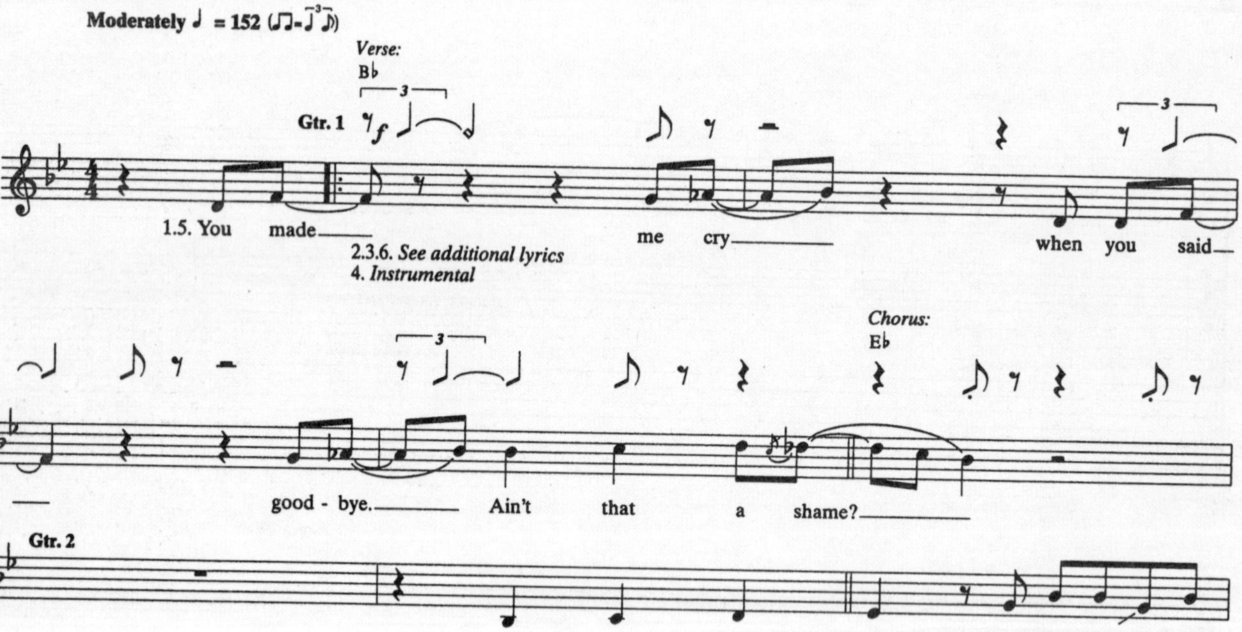

Moderately ♩ = 152

Verse:
B♭
Gtr. 1

1.5. You made me cry when you said good-bye. Ain't that a shame?
2.3.6. *See additional lyrics*
4. *Instrumental*

Chorus:
E♭
Gtr. 2

My tears fell like rain. Ain't that a shame?

Verse 2:
You broke my heart when you said we'll part.
(To Chorus:)

Verses 3 & 6:
Oh well, goodbye, although I'll cry.
(To Chorus:)

ALL I WANNA DO

Words and Music by
SHERYL CROW, WYN COOPER, KEVIN GILBERT,
BILL BOTTRELL and DAVID BAERWALD

*Gtr. III is tuned to open E ⑥ = E ⑤ = B ④ = E ③ = G♯ ② = B ① = E

end Rhy. Fig. 2
C7
D9
be- fore I die" – says the man — next to me out of no- where It's
hold
w/Rhy. Fig. 2 (Gtr. 1)
E7
a - pro- pos of no - thing. He says his name – is Wil- liam but I'm
hold
C7
D9
sure he's Bill — or Bill - y or Mac or Bud - dy. And he's
hold
w/Rhy. Fig. 2 (Gtr. 1) 3 times sim.
E7
plain ug - ly to me. And I won - der if he's e - ver had a
Gtr. III
hold

C7
D9
E7
day of fun— in his whole life.
We are drink - ing beer at
Gtr. II
C7
D9
noon on— tues - day in a bar that fac - es— a gi - ant car wash.
And the
hold

E7
good peo - ple of the world are wash - ing their cars on their lunch break,
hold
C7
D9
hos - ing and scrub - bing as best they can in skirts and suits.
Bridge:
w/Rhy. Fig. 1 (Gtr. 1)
A13
A♯13
Gtr. II
They drive their shin - y Dat - suns and Bu - icks
back to the phone com - pan - y the re - cord store too.
B C♯ E F♯
Well, they're nothing - ing like Bil - ly and me. 'Cause all I wan - na
Chorus:
Rhy. Fig. 3
(end Rhy. Fig. 3)
Gtr. I
do, is have some fun, I got a feel - ing I'm not the on - ly one. All I wan-na
Gtr. III
Rhy. Fig. 3 A
(end Rhy. Fig. 3A)
hold
hold
hold

w/Rhy. Fig. 3 A (Gtr. 3)
w/Rhy. Fig.3 (Gtr. 1) 11/2 times sim.
E7
C7
D9
To Coda
do is have some fun, I got a feel - ing, I'm not the on - ly one. All I wan-na
C7
B7
do is have some fun, un-til the sun comes up o-ver San-ta Mo-ni-ca Bou-le-vard
Gtr. III
Rhy. Fig. 4
end Rhy. Fig. 4
hold
1.
w/Rhy. Fig. 3 (Gtr. 1) sim.
E7
C7
D9
hold
hold
hold
2.
w/Rhy. Fig.3 (Gtr. 1) 2 times sim.
Gtr. II
E7
C7
D9
E7
C7
D9

Verse 2:
I like a good beer buzz early in the morning,
And Billy likes to peel the labels, from his bottles of Bud.
And shred them on the bar.
Then he lights every match in an oversized pack.
Letting each one burn down to his thick fingers.
Before blowing and cursing them out.
And he's watching the Buds as they spin on the floor.
A happy couple enters the bar dancing dangerously close to one another.
The bartender looks up from his want ads.
(To Chorus:)

ALL STAR

Words and Music by
GREG CAMP

Tune down 1/2 step:
⑥= E♭ ③= G♭
⑤= A♭ ②= B♭
④= D♭ ①= E♭

Moderately ♩ = 104

Verse 1:

G D Am C

Rhy. Fig. 1

Elec. Gtr. 1 *mf*

Some - bod - y once told me the world __ is gon - na roll me. I

w/Rhy. Fig. 1 *(Elec. Gtr. 1) 3 times*

G D Am C G D

ain't the sharp - est tool in the shed. ____ She was look - ing kind of dumb with her fin -

Am C G D Am C

ger and her thumb in the shape of an "L" on her fore - head. 2. Well, the

Verses 2 & 3:

w/Rhy. Fig. 1 *(Elec. Gtr. 1) 4 times*

G D Am C

years start com-ing and they don't stop com-ing. Fed to the rules and I hit the ground run-ning.
cool place and they say it gets cold - er. You're bun - dled up now wait till you get old - er. But the

Elec. Gtr. 2 Riff A *mf*

P.M.

TAB: 3 4 5 7 | 5 7 8 5

G
D
Am
C
F5
Did-n't make sense not to live for fun. Your brain gets smart but your head gets dumb._
me-te-or men beg to dif-fer, judg-ing by the hole in the sat-el-lite pic-ture. The ice we
So much to do, so much_to see. So what's wrong_with tak-ing the back streets? You'll
skate is get-ting pret-ty thin. The wa-ter's get-ting warm so you might as well swim. My world's on
nev-er know if you don't go. You'll nev-er shine if you don't glow.
fire, how a-bout yours? That's the way I like it and I'll nev-er get bored.
(P.M.)
Cont. in slashes

Chorus:
G
C
C#m7(♭5)
C
*Elec. Gtr. 2 & Acous. Gtr. 1
Rhy. Fig. 2
Hey now, you're an all - star. Get your game on, go play.
*Two gtrs. arr. for one.
w/Rhy. Fig. 2 (Elec. Gtr. 2 & Acous. Gtr. 1) 2 times
Hey now, you're a rock star. Get the show on, get paid.
All that glit - ters is gold. On - ly shoot - ing
F
1.
2.
Elec. Gtr. 2 & Acous. Gtr. 1
stars break the mold.
3. It's a
Interlude:
1. 2. 3.
4.
F5
Synth.
Elec. Gtr. 2
"Go for the moon."
"Go for the moon.
P.M.
P.M.

Chorus:
w/Rhy. Fig. 2 (Elec. Gtr. 2 & Acous. Gtr. 1) 3 times
G C C#m7(b5) C
Hey now, you're an all - star. Get your game on, go play.
G C C#m7(b5) C G C
Hey now, you're a rock star. Get the show on, get paid. And all that glit - ters is gold.
C#m7(b5) C G F
Elec. Gtr. 2
& Acous. Gtr. 1
On - ly shoot - ing stars. Some -
Verse 4:
w/Riff A (Elec. Gtr. 2) 3 times
G D Am C
bod - y once asked could I spare some change for gas. "I need to
Elec.
Gtr. 3
Rhy. Fig. 3
mf hold throughout
w/Rhy. Fig. 3 (Elec. Gtr. 3) 2 times
G D Am C
get my - self a - way from this place." I said, "Yep,

G
D
Am
C
what a con - cept. I could use ___ a lit - tle fuel my - self and we could
all ___ use a lit - tle change." ___ Well, the
Elec. Gtr. 3
Elec. Gtr. 2
P.M.
Verse 5:
C♯m7(♭5)
years start com-ing and they don't stop com-ing. Fed to the rules and I hit the ground run-ning.
Riff B
hold throughout
w/Riff B (Elec. Gtr. 3) 3 times
Did-n't make sense not to live for fun. Your brain gets smart but your head gets dumb._

G
C
C#m7(♭5)
C
So much to do, so much _ to see. So what's wrong _ with tak - ing the back streets? You'll
G
C
C#m7(♭5)
C
F5
Elec. Gtr. 2
nev - er know if you don't go. (Go!) You'll nev - er shine if you don't glow.
Chorus:
w/Rhy. Fig. 2 (Elec. Gtr. 2 & Acous. Gtr. 1) 5 times
G
C
C#m(♭5)
C
G
C
Hey now, you're an all - star. Get your game on. go play. Hey now, you're a rock star. Get the
C#m7(♭5)
C
G
C
C#m7(♭5)
C
show on, get paid. And all that glit - ters is gold. _____ On - ly shoot - ing
G
C
C#m7(♭5)
C
G
C
stars _ break the mold. _____ And all that glit - ters is gold. _
C#m7(♭5)
C
G
F
C
Elec. Gtr. 2 & Acous. Gtr. 1
_____ On - ly shoot - ing stars _ break the mold. _____

ALL THE YOUNG DUDES

Words and Music by
DAVID BOWIE

A Asus A D F♯m/C♯

when you're twen-ty__ five. And when they're steal-ing clothes from Mogs_ and Spogs__ and
we can love. And my broth - er's back at home with his Bea-tles and his Stones._ He

Elec. Gtr. 2

Bm D/A F♯m

Fred-die's got spots from rip - ping off the__ stars_ from his face,_ funk - y lit - tle
nev - er got it off on that rev - o - lu - tion stuff.____ What a drag.____ Too man - y

Pre-chorus:

A Asus A Em Em7

Acous. Gtr. 1

Bow - ie plays. 1. Tel - e - vi - sion man is cra - zy, say-ing we're ju - ve -
snags. 2. Well, I drunk a lot of wine and I'm feel-ing fine, gon - na

Elec. Gtr. 2

F♯ Bm Bm/A G D

nile de - lin - quent wrecks. Oh____ man, I need_ T V when I__ got
race some_ cow_ to bed. Oh,____ is that con-crete all a-round, or is it in my

A
Asus
A
T Rex?
head?
Oh broth - er, d'ya get it?
Yeah,
I'm a dude_ to bash.
I'm a dude,_ I'm bad.
Elec. Gtr. 2
P.M.
Chorus:
D
F♯m/C♯
Bm
D/A
Rhy. Fig. 2
Ah,
all the young dudes,
Hey,
dudes!
car - ry the news.
Elec. Gtr. 2
Rhy. Fig. 2A
Elec. Gtr. 1
Riff 1
Am
Am/G
F
C/E
C
G/B
C
A
end Rhy. Fig. 2
Boo - ga - loo dudes,
car - ry the news.
Where are ya?
Stand up!
C'mon!
end Rhy. Fig. 2A
end Riff 1

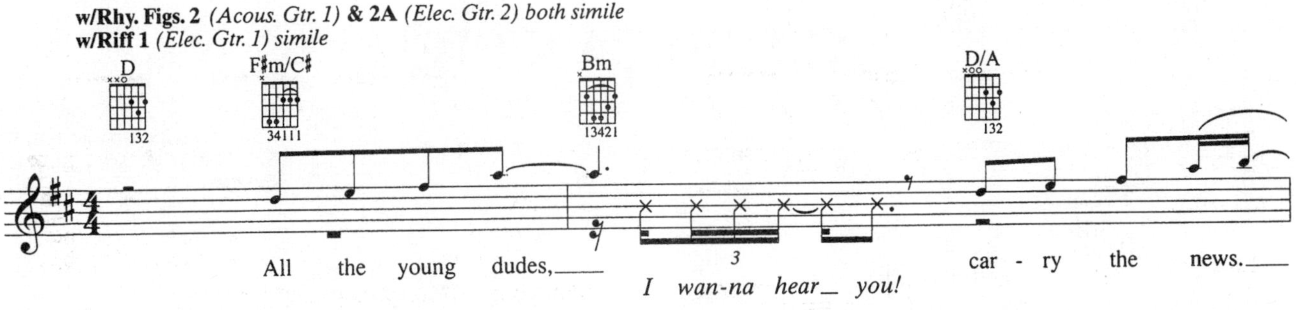
w/Rhy. Figs. 2 (Acous. Gtr. 1) & 2A (Elec. Gtr. 2) both simile
w/Riff 1 (Elec. Gtr. 1) simile
D
F#m/C#
Bm
D/A
All the young dudes,
I wan-na hear you!
car - ry the news.

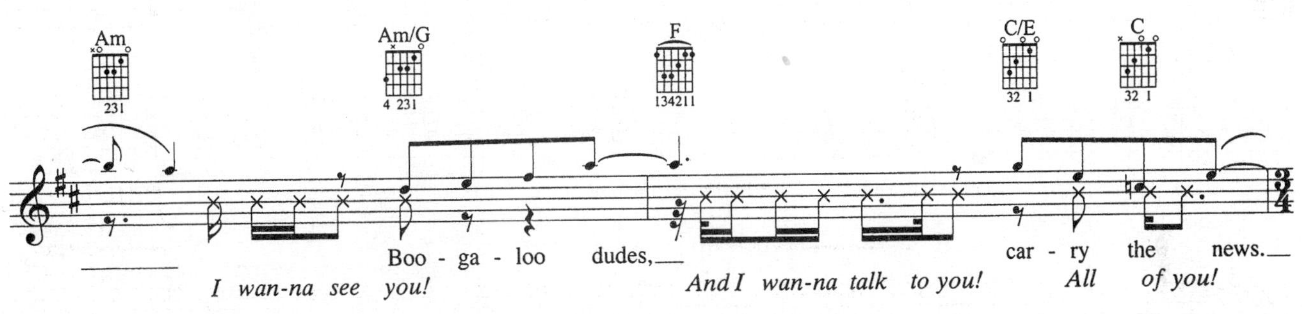
Am
Am/G
F
C/E
C
Boo - ga - loo dudes,
I wan-na see you!
And I wan-na talk to you!
car - ry the news.
All of you!

Chorus:
w/Rhy. Figs. 2 (Acous. Gtr. 1) & 2A (Elec. Gtr. 2) both simile
w/Riff 1 (Elec. Gtr. 1) simile
1.
2.
G/B C A
G/B C A
D
F#m/C#
Bm
D/A
Now!
All the young dudes,
What news?
car - ry the news.

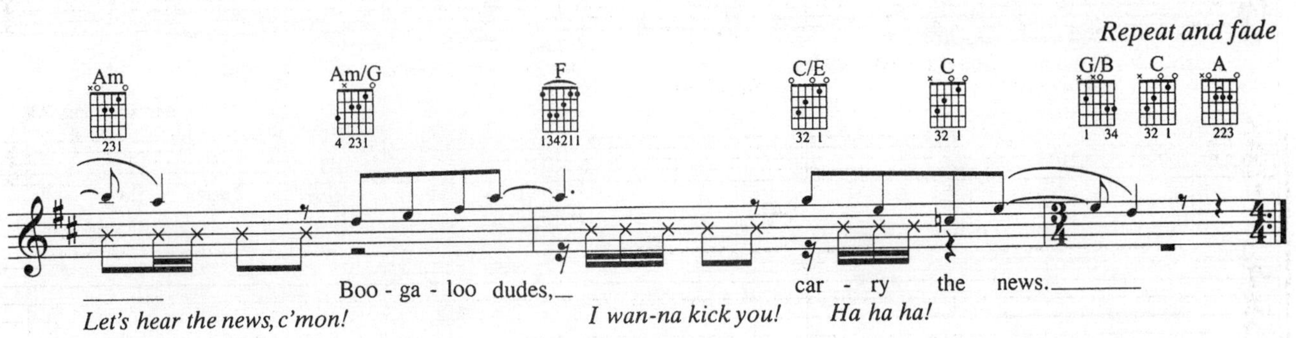
Repeat and fade
Am
Am/G
F
C/E
C
G/B C A
Boo - ga - loo dudes,
Let's hear the news, c'mon!
I wan-na kick you!
car - ry the news.
Ha ha ha!

AMERICAN PIE

Words and Music by
DON McLEAN

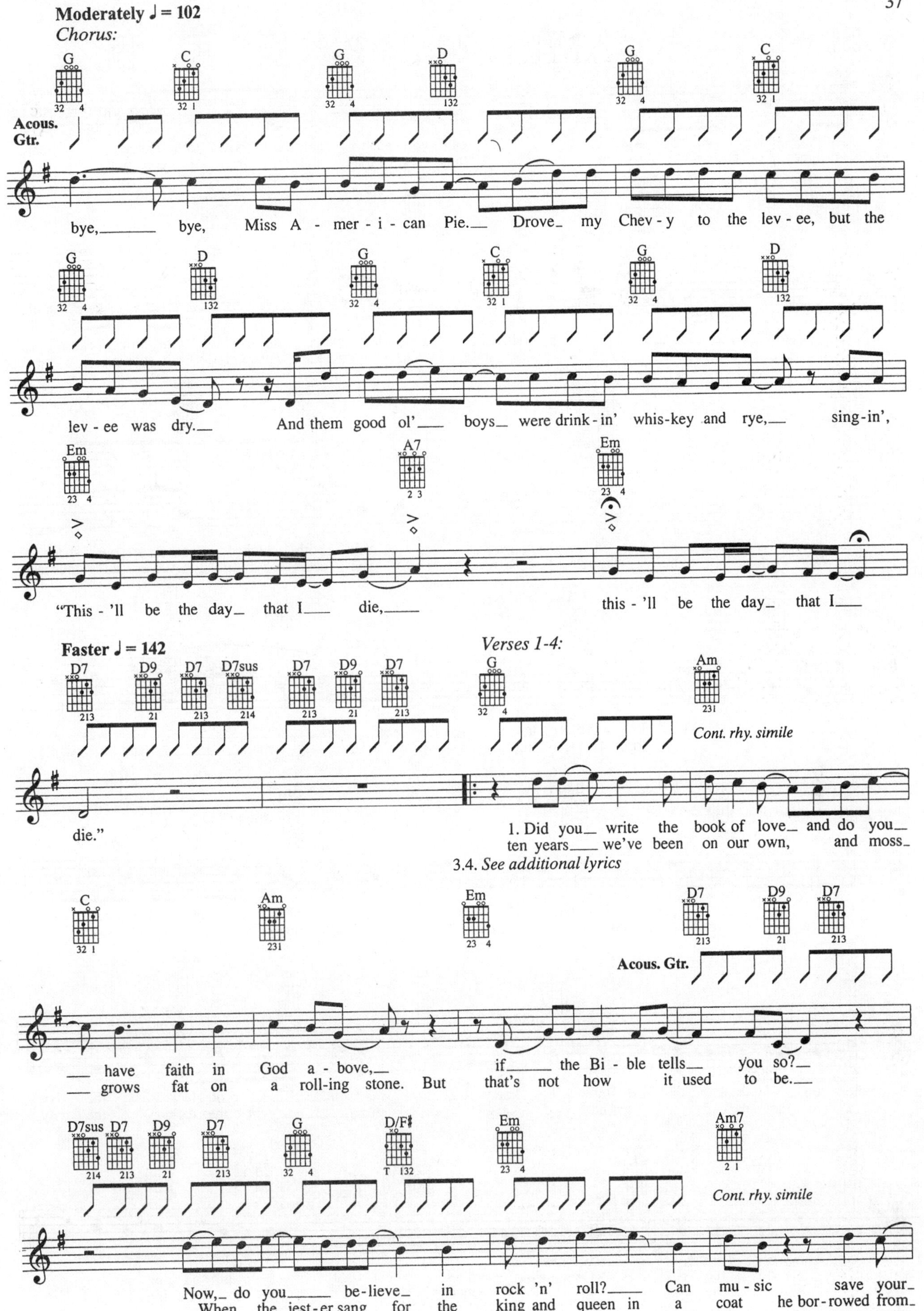
Moderately ♩ = 102
Chorus:
G C G D G C
Acous. Gtr.
bye, bye, Miss A - mer - i - can Pie. Drove my Chev - y to the lev - ee, but the
G D G C G D
lev - ee was dry. And them good ol' boys were drink - in' whis - key and rye, sing - in',
Em A7 Em
"This - 'll be the day that I die, this - 'll be the day that I
Faster ♩ = 142
Verses 1-4:
D7 D9 D7 D7sus D7 D9 D7 G Am
Cont. rhy. simile
die."
1. Did you write the book of love and do you
2. ten years we've been on our own, and moss
3.4. See additional lyrics
C Am Em D7 D9 D7
Acous. Gtr.
have faith in God a - bove, if the Bi - ble tells you so?
grows fat on a roll-ing stone. But that's not how it used to be.
D7sus D7 D9 D7 G D/F♯ Em Am7
Cont. rhy. simile
Now, do you be - lieve in rock 'n' roll? Can mu - sic save your
When the jest - er sang for the king and queen in a coat he bor - rowed from

C Em A7 A9 A7
— mor - tal soul? — And — can you teach me — how to dance — real —
— James Dean. And a voice that came — from you and me. —
D7 D9 D7 D7sus D7 Em D
Acous. Gtr.
— slow? — Well, I — know that you're — in love with him — 'cause I —
— Oh, and — while the king was look - ing down,. the
Em D7 C G/B
— saw you danc - in' in the gym. — You both kicked off — your shoes. —
jest - er stole his thorn - y crown.. The court - room — was ad - journed..
Am Asus2 Am C D7
Cont. rhy. simile
— Man, I dig those rhy - thm and blues. — I was a
— No ver - dict was re - turned. — and while
G D/F♯ Em Am
lone - ly teen - age — bronc - in' buck — with a pink car - na - tion and a
Len - in read a book — on Marx, a quar - tet prac - ticed
C G D/F♯ Em
pick - up — truck. — But I knew I — was out — of luck the day —
in the park. — And we sang dir - ges — in the dark the day —
C D7 G C G D
— the mu - sic died. — I start - ed sing - in', —
— the mu - sic died. — We were sing - in', — } "Bye, —

Chorus:
G C G D G C
Acous. Gtr.
Cont. rhy. simile
bye, Miss A - mer - i - can Pie." Drove my Chev - y to the lev - ee, but the
G D G C G D
lev - ee was dry. Them good ol' boys were drink - in' whis - key and rye, and sing - in',
Em A7 Em
"This - 'll be the day that I die, this - 'll be the day that I
1.2.3.
D7 D9 D7 D7sus D7 D9 D7
4.
D D7sus D7
Acous. Gtr. tacet
die." 2. Now, for die."
Freely (Half-time feel)
Verse 5:
G D/F♯ Em Am C
I met a girl who sang the blues and I asked her for some hap - py news. But
Em D G D/F♯ Em G/B
she just smiled and turned a - way. I went down to the sa - cred store where I
Am G/B C Em C D
heard the mu - sic years be - fore. But the man there said the mu - sic would - n't play. And

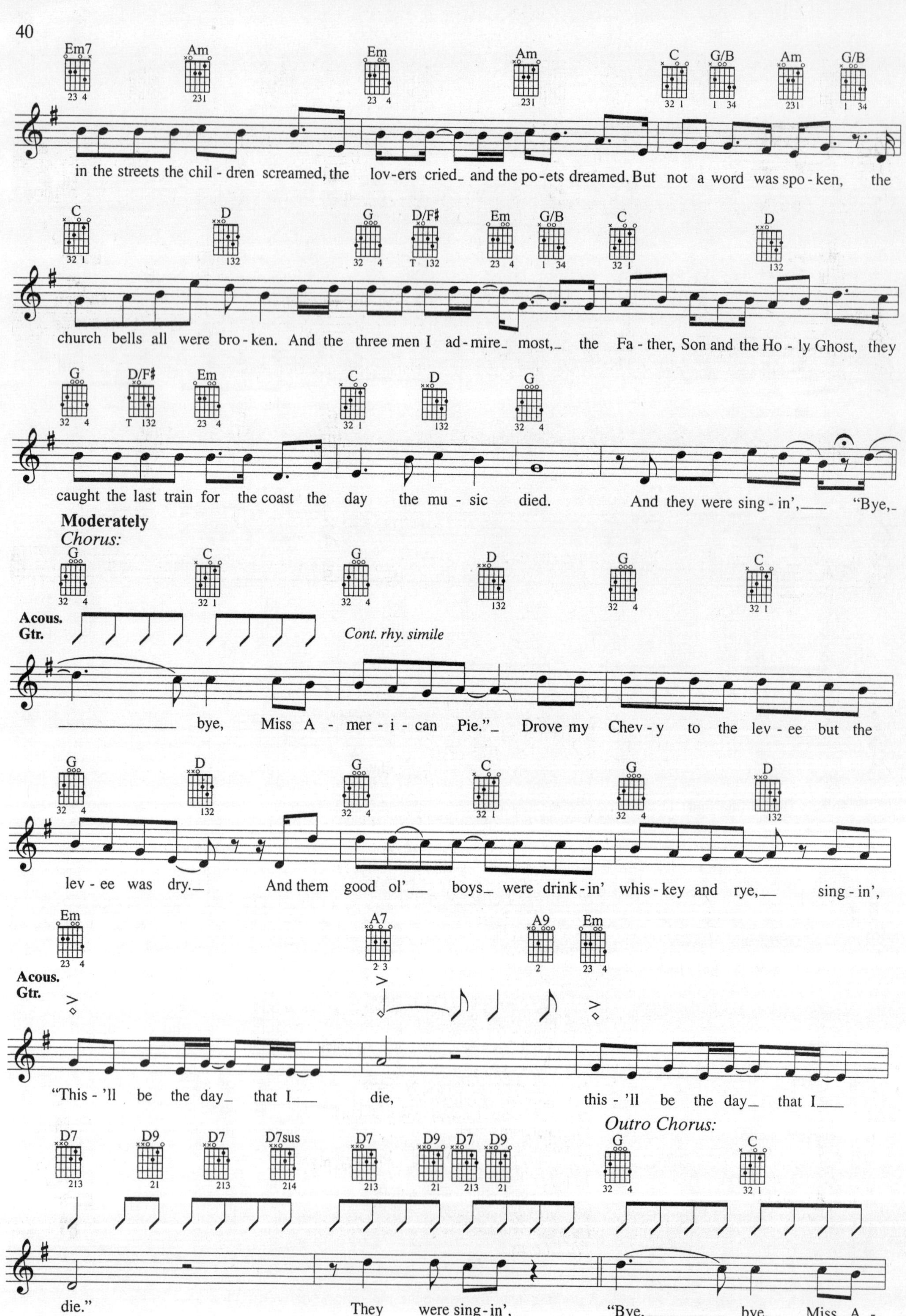
Em7
Am
Em
Am
C
G/B
Am
G/B
in the streets the chil - dren screamed, the lov-ers cried_ and the po-ets dreamed. But not a word was spo - ken, the
C
D
G
D/F♯
Em
G/B
C
D
church bells all were bro - ken. And the three men I ad-mire_ most,_ the Fa - ther, Son and the Ho - ly Ghost, they
G
D/F♯
Em
C
D
G
caught the last train for the coast the day the mu - sic died. And they were sing - in',___ "Bye,_
Moderately
Chorus:
G
C
G
D
G
C
Acous. Gtr.
Cont. rhy. simile
bye, Miss A - mer - i - can Pie."_ Drove my Chev - y to the lev - ee but the
G
D
G
C
G
D
lev - ee was dry._ And them good ol'_ boys_ were drink - in' whis - key and rye,_ sing - in',
Em
A7
A9
Em
Acous. Gtr.
"This - 'll be the day_ that I___ die, this - 'll be the day_ that I___
D7
D9
D7
D7sus
D7
D9
D7
D9
Outro Chorus:
G
C
die." They were sing - in', "Bye,___ bye, Miss A -

Verse 3:
Helter skelter in a summer swelter,
The birds flew off with the fallout shelter,
Eight miles high and falling fast.
It landed foul on the grass.
The players tried for a forward pass
With the jester on the sidelines in a cast.
Now the halftime air was sweet perfume
While sergeants played a marching tune.
We all got up to dance.
Oh, but we never got the chance.
'Cause the players tried to take the field,
The marching band refused to yield.
Do you recall what was revealed,
The day the music died?
We started singin'...
(To Chorus:)

Verse 4:
And there we were all in one place;
A generation lost in space
With no time left to start again.
So come on, Jack be nimble, Jack be quick,
Jack Flash sat on a candlestick
'Cause fire is the devil's only friend.
And as I watched him on the stage,
My hands were clenched in fists of rage.
No angel born in hell
Could break that Satan's spell.
And as the flames climbed high into the night
To light the sacrificial rite,
I saw Satan laughing with delight,
The day the music died.
He was singin'...
(To Chorus:)

AQUALUNG

Words and Music by
IAN ANDERSON and
JENNIE ANDERSON

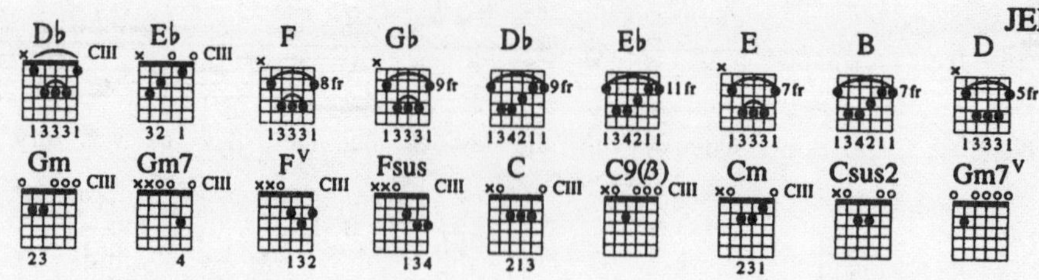

Moderately ♩ = 120

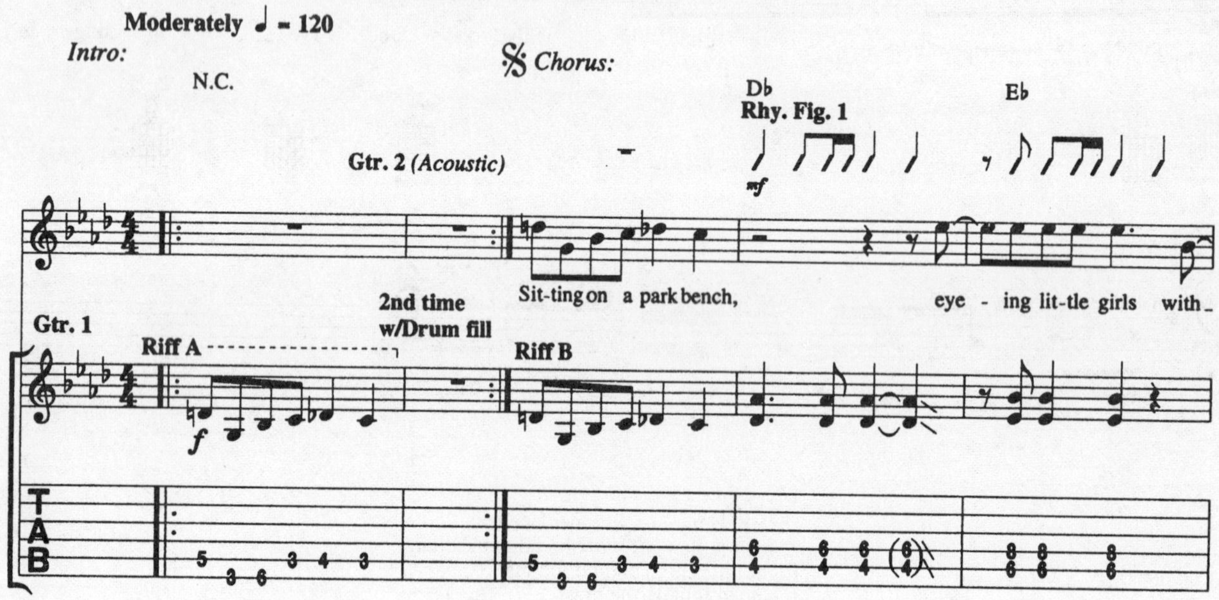

w/Riff B (Gtr. 1)
N.C.
Db
w/Rhy. Fig. 1 (Gtr. 2)
Eb
F
Eb F
Snot's run-ning his nose, greas - y fin - gers smear - ing shab-by clothes,
Eb F Gb Db I
Eb I
Db I Gb
E B D
w/Riff B
hey Ag - ua - lung.
Dry-ing in the cold sun,
w/Rhy. Fig. 1 (Gtr. 2) & Riff B (Gtr. 1)
Db
Eb
F
Eb
F
watch - ing as the fil - ly pant - ies run,
Gtr. 3
Riff C
f
3 3 3 (3)
5 5 5
7 7 7 5 7
Eb F Gb Db I
Eb I
Db I Gb
E B D
hey Aq - ua - lung.
end Riff C
5 7 8 3
5 5 5 5 3 3
3 6 6 4
w/Riff B (Gtr. 1)
N.C.
w/Rhy. Fig. 1 (Gtr. 2) & Riff C (Gtr. 3)
Db
Eb
Feel - ing like a dead duck,
spit - ting out piec - es of his
F
Eb
F Eb F Gb Db I
E I
Db I Gb
bro - ken luck,
oh Aq - ua - lung.

To Coda
E B D Gm
Rhy. Fig. 2
Gm7 F^{V} Gm7 F^{V} Gm7 F^{V} Fsus F^{V} Gm7
1. Sun streak-ing cold, an old man wand' - ring lone -
2-4. See additional lyrics
C C9(♭3) C C9(♭3) Cm C(9) Gm Gm7^{V} Gm F^{V} Gm7 F^{V}
1. 3.
Gm7 F^{V} Fsus F^{V} Gm7
end Rhy. Fig. 2
- ly. Tak-ing time the on - ly way he knows.
2. 4.
Gm7 F^{V} Fsus F^{V} Gm7 F^{V} Gm7 F^{V} Gm7 F^{V} Fsus F^{V} Gm7
Faster ♩ = 176
Verse 5:
Gm
f
Do you still re - mem -
F Gm7 F Gm Gm7^{I} Gm
- ber De - cem - ber's fog - gy freeze, when the ice that clings on
F Gm7 F Gm Gm7^{I}
2.
Fsus F Gm7
to your beard was scream-ing ag - o - ny. Hey! Then you
F Gm7 F Fsus F Gm7
4.
F Fsus F Gm7 F Gm7
Wo - o - ho ho. oh whoa.

Interlude:
F
Gm
F
Gtr. 1
C
(Doubled by 2nd guitar)
Cm
Gm
Feedback (2nd gtr.)
Feedback (1st gtr.)
8va
pp
f
F

Guitar Solo:

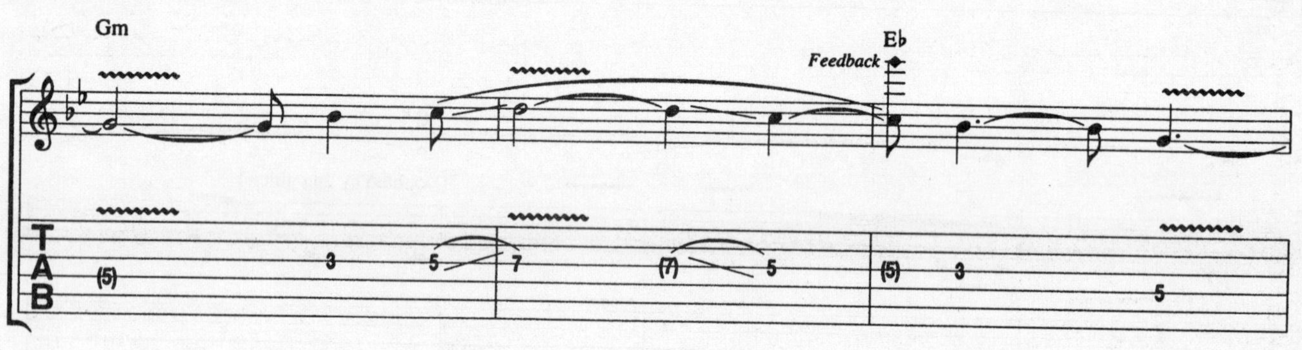

Eb
F
Gm
Eb
III pos.
F
Gm
Eb
F
Gm
Eb
F
1/3
CVI
Gm

Eb
F
T
A
B
3 5 3
5
3 5 3 5 7 5 5 5
5 7 7 6 8 (8) 10
(10) 11 13 15 13 13 15 13
13 15 13 15 (15)
Allegro (♩ = 120)
w/Rhy. Fig. 2
Gm
Gm7 F
Gm7 F Gm7 F
Fsus F Gm7
Dee dee dee dee, dee dee dee dee dee dee,
C
C9 C C9 Cm
C(9)
Gm
(Gm7 I) Gm
dee dee dee dee dee dee dee dee dee dee.
1.
Gm7 F Gm7 F Fsus F Gm7
2.
F
Gtr. 2
Gm7 F
me, yeah.
F Gm7 F Fsus F Gm7 F Gm7 F Gm7 F Gm7 F
Hmm.

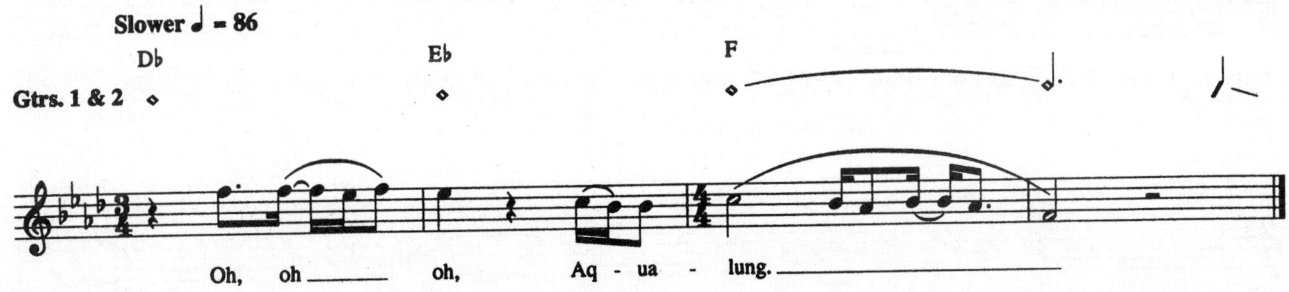

Verses 2 & 7:
Leg hurting bad, as he bends to pick a dog-end.
He goes down to the bog and warms his feet.

Verses 3 & 8:
Feeling alone, the Army's up the road.
Salvation a la mode, and a cup of tea.

Verses 4, 9 & 10:
Aqualung my friend, don't you start away uneasy.
You poor old sod, you see, it's only me.

AMANDA

Words and Music by
TOM SCHOLZ

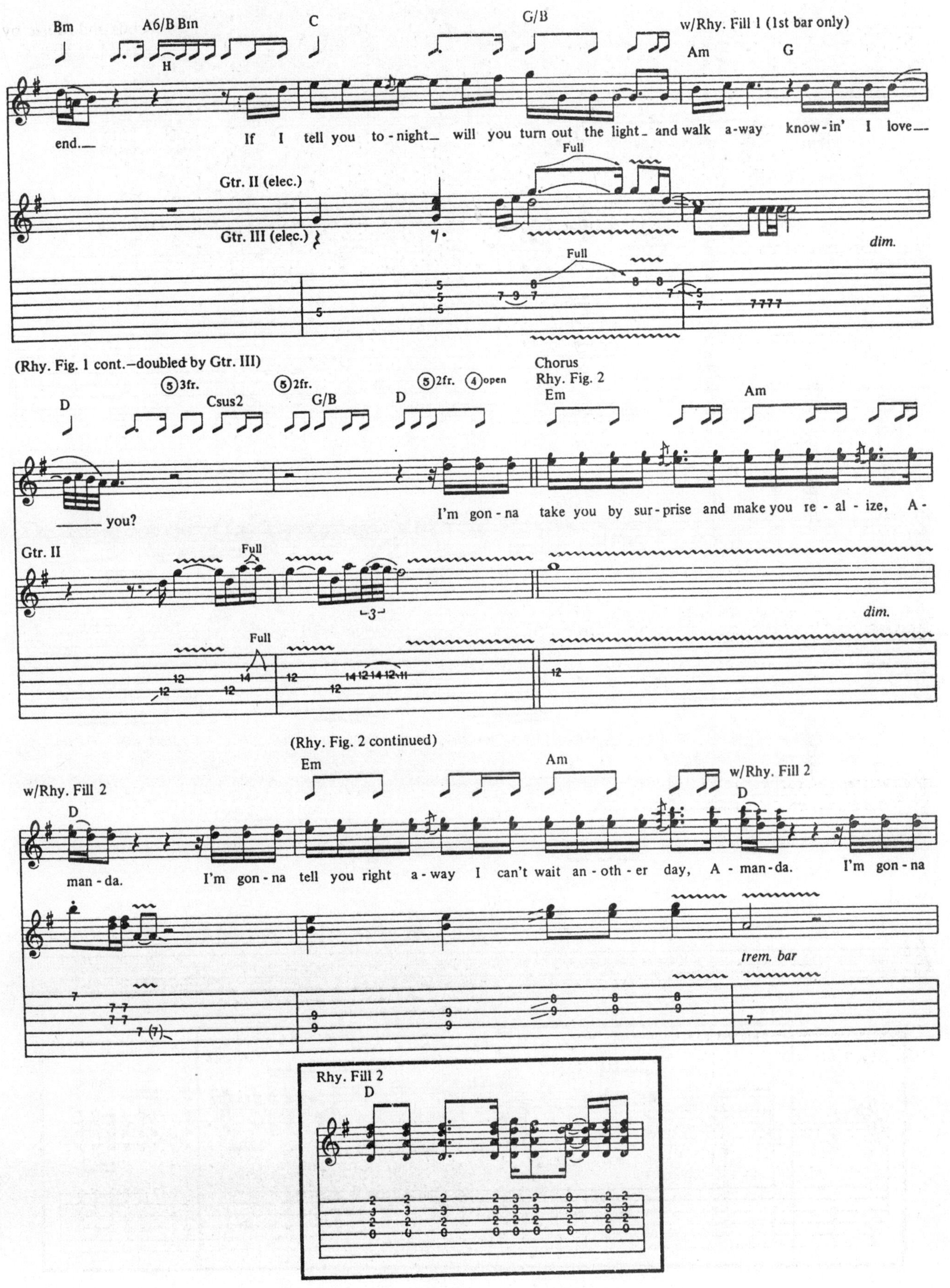
Bm
A6/B Bm
H
C
G/B
w/Rhy. Fill 1 (1st bar only)
Am
G
end.__ If I tell you to-night__ will you turn out the light__ and walk a-way know-in' I love__
Full
Gtr. II (elec.)
Gtr. III (elec.)
dim.
(Rhy. Fig. 1 cont.–doubled by Gtr. III)
D
Csus2
G/B
D
Chorus
Rhy. Fig. 2
Em
Am
__ you?
I'm gon-na take you by sur-prise and make you re-al-ize, A-
Gtr. II
Full
dim.
(Rhy. Fig. 2 continued)
w/Rhy. Fill 2
D
Em
Am
w/Rhy. Fill 2
D
man-da. I'm gon-na tell you right a-way I can't wait an-oth-er day, A-man-da. I'm gon-na
trem. bar
Rhy. Fill 2
D

(Rhy. Fig. 2 continued)
w/Rhy. Fill 2
Em
Am
Amsus2 Am D
Csus2 (type 2)
say it like a man and make you un - der - stand, A - man - da. I love you.
2nd Verse
Repeat Rhy. Fig. 1
G
C/G
G
Em
And I feel like to - day's the day. I'm look - in' for the words to say.
w/Rhy. Fill 3
BmA6/BBm
C
G/B
Am
G
Do you wan - na be free, are you read - y for me to feel this way? I don't wan - na lose
dim.
Rhy. Fill 3
Am
G
D
D7sus4

Resume Rhy. Fig. 1
D
D7sus4
G
C/G
G sus4 sus2
G
Em
ya.
So, it may be too soon, I know.
The feel - in' takes so long to
Bm
A6/B Bm
C
G/B
grow.
If I tell you to-day, will you turn me a - way and
Full
Full
Resume Rhy. Fig. 1 & Rhy. Fill 4
w/Rhy. Fill 1 (1st bar only)
Am
G
D
Csus2
G/B
D
let me go?
I don't wan - na lose you.
Gtr. II
Gtr. IV
dim.
(w/Echo device)
(Echo off)
*TAB no. on left = Gtr. IV; TAB no. on right = Gtr. II.
Rhy. Fill 4
Gtr. III
D
Csus2
G/B
D

Guitar solo
w/Rhy. Fig. 2 & Fill 1
Em
Am
w/Rhy. Fill 2
D
Gtr. II
1/2
hold
grad. release
Gtr. IV
Full
Resume Rhy. Fig. 2 & Fill 1
I'm gon - na
Fill 1

Chorus
Repeat Rhy. Fig. 2
w/Rhy. Fill 2
Em
Am
D
take you by sur-prise and make you re - al - ize, A - man - da. I'm gon - na
Gtr. II
Gtr. IV
Resume Rhy. Fig. 2
w/Rhy. Fill 2
Em
Am
D
tell you right a - way I can't wait an - oth - er day, A - man - da. I'm gon - na
Resume Rhy. Fig. 2
w/Rhy. Fill 2 & Rhy. Fill 5
Interlude
Em
Am
D
E
say it like a man and make you un - der - stand, A - man - da. Oh, girl.
pick slides
(Clean tone)
Let ring
Rhy. Fill 5
D

Bm7
E
Bm7
Bridge
E
You and I,_ I
Let ring
Let ring
Let ring
Let ring
Bm7
E
Bm7
know that we can't wait._ And I swear,_ I swear it's not a lie,_ girl. To-mor-row may be too late.___
Let ring
Let ring
Let ring
(Both gtrs.)
C
D
G5
D/F♯
Em
D
w/Rhy. Fill 6
C Gsus4/B
Am
C/G(type 2)
You, you and I,_ girl, we can share a life_ to-geth - er. It's now or nev - er, and to-mor-row may be too
(harmony vocal) and to-mor-row may be too
D
Dsus4
Csus2
G/B
D Dsus4
⑤3fr.
⑤2fr.
⑤open
3rd Verse
w/Rhy. Fig. 1
G
C/G
late,___ oh.___
late.___
And_ feel - in' the way_ I do,_
G
Em
Bm
A6/B Bm
w/Rhy. Fill 7
Am
C/G(type 2)
D/F♯(type 2)
I don't wan-na wait my whole life through_ to say___ I'm in love with you.
Rhy. Fill 6
C
Gsus4/B
Am
Rhy. Fill 7
Am
C/G

BIG YELLOW TAXI

Gtr. tuning:
⑥ = E ③ = G♯
⑤ = B ② = B
④ = E ① = E

Words and Music by
JONI MITCHELL

Moderately fast ♩ = 172
Intro:

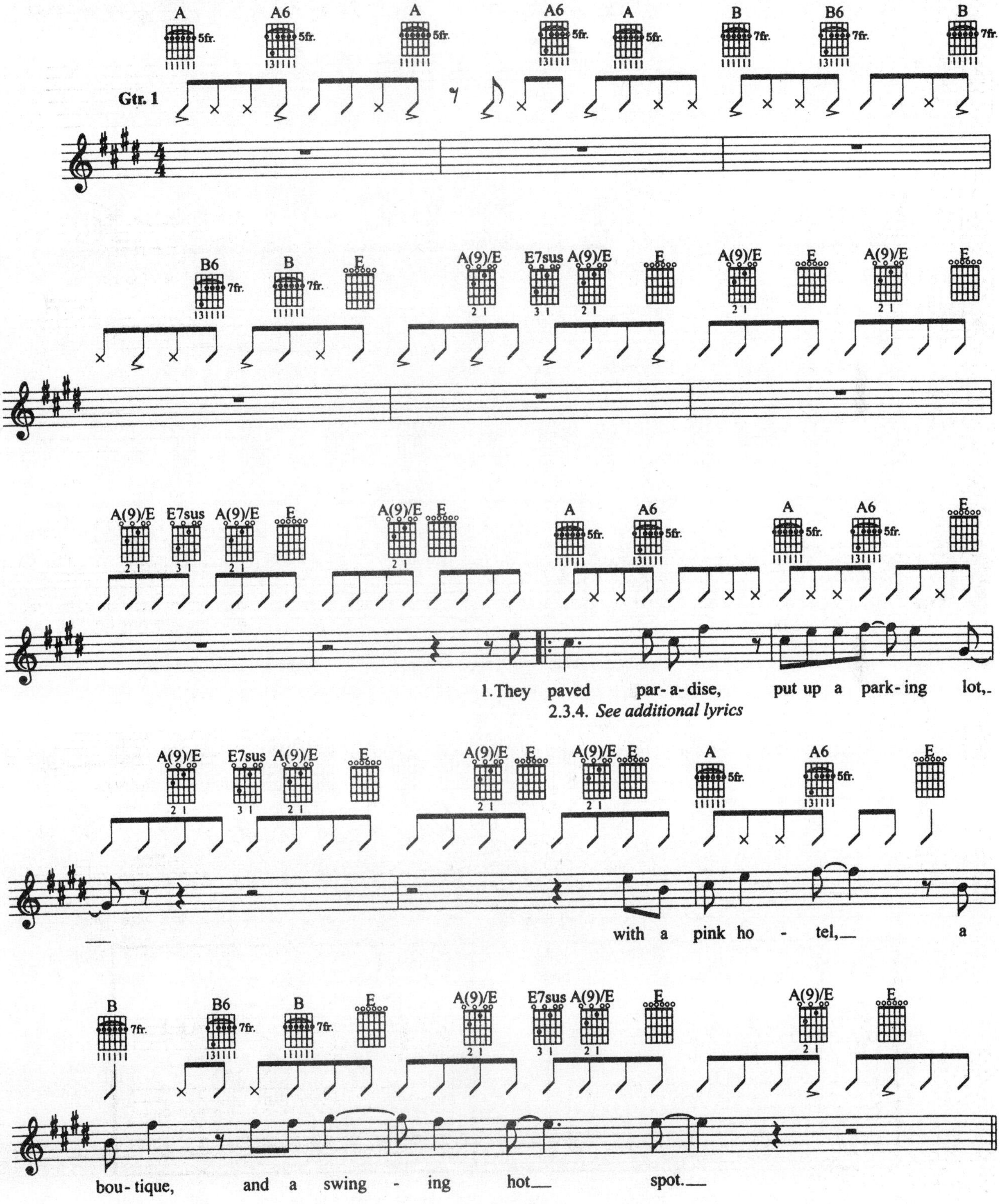

A A6 A A6 A B B6 B
Gtr. 1

B6 B E A(9)/E E7sus A(9)/E E A(9)/E E A(9)/E E

A(9)/E E7sus A(9)/E E A(9)/E E A A6 A A6 E

1. They paved par - a - dise, put up a park - ing lot,
2.3.4. *See additional lyrics*

A(9)/E E7sus A(9)/E E A(9)/E E A(9)/E E A A6 E

with a pink ho - tel, a

B B6 B E A(9)/E E7sus A(9)/E E A(9)/E E

bou - tique, and a swing - ing hot spot.

Chorus:
E5
3fr.
Emaj7
A(9)/E
E
Rhy. Fig. 1
Don't it al - ways seem__ to go that you don't know what_ you've got_
B7sus
E
A
A6
A
E
B
B6
B
E
5fr.
7fr.
__ till it's gone? They paved par - a - dise, put up a park - ing lot._
1.-3.
E
A(9)/E
E7sus
A(9)/E
end Rhy. Fig. 1
Shoo__ bop,_ bop, bop,_ bop, shoo__ bop,_
4.
_ bop, bop,_ bop.
2. They lot.
Shoo__ bop,_ bop, bop,_ bop.
I said,
w/Rhy. Fig. 1 (Gtr. 1)
don't it al - ways seem_ to go that you don't know what_ you've got__ till it's gone? They

Verse 2:
They took all the trees,
Put them in a tree museum.
And they charged all the people
A dollar and a half just to see 'em.
(To Chorus:)

Verse 3:
Hey farmer, farmer,
Put away the D.D.T., now.
Give me spots on all my apples,
But leave me the birds and the bees.
Please!
(To Chorus:)

Verse 4:
Late last night,
I heard the screen door slam,
And a big yellow taxi
Took away my old man.
(To Chorus:)

BAD RELIGION

Words and Music by
SALVATORE EMA and TOMMY STEWART

Chorus
Half-Time Feel
Bkgd. Voc.: w/ Voc. Fig. 1, 2nd time
*D5 C5
D5
bad re - li - gion,
from a bro - ken na - tion.
It's a
Rhy. Fig. 2
End Rhy. Fig. 2
*Chord symbols reflect implied tonality.
1.
End Half-Time Feel
C5
D5
con - tra - dic - tion,
and I can't take it an - y - more, yeah.
Gtr. 1: w/ Rhy. Fig. 1
2.
D5
Gtr. 1: w/ Rhy. Fig. 2
C5
I can't take it an - y fuck - ing way!
(It's a bad re - li - gion, bad
Voc. Fig. 1
(A bad re - li - gion. A bro - ken na - tion.)

D5
From a bro - ken na - ti - on.
It's a
re - li - gion, bad re - li - gion.
A bro - ken na - tion.

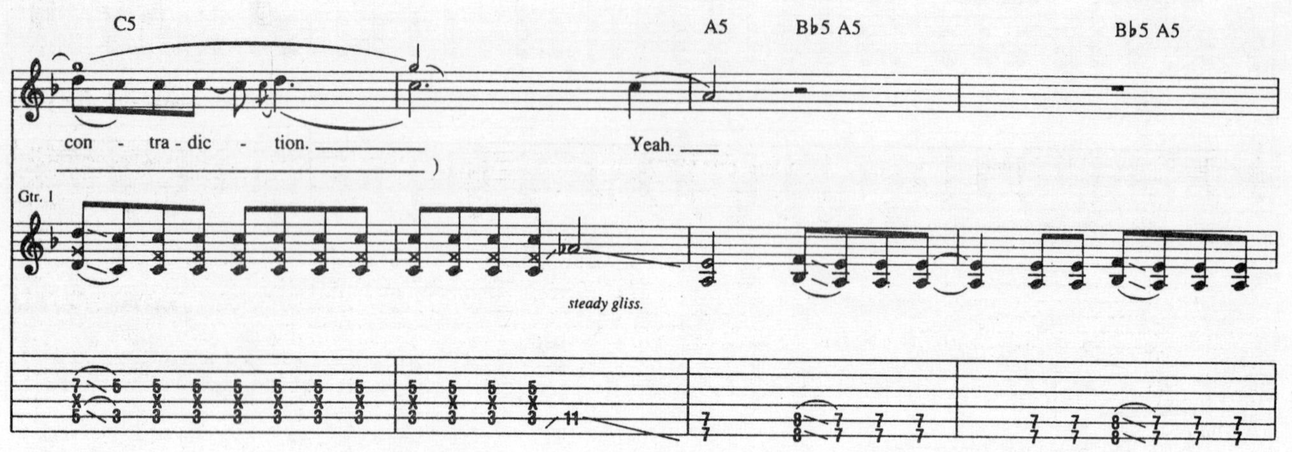
C5
A5
Bb5 A5
Bb5 A5
con - tra - dic - tion.
Yeah.
Gtr. 1
steady gliss.

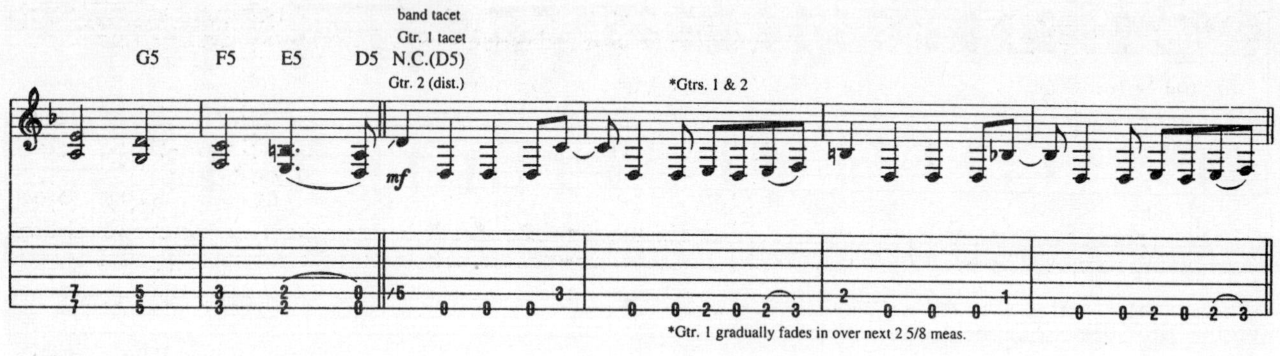
Interlude
band tacet
Gtr. 1 tacet
G5
F5
E5
D5
N.C.(D5)
Gtr. 2 (dist.)
*Gtrs. 1 & 2
mf
*Gtr. 1 gradually fades in over next 2 5/8 meas.

band enters
f

w/ Voc. ad lib
play 3 times
End Half-Time Feel
Outro
Gtr. 1: w/ Rhy. Fig. 1, 1 3/4 times
Gtr. 2 tacet
D5
Can you feel it? I got - ta live with it ev - 'ry - day. And
Gtr. 1: w/ Rhy. Fill 1
E5 F5 E5 F5 D5
I can't take the pres - sure, I'm go - ing in - sane. Now go a - way.
Gtr. 1: w/ Rhy. Fig. 1, 1st 3 meas.
Gtr. 1: w/ Rhy. Fill 1
E5 F5 E5 F5 D5
Gtr. 1: w/ Rhy. Fig. 1, 1st 3 meas.
Go a - way.
Gtr. 1: w/ Rhy. Fill 2
Gtr. 1: w/ Rhy. Fig. 1
Yeah.
Rhy. Fill 1
Gtr. 1
P.M.
Rhy. Fill 2
Gtr. 1

BE MY BABY

Words and Music by
ELLIE GREENWICH, JEFF BARRY and PHIL SPECTOR

Verse 2:
I'll make you happy, baby,
Just wait and see.
For every kiss you give me,
I'll give you three.
Oh, since the day I saw you,
I have been waiting for you.
You know I will adore you till eternity.
So, won't you please...
(To Chorus:)

BEAUTIFUL

Words and Music by
BILLY CORGAN

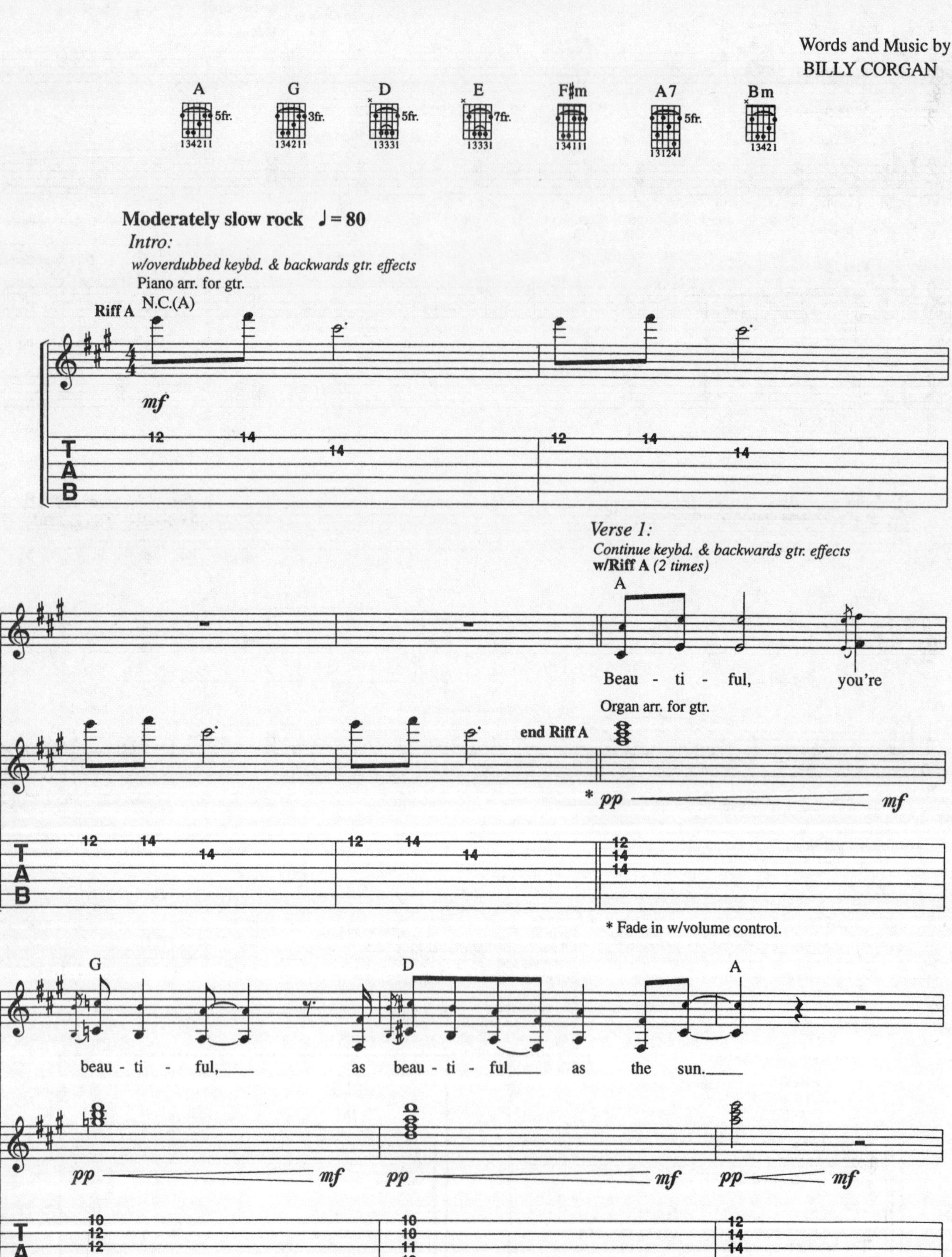

(Organ continues simile)
A
G
**Gtr. 1
Won - der - ful, you're won - der - ful, as
** This part is a representation of the overall harmony created by the various keybd., backwards gtr. & bass parts.
D
E
won - der - ful as they come. And I
Chorus:
w/Riff B (3 times)
A
E
D
A
E
can't help but feel at - tached to the feel-ings I can't e - ven match.
w/Riff B (1st bar only)
D
A
E
D
E
G
With my face pressed up to the glass, want - ing you.
Verse 2:
w/Riff C (4 times)
A
G
D
A
Beau-ti - ful, you're beau - ti - ful, as beau-ti - ful as the sky.
Riff B
Piano arr. for gtr.
Riff C
Piano arr. for gtr.

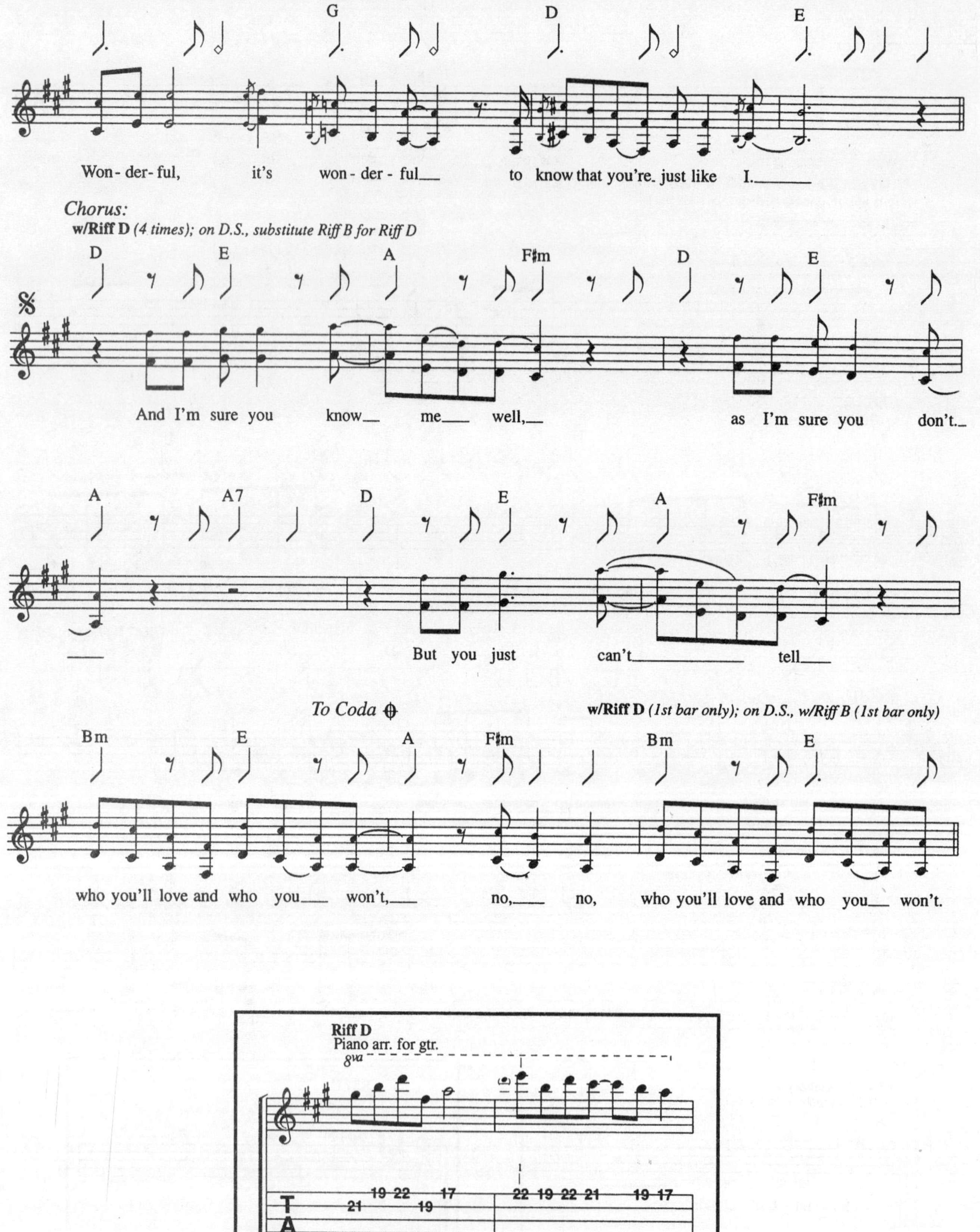

G D E

Won - der - ful, it's won - der - ful___ to know that you're just like I.______

Chorus:
w/Riff D *(4 times); on D.S., substitute Riff B for Riff D*

D E A F♯m D E

And I'm sure you know___ me___ well,___ as I'm sure you don't.___

A A7 D E A F♯m

___ But you just can't______ tell___

To Coda ⊕ **w/Riff D** *(1st bar only); on D.S., w/Riff B (1st bar only)*

Bm E A F♯m Bm E

who you'll love and who you___ won't,___ no,___ no, who you'll love and who you___ won't.

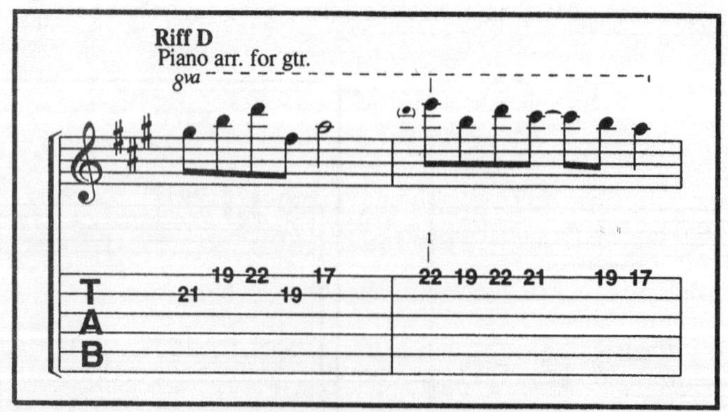

Bridge:
A
G5
N.C.(D)
(F)
I love you,
Gtr. 1
Rhy. Fig. 1
hold throughout
1/2
w/Rhy. Fig. 1 (Gtr. 1) 5 times
as you love me.
(Bkgd. vcl.) Na na na na na na na
Gtr. 3
Gtr. 2
(both notes vib.)
Bkgd. Vcl. part 1
na na na. Na na na na na na na na na na.
Riff E (both gtrs.)
w/Bkgd. Vocal part 1 (3 times)
& Riff E (Gtrs. 2 & 3) 3 times
So let the clouds roll by your face. We'll let the world spin on
to an-oth-er place. We'll climb the tall-est tree a-bove it all

w/Rhy. Fig. 1 (Gtr. 1) Riff E (Gtrs. 2&3), & Bkgd. Vocal part 1
(1st bar of each only)
w/Rhy. Fig. 1A (Gtr. 1), Riff F (Gtrs. 2&3) & Bkgd. Vocal part 2
D.S. 𝄋 al Coda
A
G5
N.C.(D)
to look down on you and me___ and them.
w/Riff B (bar 2 only)
w/Riff B
Gtr. 1
Coda
A
F♯m
Bm
E
F♯m
D
No,__ no, who you'll love and who you__ won't,__ no,___ no.
w/overdubbed keybd. & backwards gtr. effects
Rhy. Fig. 2
D
E
A
F♯m
D
E
F♯m
D
end Rhy. Fig. 2
Gtr. 2
w/heavy reverb, fast tremolo & severe e.q.
Outro:
w/Rhy. Fig. 2 (Gtr. 1) till fade, w/slight improv.
D
E
A
F♯m
D
E
Don't let your life wrap up a-round_ you.__ Don't for-get__ to call,_
Rhy. Fig. 1A
Gtr. 1
hold
Riff F
Gtr. 3
Gtr. 2
both notes vib.
Bkgd. Vocal Part 2
__ na na.

F♯m D E A F♯m
when - ev - er. I'll be here just wait - ing for you.
sim.
Begin fade
D E F♯m D E
I'll be un - der your stars for - ev - er. Nei - ther here nor there, just
A F♯m D E F♯m D
right be - side you. I'll be un - der the stairs for - ev - er. Nei - ther
Fade
E A F♯m D E F♯m D
here nor there, just right be - side you.

BLUE MONDAY

Words and Music by
DAVE BARTHOLOMEW
and ANTOINE DOMINO

F7
Thurs - day is a hard work - ing day, and Fri - day I get my
B♭
B♭7
Piano
pay.
Sat - ur - day
Chorus:
E♭
Edim7
Cont. rhy. simile
morn - ing, oh, Sat - ur - day morn - ing, all my tired - ness has gone a - way.
Gtr. 1
B♭7
E♭
Edim7
I got my mon - ey and my hon - ey, and I'm
8va

C7
F
F/E♭
B♭/D
F7/C
B♭
out on the stem___ to play.___
But Sun - day morn - ing my___ head is bad,___
Cont. in slashes
T
A
B
B♭7
Cont. rhy. simile
E♭
B♭
___ but it's worth it for the time___ that I've had.
But I've
1.
F7
B♭
got to___ get my rest,___ 'cause_ Mon - day is next.___
(F7)
2.
F7
Piano
___ 'cause___ Mon - day is next.___
N.C.
B♭7
Gtr. 1

BRIDGE OF SIGHS

Words and Music by
ROBIN TROWER

Chorus:
Cmaj7
A
G
A5
Bb5
B+
Elec. Gtr. 1
Why so un - for - giv - ing?
And why so cold?
1.
w/Rhy. Fig. 1 (Elec. Gtr. 1) simile
Cmaj7
B7
B5
Em7
A7
Been a long time cross - ing
Bridge of
Sighs.
Em7
A7
Em7
2.
Em7
A7
Em7
Sighs.
Elec. Gtr. 1
Outro:
Em7
A7
w/Riff 1 (Elec. Gtr. 4) play 3 times during 3rd - 5th repeat only.
Em7
*Elec. Gtr. 4 Riff 1
w/delay
Elec. Gtr. 1
**Elec. Gtr. 2
**Elec. Gtr. 3
*3rd - 5th times only.
**2nd - 5th times only.

1.-4.
Em7
23 44
A7
1112
Em7
2
3
1/2

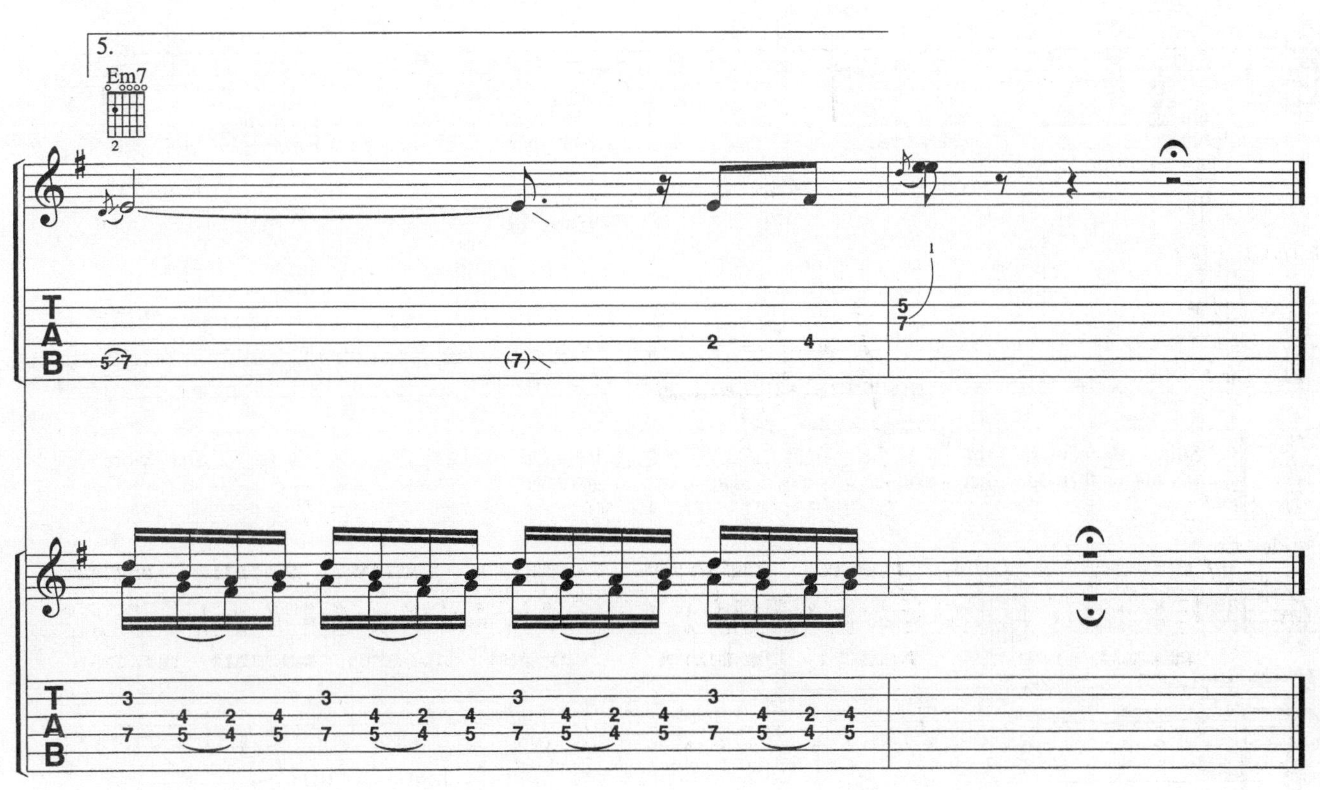

5.
Em7
2
1

BLUE VELVET

Words and Music by
BERNIE WAYNE and LEE MORRIS

B♭maj7 B♭9 E♭
feel - in' the rap - ture grow like a flame burn - ing
ah, ah. Ah,
D.S. 𝄋 al Coda
E♭m E♭m7 Dm7 D♭m7 Cm7 F
bright - ly. 3. But when she left, gone was the glow of
Coda
Fm B♭7 E♭maj7 E♭m B♭
years. And I still can see blue vel - vet through my tears.
ah. Ah,
Verse 4:
F♯ B D♯m Dm C♯m F♯
She wore blue vel - vet, but in my heart there'll al - ways
ah. Vel - vet, whoa, whoa.
B D♯m Dm C♯m F♯
be pre - cious and warm are mem - o - ry through the
Whoa, whoa, whoa, oo.
Freely
F♯m B7 (E) (Em)
years. And I still can see blue vel - vet through my
Ah.
Outro:
B D♯m Dm C♯m C B
a tempo
rit.
tears.
Bkgd. Vcl.: Blue vel - vet, oo, oo.
Verse 3:
But when she left,
Gone was the glow of blue velvet.
But in my heart there'll always be
Precious and warm memories
Through the years.
(To Verse 4:)

BORN TO BE WILD

Words and Music by
MARS BONFIRE

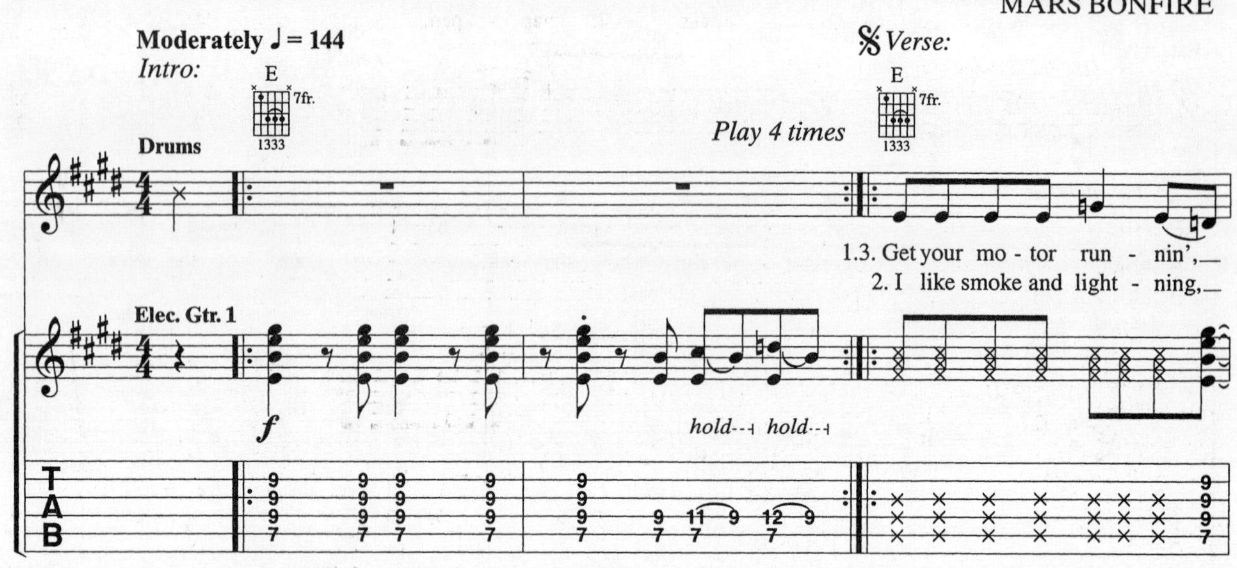

G A E G A

Yeah, darling, gon - na make it hap - pen, take the world in a

Elec. Gtr. 1 *(1st & 3rd times only)*

hold hold hold hold

Elec. Gtr. 1 *(2nd time only)*

hold hold hold hold

Substitute w/Fill 1 *(Elec. Gtr. 1) 3rd time only*

E G A E

love em - brace. Fire all of your guns at once and

hold hold

hold hold

Fill 1

Elec. Gtr. 1

1.
2.
3.
To Next Strain
(To Pre-chorus:)
G
A
E
3fr.
5fr.
7fr.
134211
1333
ex - plode in - to space.
Like a
Like a
Cont. in slashes
Pre-chorus:
Elec. Gtr. 1
Cont. rhy. simile
true na - ture's child, we were born, born to be wild. We can
climb so high, I nev - er wan - na die.
Chorus:
D
Born to be wild.
To Coda

Interlude:
E
7fr.
1333
Play 4 times
E7(♯9)
6fr.
2134
Play 4 times
E
7fr.
1333
D.S. 𝄋 al Coda
N.C.
Elec. Gtr. 1
Cont. rhy. simile
Elec. Gtr. 1
Elec. Gtr. 2
mf
w/slide
Coda
E
7fr.
1333
Elec. Gtr. 1
Cont. rhy. simile
Elec. Gtr. 2
E7(♯9)
6fr.
2134
Elec. Gtr. 1
(8va throughout)
Elec. Gtr. 2
Cont. rhy. simile
Begin fade
Fade

BURNING DOWN THE HOUSE

Words by
DAVID BYRNE

Music by DAVID BYRNE, CHRIS FRANTZ,
JERRY HARRISON and TINA WEYMOUTH

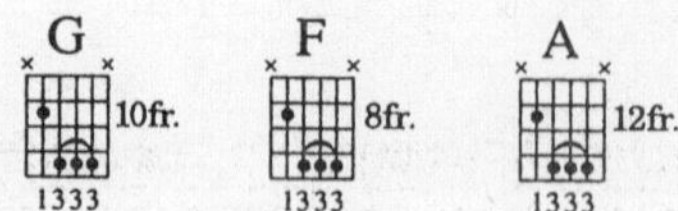

Moderately ♩ = 104

Intro:

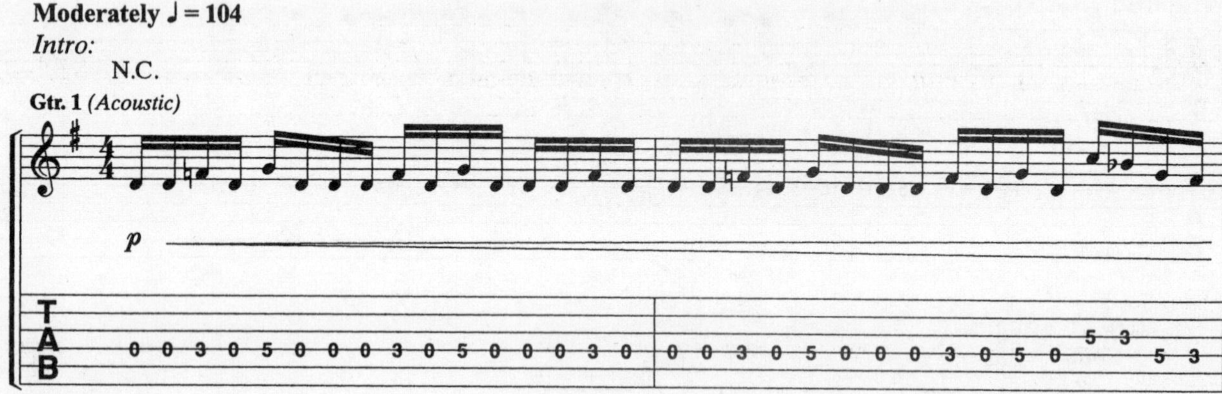

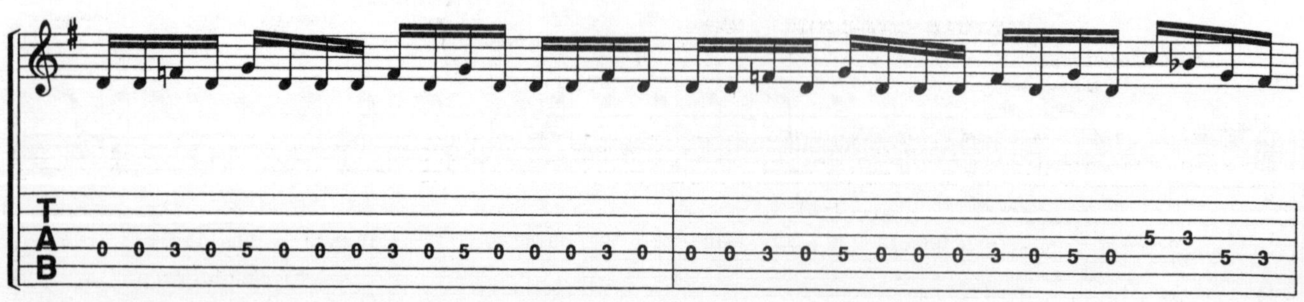

Ah.
0 0 3 0 5 0 0 0 3 0 3 0 5 0 0 0
3 0 3 0 5 0 0 0 3 0 5 0 5 3 5 3
Verse 1:
G
*Gtrs. 1 & 2
Rhy. Fig. 1
F
G
mf
1. Watch out, you might get what you're af - ter. Cool ba - bies,
F
G
F
strange but not a stran - ger. I'm an or - di - nar - y
Verses 2, 3 & 4:
w/Rhy. Fig. 1 (Gtrs. 1 & 2)
G
A
F
end Rhy. Fig. 1
G
Rhy. Fig. 2
*Gtr. 1
guy, burn - ing down the house.
2. Hold tight
3. 4. See additional lyrics
*Verse 4 only.

w/Rhy. Fig. 2 (Gtr. 1) 2 times, simile
F
end Rhy. Fig. 2
G
F
wait 'til the par - ty's o - ver. Hold tight, we're in for nas - ty weath - er.
G
F
G
A
All gtrs. out
F
There has got to be a way, burn - ing down the house.
Chorus:
* G
F
1. Here's your tick - et, pack your bags, time for jump - ing o - ver - board.
2. 3. See additional lyrics
*Harmony implied by keyboard and bass.
G
F
G
The trans - por - tà - tion is here. Close e - nough but not too far,
To Coda
F
G
F
may - be you know where you are. Fight - in' fire with fire. Uh.
Interlude:
6
G
A
F
D.S. al Coda
Burn - ing down the house.
Coda
Outro:
F
G
F
G
F
Uh.

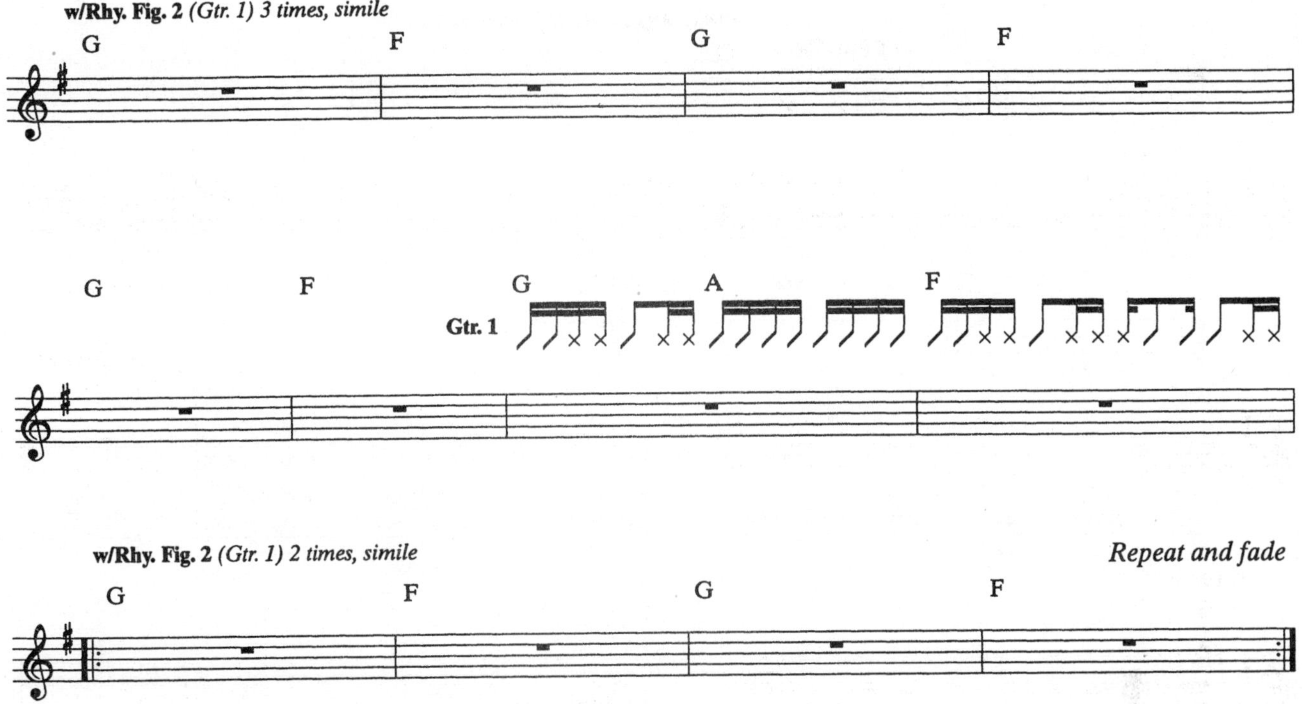

Verse 3:
All wet, hey, you might need a rain coat.
Shake down, means walking in broad daylight.
Three hundred sixty-five degrees,
Burning down the house.

Chorus 2:
It was once upon a place, sometimes I listen to myself.
Gonna come in first place.
People on their way to work;
Baby, what do you expect?
Gonna burst into flames.

Verse 4:
My house, down on the haunted alley.
That's right, don't want to hurt nobody.
Some things sure has swept me off my feet,
Burning down the house.

Chorus 3:
No visible means of support
And you have not seen nothing yet.
Everything's stuck together.
And I don't know what you expect,
Staring right into the TV set,
Fightin' fire with fire.
(To Coda)

THE BOYS ARE BACK IN TOWN

Words and Music by
PHILIP PARRIS LYNOTT

A5
D5
B5
E5
Intro
Bright Shuffle
Gtrs. 1&3 A5
Rhy. Fig. 1
B5
D5
1.,2.,3.
A5
End Rhy. Fig. 1
4.
Gtr. 2
Gtr. 2: w/ Fill 1, 3rd time
P.M.
* 1st time only
Verse
A5
C#min7
D
F#7 sus 4
1. Guess who just got back to - day. Them wild - eyed boys that had been a - way.
2. You know that chick that used to dance a lot? Every night she'd be on the floor shakin' what she got.
3. Fri - day night they'll be dressed to kill down at Dino's Bar and Grill.
2nd & 3rd time simile
let ring
Fill 1
Gtr 2:

F#7 sus 4
Bm7
Bm7/E
Gtr 3: w/ fill 2, 2nd time
A5
Have - n't changed, had - n't much _ to say, but man, I still think them _ cats are cra-zy.
Man, when I tell you she was cool, she was red hot! I mean she was steamin'!
The drink will flow and blood will spill, and if the boys wan-na fight you better let'em.
*for Bm7/E mute A string w/1st finger of left hand.
Gtr 2: 3rd time w/ Fill 4
let ring
C#m7
D
F
C#m7
They were ask - in' if you were a - round, how you was, _ where you could _ be found.
And that time over at Johnny's place, well this chick _ got up and she slapped Johnny's face.
That juke-box in the corner blastin' out my favorite song. The nights are getting warm and it won't be long.
let ring
Fill 2
Gtr 3
1/2
Fill 4
Gtr 2
let ring

F#7sus4
Bm7
Bm7/E
A5
Told them you were liv-in' down - town,
Man, we just fell a-bout the place.
Won't be long 'till sum - mer comes,
driv-in' all the old men cra - zy.
If that chick don't wan - na know, forget her.
now that the boys are here again.
The
Gtrs. 1&3: continue above
let ring
Gtr 2: 3rd time w/ Fill 5.
Chorus
Gtrs. 1&3: w/ Rhy. Fig. 1 (3 times)
B5
D5
A5
boys are back in town. The boys are back in town.
I said the
Gtr. 2
to Coda
B5
D5
A5
boys are back in town.
The boys are back in town.
The
Fill 5
Gtr 2:
T
A
B

B5
D5
boys ___ are back in town.___ The boys ___ are back in town.___ The boys ___ are back in town.___
The boys
Gtr. 3 tacet
N.C.
___ are back in town. ___
Gtr. 1
Rhy. Fig. 3
Gtr. 2
Rhy. Fig. 4
End Rhy. Fig. 3
A5
End Rhy. Fig. 4
Gtr. 2: w/ Fill 3, 2nd time
full
Fill 3
Gtr 2:

Bridge

Dsus4 D C#m7 F#7sus4 Bmin7

Spread the word __ a-round.

Gtrs 1&3:

Rhy. Fig. 2

E9sus4 F#7sus4

Guess who's back in town. _

P.M.

End Rhy. Fig. 2

Dsus4 D C#m7 F#7sus4 Bm7

You _ spread the word a-round.

Gtrs. 1&3

Gtr. 2: w/ Rhy. Fig. 2

E9sus4 F#7sus4 *D.S. al Coda*

End Rhy. Fig. 2

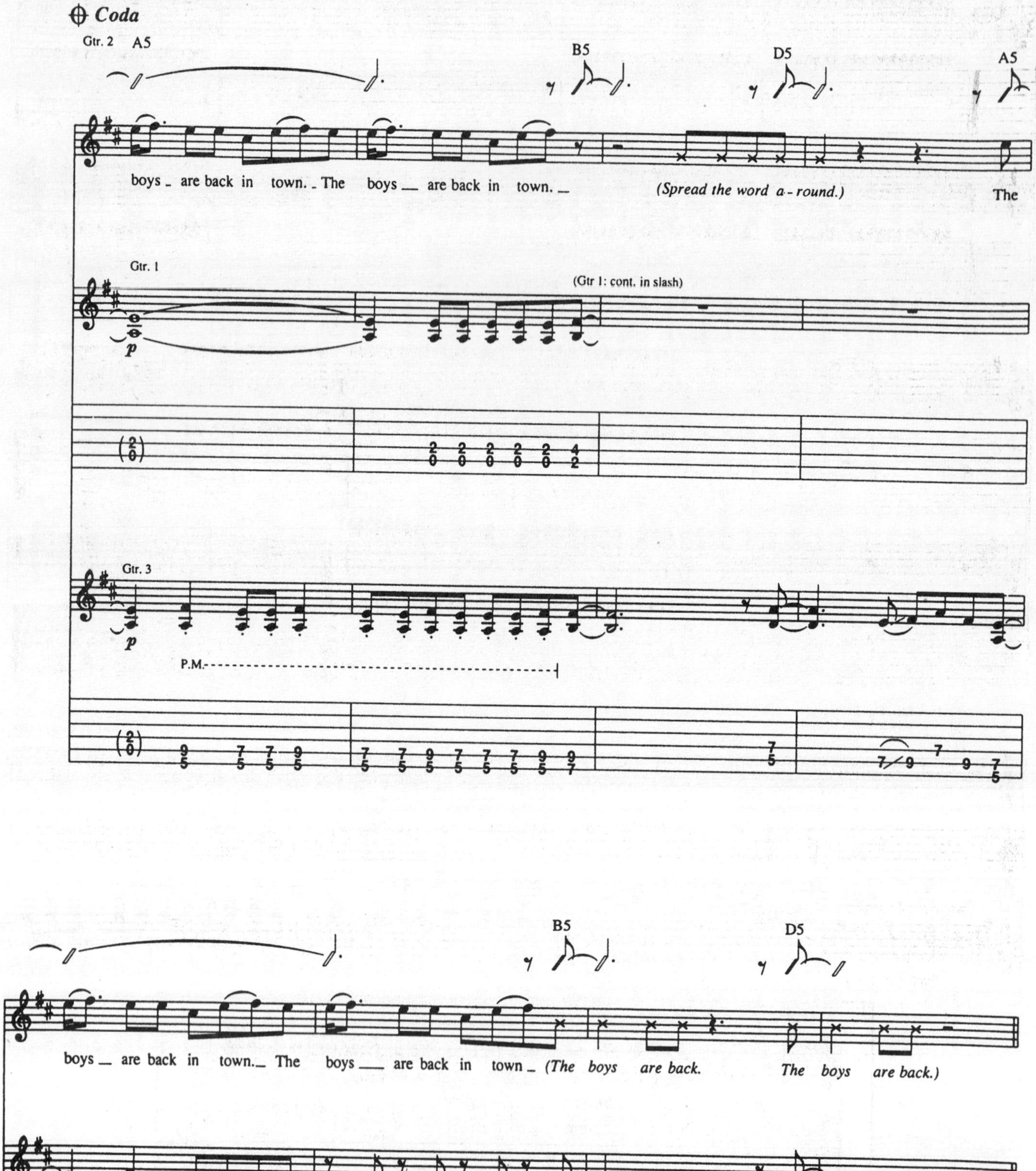

Coda

Gtr. 2 A5

B5 D5 A5

boys _ are back in town. _ The boys __ are back in town. _ *(Spread the word a - round.)* The

Gtr. 1

(Gtr 1: cont. in slash)

p

Gtr. 3

p

P.M.

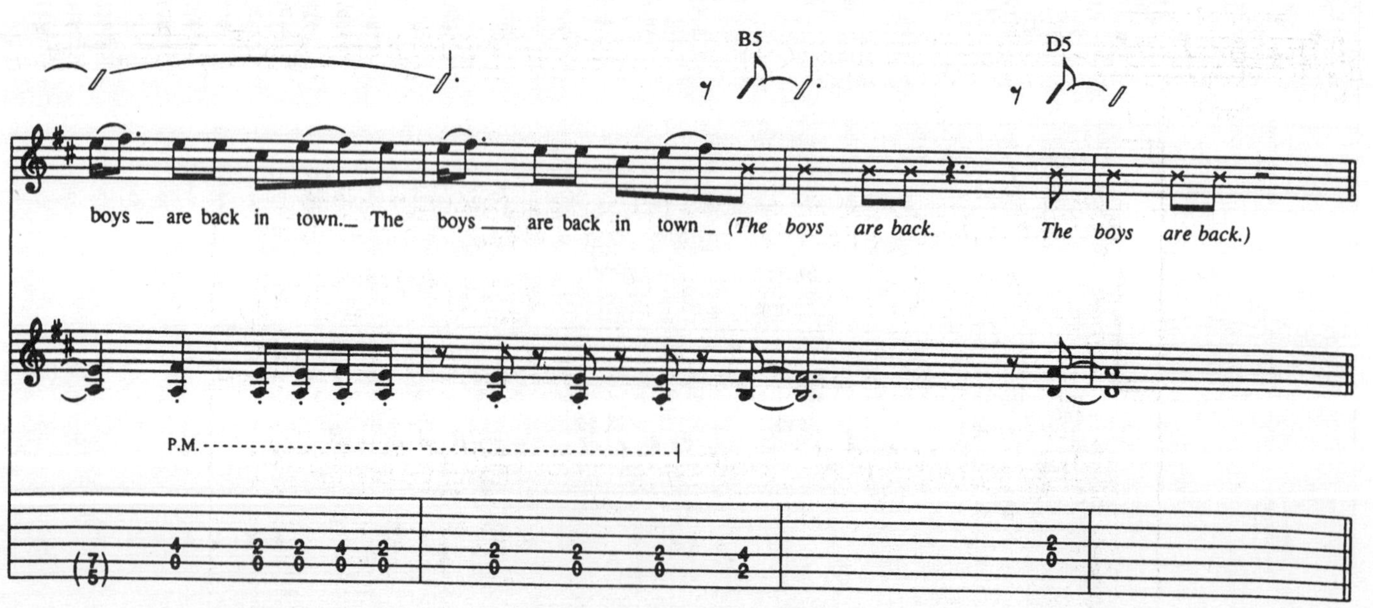

Gtr. 1
N.C.
Gtr. 2
D5
Gtr. 3:
E5
(Gtr. 1: play chords w/ Gtr. 3, 2nd time)
2nd time only
2nd time only
Gtr. 1: w/ Rhy. Fig. 3 (7 times)
Gtr. 2: w/ Rhy. Fig. 4 (7 times)
N.C.
Gtr. 3: w/ Fill 6 (2 times)
The boys are back in town a - gain.
Gtr. 4: w/ Fill 7
'Been hang - in' down at Di - no's
Fill 6
Gtr.3
TAB
Fill 7
Gtr. 4
TAB

The boys are back_ in town_ a-gain._
Gtr. 3
Gtr. 4
hold bend
full
fade

CASEY JONES

Words by
ROBERT HUNTER

Music by
JERRY GARCIA

F
B♭
Trou - ble a - head,
trou - ble be - hind,
B♭
F
C
To Coda
and you know that no - tion just crossed my mind.
end Rhy. Fig. 1
w/Riff A (Gtr. 1)
*Verse:
C
1. This old en - gine
2. 4. See additional lyrics.
3. Instrumental
*Gtr. 1 ad lib. single line and double - stop licks behind vocal.
D
F
makes it on time,
leaves cen - tral sta - tion 'bout a

G
C
D
quar - ter to nine.
Hits riv - er junc - tion at sev - en - teen to at a quar -
mf
F
E7
1. 2.
Am
G
3.
Am
D.S. 𝄋 al Coda
G
- ter to ten you know - it's trav - 'lin' a - gain.
Coda
w/Rhy. Fig. 1 (Gtr. 2, simile)
C
F
Driv-in' that train, high on co - caine, Ca - sey Jones, you'd bet - ter
Gtr. 1
G
C
watch your speed. Trou - ble a - head,

F
trou - ble be - hind, ___
and ___ you know that no - tion ___ just ___
T
A
B
C
C
Gtr. 2
___ crossed ___ my ___ mind.
Driv - in' that ___ train, ___ high ___
Gtr. 1
B♭
Cont. rhy. simile
F
___ on co - caine, ___ Ca - sey Jones ___ you'd bet - ter
C
watch your ___ speed. ___
Trou - ble a - head, ___ trou -

Verse 2:
Trouble ahead the lady in red,
Take my advise you'd be better off dead.
Switchman's sleeping train hundred and two is
On the wrong track and headed for you.
(To Chorus:)

Verse 4:
Trouble with you is the trouble with me;
Got two good eyes, but we still don't see.
Come 'round the bend, you know it's the end.
The fireman screams and the engine just gleams.
(To Chorus:)

CALIFORNIA DREAMIN'

Words and Music by
JOHN PHILLIPS and MICHELLE PHILLIPS

C#m B A B G#7sus

1.

dream - in'
(Cal - i - for - nia dream - in' on such a win - ter's day.
on such a win - ter's day. on such a win - ter's day.________)

2. Stopped in - to a church,_

2.

Flute Solo:

C#m

Cont. rhy. simile

A

—)

E G#7 C#m A G#7sus G#7 C#m B

A B G#7sus G#7 C#m B

A B G#7sus G#7

D.S. 𝄋 *al Coda*

3. All the leaves are

𝄌 *Coda*

C#m B A B C#m B

dream - in' on such a win - ter's day.________
(Cal - i - for - nia dream - in' on such a win - ter's, Cal - i - for - nia dream -

A B C#m B A B A C#m

6-str. & 12-str. Acous. Gtrs.

__ On such a win - ter's day________ On such a win - ter's day.________
- in' on such a win - ter's, Cal - i - for - nia dream - in' on such a win - ter's day.________)

Verse 2:
Stopped into a church
I passed along the way.
Well, I got down on my knees (Got down on my knees.)
And I pretend to pray. (I pretend to pray.)
You know the preacher liked the cold (Preacher liked the cold.)
He knows I'm gonna stay. (Knows I'm gonna stay.)
(To Chorus:)

Verse 3:
All the leaves are brown (All the leaves are brown)
And the sky is gray. (And the sky is gray.)
I've been for a walk (I've been for a walk)
On a winter's day. (On a winter's day.)
If I didn't tell her, (If I didn't tell her,)
I could leave today. (I could leave today.)
(To Chorus:)

CALL ME

Words by
DEBORAH HARRY
Music by
GIORGIO MORODER

Verse:
D5
5fr.
134
B♭7
13141
Elec. Gtr. 1
Cont. rhy. simile
1. Col - or___ me___ your_ col - or,___ ba - by. Col - or___ me___ your_ car.___
2. Cov - er___ me___ with_ kiss - es,___ ba - by. Cov - er___ me___ with_ love.___
Elec. Gtr. 2
Rhy. Fig. 2
end Rhy. Fig. 2
w/Rhy. Fig. 2 (Elec. Gtr. 2) simile
D5
5fr.
134
B♭7
13141
A5
5fr.
134
Col - or___ me___ your_ col - or,___ dar - ling, I know_ who_ you_ are.___
Roll me in___ de - sign - er___ sheets,_ I'll nev - er___ get e - nough._ 2. E -
Pre-chorus:
G5
3fr.
134
A5
5fr.
134
G5
3fr.
134
Elec. Gtr. 1
1. Come up___ off___ your_ col - or___ chart,_ I know_ where_ you're_ com -
mo - tions_ come,_ I___ don't___ know_ why,___ cov - er___ up___ love's_
Elec. Gtr. 2

To Next Strain
(To Chorus:)
A5
5fr.
134
C5
3fr.
- ing from. Call me al - i - bi. Call me
Chorus:
D5
F5
8fr.
G5
10fr.
Elec. Gtr. 1
Cont. rhy. simile
Call me. on the line. Call me, call me an - y,
B♭5
13fr.
an - y - time. Call me, Call me. I'll ar - rive.
1. You can
2. When you're
w/Rhy. Fig. 1 (Elec. Gtr. 2) simile
w/Fills 1 (Elec. Gtr. 1) & 1A
(Elec. Gtr. 3) both simile
call me an - y day or night, call me.
read - y, we can
share the wine, call

D5
5fr.
134
G5
10fr.
F5
8fr.
E5
7fr.
A5
12fr.
Elec. Gtr. 1
me.
*Elec. Gtr. 2
Elec. Gtr. 3
1/2
*Two gtrs. arr. for one throughout section.
*Bridge/Synth. Solo:
B5
Ooh, he speaks the lan - guag - es of love.
Rhy. Fig. 3
end Rhy. Fig. 3
*Vocal 1st time only.
w/Rhy. Fig. 3 (Elec. Gtr. 2) simile
23
Ooh, a - mo - re, chia - ma - mi,
chia - ma - mi.
Ooh, a - pelle moi,

C5
3fr.
134
mon che - rie, a - pelle moi. An - y - time,
D5
5fr.
134
an - y - place, an - y - while, an - y - where.
B♭5
134
A5
5fr.
134
An - y - time,
*Elec. Gtr. 2
*Elec. Gtr. 3
8va
hold
13
15
14 15
14 15
(13)
(15)
*This riff 1st time only.
G5
3fr.
134
an - y - place, a - ny - where, an - y day.

1.
A5
5fr.
134
Elec. Gtr. 2
Elec. Gtr. 3
2.
A5
C5
3fr.
1. Call me
**Elec. Gtr. 2
grad. bend
**Elec. Gtr. 2 only.
Chorus:
D5
F5
G5
B♭5
Elec. Gtr. 1
me on my line. Call me, call me an - y, an - y - time. Call
Call me. on my line. Call me, call me in a sleek de - sign. Call
Repeat and fade
me for a ride. Call me, call me for some o - ver - time. 2. Call
me, Call me. call me for your lov - er's, lov - er's al - i - bi. 3. Call

CAN'T CRY ANYMORE

Words and Music by
SHERYL CROW and BILL BOTTRELL

2.4.5.
G5 D5 G5 D5 Em
But
cont. w/slashes
Gtr. I
hold
Gtr. II (w/tremolo effect)
Chorus:
Am
Em
*Gtr. I
Would - n't it be good if we — could hop a flight to an - y - where. — Well, so long — to this life. —
Gtr. II
* (L) = Lower portion of chord is strummed as in Rhy. Fig. 2
(H) = Upper portion of chord is strummed as in Rhy. Fig. 2
Rhy. Fig. 3
end Rhy. Fig. 3
To Coda I
To Coda II
A
C II
So much — for pre - tend - ing, —

Rhy. Fig. 4
D5
D.S. 𝄋 al Coda I
end Rhy. Fig. 4
'Cause Bad luck's never ending.
And now I know that.
Coda I
w/Rhy. Fig. 4 simile (Gtr. 1)
'Cause Bad luck's never end ing.
It's never ending.
Guitar Solo:
w/Rhy. Fig. 1 simile (Gtr. 1)
w/ad lib. vocals
G5
Gtr. II
D5
G5
D5
G5
D5
G5
D5
G5
Em
C
D.S. 𝄋 al Coda II
2nd ending only
G5
D5
G5
D5
G5

Verse 2:
Since I left,
Been feelin' better, cause that's
What you get when you
Stay together too long.
And I can't cry anymore.

Verse 3:
And now I know that,
Money comes in.
But the fact is (there's)
Not enough to pay my taxes.
And I can't cry anymore.

Verse 4:
Well gotta brother.
He's got real problems.
Heroin now,
There's just no stopping him tonight.
And I won't cry anymore.

Verse 5:
Well it could be worse,
I could've missed my calling.
Sometimes it hurts,
But when you read the writing on the wall.
Can't cry anymore.

CAN'T GET ENOUGH OF YOU BABY

Words and Music by
SANDY LINZER and DENNY RANDELL

Tune down 1/2 step:
⑥= E♭ ③= G♭
⑤= A♭ ②= B♭
④= D♭ ①= E♭

Moderately ♩ = 124

Intro:

Organ *(arr. for gtr.)*

8va throughout

f

3

Gtr. 1

f

hold throughout

1/2 1/2 1/2

Cont. in slashes

G7 C7 G7 C7

3fr 3fr 3fr 3fr

131241 13141 131241 13141

Gtr. 2

Cont. rhy. simile

Rhy. Fig. 1

Rhy. Fig. 1A

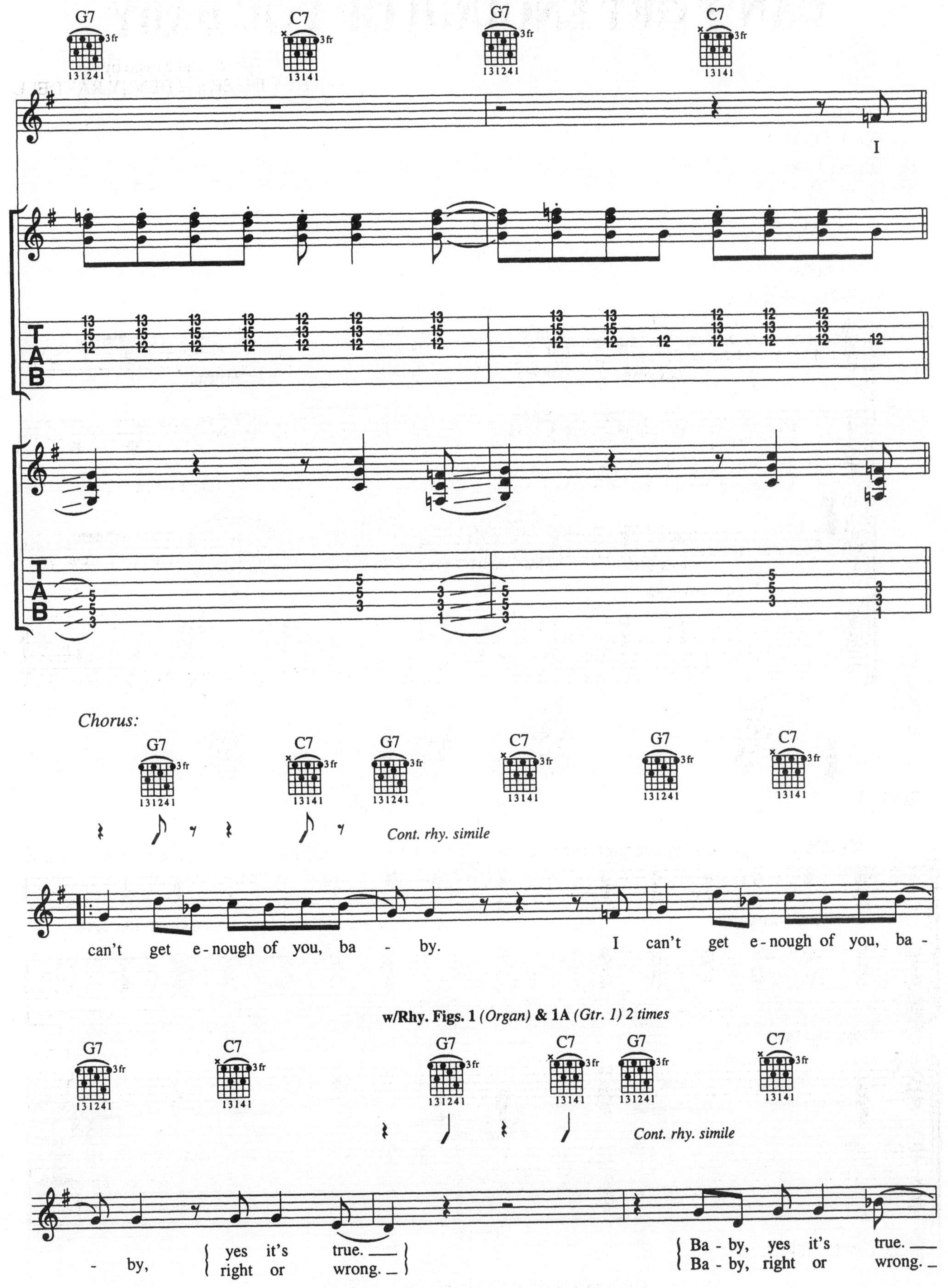
G7
C7
3fr
131241
13141
I
Chorus:
Cont. rhy. simile
can't get e-nough of you, ba - by. I can't get e-nough of you, ba -
w/Rhy. Figs. 1 (Organ) & 1A (Gtr. 1) 2 times
- by, yes it's true. right or wrong.
Ba - by, yes it's true.
Ba - by, right or wrong.

Verse:
G7
C7
Gtr. 2
1. When - (3.) ev - er we kiss, I get to
2. When you had to go, I
Cont. rhy. simile
feel - ing like this. I get to wish - ing that there were two of you.
hat - ed the thought. I on - ly wish the night was twice as long.
My
Bridge:
D
Em
heart cries out, "More, ba - by."
1. It feels so nice, I
2.3. I love you so much, I
To Coda
Am
G/B
C
1.
want your arms to wrap a - round me twice.
wish that there was more of you to touch.
Gtr. 1

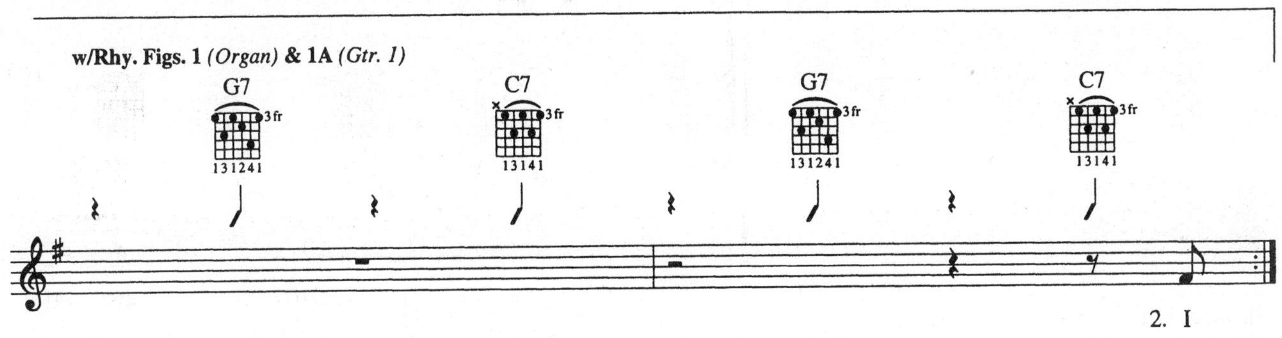
w/Rhy. Figs. 1 (Organ) & 1A (Gtr. 1)
G7
C7
G7
C7
2. I

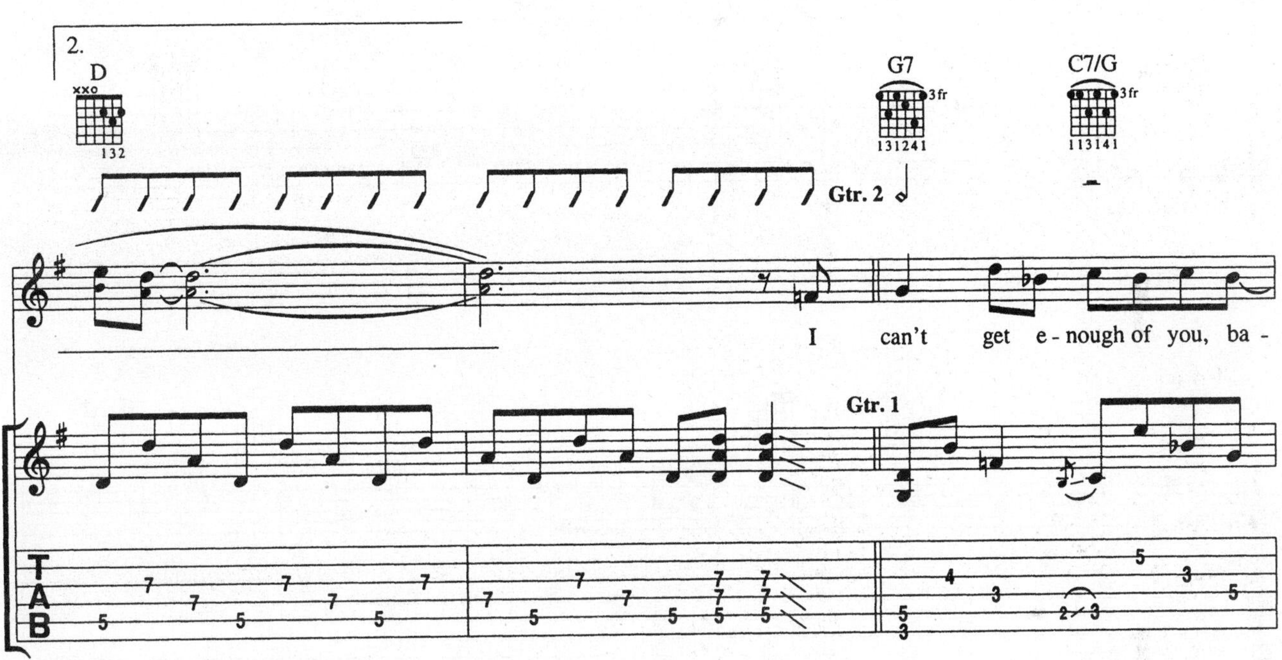
2.
D
G7
C7/G
Gtr. 2
I can't get e-nough of you, ba-
Gtr. 1

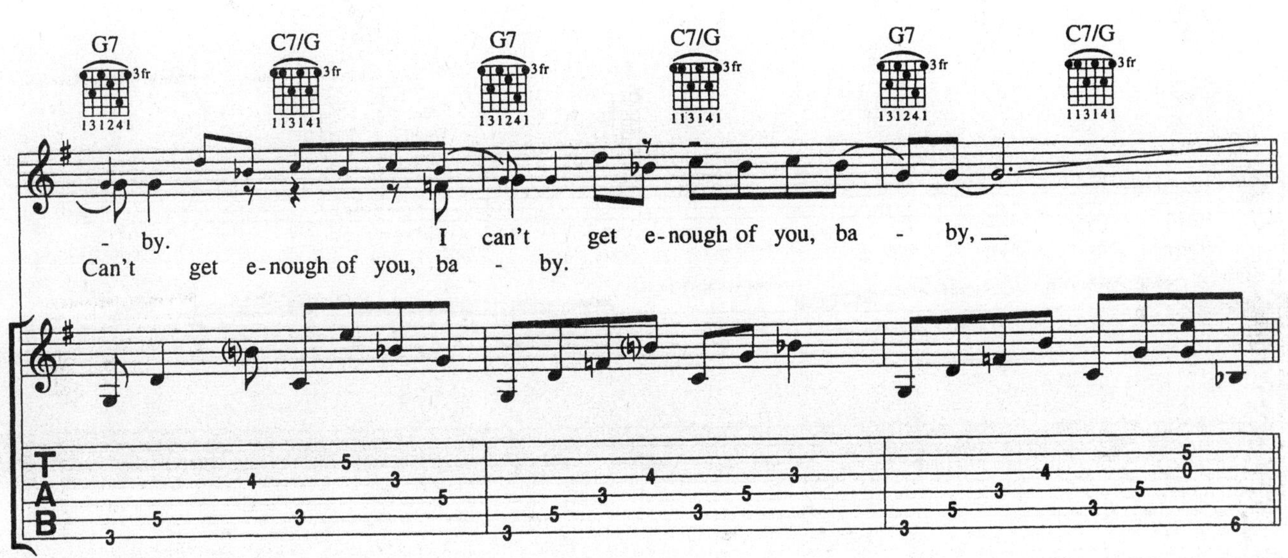
G7
C7/G
G7
C7/G
G7
C7/G
- by. I can't get e-nough of you, ba - by,
Can't get e-nough of you, ba - by.

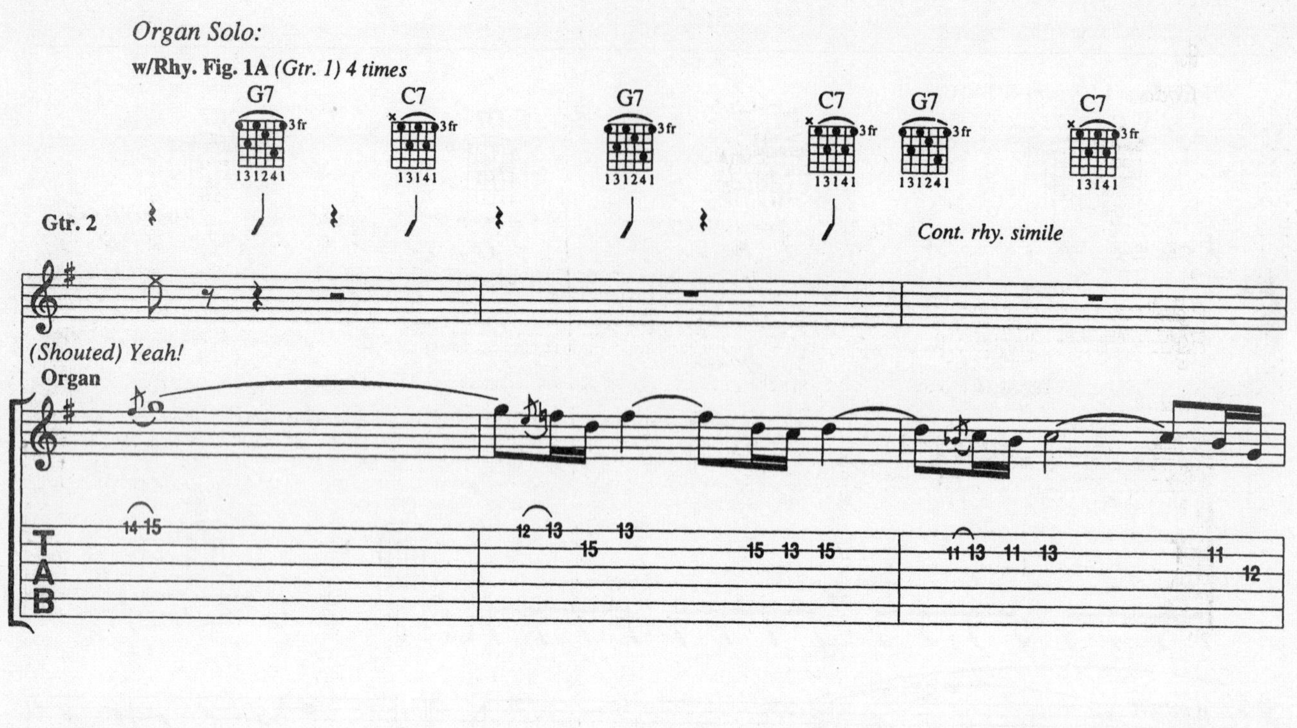
Organ Solo:
w/Rhy. Fig. 1A (Gtr. 1) 4 times
G7
C7
G7
C7
G7
C7
Gtr. 2
Cont. rhy. simile
(Shouted) Yeah!
Organ

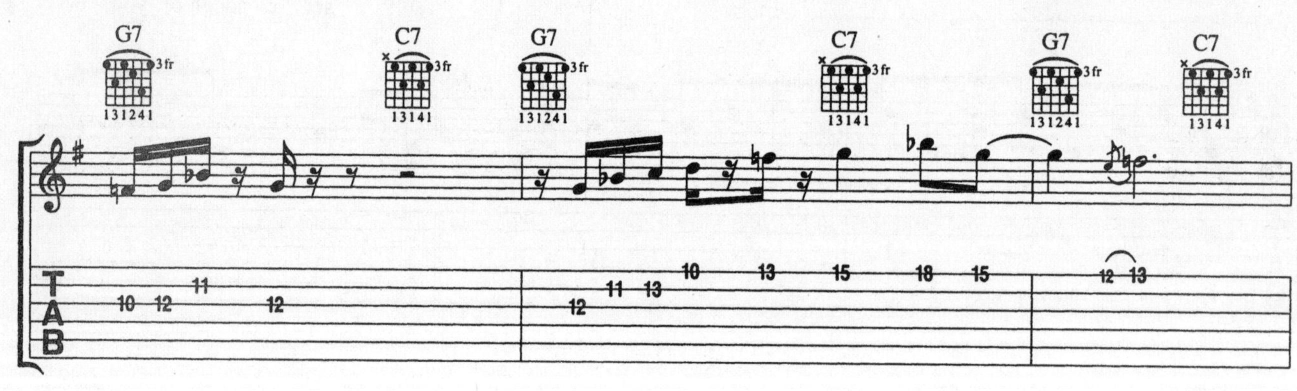
G7
C7
G7
C7
G7
C7

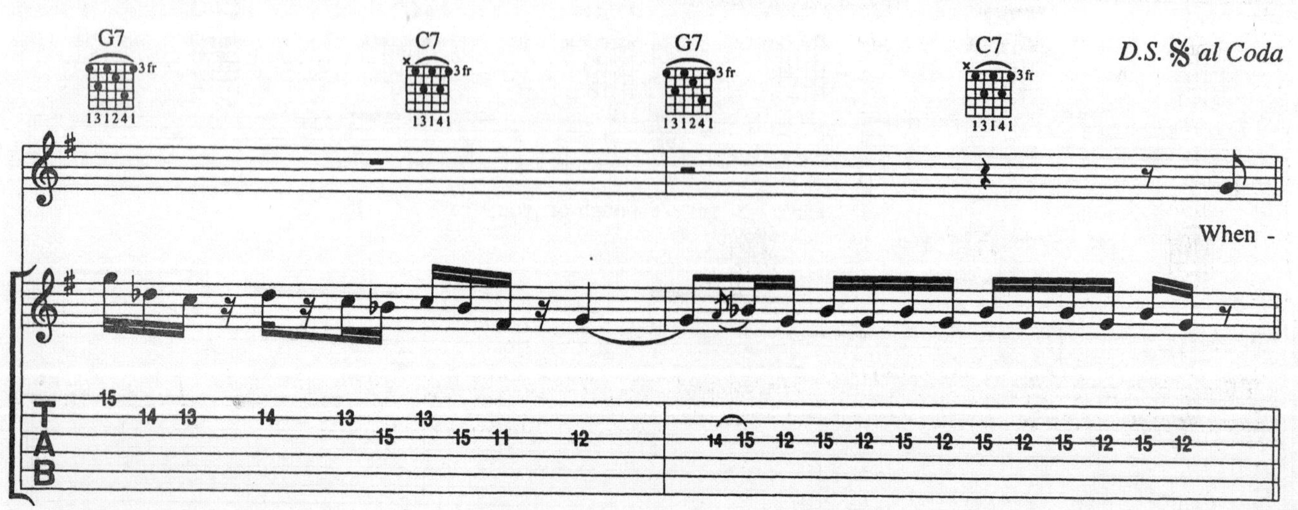
G7
C7
G7
C7
D.S. 𝄋 al Coda
When -

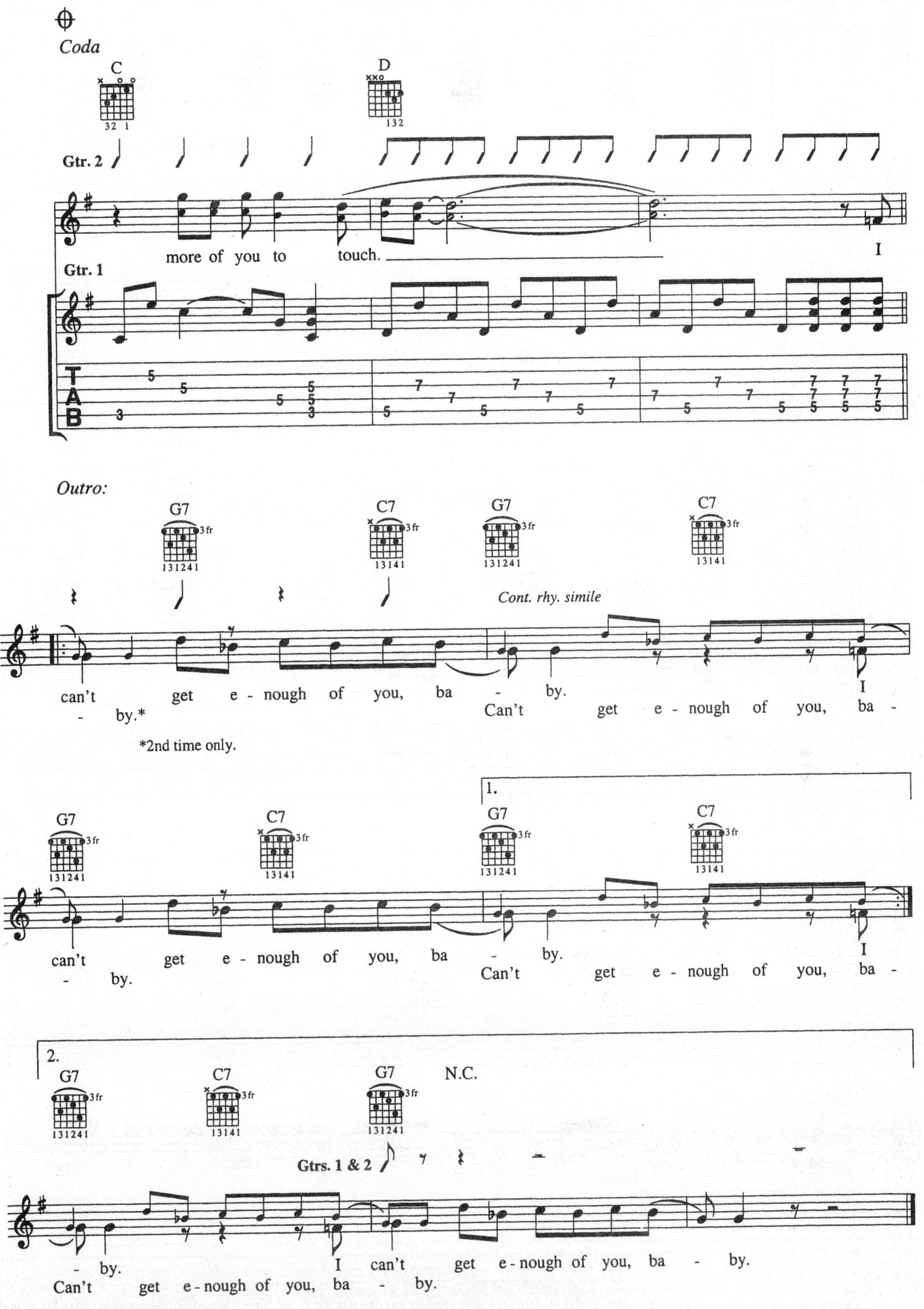
Coda
C
D
Gtr. 2
more of you to touch.
I
Gtr. 1
Outro:
G7
C7
Cont. rhy. simile
can't get e - nough of you, ba - by.
- by.*
I
Can't get e - nough of you, ba -
*2nd time only.
1.
can't get e - nough of you, ba - by.
- by.
I
Can't get e - nough of you, ba -
2.
N.C.
Gtrs. 1 & 2
- by.
I can't get e - nough of you, ba - by.
Can't get e - nough of you, ba - by.

CATHEDRAL

Words and Music by
EDWARD VAN HALEN, ALEX VAN HALEN,
MICHAEL ANTHONY and DAVID LEE ROTH

B
C
D
E
N.C.
sl.
N.C.
1.2.3.
sl.
4.
N.C.

CHANGE (IN THE HOUSE OF FLIES)

Words and Music by
CAMILO "CHINO" MORENO,
CHI CHENG, ABE CUNNINGHAM
and STEPHEN CARPENTER

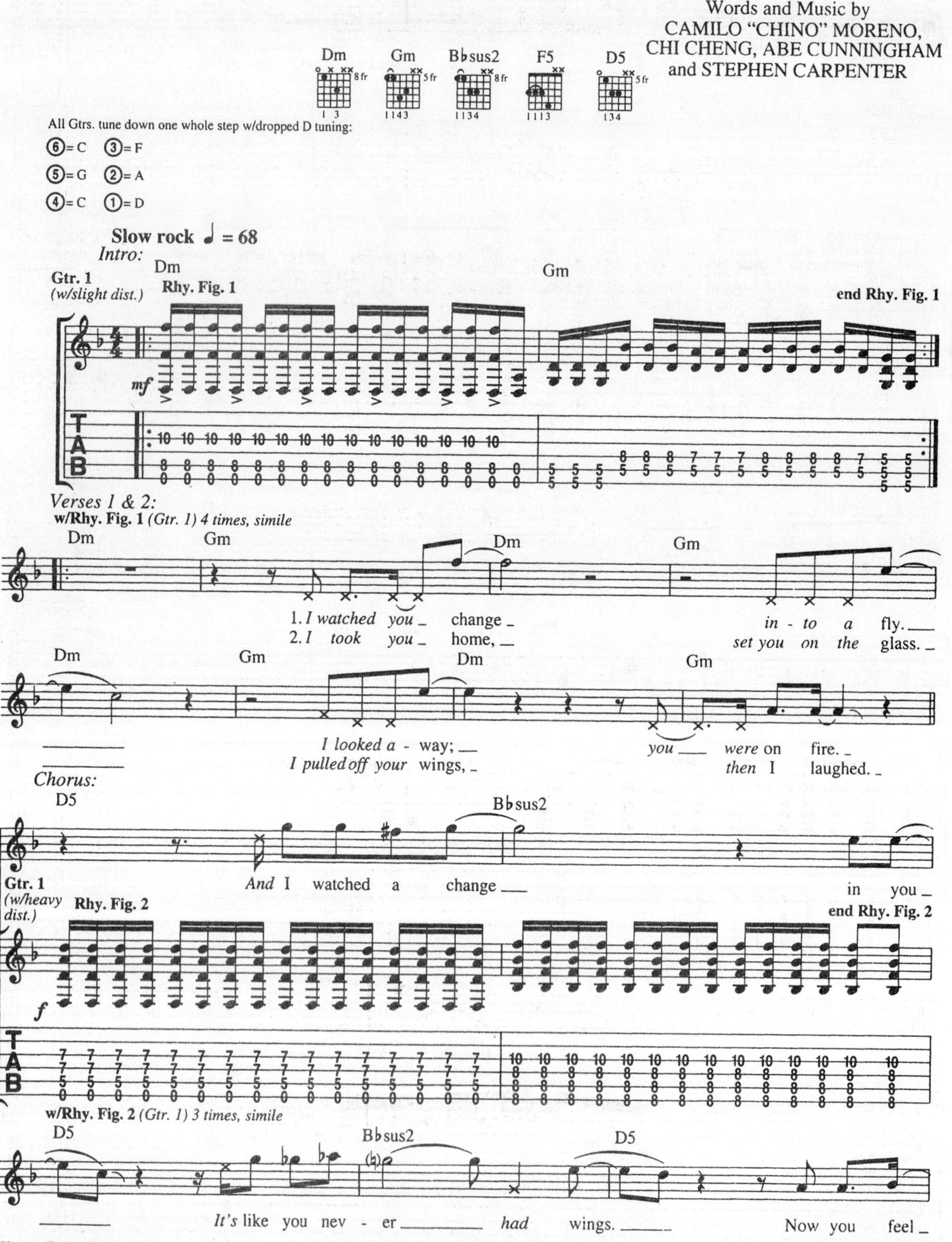

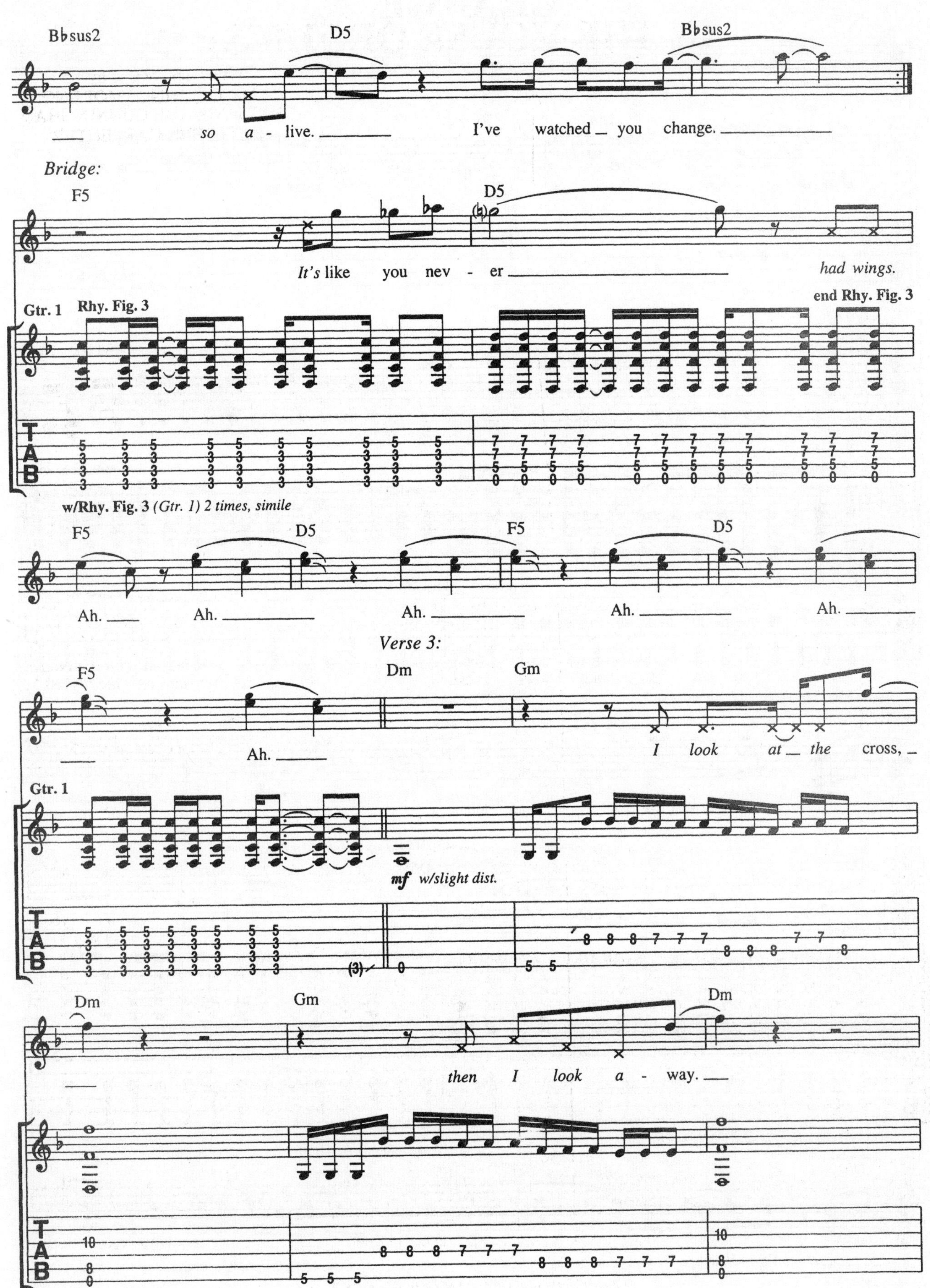

B♭sus2
D5
B♭sus2
so a - live.
I've watched you change.
Bridge:
F5
D5
It's like you nev - er
had wings.
Gtr. 1
Rhy. Fig. 3
end Rhy. Fig. 3
w/Rhy. Fig. 3 (Gtr. 1) 2 times, simile
F5
D5
F5
D5
Ah. Ah. Ah. Ah. Ah.
Verse 3:
F5
Dm
Gm
Ah.
I look at the cross,
Gtr. 1
mf w/slight dist.
Dm
Gm
Dm
then I look a - way.

Gm
Dm
Gm
Give you the lungs; blow me a-way.
Chorus:
Dm
Gm
And I watched a change in you.
Rhy. Fig. 4
end Rhy. Fig. 4
f w/heavy dist.
w/Rhy. Fig. 4 (Gtr. 1) 3 times, simile
Dm Gm Dm Gm
It's like you nev-er had wings. Now you feel so a-live.
w/Rhy. Fig. 2 (Gtr. 1) 4 times, simile
Dm Gm D5 B♭sus2
I've watched you change. Now you feel a-live.
D5 B♭sus2 D5 B♭sus2
You feel a-live. You feel a-live.
Bridge:
w/Rhy. Fig. 3 (Gtr. 1)
D5 B♭sus2 F5 D5
I've watched you change. It's like you nev-er had wings.

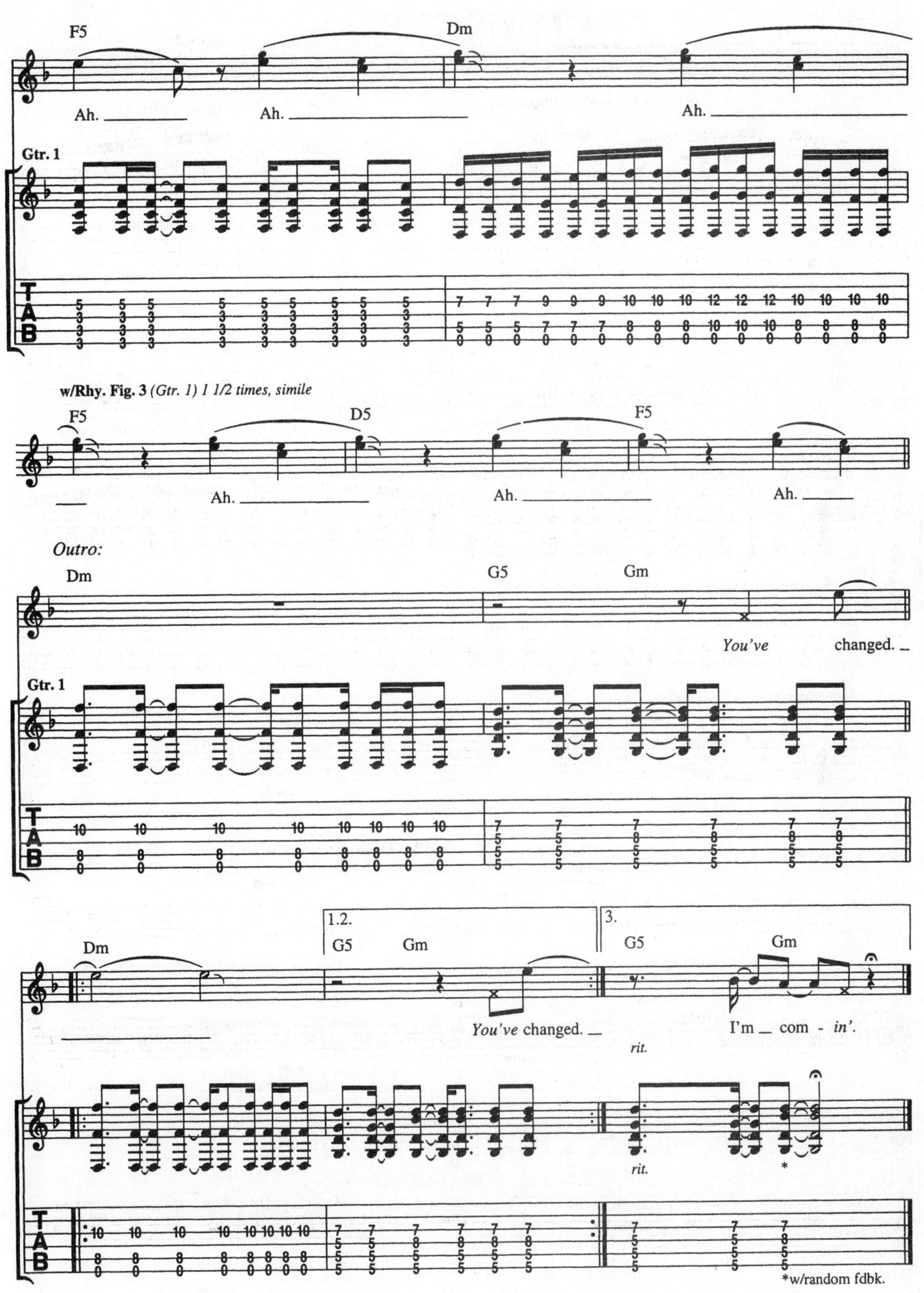
F5
Dm
Ah.
Ah.
Ah.
Gtr. 1
w/Rhy. Fig. 3 (Gtr. 1) 1 1/2 times, simile
F5
D5
F5
Ah.
Ah.
Ah.
Outro:
Dm
G5
Gm
You've changed.
Gtr. 1
1.2.
3.
Dm
G5
Gm
G5
Gm
You've changed.
I'm com - in'.
rit.
rit.
*w/random fdbk.

CHANGES

Moderately ♩ = 108
Intro:
Words and Music by
DAVID BOWIE
*Cmaj7
Db6
Dm7
Eb7
Piano (arr. for gtr.)
*Chords derived from overall tonality.
F7
D5
Piano
Elec. Gtr. 1
mf
Cont. rhy. simile
Verse:
C
1. I still don't know what I was
2. I watch the rip - ples
Sax. (arr. for gtr.)
Elec. Gtr. 1 (1st time only)

Em7
F
Cont. rhy. simile
wait - ing for___ and my time was run - ning wild._
change their size___ but nev - er leave the stream___
G
F
C
3
___ A mil - lion dead - end streets, and ev - 'ry time I thought I'd
___ of warm im - per - ma - nence._ And so the days flow
Em7
Fmaj7
got it made,_ it seemed the taste was not so sweet.
through my eyes,___ but still___ the days___ seem the same.
Pre-chorus:
G
Cmaj7
Dm7
Piano
1.So I turned my - self to face___
2. And these chil - dren___ that you___
Em7
E♭m7
Dm7
Cont. rhy. simile
3
___ me,___ but I've___ nev - er caught a glimpse
___ spit on as they try to change___ their
G
Cmaj7
Dm7
of how the oth - ers must see the fak -
worlds are im - mune___ to your___ con - sul - ta -
Em7
E♭m7
Dm7
3
er. I'm much too fast to take that test.
tions. They're quite a - ware___ what they're go - ing through.

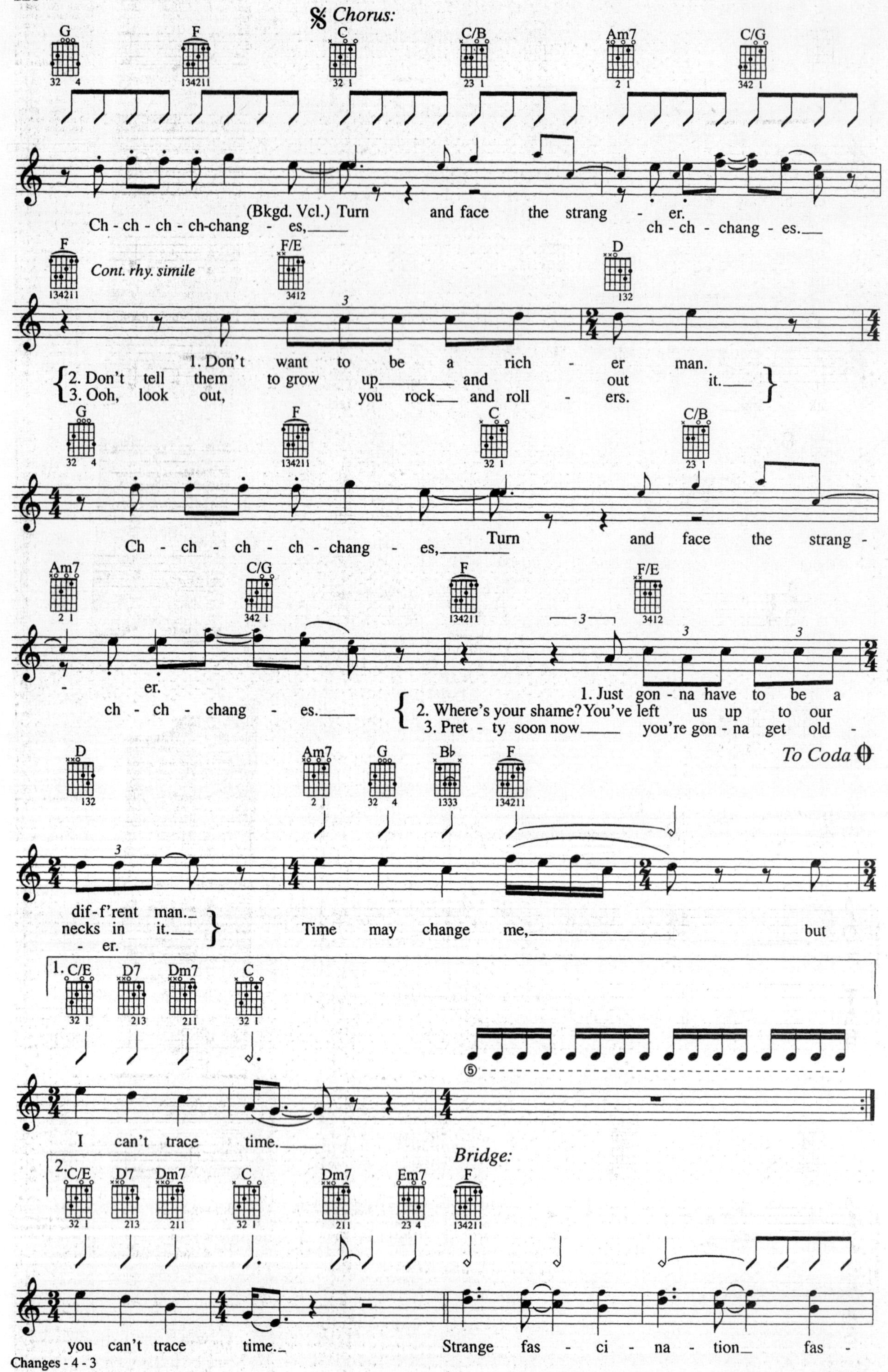
Chorus:
G F C C/B Am7 C/G
(Bkgd. Vcl.) Turn and face the strang - er.
Ch - ch - ch - ch-chang - es, ch - ch - chang - es.
F Cont. rhy. simile F/E D
1. Don't want to be a rich - er man.
2. Don't tell them to grow up and out it.
3. Ooh, look out, you rock and roll - ers.
G F C C/B
Turn and face the strang -
Ch - ch - ch - ch - chang - es,
Am7 C/G F F/E
- er.
ch - ch - chang - es.
1. Just gon - na have to be a
2. Where's your shame? You've left us up to our
3. Pret - ty soon now you're gon - na get old -
D Am7 G B♭ F
To Coda
dif - f'rent man.
necks in it.
- er.
Time may change me, but
1. C/E D7 Dm7 C
I can't trace time.
Bridge:
2. C/E D7 Dm7 C Dm7 Em7 F
you can't trace time. Strange fas - ci - na - tion fas -

C
F/C
C
F
ci - nat - ing me.
Aw, chang - es are
G
F
D.S. 𝄋 al Coda
tak - ing the pace I'm go - ing through. Ch - ch - ch - ch-chang - es,
Coda
C/E G/D Dm7 C
Am7 G B♭ F
I can't trace time. I said that time may change me, but
Freely
C/E G/D Dm7 C
Dm7
Em7
Cont. rhy. simile
I can't trace time.
Sax.
E♭7
Dm7
D♭maj7
Cmaj7
rit.

COCAINE

Words and Music by
JOHN J. CALE

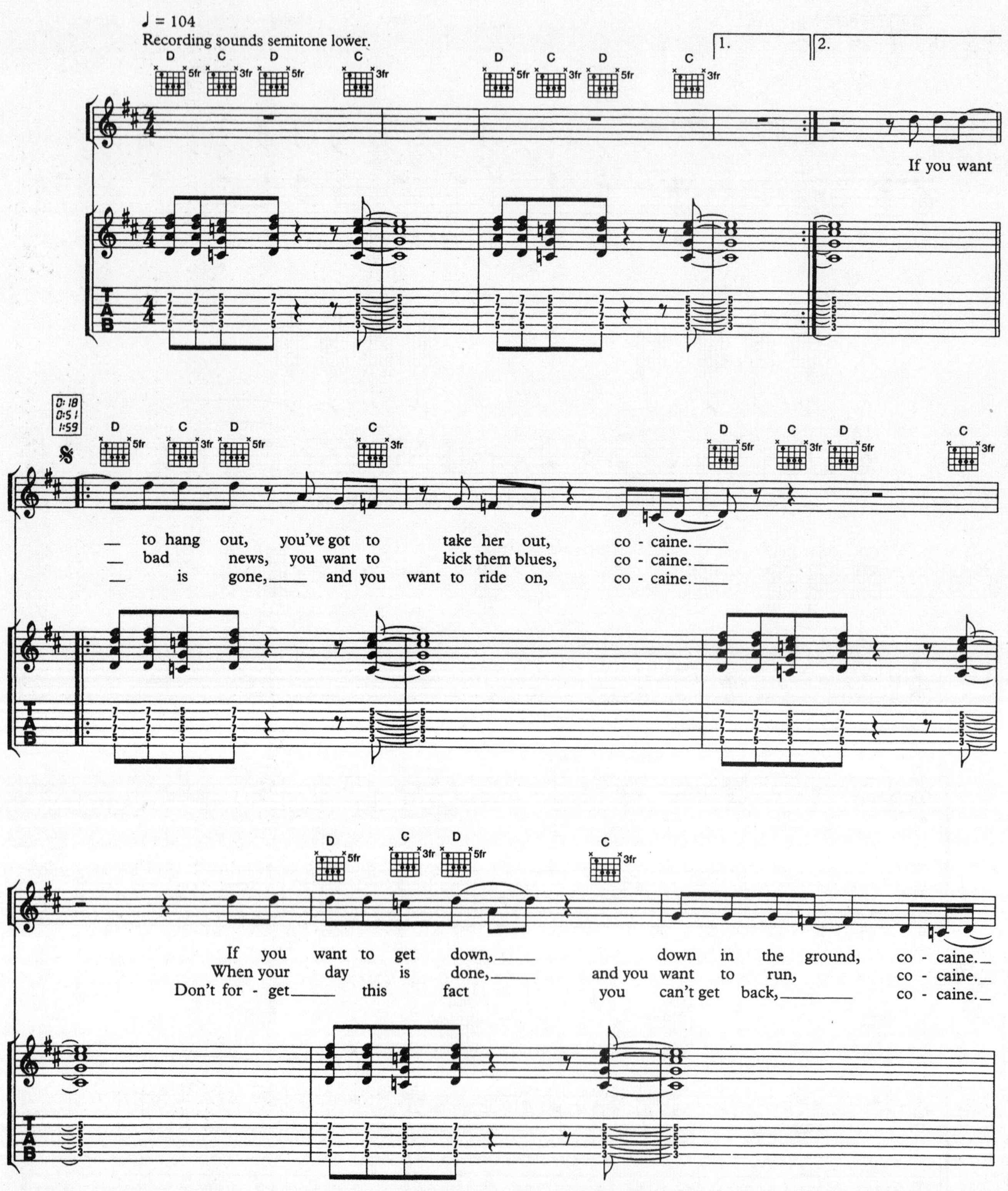

D
C
D
C
D
0:37
1:09
2:18
C
B♭
She don't lie,
she don't lie,
she don't lie,

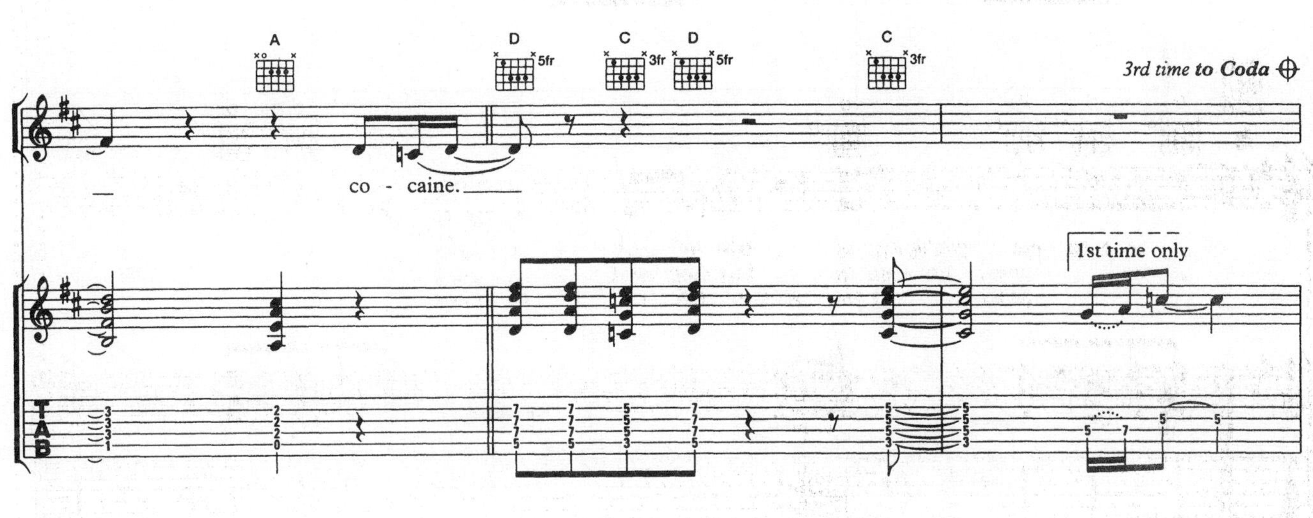
A
D
C
D
C
3rd time to Coda
co - caine.
1st time only

1.
D
C
D
C
2.
D
C
D
C
If you got

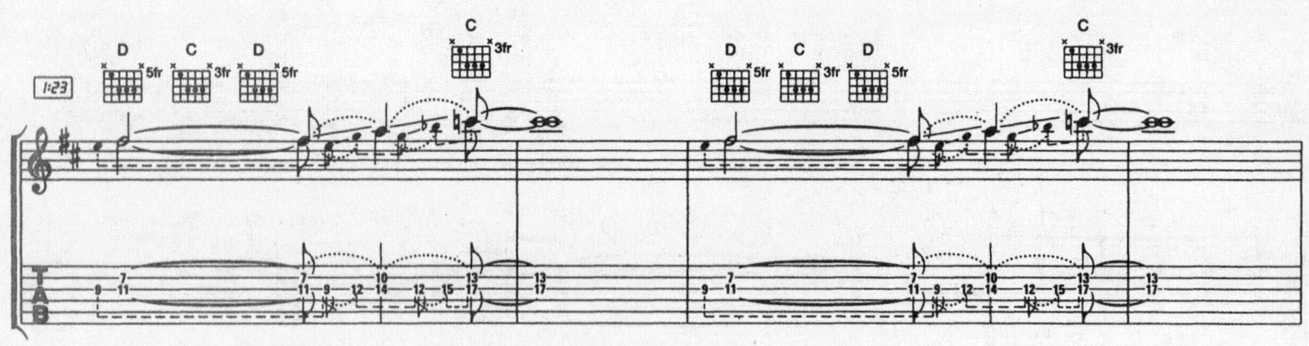
1:23
D
5fr
C
3fr
D
5fr
C
3fr
D
5fr
C
3fr
D
5fr
C
3fr

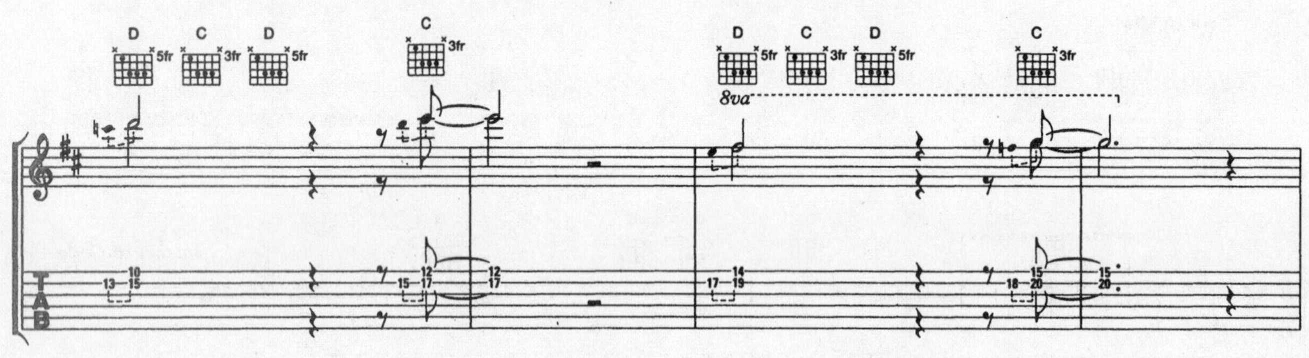
D
5fr
C
3fr
D
5fr
C
3fr
D
5fr
C
3fr
D
5fr
C
3fr
8va

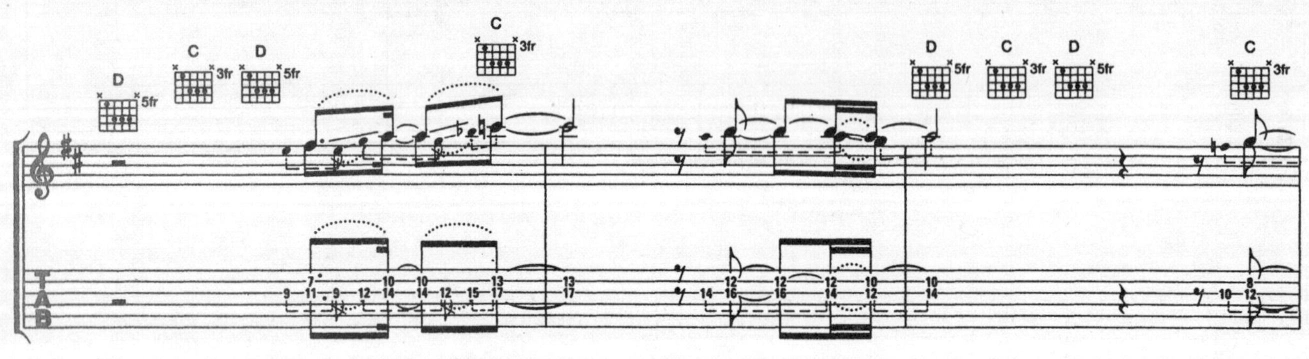
D
5fr
C
3fr
D
5fr
C
3fr
D
5fr
C
3fr
D
5fr
C
3fr

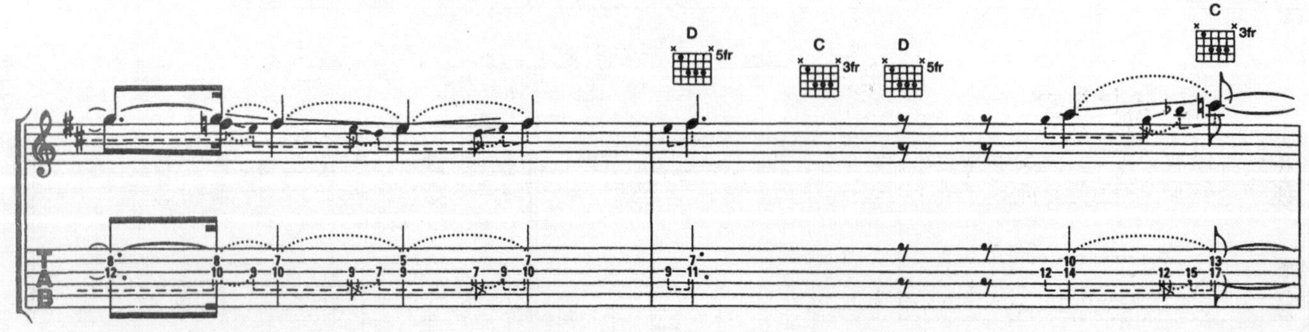
D
5fr
C
3fr
D
5fr
C
3fr

D
C
D
C
D.𝄋 al Coda
If your thing
CODA
2:28
She don't lie, she don't lie, she don't lie,
co - caine.
A
B♭
fade out

THE CHAIN

All gtrs. capo at 2nd fret to match recording
Gtr. tuning:
⑥ = D ③ = G
⑤ = A ② = B
④ = D ① = E

Words and Music by
LINDSEY BUCKINGHAM, CHRISTINE McVIE,
STEVIE NICKS, MICK FLEETWOOD and JOHN McVIE

Moderately slow
Intro:

Dm9(♭5)

Gtr. 1 *(Electric)*

Gtr. 2 *(Acous.)*

hold throughout

Dm9(♭3)
Gr. 1
1/4
1. 2. Lis - ten to the wind blow;
Gtr. 2
Rhy. Fig. 1
G
G7
5fr.
Am/C
Gm/B♭
Dm(♭3)
watch the sun rise.
down comes the night.
end Rhy. Fig. 1

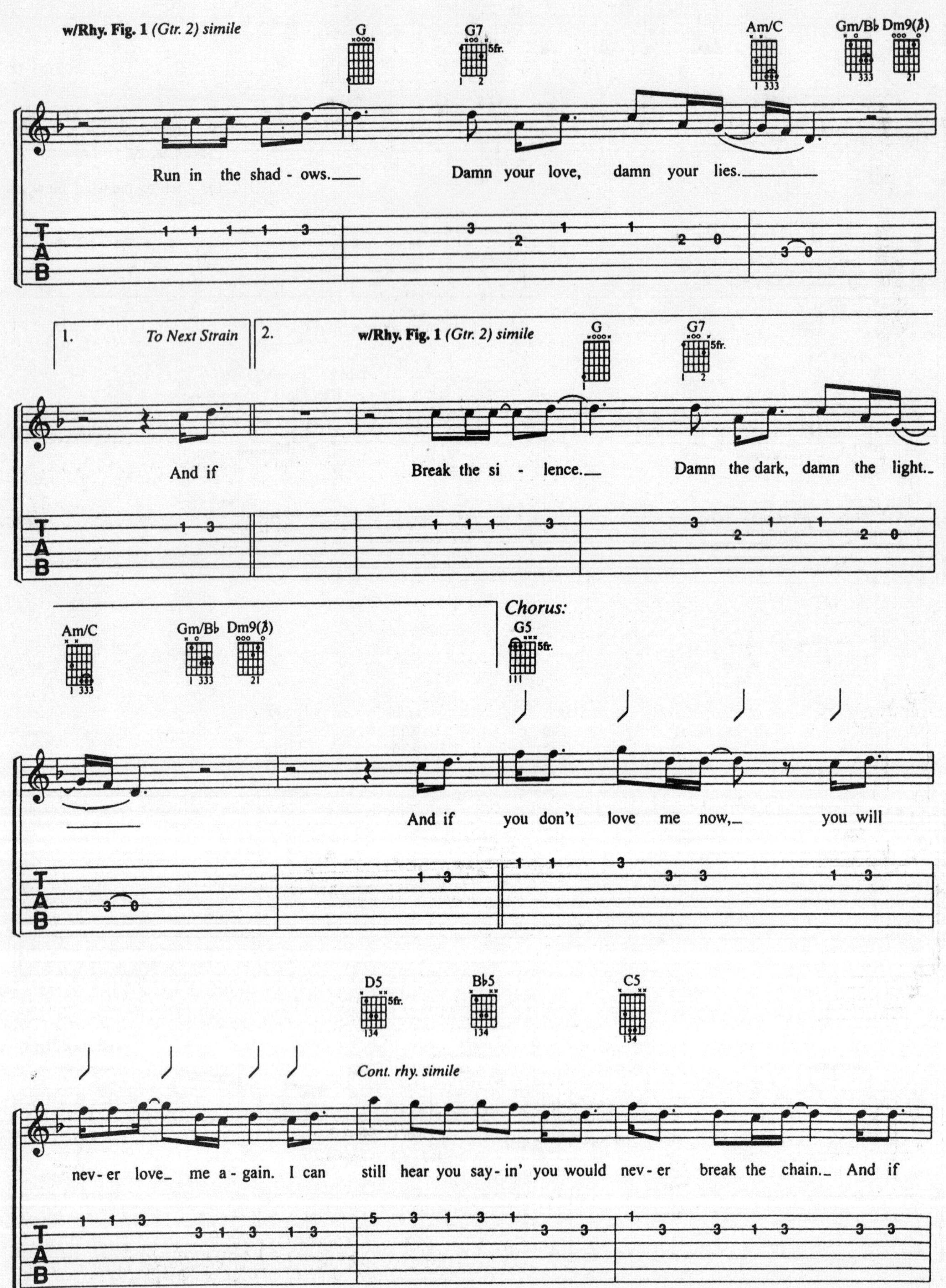

w/Rhy. Fig. 1 (Gtr. 2) simile
G
G7
5fr.
Am/C
Gm/B♭
Dm9(♮3)
Run in the shad - ows.
Damn your love, damn your lies.
1.
To Next Strain
2.
w/Rhy. Fig. 1 (Gtr. 2) simile
And if
Break the si - lence.
Damn the dark, damn the light.
Chorus:
G5
And if you don't love me now, you will
D5
B♭5
C5
Cont. rhy. simile
nev - er love me a - gain. I can still hear you say - in' you would nev - er break the chain. And if

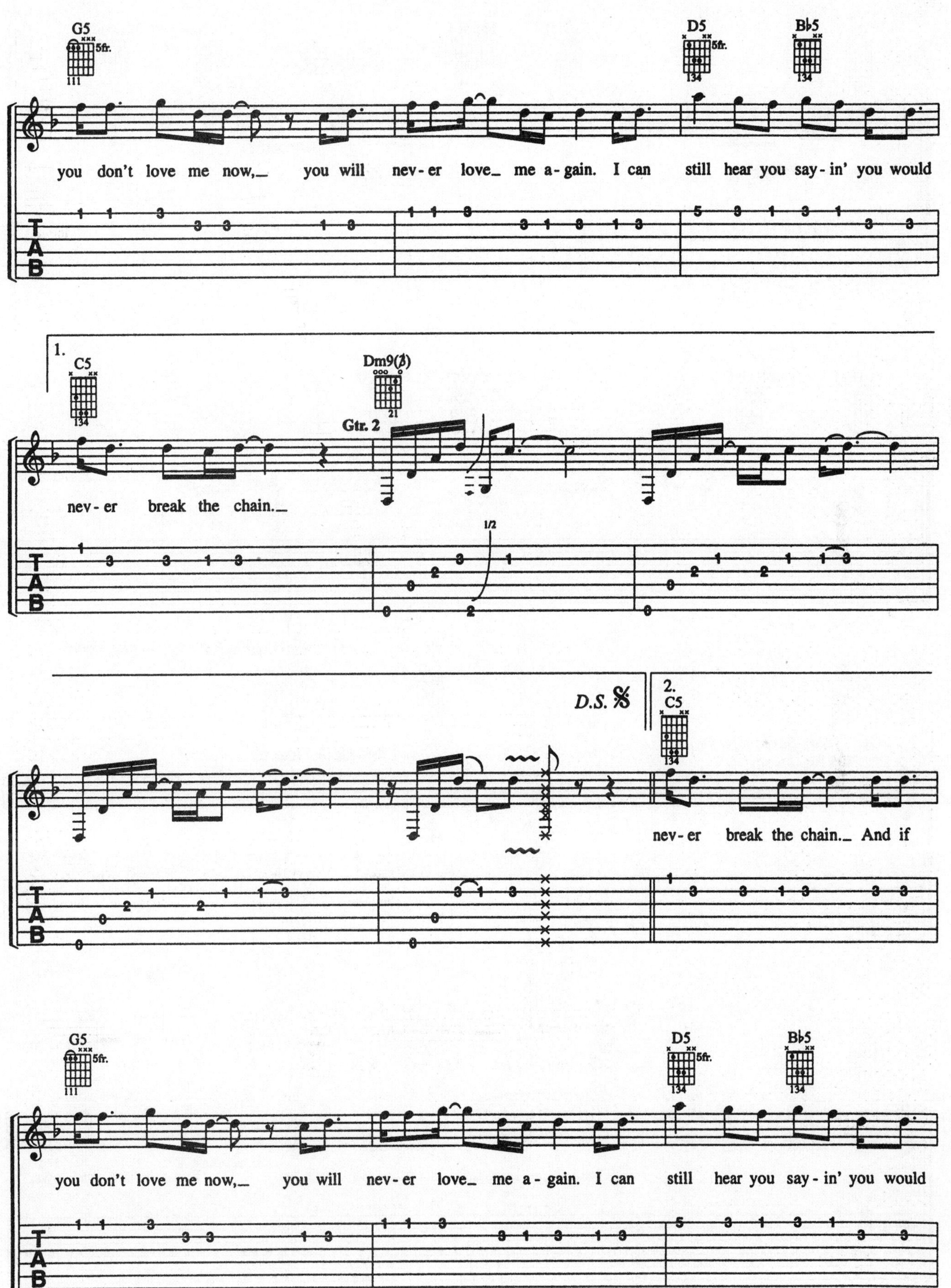
G5
5fr.
111
D5
5fr.
134
B♭5
134
you don't love me now,_ you will nev- er love_ me a- gain. I can still hear you say- in' you would
1.
C5
134
Dm9(♭3)
21
Gtr. 2
nev- er break the chain._
1/2
D.S. 𝄋
2.
C5
134
nev- er break the chain._ And if
G5
5fr.
111
D5
5fr.
134
B♭5
134
you don't love me now,_ you will nev- er love_ me a- gain. I can still hear you say- in' you would

C5
Dm9(♭)
B♭(♭5)/D
Gtr. 2
nev - er break the chain.
Gm
Dm
w/Rhy. Fig. 2 (Gtr. 3) 2 times, simile
Gtr. 3 (Elec. Bass arr. for gtr.)
Rhy. Fig. 2
end Rhy. Fig. 2
Repeat till fade
Chain, keep us to - geth - er. Run in the shad - ows.

CLOSING TIME

Words and Music by
DAN WILSON

Moderate rock ♩ = 92
Intro:
G
D5
A5
C5
*Gtr. 1
Rhy. Fig. 1
end Rhy. Fig. 1
mf semi-clean tone
*Two gtrs. arranged for one.
w/Rhy. Fig. 1 (Gtr. 1)
**Gtr. 2 Riff A
end Riff A
mf
hold throughout
**Piano arr. for gtr.
Verses 1 & 2:
w/Rhy. Fig. 1 (Gtr. 1) & Riff A (Gtr. 2) Both 8 times
1. Clos - ing time, o - pen all the doors and let you out in - to the world.
2. Clos - ing time, time for you to go out to the plac - es you will be from.
Clos - ing time, turn all of the lights on o - ver
Clos - ing time, this room won't be o - pen till your
ev - 'ry boy and ev - er - y girl.
broth - ers or your sis - ters come.
Clos - ing time,
So gath - er up your jack - ets,

A5
C5
G
D5
one last call for al - co - hol, so fin - ish your whis - key or beer.
move it to the ex - its. I hope you have found a friend.
Clos - ing time, you don't have to go home, but you can't stay here.
Clos - ing time, ev - 'ry new be - gin - ning comes from some oth - er be - gin - ning's end.
Chorus:
G5
D
Am
C
Gtr. 3
(w/distortion)
Cont. rhy. simile
I know who I want to take me home. I know who I want
to take me home. I know who I want to take me home, take me
To Coda 1.
2.
home.
Interlude 1:
B♭5
A♭5
E♭5
Cm
Gtr. 2
*Piano dbld. w/ synth.

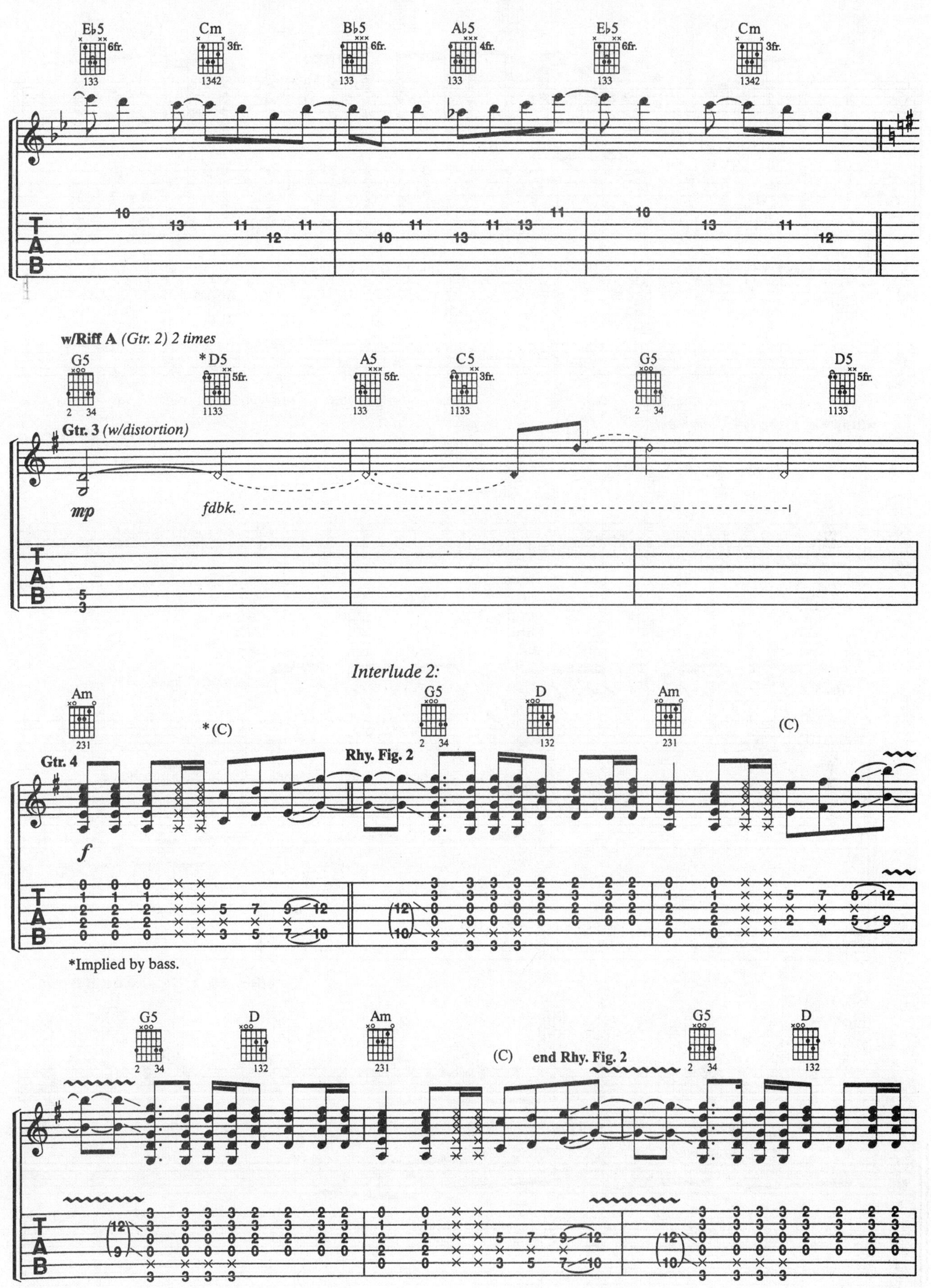

Eb5
Cm
Bb5
Ab5
Eb5
Cm
w/Riff A (Gtr. 2) 2 times
G5
*D5
A5
C5
G5
D5
Gtr. 3 (w/distortion)
mp
fdbk.
Interlude 2:
Am
*(C)
G5
D
Am
(C)
Gtr. 4
Rhy. Fig. 2
f
*Implied by bass.
G5
D
Am
(C)
end Rhy. Fig. 2
G5
D

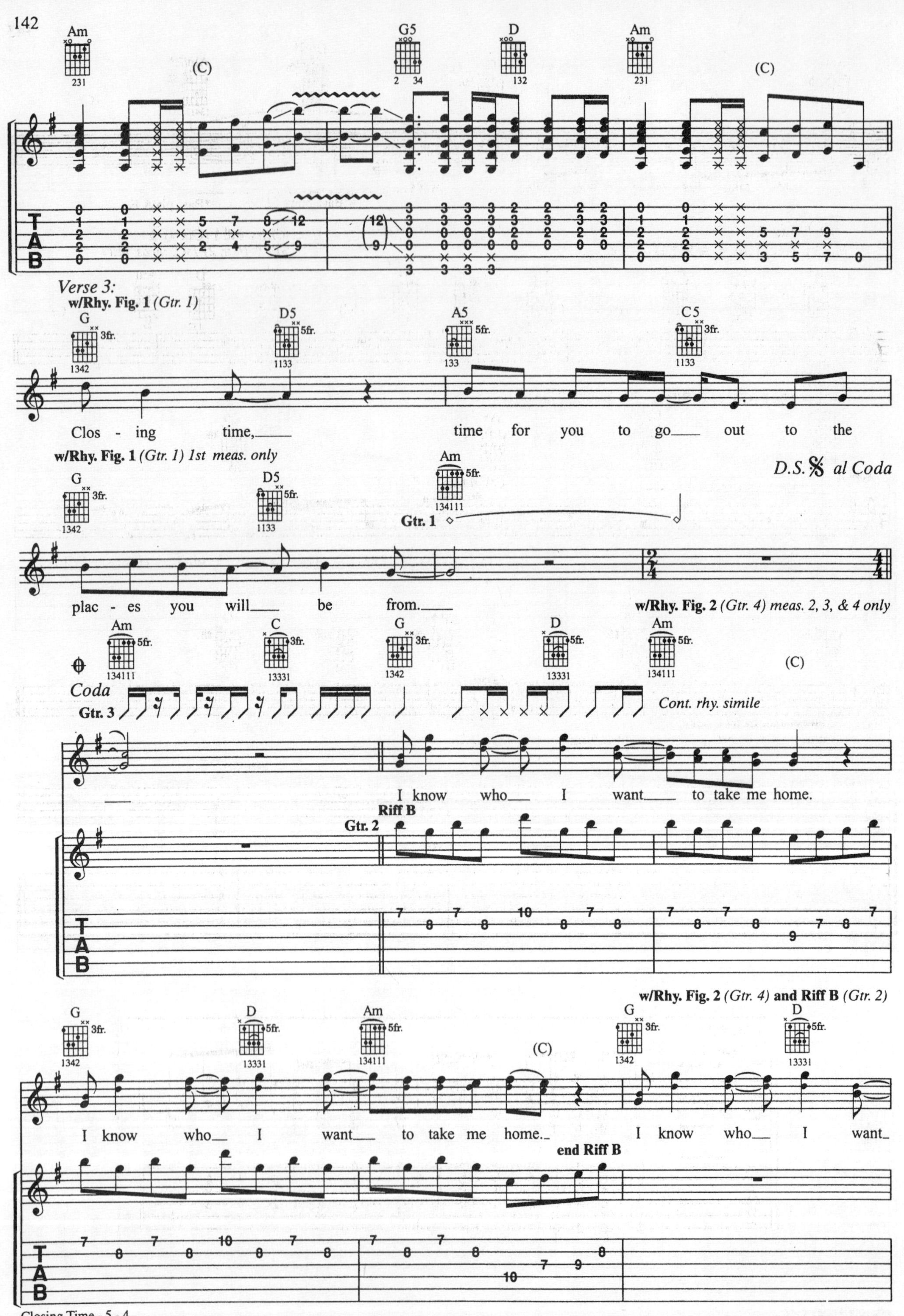
Am
G5
D
Am
(C)
Verse 3:
w/Rhy. Fig. 1 (Gtr. 1)
G
D5
A5
C5
Clos - ing time,
time for you to go out to the
w/Rhy. Fig. 1 (Gtr. 1) 1st meas. only
D.S. al Coda
plac - es you will be from.
Gtr. 1
w/Rhy. Fig. 2 (Gtr. 4) meas. 2, 3, & 4 only
Coda
Gtr. 3
Cont. rhy. simile
I know who I want to take me home.
Riff B
Gtr. 2
w/Rhy. Fig. 2 (Gtr. 4) and Riff B (Gtr. 2)
I know who I want to take me home.
I know who I want
end Riff B

Am G D/F♯* Am/E*

(C) (C)

___ to take me home, take me___ home.___

*Bass plays F♯. *Bass plays E.

Interlude 3:

w/Rhy. Fig. 2 *(Gtr. 4)* **& Riff B** *(Gtr. 2)*

w/Rhy. Fill 1 *(Gtr. 4)* **&**
Riff B *(Gtr. 2) 1st 2 meas. only*

G5 D Am (C) G5 D Am (C) G5 D Am (C)

Outro:

w/Rhy. Fig. 1 *(Gtr. 1)* **& Riff A** *(Gtr. 2) Both 2 times*

G5 (D5) A5 C5

Gtr. 4 Gtr. 4 tacet

Clos - ing time,___ ev - 'ry new be - gin - ning comes from

G D5 A5 C5 G

some oth - er be - gin - ning's end.___

Gtr. 2

rit.

Gtr. 1

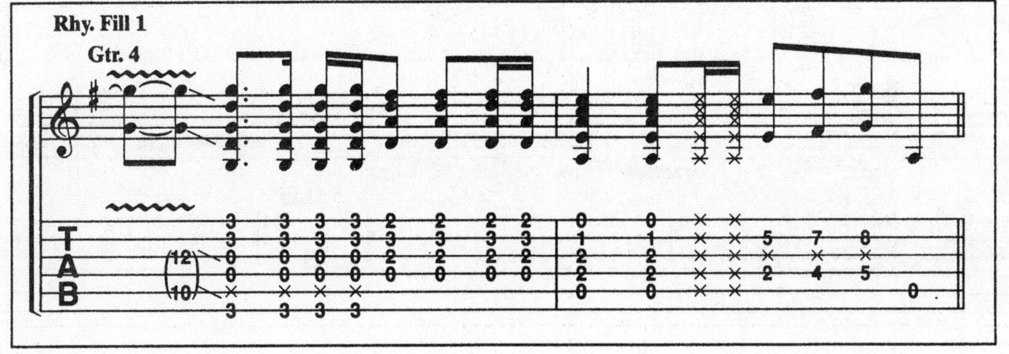

CRAZY LOVE

Words and Music by
VAN MORRISON

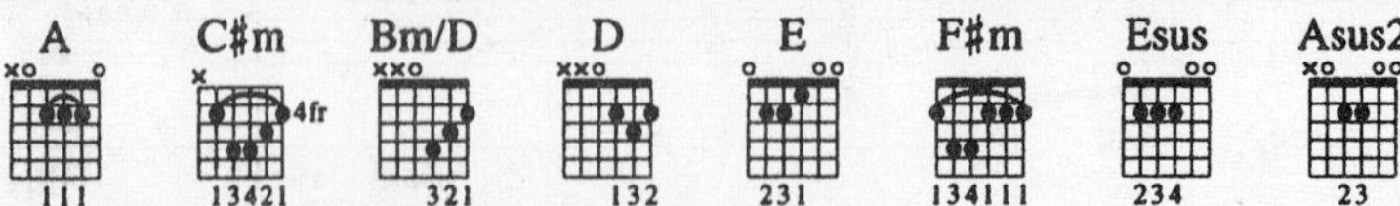

Moderately slow ♩ = 76

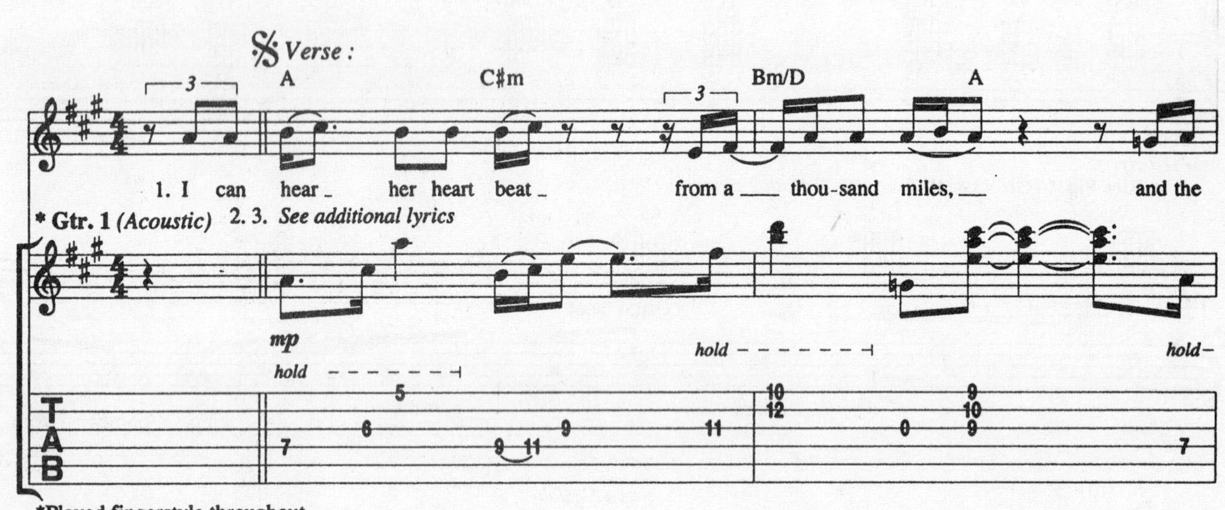

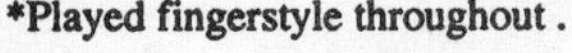

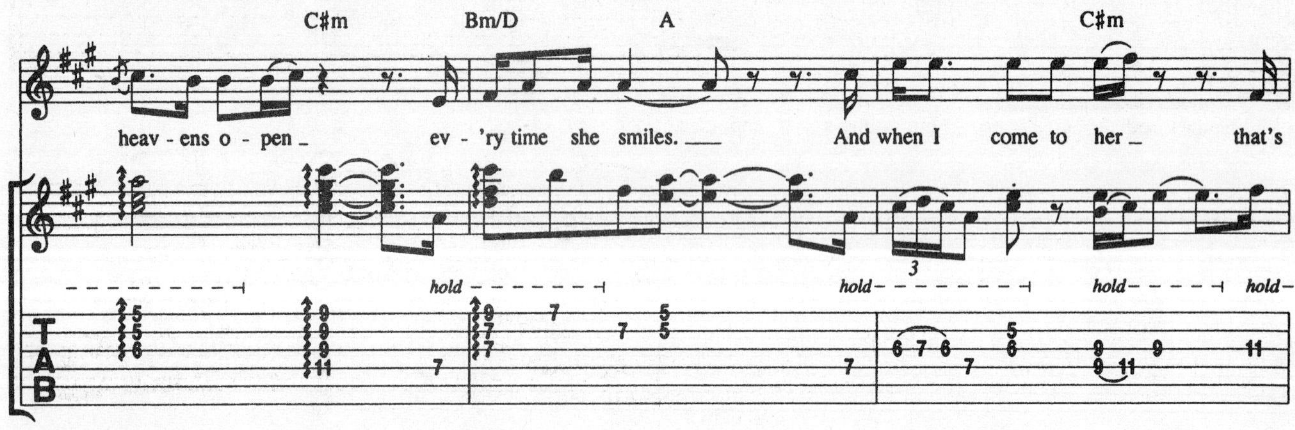

Chorus:
D
E
love, love, love, love, cra - zy love. She give me
Love, love, love, love, cra - zy love.
hold
To Coda
1.
A
C#m
F#m
A
D
N.C.(A)
love, love, love, love cra - zy love. 2. She's
Love, love, love, love, cra - zy love.
2.
D
N.C.(A)
Bridge:
E
D
A
cra - zy love. Yeah, I need her in the day - time,
cra - zy love.
I need her.
E
D
N.C.(A)
and I need her in the night.
I need her.

E D A F#m
Yeah, I want to throw_my arms___ a-round___ her_ and
I need her.
hold
hold
hold
T
A
B
Bm E A E
D.S. 𝄋 al Coda
kiss and hug_her, kiss_and hug_her tight.___
3. And when
hold
hold
hold
C#m Bm/D A
it makes___ me right-eous,
yeah, and it makes me whole.
(Ooh.___
(Ooh.___
hold
hold
hold
hold
C#m D C#m Bm A
Yeah, and it makes___ me mel-low
down in-to my soul.___ She give me
___)
(Ooh.___)
hold
hold
hold

Verse 2 :
She's got a fine sense of humor,
When I'm feeling low - down.
And when I come to her
When the sun goes down.
Take away my trouble,
Take away my grief,
Take away my heartache
In the night, like a thief.
(To Chorus :)

Verse 3 :
And when I'm returning from so far away,
She gives me some sweet lovin',
Brightens up my day.
Yeah, and it makes me righteous.
Yeah, and it makes me whole.
Yeah, and it makes me mellow
Down into my soul.
(To Chorus :)

CREEQUE ALLEY

Words and Music by
JOHN PHILLIPS and MICHELLE GILLIAM

Moderately ♩ = 120 (♫ = ♩♪)
Intro:
A7
Play 4 times
12-str. Acous. Gtr.
(w/capo II)
Cont. in slashes
Verse:
A7
12-str. Acous. Gtr.
Cont. rhy. simile
1. John and Mit-chie were get-tin' kind of itch-y just to leave the folk mu-sic be-hind.
2.3.4.6. See additional lyrics
5. Flute solo
D7
Zal and Den-ny, work-in' for a pen-ny, try'n'
A7
E7
to get a fish on the line. In a cof-fee house Se-bas-tian sat,
D7
and af-ter ev-'ry num-ber they passed the hat. Mc-
A7
Guinn and Mc-Guire's just a-get-tin' high-er in L. A., you know where that's at.

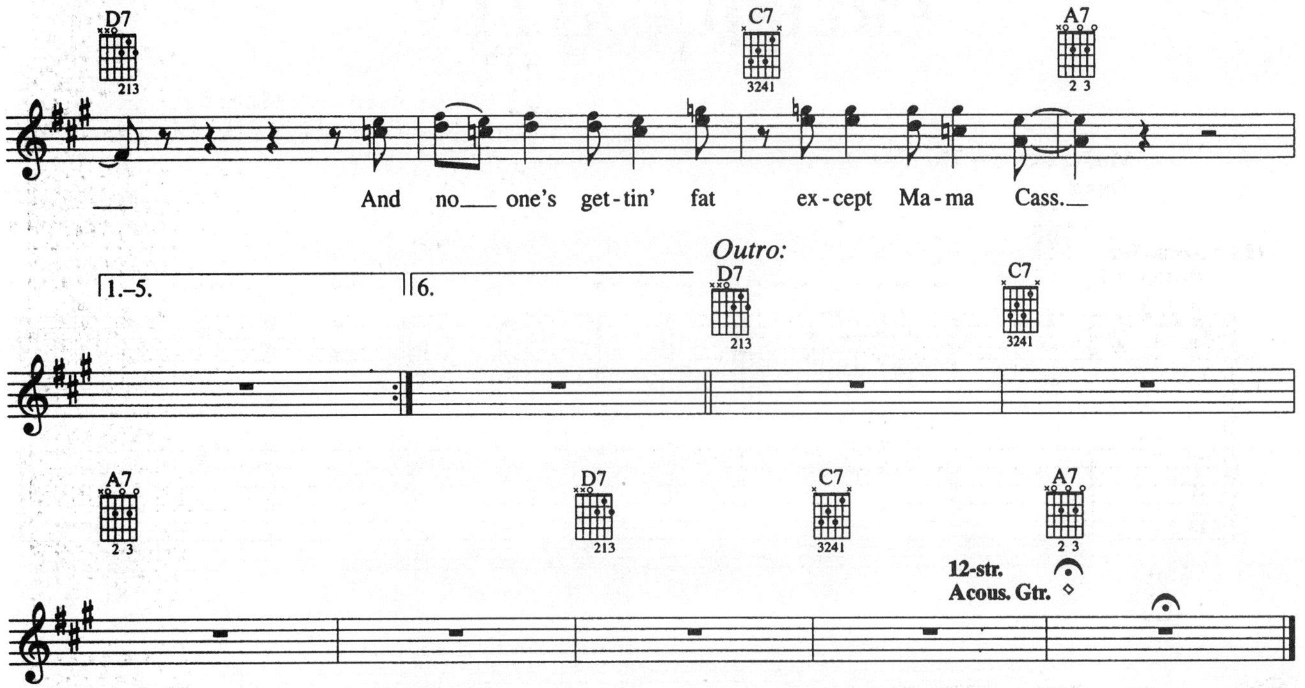

Verse 2:
Zally said, "Denny, you know there aren't many
Who can sing a song the way that you do."
"Let's go south." Denny said, "Zally, golly, don't you think that
I wish I could play guitar like you?"
Zal, Denny, and Sebastian sat, (at the Night Owl)
And after every number they passed the hat.
McGuinn and McGuire still are gettin' higher in L. A.,
You know where that's at.
And no one's gettin' fat except Mama Cass.

Verse 3:
When Cass was a sophomore, planned to go to Swarthmore,
But she changed her mind one day.
Standin' on the turnpike, thumb out to hitchhike,
Take her to New York right away.
When Denny met Cass, he gave her love bumps,
Called John and Zal and that was the Mugwumps.
McGuinn and McGuire couldn't get no higher
But that's what they were aimin' at.
And no one's gettin' fat except Mama Cass.

Verse 4:
Mugwumps, high jumps, low slumps, big bumps,
Don't you work as hard as you play?
Make-up, break-up, everything you shake up,
Guess it had to be that way.
Sebastian and Zal formed the Spoonful,
Michelle, John, and Denny gettin' very tuneful.
McGuinn and McGuire, just a-catchin' fire in L.A.,
You know where that's at.
And everybody's gettin' fat except Mama Cass.
(To Flute Solo:)

Verse 6:
Broke, busted, disgusted, agents can't be trusted,
And then she wants to go to the sea.
Cass can't make it, she says, "We'll have to fake it."
We knew she'd come eventually.
Greasin' on American Express cards, tents, low rent,
But keepin' out the heat's hard.
Duffy's good vibrations and our imaginations
Can't go on indefinitely.
And California dreamin' is becoming a reality.

CRYING

Words and Music by
ROY ORBISON and JOE MELSON

Verse 2:
I thought that I was over you,
But it's true, so true.
I love you even more than I did before,
But darling, what I can I do?
For you don't love me, and I'll always be...

Chorus 2:
Crying over you,
Crying over you.
Yes, now you're gone and from this moment on
I'll be crying, crying, crying, crying.
Yeah, crying, crying over you.

CROSS EYED MARY

Words and Music by
IAN ANDERSON

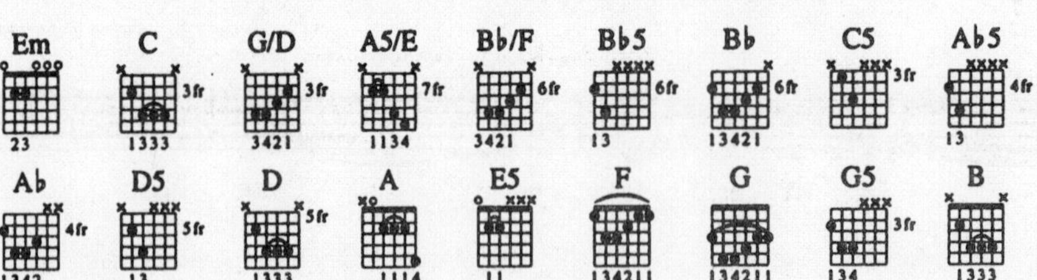

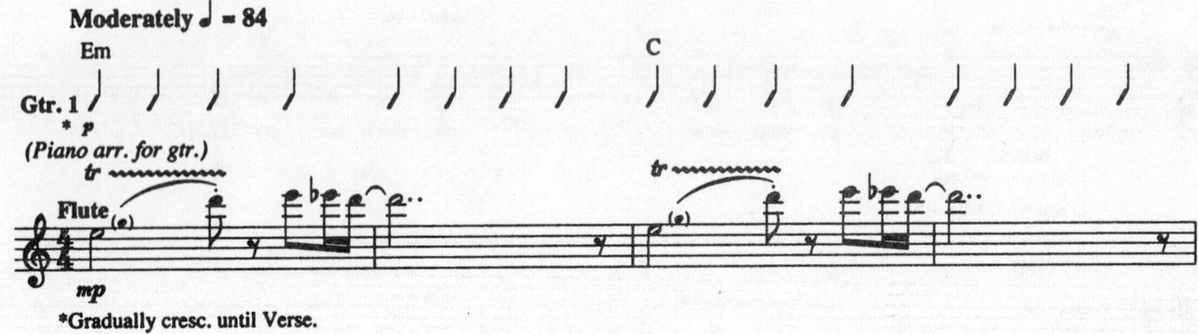

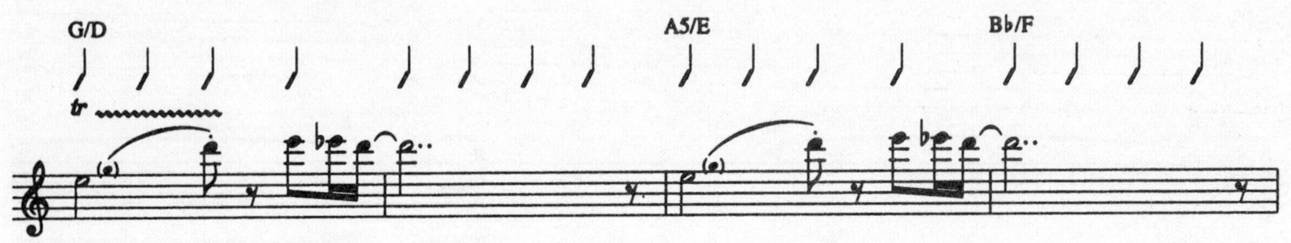

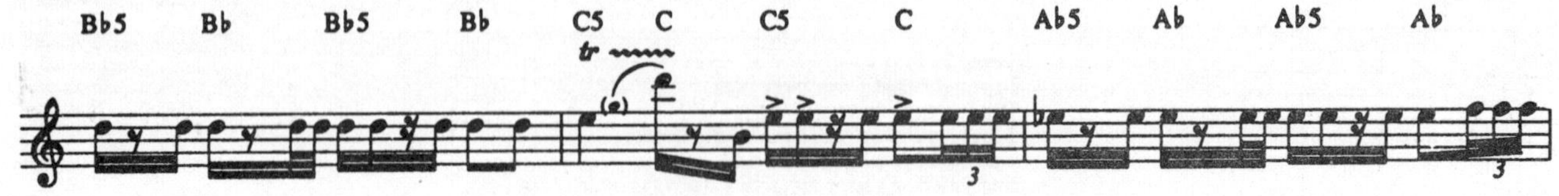

Bb
A
E5
tr
Verses 1 & 2:
Rhy. Fig. 1A
Em
F
1. Who would be a poor man, a beg-gar man, a thief,
2. See additional lyrics
Gtr. 2 Rhy. Fig. 1
G
D
end Rhy. Fig. 1A
if he had a rich man in his hand.
end Rhy. Fig. 1
w/Rhy. Figs. 1 (Gtr. 2) & 1A (Gtr. 1)
Em
F
And who would s-teal the can-dy from a laugh-ing ba-by's mouth if

G
D
he could take it from the mon-ey man?

Chorus:
N.C.(Am)
G5
N.C.(Am)
G5
Cross-eyed Mar - y, a-goes jump - ing in a-gain. She
T
A
B

N.C.(Am)
G5
N.C.(Am)
G5
signs no con - tract, but she al - ways plays the game. She
T
A
B

N.C.(B♭m)
A♭5
N.C.(B♭m)
A♭5
dines in Hamp - stead Vil-lage on ex - pense ac-count - ed gruel. And the
T
A
B

To Coda
N.C.(Bbm)
Ab5
C
D
C
B
A
B
Gtr. 2
jack - knife - bar - ber
drops her off at school.
Hey!
end Rhy. Fig. 2
Gtr. 1
Solos:
w/Rhy. Fig. 2 (Gtr. 1)
Gtr. 1
7
Verse 3:
w/Rhy. Fig. 1A (Gtr. 1, 2 times)
Em
F
Laugh-ing in the play - ground, gets no kicks from lit - tle boys, would
Gtr. 2
G
D
rath - er make it with a letch - ing grey.

Verse 2:
Laughing in the playground,
Gets no kicks from little boys,
Would rather make it with a letching grey.
Or maybe her attention is drawn by Aqualung,
Who watches the railings as they play.
(To Chorus:)

DEDICATED TO THE ONE I LOVE

Words and Music by
LOWMAN PAULING and RALPH BASS

Verses 2 & 4:
G
3fr.
134211
D7
213
Am
231
G/B
2
Nylon-str.
Gtr.
fore dawn.__ Each night be-fore_ you go to bed,__ my ba - by,__
Cont. in slashes
T
A
B
C
32 1
whis-per a lit-tle______ prayer for me, my ba - by.__ And tell__________
Eb7
4fr.
3241
D7sus
To Coda
Bridge 1:
all the stars a - bove____________ this is ded-i-cat-ed to the one I love.
Life can nev-er be ex-
Cont. rhy. simile
G7
131211
act - ly like we want it to be. I could be___ sat - is - fied__________
know - ing__ you__ love me. There's one thing I want you to do, es -
A7
2 3
pe - cial - ly for me. And it's some - thing__ that ev - 'ry - bod - y needs.__________

Verse 3:

G Am G/B C D7

Nylon-str. Gtr.

While I'm far a - way from you, my ba - by, whis-per a lit-tle

G Am G/B D7 Em Bm

prayer for me, my ba - by. Be - cause it's hard for me, my ba - by,

D7sus

Interlude:

G7

Cont. rhy. simile

and the dark - est hour is just be - fore dawn.

Bridge 2:

Bm Em G C Bm C Bm

Nylon-str. Gtr.

If there's one thing I want you to do es - pe - cial - ly for me, and it's

E♭7 D7

D.S. 𝄋 al Coda

some - thing that ev - 'ry-bod - y needs... 4. Each night be - fore you

Coda

Em C

Nylon-str. Gtr.

Cont. rhy. simile

love. This is ded-i-cat - ed, this is ded - i - cat-ed to the one I

To the one I love. To the one I

A G

Nylon-str. Gtr.

love. This is ded - i - cat - ed, this is ded - i - cat - ed. This is ded - i - cat - ed.

love. To the one I love.

DANIEL

Words and Music by
ELTON JOHN and BERNIE TAUPIN

G
E7
Am
G
I can see the red tail - lights head - ing for Spain. Oh, and
Well, Dan - iel says it's the best place he's ev - er seen. Oh, and
F
G
Am
I can see Dan - iel wav - ing good - bye. God, it looks
he should know, he's been there e - nough. Lord, I
To Coda
F
G
F/G
like Dan - iel; must be the clouds in my eyes.
miss Dan - iel. Oh, I miss him so

1.
C
G
2.3.
C
much.
Oh,
T
A
B
Chorus:
F6
C
F/C
C
Dan - iel, my brother - er, you are old - er than me. Do you still
F
C
Dm7/C
C
G/B
feel the pain of the scars that won't heal? Your eyes have died,
Am
G
F
A♭6
4fr.
Acous. Gtr.
but you see more than I.
Dan - iel, you're a
1.
D.S. 𝄋
2.
D.S. 𝄋 al Coda
C
A7
Dm7
G7
Dm7
G7
Resume rhy. fig. simile
star in the face of the sky.

Coda
C
F
Oh God, it looks like Dan - iel.
Outro:
G
F/G
C
F
Cont. Intro rhy. simile
Must be the clouds in my eyes.
Synth. Flute
13 12 15 13 12
12 14 13 12 15 13
Gsus
C
F/C
C
Acous. Gtr.
13 12 17 15 18 17 15
17

DATE RAPE

Words and Music by
BRAD NOWELL

Em
her heart_raced as he walked through the door_ and took an emp - ty seat next to her at the bar._
Rhy. Fig. 2
Gtr. 2
B
"My brand new car is parked right out - side._
Am
How'd ya like to go for a ride?"_ And she said,
Em
"Wait a min-ute I have to think."_ He said,_"That's fine._ May I please buy you a drink?"
B
One drink turned in - to three or four_ and they
C
B
left and got in - to his car___
Em
and they

C
B
Em
drove a-way some place real far.
Bridge
Em
Now, babe, the time has come. _
One night in jail, it was get-ting late. ___
End Rhy. Fig. 2
simile on repeat
Gtr. 2: w/ Rhy. Fill 1, 2nd time
B
Em
How'd ya like to have a lit-tle fun?" _ And she said, ___
He was butt-raped _ by a large in-mate, _ and he screamed. _
"If we could on-ly please be on ___ our way, _
But the guards paid no at-ten
G
D
B
Em
___ I will not run." _
- tion to his cries.
That's when things got out of con-trol.
That's when things got out of con-trol. The
Rhy. Fill 1
Gtr. 2
T
A
B

Chorus
Em B C Am E5 B C Am Em B C Am Em B C
She did-n't want to, he had his way. She said, "Let's Go." He said, "No way!"
mo-ral of the date rape sto-ry, it does not pay to be drunk and hor-ny.
Rhy. Fig. 3
B
Come on babe it's your luck-y day. Shut your mouth we're gon-na do it my way.
But that's the way it had to be. They locked him up and threw a-way the key. Well, I
To Coda
rit.
Come on ba-by don't be af-raid, if it was-n't for date rape I'd nev-er get laid.
can't take pit-ty on men of his kind, e-ven though he now takes it in the be-hind.
End Rhy. Fig. 3
rit.
Guitar Solo
A Tempo
Gtr. 2: w/ Rhy. Fig. 1, 1st 2 meas., 2 times, simile
N.C.
Em
Gtrs. 3 & 4 (dist.)
8va
loco
f
full
P.H.

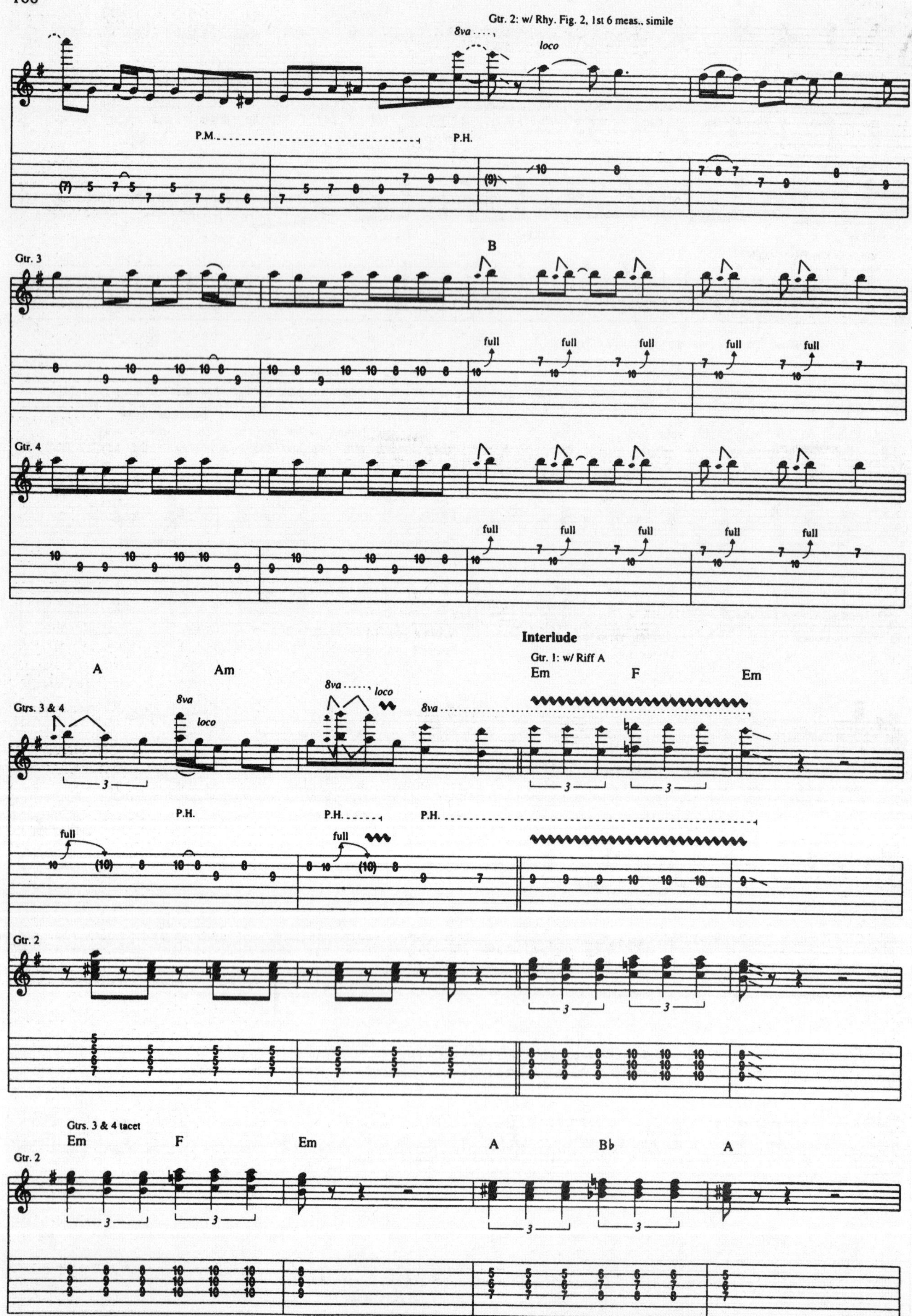

Gtr. 2: w/ Rhy. Fig. 2, 1st 6 meas., simile
8va
loco
P.M.
P.H.
Gtr. 3
B
full
Gtr. 4
Interlude
Gtr. 1: w/ Riff A
A
Am
Em
F
Em
Gtrs. 3 & 4
8va
loco
P.H.
Gtr. 2
Gtrs. 3 & 4 tacet
Em
F
Em
A
B♭
A

Gtr. 2
Em
F
Em
G
F#
F
Verse
Gtr. 2: w/ Rhy. Fig. 1, simile
Em
2. He fin-ished up and he start-ed the car. He turned a-round and drove back to the bar.
Am
B
C
B
He said, "Now ba-by don't be sad, in my o-pin-ion you weren't half-bad." She
Gtr. 2
Cmaj7
Em
picked up a rock, threw it at the car, hit him in the head, now he's got a big scar. Come on
Am
B
C
B
party people won't you lis-ten to me. Date Rape Sty-lee.
Gtr. 2: w/ Rhy. Fig. 2, simile
Em
The next day she went to her drawer, looked up her lo-cal at-tor-ney at law.

B
Am
went to the phone and filed the po - lice re - port
and then she took the guy's
Em
ass to court._ Well,
the day he stood
in front of the judge_ he
screamed,_ "She lies _ that
lit - tle slut!"_
B
The judge knew he was full of shit _
C
B
and he gave him twen - ty - five
Em
C
B
Em
D.S. al Coda
years.
And now his heart is filled with
tears. ________
Coda
Faster ♩ = 220
Gtr. 2: w/ Rhy. Fig. 3, simile
4
B
That's the way it had to be. ___
They locked him up and threw a - way the key. ___ Well, I can't take pit - y on
men of his kind, ___ e - ven though he now takes it in the be - hind. ___ DATE RAPE.
Outro
Em
Rhy. Fig. 4
Gtr. 2
B
C
G
Gtr. 1 Riff B
End Riff B

Gtr. 1: w/ Riff B
Em
B
C
G
Huh, huh, huh.
End Rhy. Fig. 4
Gtr. 2: w/ Rhy. Fig. 4, simile
Gtr. 1 tacet
Em
B
C
G
Na, na, na, na, na, na.
Na, na, na, na, na, na.
Em
B
C
G
Ba, na, na, na, na, na.
La da, da, la, la, la.
E5 B5 D5 A5 E5 B5 D5 A5 E5 B5 D5 A5
She did - n't want to, she did - n't want to, she did - n't want to,
Gtrs. 2 & 3
E5 B5 D5 A5 E5
she did - n't want to TAKE IT!

THE DISTANCE

All gtrs. tune down 1/2 step:
⑥ = E♭ ③ = G♭
⑤ = A♭ ② = B♭
④ = D♭ ① = E♭

Words and Music by
Edward Kowalczyk

*Doubled by Acous. Gtr. throughout.

Verse 1:
w/Rhy. Figs. 2 (Elec. Gtr. 2) & 2A (Elec. Gtr. 3) 4 times
Am
C
Am
C
Am
C
I've__ been__ to pret - ty build - ings,
end Rhy. Fig. 2
hold
end Rhy. Fig. 2A
Elec. Gtr. 4 out
end Rhy. Fig. 2B
Am C Am C Am C Am C
all in search_ of you.__ I__ have_ lit__ all__ the can - dles,
Verses 2 & 3:
w/Rhy. Figs. 2 (Elec. Gtr. 2) & 2A
(Elec. Gtr. 3) 4 times
Am C Am C Am C
sat in all__ the pews.__ 2. The des - ert__ had__ been done__
car__ be - came_ the church_

w/Rhy. Fig. 1 (Elec. Gtr. 1) 2 times, 2nd time only
Am C Am C Am C Am C
— be - fore,_ but I did - n't e - ven_ care.____ I got sand_ in both_
— and I,____ the wor-ship - per_ of_ si - lence there. In a mo - ment, peace_ came o -
Am C Am C Am C
— my shoes_ and scor - pi - ons in my_ hair,____ I saw___ that . . .
- ver me___ and the one who was beat - in' my heart ap - peared_ and . . .
w/Rhy. Fig. 1 (Elec. Gtr. 1)
w/Rhy. Figs. 2 (Elec. Gtr. 2), 2A (Elec. Gtr. 3), & 2B (Elec. Gtr. 4)
Chorus:
Dsus2 Am C
Oh,_ the dis - tance is____ not_ do - a - ble___ in these bod - ies_ of
Elec. Gtrs. 2, 3, & 4
Rhy. Fig. 3
end Rhy. Fig. 3
w/Rhy. Fig. 3 (Elec. Gtrs. 2, 3, & 4)
Am C Dsus2
clay, my broth - er.________ Oh,_ the dis - tance, it makes_ me un - com - f'ta - ble._
w/Rhy. Fig. 1 (Elec. Gtr. 1)
w/Rhy. Figs. 2 (Elec. Gtr. 2), 2A (Elec. Gtr. 3), & 2B (Elec. Gtr. 4)
Am C Am C Dsus
— Guess it's nat - 'ral to feel this way.__________ Oh,
Elec. Gtrs. 2, 3, & 4

1.

Elec. Gtr. 4 out

C(9) G5 Dsus D

let's hold out___ for some - thin' sweet - er,___ spread your wings___ and fly.___

T A B

3 3 3 3 3 3
3 3 3 3 3 3 3 3
2 2 0 0 0 0 0 2
0 0 0 0 0 0 0 0
3
3 3

3 3 3 3 3 3 2 2
3 3 3 3 3 3 3 3 0
2 2 2 2 2 2 2 2 2 2 2 0
0 0 0 0 0 0 0 0 0 0 0 0

w/Rhy. Figs. 2 *(Elec. Gtr. 2)* & 2A *(Elec. Gtr. 3)*

D.S. 𝄋

2.

Am C Am C C(9) G5

3. My are we locked___ in - to these___

T A B

3 3 3 3 3
3 3 3 3 3 3 3
3 3 0 0 0 0 0
2 2 0 0 0 0 0
0 0 0 0 0 0 0
3
3 3

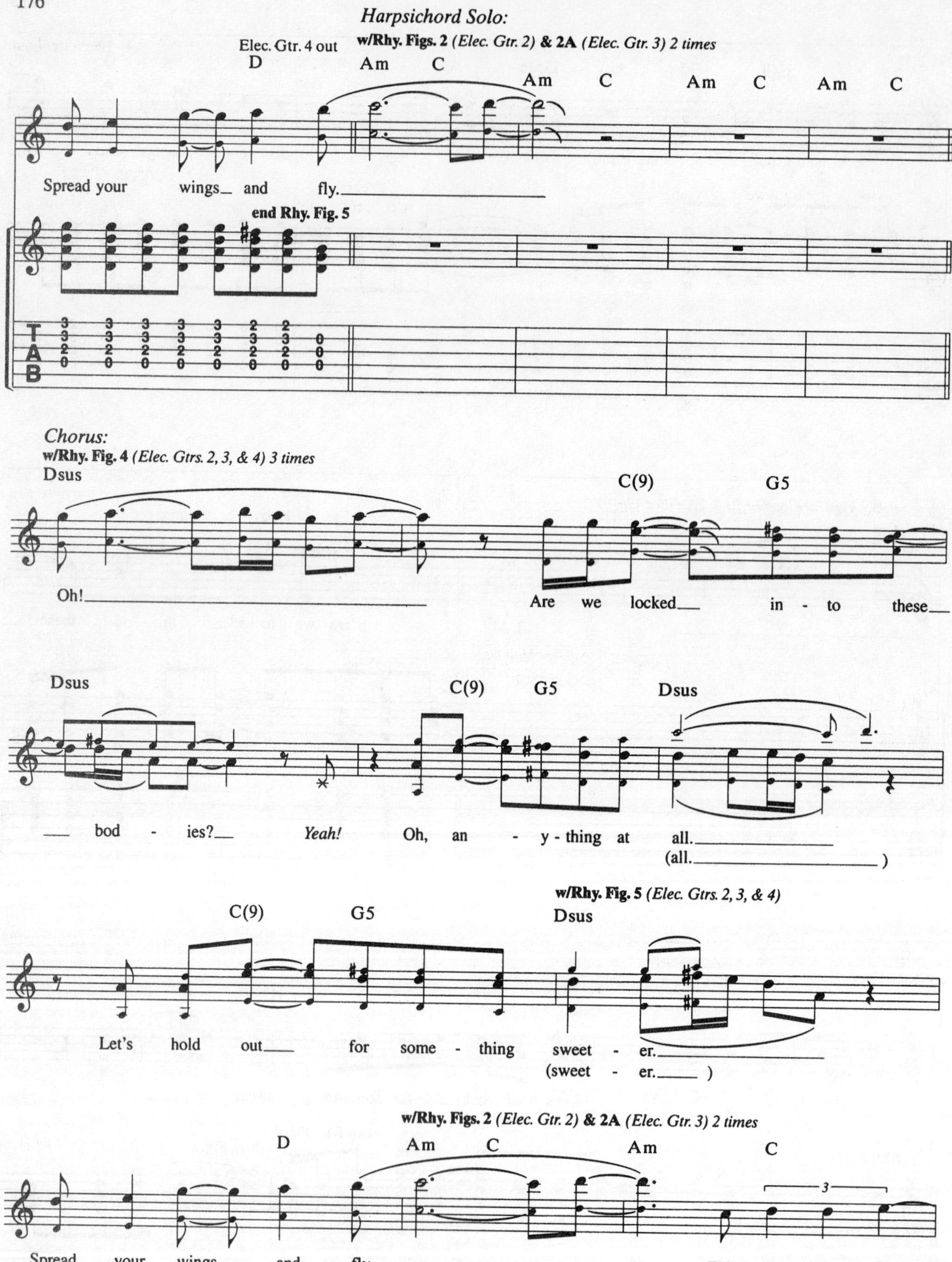
Harpsichord Solo:
Elec. Gtr. 4 out
w/Rhy. Figs. 2 (Elec. Gtr. 2) & 2A (Elec. Gtr. 3) 2 times
D
Am C
Am C Am C Am C
Spread your wings_ and fly.
end Rhy. Fig. 5
T
A
B
Chorus:
w/Rhy. Fig. 4 (Elec. Gtrs. 2, 3, & 4) 3 times
Dsus
C(9) G5
Oh!
Are we locked_ in - to these_
Dsus
C(9) G5
Dsus
_ bod - ies?_ Yeah! Oh, an - y - thing at all.
(all.)
w/Rhy. Fig. 5 (Elec. Gtrs. 2, 3, & 4)
C(9) G5
Dsus
Let's hold out_ for some - thing sweet - er.
(sweet - er._)
w/Rhy. Figs. 2 (Elec. Gtr. 2) & 2A (Elec. Gtr. 3) 2 times
D
Am C
Am
C
3
Spread your wings_ and fly.
This dis - tance is_

Outro:
w/Rhy. Figs. 2 (Elec. Gtr. 2), 2A (Elec. Gtr. 3), & 2B (Elec. Gtr. 4) till fade
Am C Am C Am C
— dream - ing, — we're al - read - y — there — to - night. —
(Let him come in - to the cit - y. Let him
Elec. Gtr. 5 (12-string)
Riff A
Am C Am C Am C
find his luck-y pen-ny. Let him put it in his pock - et and shake — it all a - round. Let him
end Riff A
w/Riff A (Elec. Gtr. 5)
w/Rhy. Fig. 1 (Elec. Gtr. 1) tacet 1st time only
Am C Am C
— dream - ing. —
come in - to the cit - y. Let him find his luck - y pen - ny. Let him
*Tacet 1st time only.
Repeat and fade
Am C Am C
This dis - tance is —
put it in his pock - et and shake — it all a - round. Let him)

DO YOU WANT TO KNOW A SECRET?

Words and Music by
JOHN LENNON and PAUL McCARTNEY

*Elec. Gtr. 2 ad lib. simile on repeats.

DOIN' TIME

Words and Music by
BRAD NOWELL, ADAM HORVITZ, ADAM YAUCH, MARSHALL GOODMAN,
GEORGE GERSHWIN, DuBOSE and DOROTHY HEYWARD and IRA GERSHWIN

Verse

Gtr. 1: w/ Rhy. Fig. 1, 2 times, 1st & 3rd times.
Gtr. 1: w/ Rhy. Fill 1, 2nd time

Gm C Gm C

1. Me and my girl we got this re - la - tion - ship.
2. Oh, take this veil from off my eyes.
3. E - vil, I've come to tell you that she's e - vil, most def - i - nite - ly.

Gm C Gm C

I love her so - bad, but she treats me like a...
My burn - ing sun will some - day rise. So
E - vil, or - n'ry, scan - dal - ous and e - vil, most def - i - nite - ly. The

Gm C Gm C

On lock down like a pen - i - ten - tia - ry, she spreads her
what am I gon - na be do - in' for a wife? Said I'm gon - na play with my - self.
ten - sion is get - ting hot - ter, I'd like to

Gm C 1., 2. Gm C

lov - in' all o - ver and when she gets home there's none left for me.
Show them now we've come off the shelf. So what.
hold her head un - der

3. Gm C

wa - ter, oh.

Verse

Gtr. 1 tacet

Gm C6 Gm C6

Me and my girl, we've got a re - la -

Gtr. 2 (clean) Rhy. Fig. 2 End Rhy. Fig. 2

mf

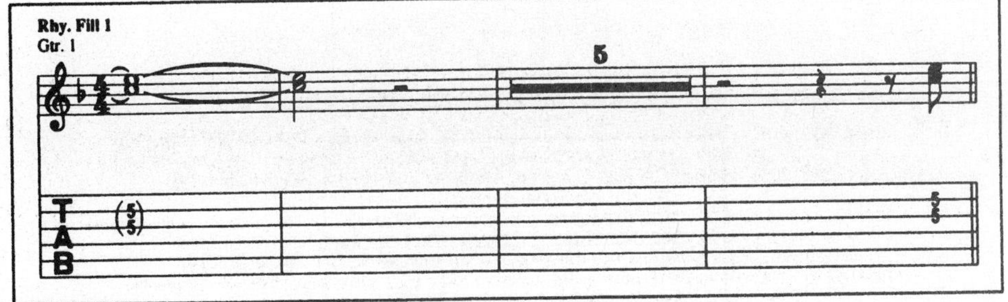

Gtr. 2: w/ Rhy. Fig. 2, 3 times, simile
Gm
C6
Gm
C6
- tion - ship, uh. Me and my girl, hmm, we got a re - la -

Gm
C6
Gm
C6
- tion - ship, mm. My girl, we got a re - la -

Gm
C6
w/ Voc. Fill 1
Gm
C6
D.S. al Coda
- tion ship, oh. And my girl, huh, got a re - la -

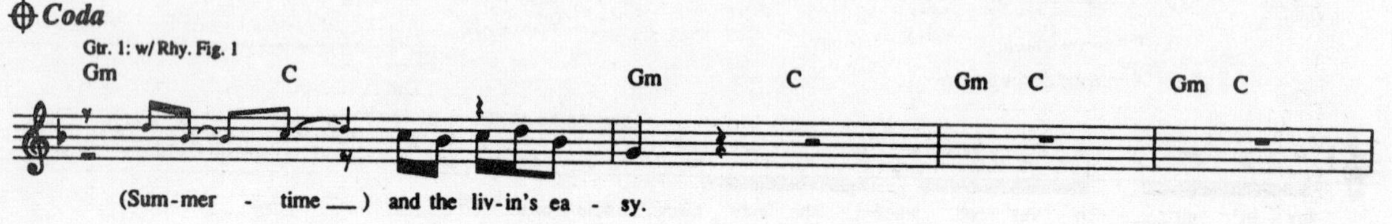
Coda
Gtr. 1: w/ Rhy. Fig. 1
Gm
C
Gm
C
Gm C
Gm C
(Sum - mer - time) and the liv - in's ea - sy.

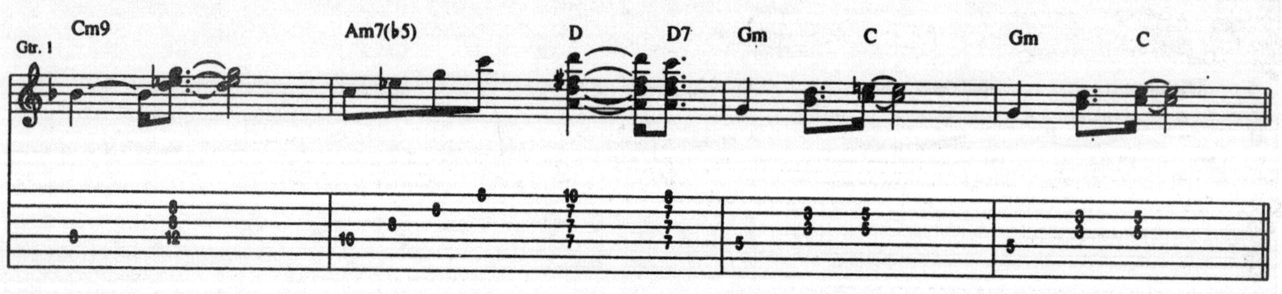
Gtr. 1
Cm9
Am7(♭5)
D
D7
Gm
C
Gm
C

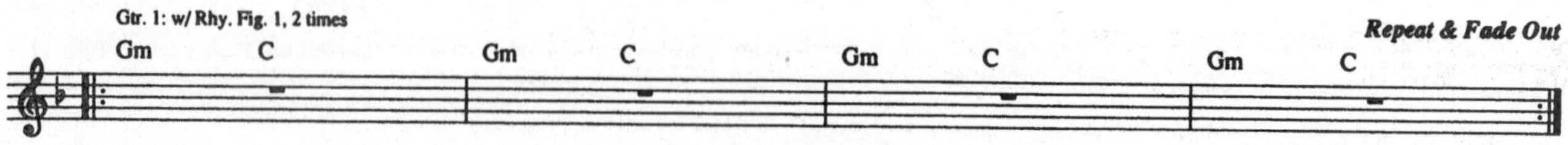
Gtr. 1: w/ Rhy. Fig. 1, 2 times
Gm
C
Gm
C
Gm
C
Gm
C
Repeat & Fade Out

Voc. Fill 1
So take a

DON'T SPEAK

Words and Music by
GWEN STEFANI and ERIC STEFANI

Cm
Gm
Fm
B♭
E♭
B♭
C
— as though your let-ting go. And if it's real, then I don't want to know.
Chorus:
Fm
B♭m
E♭
C
Gtr. 2 (Acous.)
Rhy. Fig. 2
Don't speak, I know just what you're say - ing. So, please stop ex - plain-
Gtr. 1
B♭m
C
Fm
B♭m
C
- ing. Don't tell me 'cause it hurts.

Fm
B♭m
E♭
C
Don't speak,
I know what_ your think - ing.
I don't need_ your rea-
B♭m
C
Fm
B♭m C
end Rhy. Fig. 2
- sons.
Don't tell_ me 'cause_ it hurts._
2. Our
Verse 2:
w/Rhy. Fig. 1 (Gtr. 1)
Cm
Gm
Fm
B♭
Gm
Fm
B♭
mem-o - ries,_
they can be_ in-vit - ing, but some are al - to - geth - er might - y
fright - 'ning.
As-
Cm
Gm
Fm
B♭
Gtr. 2
_ we die,_
both
you and I._
Gtr. 1

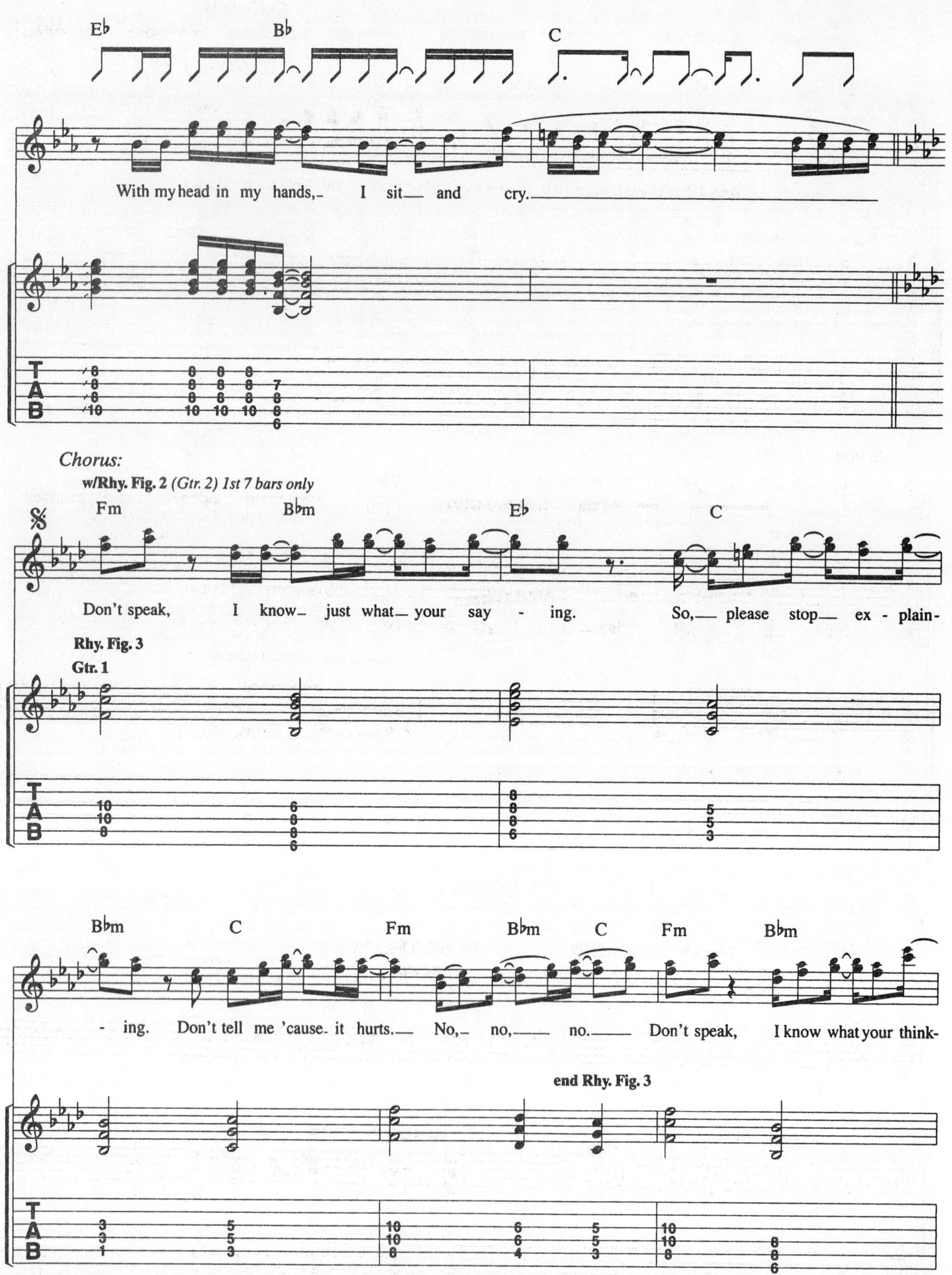
E♭
B♭
C
With my head in my hands, I sit and cry.
Chorus:
w/Rhy. Fig. 2 (Gtr. 2) 1st 7 bars only
Fm
B♭m
E♭
C
Don't speak, I know just what your say - ing. So, please stop ex - plain-
Rhy. Fig. 3
Gtr. 1
B♭m
C
Fm
B♭m
C
Fm
B♭m
- ing. Don't tell me 'cause it hurts. No, no, no. Don't speak, I know what your think-
end Rhy. Fig. 3

To Coda
F5 E♭5 C5 A♭5
Gtr. 2
E♭ C B♭m C
- ing. And I don't need your rea - sons. Don't tell_ me 'cause_ it hurts._
Gtr. 1
Bridge:
D♭ A♭ C♭ G♭
It's all end - ing._ I got - ta stop pre - tend - ing who we
D♭sus2/A D♭sus2 D♭sus2/E♭ D♭sus2 D♭sus2/E♭ A♭
are.

Guitar Solo:
Cm Gm Fm B♭ Cm Gm Fm B♭
Gtr. 2
Gtr. 3 (Acous.)
mf
rake
Gtr. 1
Cm Gm Fm B♭ Gm Cm Fm
rake
3
3

D.S. 𝄋 al Coda

Interlude:

Cm Gm Fm B♭ Fm B♭

You and me, I can see us dy - ing. Are we?

Gr. 1

TAB: 4 5 5 4 5 5 3 3 5 3 3 5 | 1 1 3 1 1 3 3 3 3 3 3 3 | 1 1 3 1 1 3 3 3 3 3 3 3

Gtr. 2 *(w/slight dist.)*

Gtr. 4 out

mf

TAB: 3 3 1 (×8) | 3 3 3 1 (×8)

w/last bar of Rhy. Fig. 2 *(Gtrs. 1 & 2)*

w/Rhy. Fig. 2 *(Gtr. 2)*
w/Rhy. Fig. 3 *(Gtr. 1) 2 times*

Coda

Fm B♭m C Fm B♭m

Don't tell me 'cause it hurts. *I know what you're say-
(Ah, ee, ah, ee, ah. Ah.

*Vocal ad lib. on repeats.

E♭ C B♭m C Fm B♭m C

- ing. So, please stop ex - plain - ing. Don't speak. Don't speak. Don't speak. No.
Ah. Ah.

Fm B♭m E♭ C

I know what you're think - ing. And I don't need your rea-
Ah, ee, ah, ee, ah. Ah. Ah.

Repeat and fade

B♭m C Fm B♭m C

- sons. I know you're good. I know you're good. I know you're real good. Oh.
)

DOMINO

Words and Music by
VAN MORRISON

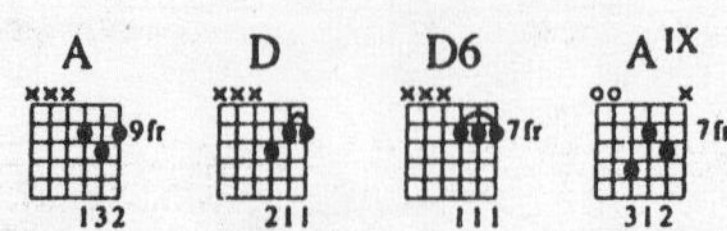

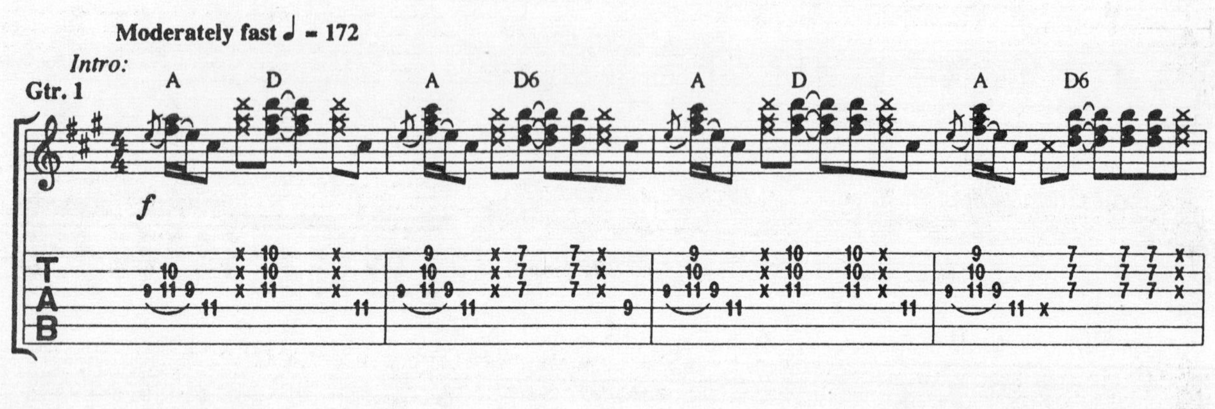

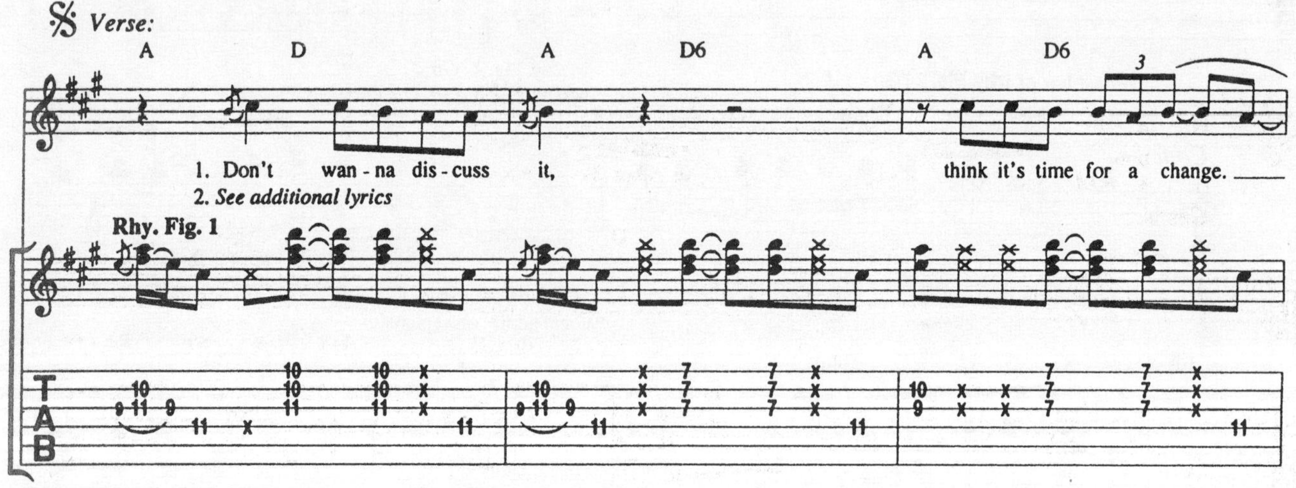

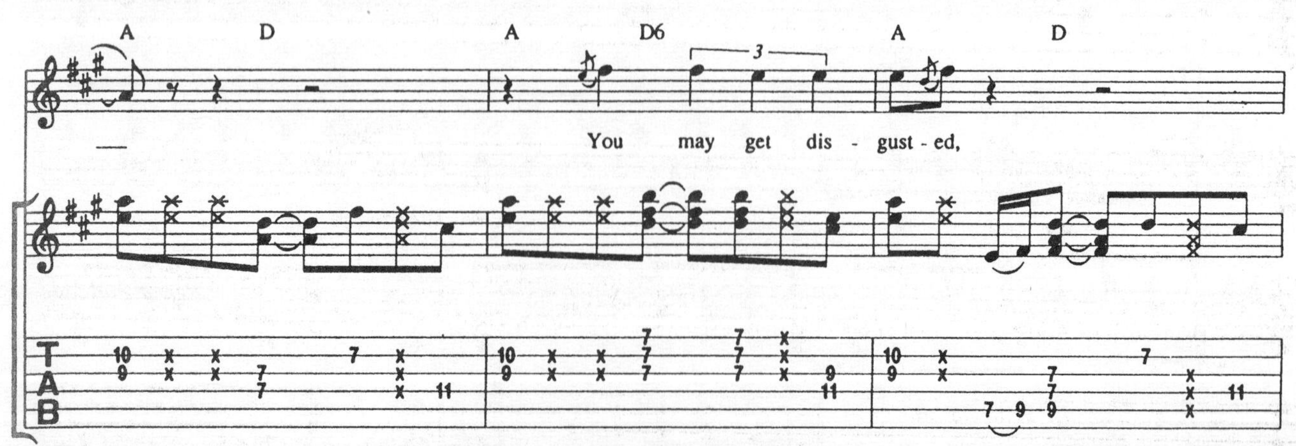

A
D6
A
start think - in' that I'm strange.
end Rhy. Fig. 1
A
D6
A
D
A
D6
That case I'll go un - der-ground, get some heav - y
A
D
A
D6
A
D
rest. Nev - er have to wor - ry,
A
D6
A
D
a - bout what is worst, or what is best. Get it!
Chorus:
A
D
A
D
A
D
Oh Dom - in - o, Al - right. Roll me o - ver, Ro - me -
A
D
A
D
A
D
o. There you go. Lord, have mer - cy. I said,

A D A D A D
Oh Dom-in-o, Roll me o-ver, Ro-me-
hold
A D A D A D
o. There you go. Say it a-gain. I said,
N.C.(B) (E) A D6 A D6
Oh, oh, Dom-in-o. I said,
(B) (E) A D6 A D6
To Coda
Oh, oh, Dom-in-o.
Dig it!
(2nd time) Hey, Mr. D.J.,
P.M.

Verse 2:
There's no need for argument.
There's no argument at all.
And if you never hear from him,
That just means he didn't call.
Or vice-a-versa, that depends on wherever you're at.
Alright.
And if you never hear from me, that just means I would rather not.
(To Chorus:)

DON'T LET ME BE MISUNDERSTOOD

Words and Music by
BENNIE BENJAMIN, SOL MARCUS
and GLORIA CALDWELL

Chorus:
Elec. Gtr. 1
I'm just a soul whose in - ten - tions are good,_ Oh, Lord, please don't let me
1.
w/Riff A (Elec. Gtrs. 1 & 2)
N.C.
be mis - un - der - stood.
2.
Bridge:
Elec. Gtr. 1
Cont. rhy. simile
stood. If I seem edg - y I want you to know
that I nev - er mean to take it out on you._ Life has its prob - lems and
*Bass plays F♯.
D.S. 𝄋 al Coda
I get my share,_ and that's one thing I nev - er mean to do,_ 'cause I love you.
Chorus:
Coda
Elec. Gtr. 1
sim - ple thing I've done. I'm just a soul whose in - ten - tions are good,_
w/Riff A (Elec. Gtrs. 1 & 2)
Repeat and fade
N.C.
oh, Lord, please don't let me be mis - un - der - stood. Yes,

DOWN ON THE CORNER

Words and Music by
JOHN C. FOGERTY

C
F
G
1333
134211
134211

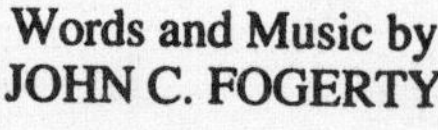

Moderately 𝅗𝅥 = 100

Intro:

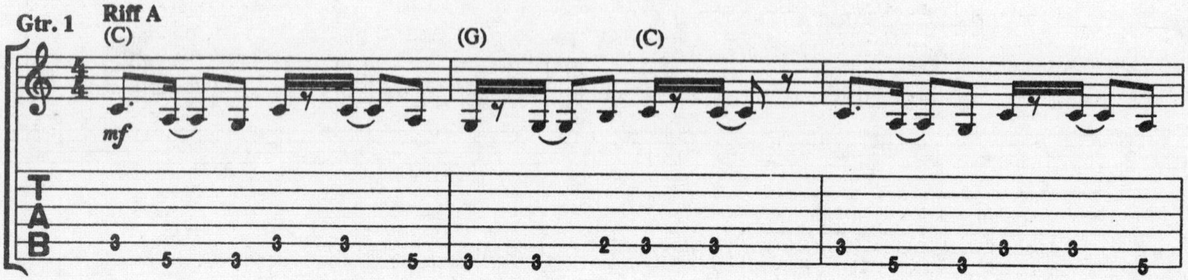

Gtr. 1
Riff A
(C)
(G)
(C)
mf

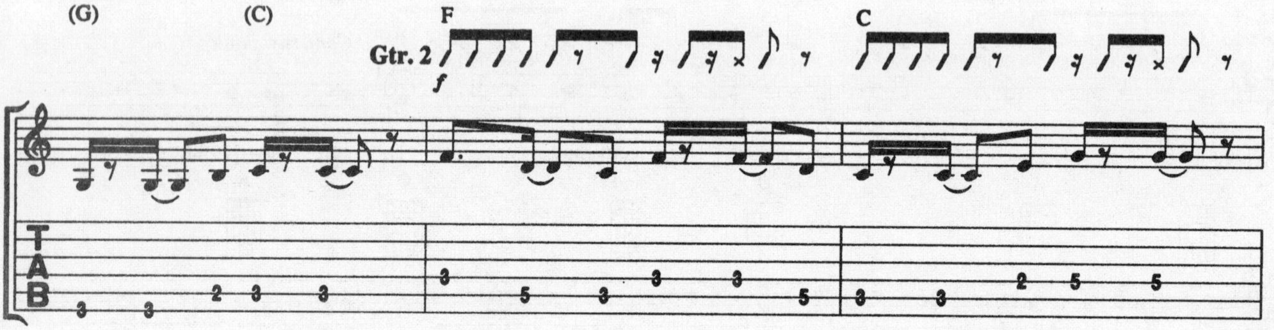

(G)
(C)
F
C
Gtr. 2
f

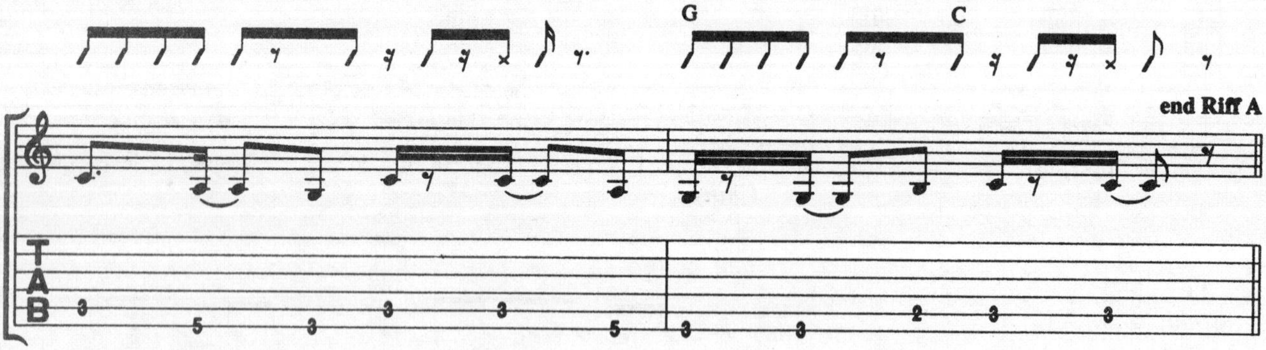

G
C
end Riff A

Verses 1 & 2:
w/Riff A *(Gtr. 1)*

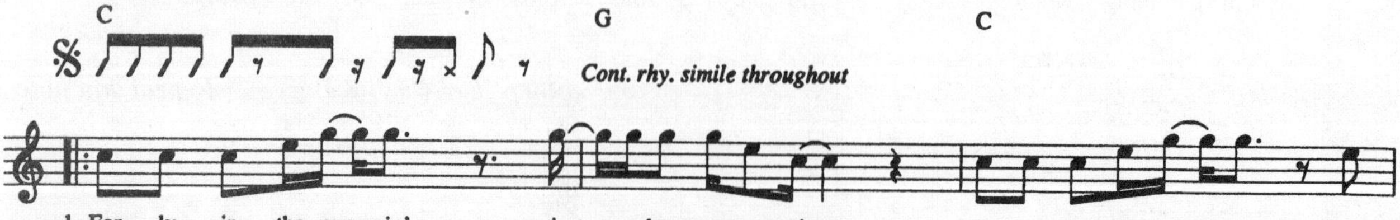

C
G
C
Cont. rhy. simile throughout

1. Ear - ly in the eve - nin' just _ a-bout sup-per time, _ o - ver by the court-house, they're
2. *See additional lyrics*

G C F C
start - ing to un - wind. _ Four kids on the cor - ner trying to bring you up; _
Chorus:
G C F C
Wil - ly picks _ a tune _ out and he blows it on the harp. Down on the cor - ner,
G C F C G C
out here in the street, Wil - ly and the Poor - boys _ are playin'; _ bring a nick - el; tap your feet.
Interlude:
C G C
Gtr. 2
T
A
B
C G C F
Riff B
C G C
end Riff B

Chorus:
F C G C
Down on the cor - ner, out here in the street; Wil - ly and the
F C G C
Poor boys ___ are playin'; _ bring a nick - el; tap your feet.
Interlude:
C G C
Verse 3:
w/Riff A (Gtr. 1, 1st 4 bars only)
C G C
You don't need a pen - ny just to hang a - round, _ but if you got a nick - el won't you
w/Riff B (Gtr. 1)
G C F C
lay your mon-ey down. _ O - ver on the cor - ner, there's a hap - py noise. _
Chorus:
G C F C
Peo - ple come _ from all ___ a - round _ to watch the mag - ic boy. _ Down on the cor - ner,
Repeat & fade
G C F C G C
out here in the street, Wil-ly and the Poor boys ___ are playin'; _ bring a nick - el; tap your feet.

Verse 2:
Rooster hits the washboard,
People just gotta smile.
Blinky thumps the gut bass
And solos for a while.
Poor-boy twangs the rhythm out,
On his kalamazoo.
And Willy goes in to a dance
And doubles on kazoo.
(To Chorus:)

DRAG THE WATERS

Words and Music by
VINCENT ABBOTT, DARRELL ABBOTT,
PHILIP ANSELMO and REX BROWN

Verses 1 & 2:
F5 E5 F5 E5 N.C. F5 E5 N.C.
1. A smack on the wrists is the words from the mouth of the out-
2. See additional lyrics
Gtr. 1
Rhy. Fig. 2
- sid-ers, law-yers, po-lice.
F5 E5 N.C.
A small price to pay for the dope
and the guns and the rape, it should all be o-kay.
C5 B5
Your
end Rhy. Fig. 2
w/Rhy. Fig. 2 (Gtr. 1)
F5 E5 N.C.
fa-ther is rich, he's the judge, he's the man, he's the god that got your sen-tence re-duced.
F5 E5 N.C.
But in the back of his mind, he well knows what he'd find if he looked

Chorus:
F5 E5
a lit - tle deep - er in you.
In you!
Gtr. 1
P.M.
F5 E5 N.C.
Drag the wa - ters some more.
Like nev - er be - fore.
P.M.
(G5)
Whoa!
Ah!
How!
P.M.
(A5)
Yeah!
How!
Yeah!
P.M.

w/Rhy. Fig. 1 (Gtr. 1) 4 times
C5/G D5/A Eb5/Bb F5 E5 F5 E5
How!
Whoa!
P.M.
P.M.
N.C. F5 E5 F5 E5 N.C. F5 E5 F5 E5
Drag the wa - ters some more.
Like nev - er be - fore.
1.
2.
N.C. F5 E5 F5 E5 N.C. N.C.
Drag the wa - ters some more.
Interlude:
F5 E5 F5 E5
Gtr. 2
f
grad. bend
w/flanging & echo effects, & wah as filter effects
hold
Gtr. 1

F5 E5
1½
grad. bend 1/2
F5 E5
Guitar Solo:
N.C.
Gtr. 2
w/flange echo & wah used as filter
P.M.
w/delay

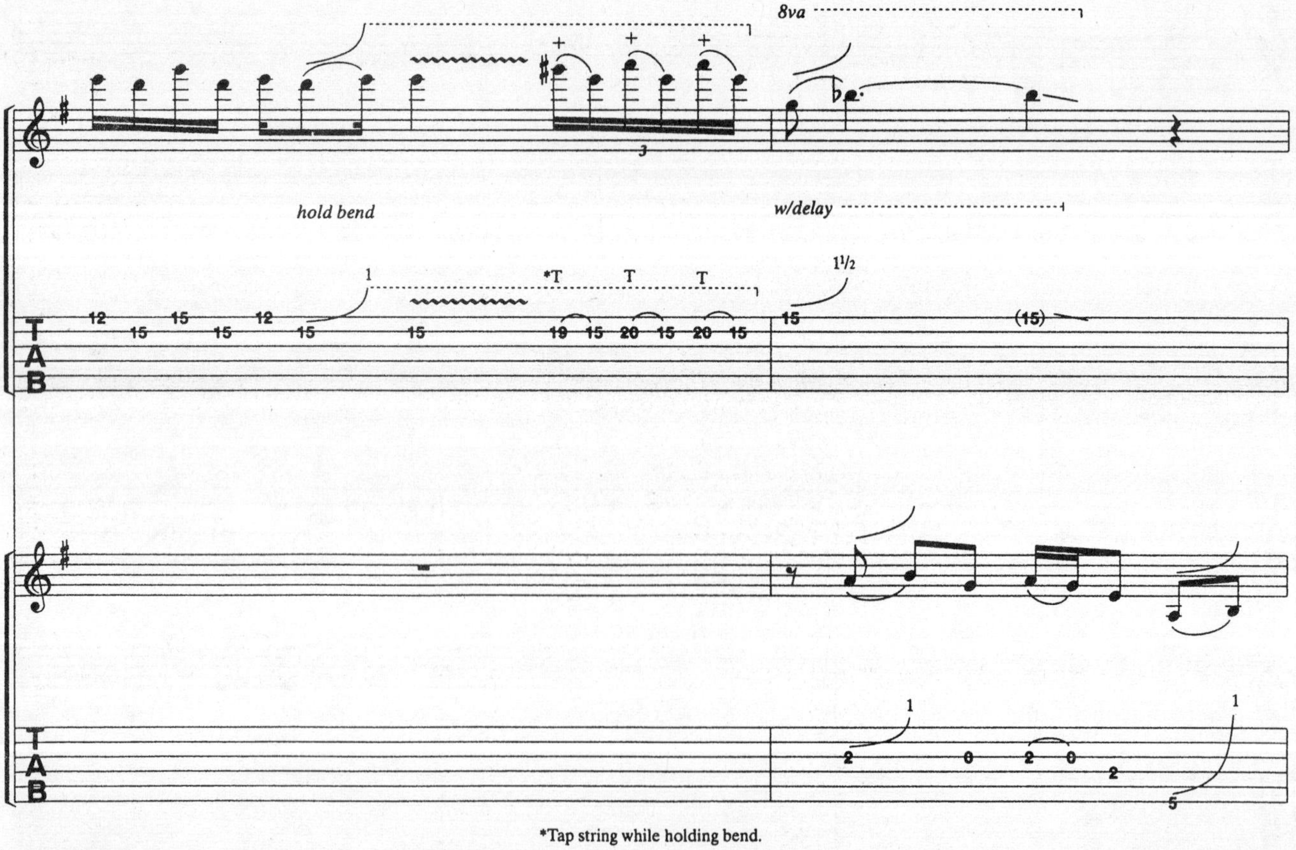

*Tap string while holding bend.

(F5) (E5)
P.M.
8va
w/delay
1½
(F5) (E5)
1½
P.M.
(8va)
w/delay
2½

Chorus:
w/Rhy. Fig. 1 (Gtr. 1) 4 times
F5 E5
F5 E5
N.C.
F5 E5
F5 E5
N.C.
Yeah!
Ha!
Drag the wa - ters some more.
Like nev - er be - fore.
8va
Gtr. 2
F5 E5
F5 E5
N.C.
F5 E5
F5 E5
N.C.
Drag the wa - ters some more.
Double-time feel
F5 E5
F5 E5
N.C.
F5 E5
F5 E5
Drag the wa - ters some more.
Gtr. 2
2½
Gtr. 1
P.M.
P.M.
P.M.
P.M.

N.C. F5 E5 F5 E5 N.C.

Like nev - er. be - fore.________ Drag the wa - ters some more.

1½ 2 1

T A B

15 (15) 15 12 15 (15)

P.M. P.M.

1 1 1 1

2 0 2 0 2 2 0 2 0 2

0 5 3 1 2 0 0 0 0 3 1 2 0 0 0 0 0 5

F5 E5 F5 E5 N.C.

1 1/2

17 15 17 15 17 17 14 (14)

P.M. P.M.

grad. bend

1 1/2 1

3 1 2 0 0 0 0 3 1 2 0 0 0 0 0 2 0 2 0 2 5 (5)

See what it is— in - side that fuck - in' lie.
Huh! Huh!
Huh! Huh! Ah!—
Outro Chorus:
Half-time feel
w/Rhy. Fig. 1 (Gtr. 1) 2 times
F5 E5 F5 E5
N.C.
Drag the wa - ters some more.—
F5 E5 F5 E5 N.C.
Like nev - er be - fore.—
F5 E5 F5 E5 N.C. F5 E5 F5 E5 G5 A5 B♭5 A5 B♭5 B5
Drag the wa - ters some more.—
Ah!
Gtr. 1
P.M.
*Gtr. 2 ad libs. trem. bar dives, pick scrapes and feedback until end.

Verse 2:
Sweet is the slice and the lips
You're gonna have that woman.
She is your favorite lay.
Promised, you swore, that no one had been there
And she was gonna keep it that way.
Let it move in, you got thin
And got high and your money went
And so did your friends.
But she's by your side and her smile
Cannot hide the premonition of the beckoning end,
The end.
(To Chorus:)

DRIVE

Words and Music by
RIC OCASEK

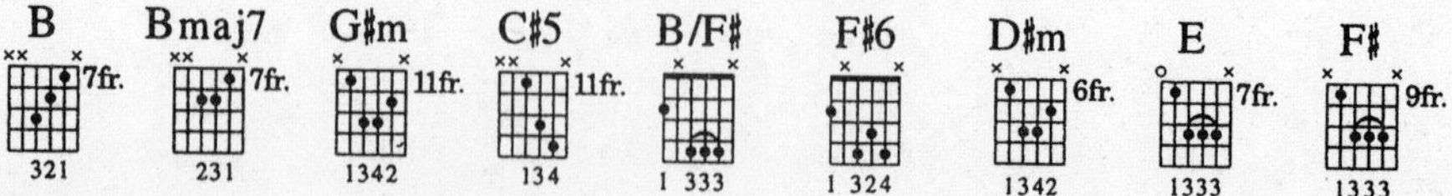

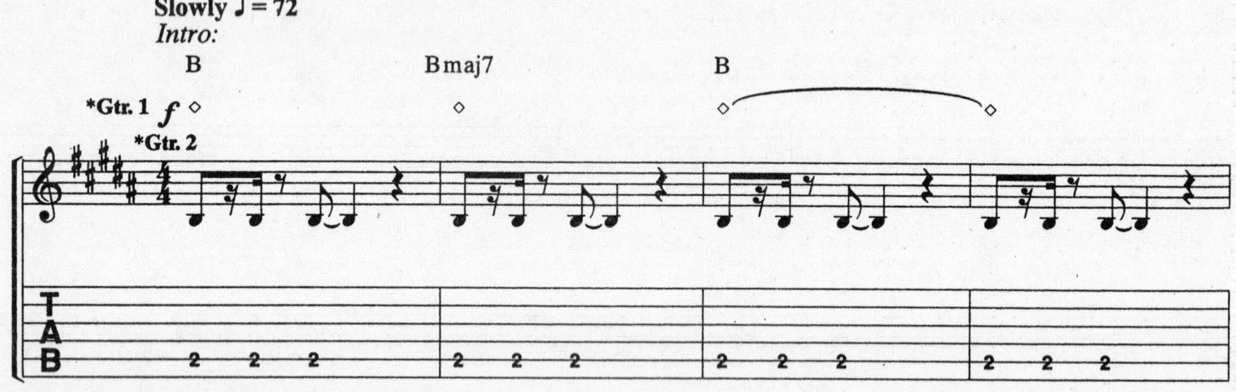

*All gtrs. are keybds. arr. for gtr. throughout.

**Rhy. Fig. 1 includes both gtrs.

Pre-Chorus:
B
G♯m
Rhy. Fig. 2
so great?
you break?
You can't go on
To Coda
C♯5
G♯m
C♯5
end Rhy. Fig. 2
think - in'
noth - in's wrong.
But now,
Chorus:
B/F♯
F♯6
B
who's gon - na drive you home
to - night?

Verse 2:
w/Rhy. Fig. 1 (Gtrs. 1 & 2) 4 times
B
Bmaj7
B
Who's gon - na pick you up__ when you___ fall?__
T
A
B
2 2 2
2 4
Bmaj7
Who's gon - na hang it up___ when_
B
Bmaj7
__ you___ call?_ Who's gon - na pay_ at - ten - tion to your_
B
___ dreams?_ Yeah, who's gon - na plug your ears_
Pre-Chorus:
w/Rhy. Fig. 2 (Gtrs. 1 & 2)
Bmaj7
B
G♯m
___ when you_______ scream?_ You can't_ go on_
C♯5
G♯m
C♯5
______ think - in' noth - in's wrong.___ But now,_

Chorus:
B/F♯
F♯6
Interlude:
B
who's gon- na drive you home
to - night?
Gtr. 3
hold throughout
G♯m
Cont. rhy. simile
B
G♯m
D♯m
Fa fa fa.
Fa fa fa.

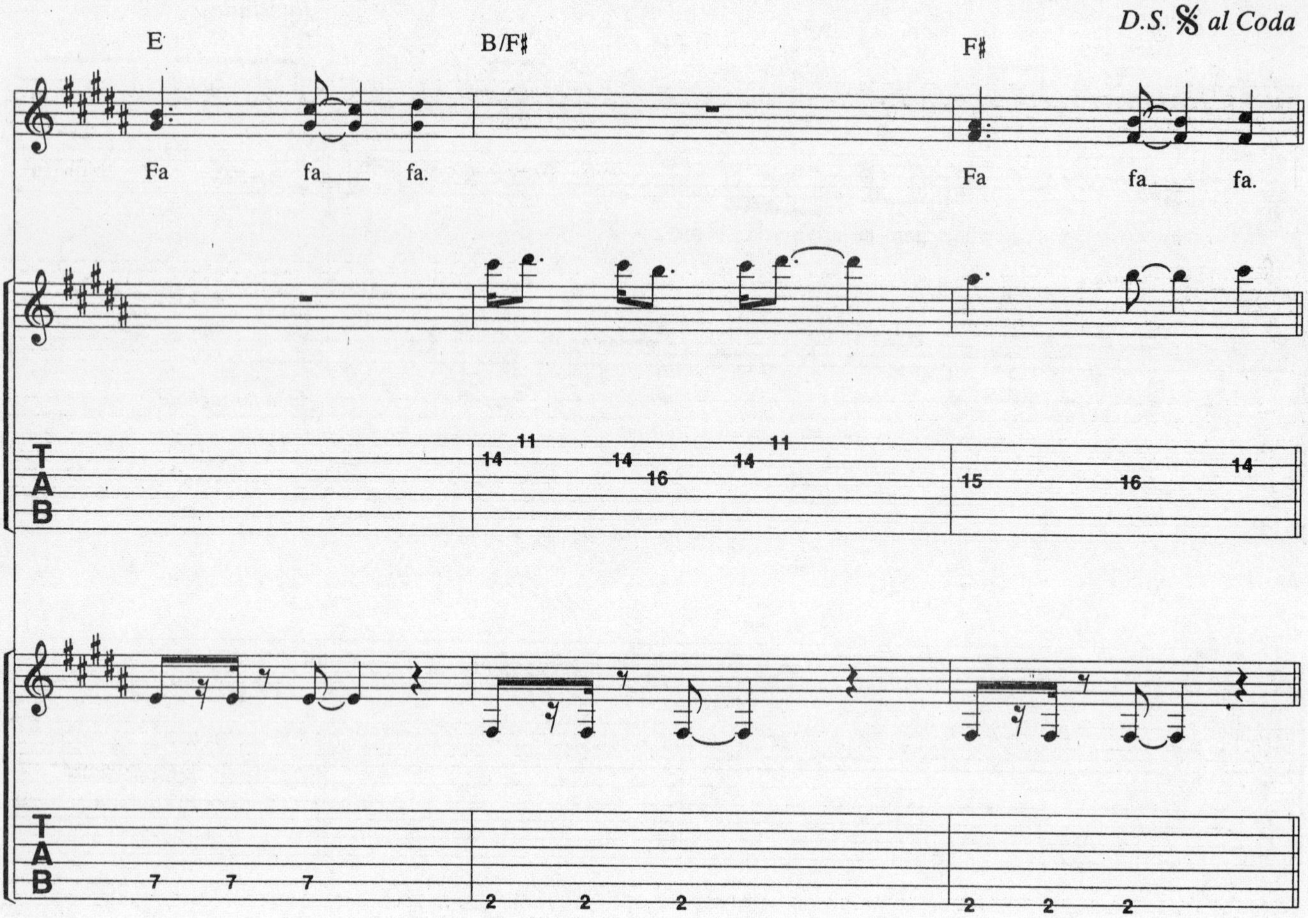

D.S. 𝄋 al Coda
E
B/F♯
F♯
Fa fa___ fa.
Fa fa___ fa.
T
A
B
14 11 14 16 14 11
15 16 14
7 7 7
2 2 2
2 2 2

Chorus:
Coda
C♯5
B/F♯
F♯6
Cont. rhy. simile
But now,___ who's gon - na drive you home_ to - night?_
T
A
B
4 4 4
2 2 2
2 2 2

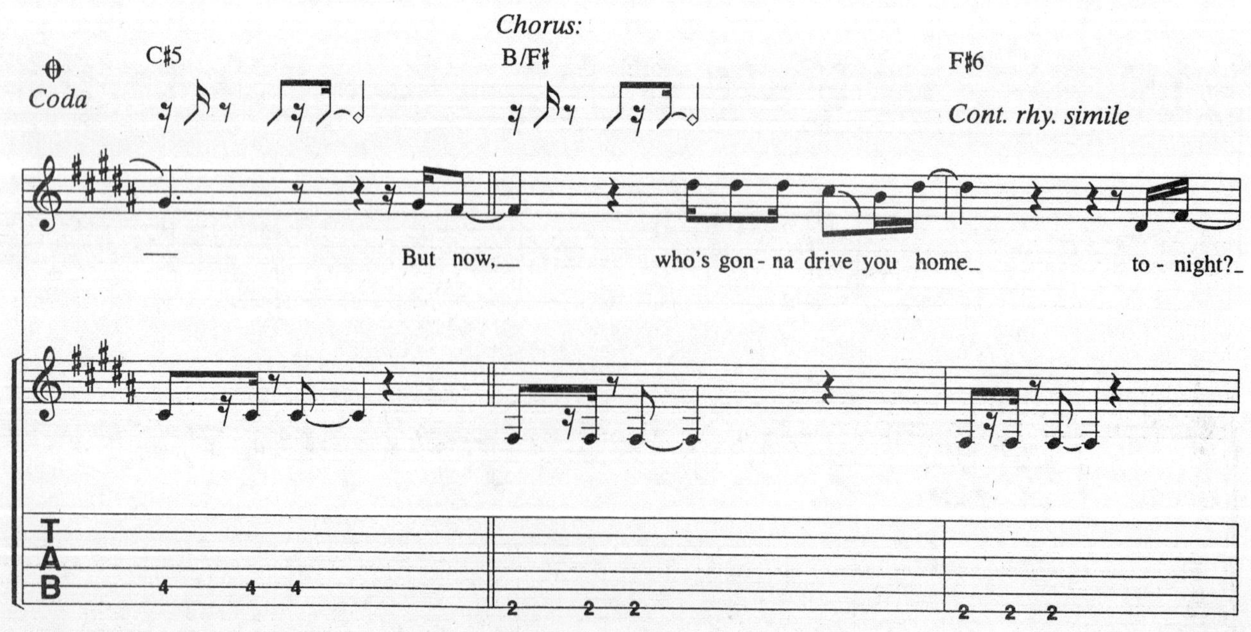

B
G♯m
C♯5
Ho,
you know you can't go on
think - in'
G♯m
B/F♯
noth - in's wrong.
Who's gon - na drive you home
F♯6
B
to - night?

ERUPTION

Words and Music by
EDWARD VAN HALEN, ALEX VAN HALEN,
MICHAEL ANTHONY and DAVID LEE ROTH

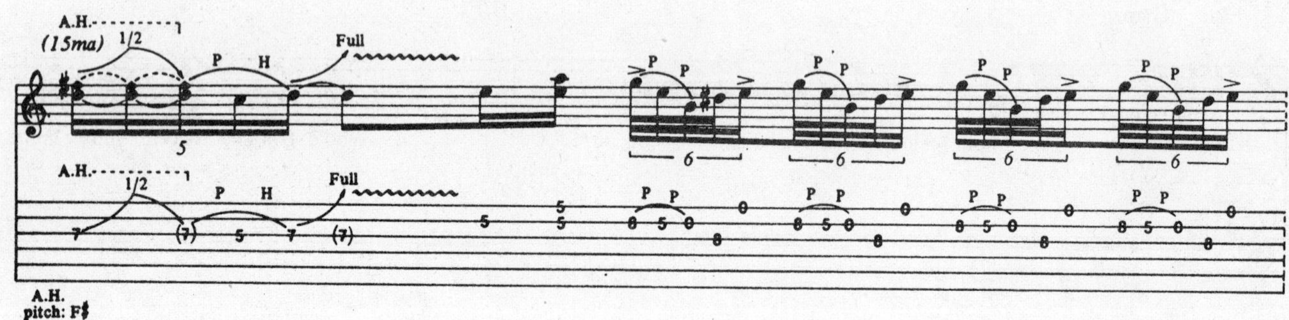

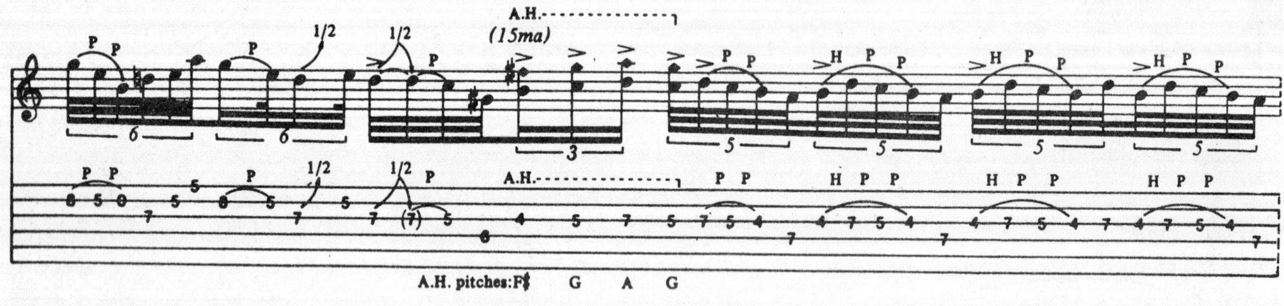

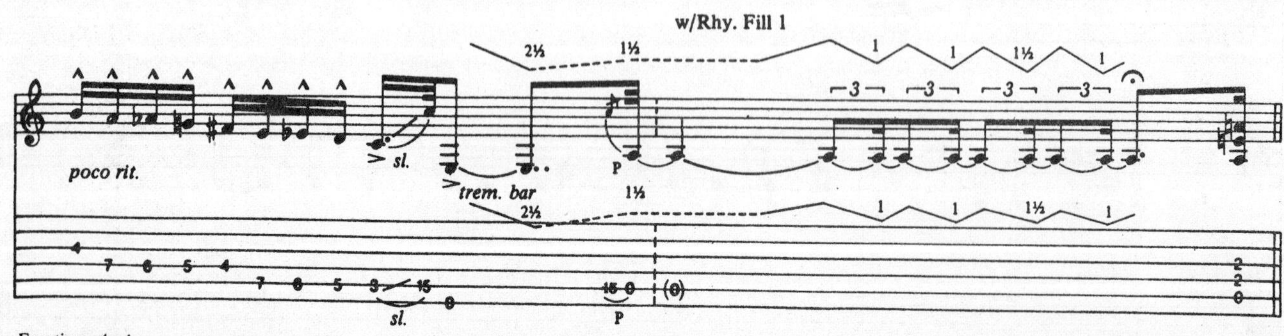

8va
A5
G5
D5
sl.
Harm.
Full
1/4
*Release finger pressure when arriving at 19fr. at end of slide to sound F♯ natural harmonic.
1½
P
H
rake
loco
trem. bar
3½
Faster (♩ = 132)
accel.
Rhy. Fill 1
Overdubbed gtr.

loco
trem. bar
dim.
*w/more intense flanging.
rake
(trills)
Faster (♩ = 146)
(C♯m)
poco rit.
* poco accel.
*w/flanger (slow sweep, medium intensity & regeneration)
& tape echo delay (approx. 150 ms. w/one repeat).
(A)
(A dim)
(B)
*Slightly rushed.

(E)
(C)
(Csus2)
(D)
(Dsus2)
(E7)
(E°)
(Am)
(D7)
(D°)
(Gm)
(D)
(C7)
(C°)
(Fm)
(C)
(B)
(Em)
*Slightly rushed.
*Harm.
(Echoplex on)
Fdbk.
trem. bar
rit.
dim.
**w/tape echo effect.
*Tap open low E at 12fr. to produce octave harmonic.
Fdbk. pitch: B
**Univox tape echo runaway feedback effect.

EUROPA
(Earth's Cry Heaven's Smile)

Words and Music by
CARLOS SANTANA and TOM COSTER

Fm7
B♭7
E♭maj7
A♭maj7
G7sus
G7
Cm
N.C.
mf
B♭7sus
B♭7
E♭maj7
A♭maj7
G7sus
G7
Cm
N.C.
B♭7sus
B♭7

E♭maj7
A♭maj7
G7sus
G7
C maj7
N.C.
Fm7
B♭7
E♭maj7
A♭maj7
G7sus
G7
Cm7
Fm7
Cm7
Fm7
Cm7

Fm7
Cm7
Fm7
Cm7
Fm7
Cm7
Fm7
Cm7
Fm7
Cm7
Fm7
slow bend

Cm7
Fm7
Cm7
Fm7
Cm7
Fm7
Cm7
Fm9/B♭
Cm7
Fm9/B♭
Cm7
Fm9/B♭
8va
Cm7
Fm9/B♭
Cm7
sim.

Fm9/B♭
Cm7
Fm9/B♭
Cm7
Fm9/B♭
Cm7
Fm9/B♭
Cm7
Fm9/B♭
Cm7
Fm9/B♭
8va
T
A
B

Cm7
Fm9/B♭
Cm7
Fm9/B♭
Cm7
8va
Begin fade
Fm9/B♭
Cm7
Fm9/B♭
Fm9/B♭
Cm7
Fade

EVERY MORNING

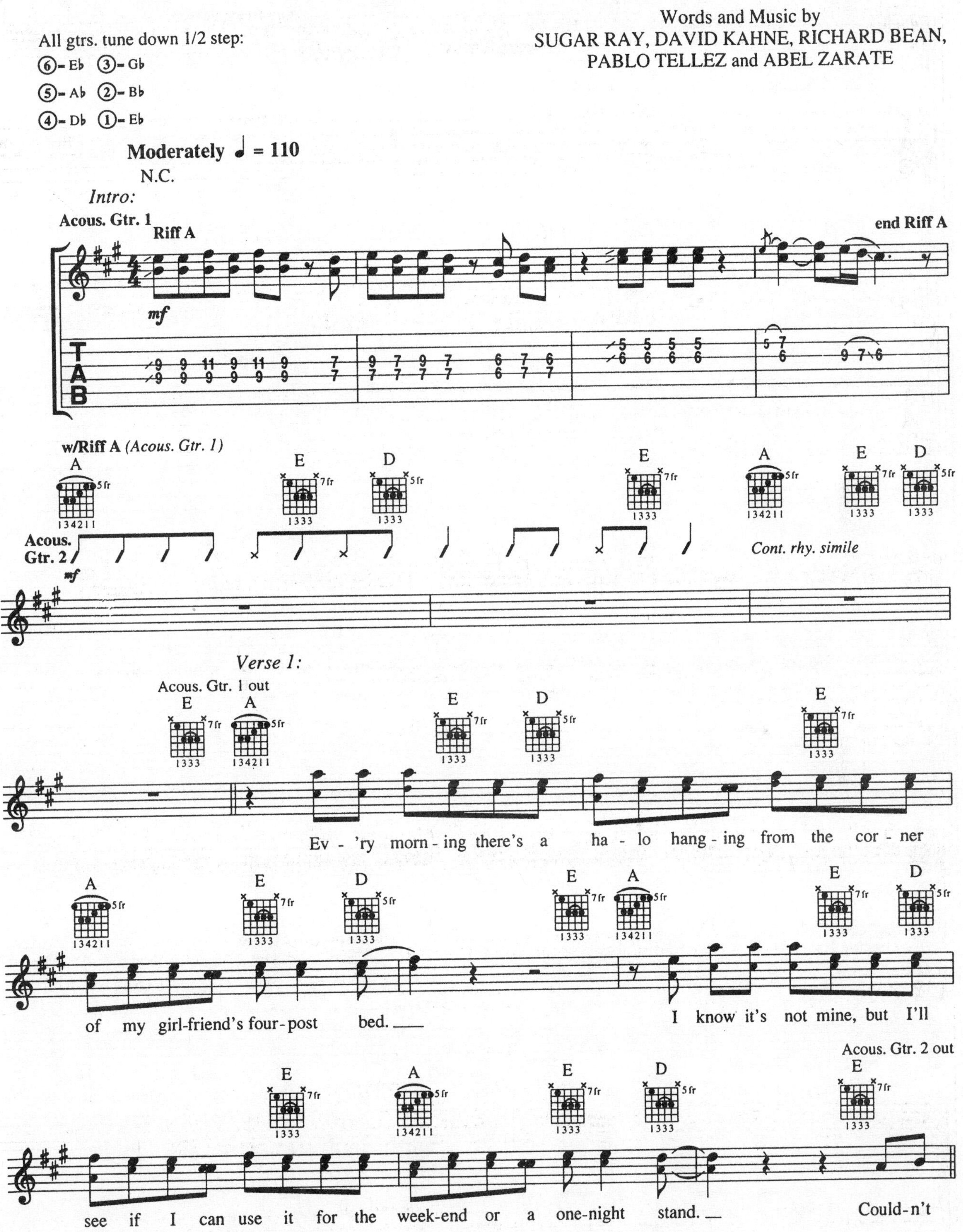

Every Morning – 7 – 1

Verse 2:
E/A
D
E/A
D
un-der-stand how to work it out. _ Once a -
Elec. Gtr. 1
clean
Elec. Gtr. 2
Rhy. Fig. 1
clean
end Rhy. Fig. 1
w/Rhy. Fig. 1 (Elec. Gtr. 2)
gain, as pre-dict-ed, left my bro-ken heart o - pen and you ripped it out. _____
Elec. Gtrs. 1 & 2 out
Pre-chorus:
A
E
D
Acous. Gtr. 2
Some-thing's got me reel - ing, don't stop me from be-liev - ing, turn me a-round a - gain. _
Said that we can do it, you know I want to do it a - gain. _

w/Fill 1 (Acous. Gtr. 1)
Chorus:
A E A E D E
Ev - 'ry morn-ing,
(Ah. Ah.
(Sug-ar Ray say.)
w/Fill 1 (Elec. Gtr. 1) w/clean tone
A E D E A E D
ev - 'ry morn-ing when I wake up,
she al-ways rights the wrong,
)
(Ah.
(Shut the door, ba - by, don't say a word.)
w/Fill 1 (Elec. Gtr. 1)
E A E D E
Cont. rhy. simile
she al - ways rights, she al-ways rights.
Ah.)
(Shut the door, ba - by, shut the door, ba - by.)
A E D E A D E
Gtr. 1
Gtr. 2
Fill 1
Acous. Gtr. 1

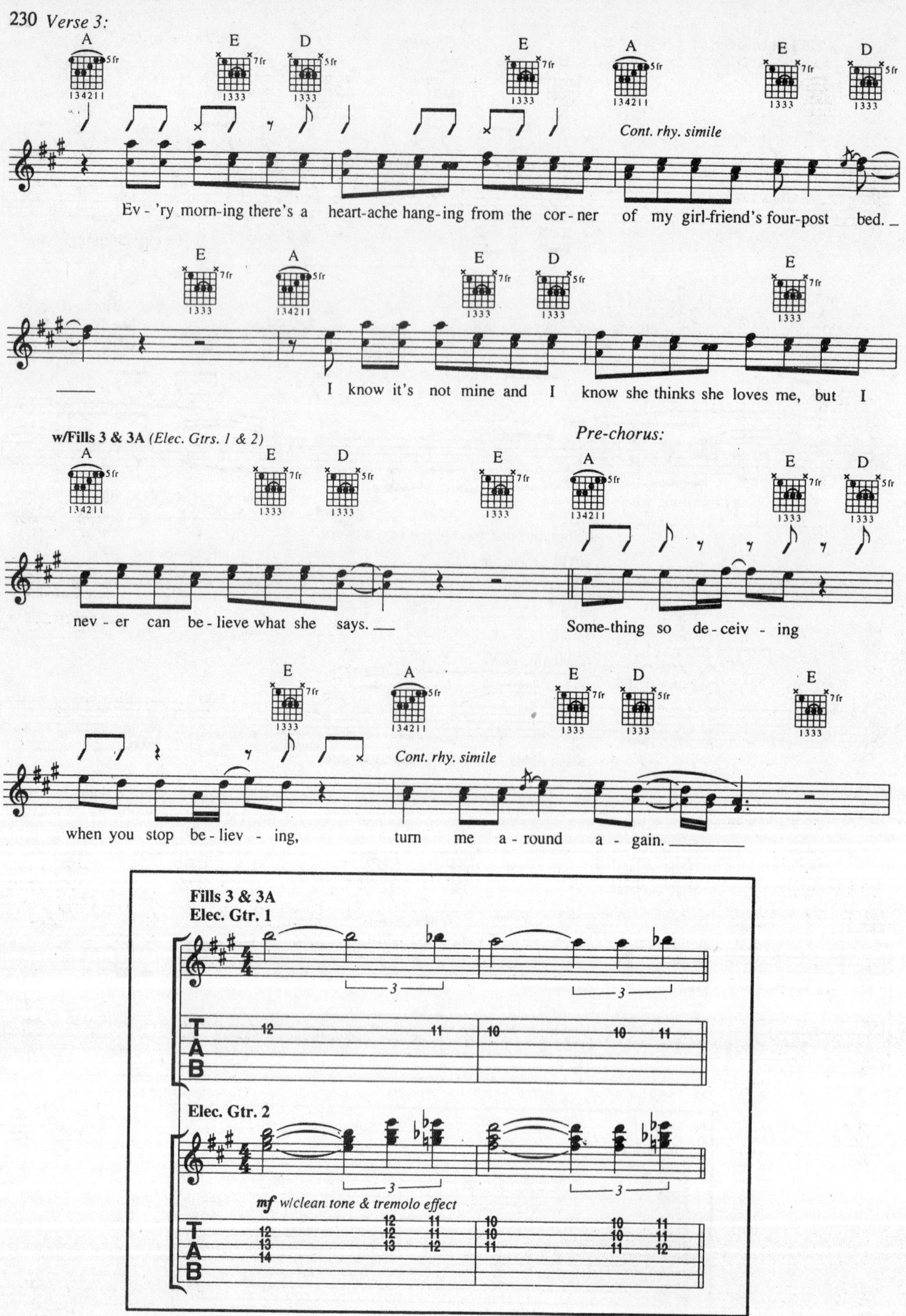
Verse 3:
A
E
D
E
A
E
D
Cont. rhy. simile
Ev - 'ry morn-ing there's a heart-ache hang-ing from the cor - ner of my girl-friend's four-post bed.
E
A
E
D
E
I know it's not mine and I know she thinks she loves me, but I
w/Fills 3 & 3A (Elec. Gtrs. 1 & 2)
Pre-chorus:
nev - er can be - lieve what she says.
Something so de - ceiv - ing
Cont. rhy. simile
when you stop be - liev - ing, turn me a - round a - gain.
Fills 3 & 3A
Elec. Gtr. 1
Elec. Gtr. 2
mf w/clean tone & tremolo effect

w/Fill 1 (Acous. Gtr. 1)
Gtr. 2
Said we could-n't do it, you know I want to do it a - gain.
Chorus:
(Ah.
Ev - 'ry morn-ing,
Ah.
ev - 'ry morn-ing when I wake up,
)
(Shut the door, ba - by, don't say a word.)
(Ah.
ev - 'ry morn-ing,
Ah.
ev - 'ry morn-ing when I wake up,
)
(Shut the door, ba - by, shut the door, ba - by.)
Bridge:
Acous. Gtrs. 1 & 2
Cont. rhy. simile
she al-ways rights the wrong for me, ba - by,
she al - ways rights the wrong for me.

Verse 4:
A
E
D
E
A
E
D
134211
1333
1333
1333
134211
1333
1333
5fr
7fr
5fr
7fr
5fr
7fr
5fr
Acous. Gtr. 2
Cont. rhy. simile
Ev - 'ry morn-ing there's a ha - lo hang-ing from the cor-ner of my girl-friend's four-post bed.
E
A
E
D
E
I know it's not mine, but I'll see if I can use it for the
Elec. Gtr. 1
Elec. Gtr. 2
A
E
D
E
week - end or a one - night stand.
(Shut the door, ba - by, don't say a word.)

Outro:
A E D E A E D
Ev - 'ry morn - ing, ev - 'ry morn - ing when I
wake up, ev - 'ry morn - ing,
(Shut the door, ba - by, shut the door, ba - by.)
w/Vocal Fill 1
turn me a - round a - gain.
(Ev - 'ry morn - ing when I wake up.)
Ev - 'ry morn - ing,
do it a - gain.
(Ev - 'ry morn - ing when I wake up.)
Cont. rhy. simile
Ev-'ry morn - ing, ev-'ry morn-ing when I wake up.
(Shut the door, ba - by, shut the door.)
Fade
Vocal Fill 1
Shut the door, ba - by, don't say a word.

EVERYTHING YOU WANT

All gtrs. tuned down 1/2 step:

⑥ = E♭ ③ = G♭
⑤ = A♭ ② = B♭
④ = D♭ ① = E♭

Words and Music by
MATTHEW SCANNELL

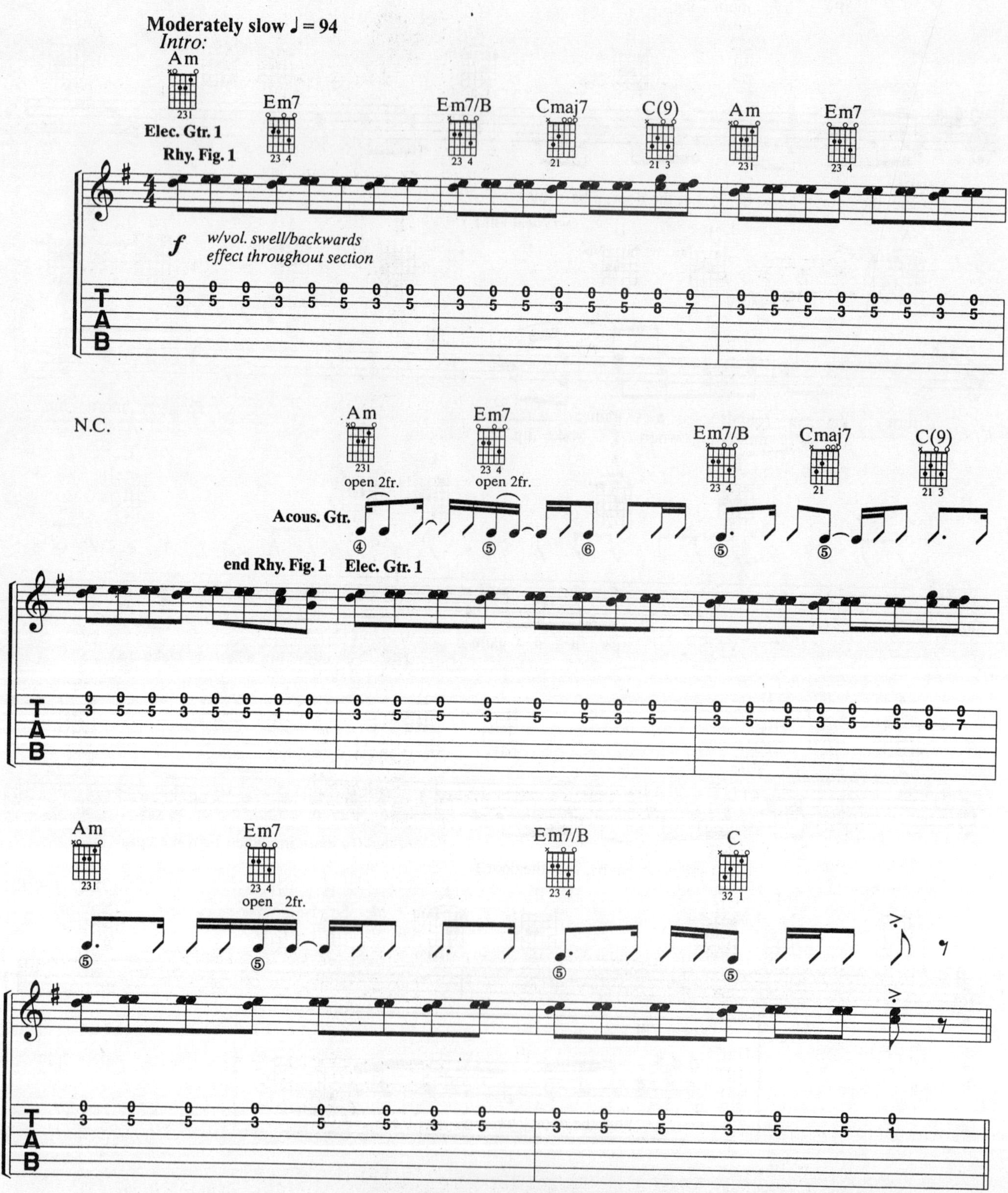

Verse 1:
w/Rhy. Fig. 1 (Elec. Gtr. 1) 2 times, simile
Am
Em7
Em7/B
Cmaj7
C(9)
Acous. Gtr. continues primary rhythm
Some - where there's speak - ing. It's al - read - y com - ing in.
Oh, and it's ris - ing at the back of your mind.
You nev - er could get it un - less you were fed it.
C
Now you're here and you don't know why.
Verses 2 - 4:
w/Rhy. Fig. 1 (Elec. Gtr. 1) Verses 2 & 3 only, 2 times, simile
Acous. Gtr. continues/resumes primary rhythm
2. But un - der skinned knees and the skid marks.
3.4. See additional lyrics
Past the plac - es where you used to learn.
w/Rhy. Fig. 1 (Elec. Gtr. 1) Verse 4 only, simile
You howl and lis - ten, lis - ten and wait for the
G/B
ech - oes of an - gels who won't re - turn. He's

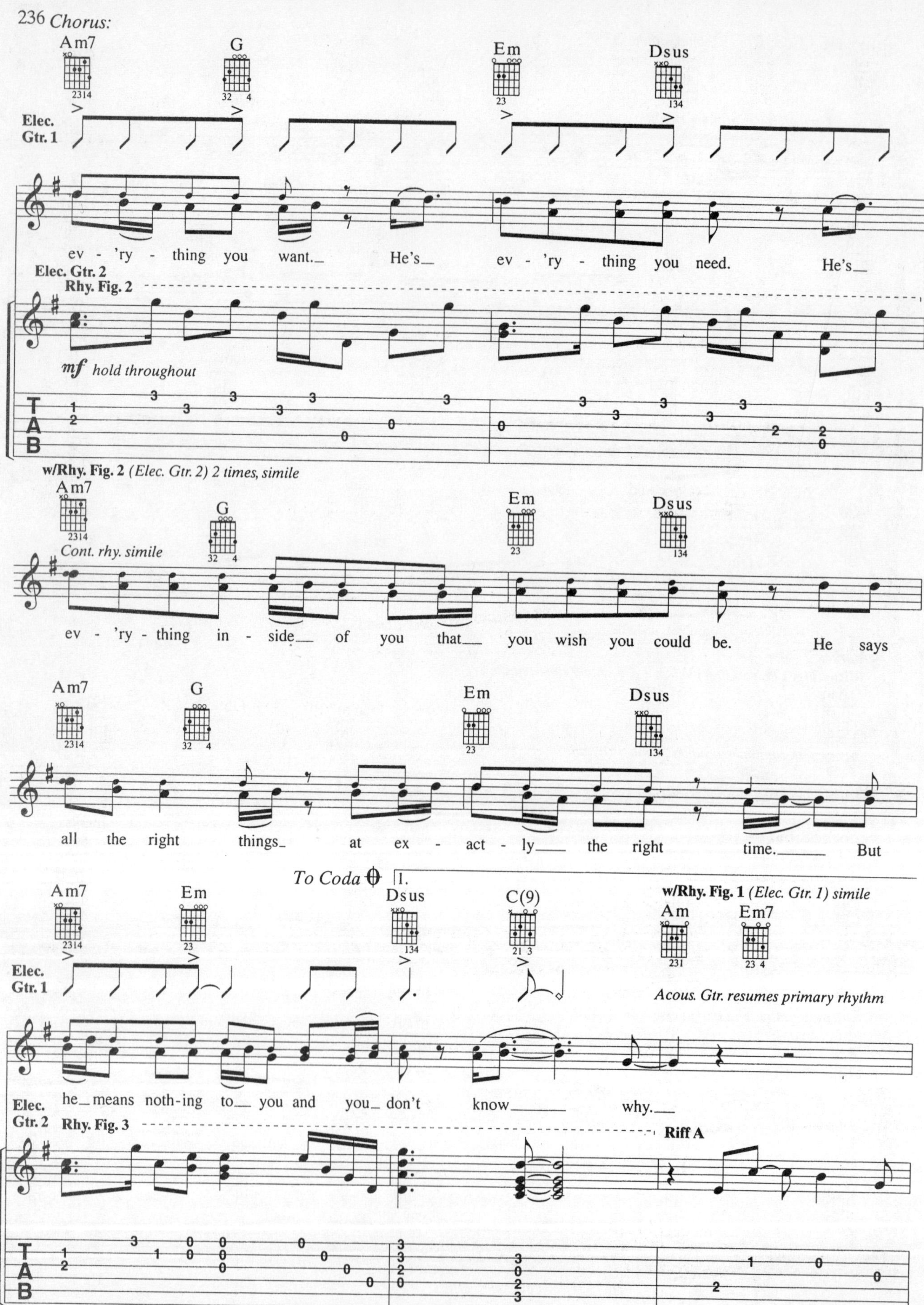
Chorus:
Am7
G
Em
Dsus
Elec. Gtr. 1
ev - 'ry - thing you want._ He's_ ev - 'ry - thing you need. He's_
Elec. Gtr. 2
Rhy. Fig. 2
mf hold throughout
w/Rhy. Fig. 2 (Elec. Gtr. 2) 2 times, simile
Cont. rhy. simile
ev - 'ry - thing in - side_ of you that_ you wish you could be. He says
all the right things_ at ex - act - ly___ the right time.___ But
To Coda
1.
C(9)
w/Rhy. Fig. 1 (Elec. Gtr. 1) simile
Am
Em7
Acous. Gtr. resumes primary rhythm
he_ means noth-ing to_ you and you_ don't know___ why._
Elec. Gtr. 2
Rhy. Fig. 3
Riff A

Em7/B
Cmaj7
C(9)
Am
Em7
Em7/B
C
Acous. Gtr.
end Riff A
2.
Bridge:
Dsus2
C(9)
Cmaj7
Em
Elec. Gtr. 1
don't know why.
But you'll just sit tight
Elec. Gtr. 2
Rhy. Fig. 4
w/Rhy. Fig. 4 (Elec. Gtr. 2) 6 times, simile
C
Em
Cont. rhy. simile
and watch it un - wind.
It's on - ly what you're
Dsus2
C(9)
Em
ask - ing for.
And you'll be just fine
C
Em
with all of your time.
It's on - ly what you're

Dsus2
C
D.S. al Coda
wait - ing___ for.
w/rotating speaker effect
Coda
Dsus2
Cmaj7
Chorus:
w/Rhy. Fig. 2 (Elec. Gtr. 2) 3 times, simile
Am7
G
Elec. Gtr. 1
don't know___ why. I___ am ev - 'ry - thing you want. I___ am
Em
Dsus
Am7
G
Cont. rhy. simile
ev - 'ry - thing you___ need. I___ am ev - 'ry - thing in - side_ of you that
Em
Dsus
Am7
G
you wish you could be. I say all the right things_ at ex -
Em
Dsus
w/Rhy. Fig. 3 (Elec. Gtr. 2) simile
Am7
Em
Elec. Gtr. 1
act - ly___ the right time.___ But I___ mean noth - ing to___ you and I___

Verse 3:
You're waiting for someone
To put you together.
You're waiting for someone
To push you away.
There's always another
Wound to discover.
There's always something more
You wish he'd say.
(To Chorus:)

Verse 4:
Out of the island,
Into the highway.
Past the places where you might have turned.
You never did notice,
But you still hide away
The anger of angels who won't return.
(To Chorus:)

EVIL WAYS

Words and Music by
SONNY HENRY

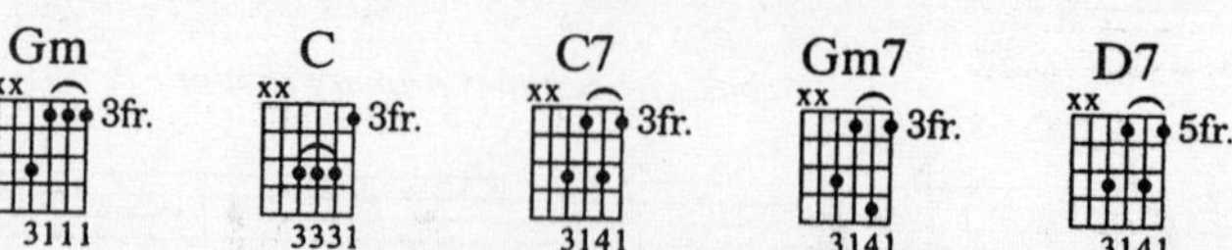

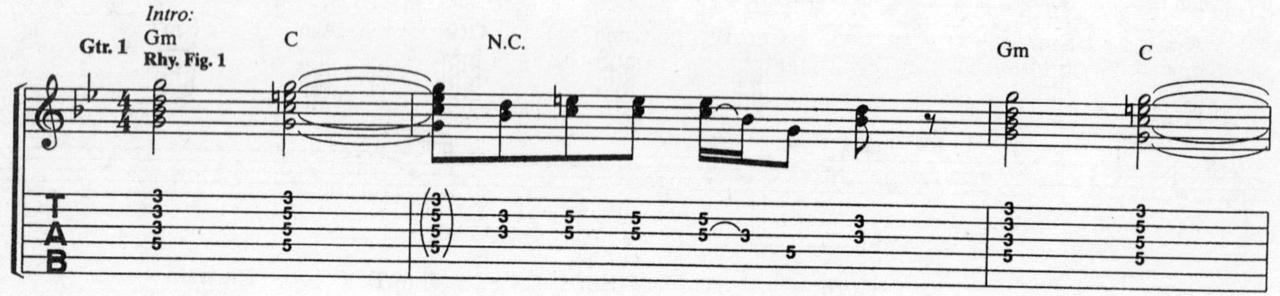

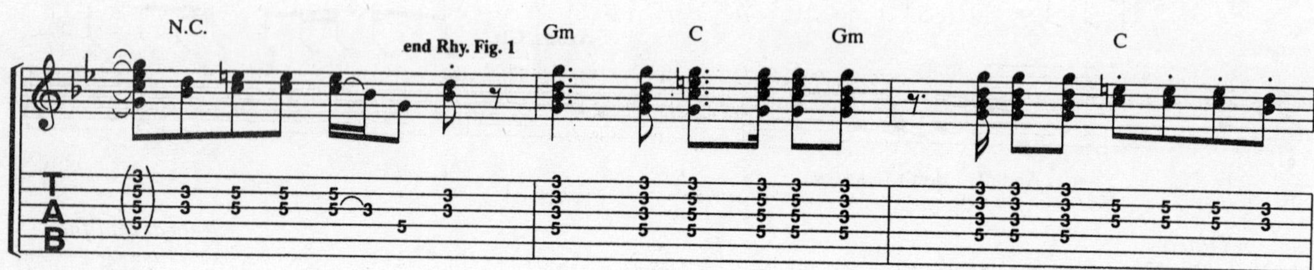

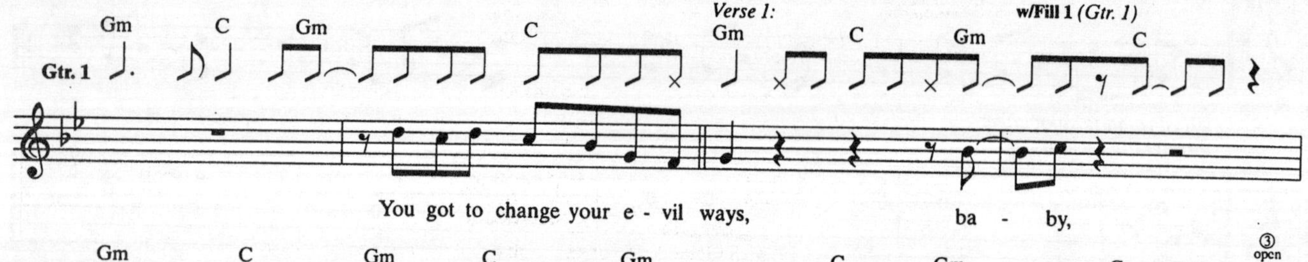

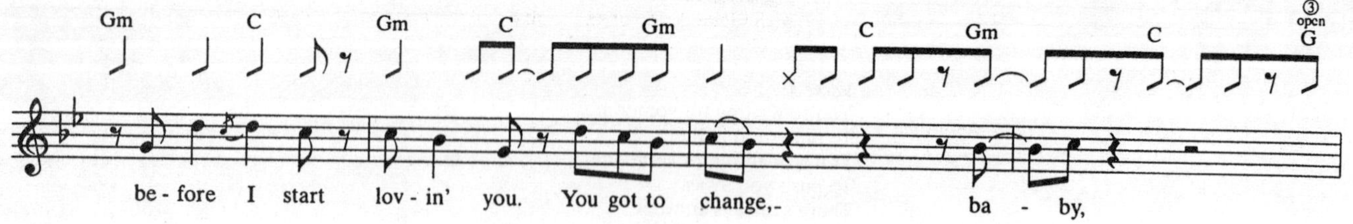

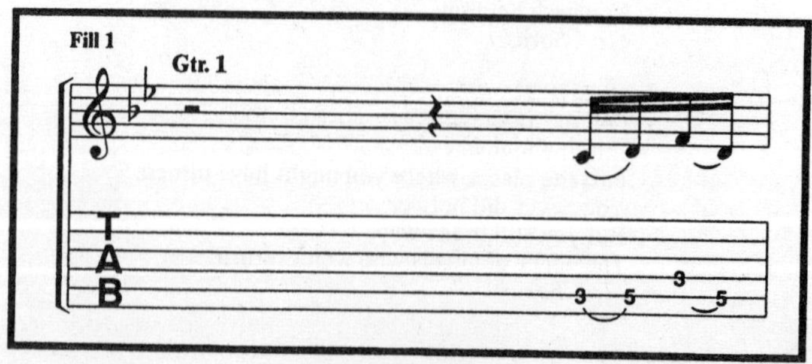

Gm C Gm C Gm C7
and ev - 'ry word — that I say is true. You got me run - nin' and hid - in' all —
Gm7 C7 Gm C7 Gm7 C7
— o - ver town. — You got me sneak - in' and a - peep - in' and run - nin' me down. — This can't go
D7 Gm C Gm C F
on. Lord. knows, you got to change, ba - by,
w/Fill 1 (Gtr. 1)
Verses 2 & 3:
Gm C Gm C Gm C Gm C
ba - by. When I come home, - ba - by,
Gm C G Gm C Gm C Gm
my house is dark — and my thoughts are cold. — You hang a - round, - ba -
C G Gm C Gm C
by, with Gene and Joan — and a - who knows who. I'm get - tin'
Gm C7 Gm7 C7 Gm C7
ti - red of wait - in' and fool - in' a - round. — I'll find some - bod - y that won't make me
Gm7 C7 D7
To Coda
feel like a clown. — This can't go on. Lord — knows you got to
Organ solo:
Play 12 times
Gm C Gm C Gm Gm C Gm C Gm
change.

w/Rhy. Fig. 1 (Gtr. 1)
Gm C N.C. Gm C N.C.
D.S. 𝄋 al Coda
When I come
Coda
N.C. Gm C7 Gm C7
Yeah, yeah, yeah!
Gm C7 Gm C7
Guitar Solo:
*Gm C Gm C
Hey, hey.
*Chords implied by organ and bass.
Gm C Gm C Gm C Gm C
Gm C Gm C Gm C

Gm
C
8va
(8va)
slow bend
hold bend
grad. dim.
Repeat and fade
T
A
B

EYES WITHOUT A FACE

Words and Music by
BILLY IDOL and STEVE STEVENS

To Coda ⊕
A 5fr. 134211
B 7fr. 134211
F♯m 134111
G♯m 4fr. 134111
Eyes with-out a face, got no hu-man grace. You're eyes with-out a face.
(Les yeux sans vis - age.)
E 231
C♯m 4fr. 13421
G♯m 4fr. 134111
B 7fr. 134211
Verse 2:
Cont. rhy. simile
I spend so much time be-liev-ing all the lies to keep the dream a-live.
D.S. 𝄋 al Coda
Now it makes me sad, it makes me mad at truth for lov-ing what was you.
⊕ Coda
Acous. Gtr.
Synth.
Elec. Gtr.
f
T
A
B
12

Interlude:
E
7fr.
1333
D
5fr.
1333
Rhy. Fig. 1
Elec. Gtr.
P.M.
P.M.
P.M.
P.M.
P.M.
When
Bridge:
w/Rhy. Fig. 1 (Elec. Gtr.) 10 times
you hear the mu-sic, you make a dip in-to some-one els-e's pock-et, then make a slip.
Steal a car, go to Las Ve-gas, ooh, gig-o-lo pool.
Hang-in' out by the state line, turn-in' ho-ly wa-ter in-to wine.
Drink-in' it down, whoo, ow.

E
7fr.
1333
D
5fr.
1333
I'm on a bus on a psy-che-del-ic trip read-in' mur-der books,_ try'n'_ to stay hip._
I'm think-in' of you, you're_ out there_ so say_ your prayers._
3
Say_ your_ prayers._ Say_ your prayers._
Ow!
Verse 3:
Resume verse fig. simile
C♯m
4fr.
13421
G♯m
134111
B
134211
231
Now I close my eyes_ and I won-der why_ I don't_ de - spise._
Now all I can do_ is love_ what was once_ so a-live_ and new._
But it's gone_ from your eyes,_ I bet - ter re-al - ize._

Chorus:
A
5fr.
134211
B
7fr.
134211
Cont. rhy. simile
Eyes with-out a face.
(Les yeux sans vis - age.)
(Les yeux sans vis -
age.)
Eyes with-out a face.
(Les yeux sans vis - age.)
Eyes with-out a face,
F♯m
134111
G♯m
4fr.
134111
got no hu - man grace.
You're eyes with - out a face,
such a hu - man waste.
You're eyes with - out a face.
Outro:
E
231
Acous. Gtr.
You know it's get - ting close.
N.C.
Synth.

FAME

Words and Music by
DAVID BOWIE, JOHN LENNON
and CARLOS ALOMAR

1.2.4.5.
3.6.
w/Rhy. Fig. 1B (Elec. Gtr. 3) 2nd & 3rd times only, simile
Cont. rhy. simile throughout
end Rhy. Fig. 1
grad. bend
1/2
end Rhy. Fig. 1A
grad. bend
1/2
Verse:
w/Rhy. Figs. 1 (Elec. Gtr. 1) & 1A (Elec. Gtr. 2) 2 times, simile
F7
3fr.
1324
(Bkgd. Vcl.) Fame.
1. Fame makes a man take things o - ver.
2. Fame; what you like is in the lim - o.
3. Is it an-y won - der I re - ject you first?
Fame.
Fame lets him loose, hard to swal - low.
Fame; what you get is no to - mor - row.
Fame, fame, fame, fame.
Fame.
Fame puts you there where things are hol - low.
Fame; what you need you have to bor - row.
Is it an-y won - der you are too cool to fool?
Fame.
Fame.
Fame.
Fame.

B♭7
6fr.
131211
Fame.
Not your brain, it's just the flame that burns your change to keep you in -
Ly-ing is fine; it's just his line to bind your time it drives you to
Bul-ly for you, chil-ly for me; got to get a rain check on
Elec. Gtr. 1
Elec. Gtr. 2
Interlude:
w/Rhy. Figs 1 (Elec. Gtr. 1) & 1A (Elec. Gtr. 2) 2 times, simile
F7
3fr.
1324
*Sane.
sane.
crime.
pain.
Fame.
Fame.
Fame.
*Substitute "Crime" during Verse 2 and "Fame" during Verse 3.
1.
2.
D.C.
3. F7
Outro:
w/Rhy. Fig. 1 (Elec. Gtr. 1) 2 times, simile
w/Rhy. Fig. 1A (Elec. Gtr. 2) from 2nd time on, twice, simile
Fame, fame, fame, fame,
*fame, fame, fame, fame, fame, fame, fame, hey, hey, hey, hey, hey,
*1st time only.
Repeat and fade
hey, hey, hey, hey, hey, hey, hey.
Fame.
What's your name?

FERRY 'CROSS THE MERSEY

Words and Music by
GERRARD MARSDEN

Verse 3:
So I'll continue to say,
Here I always will stay.
(To Chorus 3:)

All gtrs. tuned down 1/2 step:
⑥ = E♭ ③ = G♭
⑤ = A♭ ② = B♭
④ = D♭ ① = E♭

FLY

Words and Music by
MARK McGRATH, MURPHY KARGES, STAN FRAZIER,
RODNEY SHEPPARD, CRAIG BULLOCK and WILLIAM MARAGH

Moderately slow ska ♩ = 100

Intro:

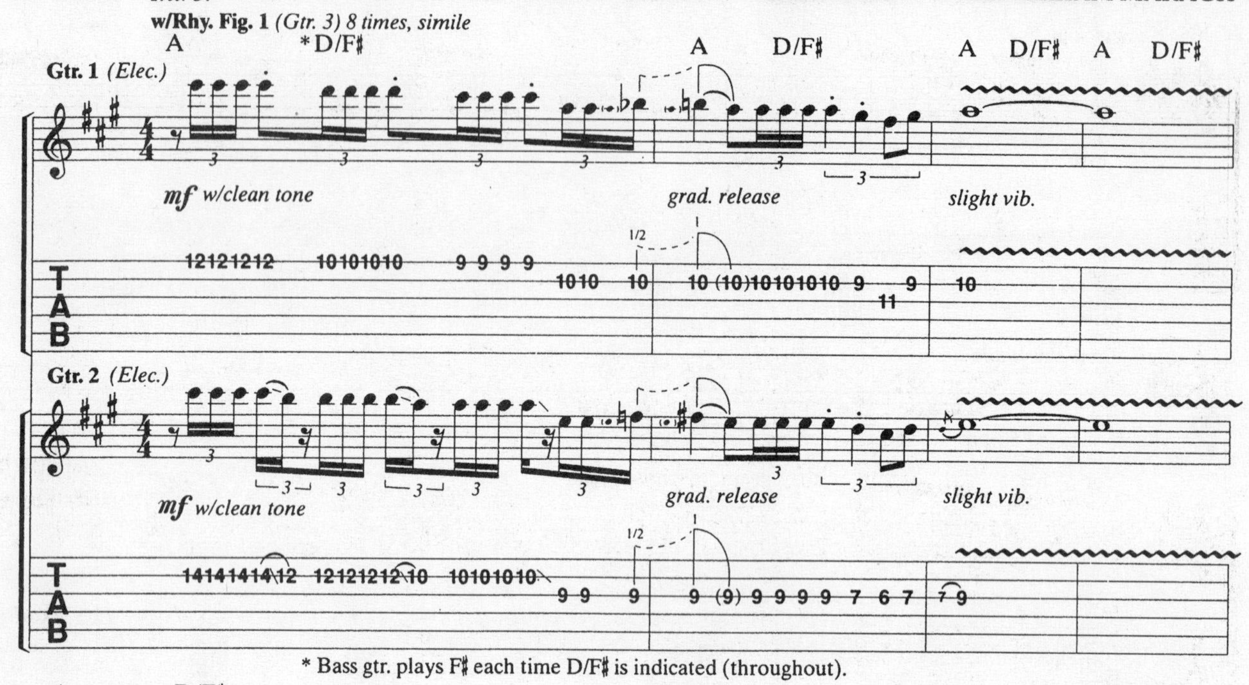

* Bass gtr. plays F♯ each time D/F♯ is indicated (throughout).

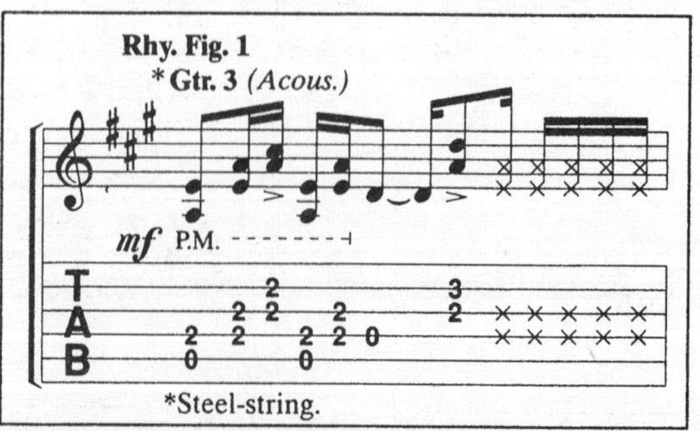

Verse 1:
A D/F♯ A D/F♯
1. All a - round the world stat - ues crum - ble for me. Who knows
Gtr. 3 Rhy. Fig. 2
P.M. P.M.
A D/F♯ A D/F♯
how long I've loved you?
end Rhy. Fig. 2
w/Rhy. Fig. 2 (Gtr. 3)
w/Rhy. Fill 1 (Gtr. 4)
Ev-'ry-where I go, peo-ple stop and they see. Twen-ty-five years old, my moth - er, God rest her soul.
Chorus:
w/Rhy. Fig. 3 (Gtr. 3) 4 times
A D A D
I just wan - na fly. Put your arms
Gtr. 4 Rhy. Fig. 4
Rhy. Fill 1
Gtr. 4 (Elec.)
mf
w/clean tone
Rhy. Fig. 3
Gtr. 3

1.
A
D
A
D
— a - round_ me, ba - by. Put your arms_ a - round_ me, ba - by.
end Rhy. Fig. 4
2.
w/Riff A1 (Gtr. 1) & Riff A2 (Gtr. 2)
A
D
A
D/F♯
— a - round_ me, ba - by. Yeah._
A
D/F♯
A
D/F♯
A
D/F♯
Verses 2 & 3:
w/Rhy. Fig. 2 (Gtr. 3) 2 times
A
D/F♯
A
D/F♯
2. Dance a lit - tle, stran - ger, show_ me where you've been.
3. See additional lyrics
A
D/F♯
A
D/F♯
Love can make you hos - tage, wan - na do it a - gain._
A
D/F♯
A
D/F♯
There's no time to think_ 'bout the start - ing or_ the end._

*Bass gtr. plays D each time Asus/D is indicated (throughout).

Interlude:
A5
Gtr. 1
f w/dist.
P.M.
P.M.
Gtr. 2
f w/dist.
P.M.
P.M.
P.M.
P.M.
*Gtr. 4
* w/chorus and compression (next 4 bars).
P.M.
P.M.
P.M.
P.M.
P.M.
P.M.

Verse 3:
All around the world statues crumble for me.
Who knows how long I've loved you?
Everyone I know has been so good to me.
Twenty-five years old,
My mother, God rest her soul.
(To Chorus:)

FOOLISH GAMES

Words and Music by
JEWEL KILCHER

Gm 3fr. 134111
B♭ 3fr. 4 111
F 10fr. 4 111
C 5fr. 4 111
C/E 12fr. 2 134
Dm 10fr. 134111

Moderately slow ♩ = 88

Intro:

Dm B♭

Rhy. Fig. 1

*Gtr. 1

mf *hold throughout*

*Piano arr. for gtr.

F C

end Rhy. Fig. 1

𝄋 *Verse:*

Dm B♭

1.You took your coat off and stood in the

2.-4. *See additional lyrics*

Rhy. Fig. 2

F C

rain, you're al-ways cra - zy like that.

end Rhy. Fig. 2

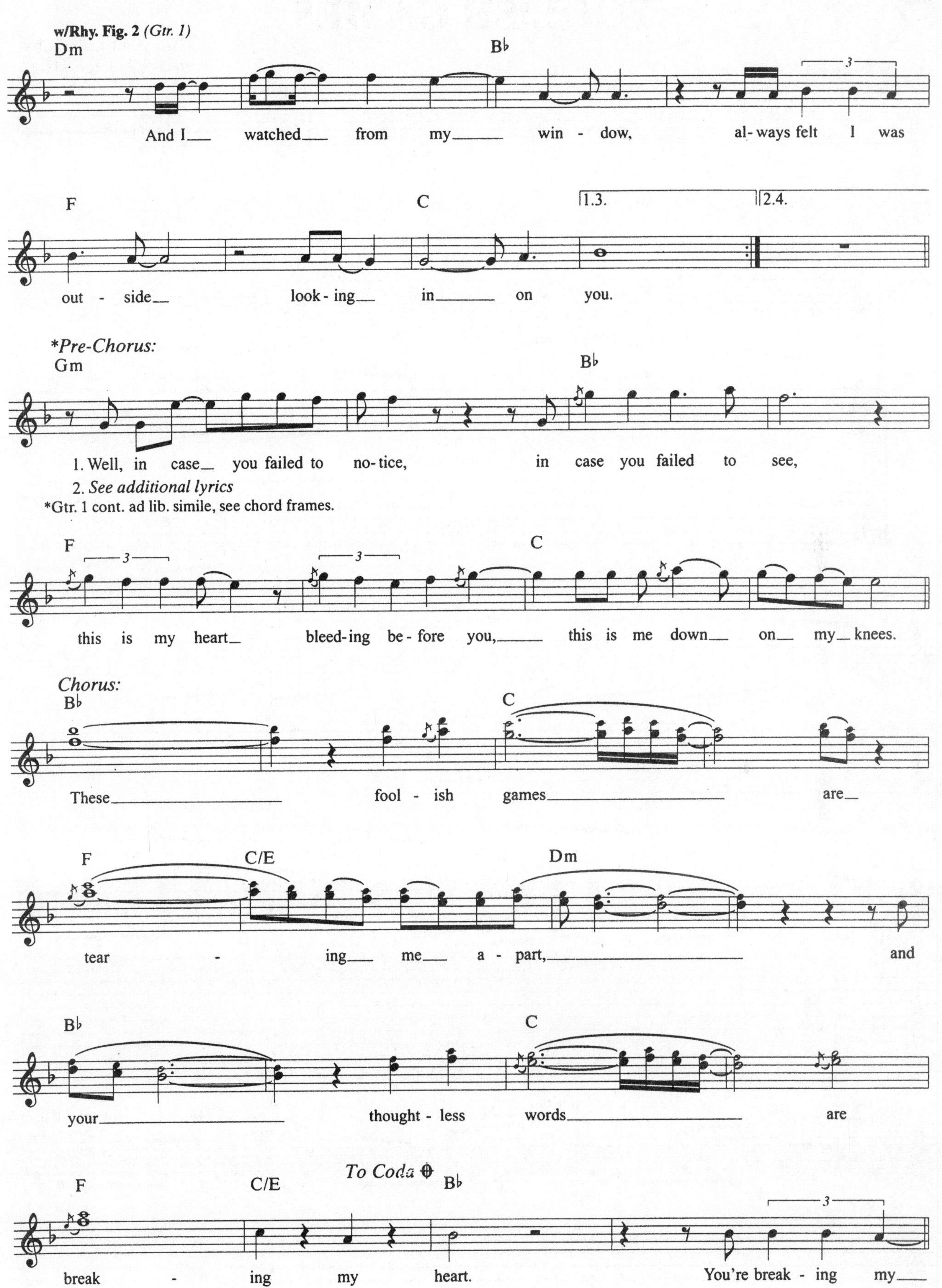
w/Rhy. Fig. 2 (Gtr. 1)
Dm
B♭
And I watched from my win - dow, al-ways felt I was
F
C
1.3.
2.4.
out - side look - ing in on you.
*Pre-Chorus:
Gm
B♭
1. Well, in case you failed to no-tice, in case you failed to see,
2. See additional lyrics
*Gtr. 1 cont. ad lib. simile, see chord frames.
F
C
this is my heart bleed-ing be-fore you, this is me down on my knees.
Chorus:
B♭
C
These fool - ish games are
F
C/E
Dm
tear - ing me a - part, and
B♭
C
your thought - less words are
F
C/E
To Coda
B♭
break - ing my heart. You're break - ing my

w/Rhy. Fig. 1 (Gtr. 1)
Dm
D.S. al Coda
6
heart.
Coda
B♭
Dm
heart.
You're break - ing my
heart.
B♭
F
C
Dm

Outro:

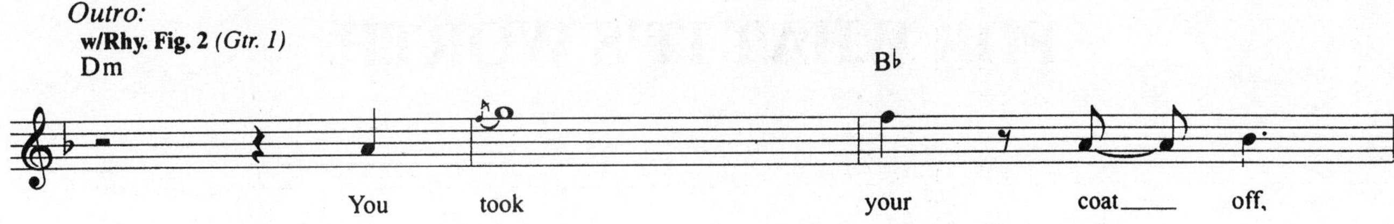

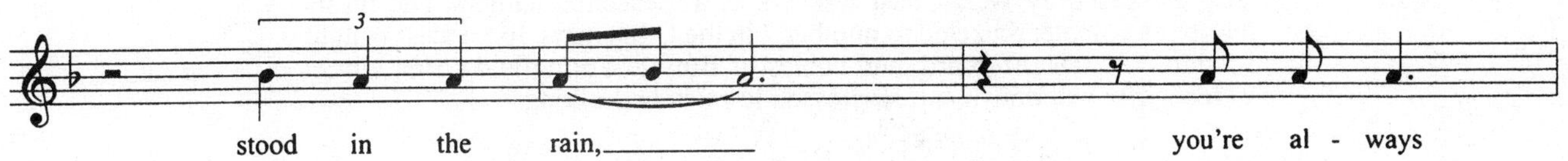

Verse 2:
You're always the mysterious one with
Dark eyes and careless hair,
You were fashionably sensitive
But too cool to care.
You stood in my doorway with nothing to say
Besides some comment on the weather.

Verse 3:
You're always brilliant in the morning,
Smoking your cigarettes and talking over coffee.
Your philosophies on art, Baroque moved you.
You loved Mozart and you'd speak of your loved ones
As I clumsily strummed my guitar.

Verse 4:
You'd teach me of honest things,
Things that were daring, things that were clean.
Things that knew what an honest dollar did mean.
I hid my soiled hands behind my back.
Somewhere along the line, I must have gone
Off track with you.

Pre-Chorus 2:
Excuse me, think I've mistaken you for somebody else,
Somebody who gave a damn, somebody more like myself.
(To Chorus:)

FOR WHAT IT'S WORTH

Buffalo Springfield's only big hit, "For What It's Worth" was written by Stephen Stills after witnessing the L.A.P.D.'s heavy-handedness at breaking up an anti-Vietnam student demonstration on Sunset Strip. Perhaps one of the mildest protest songs ever penned, "For What It's Worth" was immediately embraced by West Coast students as a 'peacenik' anthem, and on its release as a single, rocketed to number 7 in the U.S. charts. Its success caught Atlantic Records off-guard, and copies of Buffalo Springfield's first album were swiftly withdrawn and re-pressed to include the song.

Words and Music by
STEPHEN STILLS

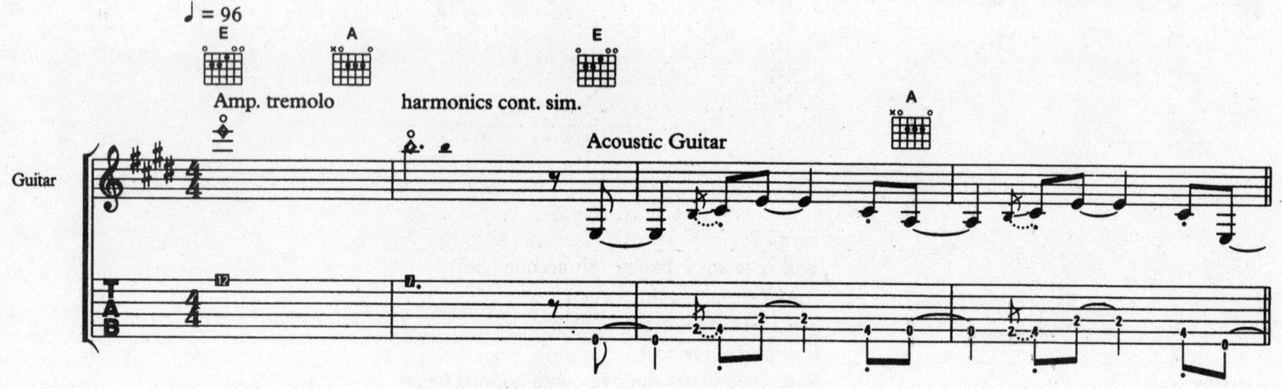

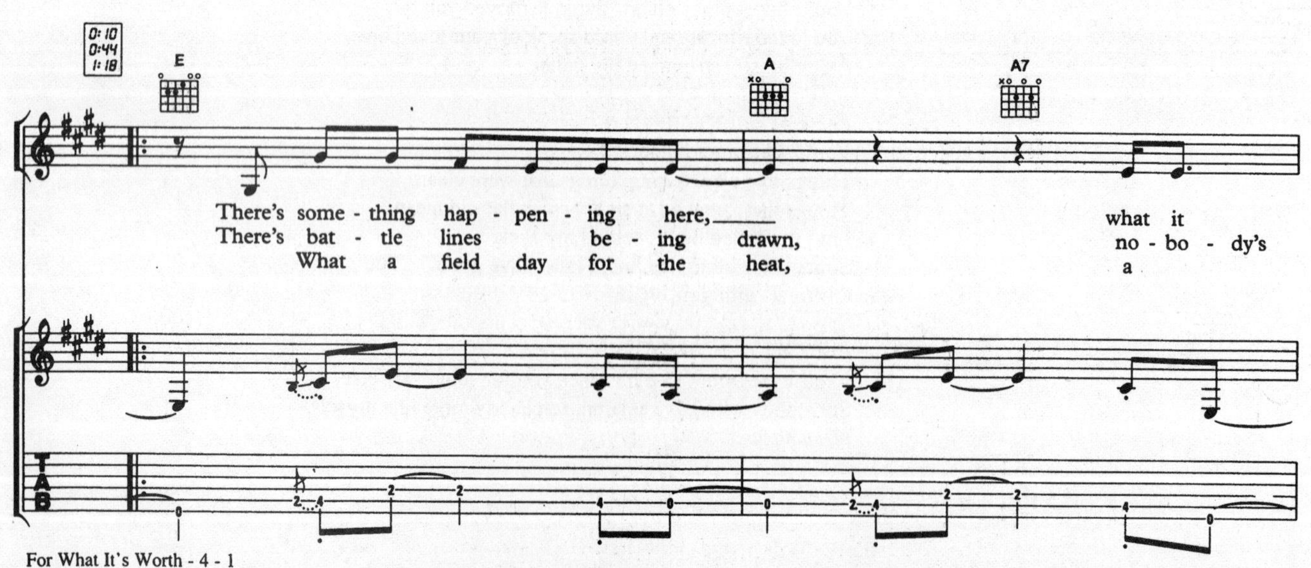

E
A
A7
E
is ain't ex - act - ly clear, there's a man with a gun ov - er there,
right if ev - ery - bo - dy's wrong, young peo - ple speak - in' their minds,
thou - sand peo - ple in the street, sing - in' songs and car - ry - in' signs,
A
A7
E
A
A7
tell - in' me I've got to be - ware. I think it's time we
get - tin' so much re - sis - tance from be - hind. I think it's time we,
most - ly sayin' 'Hoo - ray for our side'. It's time we
E
D
A
A7
stop, child - ren, what's that sound, ev - ery - bo - dy look what's go - in' down.
stop child - ren what's that sound, ev - ery - bo - dy look what's go - in' down.
stop, hey, what's that sound, ev - ery - bo - dy look what's go - in' down.
Omit 1st time
Elec. Gtr. with amp tremolo
1.
E
A
E
A
Ac. Gtr.

2.
E
A
E
A
let ring
3.
E
A
E
A
1:52
E
A7
A13sus4
E
A
A13sus4
E
Pa - ra - noi - a strikes deep, in - to your life it will creep, it
Ac. Gtr.
A7
A13sus4
E
A7
starts when you're al - ways a - fraid, step out of line, the men come and take you a - way. We'd bet - ter

2:11
E
D
A
E
D
stop, hey, what's that sound, ev-ery-bo-dy look what's go-in'. You bet-ter stop, hey, what's that sound,
Elec. Gtr.
A
E
D
ev-ery-bo-dy look what's go-in'. You bet-ter stop, hey, what's that sound,
A
A7
E
D
ev-ery-bo-dy look what's go-in'. You bet-ter stop, child-ren, what's that sound,
fade
A
A7
E
D
A7
ev-ery-bo-dy look what's go-in'.
8va

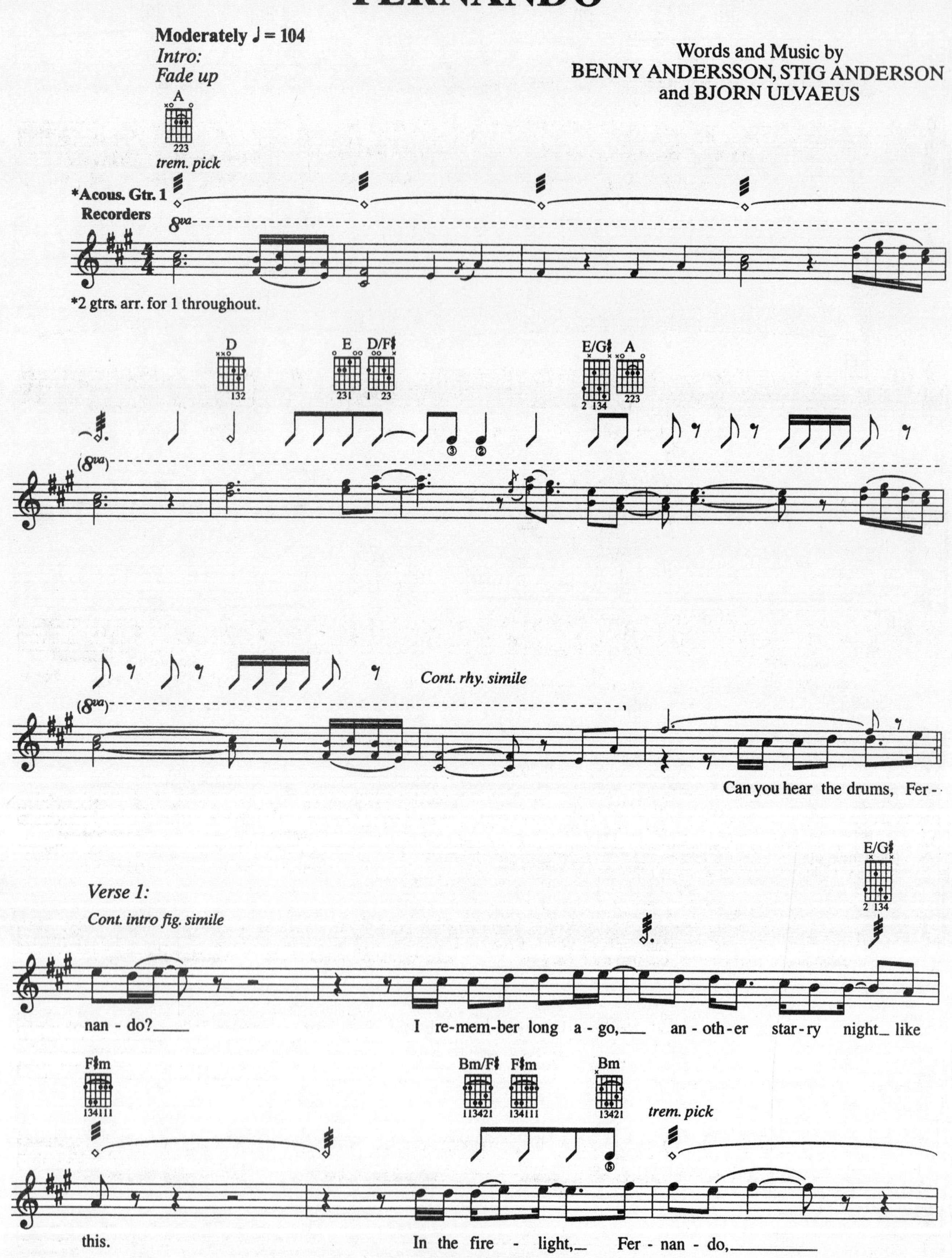
FERNANDO
Moderately ♩ = 104
Intro:
Fade up
Words and Music by
BENNY ANDERSSON, STIG ANDERSON
and BJORN ULVAEUS
A
trem. pick
*Acous. Gtr. 1
Recorders
*2 gtrs. arr. for 1 throughout.
D
E
D/F♯
E/G♯
A
Cont. rhy. simile
Can you hear the drums, Fer-
Verse 1:
Cont. intro fig. simile
E/G♯
nan - do? I re-mem-ber long a - go, an - oth - er star - ry night like
F♯m
Bm/F♯
F♯m
Bm
trem. pick
this. In the fire - light, Fer - nan - do,

*2 gtrs. arr. for 1 throughout section.

F♯m
134111
3
min - ute seemed to last e - ter - ni - ty.
have-n't seen a ri - fle in your hand.
Bm/F♯
113421
F♯m
134111
Bm
13421
I was so a - fraid, Fer - nan - do.
Can you hear the drums, Fer - nan - do?

We were young and full of life, and none of us prepared to
Do you still recall the fateful night we crossed the Rio Grande?
E
231
die. and I'm not ashamed to say the roar of guns and cannons
I can see it in your eyes, how proud you were to fight for

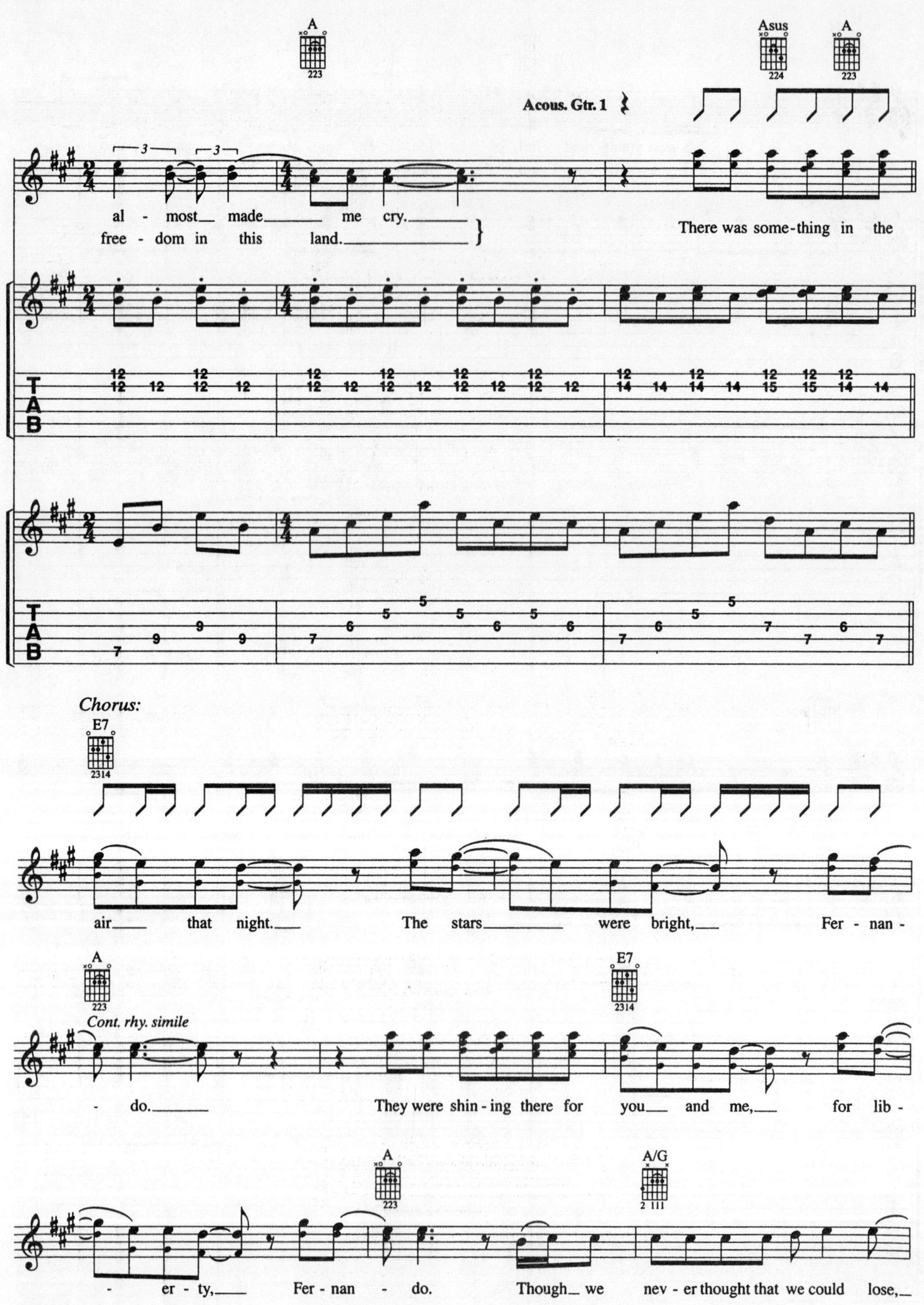
A
223
Asus
224
A
223
Acous. Gtr. 1
al - most made me cry.
free - dom in this land.
There was some-thing in the
Chorus:
E7
2314
air that night. The stars were bright, Fer - nan -
A
223
Cont. rhy. simile
- do.
They were shin - ing there for
E7
2314
you and me, for lib -
A
223
A/G
2 111
- er - ty, Fer - nan - do.
Though we nev - er thought that we could lose,

F♯
134211
B
1333
there's no re - gret.
If I had to do the
E7
2314
same a - gain, I would, my friend, Fer - nan -
A
223
To Coda
Asus
224
A
223
E7
2314
do.
If I had to do the same a - gain, I would,
D
132
E
231
D/F♯
1 23
E/G♯
2 134
A
223
Acous. Gtr. 1
my friend, Fer - nan - do.
Grad. slower
A/C♯
3111
D
132
A/C♯
3111
E
231

A tempo
A
223
trem. pick
D.S. 𝄋 al Coda
3. Now we're old and gray, Fer -
Chorus:
Coda
A
223
Asus
224
A
223
E7
2314
Acous. Gtr. 1
There was some-thing in the air that night. The stars
A
223
Cont. rhy. simile
were bright, Fer - nan - do.
They were shin - ing there for
E7
2314
you and me, for lib - er - ty, Fer - nan -
A
223
A/G
2 111
F♯
134211
- do. Though we nev - er thought that we could lose, there's no re - gret.
B
1333
E7
2314
If I had to do the same a - gain, I would,
Repeat and fade
A
223
Asus
224
A
223
my friend, Fer - nan - do.
Yes, if I had to do the

FORTUNATE SON

By
J.C. FOGERTY

C5
G5
3
ooh, they point the can - non at you, y'all.
T
A
B
Chorus:
G5
Rhy. Fig. 2
D5
D5
C5
It ain't me, it ain't me; I ain't no sen - a - tor's son.
1
(end Rhy. Fig. 2)
G5
G
w/Rhy. Fig. 2
G5
D5
Y'all. It ain't me, it ain't me;
1/2
1/2
C5
G5
I ain't no for - tu - nate one, no.
1
1/2

Verses 2 & 3:
w/Rhy. Fig. 1 (2 times)
G5
F5
C5
2. Some folks are born___ sil - ver spoon in hand,___ Lord, don't they help them -
3. See additional lyrics
G5
F5
selves, y'all.___ But when the tax___ man comes___ to the door,___
1/2
C5
G5
Lord,___ the house look a - like a rum - mage___ sale, yeah.___
1/2
Chorus:
w/Rhy. Fig. 2 (2 times)
G5
D5
C5
It ain't me,___ it ain't me;___ I ain't no mil - lion-aire's___ son___

G5
G5
D5
no, no. It ain't me, it ain't me;
C5
Substitute w/Fill 2 (2nd time)
G5
2nd time to Coda
I ain't no for - tu - nate one, no.
Interlude:
G
N.C.
Gtr.III
P.M.
Gtrs. I&II
Riff A
(end Riff A)
w/Riff A & Fill 3
D.S. al Coda
Yeah, yeah.
Fill 2
Gtr. III
Fill 3
*Gtr. IV w/distortion
dim.
*Gtr. IV is also in G tuning.

Coda G5 D5

It ain't me,___ it ain't me;___

C5 G5 w/Fill 4 G5

I ain't no for - tu - nate___ one,___ no, no, no! It ain't me,___

D5 C5 G5 *Fade out*

it ain't me;___ I ain't no for - tu - nate___ son___ son son y'all.

Gtrs. III & IV

Verse 3:
Some folks inherit star-spangled eyes.
Ooo, they send you down to war, y'all.
It ain't me.
It ain't me.
I'm no fortunate one, one.

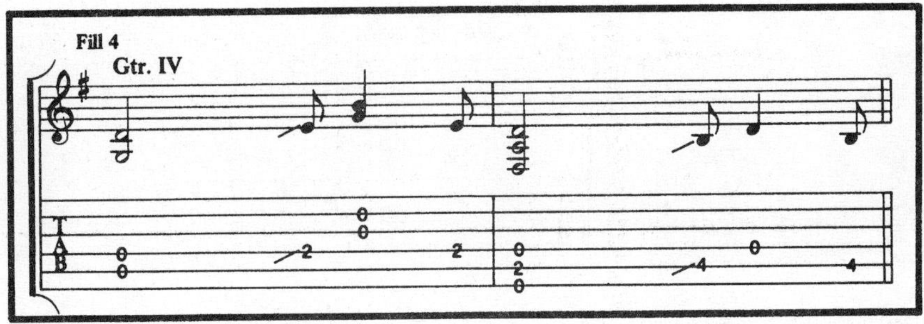

FORTY MILES OF BAD ROAD

By DUANE EDDY and AL CASEY

To Coda
1.
A
E7
A
E7
2.
A7
C
D
A
Saxophone
Elec. Gtr. 1
D
B7
E7
D.S. al Coda
Elec. Gtr. 2
1/2
D w/Riff A (Elec. Gtr. 1)
Coda
E7
A
A7
D
Elec. Gtr. 1
D7
A
E7
A
E7
Repeat and fade

FREAK ON A LEASH

Words and Music by
JONATHAN DAVIS, REGINALD ARVIZU,
BRIAN WELCH, JAMES CHRISTIAN SHAFFER
and DAVID RANDALL SILVERIA

Verse 1:
w/Riff A (Gtr. 1) 2 times
E5
F5
E5
F5
Some-thing takes a part of me.
Some-thing lost and nev-er seen.
Riff B
Gtr. 2
E5
F5
E5
Ev-'ry time I start to be-lieve,
some-thing's raped and tak-en from me,
F5
from life
Verses 2 & 3:
*w/Riff A (Gtr. 1) 2 times
E5
2.Life's got-ta al-ways be mess-in' with me.
3. Feel-ing like a freak on a leash.
end Riff B
*Substitute w/Riff B (Gtr. 2) Verse 3 only.
F5
E5
Can't it chill and let me be free?
Feel-ing like I have no re-lease.
(You ought-a see the light.)

F5
E5
Can't I take a - way all this pain?
How man - y times have I felt dis - ease?
(Show the light.)
T
A
B
10
10
12
F5
E5
I try to ev - 'ry night, all in vain,
Noth - ing in my life is
(You ought - a see the light.)
10
10
12
Slightly faster/Tempo II: ♩ = 108
Pre-chorus:
E5
D5
F5
Rhy. Fig. 1
F5
Gtr. 5
f (w/dist.)
in vain.
free, is free.
Some - times I can - not take this place.
Gtr. 4
f w/dist.
13 14 13
11 12 11
0
13
11
13 14 13
11 12 11
0
13
11
10
8
Gtr. 2
(pitches sound loco)
10
10
12
10

w/Rhy. Fig. 1 (Gtr. 5) 2 times
E5
D5
F5
E5
Some-times it's my life I can't taste.
Some-times I can-
13 14 13 13
11 12 11 0 11
13 14 13 13 10
11 12 11 0 11 8
13 14 13 13
11 12 11 0 11
9 8 7
E5
Gtr. 5
D5
F5
- not feel my face.
You'll nev - er see me fall from grace.
Gtr. 4
13 14 13 13 10
11 12 11 0 11 8
13 14 13 13
11 12 11 0 11
Chorus:
B5
F♯5
G5
F5
Rhy. Fig. 2A
w/Rhy. Figs. 2 (Gtr. 4) & 2A (Gtr. 5) 3 times
B5
Where some - thing takes a part of me.
You
Gtr. 4
Rhy. Fig. 2
4 4 4 4 4 4 4 4
4 4 4 4 4 4 4 4
4 4 4 4 4 4 4 4
3 3 3 4 4
4 4 4 5 3

F♯5
G5
F5
B5
F♯5
G5
F5
B5
and I were meant to be. Ar - chie fought for me to lay. Some-
F♯5
G5
F5
1.
To Tempo I: ♩ = 100
2.
N.C.
N.C.
slight ritard.
- thing takes a part of me. of me.
Interlude:
N.C.
Vcl. Fig. 1
Boom, da, da, boom, da, da, e - ma. Da, boom, da, da, boom, da, da, e - ma. Da
C♯5
1. 2. 3.
boom, da, da, boom, da, da, e - ma. Da, boom, da, da, boom, da, da, e - ma. Da
Gtr. 2 (left)
Gtr. 1 (right)

4.
Bridge:
C#5 D5 D#5 E5 C#5 D5 D#5 E5
Rhy. Fig. 3
Gtrs. 4 & 5
boom, da, da, boom, da, da. Go!
T
A
B
10 10 10 10 9
9 9 9 9 9
C#5 D5 D#5 E5 C#5 D5 C#5 C5
end Rhy. Fig. 3
w/Rhy. Fig. 3 (Gtrs. 4 & 5) 2 times
C#5 D5 D#5 E5 E5
So who, boy? Some, nin-ga, na, nin-ga.
C#5 D5 D#5 E5 C#5 D5 D#5 E5
Who, boy? Some things ain't, boy! Some, some, nin-ga, na, nin-ga.
C#5 D5 C#5 C5 C#5 D5 D#5 E5
Boy, some things ain't, boy! Boy, some, nin-ga, na, nin-ga.
Gtr. 2
1/2
3

C#5
D5
D#5
E5
No, some things ain't, boy!
Boy, some, nin - ga, na, nin - ga.
1/2
T
A
B
Chorus:
B5
Rhy. Fig. 4A
Gtr. 5
C#5
D5
C#5
C5
Boy, some things ain't, boy!
Some -
Gtr. 4
Rhy. Fig. 4
F#5
G5
F5
w/Rhy. Figs. 4 (Gtr. 4) & 4A (Gtr. 5) 6 times
- thing takes a part of me. You and I were meant
to be. Ar - chie fought for me to lay. Some - thing takes a part

B5
F♯5
G5
F5
B5
of me.
Part
of
me.
Gtr. 2
F♯5
G5
F5
B5
F♯5
G5
F5
Part
of
me.
Part
B5
F♯5
G5
F(♯11)
Gtr. 5
of
me.
Gtr. 2
Gtr. 4

FREE FALLIN'

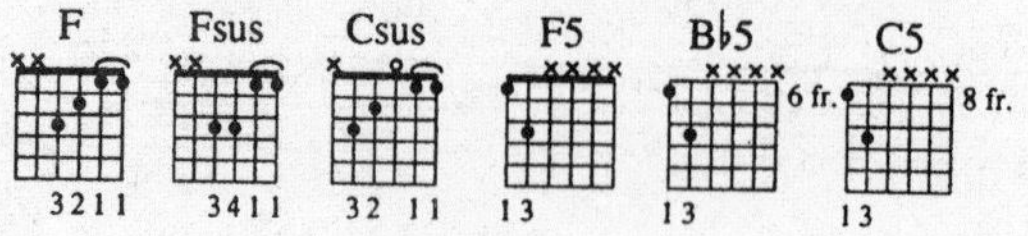

F Fsus Csus F5 B♭5 C5

3211 3411 32 11 13 13 13

6 fr. 8 fr.

Words and Music by
TOM PETTY and JEFF LYNNE

Moderate rock ♩=84

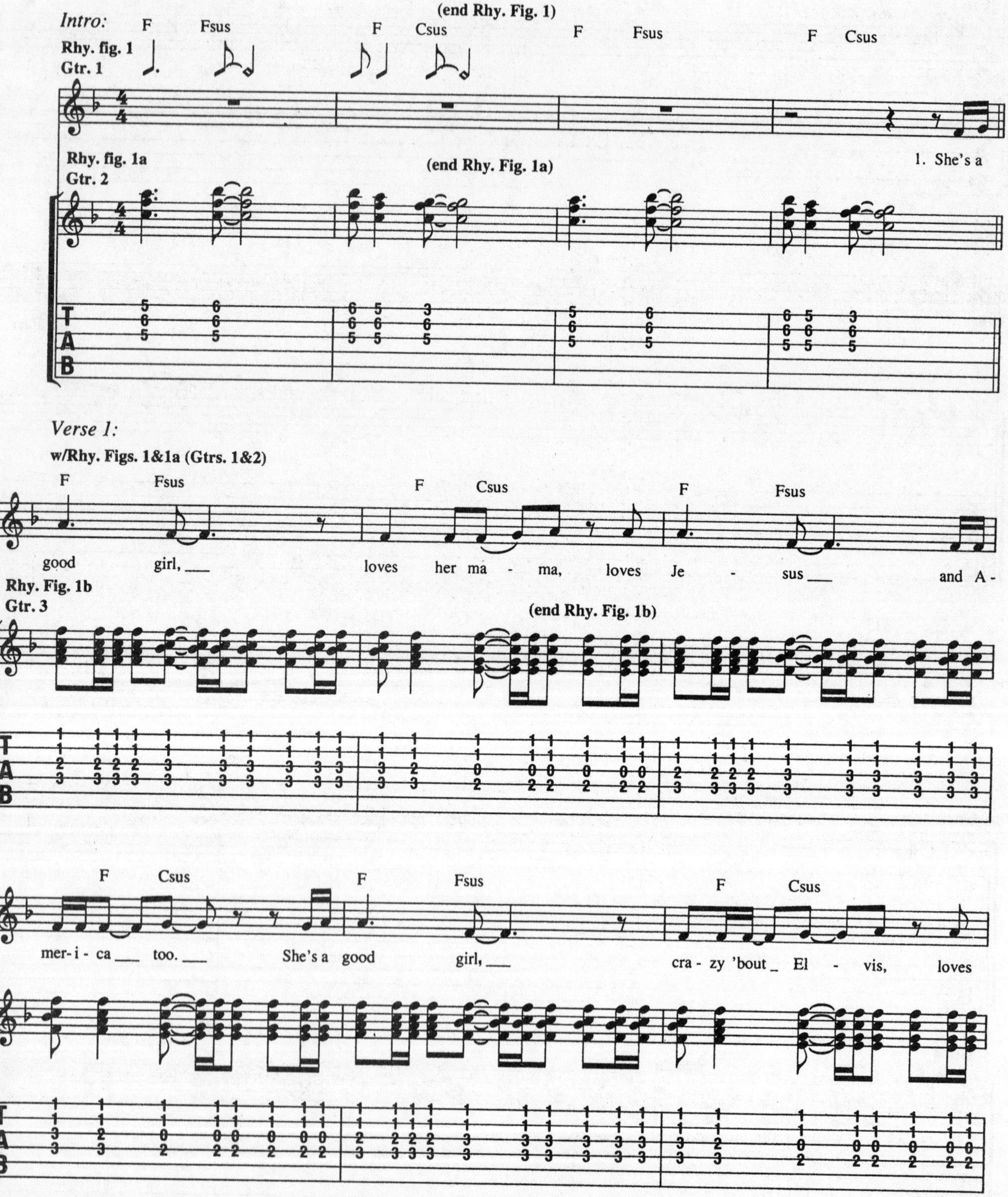

Intro:

F Fsus F Csus F Fsus F Csus

Rhy. fig. 1
Gtr. 1

(end Rhy. Fig. 1)

1. She's a

Rhy. fig. 1a
Gtr. 2

(end Rhy. Fig. 1a)

Verse 1:

w/Rhy. Figs. 1&1a (Gtrs. 1&2)

F Fsus F Csus F Fsus

good girl, ___ loves her ma - ma, loves Je - sus ___ and A -

Rhy. Fig. 1b
Gtr. 3

(end Rhy. Fig. 1b)

F Csus F Fsus F Csus
mer - i - ca ___ too. ___ She's a good girl, ___ cra - zy 'bout _ El - vis, loves

cont. Rhy. Fig. 1b
F Fsus F Csus F Fsus F Csus
hors - es and her boy-friend too.
2. It's a
w/Rhy. Figs. 1, 1a, &1b
F Fsus F Csus F Fsus
long day liv-in' in Re - se - da. There's a free - way
(3.) Vam - pires walk-in' through the val - ley move west down Ven -
(4.) See additional lyics.
F Csus F Fsus F Csus
run-nin' through the yard. And I'm a bad boy 'cause I don't e - ven miss her. I'm a
tur - a Boul-e-vard. And all the bad boys are stand-in' in the shad - ows. And the
F Fsus F Csus
bad boy for break - in her heart.
good girls are home with bro - ken hearts.
Chorus:
w/Rhy. Figs. 1, 1a, &1b
F Fsus
Now I'm free,
* Free fall - in', I'm a
F Csus F Fsus F Csus F Fsus
free fall - in'
Yeah I'm free,
free fall - in'. I'm a free fall - in', I'm a free fall - in'. I'm a free fall - in', I'm a
F Csus F Fsus
To Coda
1. F Csus
2. F Csus
free fall - in'.
3. And all the
free fall - in'. I'm a free fall - in', I'm a
* Background vocals after 4th Verse.

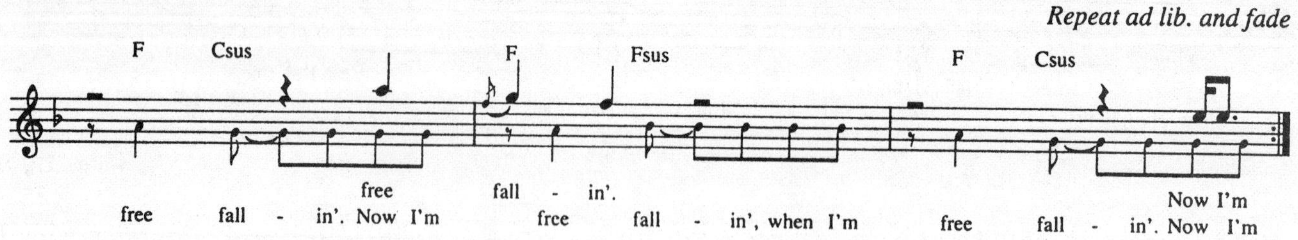

Verse 4:
I wanna glide down over Mulholland.
I wanna write her name in the sky.
I wanna free fall out into nothin'.
Gonna leave this world for awhile.
(To Chorus:)

FREE BIRD

Words and Music by
ALLEN COLLINS and RONNIE VAN ZANT

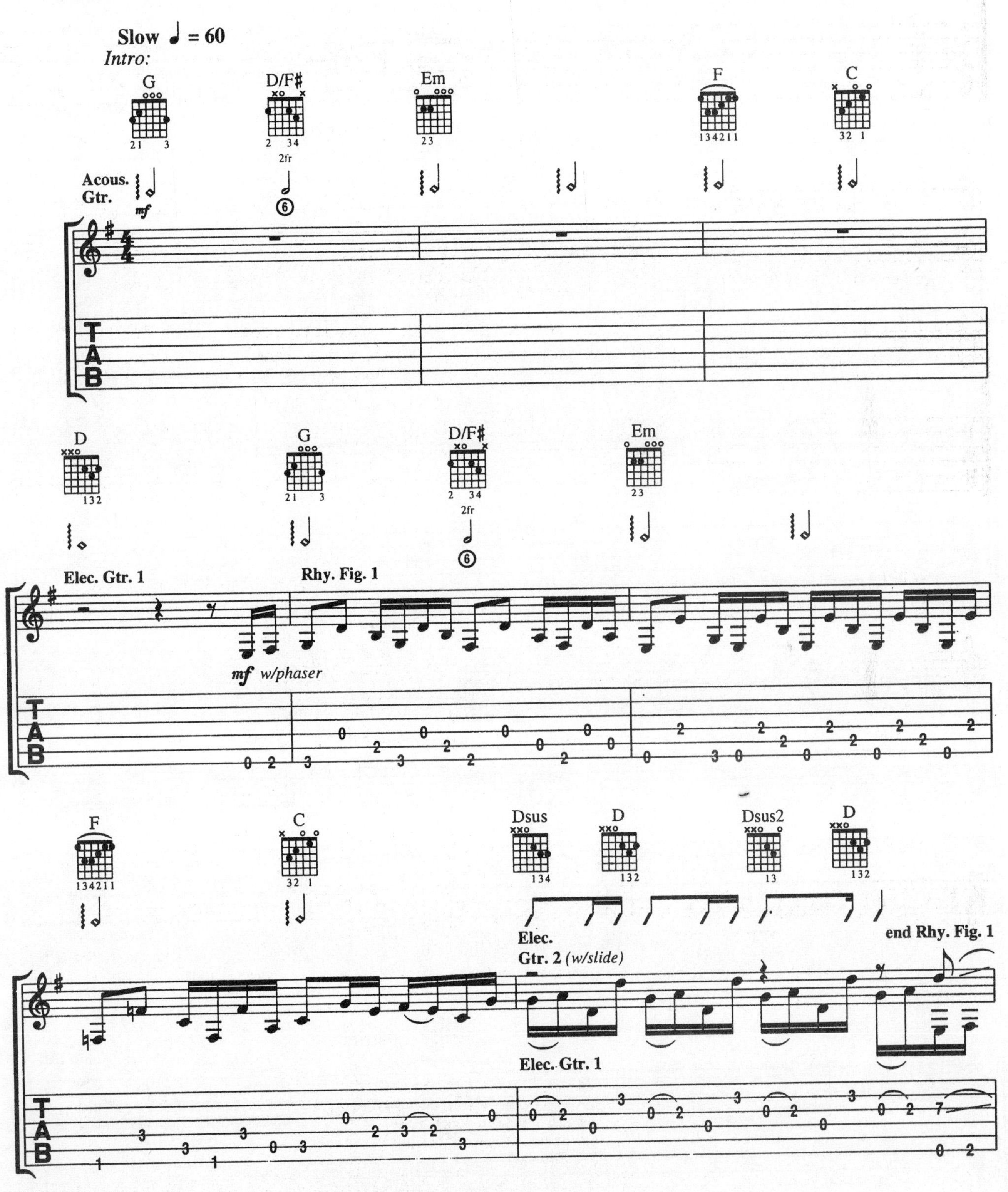

w/Rhy. Fig. 1 (Elec. Gtr. 1) 2 times
G
D/F#
Em
Rhy. Fig. 1A
Acous. Gtr.
Riff A
F
C
Dsus
D
Dsus2
D
Dsus
D
Dsus2
D
end Rhy. Fig. 1A
w/Rhy. Fig. 1A (Acous. Gtr.)
G
D/F#
Em
F
C
D
end Riff A

Verse:
w/Rhy. Figs. 1 (Elec. Gtr. 1) & 1A (Acous. Gtr.) both 4 times, simile
w/ad lib. slide gtr. (Elec. Gtr. 2) à la intro.
G
D/F#
Em
1. If I leave here to - mor - row,
2. Bye, bye, ba - by, it's been a sweet love, yeah.
F
C
D
would you still re - mem - ber me?
Though this feel - ing I can't change.
G
D/F#
Em
For I must be trav - el - ing on now,
But please don't take it so bad - ly,
F
C
D
'cause there's too man - y plac - es I've got to see.
'cause the Lord knows I'm to blame.
G
D/F#
Em
But if I stayed here with you, girl,
F
C
D
things just could - n't be the same.

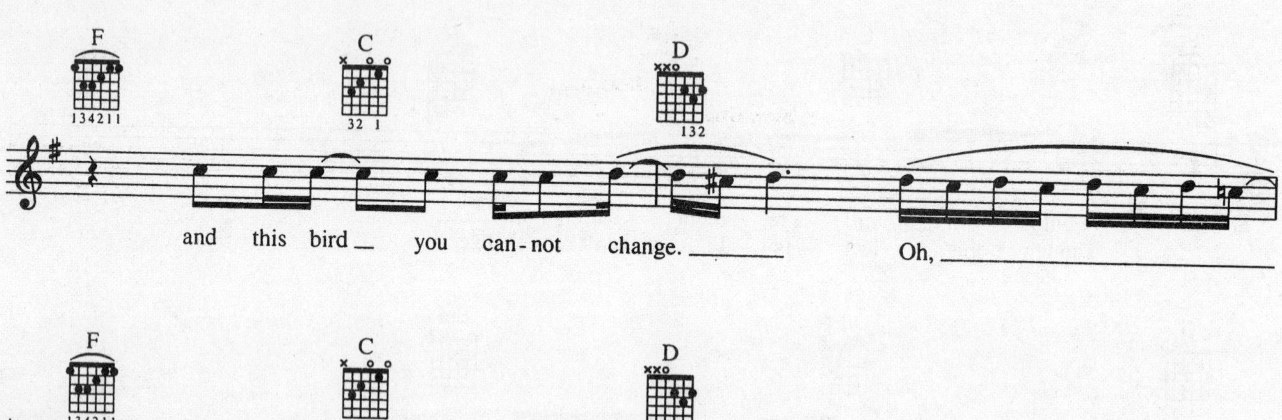

w/Rhy. Fig. 2 *(Acous. Gtr. & Elec. Gtr. 1) 2 times*

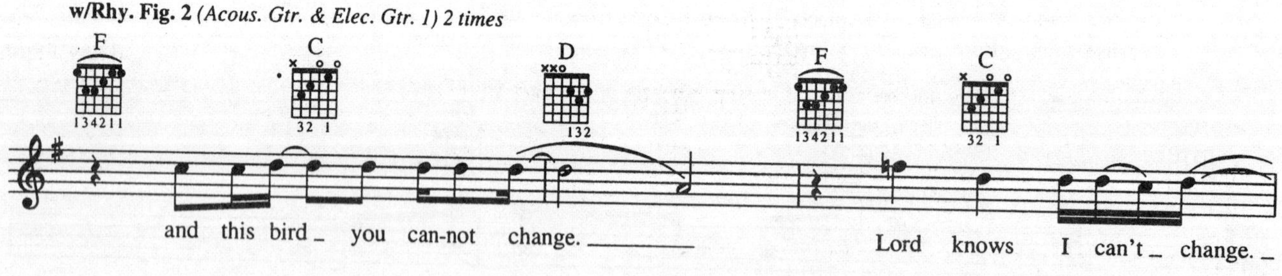

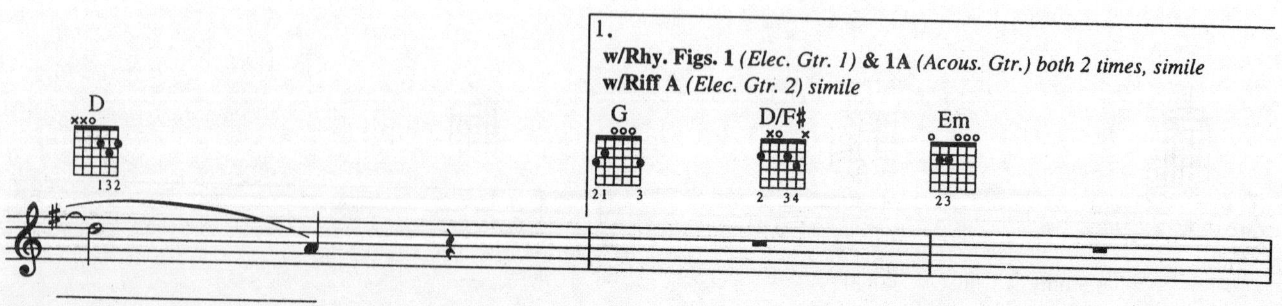

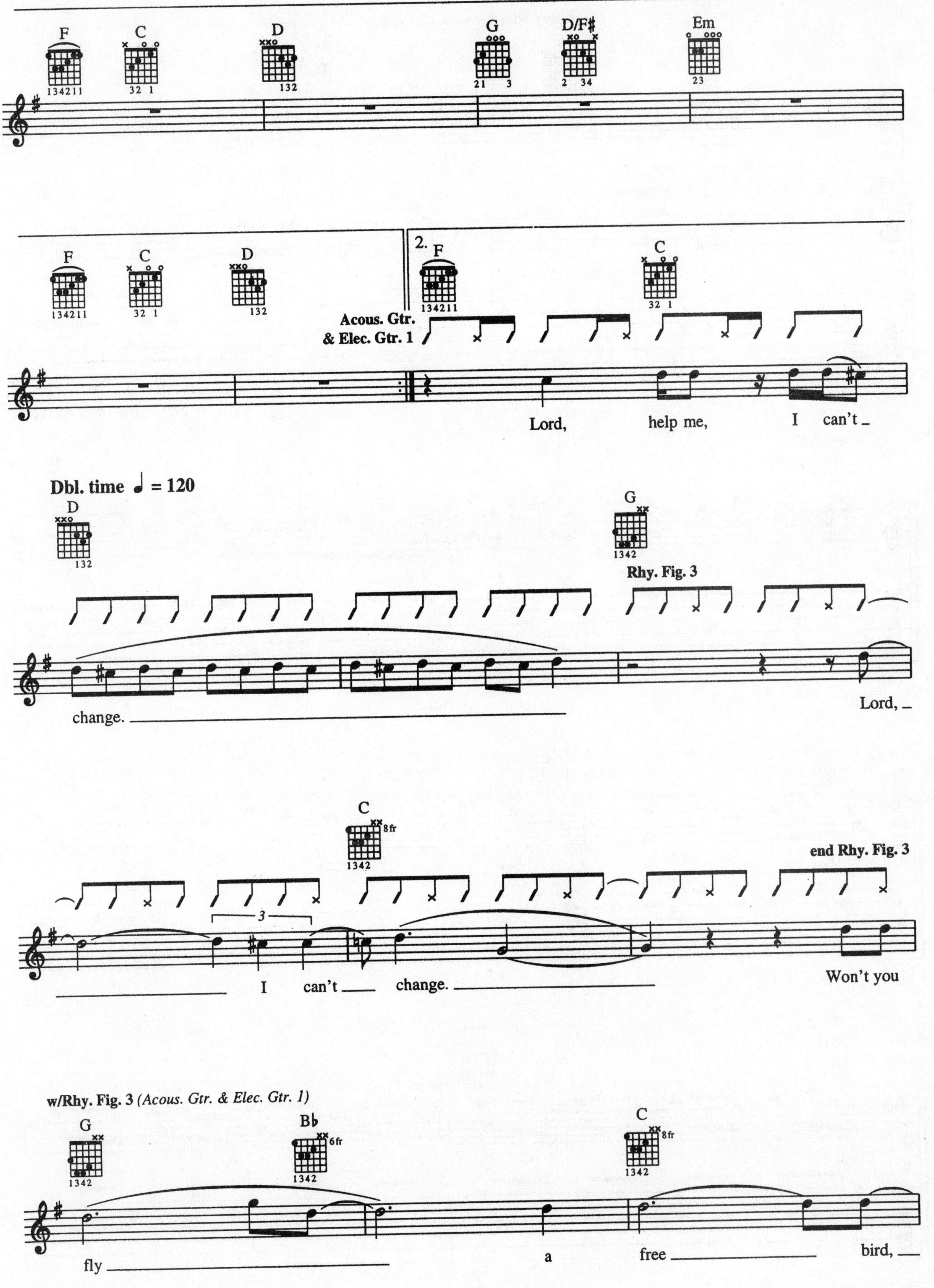
F
C
D
G
D/F♯
Em
2.
Acous. Gtr.
& Elec. Gtr. 1
Lord,
help me,
I can't
Dbl. time ♩ = 120
Rhy. Fig. 3
change.
Lord,
end Rhy. Fig. 3
I can't
change.
Won't you
w/Rhy. Fig. 3 (Acous. Gtr. & Elec. Gtr. 1)
B♭
fly
a
free
bird,

Guitar Solo:
w/Rhy. Fig. 3 (Acous. Gtr. & Elec. Gtr. 1) 4 times
G
B♭
6fr
1342
yeah.
Elec. Gtr. 3
8va throughout
f
C
8fr
T
A
B

C
8fr
1342

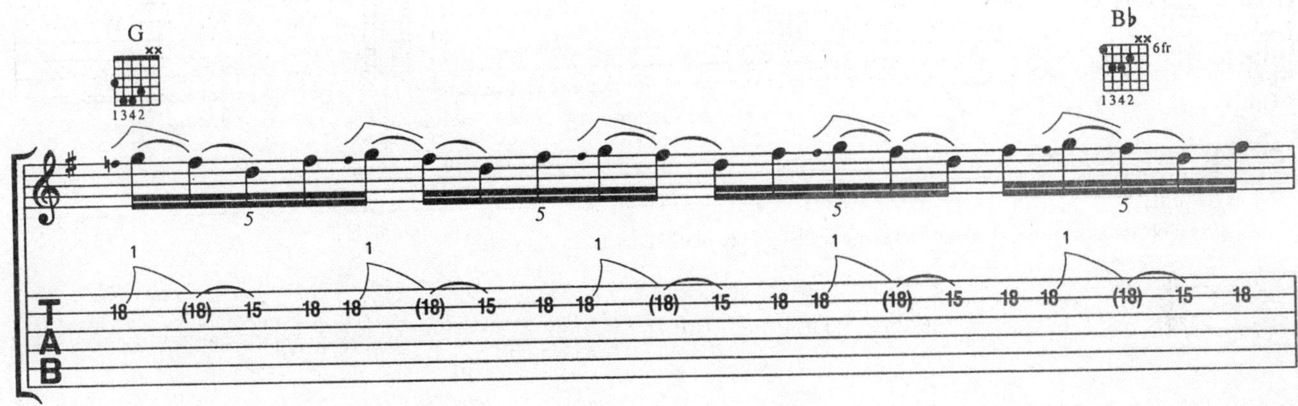
G
1342
B♭
6fr
1342

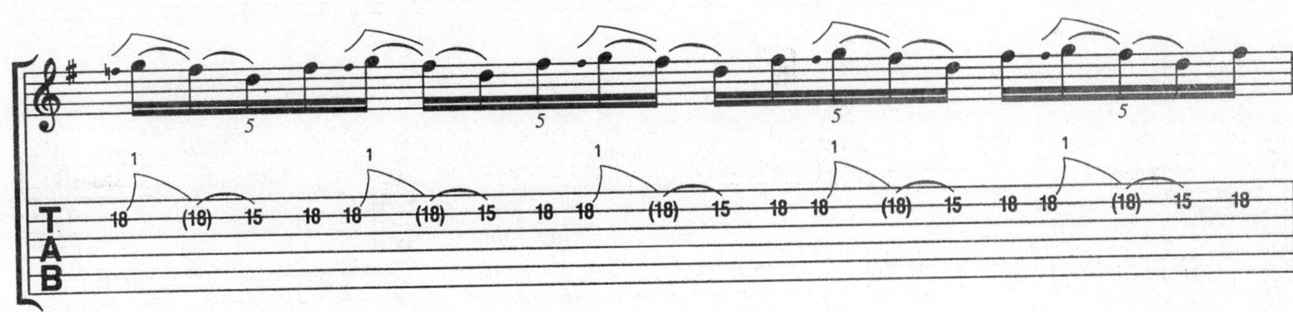

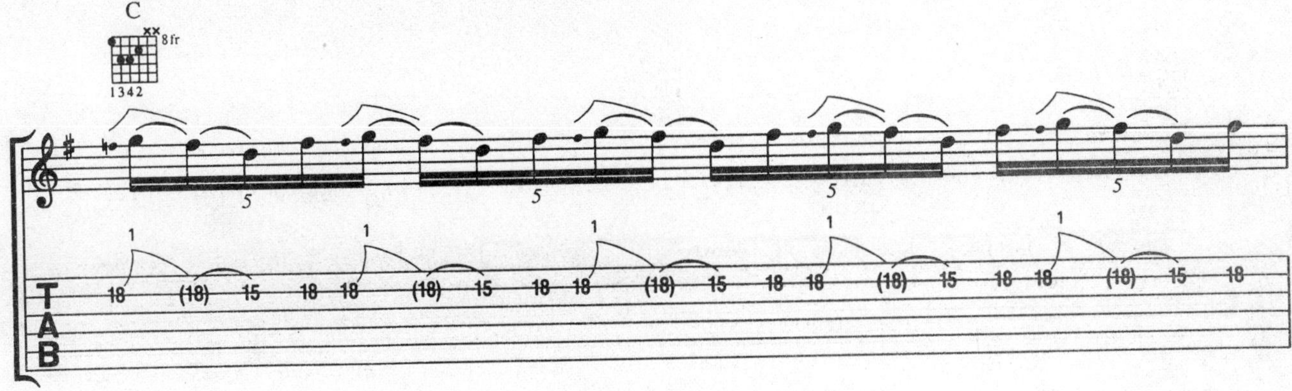
C
8fr
1342

*w/ad lib. gtr. solo (Elec. Gtr. 3) to end
G
Bb
C
Acous. Gtr. & Elec. Gtr. 1
*Ad lib. gtr. solo using G minor pentatonic scale (use previous 16 meas. as a model).
Play 4 times
open
Play 3 times
Play 4 times

Bb C Play 4 times G Bb

C Play 4 times

G Bb C

Play 8 times G5 G6 G5 G6 Bb5 Bb6 Bb5 Bb6 Bb5

C5 C6 C5 C6 C5 1.2.3. C6 C5 Bb5 4. C5 B5 Bb5 A5

Repeat and fade

G Bb C Bb

FREEDOM RIDER

Words and Music by
STEVE WINWOOD and JIM CAPALDI

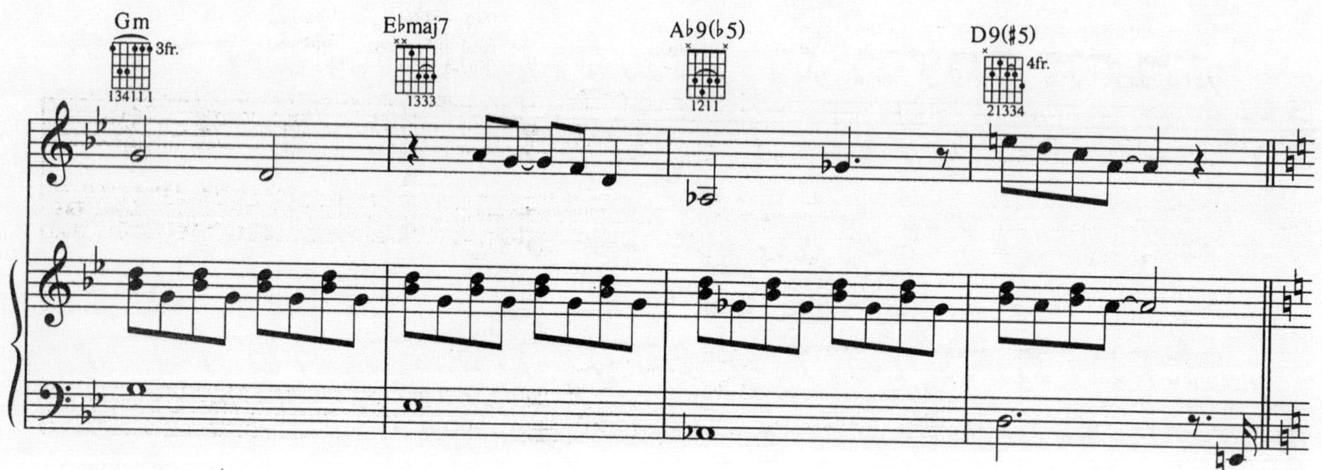

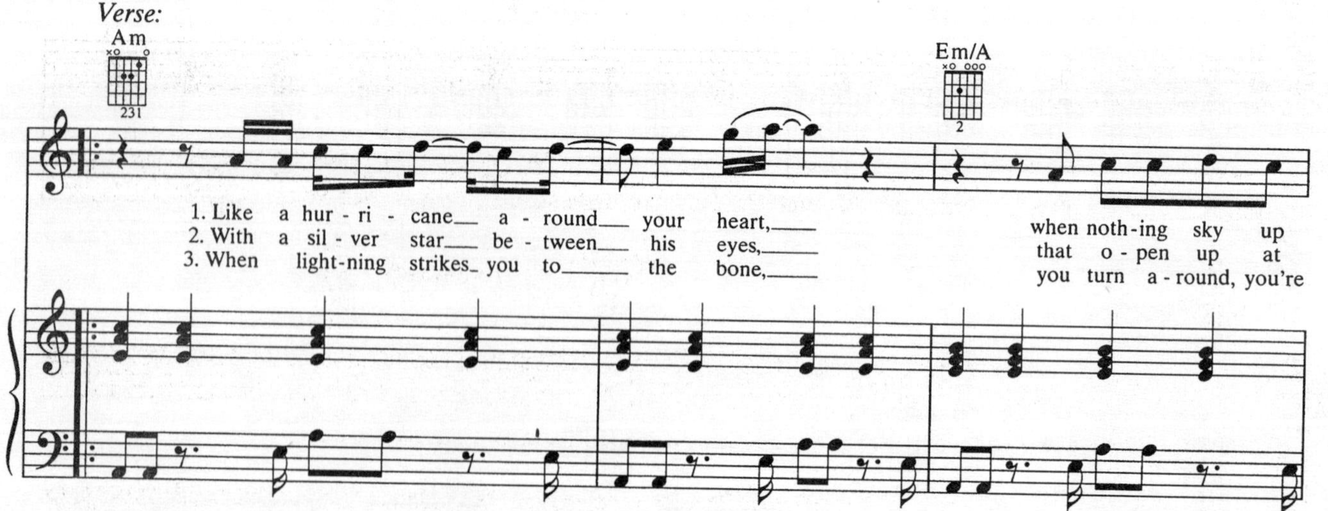

Ebm
6fr.
13421
torn a - part.
hid-den lies.
all a - lone.
He comes gath-'ring up the bits,
Big man cry-ing with de-feat,
By the time you hear that si - lent sound,
Bm7(b5)
1324
E7
2 1
Am
231
while hop-ing that the puz-zle fits.
see peo-ple gath-'ring in the street.
then your soul is in the lost and found.
He leaves you.
You feel good.
Broth - er.
Em/A
2
He leaves you.
You feel good.
Broth - er.
Ebm
6fr.
13421
Bm7(b5)
1324
To Coda
E7
2 1
Free - dom rid - er.

Tempo I
Gm
3fr.
134111
Tenor sax.
E♭maj7
1333
A♭9(♭5)
1211
D7(♭5)
113
1.
2.
Slightly faster ♩ = 112
Cm
13421
Dm
231

Dm
Em
E7
Flute Solo (ad lib.):
Am
Em/A
E♭m
6fr.
Bm7(♭5)
1.2.3.
E7(♯9)
6fr.
4.
E7(♯9)
6fr.
D.C. al Coda

Coda
E7(♯9)
6fr.
2134
Gm
3fr.
134111
Tenor sax.
E♭maj7
1333
A♭9(♭5)
1211
D7
213
Here___ it comes._
Gm
3fr.
134111
E♭maj7
1333
A♭9(♭5)
1211
1.2.3.
D7
213
Here___ it comes._

4.
D7
213
Gm
3fr.
134111
E♭maj7
1333
A♭9(♭5)
1211
D7
213
Gm
3fr.
134111
E♭maj7
1333
A♭9(♭5)
1211
Freely
D9(♭5)
4fr.
21341

FUNK #49

Words and Music by
JOE WALSH, DALE PETERS
and JAMES FOX

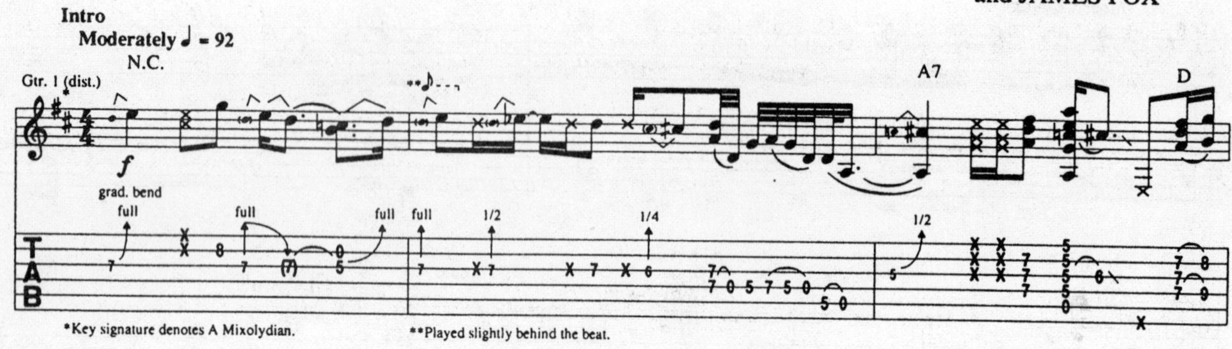

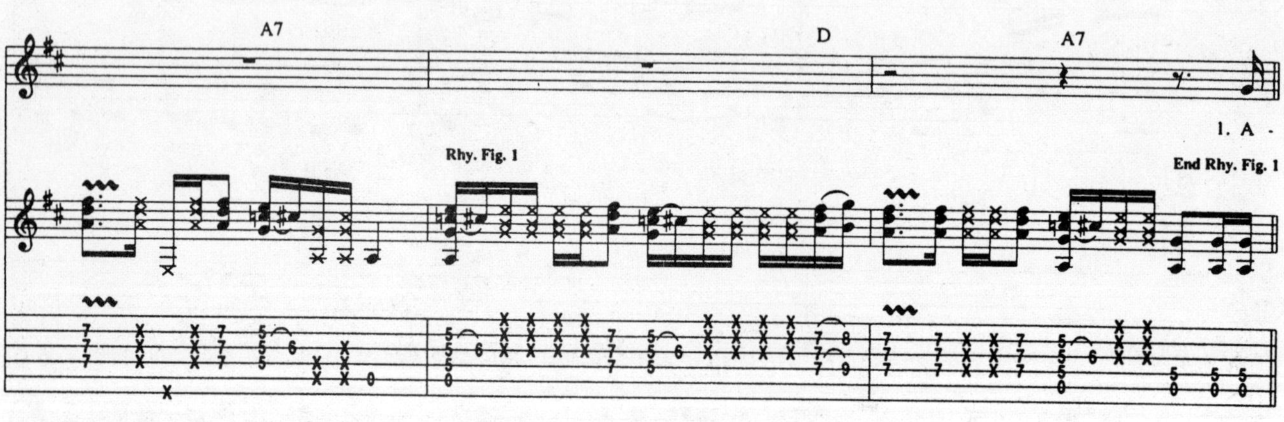

D A7

I don't think_ that's act - in' right,_ you don't think it's show - in'.
You don't think_ that I know your plan;_ what you try'n' to hand me?
If you're gon - na act this way,_ I think there's trou - ble brew - in'.

A5

* slight P.M.

* next 8 meas.

** Note in parenthesis added at random

B5

To Coda ⊕

E7♯9 A7 D

1. A7

2. A7

Drum Solo

Gtr. 1 tacet

15

Interlude

N.C.(A)

rake - - 1/4

1/2

1/4

A
D
A7
D
A7
A7
Rhy. Fig. 2
D
A7
D.S. al Coda
End Rhy. Fig. 2
Coda
Outro
Gtr. 1: w/ Rhy. Fig. 1, 4 times
A7
D
A7
D
A7
D
A7
D
A7
Gtr. 1: w/ Rhy. Fig. 2, 2 times
D
A7
D
A7
Begin Fade
Gtr. 1
P.M.
D
A7
D/A
A7
P.M.
D/A
A7
D/A
A7
D/A
A7
D
Fade Out

GIMME SOME LOVIN'

Words and Music by
STEVE WINWOOD, MUFF WINWOOD
and SPENCER DAVIS

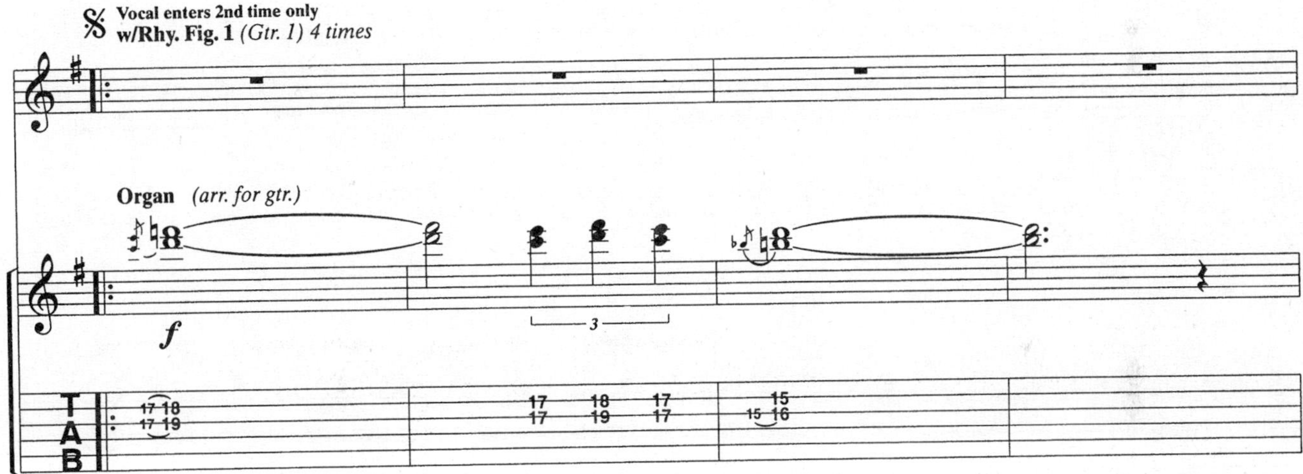

G C/G G C/G

Piano

Hey!

1. Well, my tem -
2. Well, I feel
3. Well, I feel

Gtr. 1

Verse:

G C/G G C/G G C/G G

Cont. rhy. simile

- p'ra - ture's ris - in' and my feet on the floor. Twen - ty peo - ple knock - ing 'cause they
so good, ev - 'ry - thing is sound - ing hot. You bet - ter take if eas - y 'cause the
so good, ev - 'ry - bod - y's get - tin' high. You bet - ter take it eas - y 'cause the

C/G G C/G G C/G

want - ing some more. Let me in, ba - by, I don't know what you've got. But you'd
place is on fire. Been a hard day and I don't know what to do. Wait a
place is on fire. Been a hard day, noth - ing went too good. Now, I'm

G C/G G C/G

Pre-chorus:

G

Organ

bet - ter take it eas - y, this place is hot.
Wait a min - ute, ba - by, it could hap - pen to you.
gon - na re - lax, honey, ev - 'ry - bod - y should.
} And I'm so glad we made

Gtr. 1

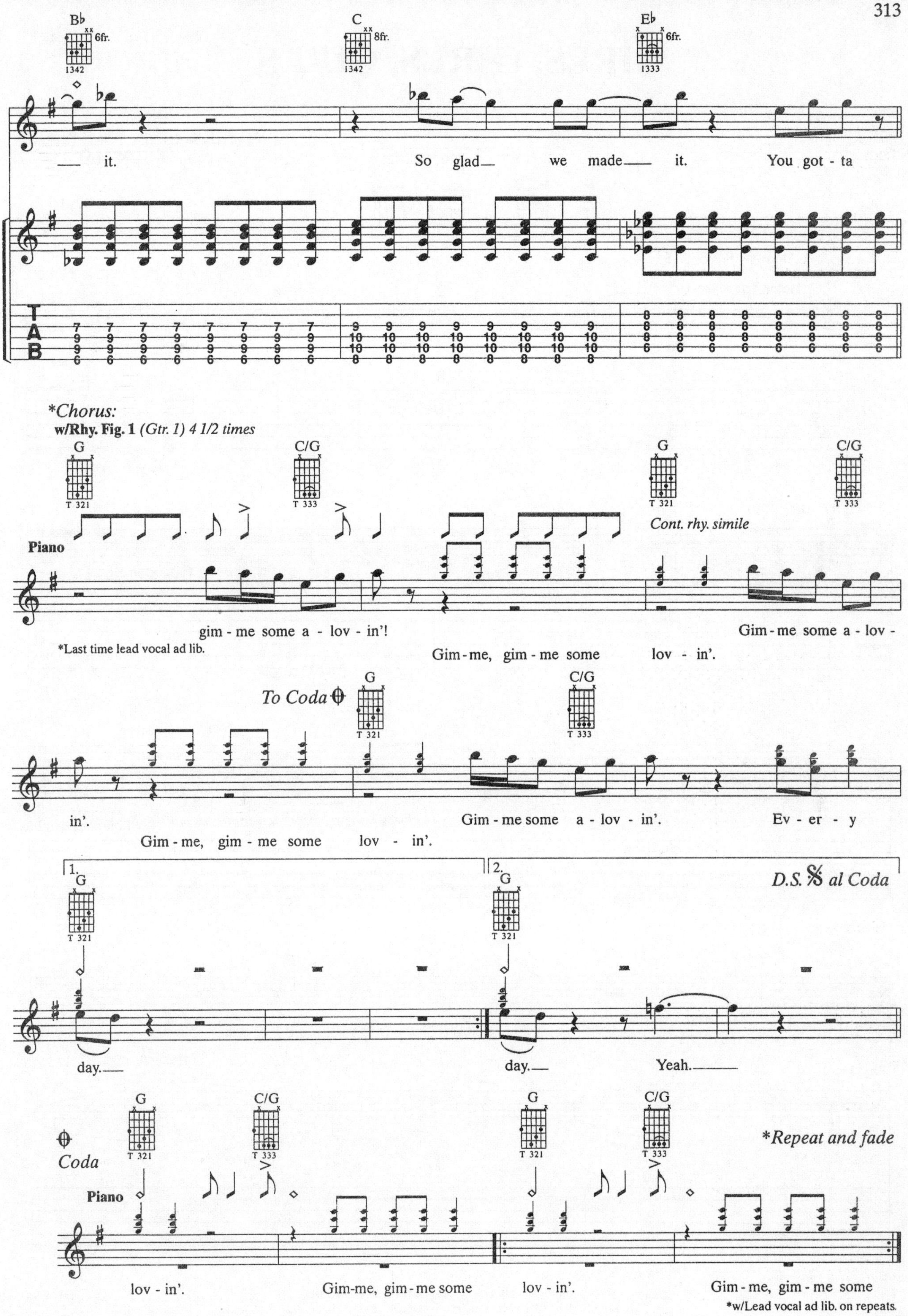

Bb C Eb

it. So glad we made it. You got-ta

*Chorus:
w/Rhy. Fig. 1 (Gtr. 1) 4 1/2 times

G C/G G C/G

Piano

Cont. rhy. simile

gim-me some a-lov-in'! Gim-me, gim-me some lov-in'. Gim-me some a-lov-

*Last time lead vocal ad lib.

To Coda

in'. Gim-me, gim-me some lov-in'. Gim-me some a-lov-in'. Ev-er-y

1. 2. D.S. al Coda

day. day. Yeah.

Coda

G C/G G C/G

*Repeat and fade

lov-in'. Gim-me, gim-me some lov-in'. Gim-me, gim-me some

*w/Lead vocal ad lib. on repeats.

GIRLS, GIRLS, GIRLS

Words by
NIKKI SIXX

Music by
NIKKI SIXX, TOMMY LEE
and MICK MARS

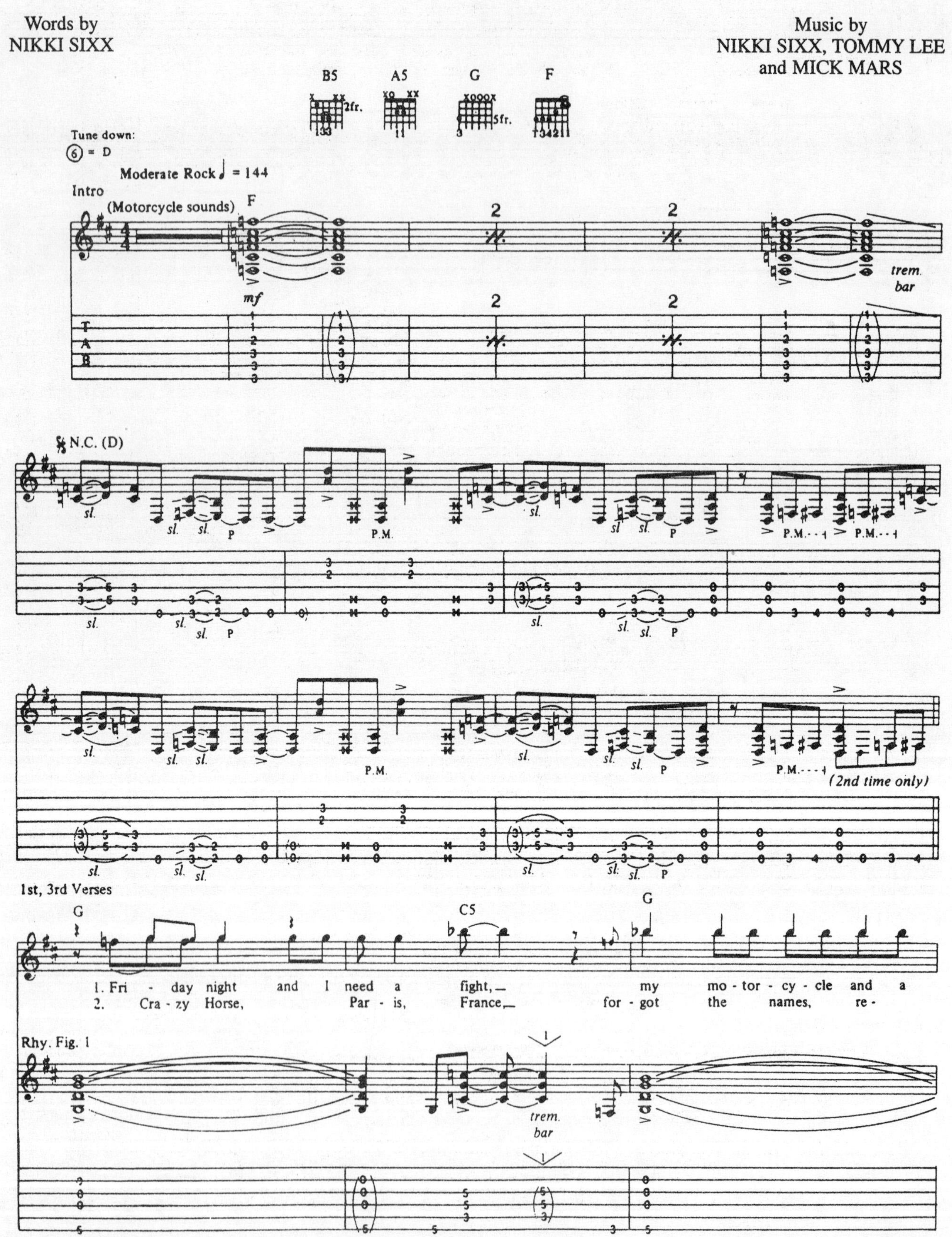

D
G
C
switch-blade knife. Hand - ful of grease and my hair feels right, but
mem-ber ro-mance. I got the pho - tos, a mén-age à trois,
trem bar
G
N.C.
Chorus
N.C. (D)
what I need to make me tight are those girls, girls, girls.
must-a broke those French-ies' laws with those girls, girls, girls. B - b - bod-
end Rhy. Fig. 1
Rhy. Fig. 2
P.M.
(G)
Long legs and bur - gun - dy lips. Girls, girls, girls.
y - shop and the Mar - ble Arch. Girls, girls, girls.
To Coda
Danc - in' down on the Sun - set Strip.
Trop - i - can - a's where I lost my heart.
P.M
P.M.

(D)
Girls, girls, girls. Red lips, fin - ger - tips.
(end Rhy. Fig. 2)
sl.
P
P.M.
2nd Verse
Repeat Rhy. Fig. 1
G
C5
D
Trick or treat, sweet to eat on Hal - low - een and New Year's Eve.
N.C.
Yan - kee girls, ya just can't be beat, but you're the best when you're off your feet.
Chorus
Repeat Rhy. Fig. 2 (1st 11 bars only)
N.C. (D)
Girls, girls, girls. At the Doll - house in Fort Lau - der - dale.
(G)
Girls, girls, girls. Rock - in' in At - lan - ta at
Tat - tle - tails. Girls, girls, girls. Rais - in' hell at the
Bridge
D5
Sev - enth Veil. Have you read the news in the So - ho Tri - bune? Ya know she
(cont. in slashes)

B5
A5
G
Rhy. gtr.
did_ me,__
well then she broke_ my heart._
I'm such a good, good
Lead gtr.
D5
boy,
I just need a new toy.
I tell ya what, girl,
(cont. in slashes)
B5
A5
G
Rhy. gtr.
dance for me._
I'll keep you o - ver - em - ployed._
Just tell_ me a
Lead gtr.
D5
sto - ry,__
you know the one I mean._
(cont. in slashes)

F
F
F
F
A.H.
(8va)
(8va)
D.S. al Coda
A.H.
Coda
(D)
Girls, girls, girls.
Hey, Tom-my, check that out man! What, Vince,
Rhy. Fig. 3
sl.
sl. P
Repeat Rhy. Fig. 3
where? Hey, right there! Hey! (whistles) Hey, ba - by, don't I know you from some-where?
Girls, girls, girls.
(end Rhy. Fig. 3) Lead gtr.
Full
Repeat Rhy. Fig. 3 (1st 2 bars only)
Girls, girls, girls.
Full
1/2
trem. bar

w/Rhy. Fig. 4
(G)
w/Rhy. Fill 1
Girls, girls, girls.
reverse rake
trem. bar
Girls, girls, girls.
trem. bar
trem. bar
Rhy. Fill 1
Rhy. Fig. 4
sl.

Guitar solo
N.C. (D)
Lead gtr.
Rhy. gtr.
Rhy. Fig. 5
trem. bar
8va

Repeat Rhy. Fig. 5 (5 times)
8va
Full
Full
loco
sl.
D5
Girls,
girls,
girls!
Lead gtr.
Rhy. gtr.
Free time
H
P

GOOD GOLLY MISS MOLLY

Words and Music by
ROBERT BLACKWELL
and JOHN MARASCALCO

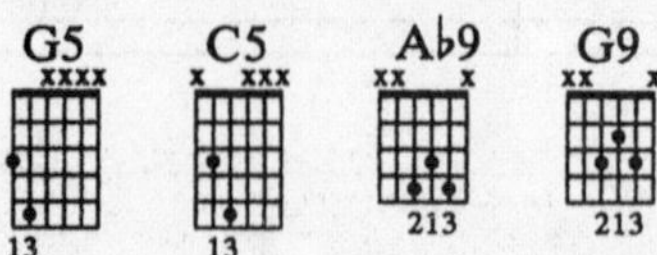

*Chords reflect overall harmony throughout.

C
G
Good gol - ly, Miss
end Rhy. Fig. 1
Chorus:
w/Rhy. Fig. 1 (Gtr. 1) 1st 11 bars only
Mol - ly, sure like to ball. Whoo,
good gol - ly, Miss Mol - ly, sure like to
C
3
G
ball. Hmm, when you're rock - in' and a - roll - in',
D
C
G5 G6 G5 G6 G5 G6 G5 G6 G5
w/Rhy. Fill 1 (Gtr. 1)
I can't hear your mam - ma call. 1.3. And from the
Verse:
G5
ear - ly, ear - ly morn - in' till the ear - ly, ear - ly night, when I caught Miss Mol - ly rock - in' at the
2. See additional lyrics

Chorus:
C
House of Blue Light. Good gol - ly, Miss Mol - ly, sure— like to
G
To Coda
D
ball.
Hoo, when you're rock - in' and a - roll - in',
C
G
I can't hear your mam - ma call.
2. Mam -
Saxophone Solo:

Verse 2:
Mamma, papa told me,
"Son, you'd better watch your step."
If they knew about Miss Molly,
I'd have to watch my pa myself.
(To Chorus:)

GOOD RIDDANCE (TIME OF YOUR LIFE)

Lyrics by BILLIE JOE
Music by BILLIE JOE and GREEN DAY

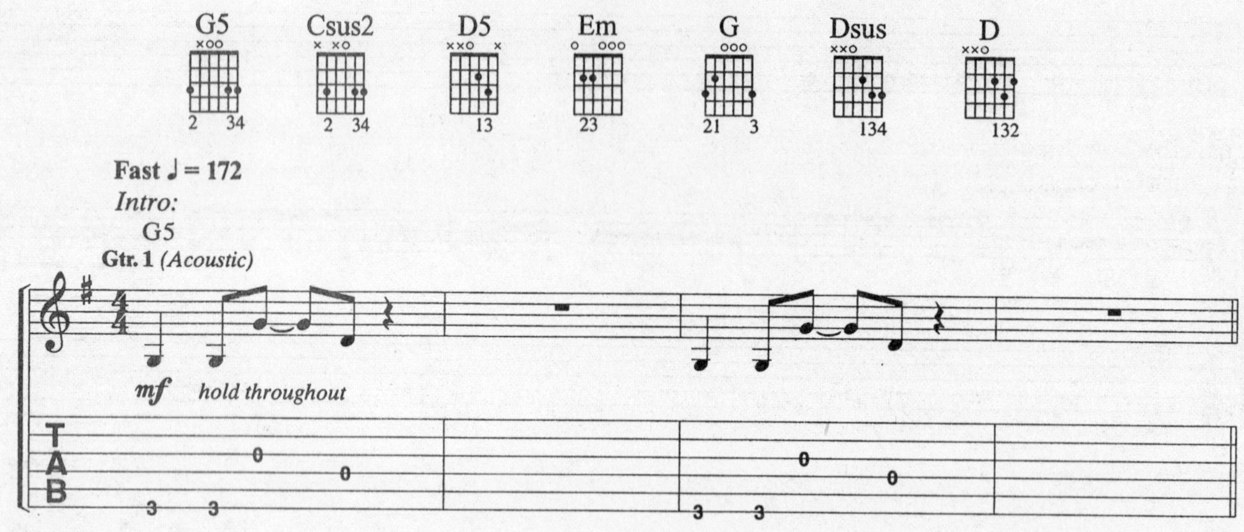

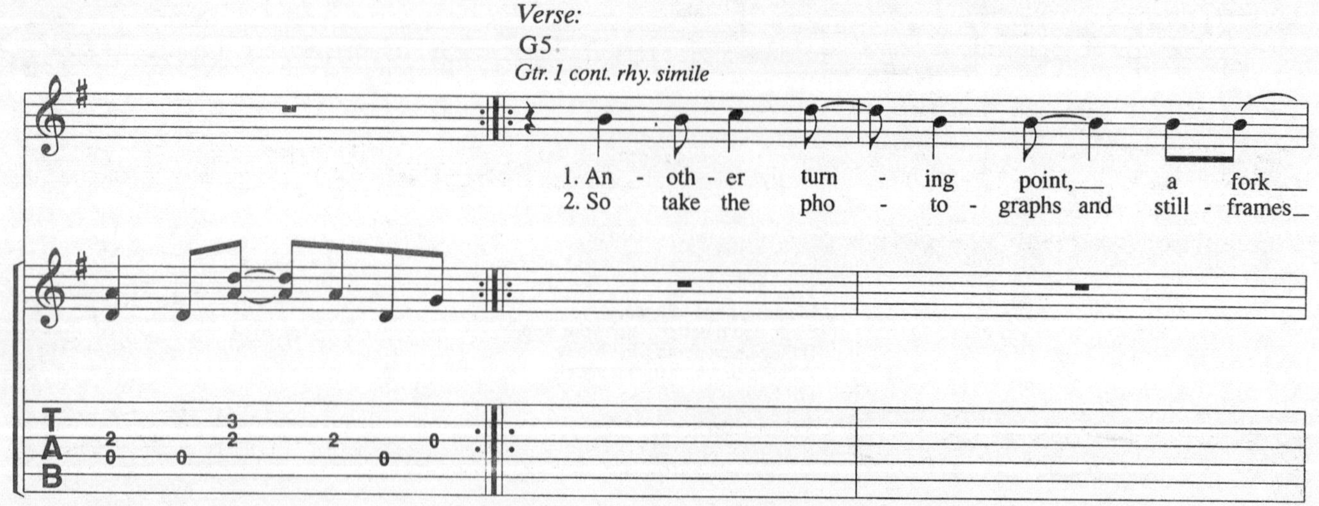

Csus2 D5 G5
stuck in the road. Time grabs you by
in your mind. Hang it on
Csus2 D5
the wrist, di - rects you where to go.
a shelf in good health and good time.
Em D5 Csus2
So make the best of this test and don't ask why.
Tat - toos of mem - o - ries, and dead skin on trial.
G5 Em D5
It's not a ques - tion, but a les -
For what it's worth, it was worth
Chorus:
Csus2 G5 Em
- son learned in time.
all the while.
It's some - thing un - pre - dict -
G5 Em G5
- a - ble, but in the end is right. I
1. 3.
Em D G5
hope you had the time of your life.

Csus2
D5
G5
Csus2
To Coda
D5
2.
D
Interlude: w/strings
G
Gtr. 1
Vocal 1st time only
of your life.
Csus2
Dsus2
D
Play 4 times
Em
D
Cont. rhy. simile
Csus2
G5
Em
D
Csus2
G5
It's
Chorus:
Em
G5
Gtr. 1
Em
G5
Cont. rhy. simile
some - thing un - pre - dict - a - ble, but in the end is right.
Em
D
I hope you had the time of your life.
G5
Csus2
D
G5
Csus2
D
D. S. al Coda
It's
Coda
D5
G5

GOT THE LIFE

Words and Music by
JONATHAN DAVIS, REGINALD ARVIZU,
BRIAN WELCH, JAMES CHRISTIAN SHAFFER
and DAVID RANDALL SILVERIA

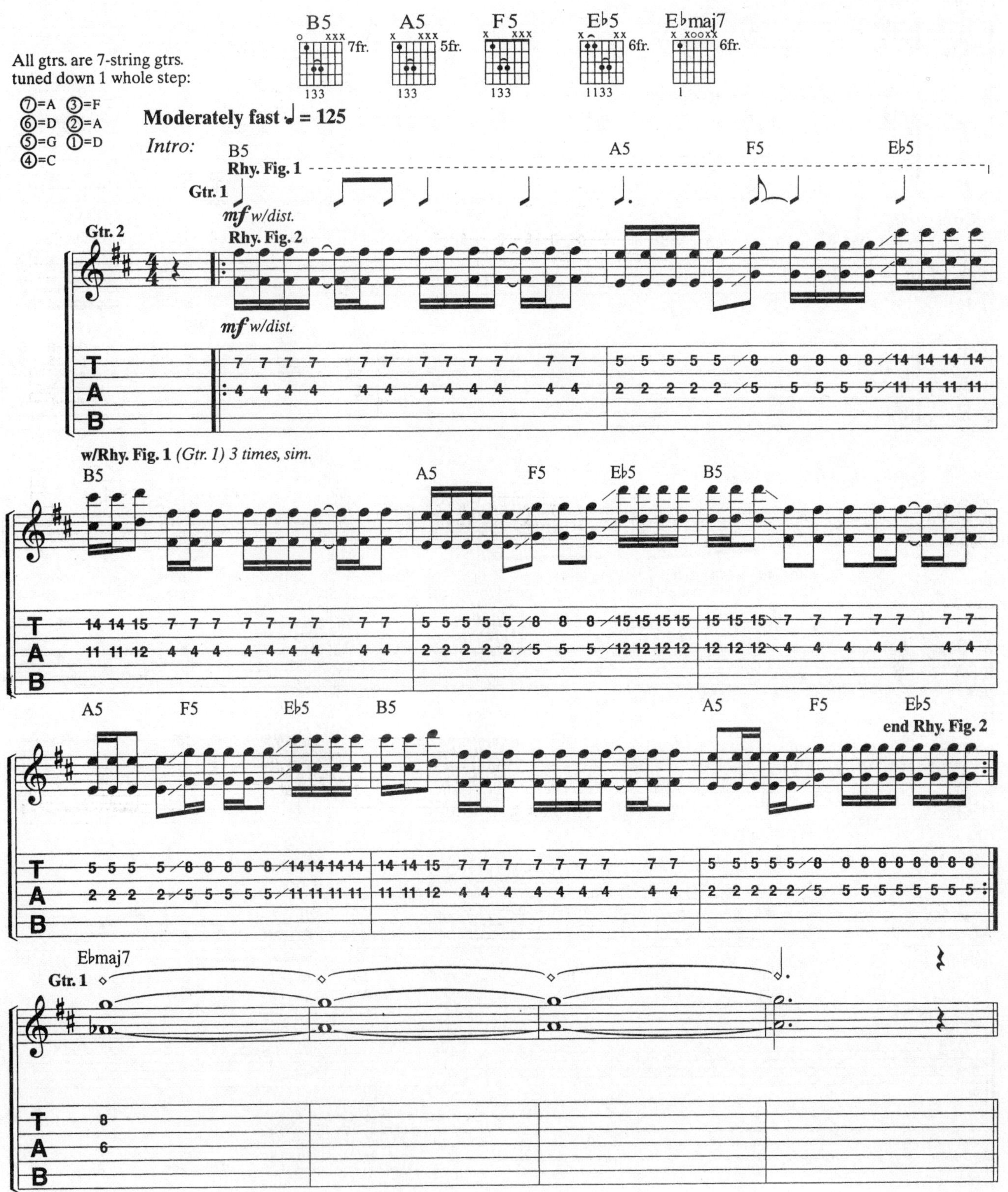

Verse:
N.C.
1. Hate some - thing, some - time, some way, some - thing kicked on the foot - ball.
2. Hate some - thing, some - where each day deal - ing with God for - give now.
Gtr. 3 (left)
8va
mf
w/whammy pedal (pitch sounds 15ma)
Gtr. 4 (right)
Rhy. Fig. 3
mf
w/Rhy. Fig. 3 (Gtr. 4) 3 times
My, some - thing in - side. I'll nev - er, ev - er fol - low. So give me___ some -
Why this sh** in - side. How an - y - one would fol - low. So give me___ noth -
(8va)
thing that is for real. I'll nev - er, ev - er fol - low.
ing, just fear.___ And
(8va)
1.

C♯5
Get your boo - gie on!
Gtr. 3
(8va)
Gtr. 5
mf
4 4 × × 2 2 4 4 × × × × 4 4 × × 4 4 × × 2 2 4 4 × × × × 4 4 × ×
Get your boo - gie on!
Gtr. 5
4 4 × × 2 2 4 4 × × × × 4 4 × × 4 4 × × 2 2 4 4 × × × × 4 4 × ×
Chorus:
w/Rhy. Fig. 1 (Gtr. 1) 7 times
w/Rhy. Fig. 2 (Gtr. 2) 2 times
2.
B5
A5
F5
E♭5
oth - er sh** will fol - low.
God breaks me and then I see
(Why?
*Gtr. 4
(8va)
loco
Gtr. 3
whammy pedal turned off
12 12 12 12 12 12 12 12 12 12
*Play 2nd time only (fdbk. note hold from Bridge ending).

B5 A5 F5 E♭5 B5
the lie. Who wants to see? God don't mind,
)
(Why?
A5 F5 E♭5 B5 A5 F5 E♭5
I've al-read-y got the life. Oh, I say.
)
B5 A5 F5 E♭5 B5
God breaks me and then I see the lie. Who
(Why?
)
To Coda
A5 F5 E♭5 B5 A5 F5 E♭5
wants to see? God don't mind, I've al-read-y got
(Why?
Interlude:
B5 A5 F5 E♭5 *B5 A5 F5 E♭5 B5
Gtr. 1
Gtr. 1 cont. in notation
the life. Oh, I say.
)
Gtr. 2
T
A
B
8
6
*Chords implied by Bass gtr.
Gtr. 2
A5 F5 E♭5 B5 A5 F5 E♭5 B5 A5 F5 E♭5
fdbk.
(0)
0
Gtr. 1
3
pp
4 4 4 4 4 4 4 4

Bridge:
B5
A5
F5
Eb5
Each day I can feel it swal - low, in - side some - thing took from me.
Gtr. 1
Riff A
w/ring modulator
8
8
9
10
B5
A5
F5
Eb5
w/Riff A (Gtr. 1)
Gtr. 2 tacet
B5
I don't feel your death - ly ways. Each day I feel so hol - low,
fdbk.
end Riff A
8
8
9
A5
F5
Eb5
B5
A5
F5
Eb5
in - side al - ways beat - ing me. Shall we nev - er see? So come dance_ with me.

N.C.

Dance_ with me. Dance_ with me. Dance_ with me. Dance_

Gtr. 3

1 1 1 1

13 (13) 13 13 (13) 13

Gtr. 4

1/2 1 1/2 1/2

12 (12) 0 3 12 (12) 0 3 12 (12) 0 3 12 (12) 0 3

D.S. 𝄋 al Coda

"Rumbutly boo. Rumbutly boo. Rumbutly boo. Rum bum ding dong ba. Rumbutly ooh. Rumbutly boo."

__ with me. Dance_with me. Dance_with me. Why?______

1 1 1

13 (13) 13 13 (13)

8va

fdbk.

1/2 1/2 1/2 1/2

12 (12) 0 3 12 (12) 0 3 12 (12) 0 3 12 (12) (12)

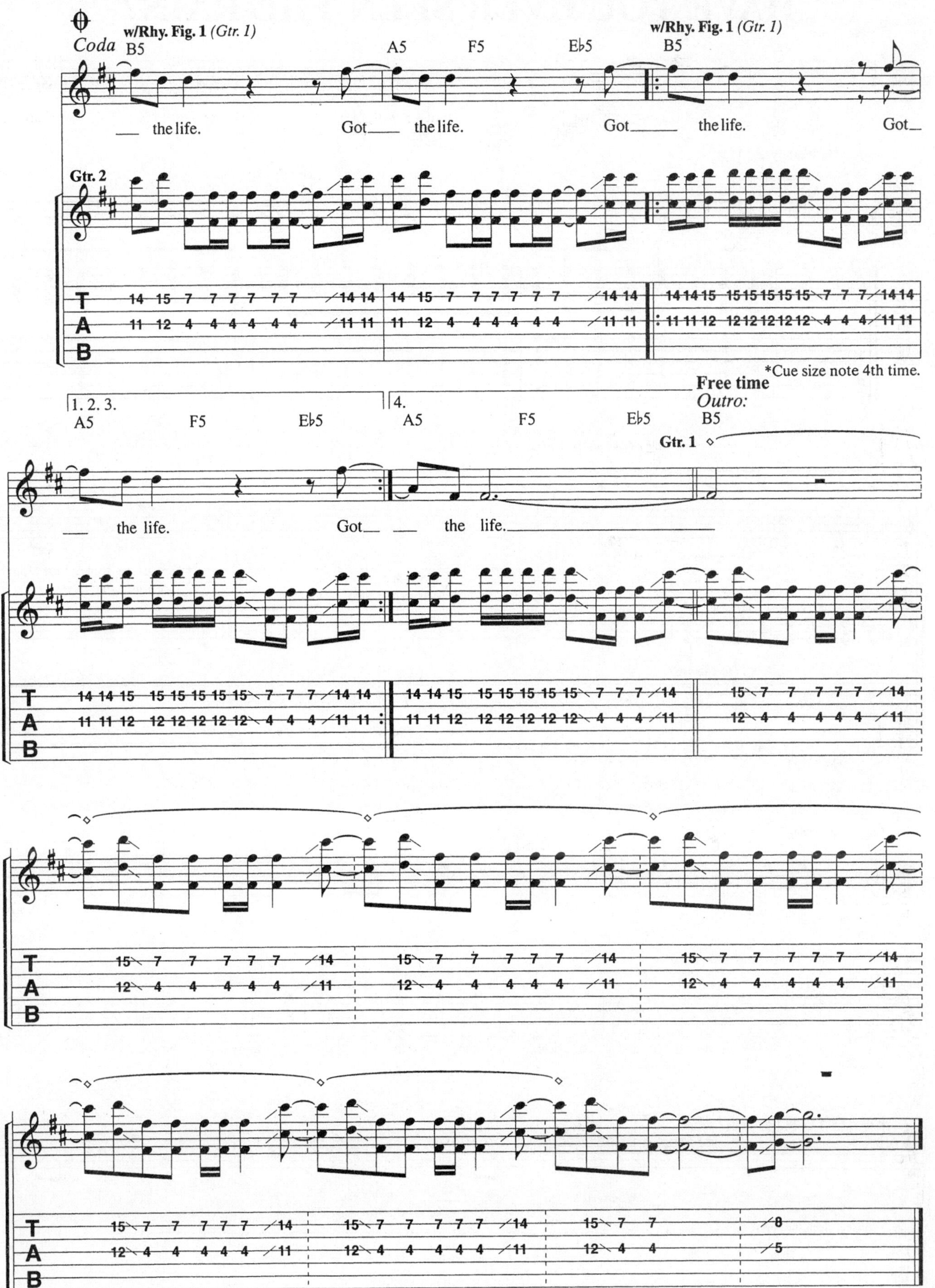
Coda
w/Rhy. Fig. 1 (Gtr. 1)
B5
A5
F5
E♭5
w/Rhy. Fig. 1 (Gtr. 1)
B5
the life.
Got
the life.
Got
the life.
Got
Gtr. 2
*Cue size note 4th time.
1. 2. 3.
4.
Free time
Outro:
A5
F5
E♭5
A5
F5
E♭5
B5
Gtr. 1
the life.
Got
the life.

HAVE YOU EVER SEEN THE RAIN?

By
J.C. FOGERTY

Verse 2:
Yesterday, and days before,
Sun is cold and rain is hard.
I know, been that way for all my time.

'Til forever, on it goes
Through the circle, fast and slow,
I know, and I can't stop. I wonder.

HEART OF GOLD

Words and Music by
NEIL YOUNG

Verse :
Em7
C
D
G
Gtr. 1
1. I wan - na live,
I wan - na give,
2. See additional lyrics
Gtr. 2 (Acoustic)
mp hold
Em
C
D
G
Em
I've been a min - er for a heart of gold.
Em
C
D
G
Em
Fm7
It's these ex - press - ions I nev - er give that keep me search-in' for a

G
C
C A G
Em
heart of — gold
and — I'm get-tin' old.
Em Em7
G
C
Keep me search-in for a heart of — gold,
an' I'm get-tin' old. —
C A G
open
1.
w/Rhy. Fig. 2 (Gtr. 1, simile)
8
2.
w/Rhy. Fig. 2 (Gtr. 1, 1st 6 bars only, simile)
6
Outro:
w/Rhy. Fig. 1 (Gtr. 1, simile)
Em7
D
Em7
D
Em7
Keep me search-in' for a heart of gold. —
You keep me search-in' an' I'm grow - in' old.
D
Em7
w/Rhy. Fig. 1 (Gtr. 1, 1st 3 bars only, simile)
Keep me search-in' for a heart of gold. —
I've been a min - er for a
G
C
G
heart of — gold,
Huh, —
huh, huh.
Mm.

Verse 2:
I've been to Hollywood, I've been to Redwood.
I cross the ocean for a heart of gold.
I've been in my mind, it's such a fine line
That keeps me searchin' for a heart of gold;
And I'm gettin' old.

HELLO MARY LOU

Words and Music by
GENE PITNEY and CAYET MANGIARACINA

A
234
C♯7
3241
I knew, Ma - ry Lou,
we'd nev - er part.
hold
F♯m
134111
B7
213 4
E7
2 1
D
132
So hel - lo, Ma - ry Lou, good - bye heart.
Verse:
Cont. rhy. simile
1. You passed me by one sun - ny day, flashed those big, brown
saw your lips, I heard your voice, be - lieve me I just
end Rhy. Fig. 1
eyes my way. And ooh, I want - ed you for - ev - er - more.
had no choice. Wild hors - es could - n't make me stay a - way.
T
A
B

A
D
Now I'm not one that gets a round,_ swear my feet's stuck
I thought a - bout a moon - lit night, my arms a - round you
hold
A
E7
A
D
to the ground._ And though I nev - er did___ need you be - fore.__
good and tight. That's all I had to see___ for me to say.__
hold
Chorus:
w/Rhy. Fig. 1 (Elec. Gtr.)
Cont. rhy. simile
A
D
I said } hel - lo, Ma - ry Lou,___ good - bye heart._
Hey, hey, }
A
E7
__ Sweet Ma - ry Lou,_ I'm so in love___ with you.___

A
C♯7
F♯m
I knew, Ma - ry Lou, we'd nev - er part. So hel - lo,
To Coda
B7
E7
A
D
A
Ma - ry Lou, good - bye heart.
Guitar Solo:
Cont. rhy. simile
Elec. Gtr.
D
f fingerstyle
hold
hold
A
E7
hold
hold
A
C♯7
F♯m
1/2
hold
D.S. al Coda
B7
E7
A
D
A
2. I

Coda
A
234
B7
213 4
E7
2 1
So hel - lo, Ma - ry Lou, good - bye
Elec. Gtr.
hold
hold
T
A
B
A
234
D
132
A
234
B7
213 4
heart. Yes, hel - lo, Ma - ry Lou,
hold
E7
2 1
A
234
D
132
A
234
Acous. Gtr.
good - bye heart.
hold

HEMORRHAGE

Lyrics and Music by
CARL BELL

Tune down 1/2 step:
⑥=E♭ ③=G♭
⑤=A♭ ②=B♭
④=D♭ ①=E♭

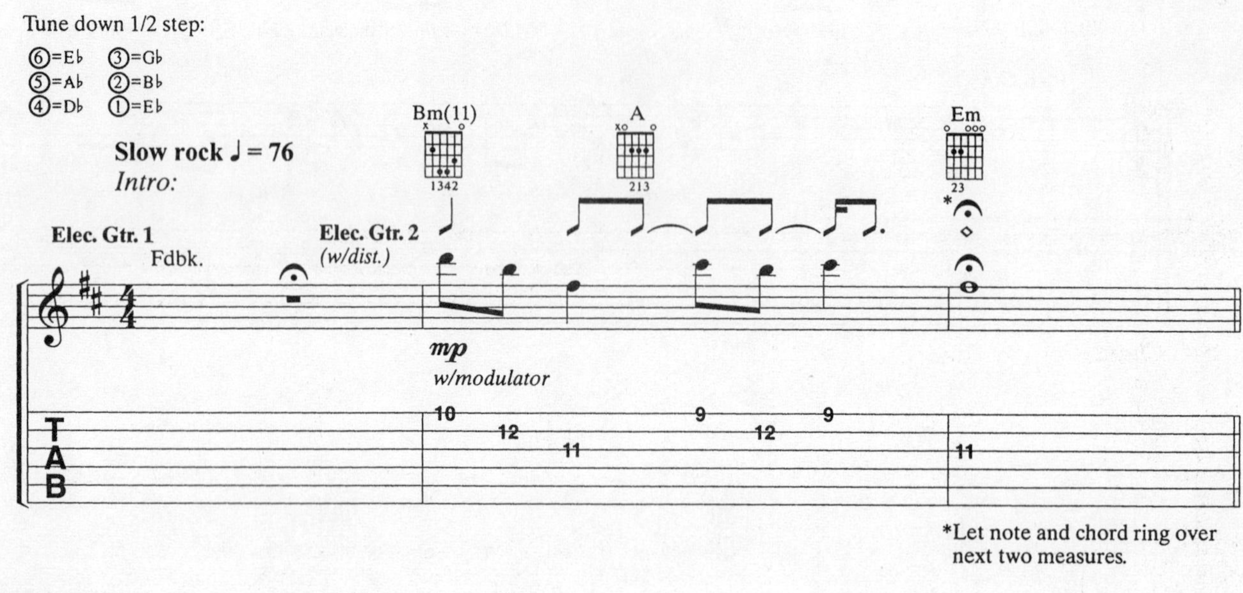

*Let note and chord ring over next two measures.

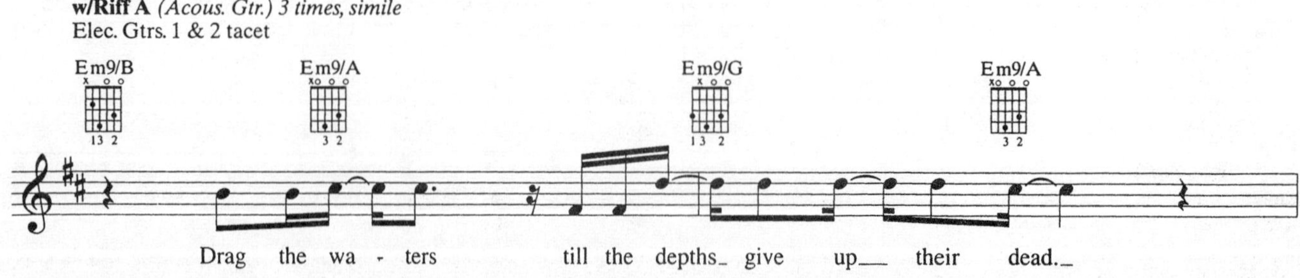

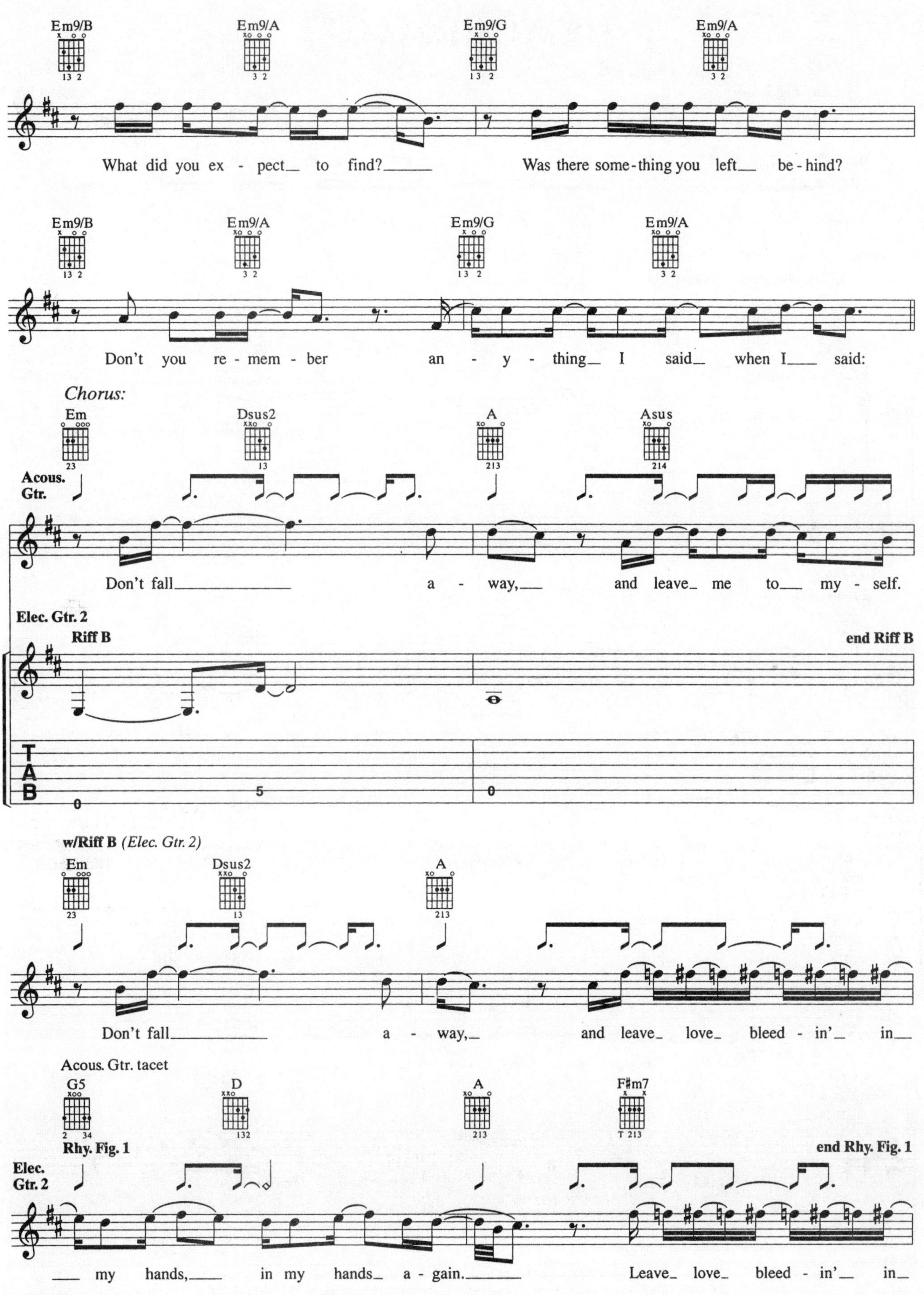
Em9/B
Em9/A
Em9/G
Em9/A
What did you ex - pect_ to find?_____
Was there some-thing you left_ be-hind?
Em9/B
Em9/A
Em9/G
Em9/A
Don't you re-mem-ber an - y - thing_ I said_ when I___ said:
Chorus:
Em
Dsus2
A
Asus
Acous. Gtr.
Don't fall____________ a - way,__ and leave_ me to__ my - self.
Elec. Gtr. 2
Riff B
end Riff B
TAB
w/Riff B (Elec. Gtr. 2)
Em
Dsus2
A
Don't fall__________ a - way,_ and leave_ love_ bleed - in'_ in__
Acous. Gtr. tacet
G5
D
A
F#m7
Rhy. Fig. 1
end Rhy. Fig. 1
Elec. Gtr. 2
___ my hands,___ in my hands_ a - gain.______ Leave_ love_ bleed - in'_ in__

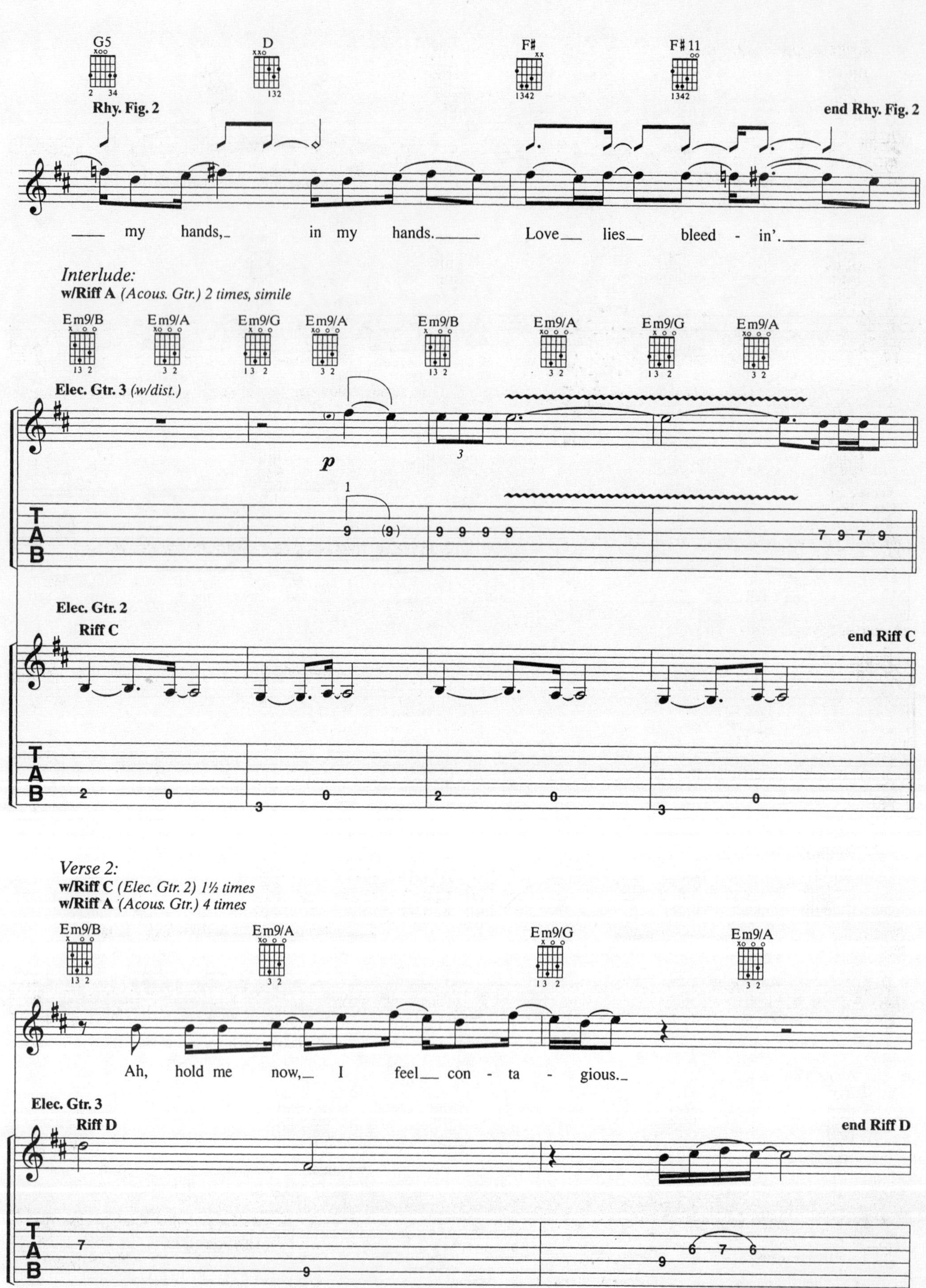
G5
D
F♯
F♯11
Rhy. Fig. 2
end Rhy. Fig. 2
___ my hands,_ in my hands.____ Love__ lies__ bleed - in'.________
Interlude:
w/Riff A (Acous. Gtr.) 2 times, simile
Em9/B
Em9/A
Em9/G
Em9/A
Em9/B
Em9/A
Em9/G
Em9/A
Elec. Gtr. 3 (w/dist.)
p
Elec. Gtr. 2
Riff C
end Riff C
Verse 2:
w/Riff C (Elec. Gtr. 2) 1½ times
w/Riff A (Acous. Gtr.) 4 times
Em9/B
Em9/A
Em9/G
Em9/A
Ah, hold me now,_ I feel__ con - ta - gious._
Elec. Gtr. 3
Riff D
end Riff D

w/Riff D (Elec. Gtr. 3) 2 times
Em9/B
Em9/A
Em9/G
Em9/A
Am I the on - ly place_ that you've left_ to_ go?_
She cries her life_ is like some mov - ie, black_ and white._
Elec. Gtr. 3 tacet
Dead ac - tors fak - in' lines._ O - ver and o - ver and o - ver a - gain,_ she cries:
Elec. Gtr. 2
Chorus:
Acous. Gtr. tacet
E5
D5
A
Elec. Gtr. 2
Rhy. Fig. 3
Don't fall_ a - way,_ and leave_ me to_ my - self.
F♯m7
end Rhy. Fig. 3
Don't fall_ a - way,_ leave_ love_ bleed - in'_ in_

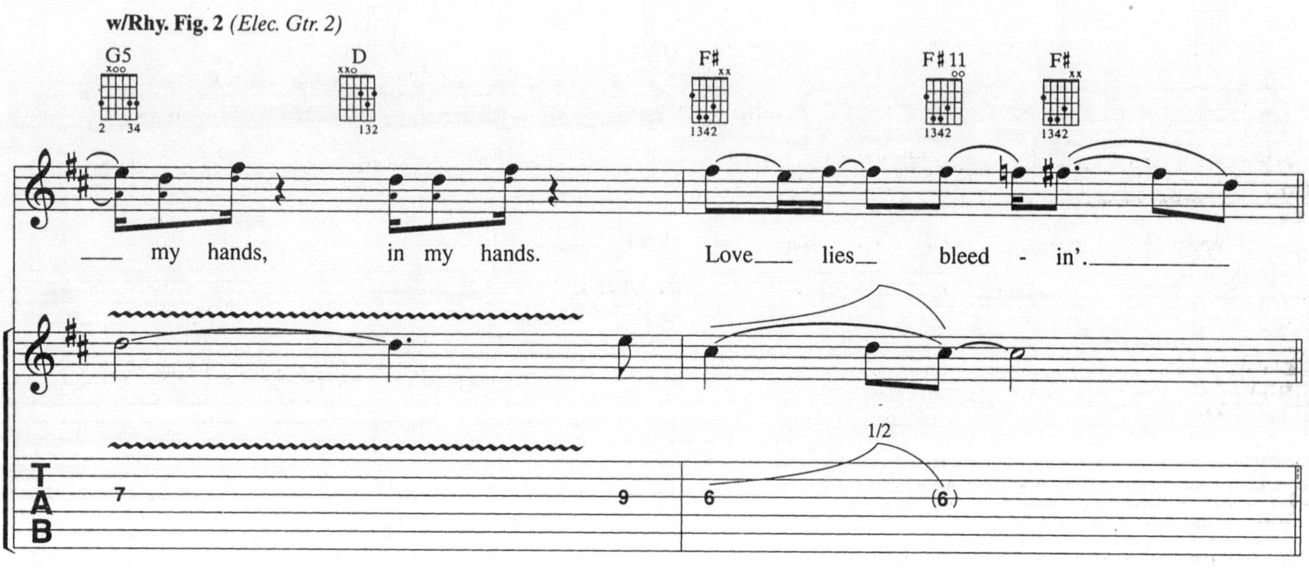

Bridge:

Elec. Gtr. 3 tacet

E5
F♯5
You don't re - mem - ber, but I do. You
Guitar Solo:
Elec. Gtr. 2 tacet
Em9/B
Em9/A
nev - er e - ven tried.
Elec. Gtr. 1
mf
Em9/G
Em9/A
Em9/B
Em9/A

Em9/G
Em9/A
Em9/B
Em9/A
Em9/G
Em9/A
Em9/B
Em9/C♯
Em9/D
Em9/F♯
Elec. Gtr. 1
Elec. Gtr. 2
Chorus:
w/Rhy. Fig. 3 (Elec. Gtr. 2)
Elec. Gtr. 1 tacet
E5
D5
A
D5
A
Don't fall a - way, and leave me to my - self.
Elec. Gtr. 3
loco

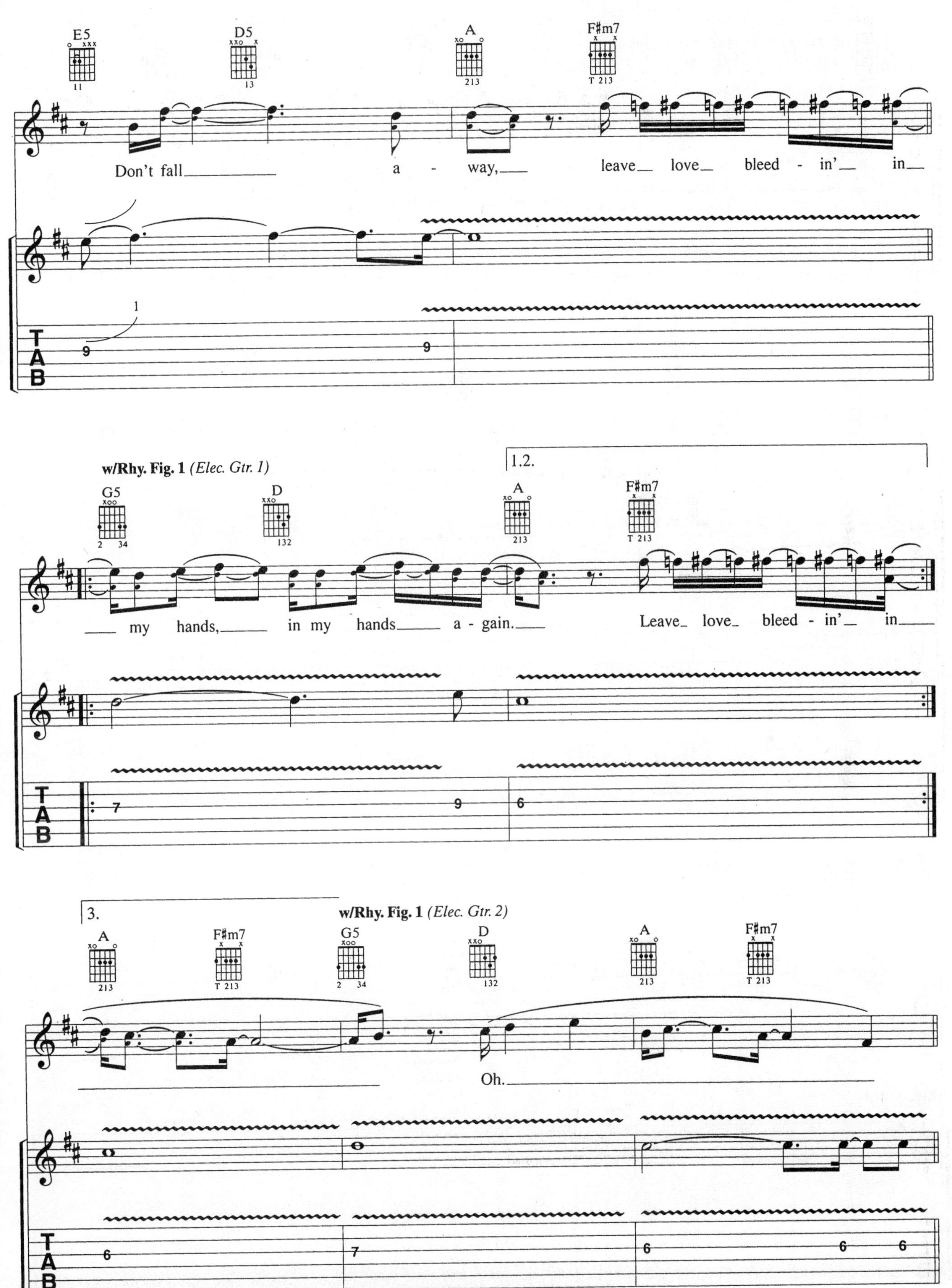
E5
D5
A
F♯m7
Don't fall a - way, leave love bleed - in' in
w/Rhy. Fig. 1 (Elec. Gtr. 1)
1.2.
G5
D
my hands, in my hands a - gain. Leave love bleed - in' in
3.
w/Rhy. Fig. 1 (Elec. Gtr. 2)
Oh.

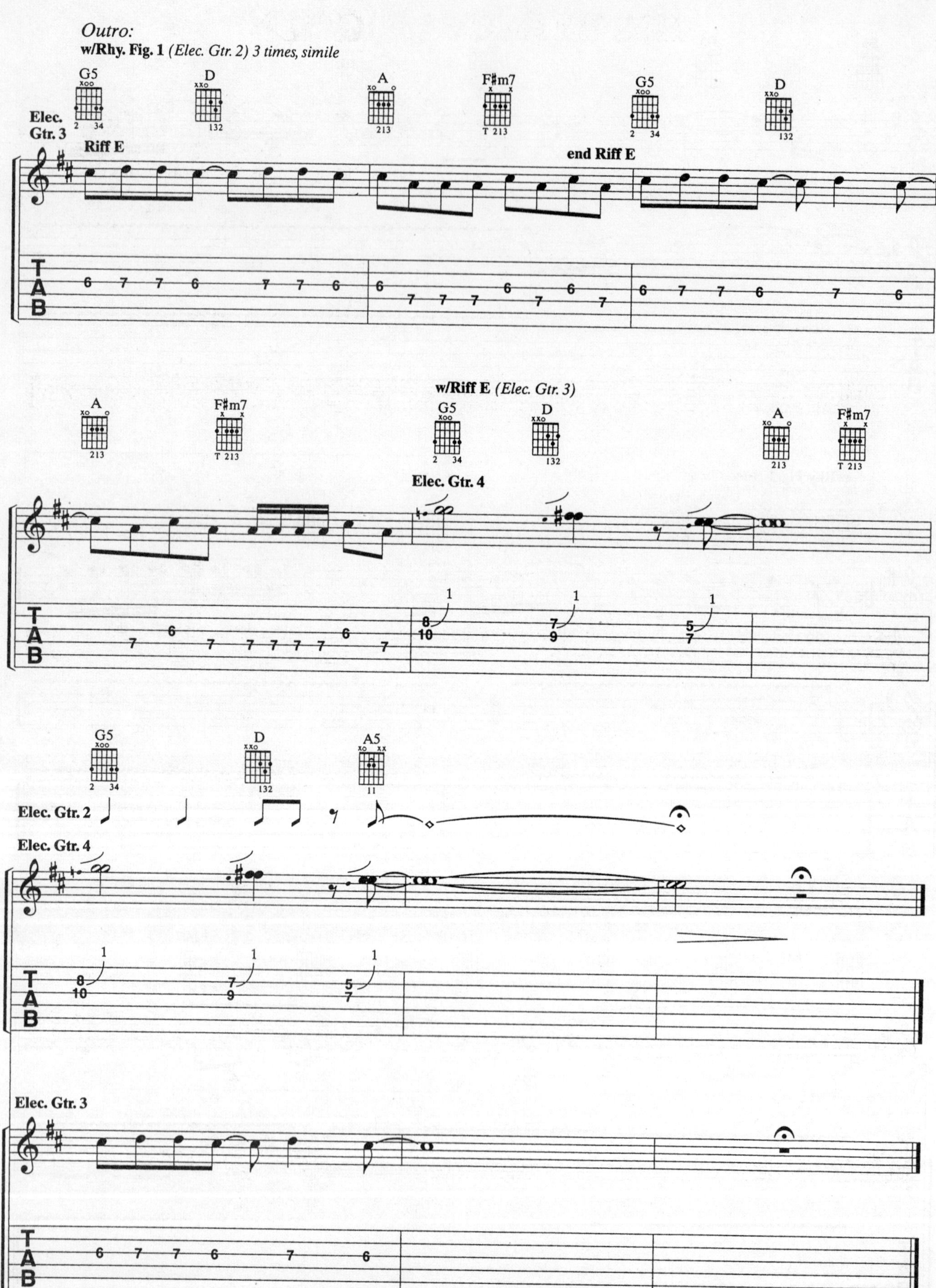

Outro:
w/Rhy. Fig. 1 (Elec. Gtr. 2) 3 times, simile
G5
D
A
F♯m7
Elec. Gtr. 3
Riff E
end Riff E
w/Riff E (Elec. Gtr. 3)
Elec. Gtr. 4
A5
Elec. Gtr. 2
Elec. Gtr. 4
Elec. Gtr. 3

HIGHER AND HIGHER

Words and Music by
GARY JACKSON, CARL SMITH
and RAYNARD MINER

G
C G
quench my de - si - re, and I'll be at
G6
G G6 G G6
your side for - ev - er more.
D
1.
2.
2. You know your love 1. Now, once,
Verse:
Cont. rhy. simile
G
2. See additional lyrics
I was down - heart - ed,
C G
G6
G G6 G G6
dis - ap - point - ment was my clos - est friend.
D
But then you came,
G
C G
and he soon de - part - ed, and you know he nev -
G6
G G6 G G6
D
er showed his face a - gain.
Chorus:
Vocal ad lib. on repeats
That's why your love keep on

G C6 G6
lift - ing me high - er,
1.3. To Coda
G G6 G D
high - er and high - er.
I said your love
2.
Interlude:
G
8va
Horns
C6 G6 G G6 G G6
(8va)
D
(8va)
1.
2. D.S. al Coda
I'm so
Coda Outro:
G
sock it to me. Uh huh, lift me up a - wom - an,
C G G6
keep my love go - ing, now,
G G6 G G6 D
*Repeat and fade
high - er and high - er.
*w/ad lib. vocal on repeat.

Chorus 2:
You know your love keeps on lifting higher,
Higher and higher.
I said your love keeps on lifting me
Higher and higher.
(To Verse 1:)

Verse 2:
I'm so glad I finally found you;
Yes, that one in a million girl.
And with my loving arms around you,
Honey, I can stand up and face the world.
Let me tell you, your love...
(To Chorus:)

HONKY TONK

By BERISFORD SHEPHERD, HENRY GLOVER,
CLIFFORD SCOTT, BILL DOGGETT and BILLY BUTLER

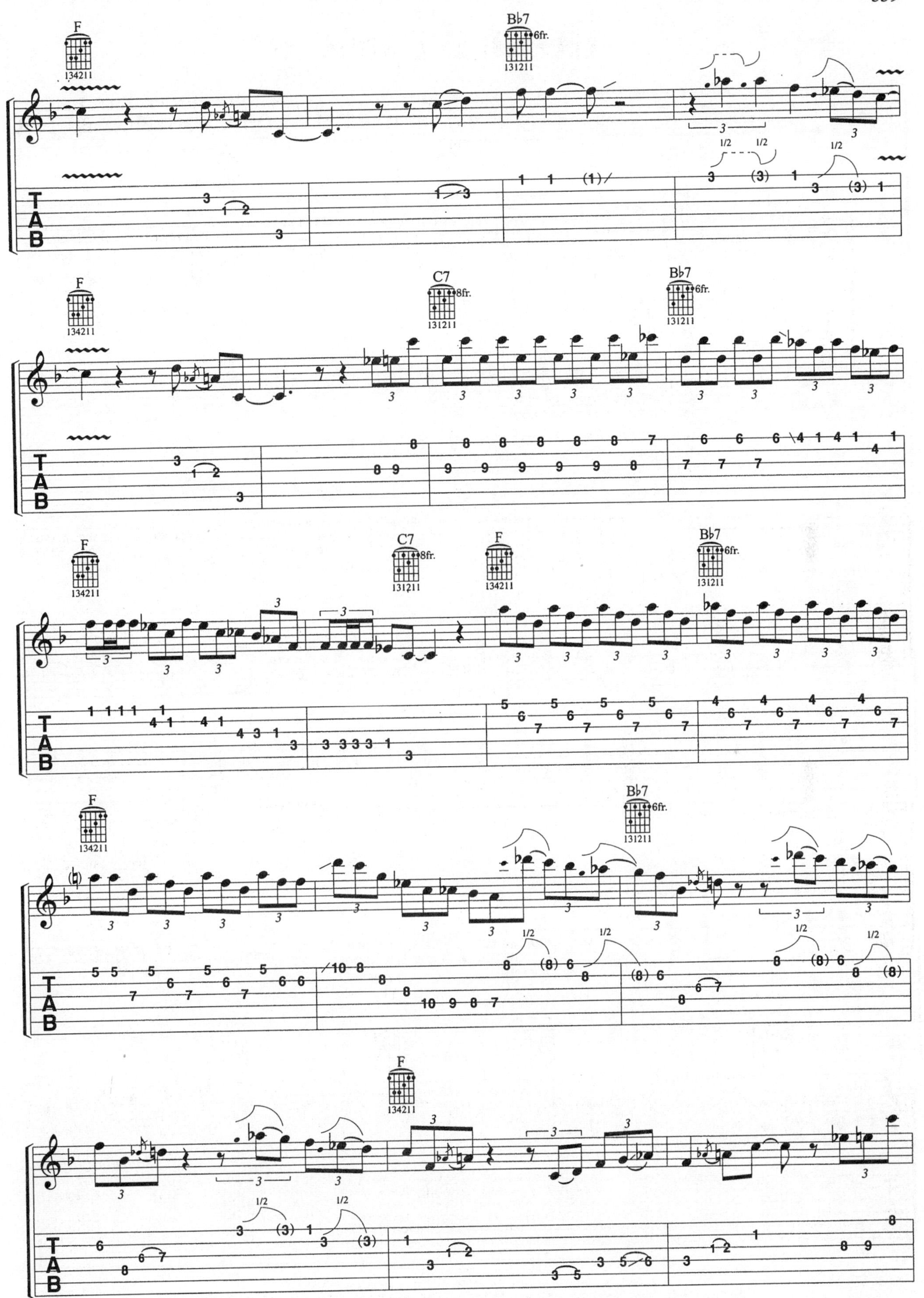
F
134211
B♭7
6fr.
131211
C7
8fr.
1/2
T
A
B

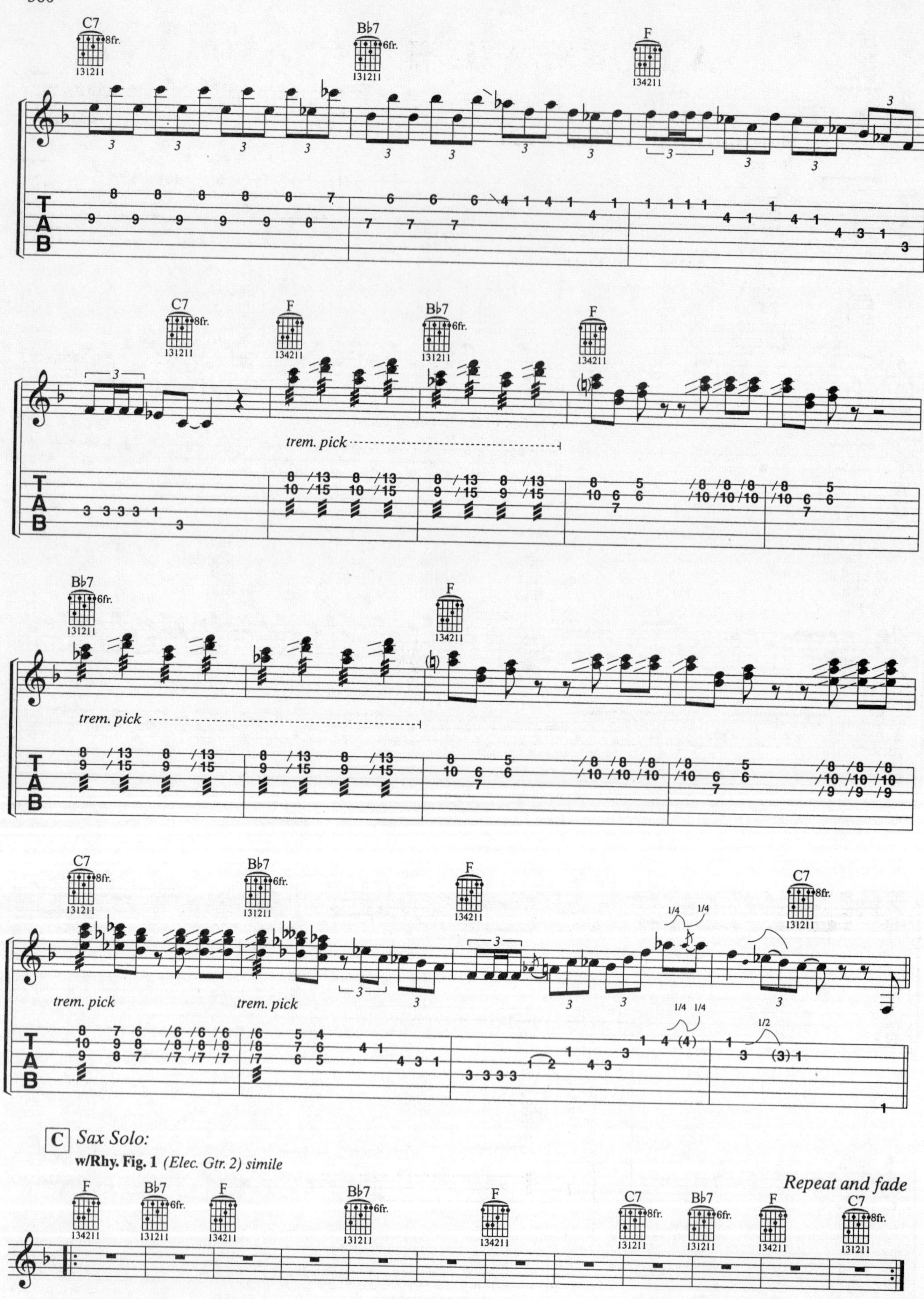
C7
8fr.
131211
B♭7
6fr.
F
134211
trem. pick
C
Sax Solo:
w/Rhy. Fig. 1 (Elec. Gtr. 2) simile
Repeat and fade

A HORSE WITH NO NAME

Words and Music by
DEWEY BUNNELL

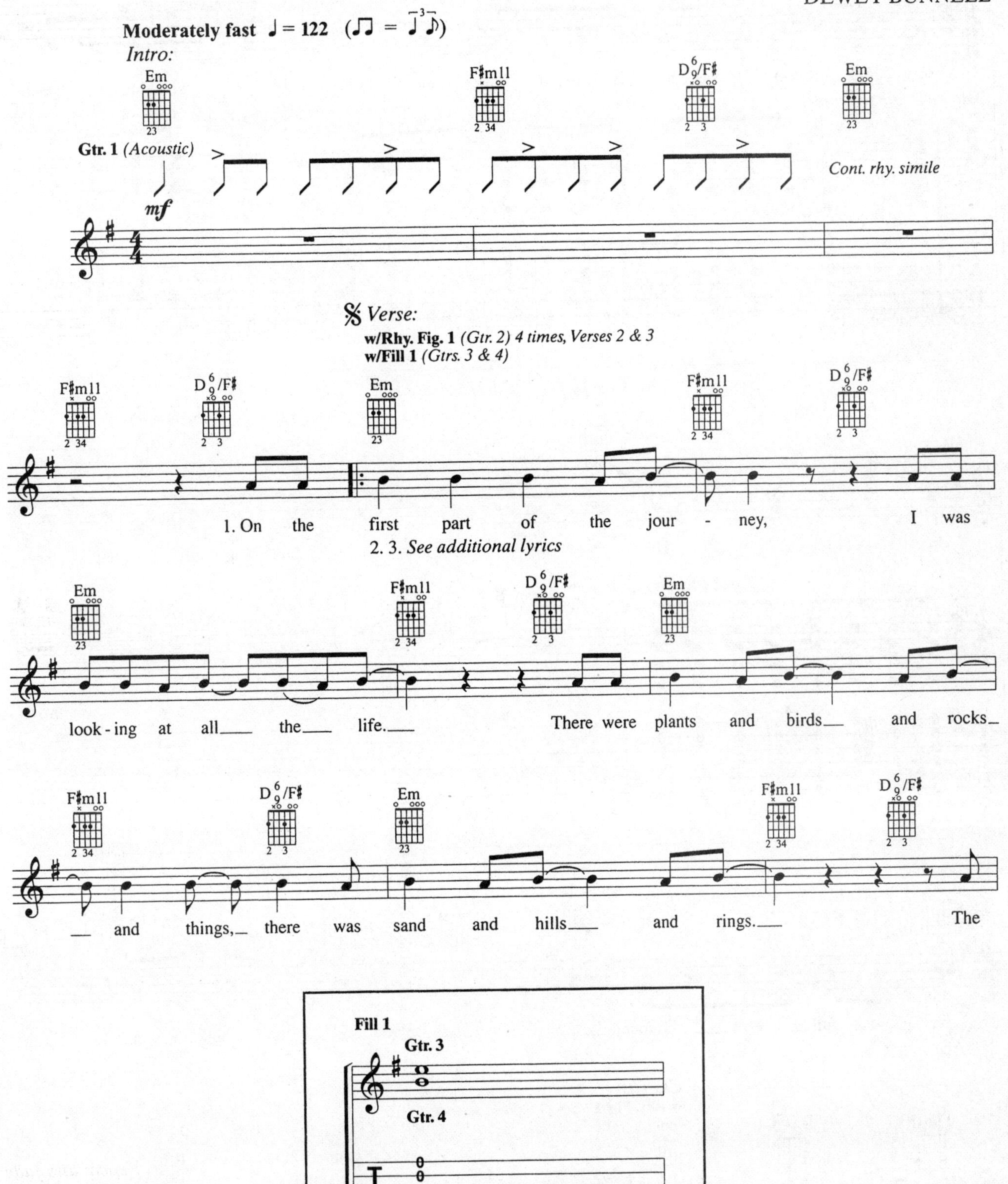

Em
F♯m11
D 6/9/F♯
1. 3.
first thing I met was a fly with a buzz__ and the sky with no__ clouds..
Gtr. 2 (12-string Acoustic)
Rhy. Fig. 1
w/Rhy. Fig. 1 (Gtr. 2) 2 times, simile
The heat was hot__ and the ground was dry,__ but the
(Ah. Ah.
end Rhy. Fig. 1
*Background vocals Verse 2 only.
To Next Strain (To Chorus:)
2.
w/Rhy. Fig. 1 (Gtr. 2)
air was full__ of__ sound.__ I've sad to think__ it was
Ah. Ah.)
Chorus:
w/Rhy. Fig. 1 (Gtr. 2) 8 times, simile
dead. You see I've been through the des - ert on a horse with no name,__ it felt

Em
F♯m11
D 6/9/F♯
good to be out of the rain.
In the des - ert you can re -
mem - ber your name 'cause there ain't no one for to give you no pain. La,
la, la, la, la, la, la, la, la, la, la, la. La,
To Coda
1.
la, la, la, la, la, la, la, la, la, la, la. 2. Af - ter
2.
Em7
F♯m7
5fr.

Em9
F♯m7
5fr.
Em7
Gtr. 2
8va
F♯m7
Em9
D.S. 𝄋 al Coda
3. Af - ter
(8va)
Gtr. 3 (Acoustic)
mf
Gtr. 4 (Acoustic)
mf

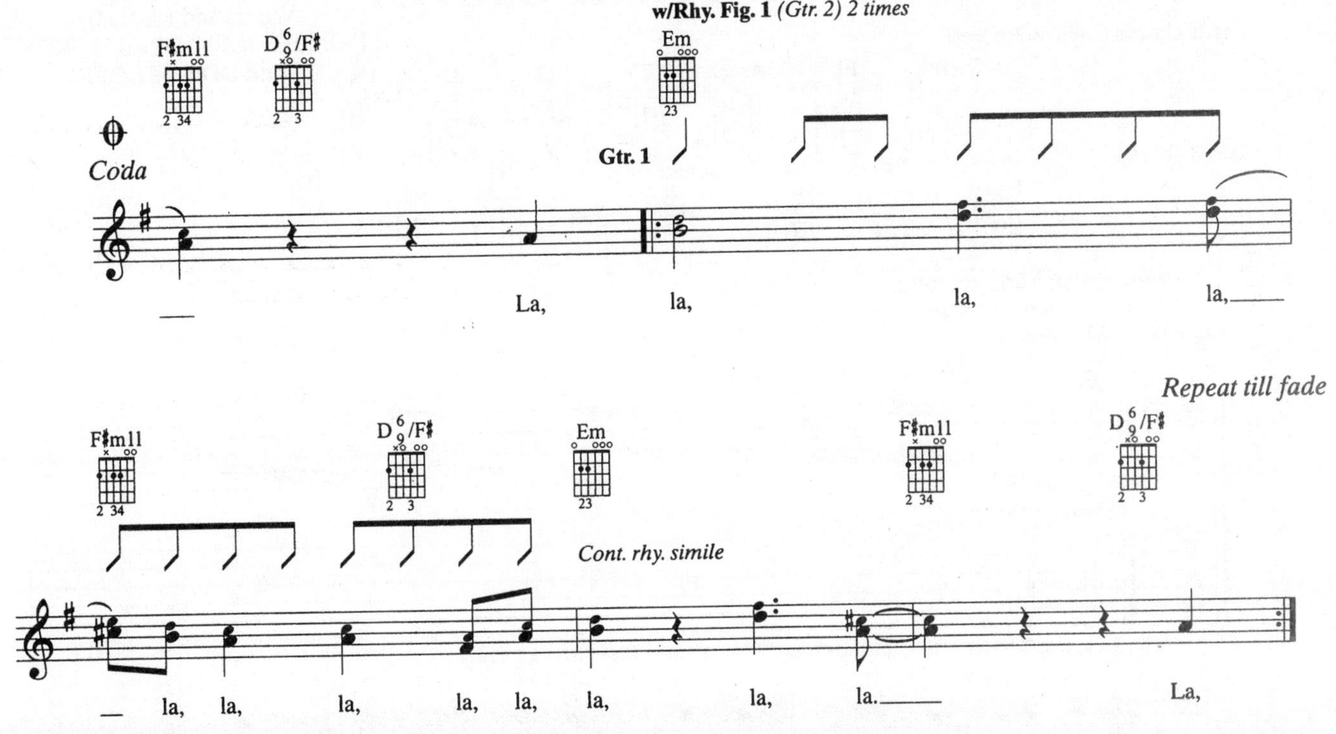

Verse 2:
After two days in the desert sun,
My skin began to turn red.
After three days in the desert fun,
I was looking at a river bed.
And the story it told of a river that flowed
Made me sad to think it was dead.
(To Chorus:)

Verse 3:
After nine days I let the horse run free
'Cause the desert had turned to sea.
There were plants and birds and rocks and things,
There was sand and hills and rings.
The ocean is a desert with its life underground
And a perfect disguise above.
Under the cities lies a heart made of ground,
But the humans will give no love.
(To Chorus:)

HOTEL CALIFORNIA
Words and Music by
DON HENLEY, GLENN FREY
and DON FELDER
Gtr. 1 chords (capo at 7th fret)
Bm F#7 Asus2 E9 G D Em7
Gtr. 3 chords
Bm F#7 A Asus2 E9 G D Em7
Moderately slow ♩ = 74
*Gtr. 1 (Acoustic 12-string)
Intro:
Rhy. Fig. 1
mp
hold throughout
*Gtr. 1 capo at 7th fret. All notes shown as "7" in tab are played as open strings.
end Rhy. Fig. 1
Verses 1 & 2:
w/Rhy. Fig. 1 (Gtr. 1)
Rhy. Fig. 2
†Gtr. 3 (Acoustic)
1. On a dark des-ert high - way, cool wind in my hair,
2. See additional lyrics
Gtr. 2
Riff A
mf
P.M.
†Gtr. 3 tacet on Verse 1, play Rhy. Fig. 2 on Verse 2.

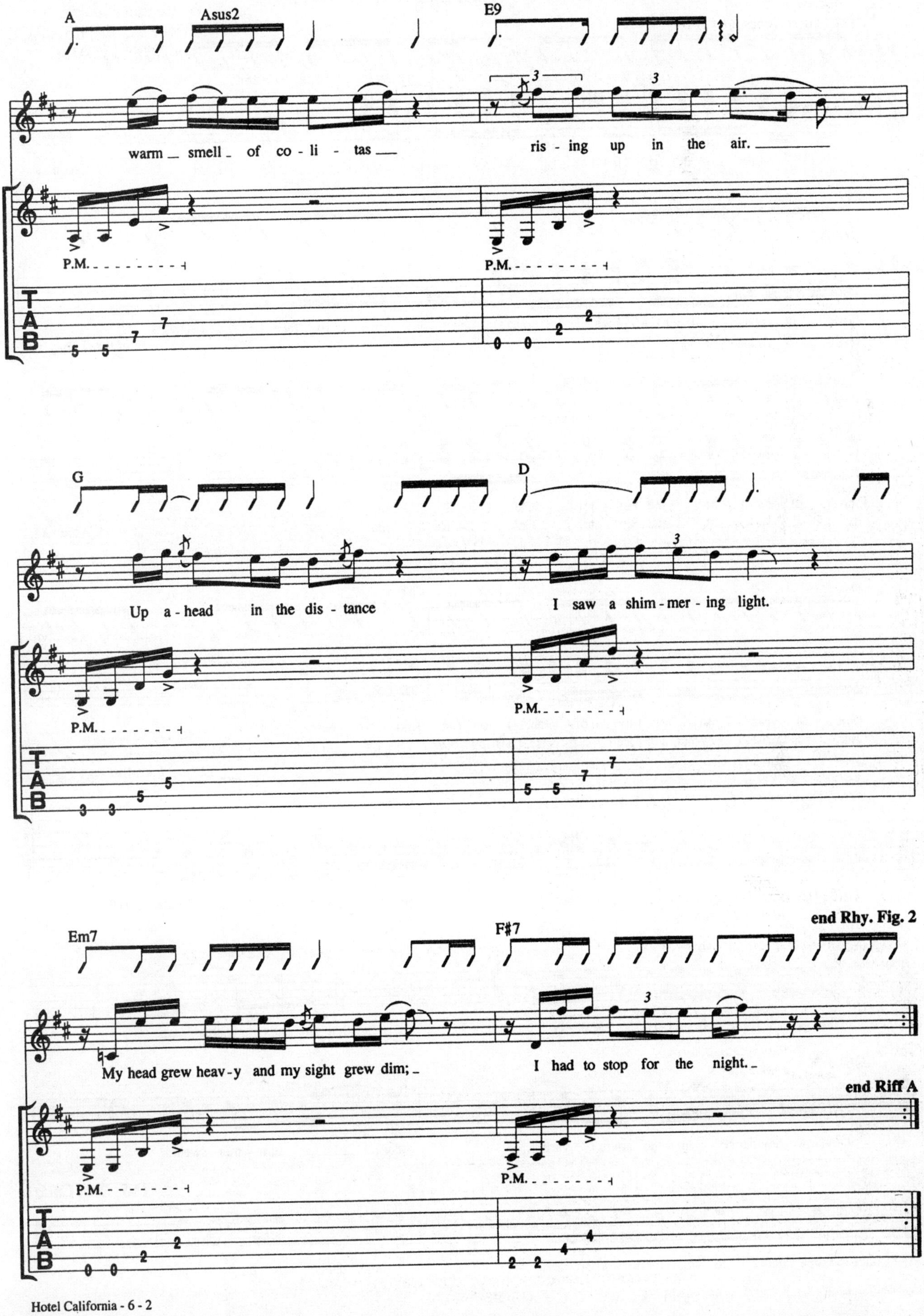

A
Asus2
E9
warm smell of co-li-tas
ris-ing up in the air.
P.M.
P.M.
G
D
Up a-head in the dis-tance
I saw a shim-mer-ing light.
P.M.
P.M.
Em7
F#7
end Rhy. Fig. 2
My head grew heav-y and my sight grew dim;
I had to stop for the night.
end Riff A
P.M.
P.M.

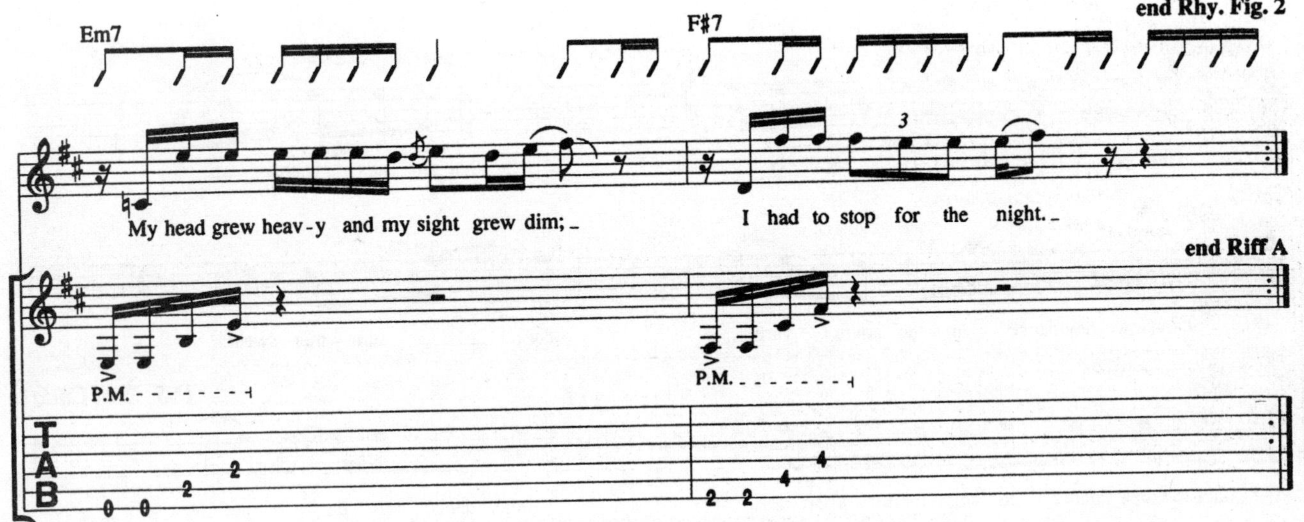

Chorus:
Gtrs. 1 & 3
G
D
Wel - come _ to the Ho - tel Cal - i - for - nia, such a
F#7
Bm
love - ly place _ (such a love - ly place) _ such a love - ly face. _
(2nd time) They're
G
D
Plen - ty of room _ at the Ho - tel Cal - i - for - nia. An - y
liv - ing it up ___ at the Ho - tel Cal - i - for - nia. What a
To Coda
Em7
F#7
time _ of year _ (an - y time _ of year _) you can find _ it here. _
nice _ sur - prise. _ (What a nice _ sur - prise. .) Bring your
Verses 3 & 4:
w/Rhy. Figs. 1 (Gtr. 1) 2 (Gtr. 3) & Riff A (Gtr. 2)
Bm
F#7
3. Her mind is Tif - fa - ny twist - ed. She got the Mer - ce - des __ bends. _ (Uh)
4. See additional lyrics
Asus2
E9
She got a lot of pret - ty, pret - ty boys _ that she calls friends. ______
G
D
How they dance in the court - yard; _ sweet ______ sum - mer sweat.
Em7
F#7
D.S. al Coda
Some dance to re - mem - ber; ______ some dance to for - get. __

Verses 5 & 6:
w/Rhy. Fig. 1 (Gtr. 1)
Coda
F#7
Bm
al - i - bis.
5. Mir - rors on the ceil - ing,
6. See additional lyrics
F#7
Asus2
the pink cham - pagne on ice,
An' she said,
"We are all just pri - son - ers here
E9
G
D
of our own de - vice."
An' in the mas-ter's cham - bers
they gath - ered for the feast.
Em7
F#7
They stab it with their steel - y knives but they just can't kill the beast.
Play 3 times
Guitar Solo:
w/Rhy. Figs. 1 (Gtr. 1) 2 (Gtr. 3) & Riff A (Gtr. 2)
Bm
F#7
A
E
G
D
Em
F#7
Outro:
w/Rhy. Figs. 1 (Gtr. 1) and 2 (Gtr. 3)
Bm
F#7
Gtr. 2
Gtr. 4
Gtr. 5
Gtr. 6

A
E9
1
1/2
TAB
G
D

Verse 2:
There she stood in the doorway;
I heard the mission bell.
And I was thinking to myself.
This could be heaven, or this could be hell.
Then she lit up a candle and she showed me the way.
There were voices down the corridor,
I thought I heard them say:
(To Chorus:)

Verse 4:
So I called up the captain,
"Please bring me my wine."
And he said, "We haven't had that
Spirit here since nineteen-sixty-nine."
And still those voices are calling from far away.
Wake you up in the middle of the night
Just to hear them say:
(To Chorus:)

Verse 6:
Last thing I remember,
I was running for the door.
I had to find the passage back
To place I was before.
"Relax," said the night man,
"We are programmed to receive.
You can check out anytime you like,
But you can never leave."

THE HOUSE OF THE RISING SUN

Words and Music by
ALAN PRICE

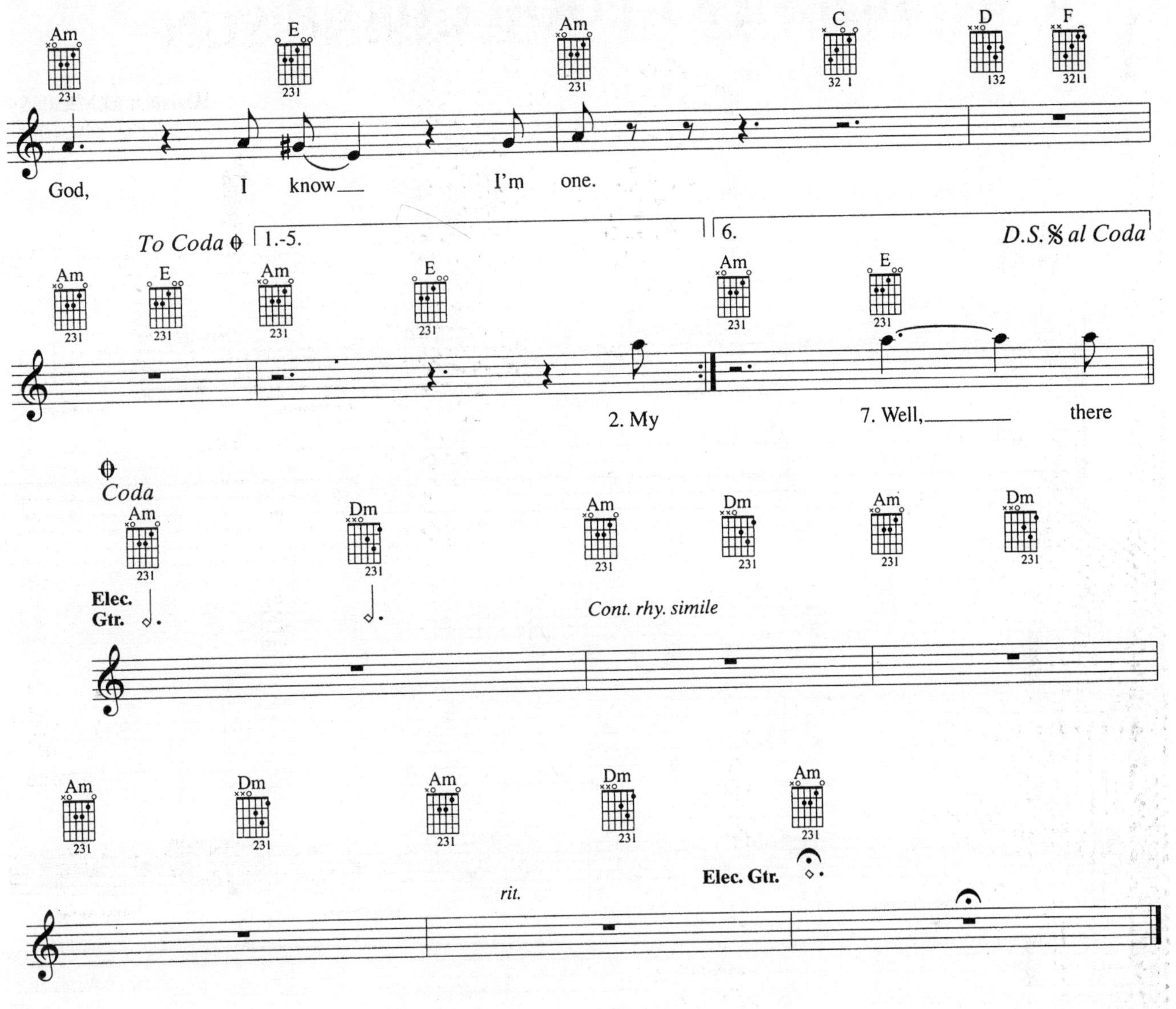

Verse 2:
My mother was a tailor,
She sewed my new blue jeans.
My father was a gambling man
Down in New Orleans.

Verse 3:
Now, the only thing a gambler needs
Is a suitcase and a trunk.
And the only time he's satisfied
Is when he's all drunk.
(To Organ Solo:)

Verse 5:
Oh mother, tell your children
Not to do what I have done.
Spend your life in sin and misery
In the house of the Rising Sun.

Verse 6:
Well, I got one foot on the platform,
The other foot on the train.
I'm going back to New Orleans
To wear that ball and chain.

HOUSE AT POOH CORNER

Words and Music by
KENNY LOGGINS

*2 gtrs. arr. for 1.

E
F#m
G#m
C#m7
Pos - ing our _ ques - tions to Owl ___ and E - yore _ as our _ days _
end Rhy. Fig. 1
Rhy. Fig. 2
Pre-Chorus:
A
B
E
C#m7
___ dis - ap - peared _ all too soon. _
1. But I've wan - dered much fur - ther to - day _
2. See additional lyrics
end Rhy. Fig. 2
Gtrs. 1 & 2
G#m
A
F#
B
___ than I _ should, and I can't seem to find _ my way back _ to the wood. So,
Chorus:
E
G#m
F#m
B
A
E
G#m
help me if ___ you can, ___ I've got _ to get back to the house _ at Pooh Cor -

F#m
B
A
E
G#m
F#m
B
A
- ner by _ one.
You'd be sur - prised, _ there's so much _ to be done;
G#m
E
G#m
count all the bees _ in the hive,
chase all the clouds _ from the sky.
To Coda
C#m7
A
G#m
C#m
Back to the days _ of
Chris - to - pher _ Rob - in and Pooh. _
(Chase the clouds a - way. _______
Ooh.)

Guitar Solo:
1.
2.
Dmaj7
A
Gtr. 1
Rhy. Fig. 3
Gtr. 2
hold
hold
G
E
F♯m
G♯m
A
Bm
C♯m
D
E7
end Rhy. Fig. 3
w/Rhy. Fig. 3 (Gtr. 1)
A
G
E
F♯m
G♯m
A
Bm
C♯m
D
E7

Gtr. 1
D
G
F♯
B
Gtr. 2

w/Rhy. Fig. 2 (Gtrs. 1 & 2)
E
F♯m
G♯m
C♯m7
A
B
La la la la___ la___ la___ la la la.___ La la la la___ la la.___

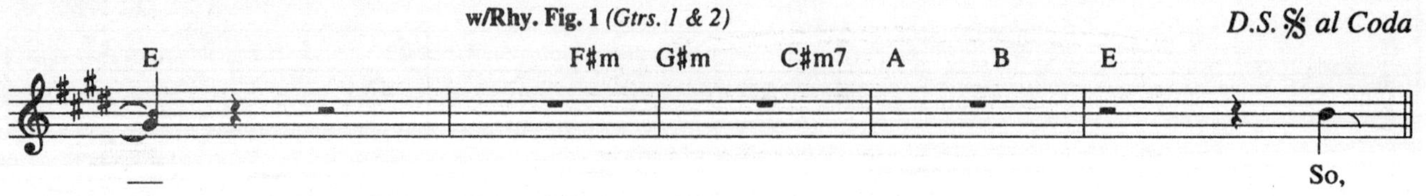
w/Rhy. Fig. 1 (Gtrs. 1 & 2)
D.S. 𝄋 al Coda
E
F♯m
G♯m
C♯m7
A
B
E
So,

Coda
A
G♯m
C♯m
B/D♯
F♯m
G♯m
A
G♯m
Back to the days___ of Chris-to-pher_ Rob - in. Back to the ways___ of
way.________ Back to the day.______________
Gtrs. 1 & 2

C#m B/D# F#m G#m A G#m C#m
Chris-to-pher _ Rob - in. Back to the ways _ of Pooh.
Back to the way.)
Gtr. 1
Gtr. 2
hold
hold

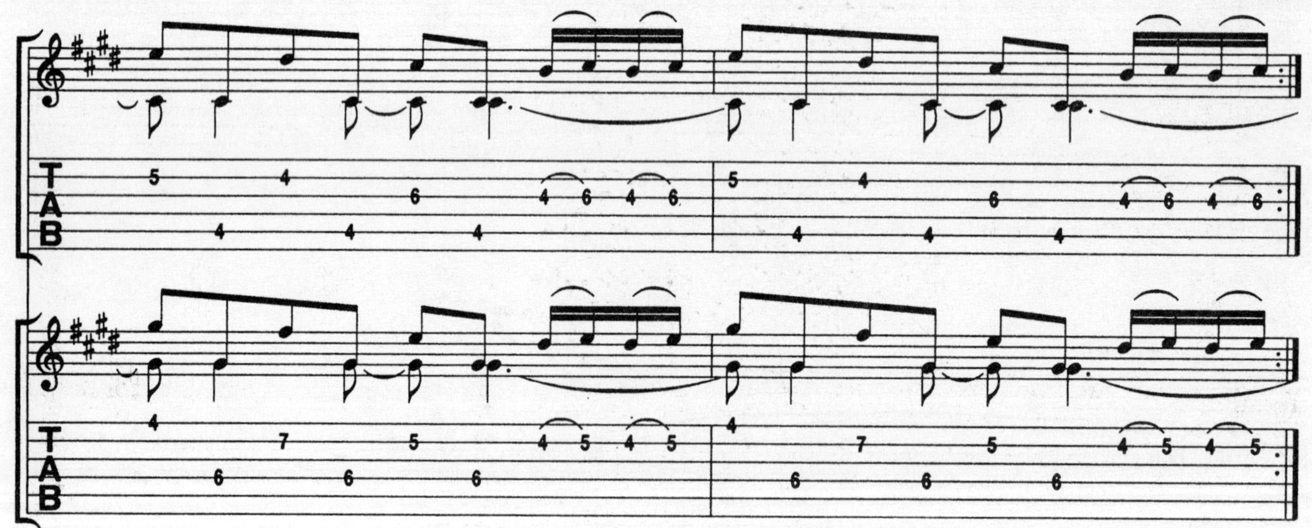

Verse 2:
Winnie the Pooh doesn't know what to do,
Got a honey jar stuck on his nose.
He came to me asking help and advice,
And from here, no one knows where he goes.

Pre-Chorus 2:
So, I sent him to ask of the owl, if he's there,
How to loosen a jar from the nose of a bear.
(To Chorus:)

I GOT YOU BABE

Words and Music by
SONNY BONO

Chorus:
w/Fill 2 (Oboe) 3 times
Cont. rhy. simile
I got you, babe. I got you, babe. 2. They
Bridge:
w/Fill 3 (Elec. Gtr. 2) 4 times
Elec. Gtr. 1
Resume rhy. fig. simile
you, babe. I got flow - ers in the spring. I got you to wear
w/Fill 4 (Elec. Gtr. 2) 3 times
my ring. And when I'm sad, you're a clown, and if I get scared, you're al-ways a -
Verse 3:
w/Fill 5 (Elec. Gtr. 2)
Cont. rhy. simile
round. So let them say your hair's too long, 'cause I don't care, with you I can't be
w/Fill 5 (Elec. Gtr. 2)
wrong. Then put your lit-tle hand in mine, there ain't no hill or moun-tain we can't climb. Babe,
Fill 2
Oboe (arr. for gtr.)
Fill 3
Elec. Gtr. 2
Fill 4
Elec. Gtr. 2
Fill 5
Elec. Gtr. 2

Chorus:
w/Fill 6 (Oboe) 3 times
F♯ B/F♯ F♯ B/F♯ F♯ B/F♯ F♯ B/F♯ F♯ C♯
Cont. rhy. simile
I got you, babe. I got you, babe.
w/Fill 7 (Elec. Gtr. 2) 5 times
F♯ B/F♯ F♯ C♯ F♯ B/F♯
I got you to hold my hand. I got you to un - der - stand. I got you to walk with me.
F♯ C♯ F♯ B/F♯ F♯ C♯
I got you to talk with me. I got you to kiss good-night. I got you to hold me tight.
F♯ B/F♯ F♯ C♯ F♯ B/F♯
I got you, I won't let go. I got you to love me so.
Freely
F♯ C♯ B F♯
Elec. Gtr. 1
I got you, babe.
Outro:
w/Fill 7 (Elec. Gtr. 2)
Repeat and fade
F♯ B/F♯ F♯ C♯
a tempo
Resume rhy. fig. simile
(2nd time) you, babe. I got you, babe. I got
Fill 6
Oboe
Fill 7
Elec. Gtr. 2
TAB

I ONLY HAVE EYES FOR YOU

Words by
AL DUBIN

Music by
HARRY WARREN

w/Bkgd. Vocal Fig. 1 (2 times)
C5 (B♭) C5 (B♭) C5 (B♭)
Bkgl. Vocal Fig. 1
Doo wop she bop. Doo wop she bop. Are the stars out
C5 (B♭) C5 (B♭) C C7
to-night? I don't know if it's cloud-y or bright. I
Chorus:
F Am G♯
on-ly have eyes for you, dear.
Gtr. 2
hold
hold
Verses 2 & 3:
C (B♭) C (B♭)
w/Bkgd. Vocal Fig. 1 (2 times)
w/Riff A (Gtr. 2) 2 times
2. The moon may be high.
3. See additional lyrics
C (B♭) C C7
but I can't see a thing in the sky. I / But they
Chorus:
F D7XIII To Coda
on-ly have eyes for you.
all dis-ap-pear from view. (And I)
Gtr. 2
8va

Verse 3:
You are here and so am I.
Maybe millions of people go by.
But they all disappear from view.
(To Chorus:)

I WANT TO HOLD YOUR HAND

Words and Music by
JOHN LENNON and PAUL McCARTNEY

D
E5
B7
some - thing,
me,
I wan - na hold your hand.
you'll let me hold your hand.
hold
C
D
G
3fr.
Em
To Coda
I wan - na hold your hand.
And let me hold your hand.
I wan - na hold your
I wan - na hold your
1.
2.3.
Bridge:
Dm
Elec. Gtr. 2
hand.
2. Oh
hand.
And when I
hold throughout
Cont. rhy. simile
Am
*Harmony 1st 7 measures, 2nd time only.
touch you I feel hap - py in - side.
It's such a

G
C
C5
D5
Elec. Gtr. 2
feel - ing that my love, I can't hide, I can't hide,
I can't hide.
1.
D.S. 𝄋
2.
D.S. 𝄋 al Coda
3. Yeah,
4. Yeah,
Coda
B7
D
hand.
I wan-na hold your hand.

I WANNA BE SEDATED

Words and Music by
JEFFREY HYMAN, JOHN CUMMINGS
and DOUGLAS COLVIN

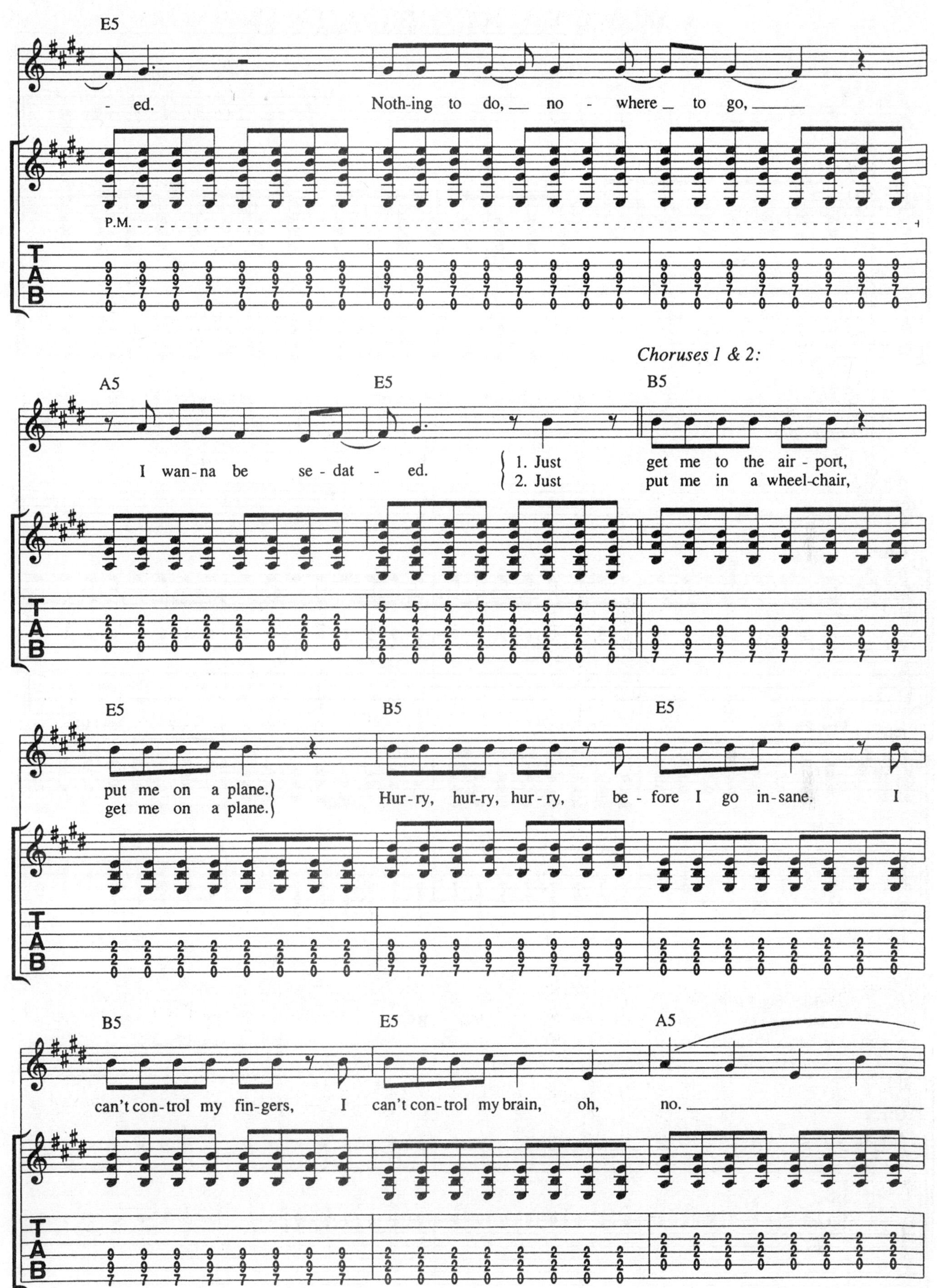
E5
-ed. Noth-ing to do, no - where to go,
P.M.
Choruses 1 & 2:
A5
E5
B5
I wan-na be se-dat - ed.
1. Just get me to the air - port,
2. Just put me in a wheel-chair,
E5
B5
E5
put me on a plane.
get me on a plane.
Hur-ry, hur-ry, hur-ry, be-fore I go in-sane. I
B5
E5
A5
can't con-trol my fin-gers, I can't con-trol my brain, oh, no.

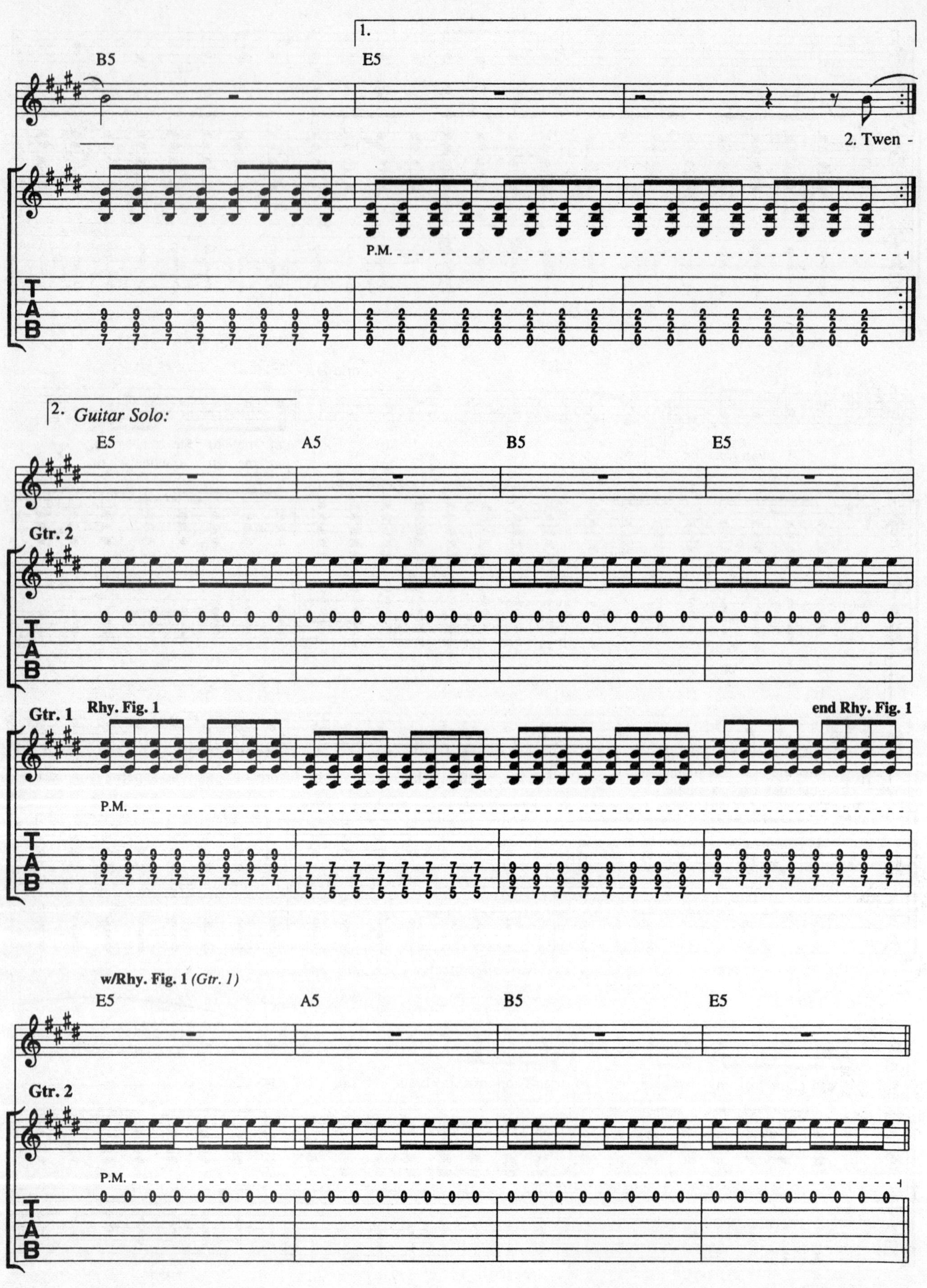
1.
B5
E5
2. Twen -
P.M.
2. Guitar Solo:
E5
A5
B5
E5
Gtr. 2
Gtr. 1
Rhy. Fig. 1
end Rhy. Fig. 1
P.M.
w/Rhy. Fig. 1 (Gtr. 1)
E5
A5
B5
E5
Gtr. 2
P.M.

E5
3. Twen -
Gtr. 2
Gtr. 1
P.M.
Verses 3 & 4:
F#5
B5
(4.) ty, twen-ty, twen-ty-four hours to go, I wan-na be se-dat-
Gtr. 1
P.M.
F#5
- ed. Noth-ing to do, no - where to go,
Gtr. 1
P.M.

Choruses 3 & 4:
B5
F#5
C#5
I wan-na be sed-dat - ed. Just put me in a wheel-chair,
F#5
C#5
F#5
get me to the show. Hur-ry, hur-ry, hur-ry, be-fore I go lo-co. I
C#5
F#5
B5
can't con-trol my fin-gers, I can't con-trol my toes, oh, no.
To Coda
D.S. al Coda
C#5
F#5
4. Twen -
P.M.

Coda
F#5
B5
C#5
F#5
Ba ba ba ba, ba ba ba ba ba, I wan-na be se-dat - ed.
Rhy. Fig. 2
end Rhy. Fig. 2
P.M.
w/Rhy. Fig. 2 (Gtr. 1) 2 times
F#5
B5
C#5
F#5
Ba ba ba ba, ba ba ba ba ba, I wan-na be se-dat - ed.
F#5
B5
C#5
F#5
Ba ba ba ba, ba ba ba ba ba, I wan-na be se-dat - ed.
Gtr. 2
w/Rhy. Fig. 2 (Gtr. 1) first 3 measures
F#5
B5
C#5
F#5
Ba ba ba ba, ba ba ba ba ba, I wan-na be se-dat - ed.

I WILL FOLLOW HIM

Music by J.W. STOLE and DEL ROMA
Original Words by JACQUES PLANTE
English Lyric by NORMAN GIMBEL
and ARTHUR ALTMAN

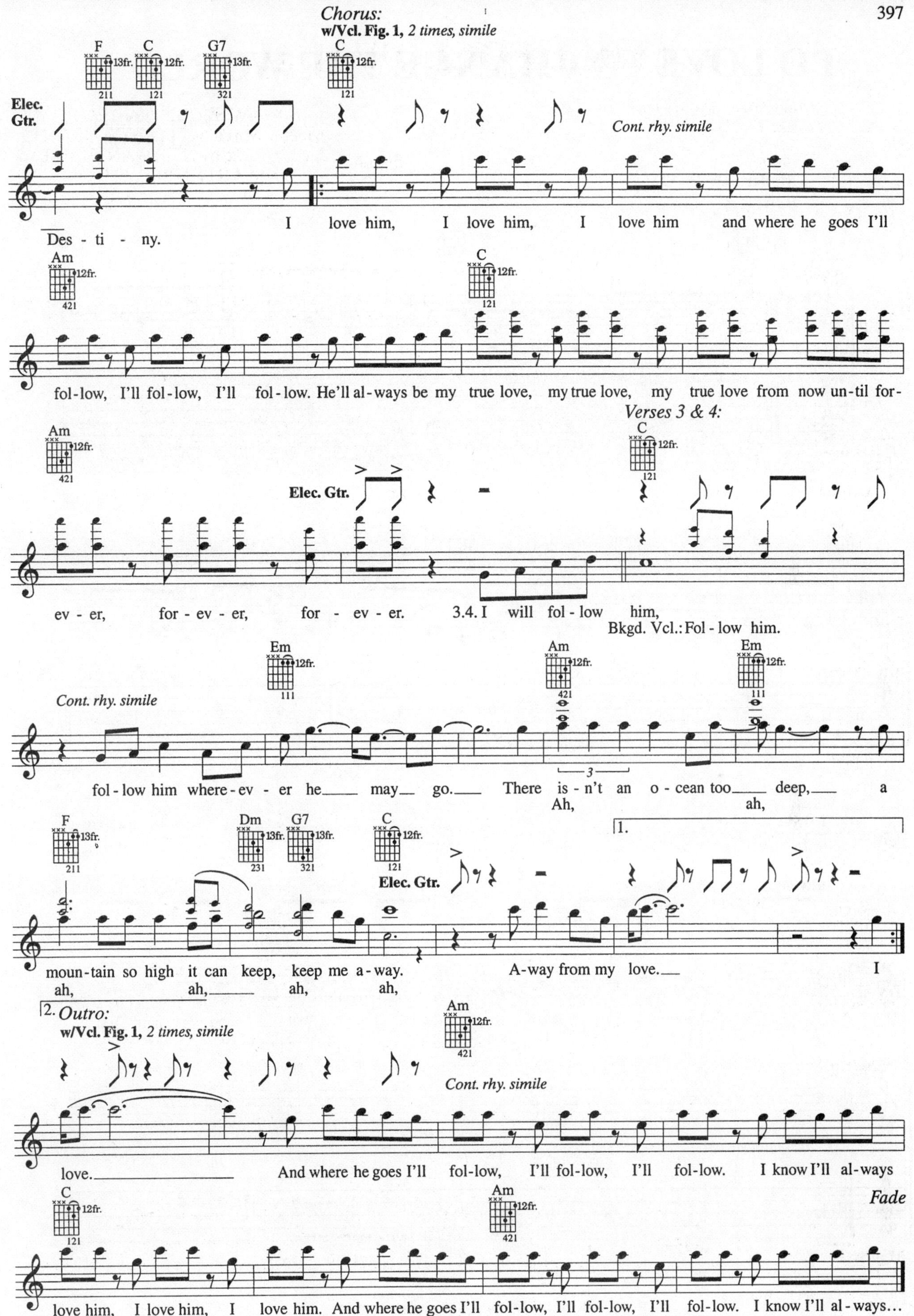
Chorus:
w/Vcl. Fig. 1, 2 times, simile
F C G7 C
Elec. Gtr.
Cont. rhy. simile
Des - ti - ny.
I love him, I love him, I love him and where he goes I'll
Am C
fol-low, I'll fol-low, I'll fol-low. He'll al-ways be my true love, my true love, my true love from now un-til for-
Am
Verses 3 & 4:
C
Elec. Gtr.
ev - er, for - ev - er, for - ev - er. 3.4. I will fol - low him,
Bkgd. Vcl.: Fol - low him.
Em Am Em
Cont. rhy. simile
fol - low him where - ev - er he may go. There is - n't an o - cean too deep, a
Ah, ah,
F Dm G7 C
Elec. Gtr.
1.
mount-tain so high it can keep, keep me a - way. A - way from my love. I
ah, ah, ah, ah,
2. Outro:
w/Vcl. Fig. 1, 2 times, simile
Am
Cont. rhy. simile
love. And where he goes I'll fol-low, I'll fol-low, I'll fol-low. I know I'll al-ways
C Am
Fade
love him, I love him, I love him. And where he goes I'll fol-low, I'll fol-low, I'll fol-low. I know I'll al-ways...

I'D LOVE TO CHANGE THE WORLD

Words and Music by
ALVIN LEE

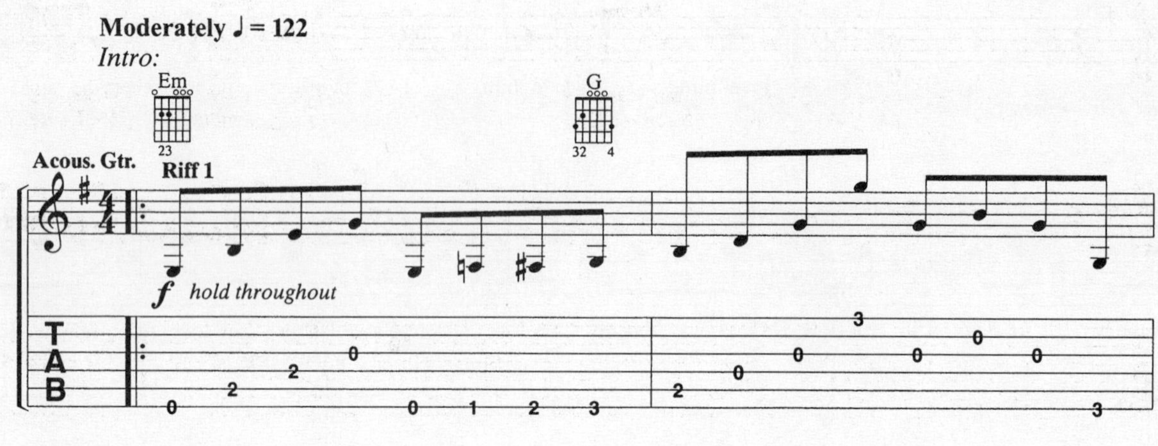

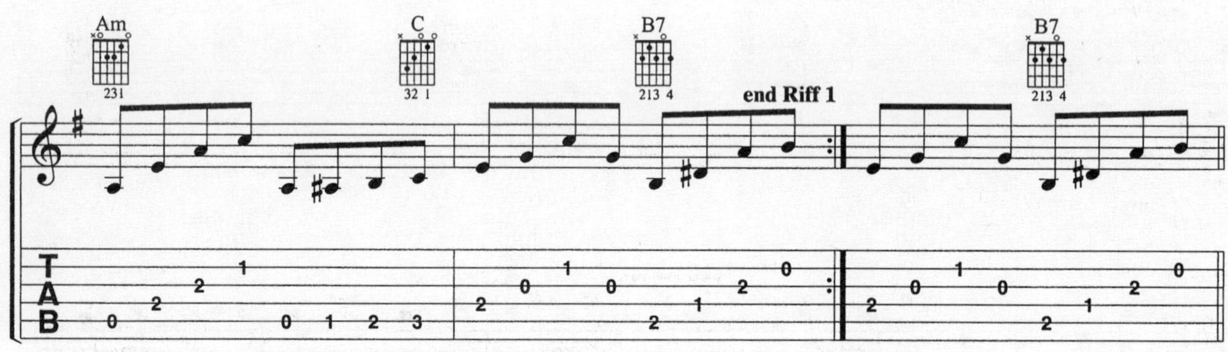

*Verse 2 only.

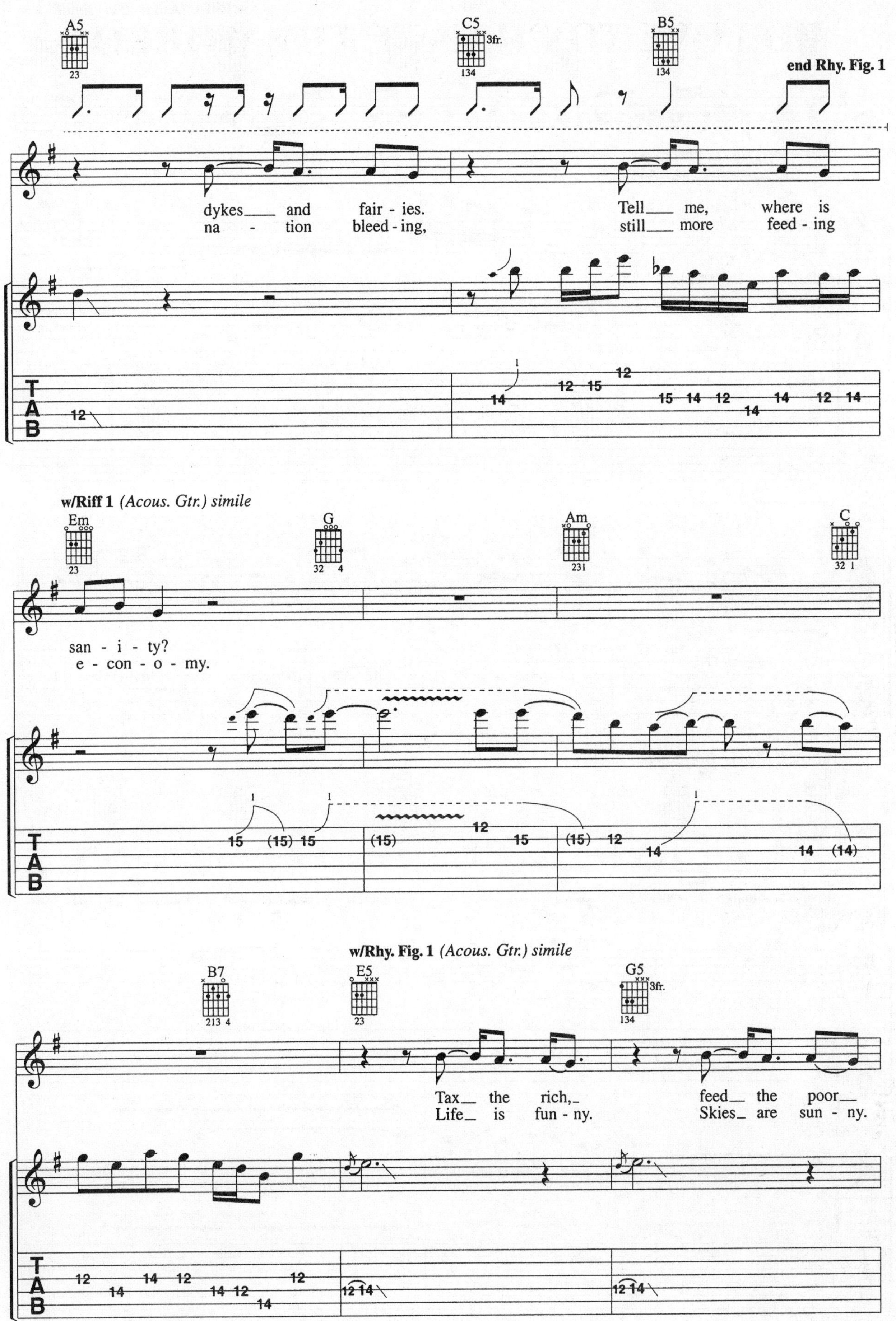
A5
C5
3fr.
B5
end Rhy. Fig. 1
dykes___ and fair - ies.
Tell___ me, where is
na - tion bleed - ing,
still___ more feed - ing
w/Riff 1 (Acous. Gtr.) simile
Em
G
Am
C
san - i - ty?
e - con - o - my.
w/Rhy. Fig. 1 (Acous. Gtr.) simile
B7
E5
G5
3fr.
Tax___ the rich,___
feed___ the poor___
Life_ is fun - ny.
Skies_ are sun - ny.

*1st time only.
**2nd time only; 3rd time ad lib. simile.

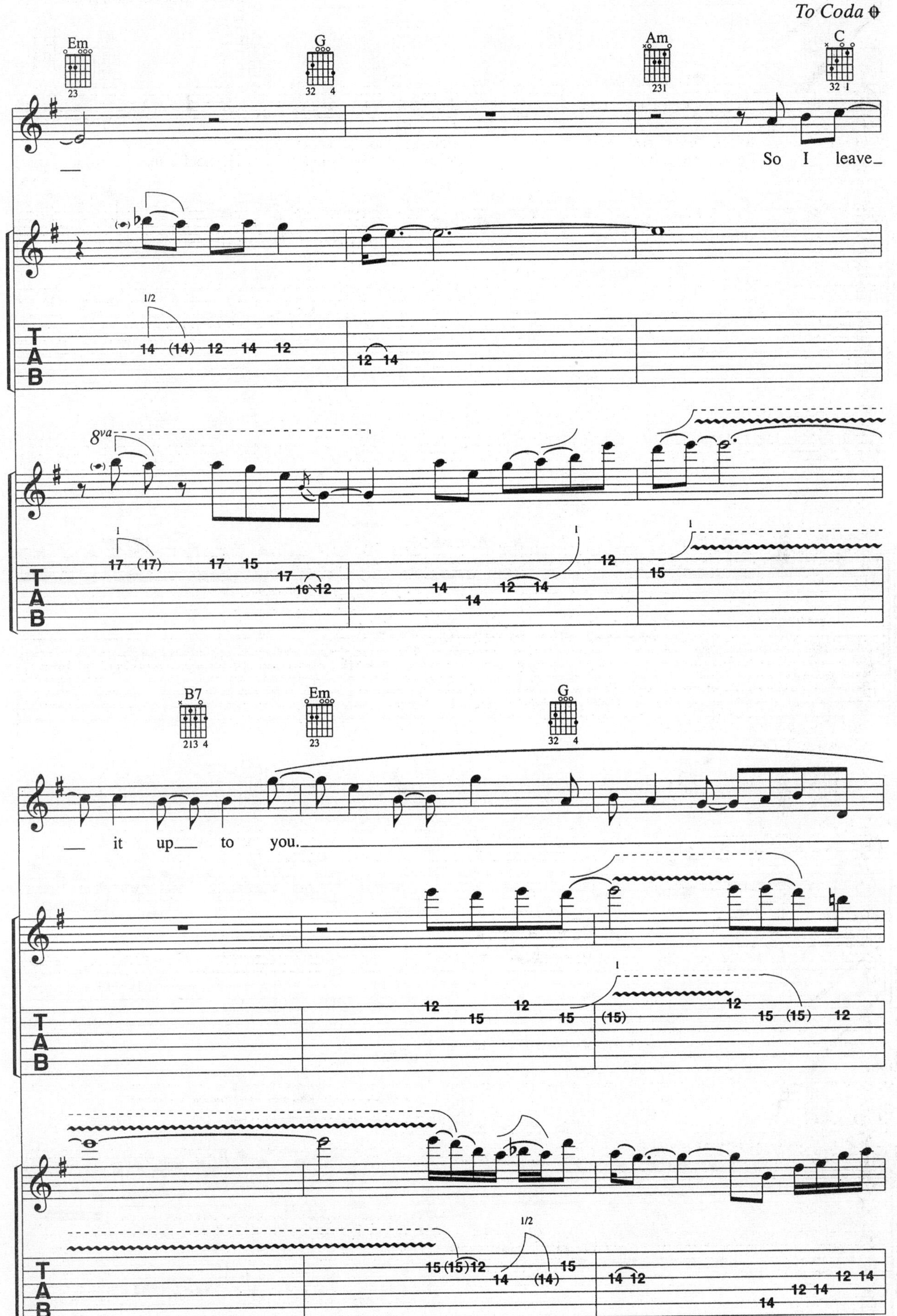
To Coda
Em
G
Am
C
So I leave
B7
Em
G
it up to you.

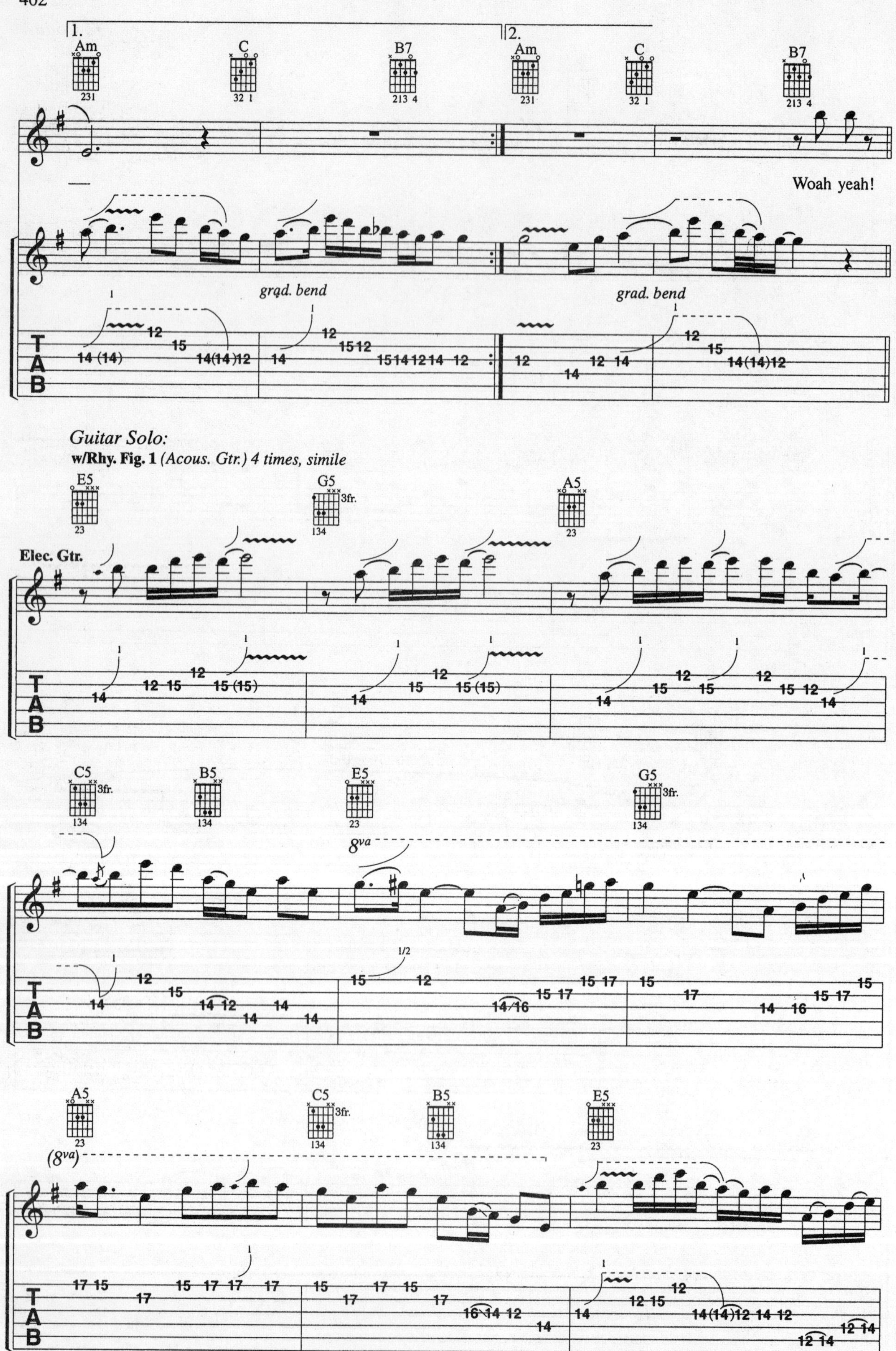
1.
Am
C
B7
2.
Am
C
B7
Woah yeah!
grad. bend
grad. bend
Guitar Solo:
w/Rhy. Fig. 1 (Acous. Gtr.) 4 times, simile
E5
G5
A5
Elec. Gtr.
C5
B5
E5
G5
8va
A5
C5
B5
E5
(8va)

G5
A5
C5
B5
E5
Bridge:
w/Rhy. Fig. 1 (Acous. Gtr.) 2 times, simile
World_ pol - lu - tion
is no so - lu - tion.
Riff 2
Elec. Gtr.
grad. bend

A5
C5
3fr.
B5
In - sti - tu - tion,
e - lec - tro - cu - tion.
grad. release
end Riff 2
w/Riff 2 (Elec. Gtr. 1) simile
E5
G5
A5
C5
B5
There's black or white,
rich or poor.
Gov-er - nors,
stop the war.
Interlude:
w/Riff 1 (Acous. Gtr.) 2 times, simile
Em
G
Am
C
Elec. Gtr.
B7
Em
G
8va

Am
C
B7
D.S. % al Coda
Coda
w/Riff 1 (Acous. Gtr.) simile
C
B7
Em
G
Acous. Gtr.
I'd
it up to you.
Elec. Gtr.
Am
C
B7
Em
Acous. Gtr.
What's go-ing on?
8va

I'M WALKIN'

Words and Music by
ANTOINE DOMINO
and DAVE BARTHOLOMEW

Verse:
Both gtrs.
Ab
Db7
Cont. rhy. simile
(3.) walk - in', yes, in - deed, I'm talk - in' 'bout
2.4. Instrumental
Ab Db7 Ab7
you and me, I'm hop - in' that you'll come back to me. Mmm.
Eb7 Ab
I'm lone - ly as I can be, I'm wait -
Db7 Ab
in' for your com - pa - ny, I'm hop - in' that
Db7 Ab Eb7
you'll come back to me. Now,
Bridge:
Db7 Ab Db7
Cont. rhy. simile
what you gon - na do when the well runs dry? You gon - na run a -
Ab Db7 Ab
way and hide. And I'm gon - na run right by your side. For
Eb7 Ab
you, pret - ty ba - by, I'd e - ven die. I'm walk - in',
Db7
Cont. rhy. simile
Ab
yes, in - deed, now I'm talk - in' 'bout you and me, I'm hop - in' that
Db7
To Coda
Ab
1.3.
Eb7
D.S. al Coda
(After 3rd ending)
2.
Eb7
you'll come back to me. 3. I'm
Coda
Gtr. 1
Ab
Gtr. 2
TAB

IN THE SUMMERTIME

Words and Music by
RAY DORSET

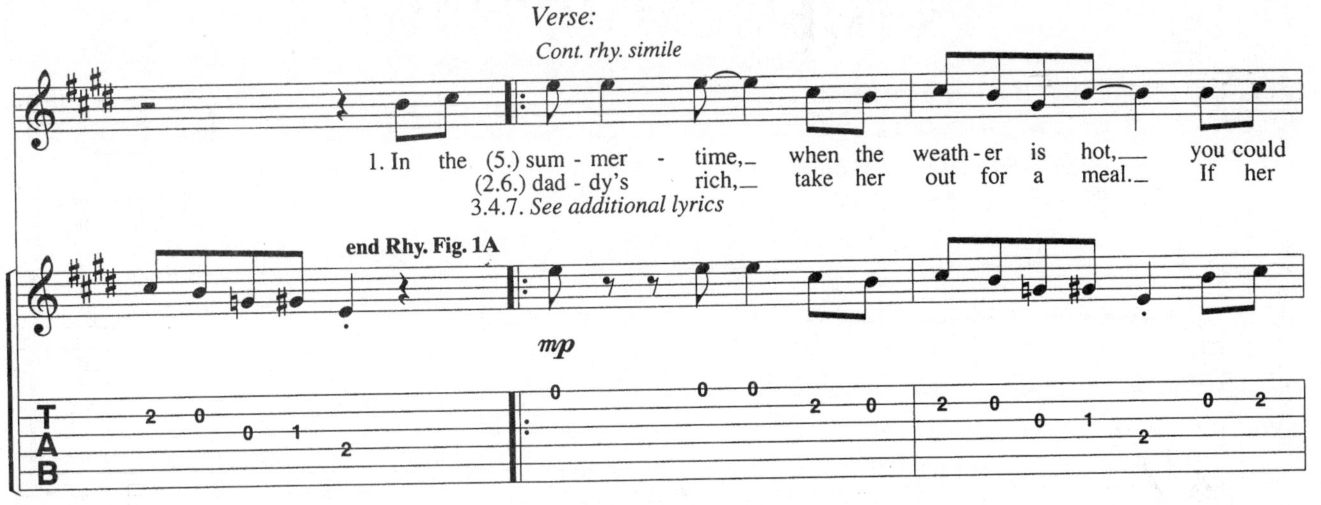
Verse:
Cont. rhy. simile
1. In the (5.) sum - mer - time, when the weath - er is hot, you could
(2.6.) dad - dy's rich, take her out for a meal. If her
3.4.7. See additional lyrics
end Rhy. Fig. 1A
mp

A
213
stretch right up and touch the sky. When the weath - er is fine, you got
dad - dy's poor, just do what you feel. Speed a - long the lane, do a
mf hold

E
231
B
1333
wom - en, you got wom - en on your mind.
turn or re - turn the twen - ty - five.
Have a drink, have a drive,
When the sun goes down, you can

1.2.4.5.6.
A
213
E
231
go out and see___ what you can find.
make it, make it good and you'll get by.
2.6. If her
3.7. We're not
5. In the
3.7.
E
231
To Coda
Interlude:
Cont. rhy. simile
phy.
Sing a - long with us.___ Di, di,
di, di, di.___ Da, di, da, da, da,___ yeah, we're hap - hap - py.___
A
213
E
231
Da, da, da, di, da, do, di, da, da, da, da, da.
hold

Verses 3 & 7:
We're not bad people, we're not dirty, we're not mean.
We love everybody, but we do as we please.
When the weather is fine,
We go fishing or go swimming in the sea.
We're always happy,
Life's for living, yeah, that's our philosophy.
(To Interlude:)

Verse 4:
When the winter's here, yeah, it's party time.
Bring your bottle the way you like
'Cause it'll soon be summertime.
When we see her again,
We'll go divin' on the reef,
We'll settle down.
(To Verse 5:)

I WANT TO WALK YOU HOME

Words and Music by
ANTOINE DOMINO

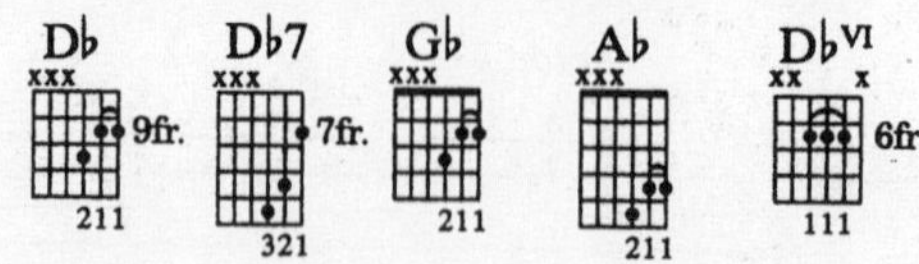

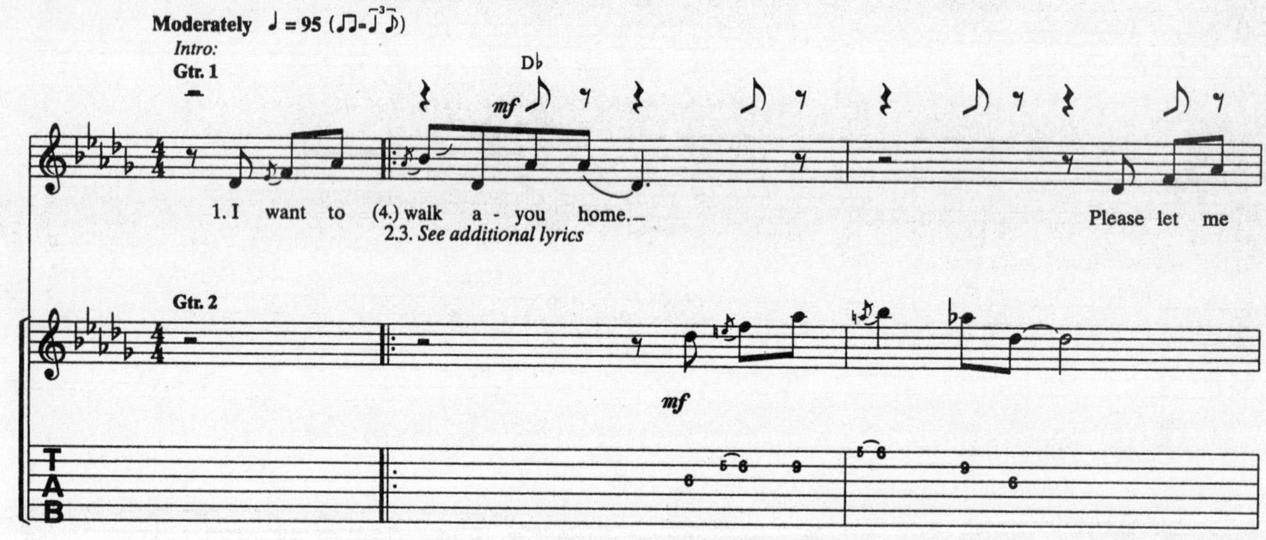

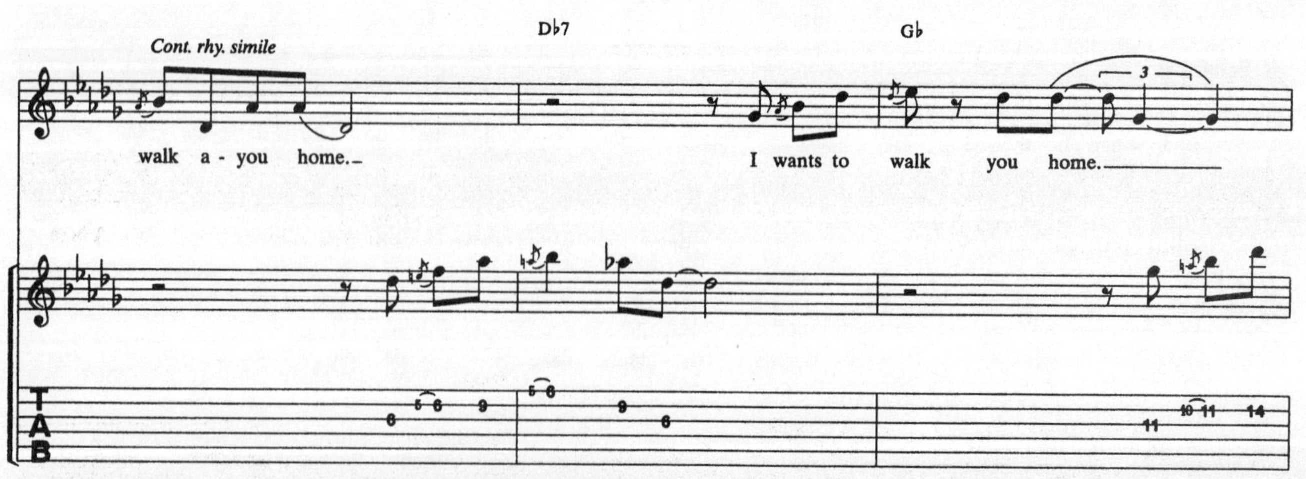

D♭
Please let me walk a - you home.
You
T
A
B
Gtrs. 1 & 2
A♭
G♭
look so good to me,
ooh,
wee,
I
1. 2. 3.
D♭
wish I was the luck - y guy
who could walk you right on down the aisle. 2. I love the
4.
D♭
saw you walk - ing all a - lone,
that's why I want to walk you home.
That's
Play 3 times
Freely
D♭VI
why I want to walk you home.
That's
why I want to walk you

Verse 2:
I love the way you walk.
I love to hear you talk.
I love the way you walk.
I love to hear you talk.
I'm not trying to be smart,
I'm not trying to break your heart,
But if I ask you for a date,
Will you tell me that I'm not too late?

Verse 3:
I want to hold your hand.
Please let me hold your hand.
I wants to hold your hand.
Please let me hold your hand.
You look so good to me, ooh-ee,
I saw you walking all alone,
That's why I want to walk you home.
So let me...
(To Verse 4:)

IN-A-GADDA-DA-VIDA

Words and Music by
DOUG INGLE

Chorus:
N.C.
G
3fr.
134211
Elec. Gtr. 1
Oh, won't_ you
E7
21
come with me___ and take my hand.___
A
5fr.
F♯7
131211
Oh, won't_ you come with me___ and walk this
B
1333
Dm
231
land.___ Please take_ my hand___

1.
w/Riff A (Elec. Gtr. 1) & Rhy. Fig. 1 (Elec. Gtr. 2) both 2 times
D7(♯9)
3fr.
314
Let me tell__ you, babe.
2.
w/Riff A (Elec. Gtr. 1) & Rhy. Fig. 1 (Elec. Gtr. 2) both 4 times
D7(♯9)
3fr.
314
Hup, hup!
Interlude:
D7(♯9)
3fr.
314
Drums
4
Elec. Gtr. 1
hold
Outro:
w/Intro Organ riff
Dm
231
Elec. Gtr. 1
N.C.

IRONIC

Lyrics by
ALANIS MORISSETTE

Music by
ALANIS MORISSETTE
and GLEN BALLARD

D/F♯
G6
D/F♯
Em7
lot - ter - y and died the next day. It's a
suit - case and kissed his kids good - bye. He wait - ed his
smok - ing sign on your cig - a - rette break. It's like
D/F♯
G6
D/F♯
Em7
black fly in your Char - don - nay. It's a
whole damn life to take that flight. And as the
ten thou - sand spoons when all you need is a knife. It's meet -

D/F♯
G6
D/F♯
Em7
death row___ par - don___ two min-utes too___ late.
plane crashed___ down___ he thought, "Well, is - n't this nice?"
ing the man of my dreams_ and meet - ing his beau - ti - ful___ wife.
And is - n't it i -
1.
D/F♯
G6/9
D/F♯
Em7
To Next Strain
(To Chorus:)
- ron-ic? Don't you___ think?_ It's like rain___
Rhy. Fig. 2
end Rhy. Fig. 2

2.3. w/Rhy. Fig. 2 (Gtr. 1) 2 times, simile
D/F♯
G6
Em7
- ron-ic? Don't you think? A lit-tle too i - ron-ic, and yeah, I
Gtr. 2
Chorus:
D
G
Gtrs. 1 & 2
real - ly do think. It's like rain on your
wed - ding day. It's a free ride when you've
al - read - y paid. It's the good ad - vice that you

D
Em7
F
C
To Coda
just did - n't take.
And who would of thought? It fig - ures.
1.
Dsus
2.
Dsus
2. Mis - ter
Well,
Bridge:
Cmaj7
D6(11)
4fr.
Gtr. 1
life has a fun-ny way of sneak-ing up on you when you think ev - 'ry-thing's o - kay, and
Gtr. 2
Riff A
Cmaj7
D6(11)
4fr.
ev - 'ry-thing's go-ing right.
And yeah, well,

Cmaj7
D6(11)
4fr.
life has a fun-ny way___ of help-ing you out___ when you think_ev-'ry-thing's_ gone_ wrong_ and
TAB
D(11)
D.S. 𝄋 al Coda
ev - 'ry-thing blows_ up in__ your face.
3. A
Gtrs. 1 & 2
end Riff A
Outro:
w/Rhy. Fig. 1 (Gtr. 1) 3 times
w/Riff A (Gtr. 2)
Coda
Dsus
Ah da di___ yeah,___ yeah, yeah,_
_ yeah. Ooh,___ yeah.___
Ya da di___
w/Rhy. Fig. 1A (Gtr. 1)
_ yeah,___ yeah, yeah,_ yeah,_ yeah, hey.___

IT'S MY PARTY

Words and Music by
HERB WIENER, JOHN GLUCK and WALLY GOLD

Verse:
A
C
1. No - bod - y knows where my John - ny has gone, but
2. Play all my re - cords. Keep danc - ing all night, but
3. Ju - dy and John - ny just walked through the door,
A
D
F
Ju - dy left the same time.
leave me a - lone for a while.
like a queen with her king.
Why was he
Till John - ny's
Oh, what a
A
B
hold - ing her hand when he's sup - posed to be
danc - ing with me, I've got no rea - son to
birth - day sur - prise; Ju - dy's wear - ing his
w/Piano Fig. 1 (simile)
Chorus:
E9
6fr.
A
A+
mine.
smile.
ring.
It's my par - ty and I'll cry if I want to, cry
D
Dm
A
F♯m
if I want to, cry if I want to. You would cry
To Coda
1. w/Piano Fig. 1 (simile)
2. w/Piano Fig. 1 (simile)
Bm
E
A
E
D
A
E
E
too, if it hap-pened to you.

Horn Soli:
A
A+
D
Dm
8va
F♯m
Bm
E
w/Piano Fig. 1 (simile)
D.S. 𝄋 al Coda
Coda
Oh,
it's my par - ty and I'll
Chorus:
w/Horn Fig. 1 (simile)
cry if I want to, cry if I want to, cry if I want to.
Repeat and fade
w/Horn Fig. 2 (simile)
You would cry too, if it hap-pened to you.

JAMES BOND THEME

Music by MONTY NORMAN

B
Swing feel
Em
Em(♯5)
Em6
Horns
Elec. Gtr.
1.
2.

C Elec. Gtr. tacet
A9
Horns
Em6/B
6fr.
Midtro:
D.S. % al Coda
Em
Em(#5)
Em6
Em(#5)
Coda
Elec. Gtr.
Outro:
N.C.
7fr.
Elec. Gtr.
Horns
Cont. in slashes
Em9(maj7)

JOHN BARLEYCORN
(Must Die)

Words and Music by
STEVE WINWOOD

Slowly 𝅗𝅥 = 80
Intro:

*Capo 7th fret to match pitch of recording.

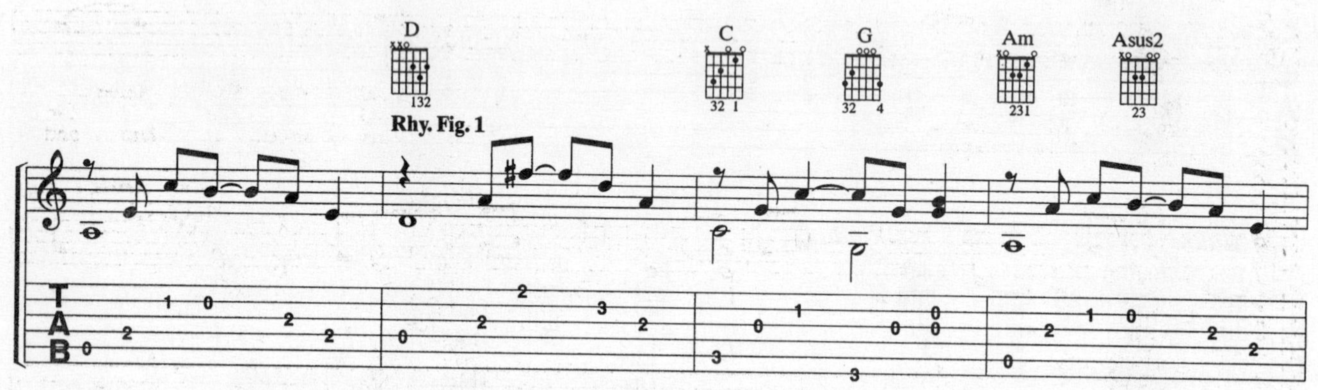

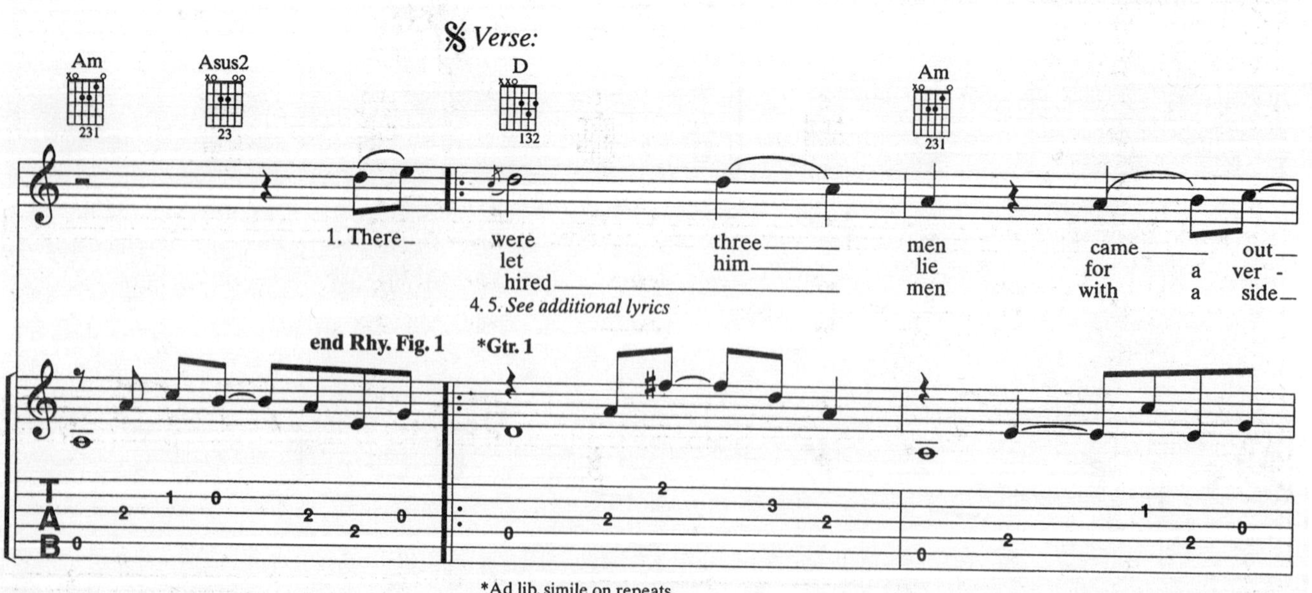

*Ad lib. simile on repeats.

C
G
Am
Asus2
Am
Asus2
D
of the west,
their for - tunes
y long time,
till the rains from
so sharp
to cut him off
C
G
Am
Asus2
Am
Asus2
D
for to try.
And these three
heav-en did fall.
And lit - tle Sir
at the knee.
They rolled him and
Am
C
G
Am
Asus2
men made a sol - emn vow:
John sprung up his head,
tied him, by the way,
P.M.

Am
Asus2
D
C
G
John Bar - ley - corn must die.
and so a mazed them all.
serv - ing him most bar - b'rous - ly.
Am
Asus2
Am
Asus2
C
They've plowed, they've
They've let him
They've hired
G/B
Am/E
Asus2
Am
sown, they've har - rowed him in,
stand till mid - sum - mer's day,
men with the sharp pitch - forks
threw
till he
who

C
D/A
D
Esus
clods up - on his head.
looked both pale and drawn.
pricked him to the heart.
E
Esus
E
Dm/A
And these three
And lit - tle Sir
And the load - er, he has
To Coda
Am
C
G
Am
Asus2
Am
Asus2
men made a sol - emn vow:
John's grown a long, long beard,
served him worse than that,
John and
for he's

D
C
G
Am
Asus2
Bar - ley - corn was dead.
so be - come a man.
bound him to the cart.
Flute Solo:
w/Rhy. Fig. 1 (Gtr. 1) 4 times, simile
1.-3.
4.
D.S. 𝄋 al Coda
2. They've
3. They've
4. They've
5. And

*Based on overall tonality.

Verse 4:
They've wheeled him around and around the field
Till they came unto a barn.
And there they made a solemn oath
On poor John Barleycorn.
They've hired men with the crabtree sticks
To cut him skin from bone.
And the miller, he has served him worse than that,
For he's ground him between two stones.
(To Flute Solo:)

Verse 5:
And little Sir John and his nut-round bowl
And his brandy in the glass.
And little Sir John and his nut-round bowl
Proved the strongest man at last.
The huntsmen, he cut off the fox,
More so loudly to blow his horn.
And the tinker, he can't mend kettle nor pot
Without a little Barleycorn.

JUMP

Words and Music by
EDWARD VAN HALEN, ALEX VAN HALEN,
MICHAEL ANTHONY and DAVID LEE ROTH

Jump - 6 - 1

(1st,) 2nd Verses
w/Riff A (2 times)
G/C C F/C G/C C F/C C/F Gsus4
ba - by, just_ how you_ feel._
are you?_ Who said that? Ba - by, how_ you been?_
You got to
You say you don't
G/C C F/C G/C C F/C C/F Gsus4
roll with the punch-es to get to what's real._
know, you won't_ know_ un-til you be - gin._
Ah, can't you
So, can't you
Pre-chorus
N.C.(Am)
(F) (C/E) (Dm)
see me stand - in' here? I got my back a - gainst the rec - ord ma - chine._
Gtr. II
slight vib. w/bar
P.M.
sl.
(F) (C/E) (Dm)
I ain't the worst that you've seen._
Ah, can't you see what I mean?_
slight vib. w/bar
P.M.
sl.
(F) (C/E) (G)
Ah, might as well_ jump._
(Gtr. II out)
slight vib. bar
P.M.
sl.

Chorus
w/Riff A
G/C C F/C G/C C F/C C/F Gsus4
(Jump!)
1. Might as well jump.
2. Go a-head and jump.
Go a-head and jump.
Might as well jump.
1st time w/Riff A1
2nd time w/Riff A
G/C C F/C G/C F/C C F/C C/F Gsus4 C/F Gsus4
(Jump!)
Go a-head and jump.
2. How old
Jump!
Guitar solo
*Bbm Gb Ab Db Bbm Gb Ab
**Gtr. III
8va
loco
rake
Full
1/2
(15ma)
A.H.
semi-harm.
*Chord names derived from bass and synth. (next 8 bars).
**Tune down 1/2 step. Music sounds as written.
Db Bbm Gb Ab
13:8
Db Bbm Gb Ab Db
9:8
P.M.
Riff A1
G/C C F/C G/C F/C C F/C C/F Gsus4
Gtr. I
8va
loco

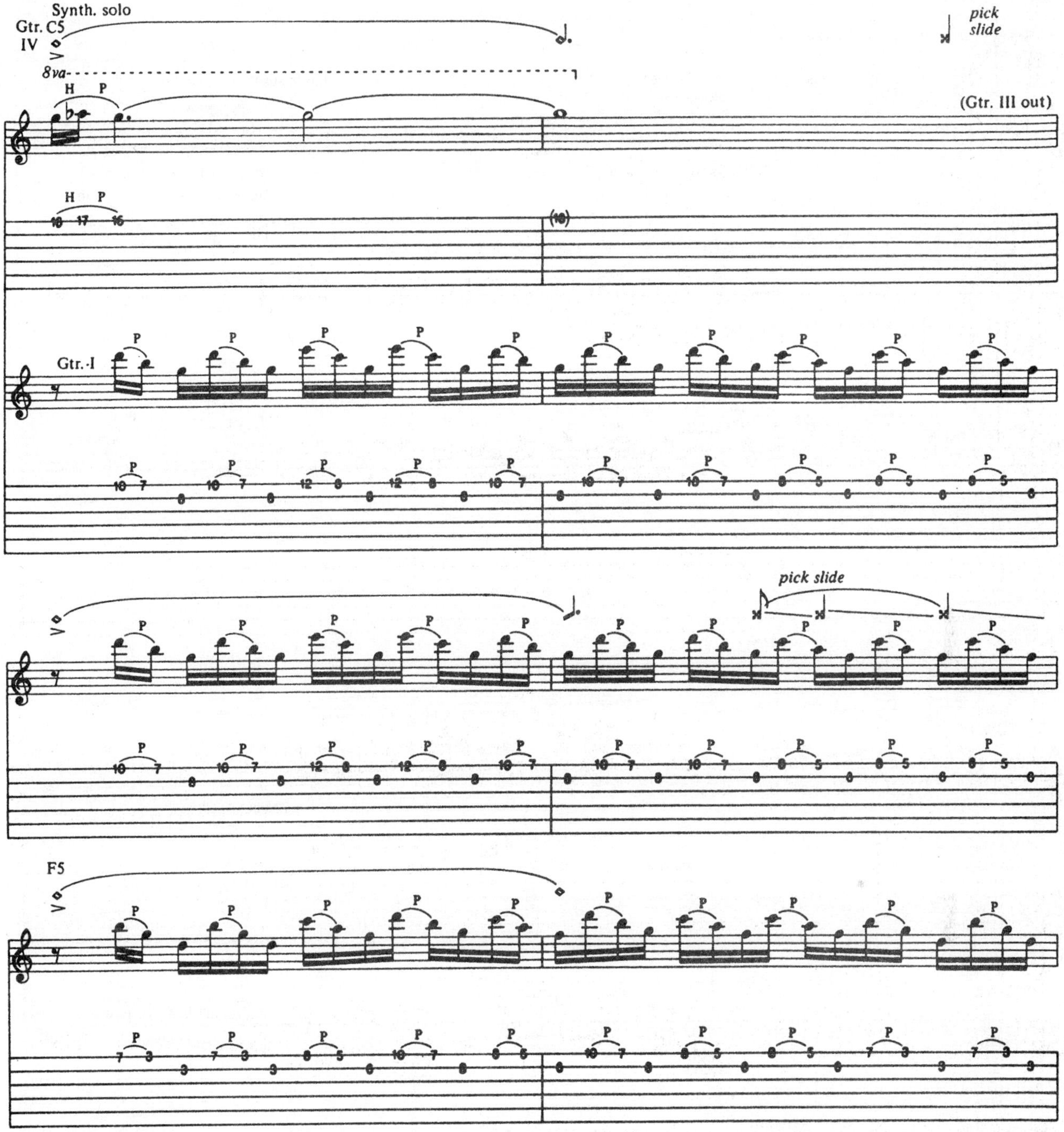

Synth. solo

Gtr. IV C5

8va

(Gtr. III out)

pick slide

Gtr. I

pick slide

F5

G5

pick slides

Bb5
8va
pick slide
*T =Tap w/R.H. index finger.
Ⓣ=Tap w/R.H. ring finger.
Ⓟ=Pull-off to R.H. index finger.
Asus4
8va
pick slide
Absus2
8va
G5
loco
C5
(Gtr. IV out)
w/Riff A
G/C C F/C G/C C F/C
1. C/F Gsus4
2. C/F Gsus4
Might as well_
Out-chorus
w/Riff A (3 times)
G/C C F/C G/C C F/C C/F Gsus4
jump. (Jump!) Go a-head and jump._ Get in and
Gtr. II
P.M.

G/C
C
F/C
G/C
C
F/C
C/F
Gsus4
jump. (Jump!)
Go a-head and
jump.
Jump!
P.M.
P.M.
Jump!
Jump!
Begin fade
w/Riff B
w/Riff A
Jump!
P.M.
Fade out
w/Riff B

JUST A GIRL

Words and Music by
GWEN STEFANI and THOMAS DUMONT

Bm
A
G
A
don't let me out of your sight. Oh,
Rhy. Fig. 4
end Rhy. Fig. 4
w/Rhy. Fig. 3 (Gtrs. 1 & 2) 2 times, simile
Substitute w/Rhy. Fig. 4
(Gtrs. 1 & 2) 2nd and 3rd times, simile
To Coda
I'm just a girl, all pret-ty and pe - tite. So don't let me have an - y rights.
1.
G5
C5
w/Rhy. Fig. 1 (Gtr. 1)
N.C.(D)
Oh, I've had it up to here. 2. The
(Oh.)
Rhy. Fig. 5
Gtrs. 1 & 2
Gtr. 2 out
end Rhy. Fig. 5
P.M.
2.
w/Rhy. Fig. 3 (Gtrs. 1 & 2)
w/Rhy. Fig. 4 (Gtrs. 1 & 2) simile
I'm just a girl, take a good look at me. Just your typ - i - cal pro - to - type.
w/Rhy. Fig. 5 (Gtrs. 1 & 2)
Oh, I've had it up to here.
(Oh.)

Interlude:
w/Rhy. Fig. 3 (Gtrs. 1 & 2) 4 times, simile
Bm A G A Bm A G A
Riff 1
*Gtr. 3
end Riff 1
mf
*Keyboard arr. for gtr. w/envelope filter.
Gtr. 3 out
Bm A/C♯* G/D* A/E* Bm A G A
Riff 2
end Riff 2
*Chord inversions implied by bass.
end double-time feel
w/Rhy. Fig. 5 (Gtrs. 1 & 2)
G5 C5
w/Rhy. Fig. 1 (Gtrs. 1 & 2)
N.C.(D)
Oh, am I mak - ing my - self clear?
(Oh,)
Verse 3:
w/Rhy. Fig. 1 (Gtrs. 1 & 2) 2 times
3. I'm just a girl. I'm just a girl in the world.
w/Rhy. Fig. 2 (Gtrs. 1 & 2)
D.S. al Coda
That's all that you'll let me be. 3. Oh,
Chorus 4:
w/Rhy. Fig. 3 (Gtrs. 1 & 2) 4 times, simile
w/Riff 1 (Gtr. 3)
w/Riff 2 (Gtr. 3)
Coda
Bm A G A Bm A
I'm just a girl, my a - pol - o - gies. What I've be - come is so bur - den-

Verse 2:
The moment that I step outside,
So many reasons for me to run and hide.
I can't do the little things I hold so dear.
It's all those little things that I fear.

Chorus 2:
'Cause I'm just a girl, I'd rather not be,
'Cause they won't let me drive late at night.
Oh, I'm just a girl. Guess I'm some kind of freak,
'Cause they all sit and stare with them eyes. Oh, . . .
(To Interlude:)

Chorus 3:
Oh, I'm just a girl, livin' in captivity.
Your rule of thumb makes me worry some.
Oh, I'm just a girl, oh, what's my destiny?
What I've succumbed to is making me numb. Oh . . .
(To Coda)

KEEP A KNOCKIN'

Words and Music by
RICHARD PENNIMAN

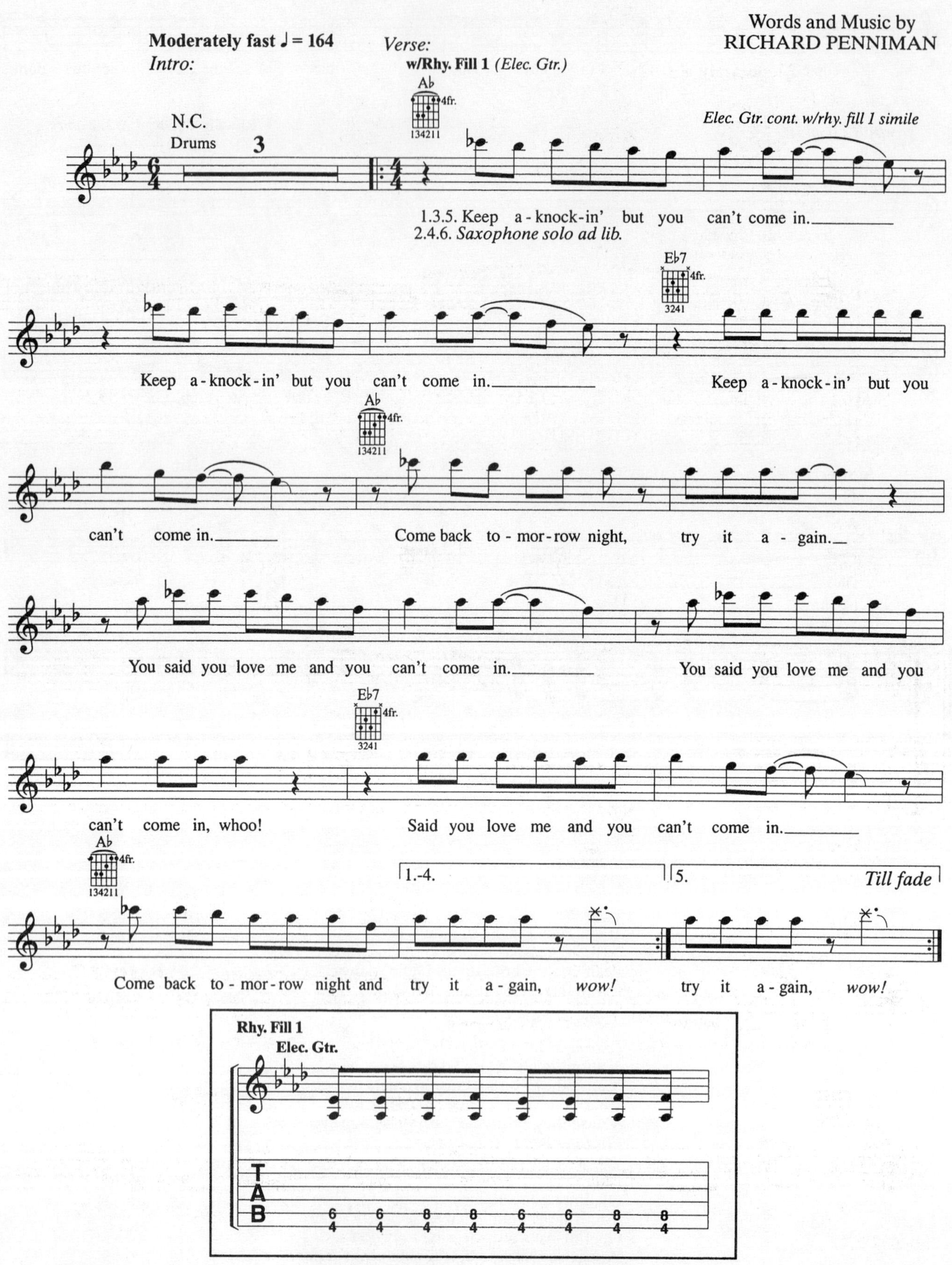

KRYPTONITE

Music by MATT ROBERTS,
BRAD ARNOLD and TODD HARRELL
Lyrics by BRAD ARNOLD

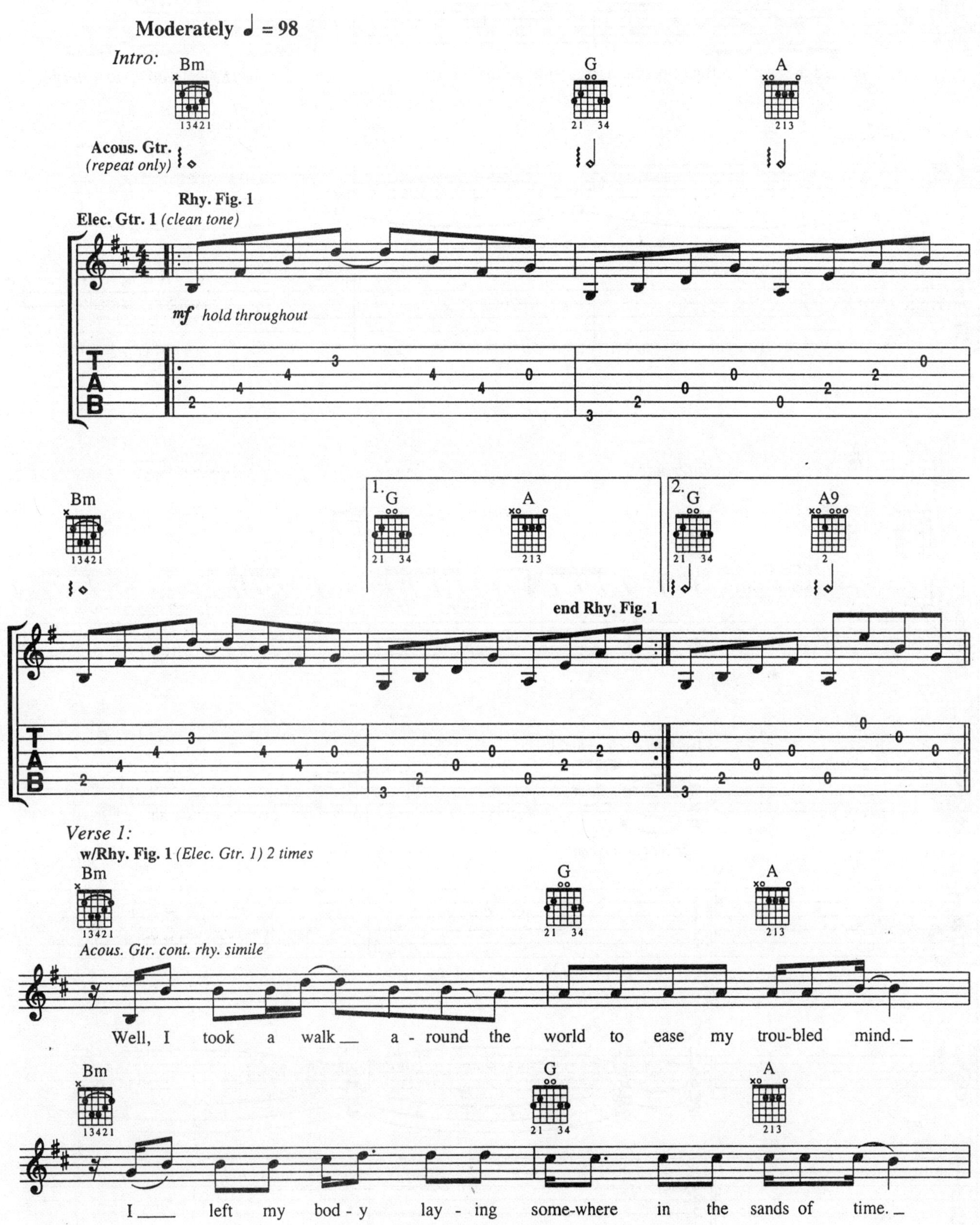

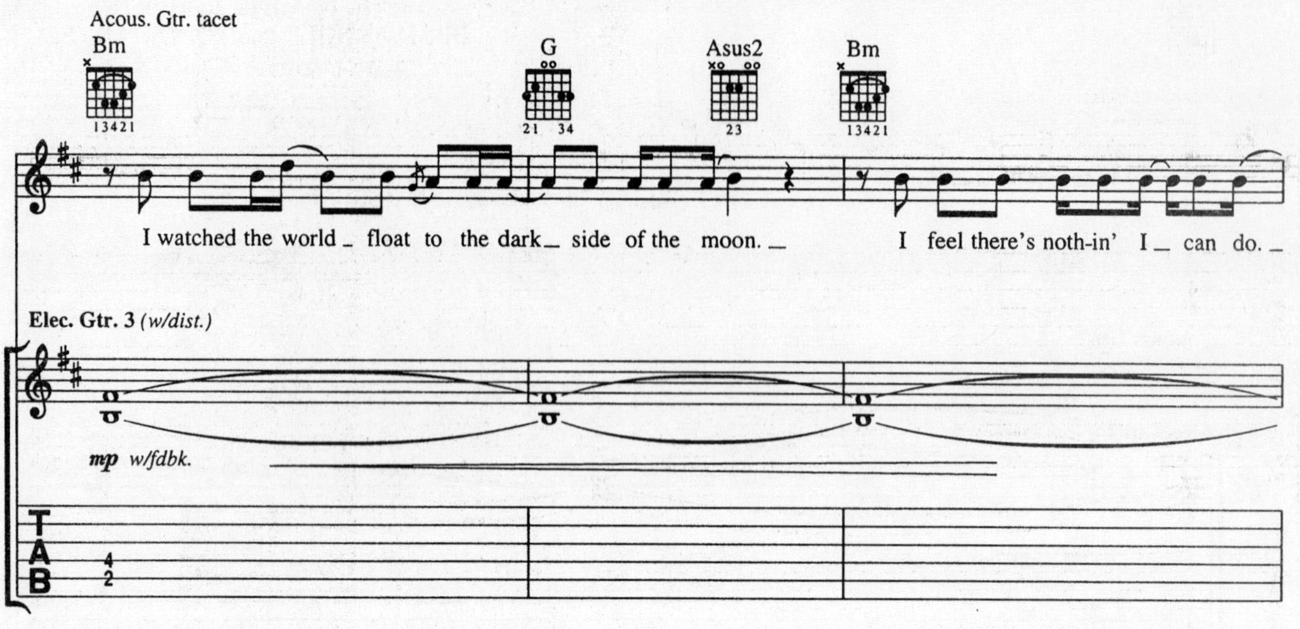

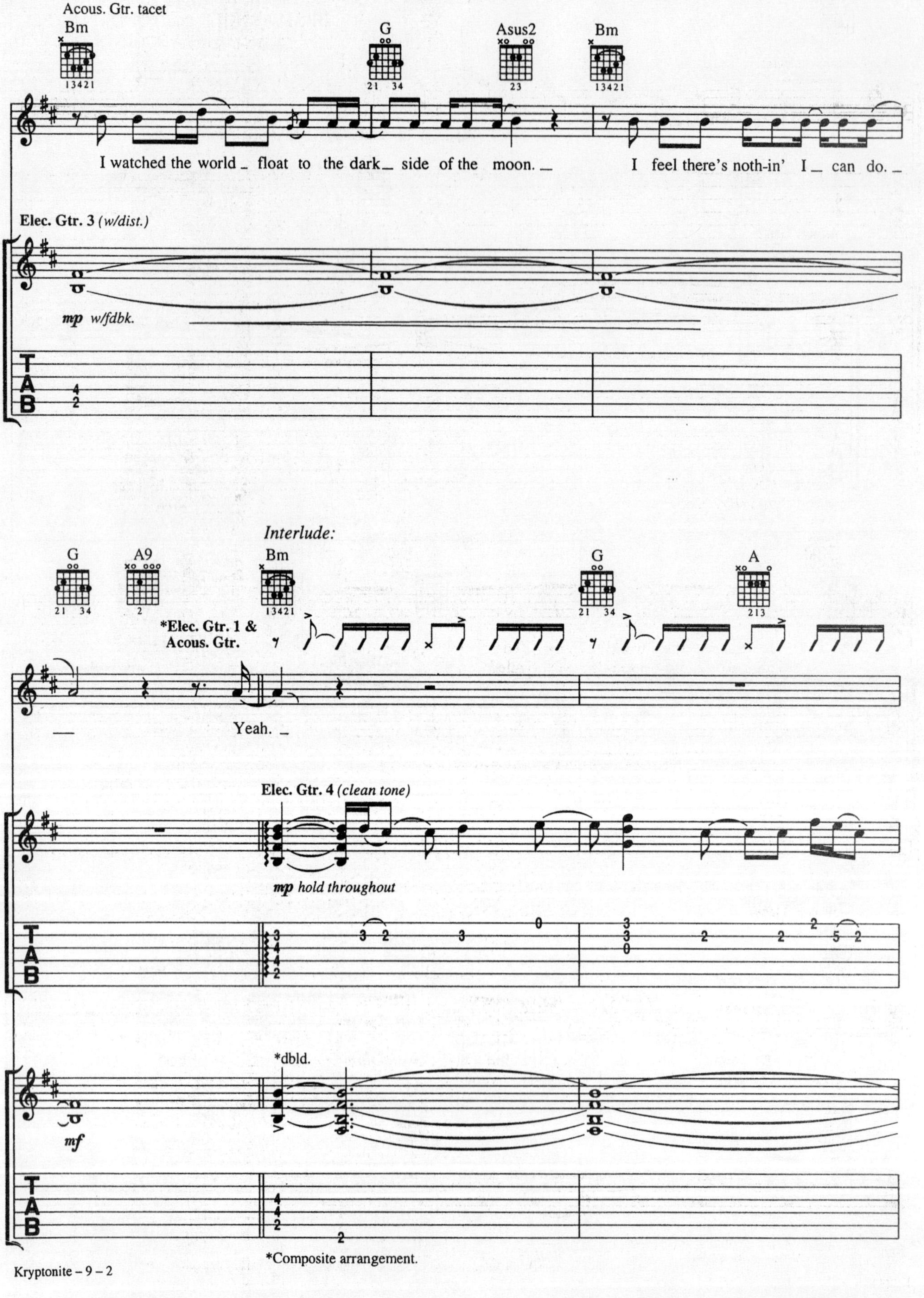

Interlude:

G A9 Bm G A

*Elec. Gtr. 1 & Acous. Gtr.

Yeah. _

Elec. Gtr. 4 *(clean tone)*

mp hold throughout

*dbld.

mf

*Composite arrangement.

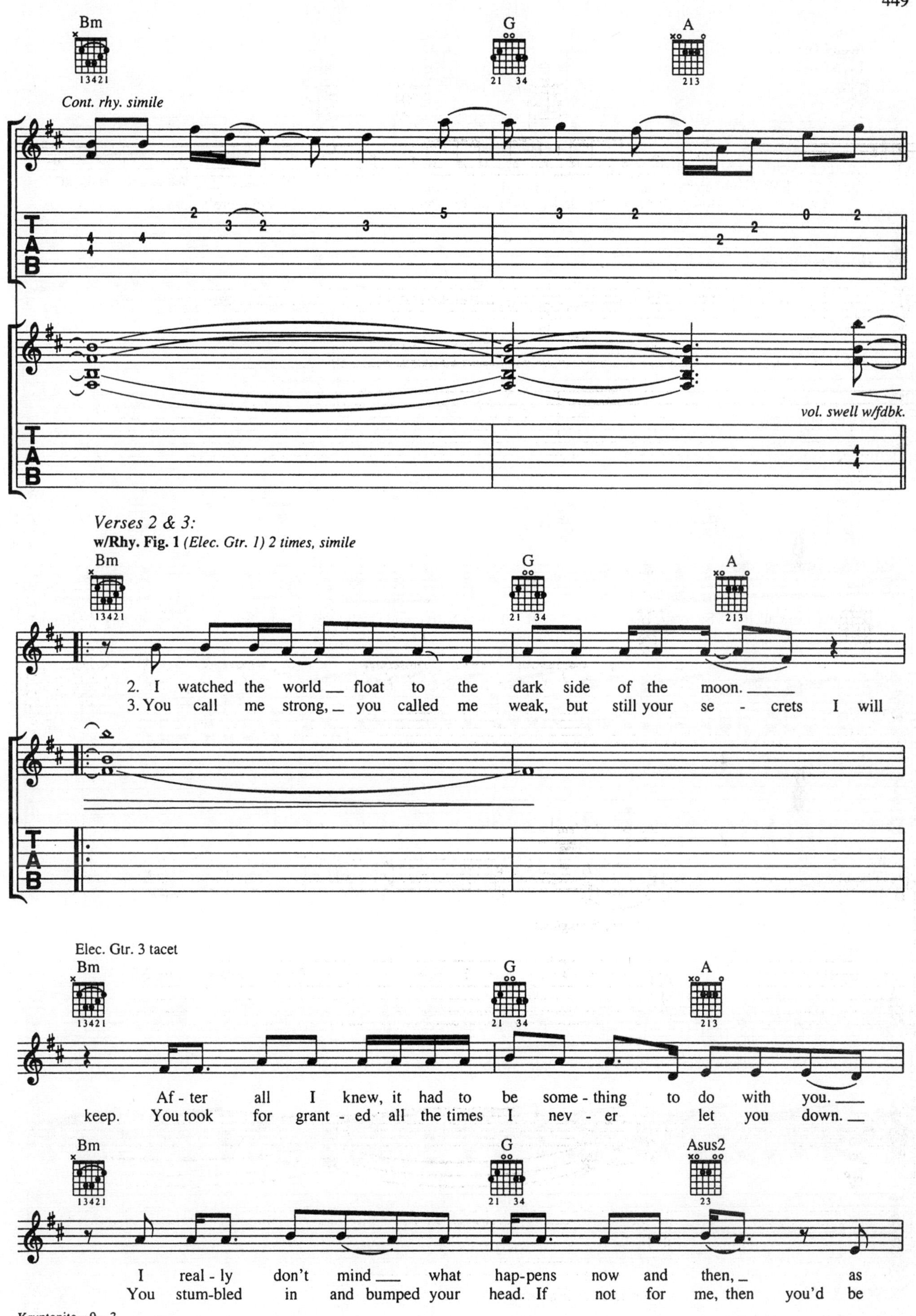
Bm
G
A
Cont. rhy. simile
vol. swell w/fdbk.
Verses 2 & 3:
w/Rhy. Fig. 1 (Elec. Gtr. 1) 2 times, simile
2. I watched the world float to the dark side of the moon.
3. You call me strong, you called me weak, but still your se - crets I will
Elec. Gtr. 3 tacet
Af - ter all I knew, it had to be some - thing to do with you.
keep. You took for grant - ed all the times I nev - er let you down.
Asus2
I real - ly don't mind what hap-pens now and then, as
You stum-bled in and bumped your head. If not for me, then you'd be

Chorus:
Bm
G
Asus2
B5
long as you'll be my friend in the end.
dead. I picked you up and put you back on sol - id ground.
If I go cra - zy, then will
*Elec. Gtr. 3
mp
f
fdbk./vol. swell
P.M. single notes throughout
*Two gtrs. arr. for one.
G5
A5
B5
E5
F#5
you still call me Su - per - man?
If I'm a - live and well, will
you be there hold - ing my hand?
no P.M.
B5
G5
A5
I'll keep you by my side with my su - per - hu - man might.

B5
7fr
133
E5
22
F♯5
133
Kryp - to - nite.
Elec. Gtr. 5 (w/dist.) on repeat
mf
21
1. Interlude:
Bm
13421
G
21 34
A
213
Elec. Gtr. 1
mp
Cont. rhy. simile
Elec. Gtr. 4
mp
hold throughout
w/flanger

2.3.
B5
7fr
133
G5
133
A5
5fr
133
Elec. Gtr. 3
vocals on D.S.
Whoa, _ whoa _
Elec. Gtr. 5
Elec. Gtr. 4
(on D.S.)
mp hold throughout
B5
7fr
133
E5
22
F♯5
133
whoa.
Whoa, _ whoa, _

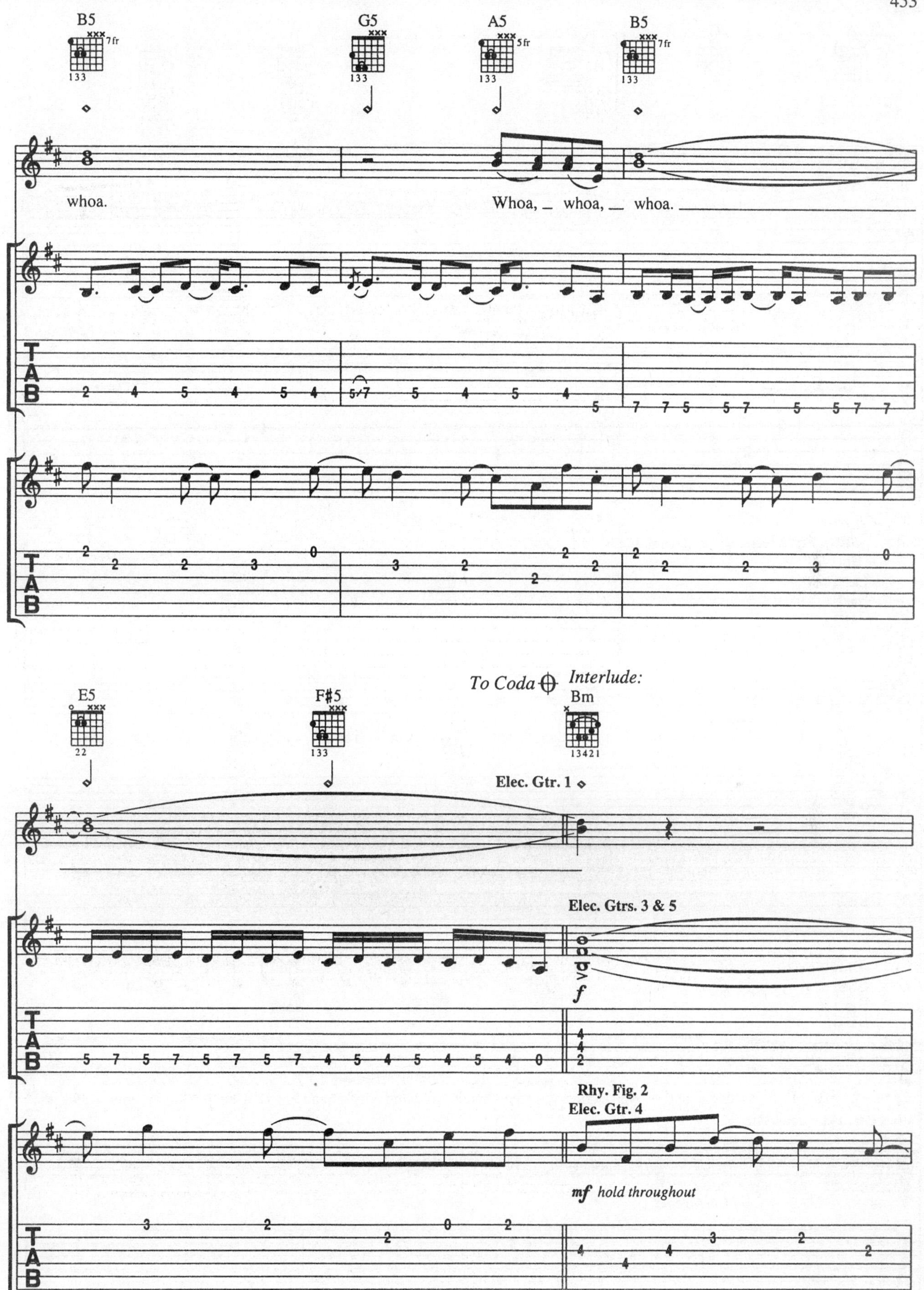
B5
G5
A5
B5
7fr
5fr
133
whoa.
Whoa, _ whoa, _ whoa.
E5
F#5
To Coda
Interlude:
Bm
22
13421
Elec. Gtr. 1
Elec. Gtrs. 3 & 5
Rhy. Fig. 2
Elec. Gtr. 4
mf hold throughout

A
G
Bm
A
G
end Rhy. Fig. 2
Chorus:
w/Rhy. Fig. 2 (Elec. Gtr. 4) 2 times, simile
Bm
A
G
If I go cra - zy, then will you still call me Su - per - man?
Bm
A
G
Bm
If I'm a - live and well, will you be there hold - ing my hand? I'll keep you by my side with
Elec. Gtr. 1 & Acous. Gtr.
mp
hold throughout

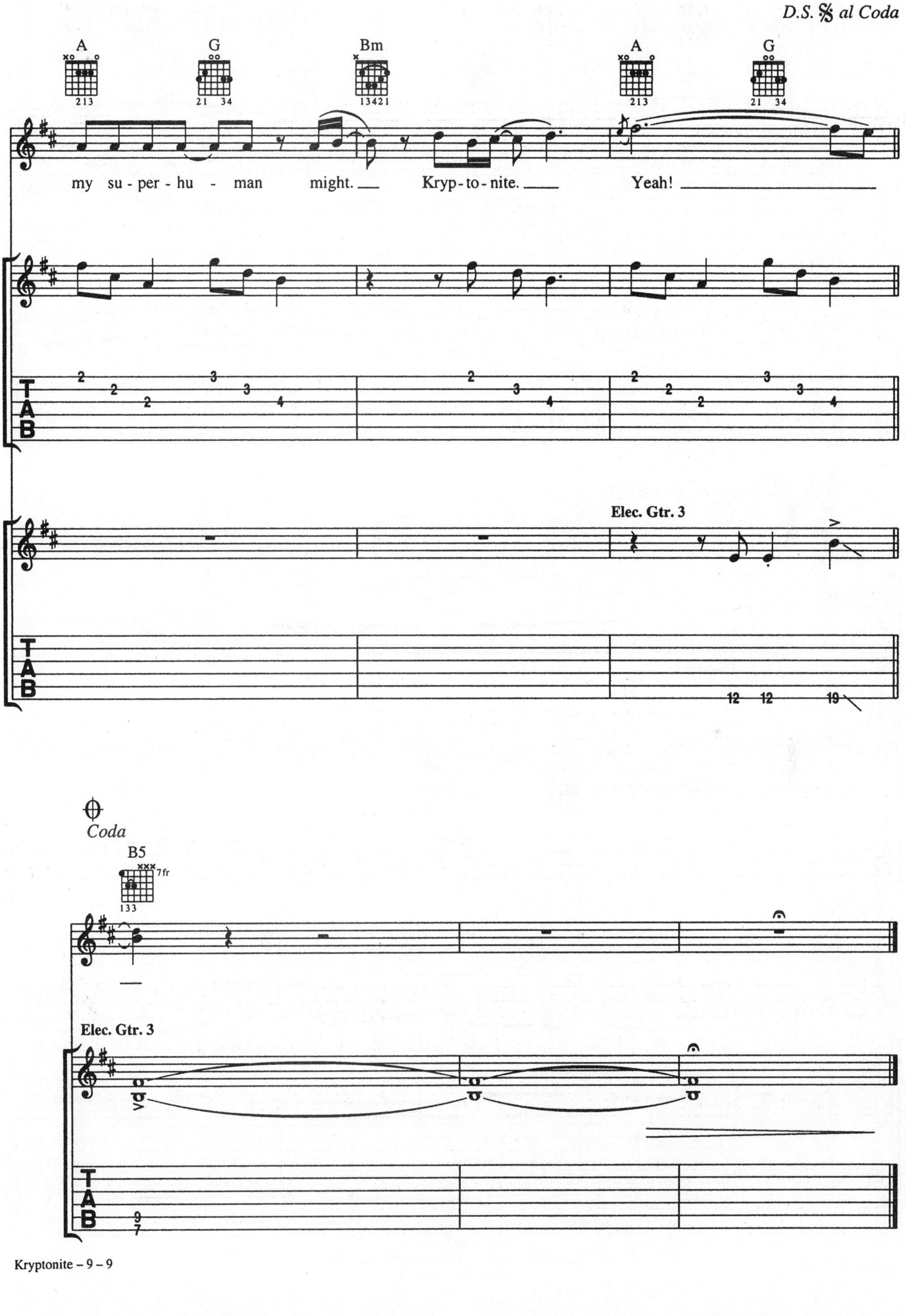

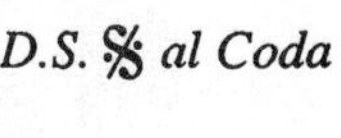

A G Bm A G

my su - per - hu - man might. Kryp - to - nite. Yeah!

Elec. Gtr. 3

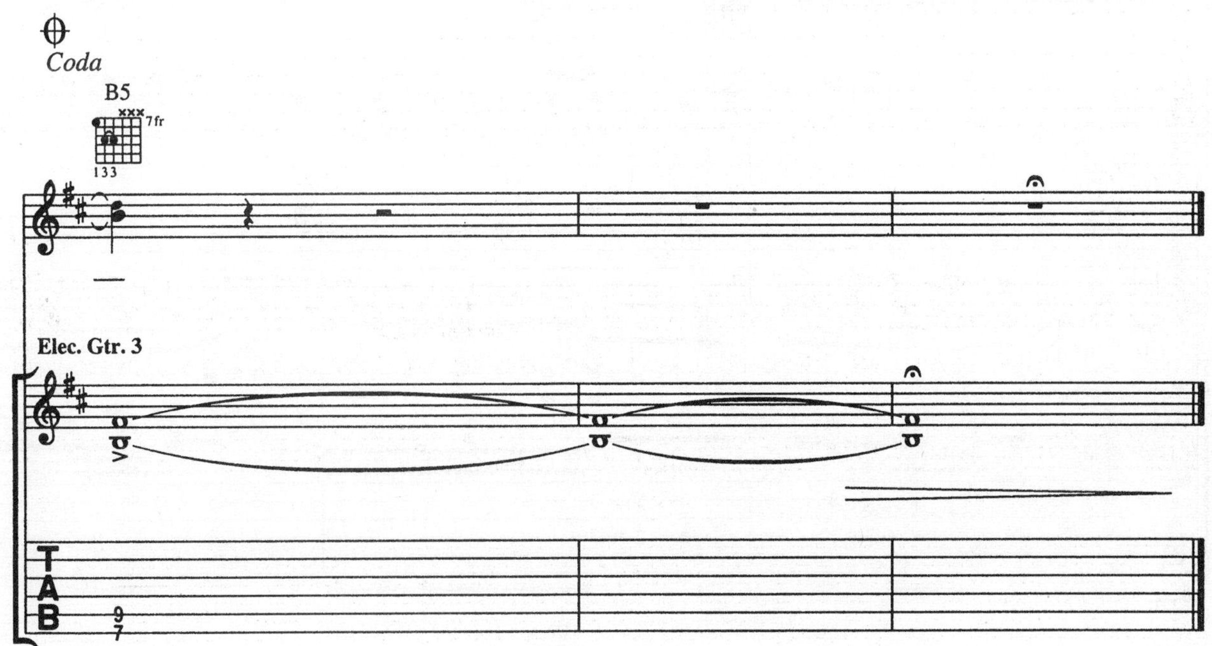

LAYLA

Words and Music by
ERIC CLAPTON and JIM GORDON

C
Dm
B♭
C
Dm
Riff E1
Elec. Gtr. 4
end Riff E1
Elec. Gtr. 1
Riff E2
end Riff E2
Riff E3
Elec. Gtrs. 2 & 3
end Riff E3
Elec. Gtr. 5
Elec. Gtr. 6
end Riff D

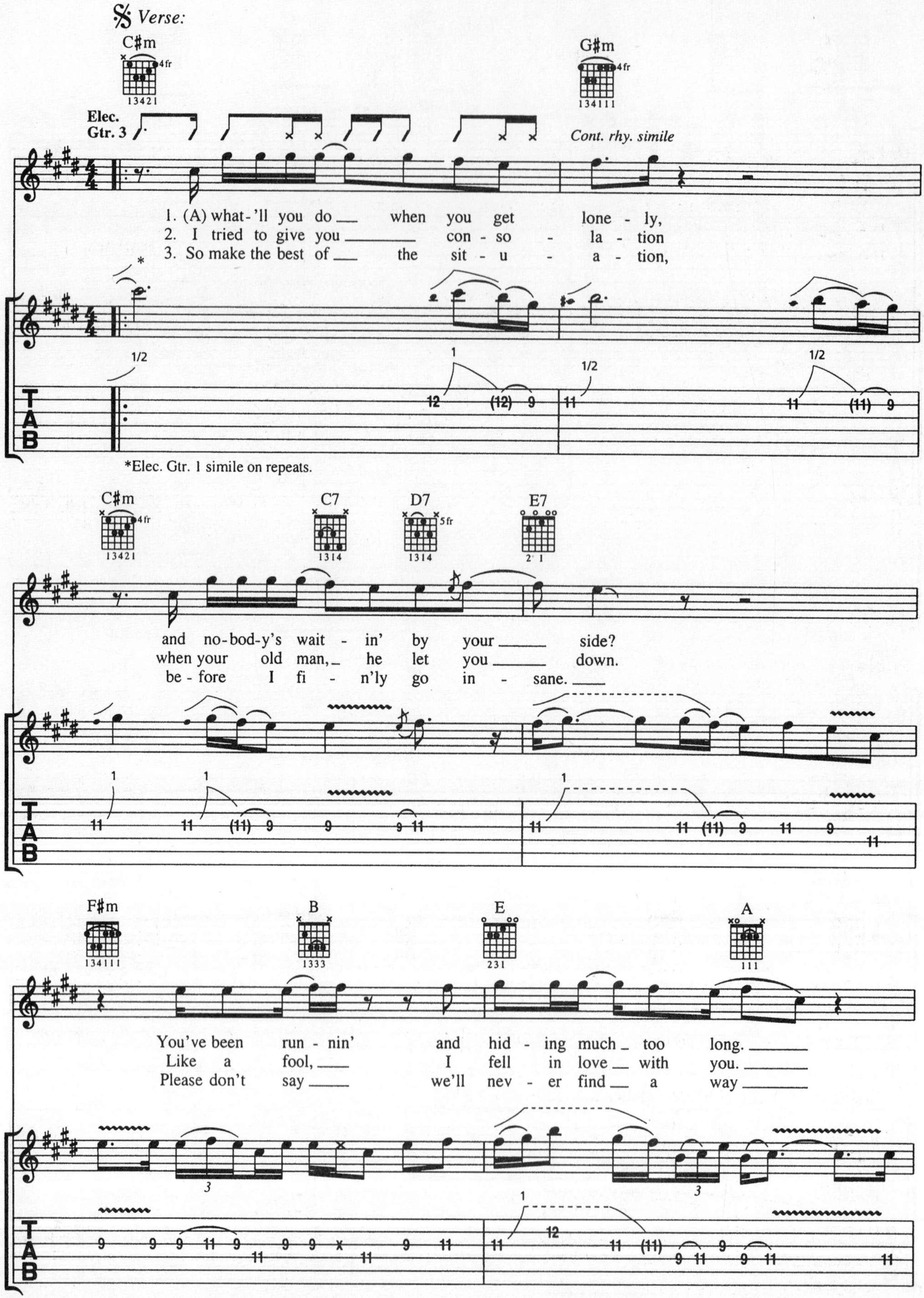
Verse:
C#m
G#m
Elec. Gtr. 3
Cont. rhy. simile
1. (A) what-'ll you do when you get lone - ly,
2. I tried to give you con - so - la - tion
3. So make the best of the sit - u - a - tion,
*Elec. Gtr. 1 simile on repeats.
C#m
C7
D7
E7
and no-bod-y's wait - in' by your side?
when your old man, he let you down.
be - fore I fi - n'ly go in - sane.
F#m
B
E
A
You've been run - nin' and hid - ing much too long.
Like a fool, I fell in love with you.
Please don't say we'll nev - er find a way

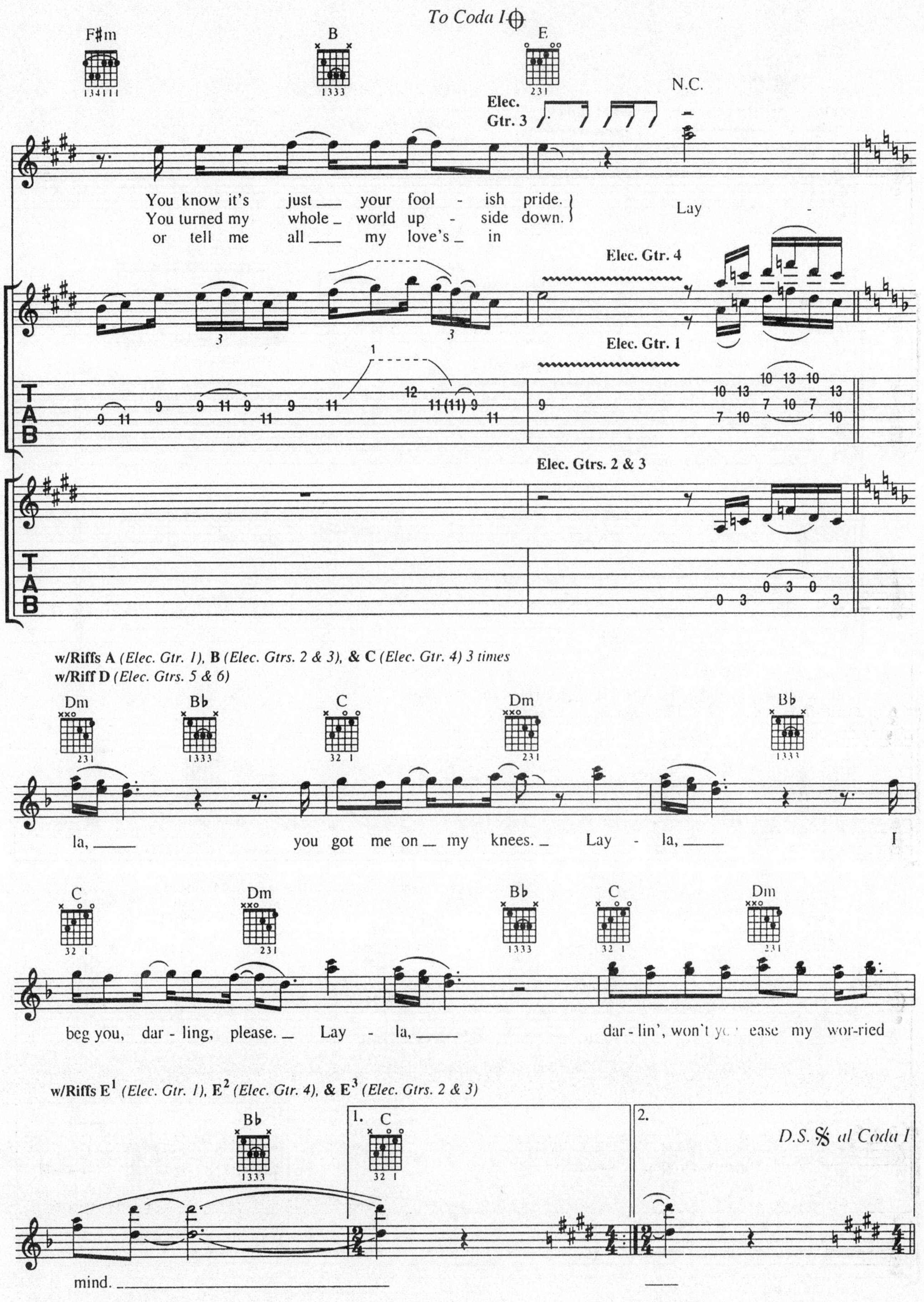
To Coda I
F♯m
B
E
N.C.
Elec. Gtr. 3
You know it's just your fool - ish pride.
You turned my whole world up - side down.
or tell me all my love's in
Lay -
Elec. Gtr. 4
Elec. Gtr. 1
Elec. Gtrs. 2 & 3
w/Riffs A (Elec. Gtr. 1), B (Elec. Gtrs. 2 & 3), & C (Elec. Gtr. 4) 3 times
w/Riff D (Elec. Gtrs. 5 & 6)
Dm
B♭
C
la, you got me on my knees. Lay - la, I
beg you, dar - ling, please. Lay - la,
dar - lin', won't you ease my wor-ried
w/Riffs E1 (Elec. Gtr. 1), E2 (Elec. Gtr. 4), & E3 (Elec. Gtrs. 2 & 3)
1.
2.
D.S. al Coda I
mind.

Coda I
E
N.C.
Elec. Gtr. 3
Cont. in notation
vain. Lay -
Elec. Gtr. 4
Elec. Gtr. 1
Elec. Gtrs. 2 & 3
Chorus:
w/Riffs A (Elec. Gtr. 1), B (Elec. Gtrs. 2 & 3), & C (Elec. Gtr. 4) 4 times
w/Riff D (Elec. Gtrs. 5 & 6) 1st 4 meas. only, 2 times
Dm Bb C Dm
la, you got me on my knees. Lay -
Bb C Dm Bb
la, I beg you, dar - lin', please. Lay - la,
C Dm Bb
1.
C Dm
dar - lin', won't you ease my wor-ried mind. Lay -

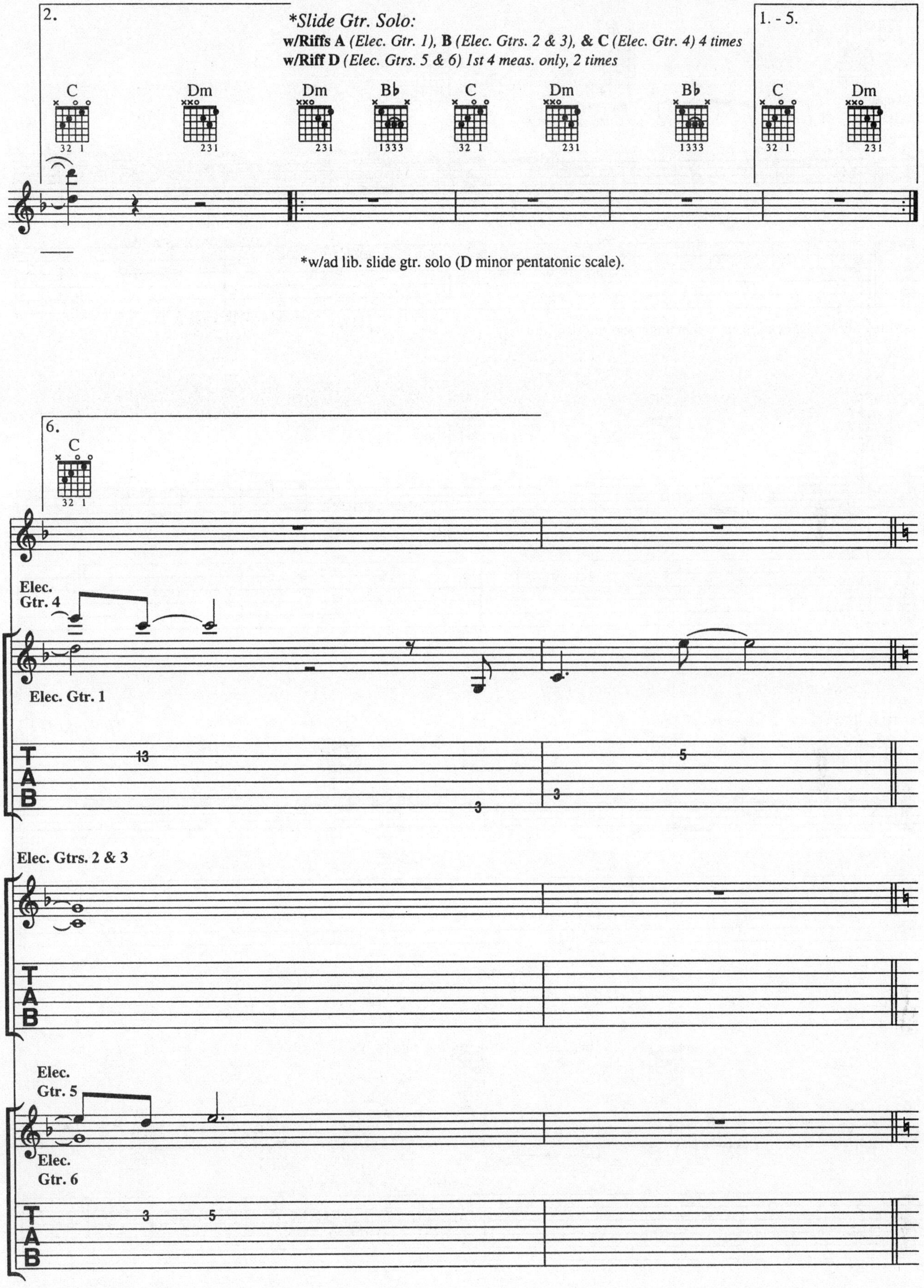

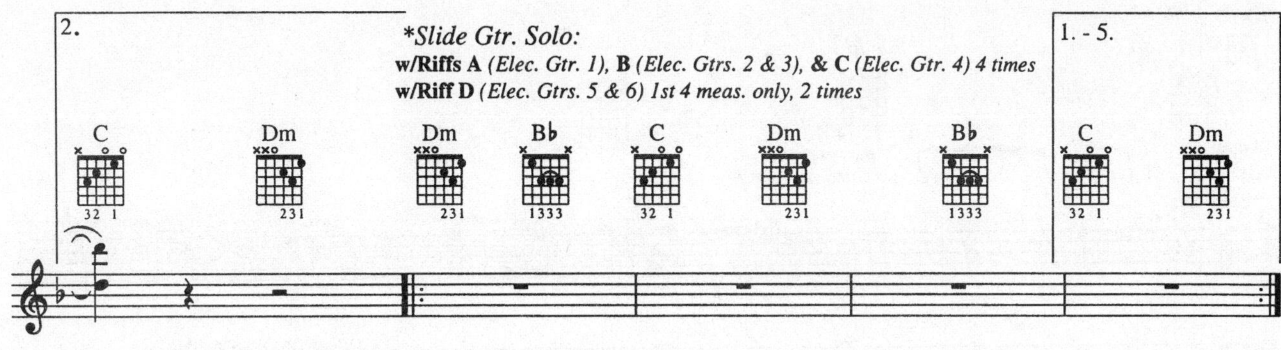

*w/ad lib. slide gtr. solo (D minor pentatonic scale).

6.

C

Elec. Gtr. 4

Elec. Gtr. 1

13 3 3 5

Elec. Gtrs. 2 & 3

Elec. Gtr. 5

Elec. Gtr. 6

3 5

𝄋𝄋 *Outro:*

A C   C/E   F

Acous. Gtr.

Cont. rhy. simile

*Elec. Gtr.

*Elec. Gtr. is a composite gtr. combining piano and elec. gtrs.

C   C/E   F

B♭9(♭5)   C

To Coda II 𝄌

Bb9(b5)
C
C/E
F
Bb9(b5)
C
G/B
C
Am
Dm
G

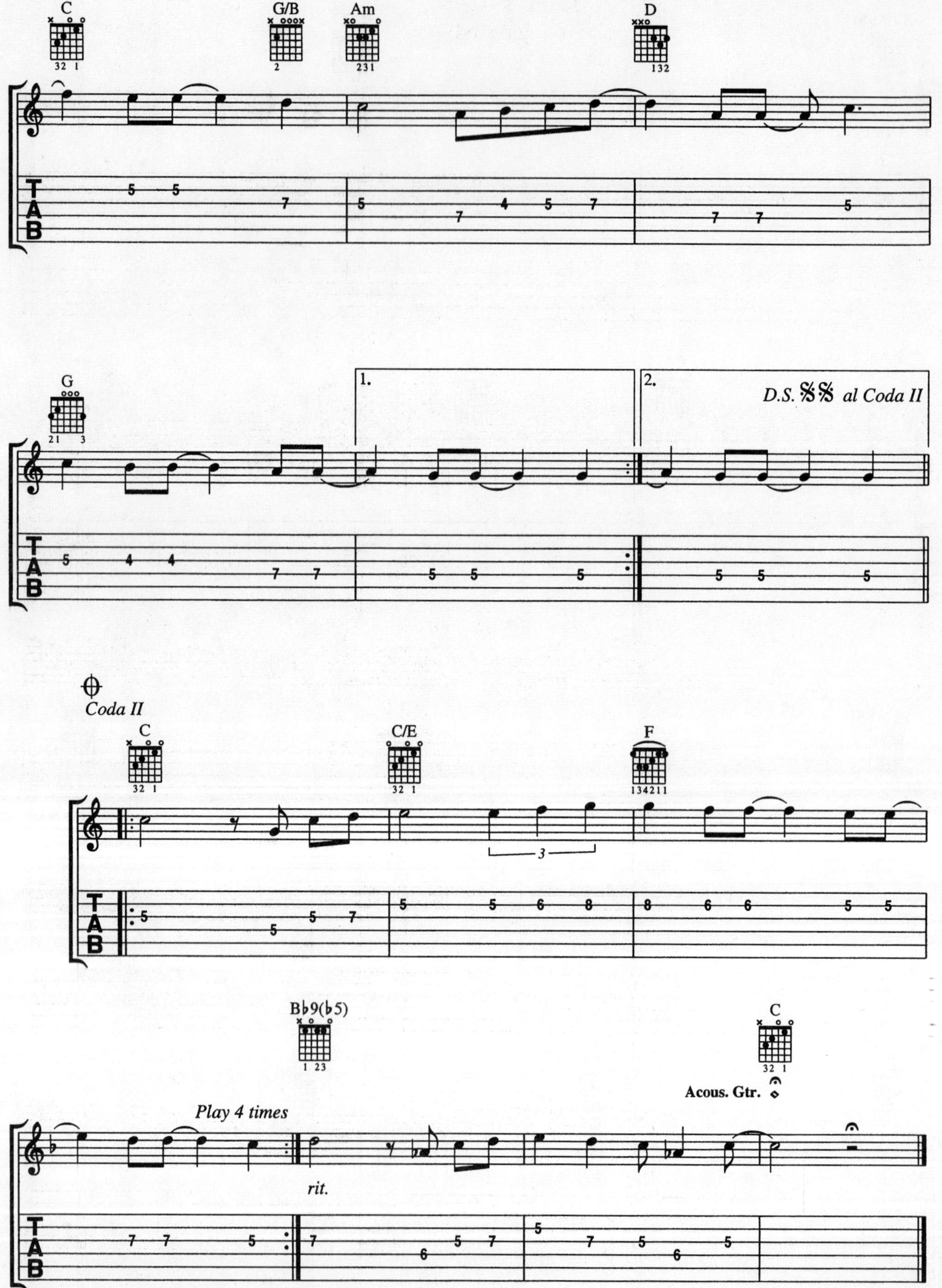
C
G/B
Am
D
G
1.
2.
D.S. 𝄉𝄉 al Coda II
Coda II
C
C/E
F
B♭9(♭5)
C
Play 4 times
rit.
Acous. Gtr.

LAYLA
(Unplugged)

Words and Music by
ERIC CLAPTON and JIM GORDON

1st Verse
C#m7
G#7
C#m7
C
D
1. What _ will you do when you get lone - ly? _____
No _ one wait-ing by your
E
E7
F#m
B
E
A
_ side. ____
You've _ been run- nin' _
hid - in' much too long, _
F#m
B
E
A
you know it's just your fool - ish pride. __
Lay - la, ___
Chorus
D5
Dm (C)
B♭
C
D5
N.C.
Dm
(C)
B♭
got me on my knees. Lay - la, _____

C
D5
N.C.
(C)
Dm
D5
N.C.
D5
beg - gin' darl - in', please. _ Lay - la, ____
darl - in' won't you ease my wor - ried
Dm
(C)
B♭
C
N.C.
(A)
(C)
mind. ___
2nd and 3rd Verses
C#m7
G#7
C#m7
C
D
2. Tried to give you _ con - sol - a - tion, __
3. Make the best of the sit - u - a - tion, __
your old man had let you
before I fin - ally go in-
E
E7
F#m
B
E
A
down. __
sane. __
Like _ a _ fool,
Please _ don't say
I fall in love __ with you.
we'll nev - er find __ a way.
Tom (6)
Tom (6)

F#m
A
E
You turned my whole world up - side down.
Tell me all my love's in vain.
Lay - la,
Chorus
Dm (C) B♭
C Dm N.C.
D5 Dm (C) B♭
got me on my knees Lay - la,
C D5 N.C. D5 Dm (C) B♭
beg - gin' dar - lin', please. Lay - la,
To Coda
C D5 N.C. D5
dar - lin', won't you ease my wor - ried
1.
Dm (C) B♭
C N.C.
mind.

2.
Dm (C)
B♭
C
D5
Dm Dsus2
D5
mind.
Lay-
Chorus
Dm (C)
B♭
C
D5
N.C.
Dm (C)
B♭
la;
got me on my knees, lay - la,
C
D5
N.C.
D5 (C)
B♭
C
Dm
N.C.
beg - gin' dar - lin, please. Lay - la,
dar - lin', won't you ease my wor - ried
Dm (C)
B♭
C
D5
N.C.
mind.
1/4

Guitar Solo
Dm
(C)
B♭
C
1/4
1/2

(C) B♭ C Dm N.C.

Lay - la

1/4

Coda

Dm (C) B♭ C D Dm (C) B♭

mind. Lay - la,

C Dm N.C. D5 Dm (C) B♭ C D5 N.C.

got me on my knees. Lay - la, beg - gin' dar - lin'', please Lay - la,

D5 Dm (C) B♭ C

ritard poco a poco

dar - lin', won't you ease my wor - ried

Rubato

(Dm)

N.C.

mind.

LET IT BE ME

English Words by MANN CURTIS
French Words by PIERRE DELANOE

Music by
GILBERT BECAUD

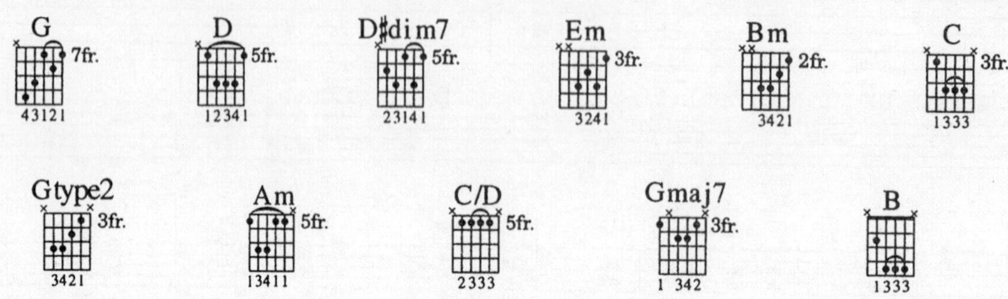

Moderately slow ♩ = 84

Intro:

Verse 1:

Em
Bm/D*
C
I want to stay a - round you. And so I
* Bass plays D.
end Rhy. Fig. 1
Gtype2
Am
C/D
Gtype2
beg you, let___ it be me.
Verses 2, 3 & 4:
w/Rhy. Fig. 1 (Gtr. 2)
G
D
D♯dim7
Em
2. Don't take this heav - en from one, if you must
3. 4. See additional lyrics
* 2nd time simile.

To Coda
Bm/D*
C
G
cling to some - one. Now and for - ev - er,
* Bass plays D.
Bridge:
Gtr. 2
Am
C/D
G
C
let it be me. Each time we
Bm
C
Gmaj7
meet, love, I find com - plete love.

Verses 3 & 4:
So never leave me lonely,
Tell me you love me only
And that you'll always
Let it be me.
(To Bridge:)

LICK IT UP

Words and Music by
PAUL STANLEY and VINCENT CUSANO

Intro

Moderate Rock ♩ = 120

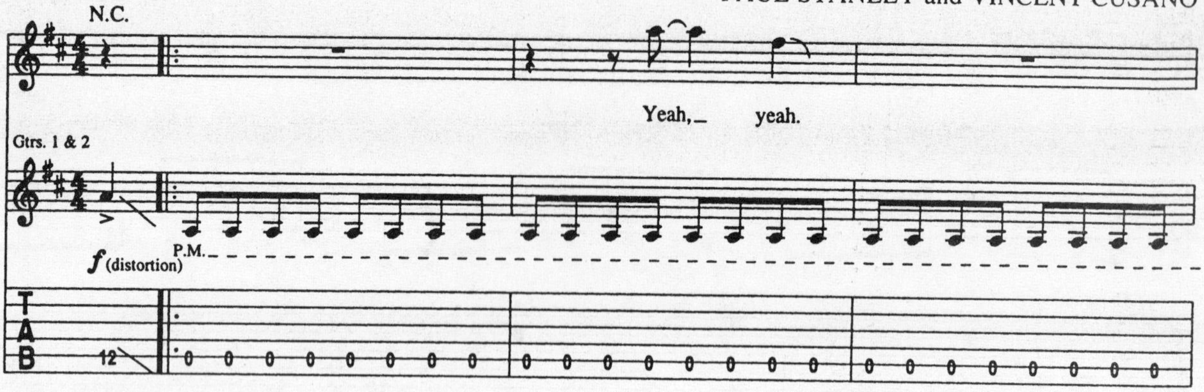

N.C.

Yeah, yeah.

Gtrs. 1 & 2

f (distortion)

P.M.

Verse

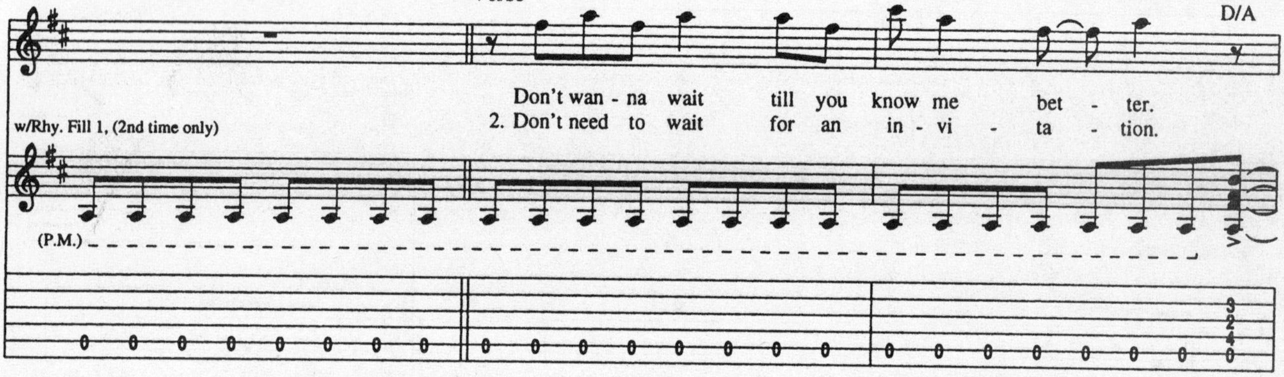

D/A

Don't wan - na wait till you know me bet - ter.
2. Don't need to wait for an in - vi - ta - tion.

w/Rhy. Fill 1, (2nd time only)

(P.M.)

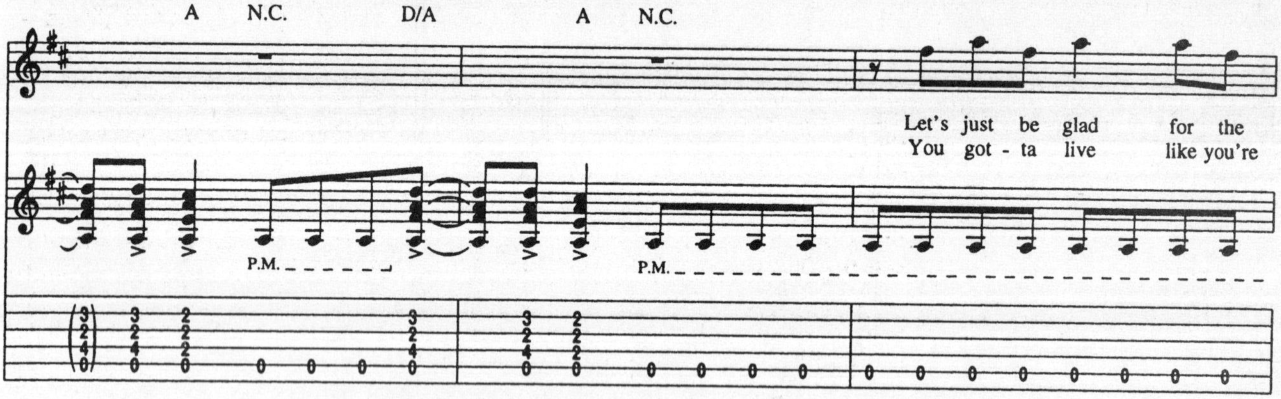

A N.C. D/A A N.C.

Let's just be glad for the
You got - ta live like you're

P.M.

P.M.

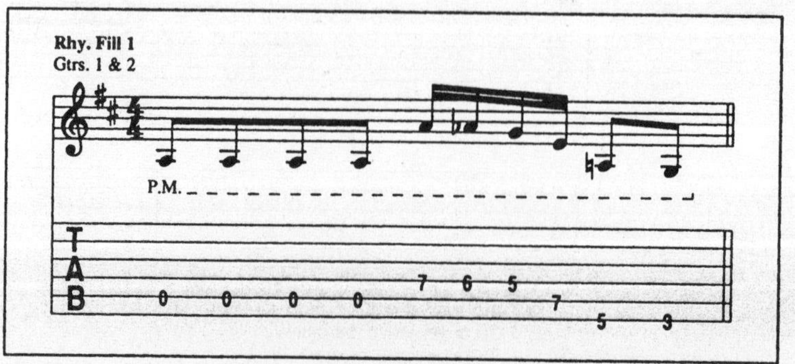

D/A
A N.C.
D/A
A N.C.
*G/A
time to - geth - er.
on va - ca - tion.
(P.M.)
P.M.
P.M.
*Bass plays A
Pre Chorus
G
D/A
Life's such a treat and it's time you taste it.
There's some - thing sweet you can't buy with mon - ey. Lick
A N.C.
D/A
A N.C.
*G/A
it up. Woa. Lick it up.
There ain't no rea - son on
It's all you need so be -
P.M.
P.M.
*Bass plays A
F5
G5
N.C.
earth to waste it.
lieve me hon - ey.
It ain't a crime to be good to your - self.

Chorus
D/A A N.C. D/A A N.C. G D A N.C.
Lick it up. Lick __ it up. Ah, ah, ah. It's on - ly right _ now.
Rhy. Fig. 1
End Rhy. Fig. 1
P.M.
w/Rhy. Fig. 1, 2 3/4 times
w/Rhy. Fill 2, 2nd & 3rd time
Lick it up. Lick __ it up. Ah, ah, ah. Ooh, yeah.
w/Rhy. Fill 2, 2nd & 3rd time
Lick it up. Lick __ it up. Ah, ah, ah. Come on, come on.
To Coda
w/Rhy. Fill 3, 1st & 2nd times
w/Rhy. Fill 2, 3rd time
Lick it up. Lick __ it up. Ah, ah, ah. Ooh.
2. Come on. _
Rhy. Fill 2
Gtrs. 1 & 2
1/2
1/4
Rhy. Fill 3
Gtrs. 1 & 2

Bridge
D/F# G5 D/F# G5 A N.C. D/F# G5 D/F# G5 A N.C.
It's on - ly right _ now.
It's on - ly right now.
Rhy. Fig. 2
End Rhy. Fig. 2
P.M.
w/Rhy. Fig. 2
D/F# G5 D/F# G5 A N.C. D/F# G5 D/F# G5 A N.C.
Ooh yeah, ooh yeah, ooh yeah, _ ooh yeah. Yeah, _ yeah. _
Interlude
*G/A D/A N.C. A N.C. G/A D/A N.C. A N.C.
let ring
w/chorus
*Bass plays A
G/A D/A N.C. A N.C. G/A D/A N.C. E
D.S. al Coda
N.C.
steady gliss.
Oh. _
Woa.
Coda
Chorus
w/Rhy. Fig. 1, 1st 3 bars
D/A A N.C. D/A A N.C. G D A N.C.
w/Rhy. Fill 2
Fade out
Lick it up. Lick _ it up. Ah, ah, ah. Yeah, yeah, _ yeah.

LIGHTNING STRIKES

Words and Music by
LOU CHRISTIE and TWYLA HERBERT

Bridge:
C
Dm
G
C
Elec. Gtr. (w/fast vibrato)
Cont. rhy. simile
1. Ev - 'ry boy wants a girl he can trust to the ver - y end.
2. When I set - tle down, I want one ba - by on my mind.
3. See additional lyrics
Ba - by, that's you, won't you wait but 'til then? When
For - give and for - get and I'll make up for all lost time. If she's
To Coda
I see lips beg - gin' to be kissed I can't stop, I can't stop my - self.
put to-geth-er fine, then she's read - ing my mind. I can't stop, I can't stop my - self.
Bkgd. Vcl.: Stop, stop, stop, stop.
Elec. Gtr.
mf
Cont. in slashes
Chorus:
Fm
Gm
Light - ning strik - ing a - gain.
Light - ning strik - ing a - gain.
1.
Cont. rhy. simile

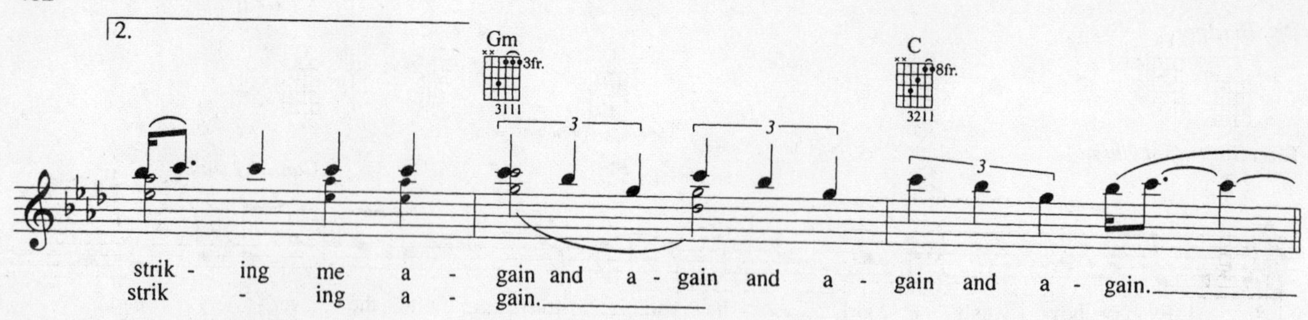
2.
Gm
3fr.
3111
C
8fr.
3211
3
3
3
strik - ing me a - gain and a - gain and a - gain and a - gain.
strik - ing a - gain.

Interlude:
E♭
6fr.
1333
D♭
4fr.
1333
A♭
4fr.
134211
Acous. Gtr. resume intro fig.
Bkgd. Vcl.: Ba - by, ah, oo,
Elec. Gtr.
mp
T
A
B

D♭
4fr.
1333
A♭
4fr.
134211
E♭
6fr.
1333
D♭
4fr.
1333
A♭
4fr.
134211
ba - by, ah, oo, ba - by, ah,
T
A
B

Chorus:
E♭
6fr.
1333
Gm7
2 3333
C
32 1
Fm
3111
Acous. Gtr. & Piano
Elec. Gtr. resume chorus figure simile
oo,
Light - ning
Light - ning
T
A
B
6
6 6 6 6 6 6 6 6
6 6 6 6 6 6 6 6
Gm
3fr.
3111
C
8fr.
3211
Fm
3111
strik - ing a - gain.
strik - ing a - gain.
Light - ning
Light - ning
D.S.𝄋 al Coda
Gm
3fr.
3111
C
8fr.
3211
strik - ing a - gain.
strik - ing a - gain.
Coda
Chorus:
Fade
Fm
3111
Elec. Gtr.
Gm
3fr.
3111
Light - ning strik - ing a - gain.
Light - ning strik - ing a - gain.
Bridge:
There's a chapel in the pines
Waiting for us around the bend.
Picture in your mind
Love forever, but 'til then,
If she gives me a sign that she wants to make time, (Stop!)
I can't stop, (Stop!) I can't stop myself. (Stop! Stop!)
(To Chorus:)

LISTEN TO THE MUSIC

Words and Music by
TOM JOHNSTON

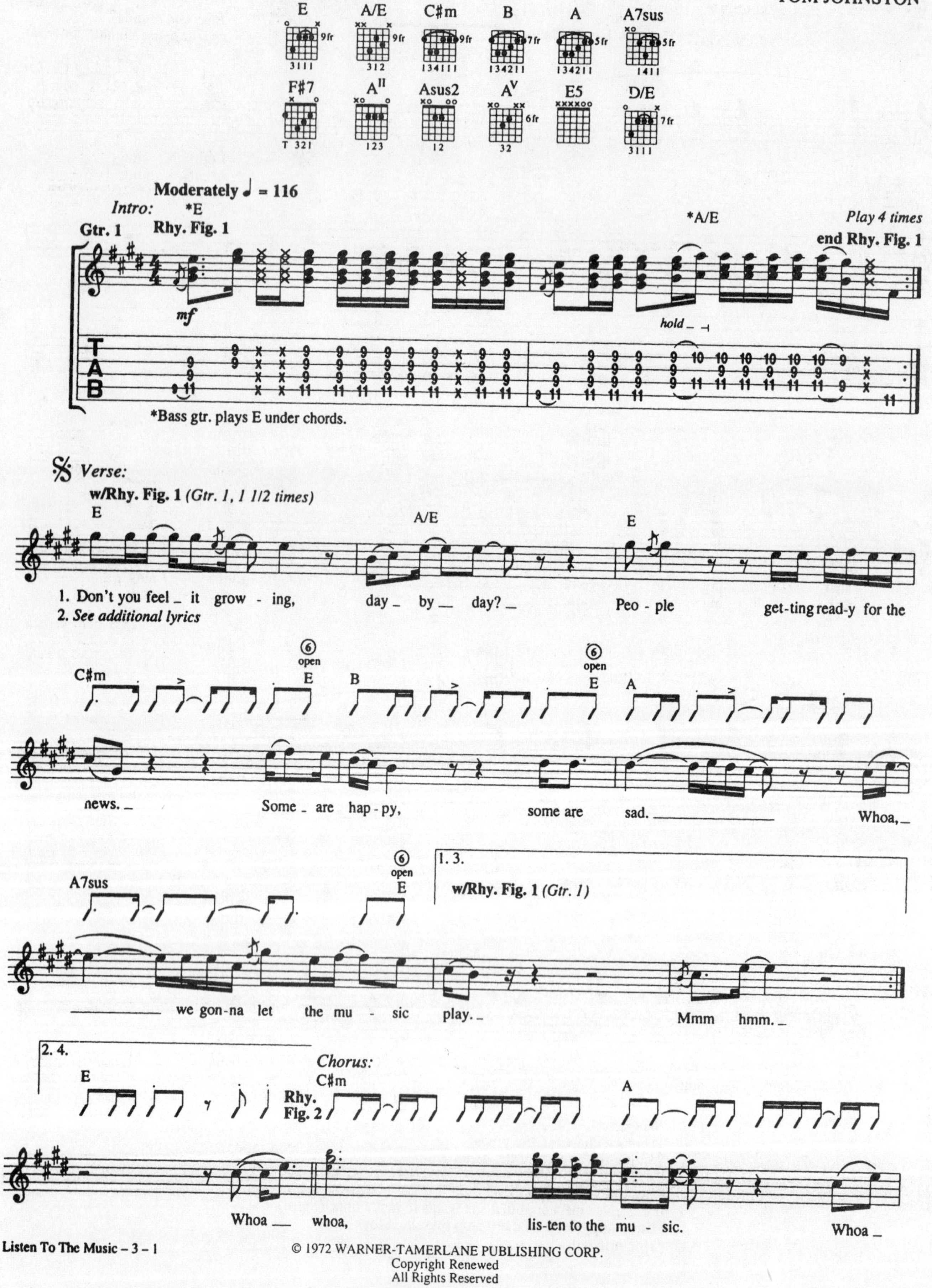

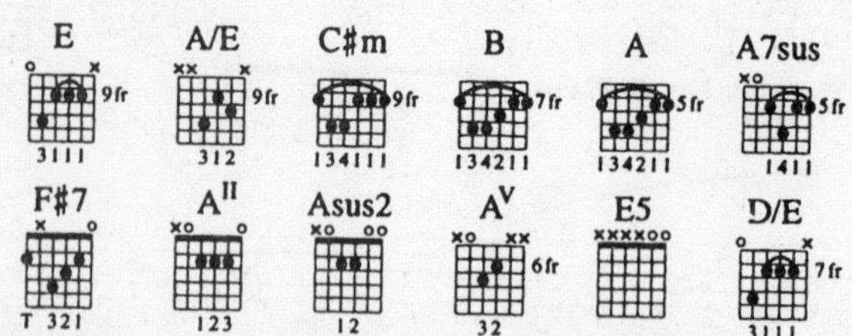

Moderately ♩ = 116

Intro:

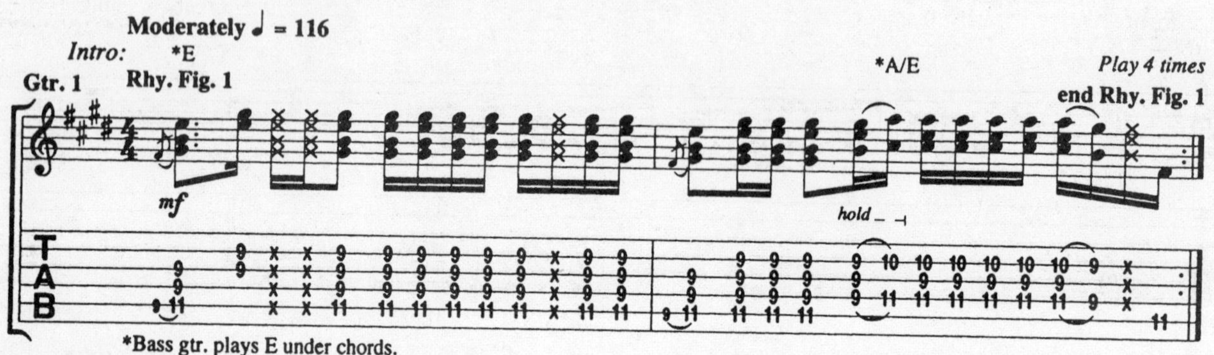

*Bass gtr. plays E under chords.

𝄋 *Verse:*

w/Rhy. Fig. 1 *(Gtr. 1, 1 1/2 times)*

E A/E E

1. Don't you feel _ it grow - ing, day _ by _ day? _ Peo - ple get-ting read-y for the
2. *See additional lyrics*

C#m ⑥ open E B ⑥ open E A

news. _ Some _ are hap - py, some are sad. _ Whoa, _

A7sus ⑥ open E

_ we gon-na let the mu - sic play. _

1. 3.
w/Rhy. Fig. 1 *(Gtr. 1)*

Mmm hmm. _

2. 4.
E

Chorus:
C#m
Rhy. Fig. 2
A

Whoa _ whoa, lis-ten to the mu - sic. Whoa _

Cont. rhy. simile
C#m
A
C#m
A
whoa, lis-ten to the mu - sic. Whoa whoa, lis-ten to the mu - sic. all the time.
To Coda
D.S. al Coda
w/Rhy. Fig. 1 (Gtr. 1 2 times)
F#7
A11
Asus2
A11
Asus2 A V E5 G# E5
6fr
end Rhy. Fig. 2
hold hold
4
Bridge:
Coda
Asus2 A V E5 G# E5
6fr
hold hold
E
D/E
Like a la - zy flow - ing riv - er,
hold
A
E
sur-round - ing cas - tles in the sky.
hold hold hold
D/E
And the crowd is grow - ing big - ger,
hold

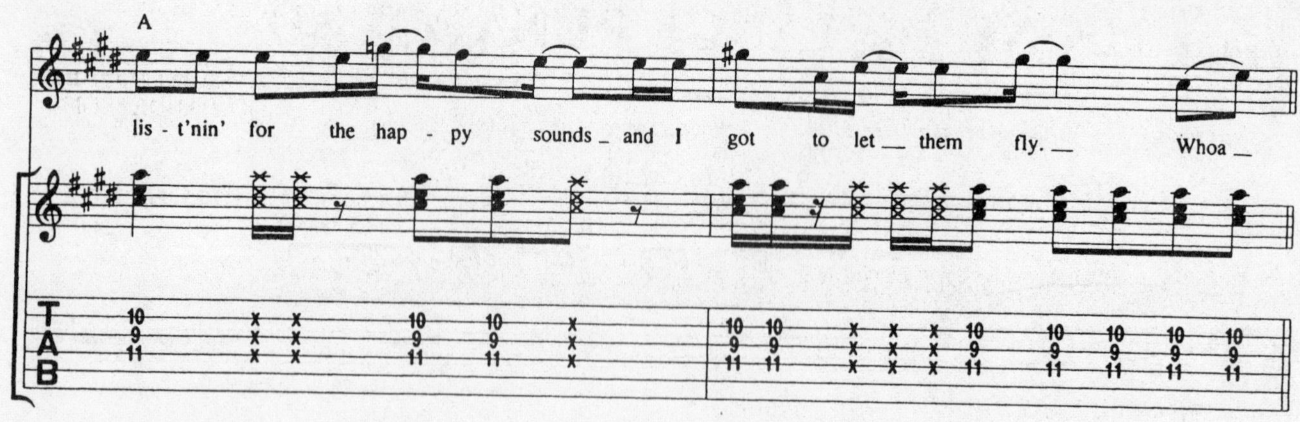
A
lis - t'nin' for the hap - py sounds _ and I got to let _ them fly. _ Whoa _
T
A
B

Chorus:
w/Rhy. Fig. 2 (Gtr. 1, simile)
C#m
A
C#m
whoa, lis - ten to the mu - sic. _ Whoa _ whoa, lis - ten to the

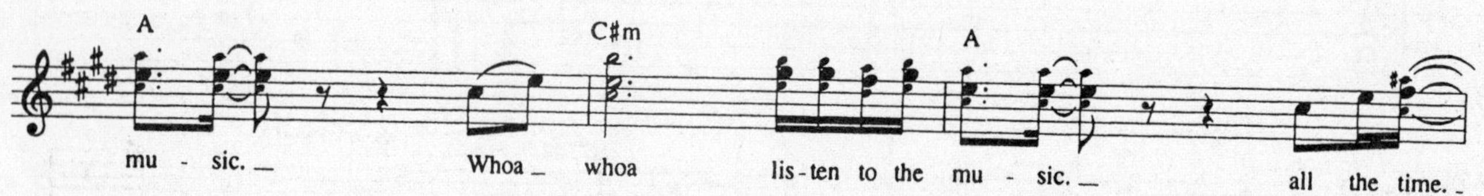
A
C#m
A
mu - sic. _ Whoa _ whoa lis - ten to the mu - sic. _ all the time. _

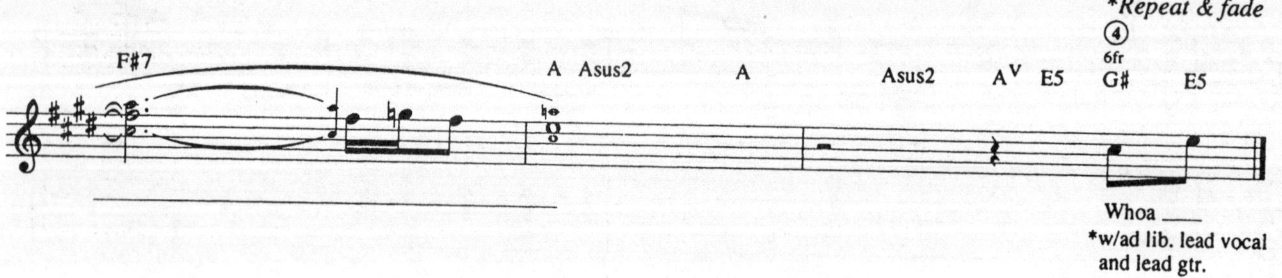
*Repeat & fade
F#7
A Asus2
A
Asus2
A E5
G#
E5
6fr
Whoa ___
*w/ad lib. lead vocal and lead gtr.

Verse 2:
What the people need is a way to make 'em smile.
It ain't so hard to do if you know how.
Gotta get a message, get it on through.
Oh, now mama's goin' to after 'while.
(To Chorus:)

Verse 3:
Well I know, you know better everything I say.
Meet me in the country for a day.
We'll be happy, and we'll dance.
Lord, we're gonna dance the blues away.
If I'm feeling good to you, and you're feeling good to me,
There ain't nothing we can't do or say.
Feeling good, feeling fine.
Whoa, baby, let the music play.
(To Chorus:)

LONG DISTANCE RUNAROUND

Words and Music by
JON ANDERSON

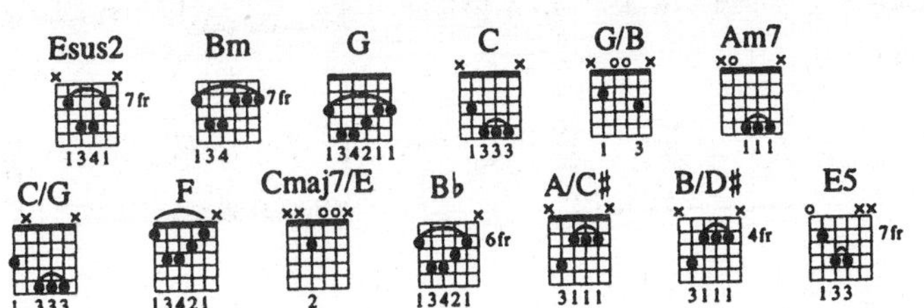

Moderately fast ♩ = 176

Intro:

TAB
TAB
TAB
TAB

Bm
Half - time
Verse:
Esus2
Bm
Cont. rhy. simile
Esus2
1. 3. Long dis-tance run - a - round, long time
2. 4. See additional lyrics
Bm
wait-ing to feel the sound.
I still remem - ber the

G
To Coda 1
dream there, I still re-mem - ber the time you said good - bye.
C
G/B
Am7
C/G
F
Cmaj7/E
B♭
Did we real-ly tell lies?
Let-tin' in the sun - shine.
Did we real-ly count to
To Coda 2
1.
2.
D.S. al Coda 1
one hun - dred? hun - dred?
Coda 1
G
A
12 fr
Interlude:
Double - time
N.C.
Gtr. 2
Cont. in notation
time you said good - bye.
Gtr. 1

Verses 2 & 4:
Cold summer listening,
Hot colour melting the anger to stone.
I still remember the dream there,
I still remember the time you said goodbye.
Did we really tell lies?
Lettin' in the sunshine.
Did we really count to one hundred?

(To Interlude:)
(To Coda 2:)

LIVIN' ON A PRAYER

Words and Music by
JON BON JOVI, RICHIE SAMBORA
and DESMOND CHILD

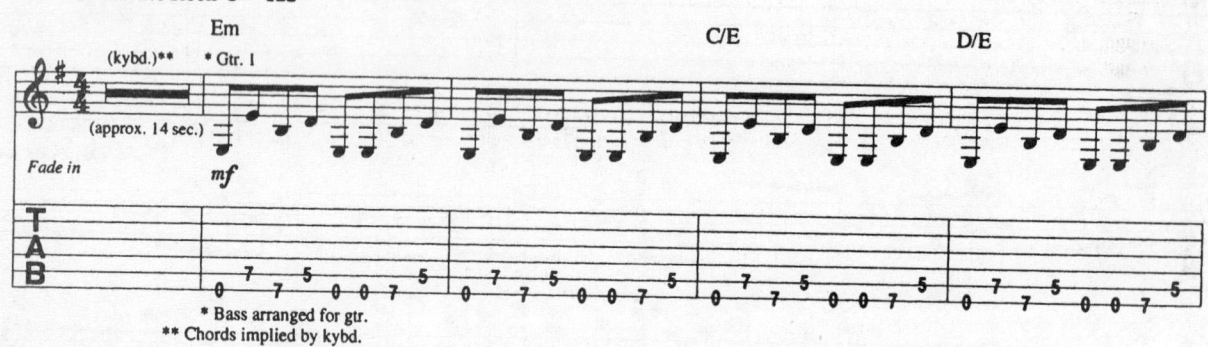

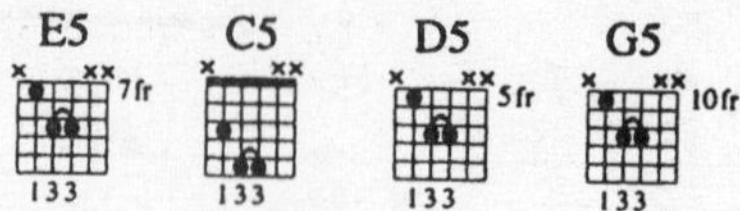

Intro

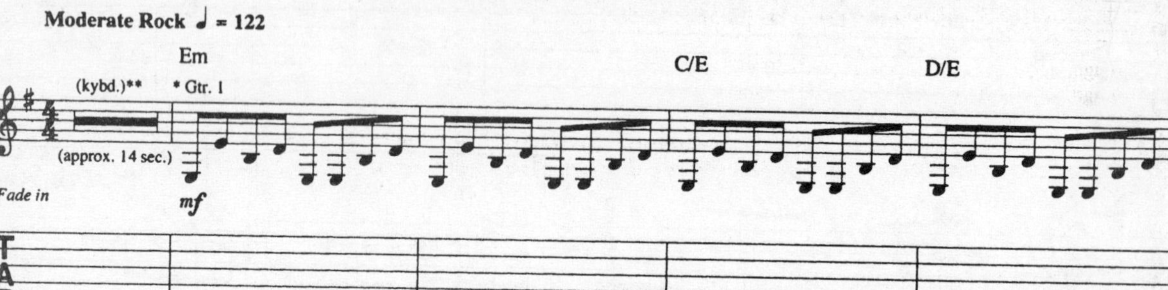

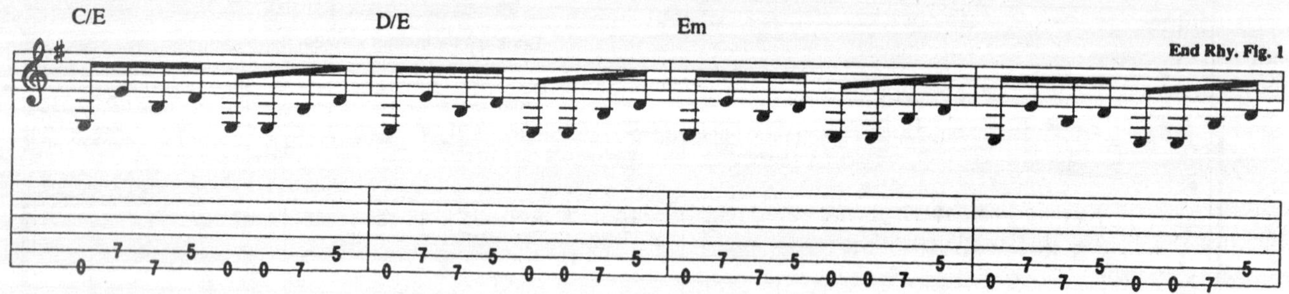

Verse
Gtr. 2 tacet, 1st time
Gtr. 2: w/ Rhy. Fig. 1, 2 times, 2nd time
(N.C.)Em
1. Tom-my used to work on the docks. Un-ion's been on strike, he's down on his luck, it's
2. Tom-my's got his six string in hock. Now he's hold-ing in when he used to make it talk so
Gtr. 3: w/ Fill 1, 2nd time
C5
D5
N.C.(Em)
tough, so tough.
tough, mmm, it's tough.
Gi-na works the din-er all day.
Gi-na dreams of run-ning a-way.
Gtr. 2
Work-ing for her man, she brings home her pay for love, mmm, for love.
When she cries in the night, Tom-my whis-pers; "Ba-by, it's o-kay, some-day."
Pre-Chorus
C5 D5 E5 C5 D5
She says we've got to hold on to what we've got. It does-n't make a dif-f'rence if we
We've got to
* w/ out talk box.
Fill 1
Gtr. 3 (dist.)
8va
w/ talk box
f
full
full
w/ bar
T
A
B

E5 C5 D5 E5 D5 C5 D5
make it or not. We've got each oth - er, and that's a lot for love. We'll give it a shot.
Chorus
E5 C5 D5 G5 C5 D5 E5 C5
Whoa, we're half way there. Whoa, liv - in' on a prayer. Take my hand, we'll
P.M.
D5 G5 C5 D5 Csus2 D G
make it, I swear. Whoa, liv - in' on a prayer. Liv - in' on a prayer.
8va
loco
P.H.
(cont. in slash)
Guitar Solo
E5 C5 D5 G5 C5 D5
Gtr. 1
Gtr. 2
w/ out talk box
P.H.
rake
full
full full
pitch: C♯ D♯ C♯

(cont. in notation)
E5 C5 D5 G5 C5 E5
P.M.
1/2
rake
full full
Gtr. 2 tacet
C5 D5 E5 D5 C5
Ooh, we've got to hold on, ready or not. You live for the fight when that's
Gtr. 1
P.M.
8va
Gtr. 2
full
Outro-Chorus
D5 G5 Eb5 F5 Bb5 Eb5 F5
all that you've got. Whoa, we're half way there. Whoa, liv - in' on a prayer.
Play 2 Times and Fade
G5 Eb5 F5 Bb5 Eb5 F5
Take my hand and we'll make it, I swear. Whoa, liv - in' on a prayer.

LOCOMOTIVE BREATH

Words and Music by
IAN ANDERSON

Verse 2:
See's his children jumping off
At stations one by one.
His woman and his best friend
In bed and having fun.
Oh, he's crawling down the corridor
On his hands and knees.

Verse 4:
He hears the silence howling,
Catches angels as they fall.
And the all-time winner
Has got him by the balls.
Oh, he picks up Gidgeon's Bible,
Open at page one.

Chorus 3:
I thank God he stole the handle,
And the train, it won't stop going;
No way to slow down.
(To Outro:)

LONG TRAIN RUNNIN'

Words and Music by
TOM JOHNSTON

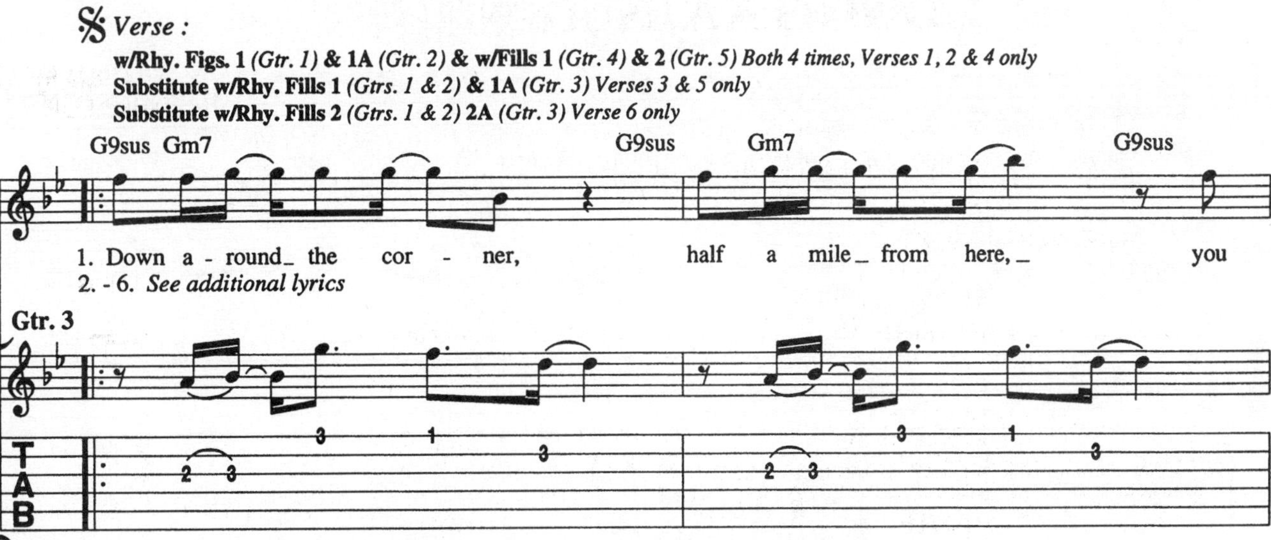
Verse :
w/Rhy. Figs. 1 (Gtr. 1) & 1A (Gtr. 2) & w/Fills 1 (Gtr. 4) & 2 (Gtr. 5) Both 4 times, Verses 1, 2 & 4 only
Substitute w/Rhy. Fills 1 (Gtrs. 1 & 2) & 1A (Gtr. 3) Verses 3 & 5 only
Substitute w/Rhy. Fills 2 (Gtrs. 1 & 2) 2A (Gtr. 3) Verse 6 only
G9sus Gm7
G9sus
Gm7
G9sus
1. Down a - round_ the cor - ner, half a mile_ from here,_ you
2. - 6. See additional lyrics
Gtr. 3

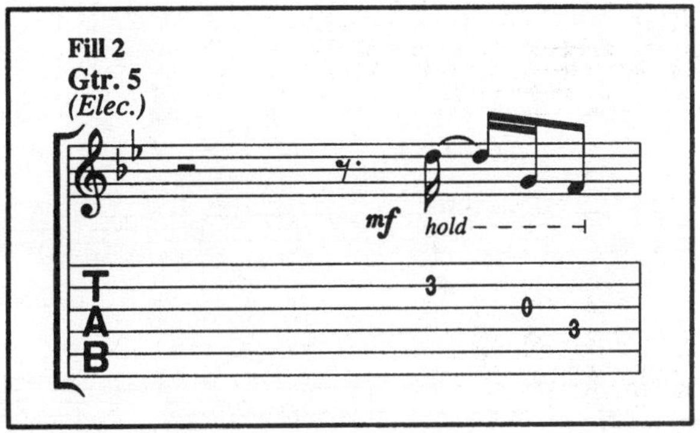
Fill 2
Gtr. 5
(Elec.)
mf
hold

Rhy. Fills 1 & 1A
Gm7
Gbm7 Gm7
Cm7
Gtrs. 1 & 2
Gtr. 3

Rhy. Fills. 2 & 2A
Gm7
Gbm7 Gm7
Gbm7 Gm7
Gbm7 Gm7 Gm7 type2
Gtrs. 1 & 2
Gtr. 3

Gm7
G9sus
Gm7
G9sus
see them old trains run - nin', and you watch them dis - ap - pear. _ With - out

Cm7
Cm6
Gtrs. 1 & 2
love, _
where would you _ be now_

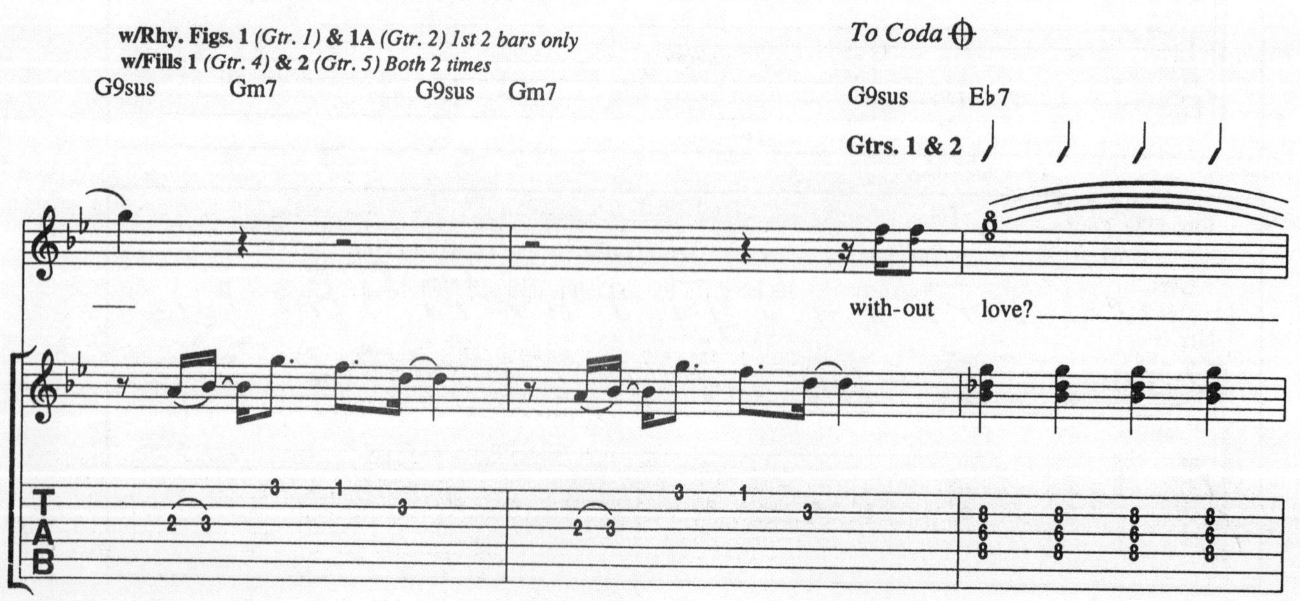

w/Rhy. Figs. 1 (Gtr. 1) & 1A (Gtr. 2) 1st 2 bars only
w/Fills 1 (Gtr. 4) & 2 (Gtr. 5) Both 2 times
G9sus
Gm7
G9sus
Gm7
To Coda
G9sus
E♭7
Gtrs. 1 & 2
with - out love?

w/Fills 1 (Gtr. 4) & 2 (Gtr. 5) Both 2 times
Gm/D
D7
G9sus Gm7
G9sus
1. - 4.
5.
D.S. 𝄋 al Coda
Gm7
G9sus
G9sus Gm7
G9sus
Coda
Freely
Eb7
Gm/D
D7
Cm7
Gtrs. 1 & 2
Gtr. 3
love,
ooh,
where would you be
now?
Gtr. 3
Gtr. 1

Outro:

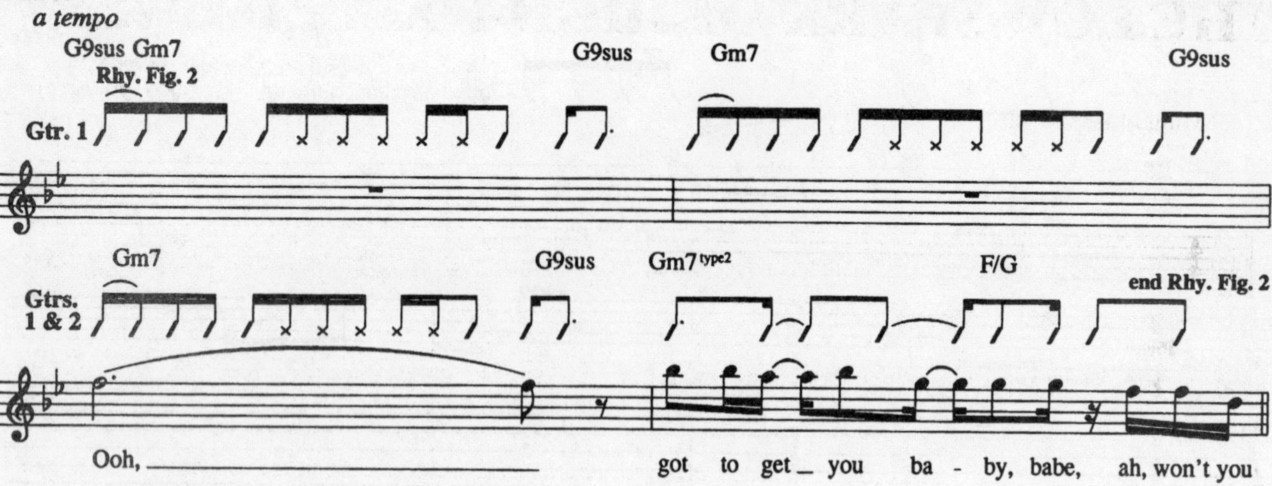

Verse 2:
You know I saw Miss Lucy,
Down along the tracks;
She lost her home and her family,
And she won't be comin' back.
Without love, where would you be right now,
Without love?
(To Verse 3:)

Verses 3 & 5:
Well, the Illinois Central
And the Southern Central freight
Gotta keep on pushin', mama,
'Cause you know they're runnin' late.
Without love, where would you be now,
Without love?
(1st time to Verse 4:)
(2nd time to Verse 6:)

Verse 4:
Harmonica Solo:
(To Verse 5:)

Verse 6:
Where pistons keep on churnin'
And the wheels go 'round and 'round,
And the steel rails are cold and hard
For the miles that they go down.
Without love, where would you be right now,
Without love?
(To Coda)

THE LOW SPARK OF HIGH-HEELED BOYS

Words and Music by
STEVE WINWOOD and JIM CAPALDI

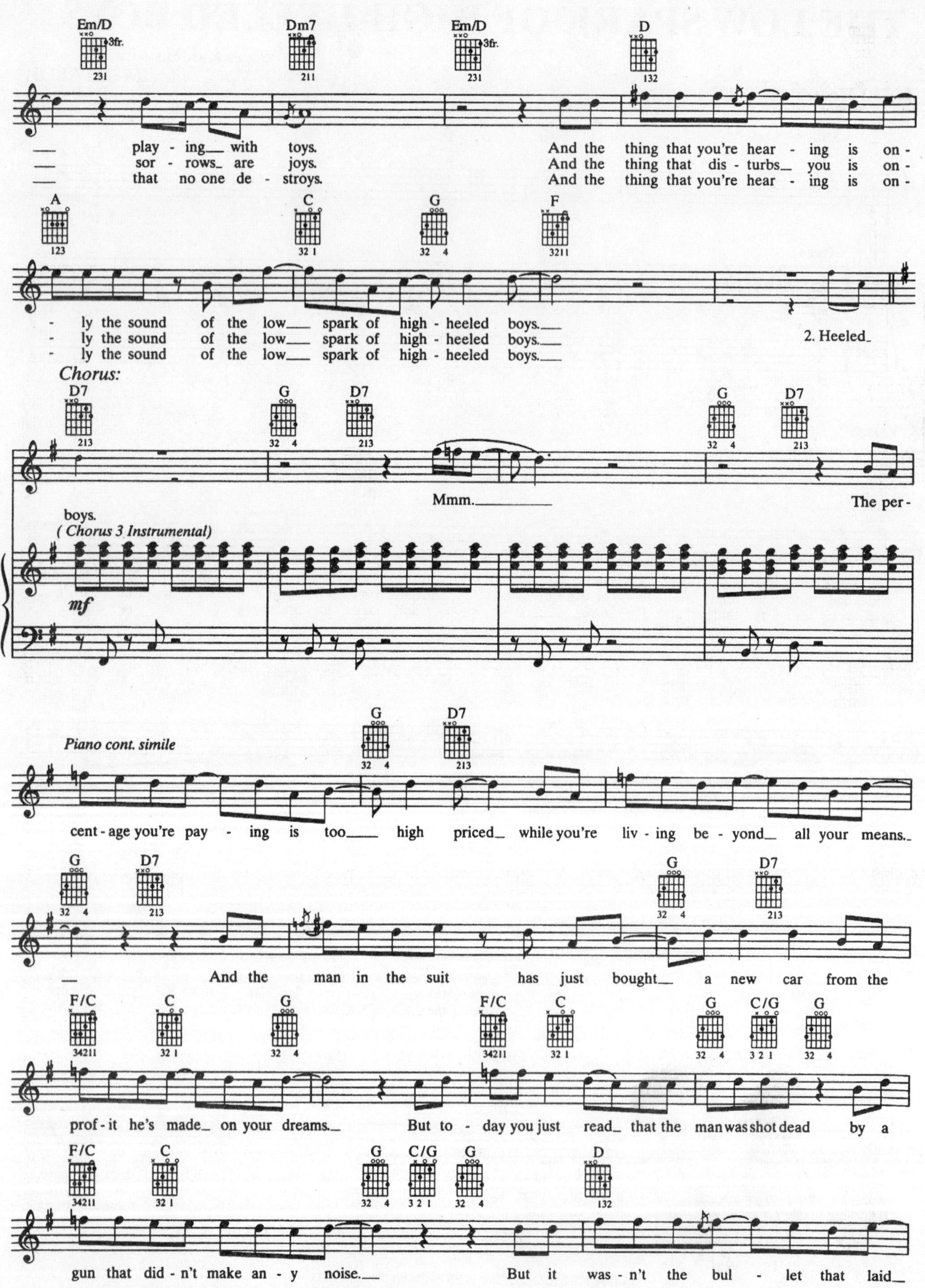
Em/D Dm7 Em/D D
play - ing with toys. And the thing that you're hear - ing is on -
sor - rows are joys. And the thing that dis - turbs you is on -
that no one de - stroys. And the thing that you're hear - ing is on -
A C G F
- ly the sound of the low spark of high - heeled boys.
- ly the sound of the low spark of high - heeled boys.
- ly the sound of the low spark of high - heeled boys.
2. Heeled
Chorus:
D7 G D7 G D7
boys.
Mmm.
The per-
(Chorus 3 Instrumental)
mf
Piano cont. simile
G D7
cent - age you're pay - ing is too high priced while you're liv - ing be - yond all your means.
G D7 G D7
And the man in the suit has just bought a new car from the
F/C C G F/C C G C/G G
prof - it he's made on your dreams. But to - day you just read that the man was shot dead by a
F/C C G C/G G D
gun that did - n't make an - y noise. But it was - n't the bul - let that laid

A
C
G
F
him to rest, was the low spark of high - heeled boys.
High-heeled
Dm7
Em/D
Dm7
To Coda
Em/D
boys.
Repeat as desired for solos
Dm7
Em/D
Dm7
Em/D
Piano cont. simile
Dm7
Em/D
Dm7
1. Em/D
D.S.
2. Em/D
D.S. al Coda
2. If
3. If I
Repeat and fade
Coda
Em/D
Dm7
Em/D
Dm7
Em/D

LOSER

Music by MATT ROBERTS,
BRAD ARNOLD and TODD HARRELL
Lyrics by BRAD ARNOLD

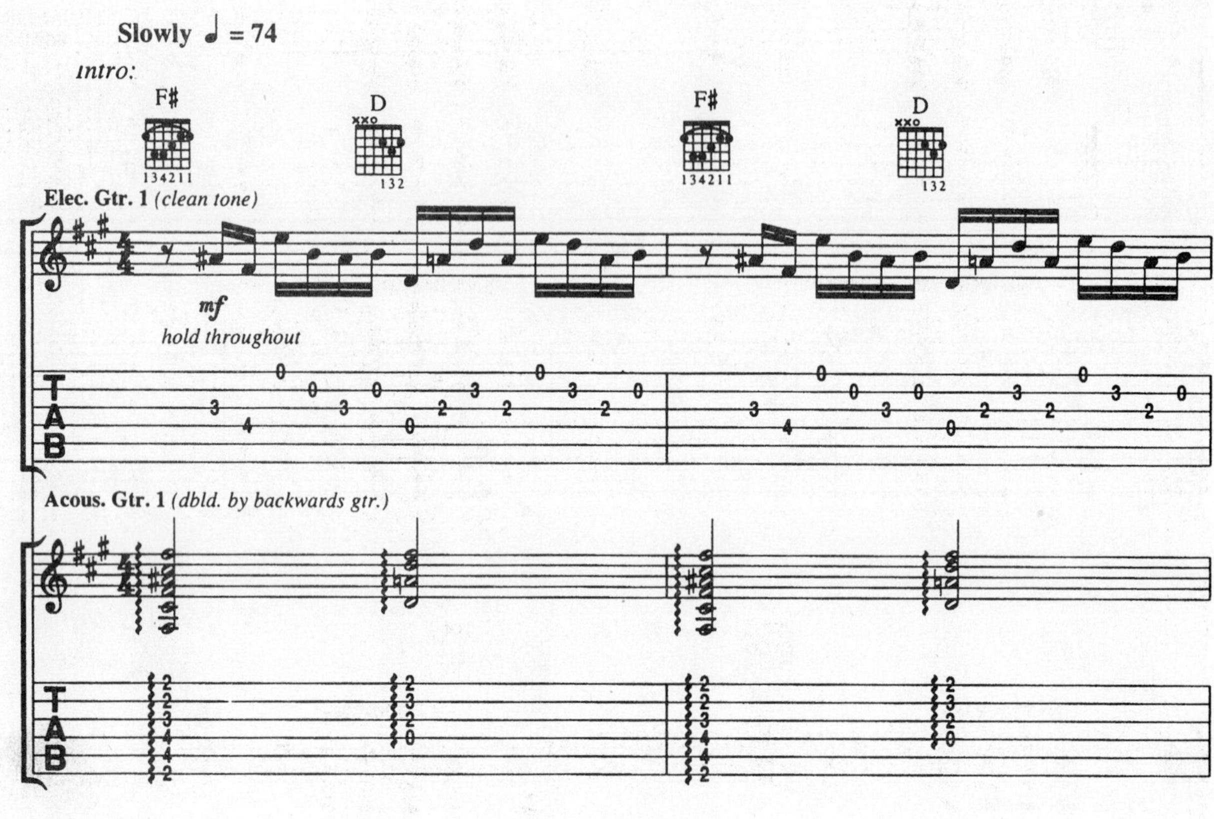

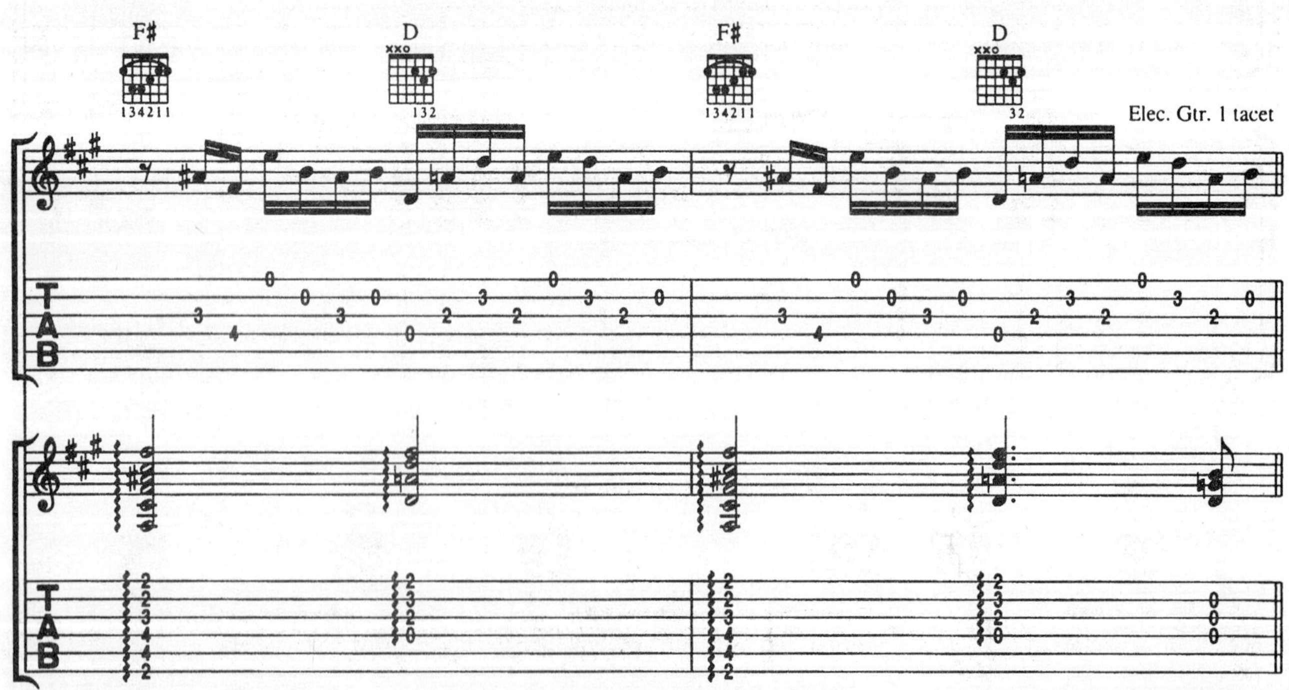

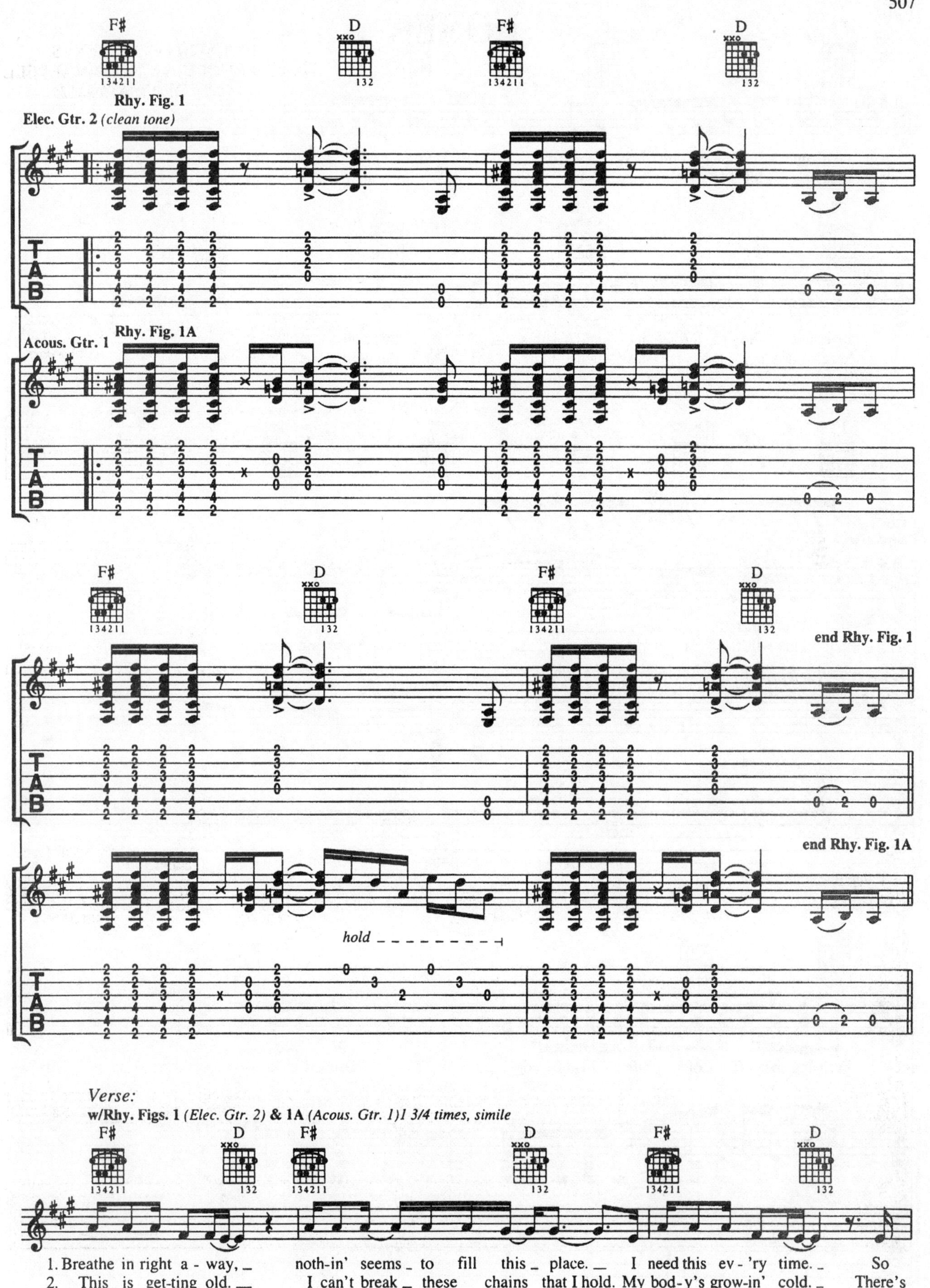
F#
D
F#
D
134211
132
Rhy. Fig. 1
Elec. Gtr. 2 (clean tone)
Acous. Gtr. 1
Rhy. Fig. 1A
end Rhy. Fig. 1
end Rhy. Fig. 1A
hold
Verse:
w/Rhy. Figs. 1 (Elec. Gtr. 2) & 1A (Acous. Gtr. 1) 1 3/4 times, simile
1. Breathe in right a - way, _ noth-in' seems _ to fill this _ place. _ I need this ev - 'ry time. _ So
2. This is get-ting old. _ I can't break _ these chains that I hold. My bod-y's grow-in' cold. _ There's

F#
D
take your lies, _ get off my _ case. ___ Some-day I will find ___ a
noth-ing left _ of this mind or my soul. Ad - dic - tion needs a pac - i - fi - er. The
love that flows _ through me like _ this. ___ And this will fall _ a - way. ___
buzz of this poi - son is tak - ing me high - er. And this will fall _ a - way. ___
Chorus:
Dsus2
E5
F#5
Acous. Gtr. 1 & Elec. Gtr. 2
Vcl. Fig. 1
This will fall a - way. ___
This will fall a - way. ___
You're get-ting clos - er to
*Elec. Gtrs. 3 & 4 (w/dist.)
Rhy. Fig. 2
A.H.
*Composite arrangement.
D5
push-ing me off _ of life's _ lit-tle edge. ___ 'Cause I'm a los - er, the

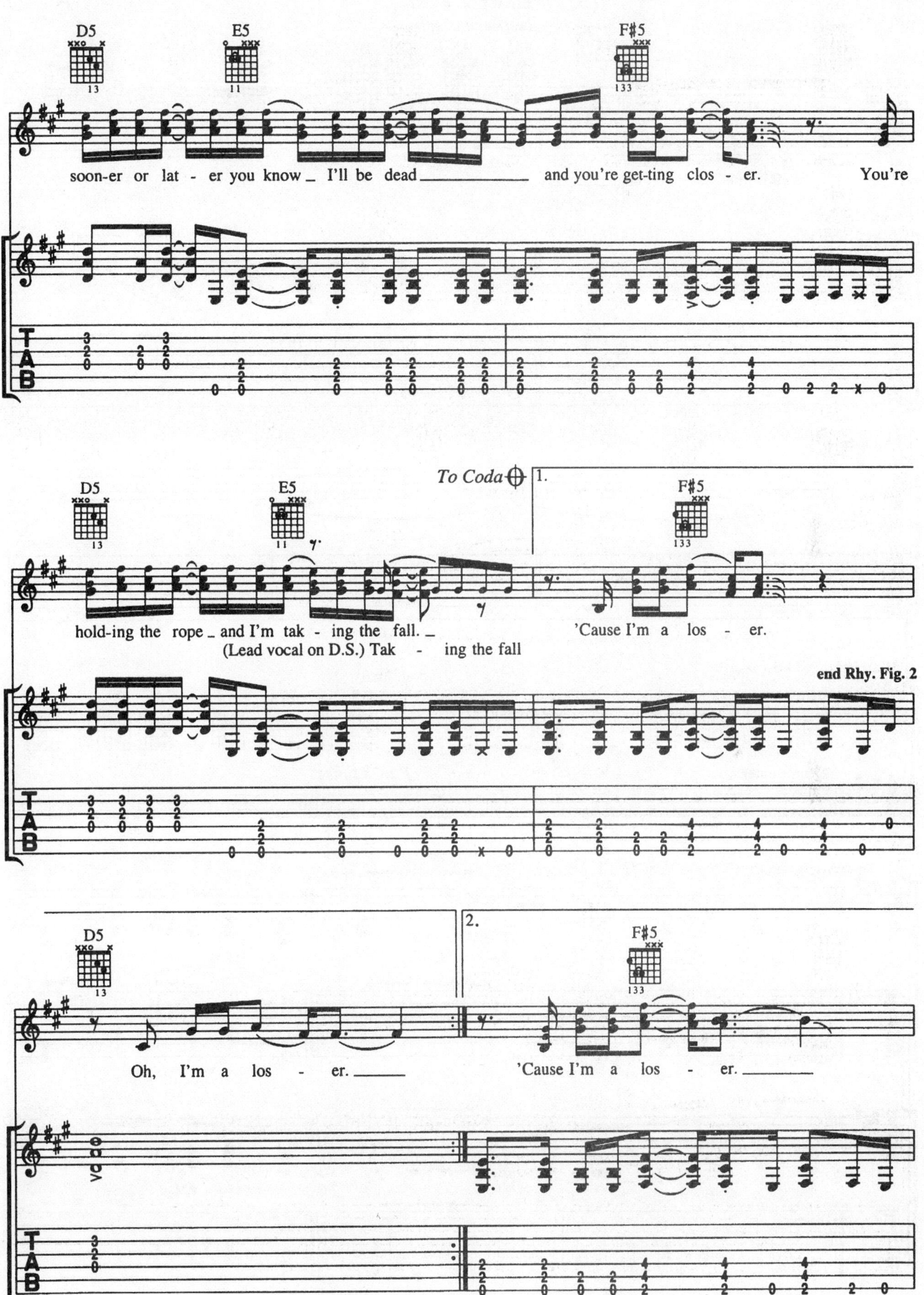
D5
E5
F#5
soon-er or lat - er you know I'll be dead and you're get-ting clos - er. You're
To Coda
1.
hold-ing the rope and I'm tak - ing the fall.
(Lead vocal on D.S.) Tak - ing the fall
'Cause I'm a los - er.
end Rhy. Fig. 2
2.
Oh, I'm a los - er.
'Cause I'm a los - er.

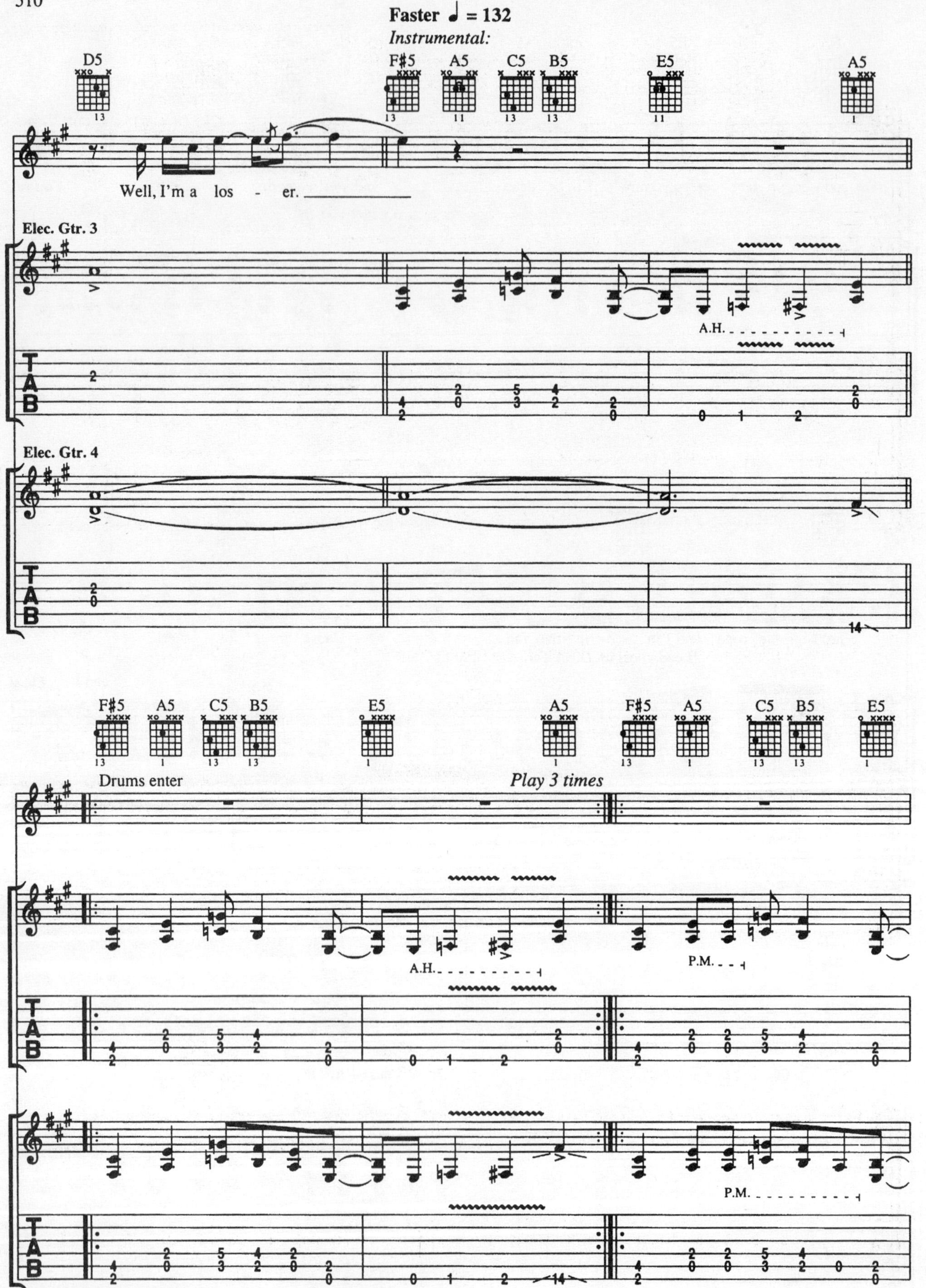
Faster ♩ = 132
Instrumental:
D5
F#5
A5
C5
B5
E5
A5
Well, I'm a los - er.
Elec. Gtr. 3
A.H.
Elec. Gtr. 4
F#5
A5
C5
B5
E5
A5
F#5
A5
C5
B5
E5
Drums enter
Play 3 times
A.H.
P.M.
P.M.

F5
F♯5
A5
F♯5
A5
C5
B5
E5
1.
F5
F♯
A5
2.
Slower ♩ = 74
Solo:
w/Rhy. Figs. 1 (Elec. Gtr. 2) & 1A (Acous. Gtr. 1) 2 times, simile
F♯
D
F♯
D
Bass Gtr. (arr. for gtr.)
w/effect
F♯
D
F♯
D

F#
D
134211
132
D.S. 𝄋 al Coda
Elec. Gtrs. 3 & 4
Coda
E5
F#5
D5
'Cause I'm a los - er.
Yeah, y - yeah, y - yeah, y - yeah, y - yeah.
Elec. Gtrs. 3 & 4

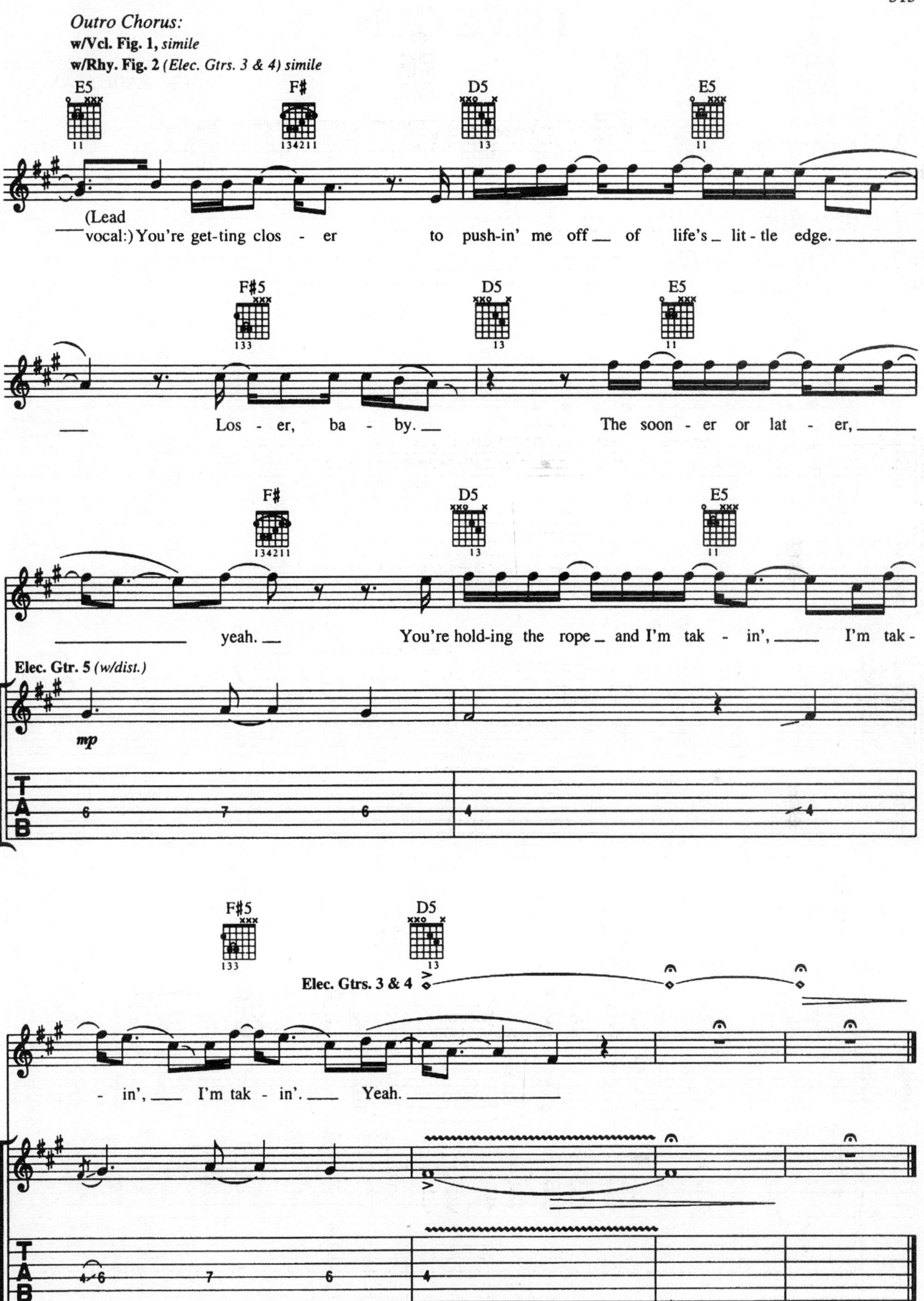
Outro Chorus:
w/Vcl. Fig. 1, simile
w/Rhy. Fig. 2 (Elec. Gtrs. 3 & 4) simile
E5
F#
D5
E5
(Lead vocal:) You're get-ting clos - er to push-in' me off of life's lit-tle edge.
F#5
D5
E5
Los - er, ba - by. The soon - er or lat - er,
F#
D5
E5
yeah. You're hold-ing the rope and I'm tak - in', I'm tak-
Elec. Gtr. 5 (w/dist.)
mp
F#5
D5
Elec. Gtrs. 3 & 4
- in', I'm tak - in'. Yeah.

LOVE GUN

Words and Music by
PAUL STANLEY

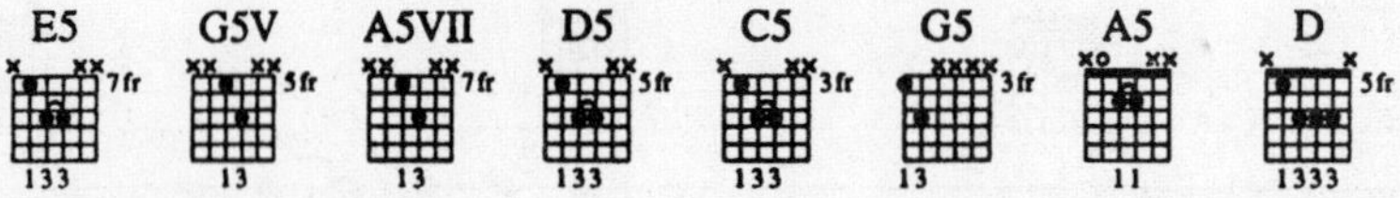

E5
G5V
A5VII
D5
C5
G5
A5
D
7fr
5fr
7fr
5fr
3fr
3fr
5fr
133
13
13
133
133
13
11
1333

Tune Down 1/2 Step
①= E♭ ④= D♭
②= B♭ ⑤= A♭
③= G♭ ⑥= E♭

Intro

Fast rock shuffle ♫ = ♩ ♪ (triplet) = 152

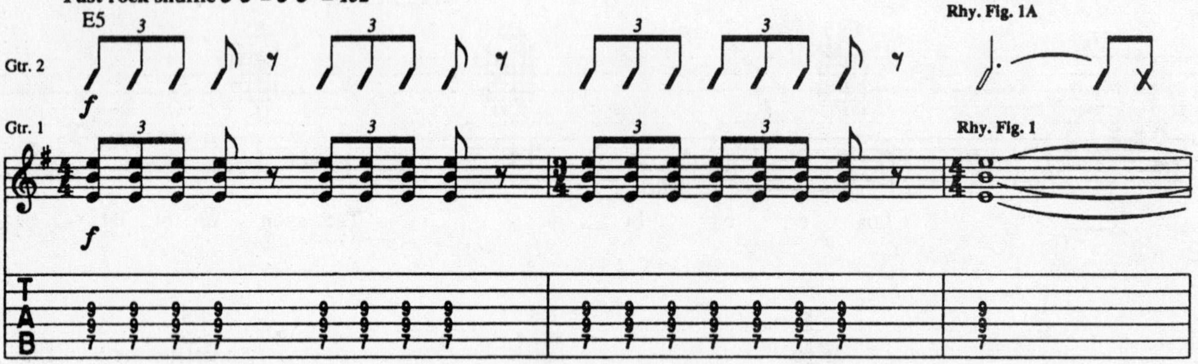

E5
Gtr. 2
Gtr. 1
Rhy. Fig. 1A
Rhy. Fig. 1
f
T
A
B

G5V
A5VII
G5V
D5
C5
D5
E5
D5
E5

End Rhy. Fig. 1A
G5V
A5VII
G5V
D5
C5
D5
E5
D5
End Rhy. Fig. 1

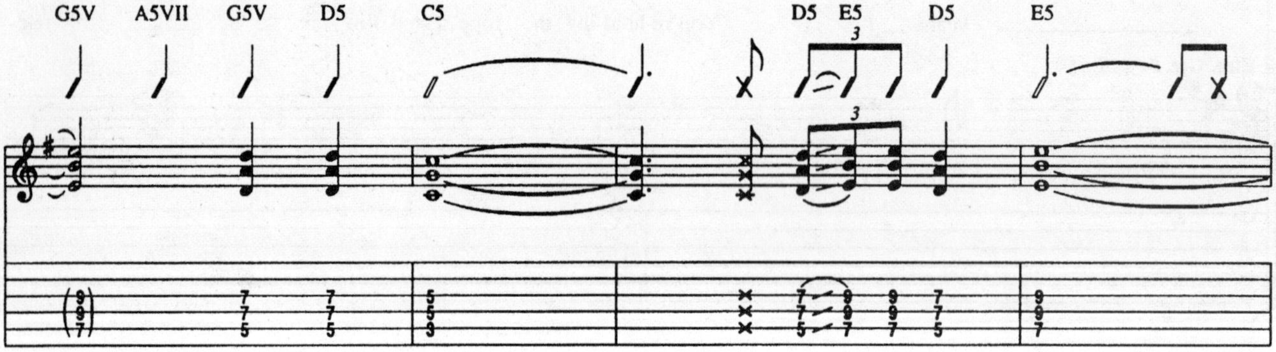

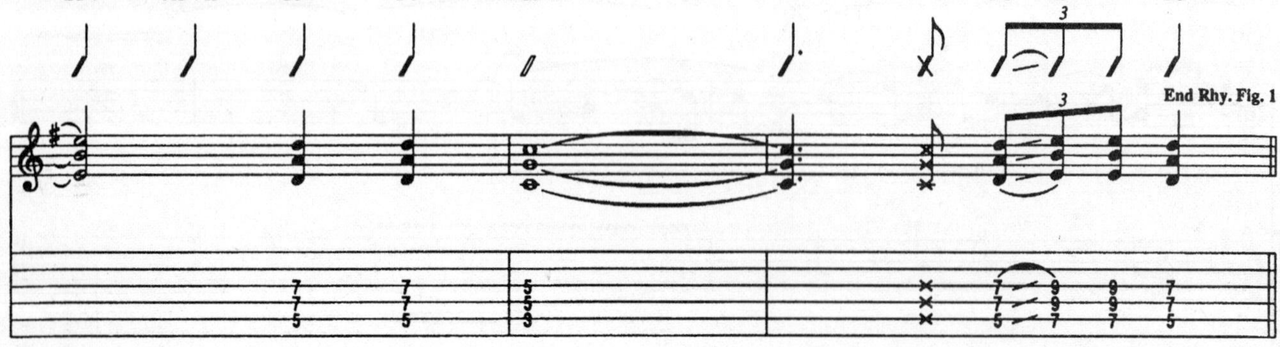

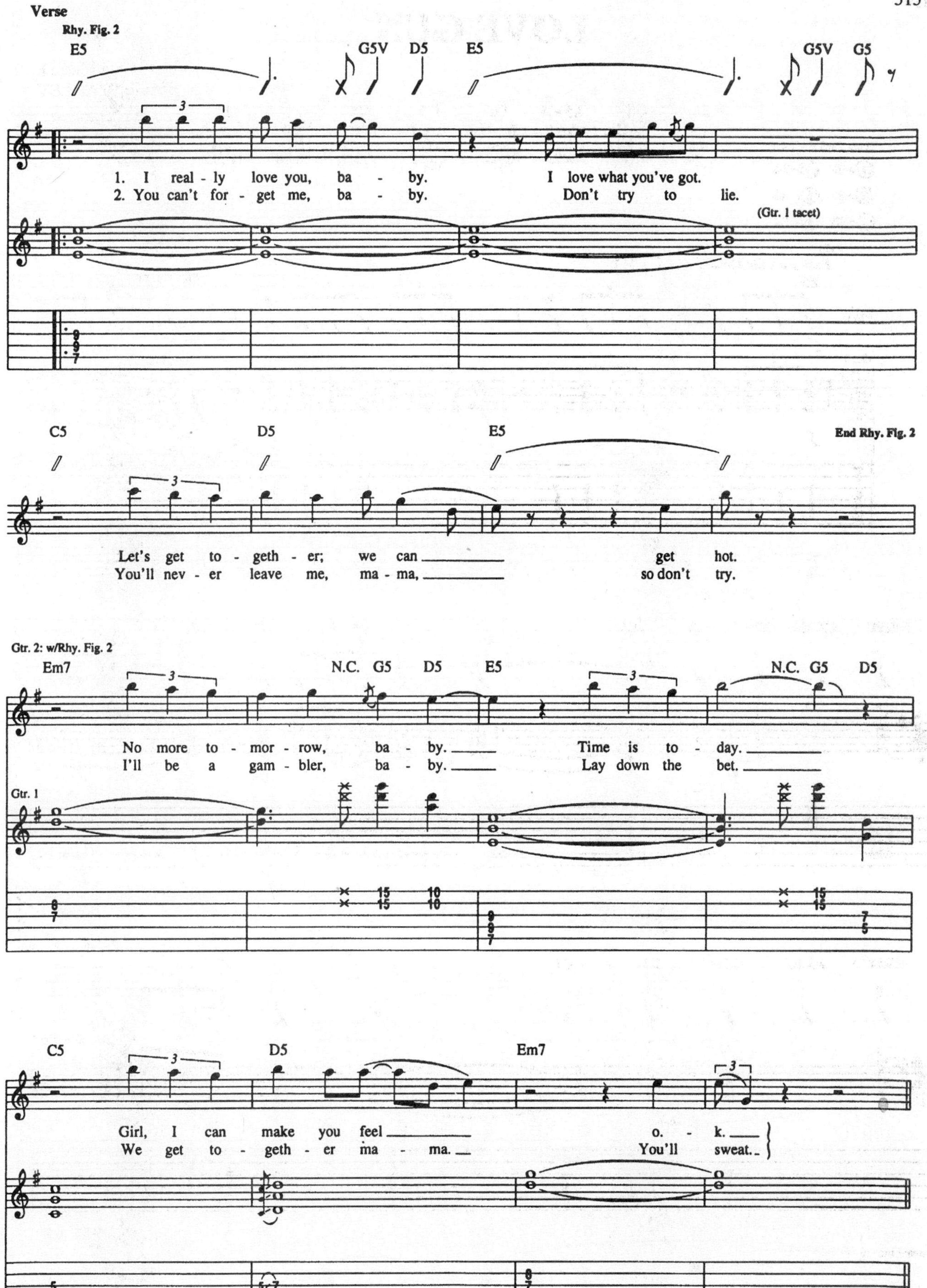
Verse
Rhy. Fig. 2
E5
G5V
D5
E5
G5V
G5
1. I real - ly love you, ba - by. I love what you've got.
2. You can't for - get me, ba - by. Don't try to lie.
(Gtr. 1 tacet)
C5
D5
E5
End Rhy. Fig. 2
Let's get to - geth - er; we can get hot.
You'll nev - er leave me, ma - ma, so don't try.
Gtr. 2: w/Rhy. Fig. 2
Em7
N.C.
G5
D5
E5
N.C.
G5
D5
No more to - mor - row, ba - by. Time is to - day.
I'll be a gam - bler, ba - by. Lay down the bet.
Gtr. 1
C5
D5
Em7
Girl, I can make you feel o. - k.
We get to - geth - er ma - ma. You'll sweat.

Pre Chorus
A5
D
E5
No place for hid - ing, ba - by.
No place to run.
A5
D
E5
You pulled the trig - ger of my
love
Chorus
Gtrs. 1 & 2: w/Rhy. Fig. 1 & 1A
E5
G5
A5
G5
D5
C5
D5 E5 D5
gun.
Love
gun.
Love
(Love.
gun.
gun.
Love
gun.
Love
gun.)
Gtrs. 1 & 2: w/Rhy. Figs. 1 & 1A
Love
gun.
Love
gun.

Interlude
Rhy. Fig. 3
End Rhy. Fig. 3
E5
Gtrs. 1 & 2
Gtr. 3
f (distortion)
Gtrs. 1 & 2: w/Rhy. Fig. 3
E5
8va
Love
Chorus
Gtrs. 1 & 2: w/Rhy. Fig. 1 & 1A, 3 times
E5 G5 A5 G5 D5 C5 D5 E5 D5
gun. Love gun. Love
(Love gun.
(8va)
P.H.
loco
full full full full full full
Sounding: (E) F♯

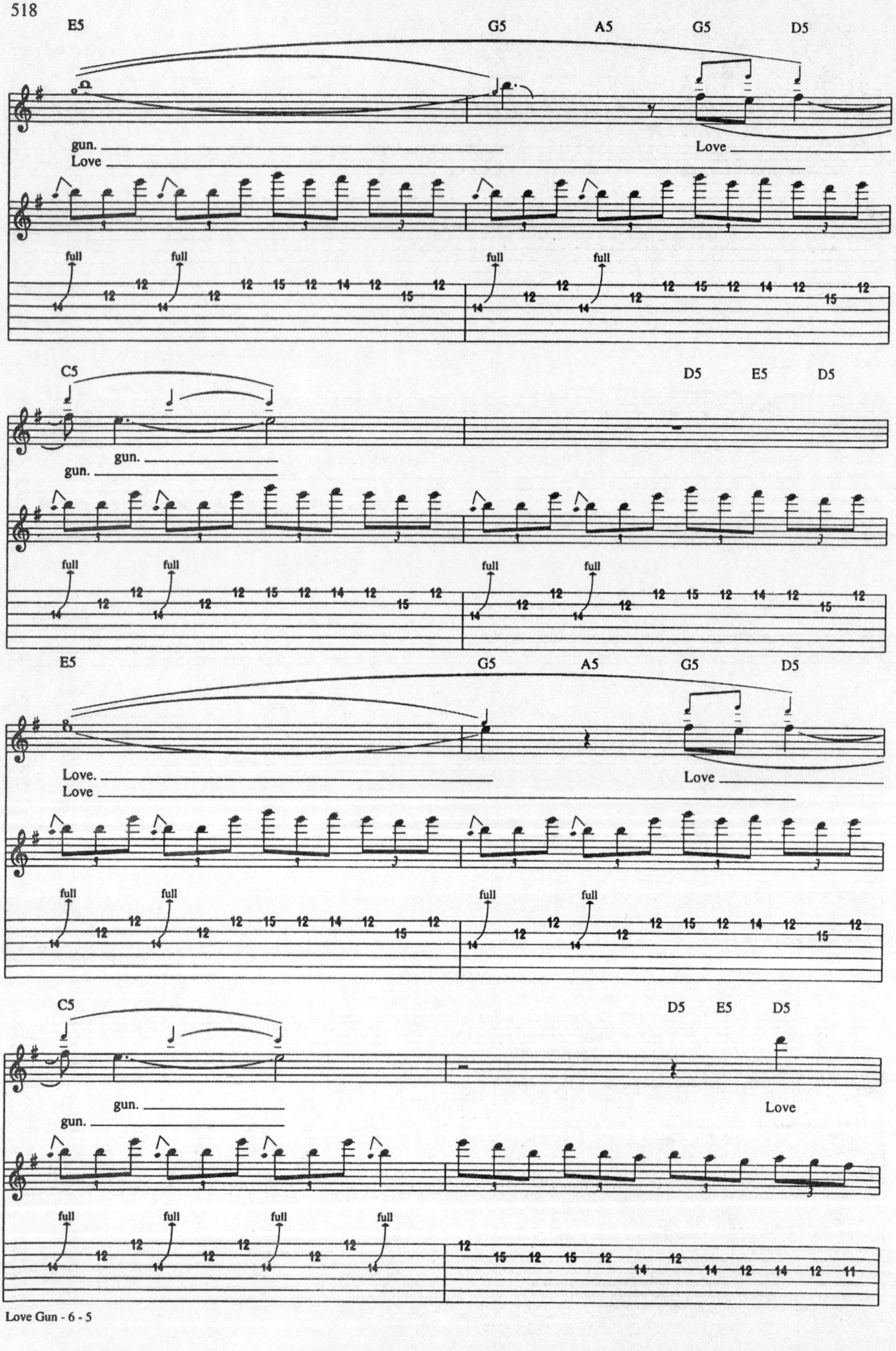

E5 G5 A5 G5 D5

gun. Love
Love

full full 14 12 12 14 12 12 15 12 14 12 15 12
full full 14 12 12 14 12 12 15 12 14 12 15 12

C5 D5 E5 D5

gun.
gun.

full full 14 12 12 14 12 12 15 12 14 12 15 12
full full 14 12 12 14 12 12 15 12 14 12 15 12

E5 G5 A5 G5 D5

Love. Love
Love

full full 14 12 12 14 12 12 15 12 14 12 15 12
full full 14 12 12 14 12 12 15 12 14 12 15 12

C5 D5 E5 D5

gun. Love
gun.

full full full full 14 12 12 14 12 12 14 12 12 14
12 15 12 15 12 14 12 14 12 14 12 11

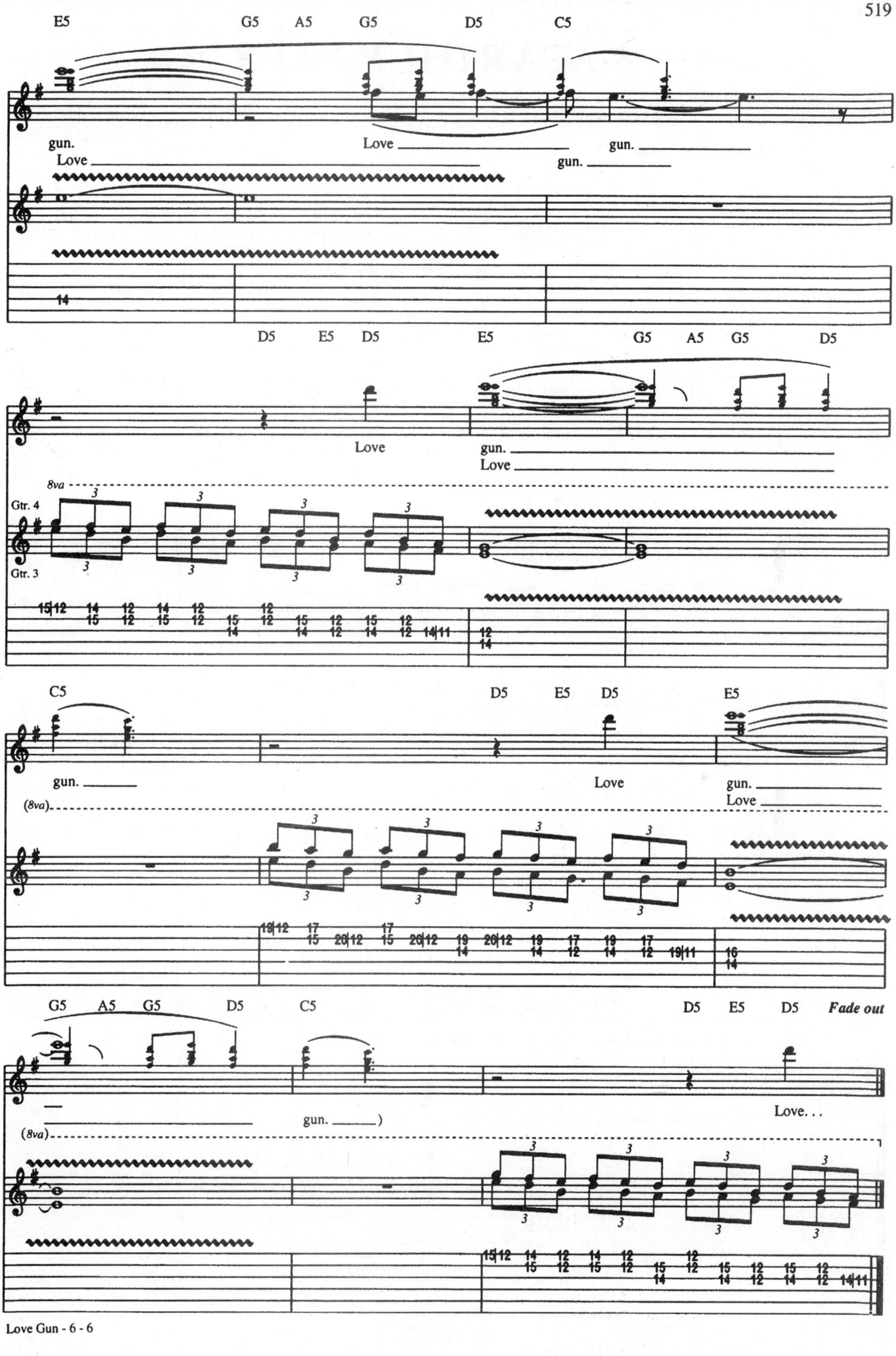

E5 G5 A5 G5 D5 C5

gun. Love ___ gun. ___
Love ___ gun. ___

D5 E5 D5 E5 G5 A5 G5 D5

Love gun. ___
Love ___

8va

Gtr. 4

Gtr. 3

C5 D5 E5 D5 E5

gun. ___ Love gun. ___
Love ___

(8va)

G5 A5 G5 D5 C5 D5 E5 D5 *Fade out*

___ gun. ___) Love. . .

(8va)

MACARTHUR PARK

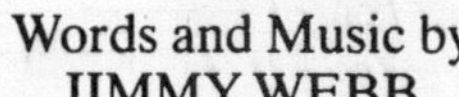

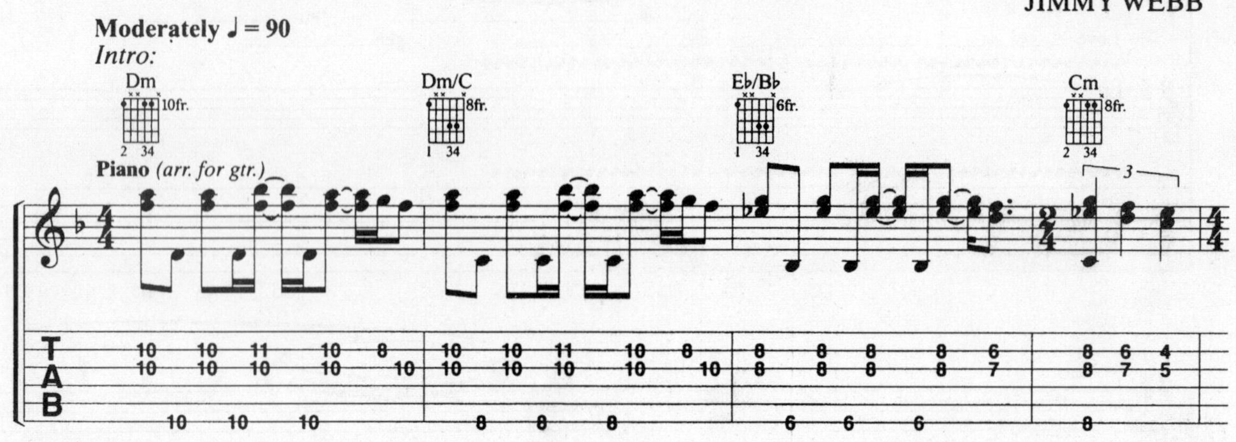

Eb/Bb
Gm
Gm/F
as we fol-lowed in the dance.
wave on the ground a-round your knees.
Ab
Bb/Eb
Gm/Ab
Ab/Db
Db/Eb
Eb/F
Dm
Acous. Gtr. 1 & Elec. Gtr. cont. simile
Be-tween the part-ed pag-es and were
The birds like ten-der ba-bies in your
Dm/C
Eb/Bb
Gm
pressed in love's hot fe-vered iron like a stri-ped pair of pants.
hands and the old men play-ing check-ers by the trees.
Chorus:
Gm/F
Ab
Bb/Ab*
C
Acous. Gtr. 1
Mac-Ar-thur's Park is melt-ing in the dark.
*Bass plays Ab.
Cmaj7
Cont. rhy. simile
C11
Fmaj7
All the sweet green ic-ing flow-ing down.
Some-one left the cake out in the rain.
C/E*
Dm7
I don't think that I can take it 'cause it took so long to bake it. And I'll
*Bass plays E.

C/E*
F
Eb
Cm7
never have that rec-i-pe a-gain. Oh, no!
*Bass plays E.
1.
Db
Eb/Ab
Eb/F
Db/Ab
2.
Ab
Bb/Eb
Gm7
Dm
Piano
C
Am7
F(9)
Bm7
Am7/F
Em7
Am7/F
Bb
Eb/Bb
Interlude:
Ab
Abmaj7
Ab7
Dbmaj7
Eb/Db
F
Strings
Acous. Gtr. 2
(nylon-string)
Verses 3 & 4:
F
Fmaj7
Bbmaj7
Bb6
Cont. rhy. simile
3. There will be an-oth-er song for me for I will sing it.
4. Take my life in-to my hands and I will use it.
Elec. Gtr.
mp
Cont. rhy. simile

Bbdim7
F(9)
F
There will be an - oth - er dream_ for me.___ Some - one will bring______ it.
I will win the wor - ship in their eyes and I will lose______ it.
F(9) F Fmaj7 Bbmaj7 Em7(b5)
I will drink the wine while it is warm______ and nev - er let__ you catch__ me
I will have the things that I de - sire,______ and my pas - sion flow like
Am7 D7sus D7 C6 D7 Gm7
look - ing at____ the sun._ And af - ter all__ the loves______ of my
riv - ers through_ the sky._ And af - ter all__ the loves______ of my
C11 C7(b9) Fmaj7 Bbmaj7
life, af - ter all__ the loves__ in my life,______ you'll__ Still be the
life, oh, af - ter all__ the loves__ in my life,___ I'll be think - ing
Ebmaj7
1. C11
2. C11
one.______ 4. I will and won - der - ing___
of you,______
Piano resumes Intro fig.
Dm Dm/C Eb/Bb Gm
Acous. Gtr. 1
Cont. rhy. simile
why.
Gm/F Ab Bb/Eb Gm/A Ab/Eb Db/Eb Eb/F C/D C/F
Piano
TAB

Double time
Instrumental Interlude:
Acous. Gtr. 1 & Elec. Gtr.
Cont. rhy. simile
Gm
Am
5fr.
Bb
6fr.
C
8fr.
Dm
Em
3fr.
F
5fr.
G
7fr.
Am7
A
Eb/Bb
G7
Cm
Fm
Ebm7
Ab7sus
4fr.

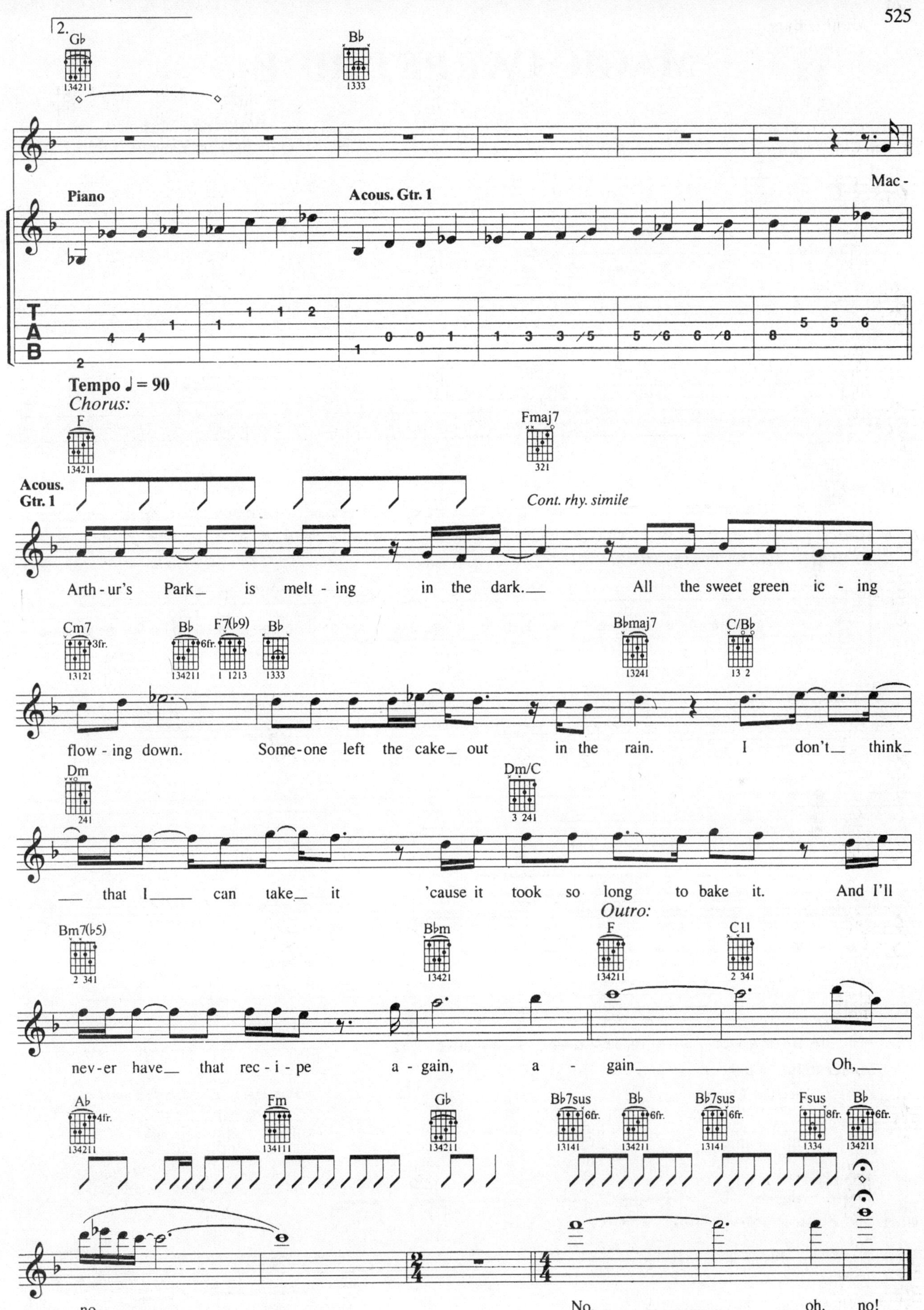
2.
Gb
Bb
Mac-
Piano
Acous. Gtr. 1
Tempo ♩ = 90
Chorus:
F
Fmaj7
Acous. Gtr. 1
Cont. rhy. simile
Arth-ur's Park is melt-ing in the dark. All the sweet green ic-ing
Cm7
Bb
F7(b9)
Bb
Bbmaj7
C/Bb
flow-ing down. Some-one left the cake out in the rain. I don't think
Dm
Dm/C
that I can take it 'cause it took so long to bake it. And I'll
Outro:
Bm7(b5)
Bbm
F
C11
nev-er have that rec-i-pe a-gain, a-gain Oh,
Ab
Fm
Gb
Bb7sus
Bb
Bb7sus
Fsus
Bb
no. No, oh, no!

MAGIC CARPET RIDE

Words and Music by
RUSHTON MOREVE and JOHN KAY

D C G
10fr. 8fr. 3fr.
3211
On a cloud of sound I drift in the night._ An-y place it goes is right.
Chorus:
w/Rhy. Fig. 1 (Elec. Gtr. 1) 4 times
Goes far, flies near, to the stars a-way from here. Well, you_ don't know what
we can find. Why don't you come with me, lit-tle girl, on a mag-ic car-pet ride?
Fade 3rd time
You_ don't know what we can see. Why don't you tell your dreams to me?
Fan-ta-sy will set you free._ Close your eyes, girl. Look in-side, girl. Let the sound take you a-
Elec. Gtr. 1 tacet
Organ
Bb
6fr.
way._
To Coda
w/Rhy. Fig. 2 (Elec. Gtr. 1) simile
Last
Elec. Gtr. 1
Rhy. Fig. 2
T
A
B

Verse 2:
w/Rhy. Fig. 1 (Elec. Gtr. 1) 3 times
D
C
G
night I held A - lad - din's lamp,
and so I wished that I could stay.
Be - fore the thing could an - swer me, well,
some - one came and took the lamp a - way.
D.S. % al Coda
I looked a - round,
a lous - y can - dle's all I found. Well,
Coda
E
Elec. Gtr. 1
Double time (♩ = 216)
Interlude:
w/bkgd. noise & fdbk.
Play 51 times
w/Rhy. Fig. 3 (Elec. Gtr. 1) 4 times
Rhy. Fig. 3
Elec. Gtr. 2
w/slide
D.S.% and fade

MISIRLOU

Title and Music by NICHOLAS ROUBANIS

Moderately fast ♩ = 160
Intro:

*Play ⑥ string in a sixteenth-note pattern and slide down from fret 7.

E
231

TAB
7 5 7 5 7 5 5 5 5 4 4 0 0 | 4 4 4 4 4 4 4 4 4 4 4 4 4 4 4 4 | 4 4 4 4 4 4 4 4 4 4 4 4 4 4 0

F
1342

E
231

3

TAB
7 7 7 7 5 5 7 7 5 7 5 5 4 4 4 4 | 5 4 5 4 5 4 1 4 | 0 0 0 0 0 0 0 0 0 0

B

*

Elec. Gtr. 2 cont. rhy. simile

trem. pick

TAB
12 12 12 / 12 12 12 | 0 0 0 0 / 0 0 0 0 1 4 4 4 4 5 5 5 5 | 7 7 7 7 7 7 7 8 8 11 11 11 11 8 8 0 0

*Play ① & ② strings in a sixteenth-note pattern and slide down from fret 12.

**Play ① string in a sixteenth-note pattern and slide down from fret 7.

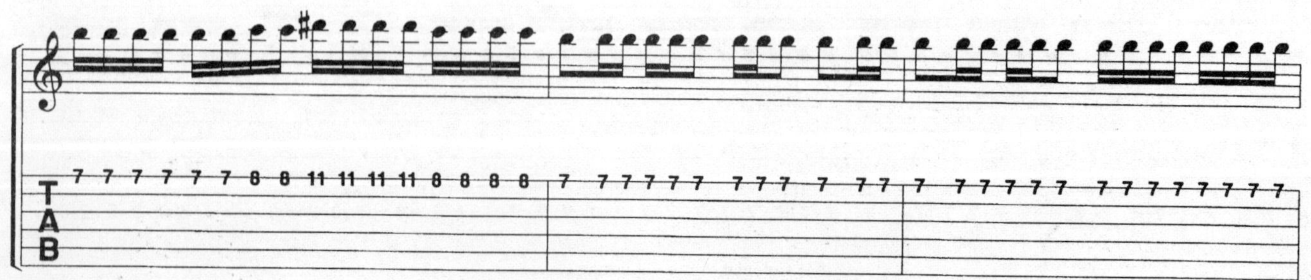

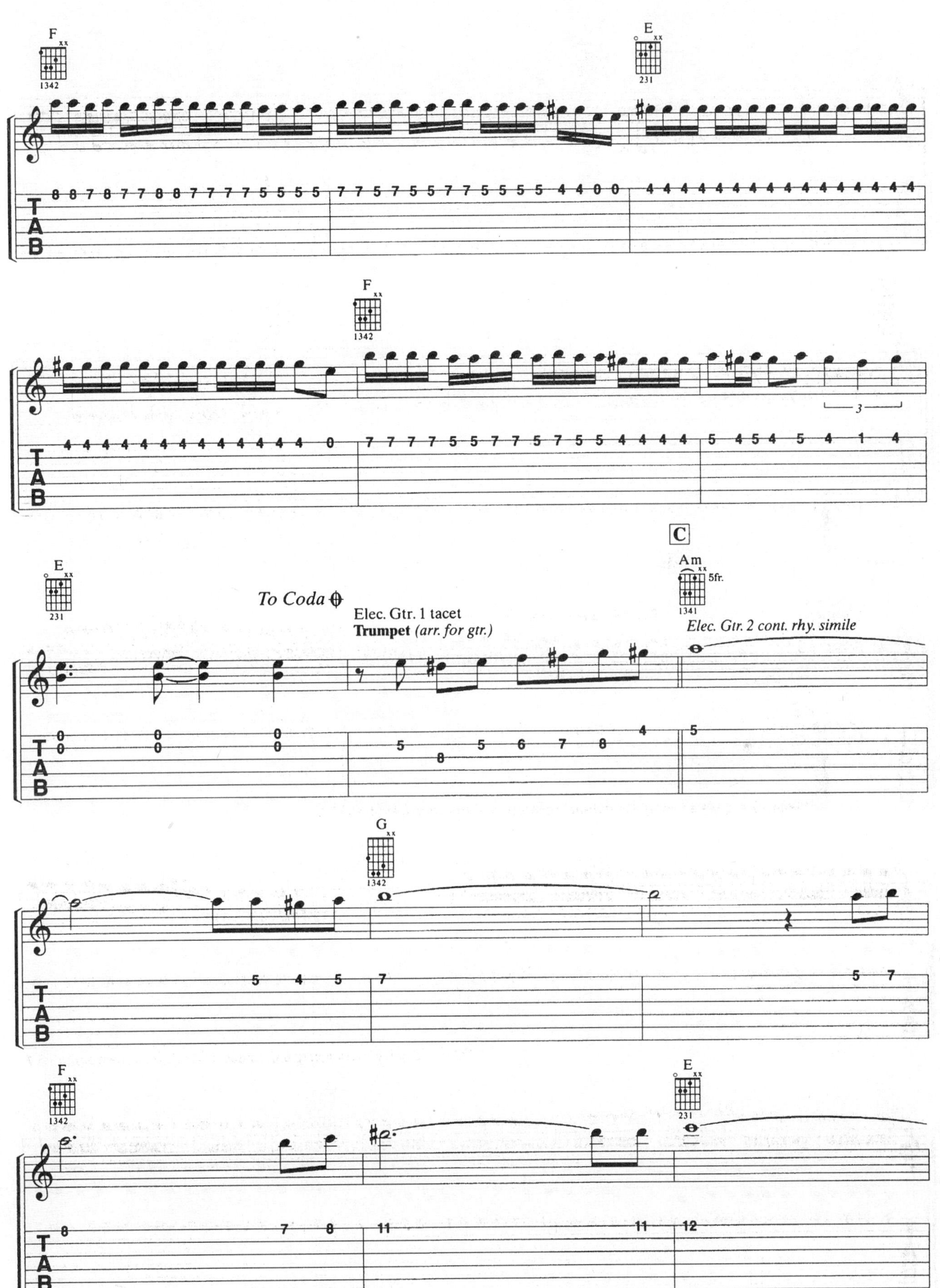
F
E
To Coda
Elec. Gtr. 1 tacet
Trumpet (arr. for gtr.)
C
Am
5fr.
Elec. Gtr. 2 cont. rhy. simile
G

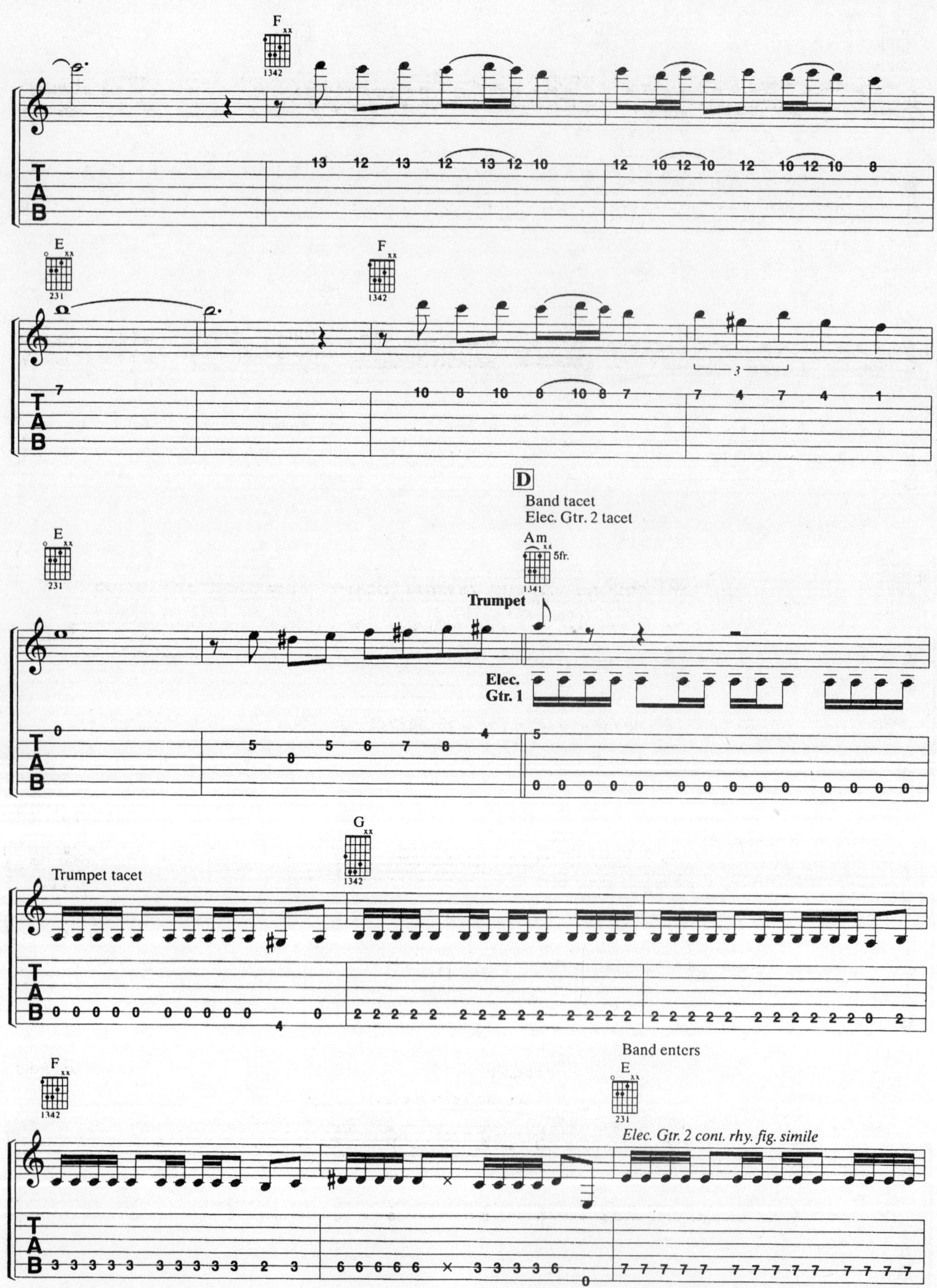
F
1342
13 12 13 12 13 12 10
12 10 12 10 12 10 12 10 8
E
231
F
1342
7
10 8 10 8 10 8 7
7 4 7 4 1
3
D
Band tacet
Elec. Gtr. 2 tacet
E
231
Am
5fr.
1341
Trumpet
Elec. Gtr. 1
0
5 8 5 6 7 8 4
5
0 0 0 0 0 0 0 0 0 0 0 0 0 0
Trumpet tacet
G
1342
0 0 0 0 0 0 0 0 0 0 4 0
2 2 2 2 2 2 2 2 2 2 2 2 2 2
2 2 2 2 2 2 2 2 2 2 2 0 2
F
1342
Band enters
E
231
Elec. Gtr. 2 cont. rhy. fig. simile
3 3 3 3 3 3 3 3 3 3 2 3
6 6 6 6 6 × 3 3 3 3 6 0
7 7 7 7 7 7 7 7 7 7 7 7 7 7

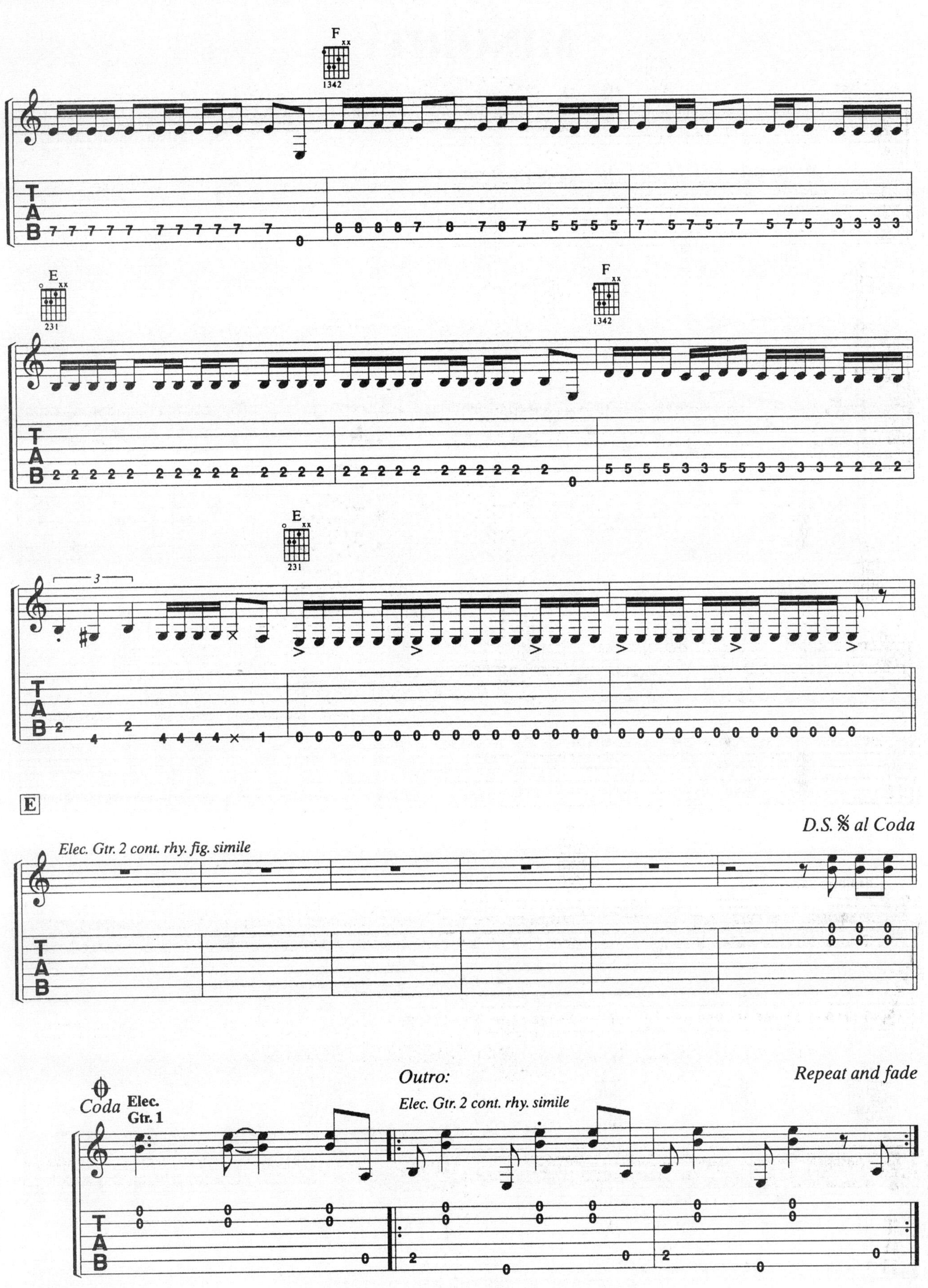
F
1342
E
231
F
1342
E
231
E
D.S. 𝄋 al Coda
Elec. Gtr. 2 cont. rhy. fig. simile
Coda
Elec. Gtr. 1
Outro:
Elec. Gtr. 2 cont. rhy. simile
Repeat and fade

MINORITY

Lyrics by BILLIE JOE
Music by GREEN DAY

Moderately ♩ = 132

Intro:

C G Fmaj7 C G F C

Acous. Gtr. Rhy. Fig. 1 — end Rhy. Fig. 1

mf *fingerstyle* — *Cont. in slashes*

Chorus:

C F G F C F

Elec. Gtr. 1 & Acous. Gtr. — *Cont. rhy. simile*

I want to be the mi - nor - i - ty. I don't need your au -

G F C F G F

thor - i - ty. Down with the mor - al ma - jor - i - ty. 'Cause

C F G F *Verse:* C G

Acous. Gtr.

I want to be the mi - nor - i - ty. 1. I pledge al - le - giance
(2.3.) light, one mind

Fmaj7
C
G
F
G
Cont. rhy. simile
to the un - der - world. One na - tion un - der - dog there of which I stand a - lone. A
flash-ing in the dark. Blind-ed by the si - lence of a thou - sand bro - ken hearts. "For
C
G
Fmaj7
C
F
face in the crowd, un - sung a - gainst the mold. With - out a doubt, sin - gled out, the
cry - ing out loud," she screamed un - to me. A free - for - all, f*** 'em all.
Chorus:
G
C
C
F
G
F
Elec. Gtr. 1 & Acous. Gtr.
on - ly way I know. "You are your own sight." 'Cause I want to be the mi - nor - i - ty.
C
F
G
F
C
F
Cont. rhy. simile
I don't_ need your au - thor - i - ty. Down with the mor - al ma -
To Coda
G
F
C
F
G
F
jor - i - ty. 'Cause_ I want to be the mi - nor - i - ty.

Bridge:
Am
E
F
C
Am
E
Elec. Gtr. 1 & Acous. Gtr.
1. Stepped out of the line___ like a sheep runs
2. Instrumental.
F
G
Am
E
F
C
from the herd. March - ing out of time___
Am
F
G
1.
B
to my own beat now.__ The on - ly way I know. 2. One
2.
Interlude:
D.S. 𝄋 al Coda
G
B
C
G
Fmaj7
C
G
Fmaj7
G
Cont. rhy. simile
3. One
G
F
C
F
G
F
Coda
nor - i - ty. I want to be the mi - nor - i - ty.
Elec. Gtr. 2
mf

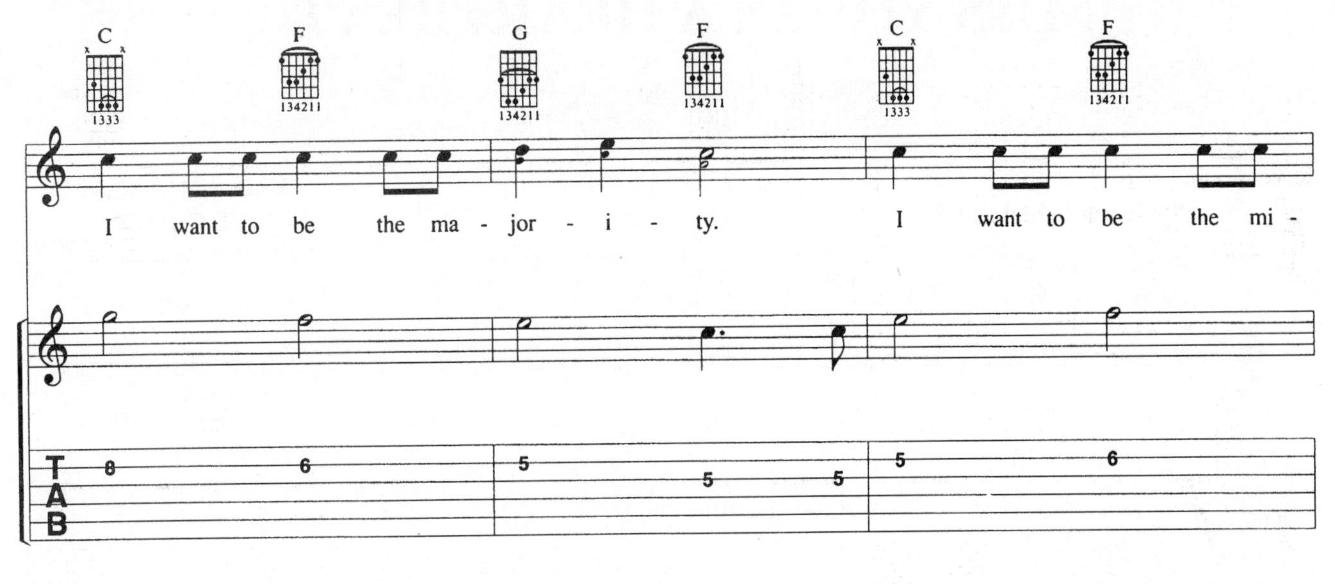
C
F
G
F
C
F
1333
134211
134211
134211
1333
134211
I want to be the ma - jor - i - ty. I want to be the mi -
T
A
B
8 6 5 5 5 5 6

G
F
C
F
G
F
134211
134211
1333
134211
134211
134211
nor - i - ty. I want to be the mi - nor - i - ty.
T
A
B
6 8 8 8 8 8 8

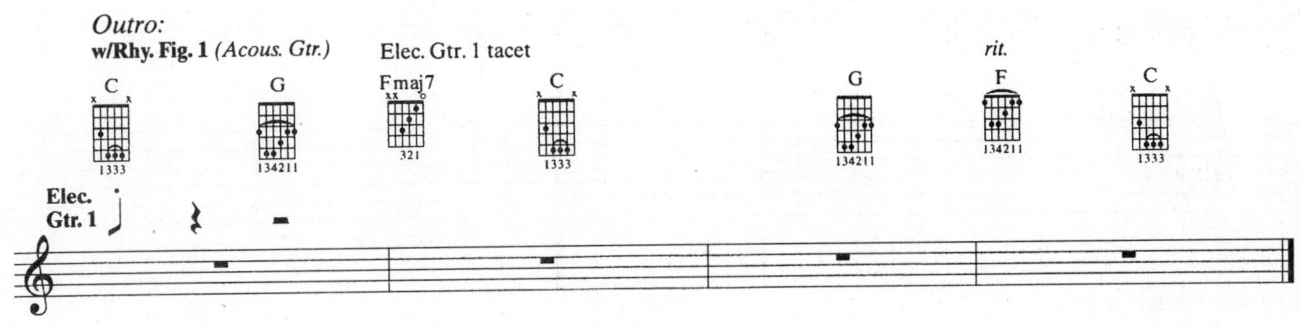
Outro:
w/Rhy. Fig. 1 (Acous. Gtr.)
Elec. Gtr. 1 tacet
rit.
C
G
Fmaj7
C
G
F
C
1333
134211
321
1333
134211
134211
1333
Elec.
Gtr. 1

MISS YOU IN A HEARTBEAT

F
Eb
Ab
Bb
Gm
3fr.
4fr.
134211
43121
134211
1333
133111

Words and Music by
PHIL COLLEN

Slow rock ballad ♩ = 67
Intro:
(Piano)
(Bb)
(F)
(Eb)
(Bb)
(F)
(Gm)
I be -

Verse 1:
(Bb)
(F)
(Eb)
(Bb)
(F)
lieve
that there's some - thing deep in - side
that should - n't be from time to

(Gm)
(Bb)
(F)
(Eb)
time.
I sure found out,
for love was such a crime.

Pre-Chorus 1:
Rhy. Fig. 1
(Bb)
(F)
(Gm)
F
Eb
Gtr. 2*
The more you care, the more you fall.
No need to wor - ry, no
Gtr. 1 w/o distortion
Rhy. Fig. 1A
*Acoustic gtr.

Ab
Eb
Bb
F
(end Rhy. Fig. 1)
need to turn _ a - way, 'cause it don't mat - ter ______ an - y - way, ba - by.
(end Rhy. Fig. 1A)
Chorus 1:
Rhy. Fig. 2
Bb
F
Gm
Eb
Bb
F
Oooh, ___ I miss you in a heart - beat. Oooh, ______ I
Rhy. Fig. 2A
hold
hold
hold
hold
hold
Gm
Bb
F
Gm
Eb
miss you right a-way. _ Oooh, ___ I miss you in a heart - beat. It ain't _
hold
hold
hold
hold
hold

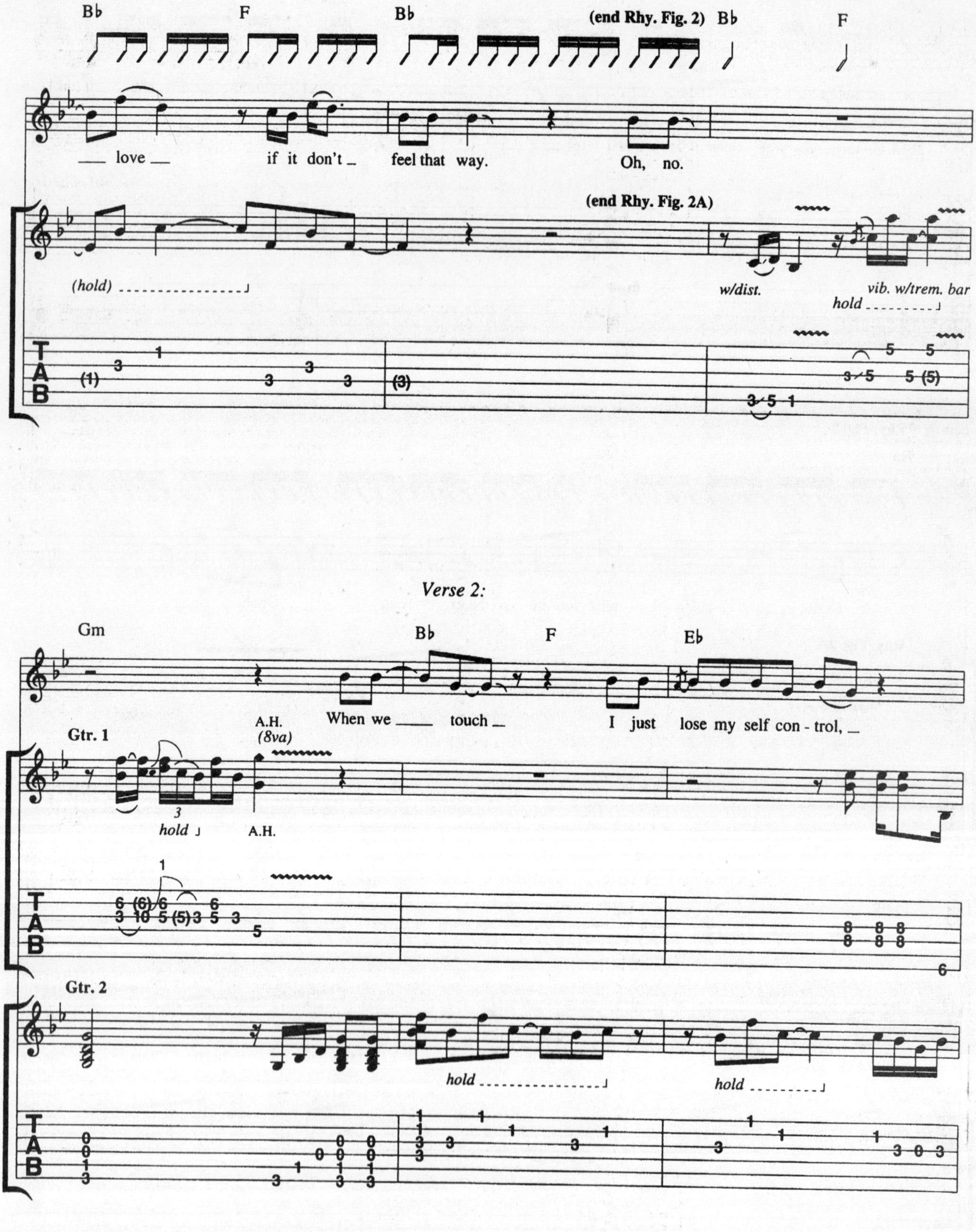

Verse 2:

Gm B♭ F E♭

When we ___ touch — I just lose my self con - trol, —

Gtr. 1

A.H. (8va)

hold A.H.

Gtr. 2

hold hold

B♭
F
Gm
B♭
F
a sad sen - sa - tion I can't hide. _
To love _ is ea - sy, it ain't
hold
hold

E♭
B♭
F
Gm
ea - sy to walk a - way. _
I keep the faith and there's a rea - son why. _
Yeah.
hold
hold

Pre-Chorus 2:
w/Rhy. Fig. 1 & 1A
F Eb Ab Eb Bb
No need to wor-ry, no need to turn _ a - way 'cause it don't mat - ter ______ any - y -
Chorus 2:
w/Rhy. Fig. 2 & 2A
F Bb F Gm Eb
way, ba - by. Oooh, _____ I miss you in a heart - beat.
Bb F Gm Bb F
Oooh. _______ Yeah, ___ I miss you right a - way. _ Oooh, _____ I
Gm Eb Bb F Bb
miss you in a heart - beat. 'Cause it ain't _ love _ if it don't _ feel that way. Now,
Bridge:
Gtr. 1
Gm F Eb F Gm F
I ain't big on prom-is-es. ___ I'll be true to you. _____ I'll do 'bout an-y-thing, _ yeah,
Gtr. 2
hold
hold
hold

Guitar Solo:
Gtr. 1 tacet (4 measures)
E♭
F
B♭
F
Gm
for some-one like, ba-by for you.
hold
Gtr. 3 (nylon str.)
B♭
F
Gtr. 2
Gtr. 3
w/Rhy. Fig. 1A (Gtr.1)
Gm
F
E♭
1/2
hold
hold

Ab
Eb
Bb
F
Chorus 3:
w/Rhy. Fig. 2 & 2A (first 7 bars)
Bb F Gm Eb Bb F
(Oooh,) I miss you in a heart - beat. (Oooh.)
Yeah, I'd
Gm Bb F Gm Eb
miss you right a - way. (Oooh,) Oh, miss you in a heart - beat. 'Cause it ain't
(I miss you in a heart - beat.)
rit.
Bb F Bb
Gr. 2
love if it don't feel that way.
Gtr. 1
rit.

MOONDANCE

Words and Music by
VAN MORRISON

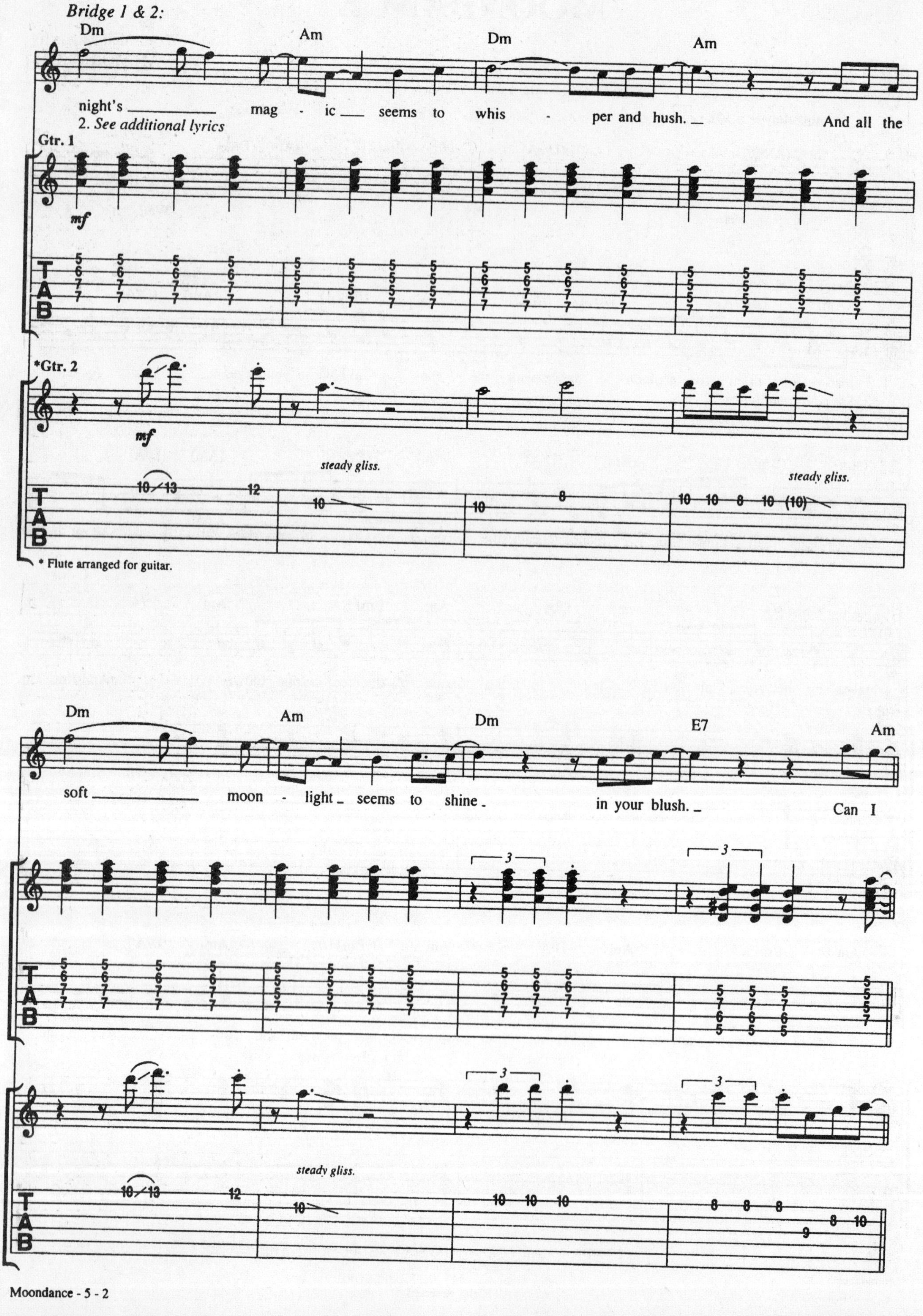
Bridge 1 & 2:
Dm
Am
Dm
Am
night's ___ mag - ic ___ seems to whis - per and hush. ___ And all the
2. See additional lyrics
Gtr. 1
mf
*Gtr. 2
mf
steady gliss.
steady gliss.
* Flute arranged for guitar.
Dm
Am
Dm
E7
Am
soft ___ moon - light ___ seems to shine ___ in your blush. ___ Can I
steady gliss.

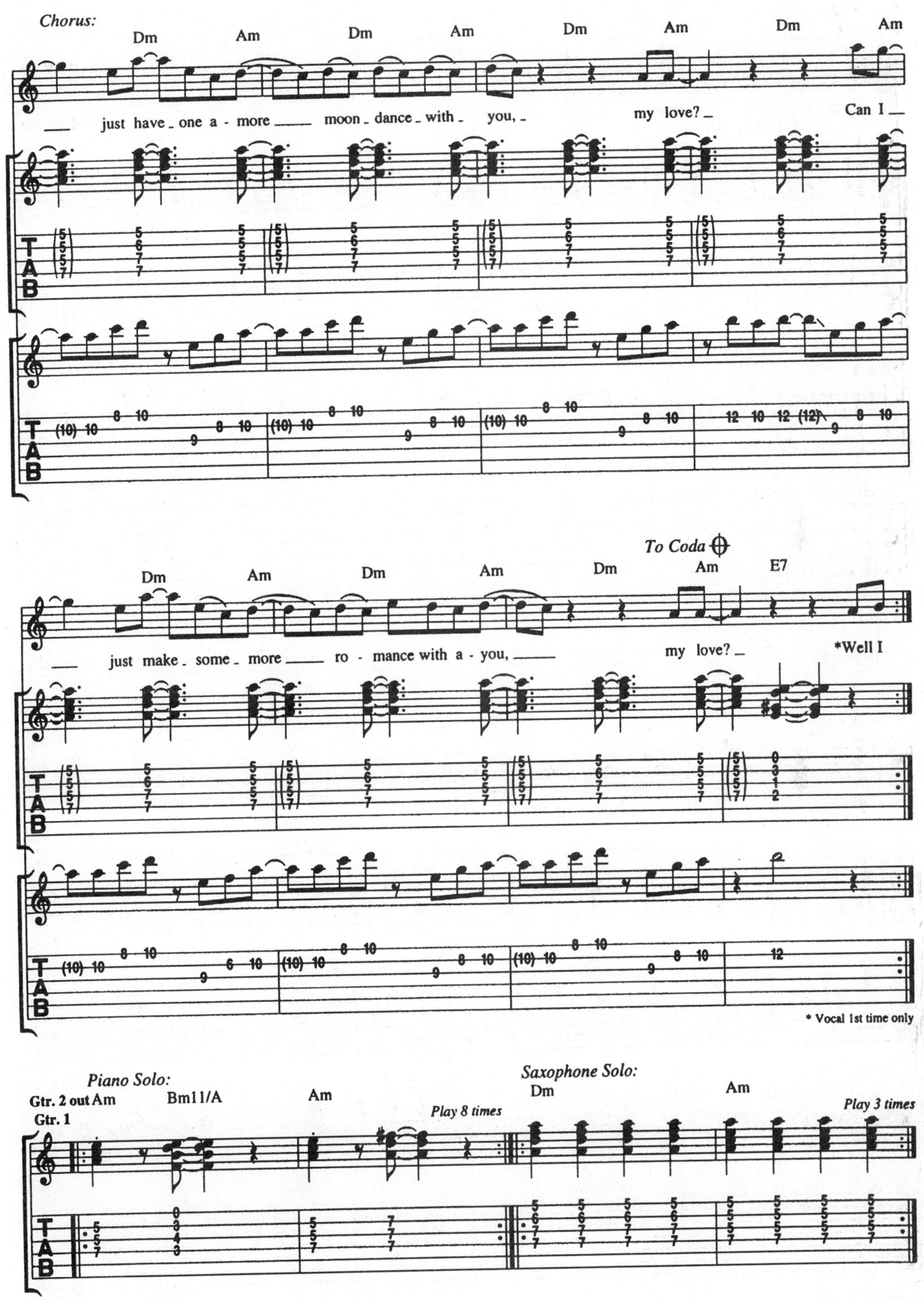
Chorus:
Dm Am Dm Am Dm Am Dm Am
just have - one a - more moon - dance - with - you, - my love? - Can I
To Coda
Dm Am Dm Am Dm Am E7
just make - some - more ro - mance with a - you, my love? - *Well I
* Vocal 1st time only
Piano Solo:
Gtr. 2 out Am Bm11/A Am
Gtr. 1
Play 8 times
Saxophone Solo:
Dm Am
Play 3 times

D.S. al Coda
Dm
E7
Am
Dm
Am
E7
Play 7 times
3. Well it's a
Coda
Outro:
E7
Am
Bm11/A
Am
D/A
One more moon - dance with you in the
Gtr. 2 out
Am
Bm11/A
Am
D/A
Am
Bm11/A
Am
D/A
moon - light on a mag - ic night.

Verse 2:
Well I wanna make love to you tonight,
I can't wait 'til the morning has come.
And I know now the time is just right
And straight into my arms you will run.
And when you come, my heart will be waiting
To make sure that you're never alone.
There and then all my dreams will come true, dear,
There and then I will make you my own.

Bridge 2:
And everytime I touch you, you just tremble inside.
And I know how much you want me that you can't hide.

(To Chorus:)

MORE THAN A FEELING

Interlude
Gtr. 3 (dist.)
Am
Em/G
Gtr. 4 w/ Fill 2
D
G
C
Em
D
C5
Rhy. Fig. 1A
Gtrs. 1 & 2
End Rhy. Fig. 1A
Rhy. Fig. 2
Gtrs. 1 & 4
End Rhy. Fig. 2
Chorus
Gtrs. 1 & 4: w/ Rhy. Fig. 2A, 3 1/2 times
Gtr. 3 tacet
It's more than a feel - ing when I
(More than a feel - ing.)
Rhy. Fig. 2A
Gtrs. 1 & 4
End Rhy. Fig. 2A
To Coda 2
hear that old song they used to play.
(More than a feel - ing.)
And I be - gin dream - in' till I
(More than a feel - ing.
To Coda 1
Bridge
Gtr. 4 tacet
Eb
Em7
Asus4 A
Asus2
A
G
see Mar - y Ann walk a - way.
)
I see my Mar - y Ann walking a - way.
Gtrs. 1 & 4
Gtrs. 1 & 2
let ring
Fill 2
Gtr. 4 (dist.)
mf

D/F# Em7 D
Gtr. 2: w/ Fill 3
Cadd9 G/B G D5 Cadd9 G/B G
*Gtrs. 1 & 2
let ring throughout
*Gtr. 1 to right of slash in Tab.
Verse
Gtr. 2 tacet
Gtr. 1: w/ Rhy. Fig. 1, 3 1/2 times
D5 Dsus4 D Cadd9 G/B G D5 Dsus4 D Cadd9 G/B G
2. So man-y peo-ple have come and gone, their fac-es fade as the years go by. Yet
D5 Dsus4 D Cadd9 G/B G D5 Dsus4 D Cadd9 G/B
I still re-call as I won-der on, as clear as the sun in the sum-mer sky.
let ring
Interlude
Gtr. 1: w/ Rhy. Fig. 1A
Am Em/G
Gtr. 4: w/ Fill 2
D
Gtrs. 1 & 4: w/ Rhy. Fig. 2, 2 times
G C Em D C5 G C Em D C5
D.S. al Coda
It's
Gtr. 3
f
1/2
fdbk.
Gtr. 5 (dist.)
full
pitch: G
Fill 3
Gtr. 2
p
Harm.
w/ bar
T
A
B

Coda 1
Bridge
Gtr. 4 tacet
Em7
Asus4 A
Asus2
A
Gtr. 2 tacet
Bm
B5
A5
G
D/F#
I see my Mar - y Ann walk-ing a - way.
Hey!
Gtrs. 1 & 2
Gtrs. 1 & 4
P.M.
Asus4
A
Guitar Solo
D
G/D
G5
D/F#
A
Gtrs. 1 & 4
Gtr. 3
Gtrs. 1 & 4 (cont. in slash)
full
D
G/D G5
D/F#
A
D
G5
B5
A
G5type 2
Gtr. 5
full
full
Gtr. 3
full
full

D G/D Bm G/D Em G/D Asus4 A
Gtr. 3: w/ Fill 4
G
G5 D Em7
(cont. in notation)
Gtrs. 3 & 5
Gtr. 5
8va
loco
full
Gtrs. 1, 3, 4 & 5
D
Gtrs. 3, 4 & 5
Cadd9 G/B G
Gtrs. 3, 4 & 5 tacet
Gtr. 2: w/ Fill 5
D5
Cadd9 G/B G
fdbk.
pitches: D, F♯
Gtr. 1
let ring throughout
Verse
Gtr. 1: w/ Rhy. Fig. 1, 7 1/2 times
D5 Dsus4 D Cadd9 G/B G
Gtr. 2 tacet
D5 Dsus4 D Cadd9 G/B G
3. When I'm tired and think - in' cold, I hide in my mu - sic, for - get the day. And
D5 Dsus4 D Cadd9 G/B G
D G/D Cadd9 G/B Cadd9 A
open
Gtr. 4
P.M.
dream of a girl I used to know, I close my eyes and she slipped a - way.
Fill 4
Gtr. 3
1/2
Fill 5
Gtr. 2
Harm.
w/ bar

Gtr. 4: w/ Fill 6

Dsus2 Dsus4 D Dsus2 Cadd9 G/B D5 Dsus4 Cadd9 G/B G

She slipped a - way...

Gtrs. 3 & 4

f

D Dsus4 Cadd9 G/B D Dsus4 Cadd9 G/B

Gtrs. 1, 3 & 4

Interlude

Gtrs. 1 & 4: w/ Rhy. Fig. 3

Am Em/G D

Gtr. 3

1/2 1/2 1/2

Gtr. 5

full full full

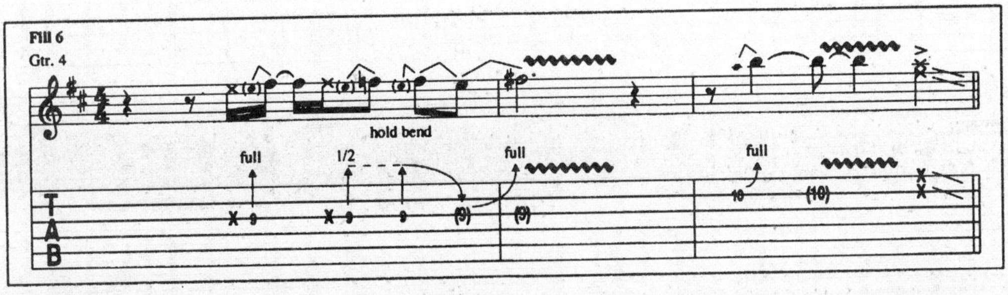

Fill 6

Gtr. 4

hold bend

full 1/2 full full

Rhy. Fig. 3

End Rhy. Fig. 3

Gtrs. 1 & 4

mf let ring

Gtrs. 1 & 4: w/ Rhy. Fig. 2
G
C
Em
D
C5
Gtrs. 1 & 4: w/ Rhy. Fig. 2A
Gtrs. 3 & 5
fdbk.
pitch: G
D.S. al Coda 2
Coda 2
It's
see Mar - y Ann _ walk a - way.
Gtrs. 1 & 4
Gtr. 3: w/ Fill 7
D5
Repeat and Fade
Fill 7
Gtr. 3
(sustain till fade)
w/ bar
Harm.

MOUTH FOR WAR

Words and Music by
VINCENT PAUL ABBOTT, DARRELL LANCE ABBOTT,
REX ROBERT BROWN and PHILIP HANSEN ANSELMO

G5 B5 N.C. G5 B5 N.C. G5
E5
G5 B5 N.C. G5
(8va)
N.C.
8va
E5
end Rhy. Fig. 2
loco
harm.
*Fret top 2 stgs. against front edge of neck pickup.
Half time ♩ = 80
Rhy. Fig. 3
Bb5 B5 C5 A5 Bb5 G5 A5 F#5 G5 Bb5 B5 C5 A5 Bb5 G5
P.M.
N.C.
E5
end Rhy. Fig. 3
Rhy. Fill 1
Re - venge!
Verse 1:
w/Rhy. Fig. 3 (Gtr. 1) 3½ times
I'm scream - ing re - venge a - gain.
Wrong.
I've been wrong for far too long.
Been con - stant - ly so frus - trat - ed,
I've moved moun - tains with less.

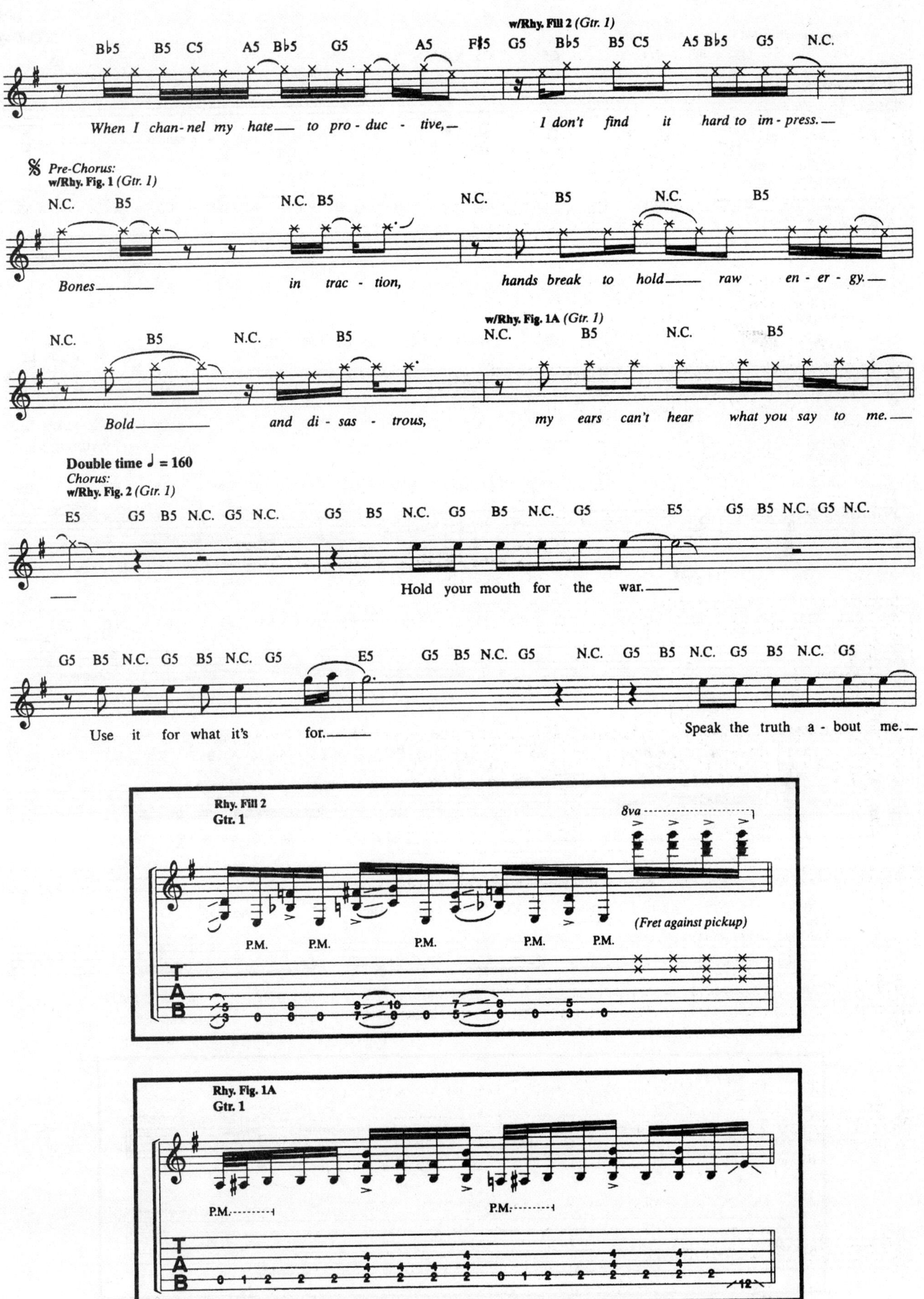
w/Rhy. Fill 2 (Gtr. 1)
B♭5 B5 C5 A5 B♭5 G5 A5 F♯5 G5 B♭5 B5 C5 A5 B♭5 G5 N.C.
When I chan-nel my hate to pro-duc-tive, I don't find it hard to im-press.
Pre-Chorus:
w/Rhy. Fig. 1 (Gtr. 1)
N.C. B5 N.C. B5 N.C. B5 N.C. B5
Bones in trac-tion, hands break to hold raw en-er-gy.
w/Rhy. Fig. 1A (Gtr. 1)
N.C. B5 N.C. B5 N.C. B5 N.C. B5
Bold and di-sas-trous, my ears can't hear what you say to me.
Double time ♩ = 160
Chorus:
w/Rhy. Fig. 2 (Gtr. 1)
E5 G5 B5 N.C. G5 N.C. G5 B5 N.C. G5 B5 N.C. G5 E5 G5 B5 N.C. G5 N.C.
Hold your mouth for the war.
G5 B5 N.C. G5 B5 N.C. G5 E5 G5 B5 N.C. G5 N.C. G5 B5 N.C. G5 B5 N.C. G5
Use it for what it's for. Speak the truth a-bout me.
Rhy. Fill 2
Gtr. 1
8va
(Fret against pickup)
P.M. P.M. P.M. P.M. P.M.
Rhy. Fig. 1A
Gtr. 1
P.M.
P.M.

Substitute w/Rhy. Fill 3 (Gtr. 1) 2nd time only
To Coda
E5 G5 B5 N.C. G5 N.C. E5
De - ter - mined.
Half time ♩ = 80
w/Rhy. Fig. 3 (Gtr. 1)
B♭5 B5 C5 A5 B♭5 G5 A5 F♯5 G5 B♭5 B5 C5 A5 B♭5 G5 N.C. E5
w/Rhy. Fill 1 (Gtr. 1)
B♭5 B5 C5 A5 B♭5 G5 A5 F♯5 G5 B♭5 B5 C5 A5 B♭5 G5 N.C. E5
Pos - sessed.
Verse 2:
w/Rhy. Fig. 3 (Gtr. 1) 3½ times
B♭5 B5 C5 A5 B♭5 G5 A5 F♯5 G5 B♭5 B5 C5 A5 B♭5 G5 N.C. E5
I feel a con-quer-ing will down in-side me.
B♭5 B5 C5 A5 B♭5 G5 A5 F♯5 G5 B♭5 B5 C5 A5 B♭5 G5 N.C. E5
Strength.
The strength of man-y to crush who might stop me.
B♭5 B5 C5 A5 B♭5 G5 A5 F♯5 G5 E5 B♭5 B5 C5 A5 B♭5 G5 N.C. E5
My strength is in num - ber,
and my soul lies in ev - 'ry - one.
w/Rhy. Fill 2 (Gtr. 1)
D.S. 𝄋 al Coda
B♭5 B5 C5 A5 B♭5 G5 A5 F♯5 G5 B♭5 B5 C5 A5 B♭5 G5 N.C.
The re-leas-ing of an - ger
can bet-ter an-y med-i-cine un-der the sun.
Rhy. Fill 3
Gtr. 1
T
A
B

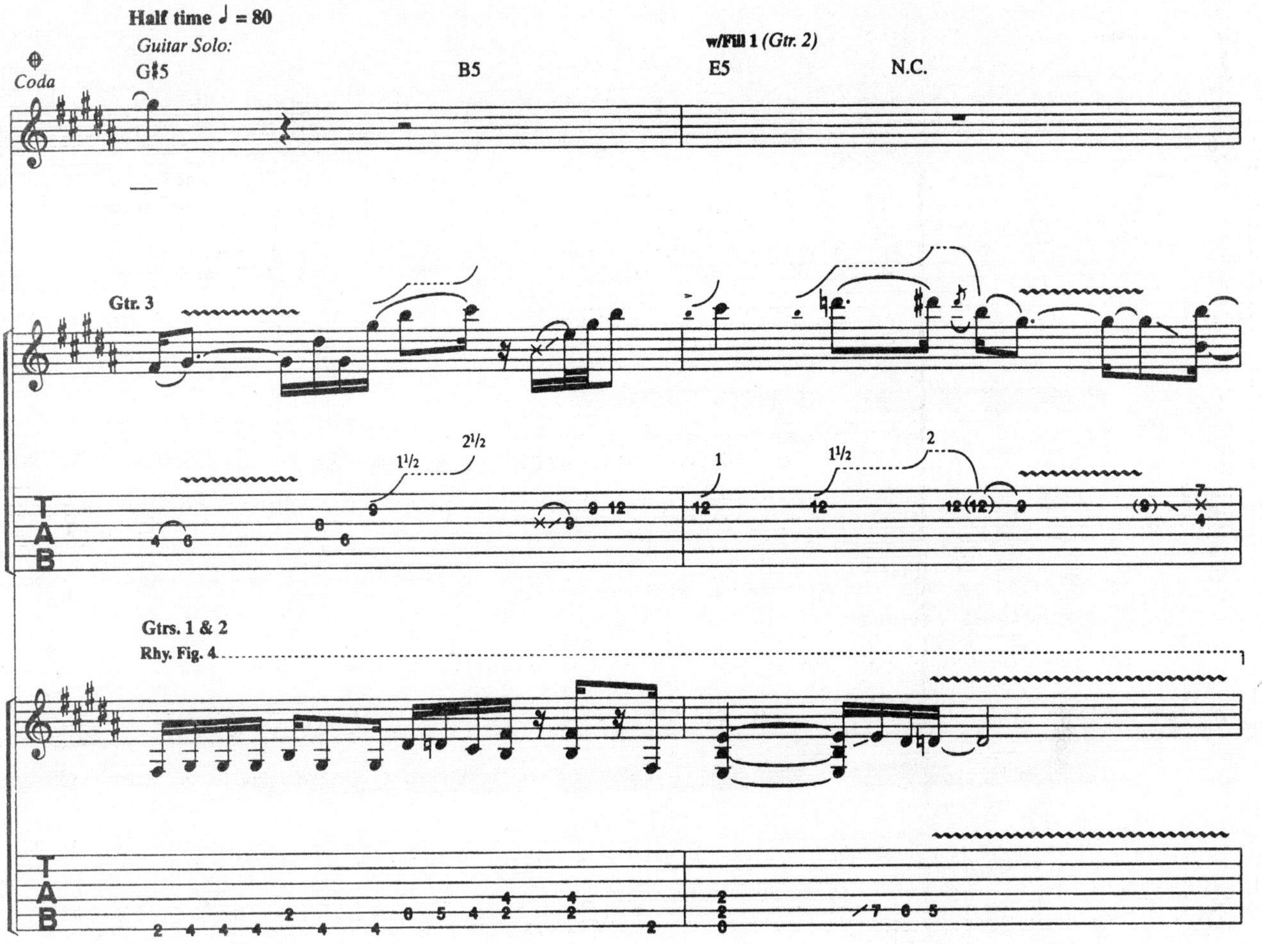

Half time ♩ = 80

Guitar Solo:

Coda

G♯5 B5 E5 N.C.

w/Fill 1 (Gtr. 2)

Gtr. 3

Gtrs. 1 & 2

Rhy. Fig. 4

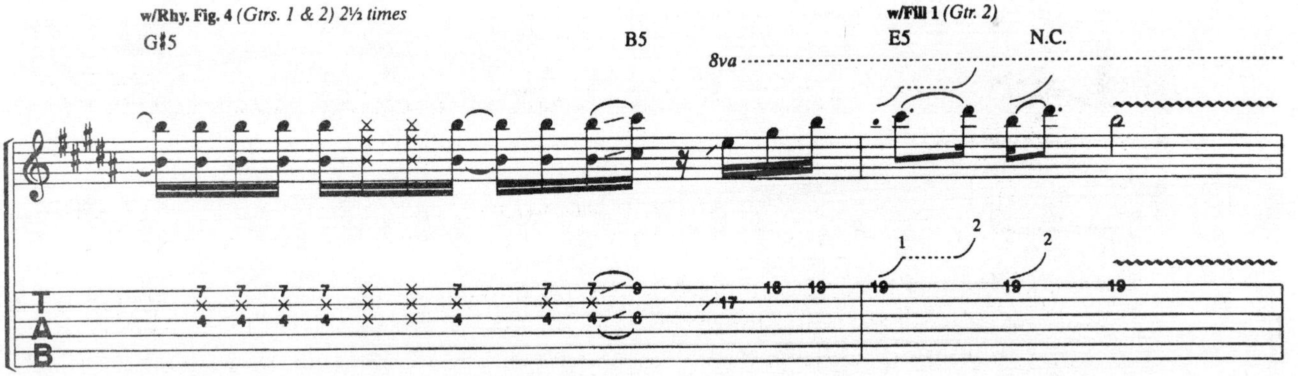

w/Rhy. Fig. 4 (Gtrs. 1 & 2) 2½ times

G♯5 B5 E5 N.C.

w/Fill 1 (Gtr. 2)

8va

G♯5
(8va)
B5
E5
N.C.
loco
trem. bar
P.M.
w/Rhy. Fill 4 (Gtr. 1) & 4A (Gtr. 2)
E5
8va
D5
Bridge:
F♯5 G♯5
B5
G♯5 D♯5
D5 C♯5 B5
F♯5
E5
D♯5 D5
There comes a time with-in ev-'ry-one
Gtr. 3
Gtrs. 1 & 2
(15ma)
harm.
*w/delay.
Rhy. Fill 4
Gtr. 1
Rhy. Fill 4A
Gtr. 2

F♯5 G♯5
B5 G♯5
D♯5 D5 C♯5 B5
F♯5 E5
D5
to close your eyes — to what's real. —
P.M.
Double time ♩ = 160
G♯5
F♯5 G♯5
F♯5 G♯5
F♯5 G♯5
F♯5
Yeah! —
G♯5
F♯5 G♯5
F♯5 G♯5
F♯5 G♯5
F♯5
Ow!
Verses 3 & 4:
G♯5
Bm/D
3. No com - pre - hen - sion to fail. (w/delay)
4. Like — a knife in - to flesh, (w/delay)
P.M.

G♯5
I vac - uum the wind for my
af - ter life is to
P.M.
Am/C
G♯5
sail.
death.
Can't be the
Pull - ing and
P.M.
Bm/D
rest, let oth - ers waste my time.
push - ing the rest of du - ra - tion,

1.
G♯5
Am/C
Own - ing suc - cess is the bot - tom line.
no one can piss on this
P.M.
G♯5
F♯5 G♯5
F♯5
2.
Dm/F
G♯5
F♯5
de - ter - mi - na - tion.
Play 14 times
G♯5
F♯5 G♯5
F♯5 G♯5
F♯5 G♯5
Uh!

MRS. BROWN YOU'VE GOT A LOVELY DAUGHTER

Words and Music by
TREVOR PEACOCK

C Em Dm G C Em Dm G
her. Tell her she can keep them just the same.
you, tell her that I'm well and feel - ing fine.
C Em Dm G Am C
Things have changed,
Don't let on,
Am C Am
she does - n't love me now. She's made it
don't say she's broke my heart. I'd go down
C G To Coda Bb
clear e - nough, it ain't no good to pine.
on my knees, but it's no good to pine.
Bridge:
Eb Gm Ab Bb
Walk - ing a - bout, e - ven in a crowd. Well,
Gb Bbm Bb
you'd pick her out. Makes a bloke feel
1. G 2. G D.S. al Coda
Elec. Gtr. 5fr. 7fr. 9fr.
so proud. so proud.
Coda G
Repeat and fade
Outro:
C Em Dm G C Em Dm G
Mis - sus Brown, you've got a love - ly daugh - ter.
(Love - ly daugh - ter.)

MY BEST FRIEND'S GIRL

Words and Music by
RIC OCASEK

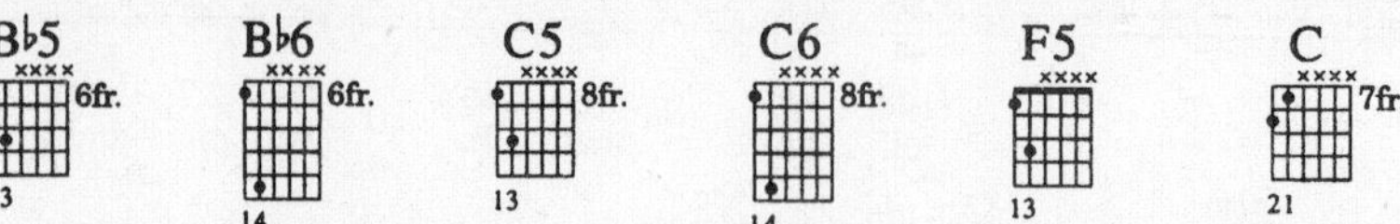

Moderately ♩ = 116
Intro:

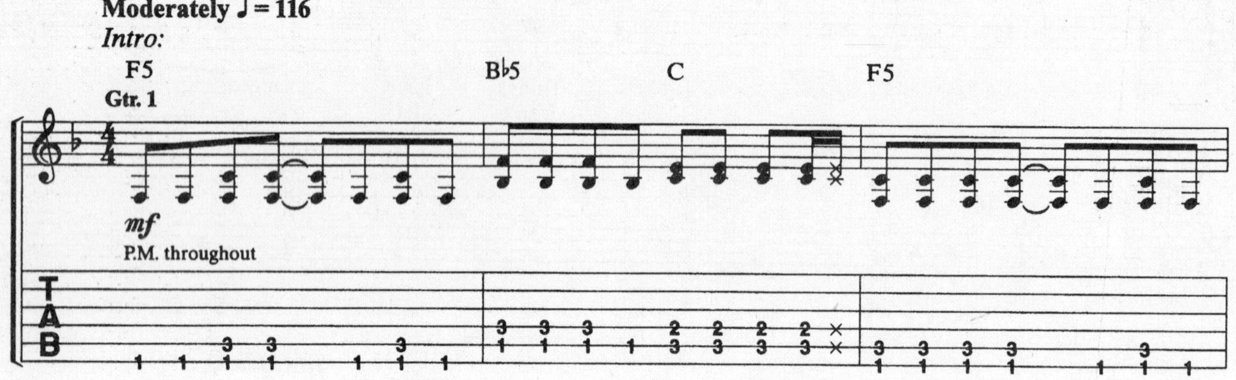

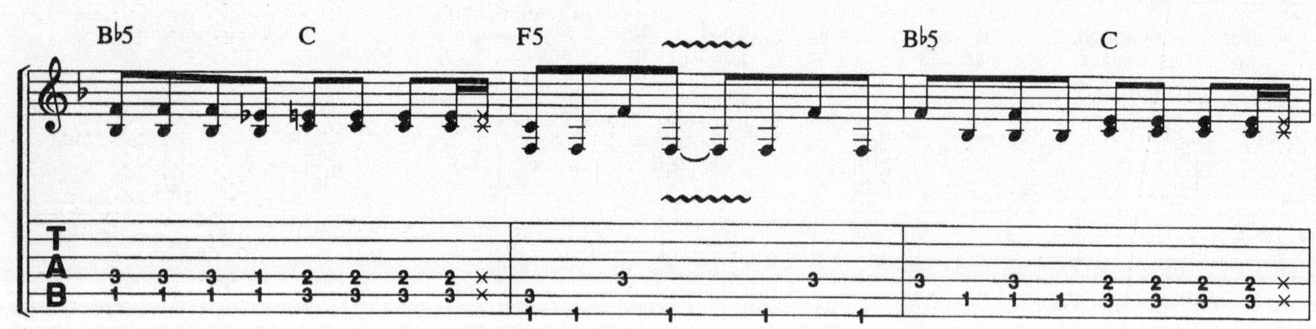

B♭5
C
F5
B♭5
C
with your suede - blue
eyes.
And ev - 'ry
F5
B♭
C
F5
new boy that you meet,
he does - n't know the real sur - prise.
Pre-Chorus:
w/Rhy. Fig. 1 (Gtr. 1)
B♭5
C
F5
B♭5
C
Here she comes a - gain. When she's danc - in' 'neath the star - ry sky,
end Rhy. Fig. 1
Gtr. 2
Riff A
1/2

F5
B♭5
C
F5
ooo,_
she'll make you flip.
When she's
Here she comes a - gain._
B♭5
C
F5
danc - in' 'neath the star - ry sky,
I kind - a like it when she dips.
end Riff A
Chorus:
B♭5 B♭6 B♭5 B♭6 B♭5 C5 C6 C5 C6 B♭5 B♭6 B♭5 B♭6 C5
Rhy. Fig. 3
Gtr. 1
She's my best friend's girl.
Gtr. 2
Rhy. Fig. 3A
P.M.
P.M.

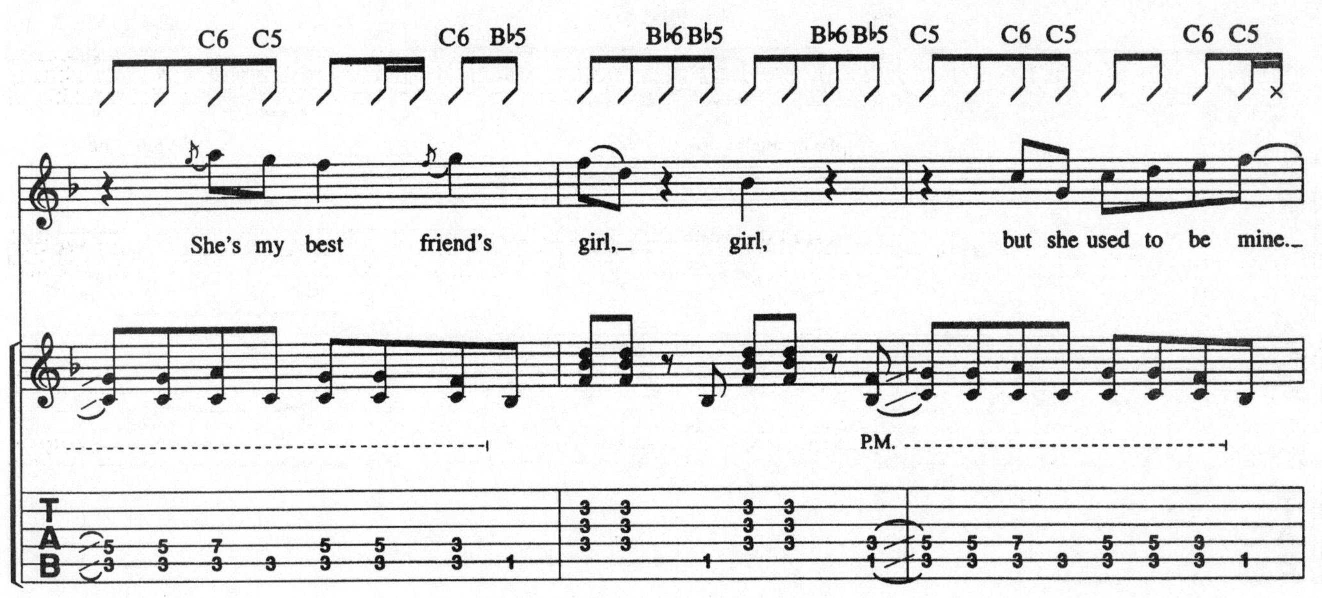

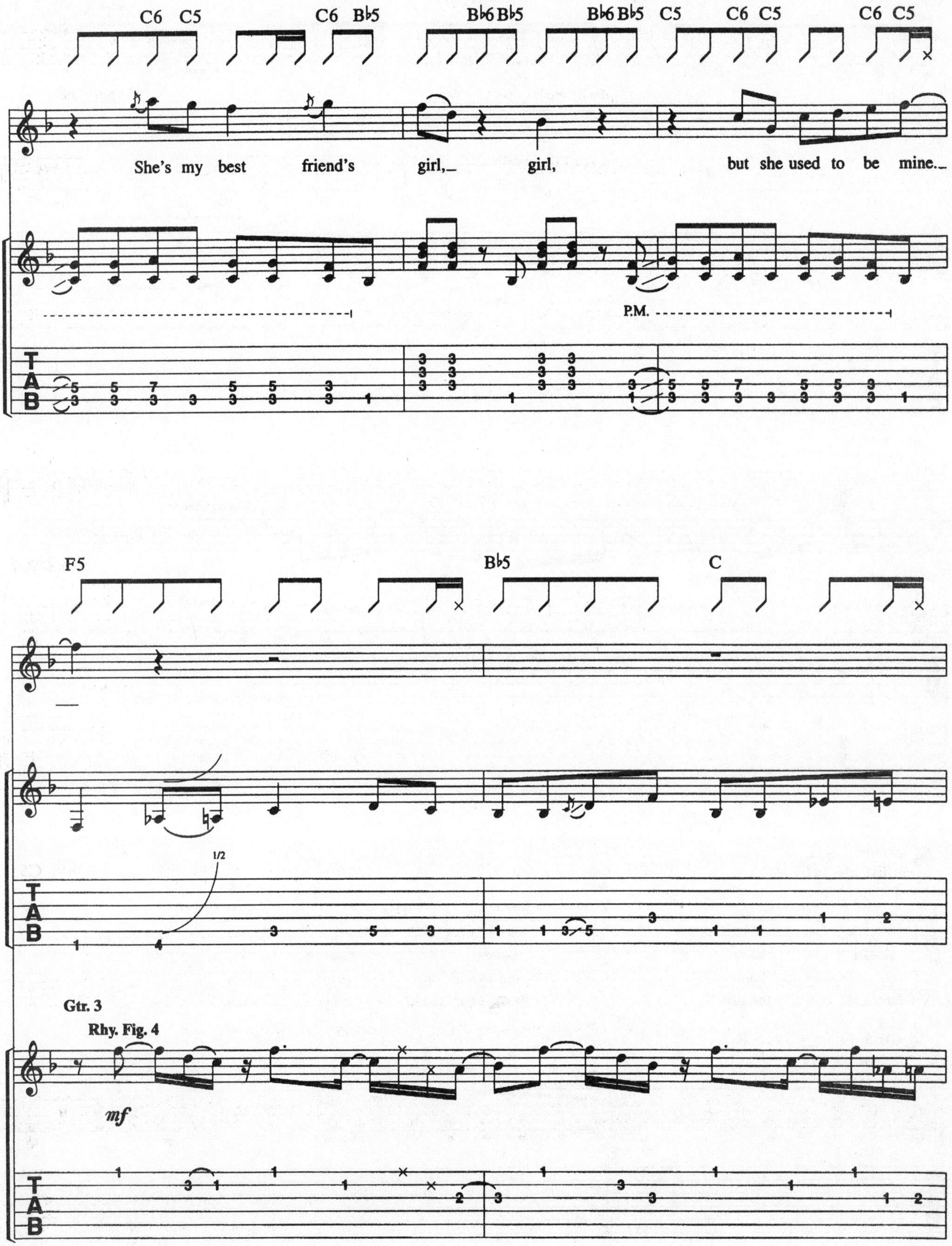

F5 B♭5 C

1/2

Gtr. 3

Rhy. Fig. 4

mf

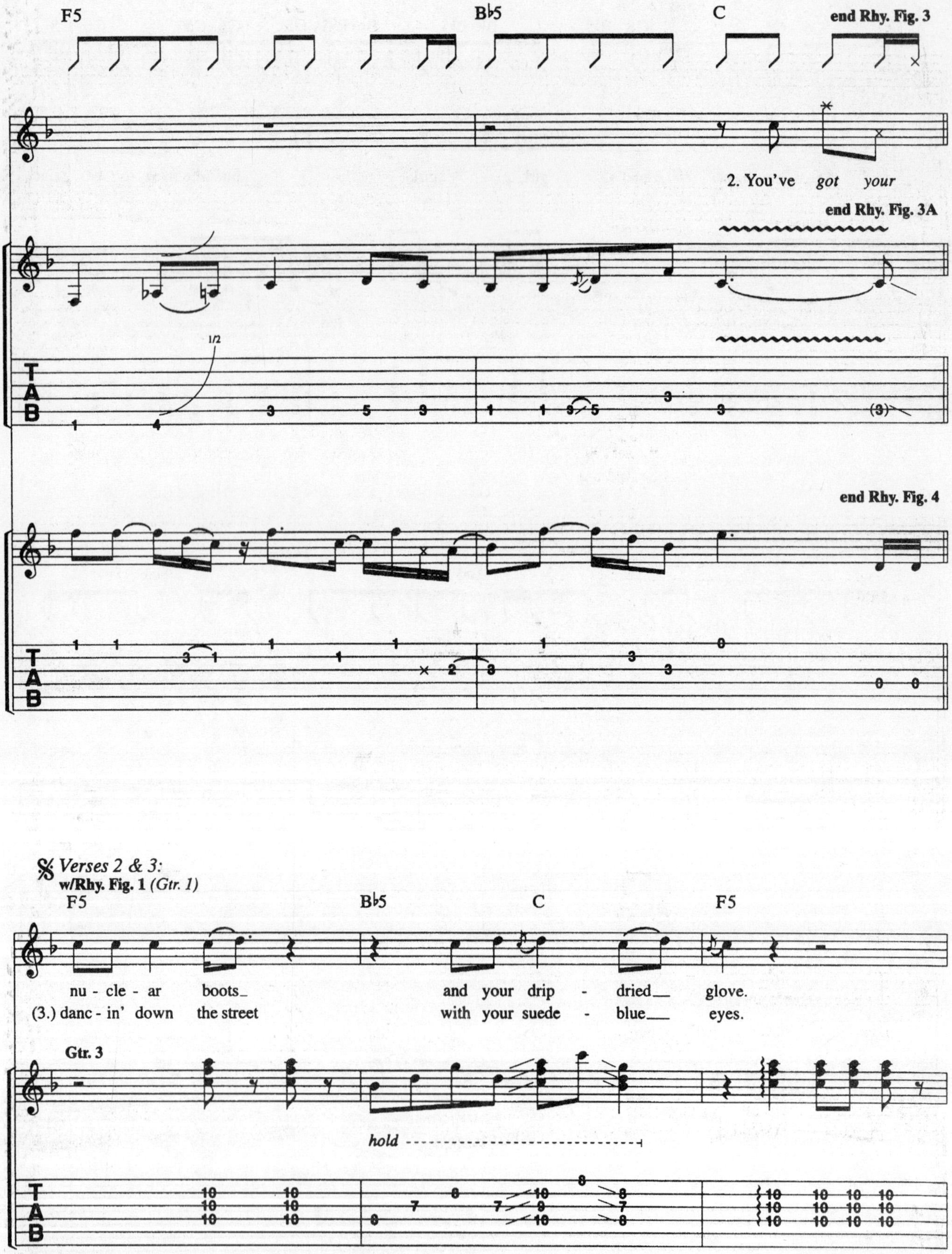

F5 B♭5 C

end Rhy. Fig. 3

2. You've *got your*

end Rhy. Fig. 3A

1/2

end Rhy. Fig. 4

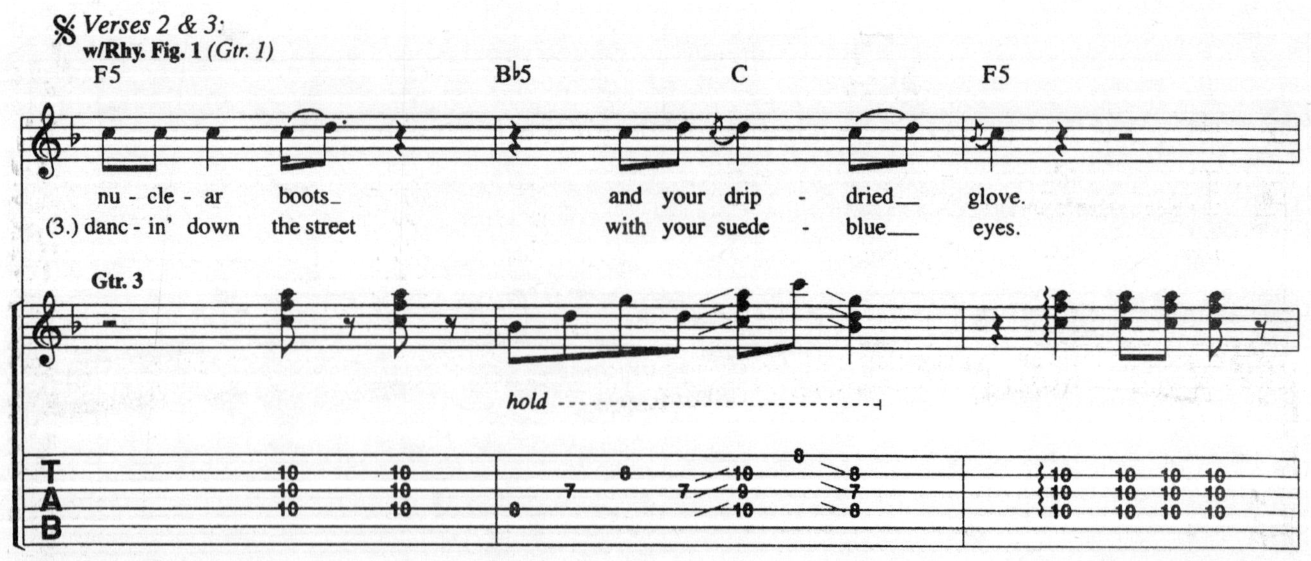

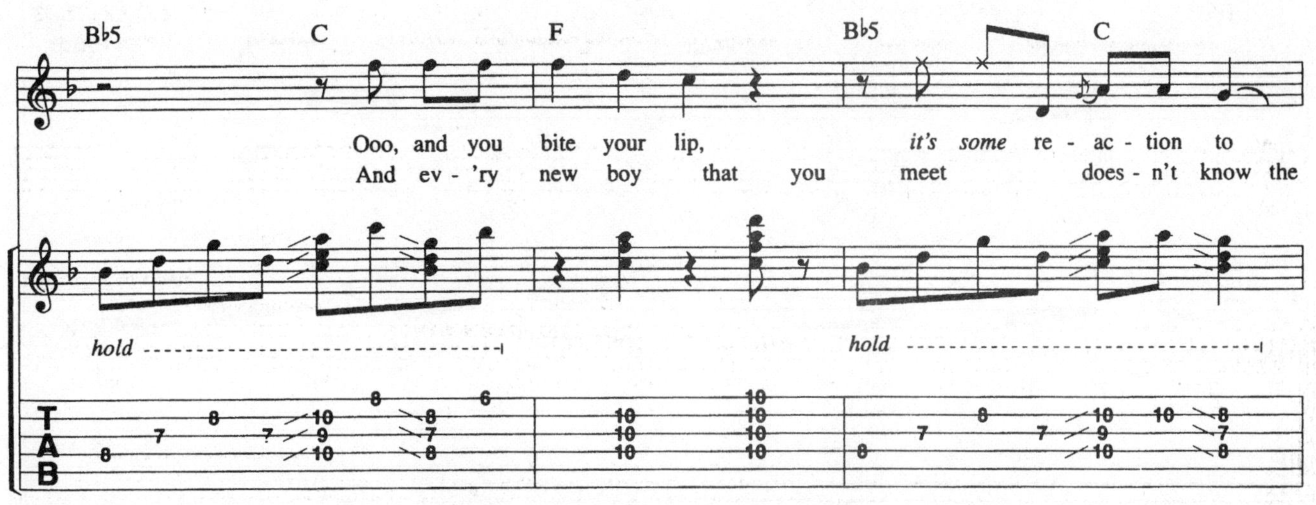
Bb5
C
F
Bb5
C
Ooo, and you bite your lip, it's some re - ac - tion to
And ev - 'ry new boy that you meet does - n't know the
hold
hold

Pre-Chorus:
w/Fill 1 (Gtr. 2)
w/Rhy. Fig. 1 (Gtr. 1) & Riff A (Gtr. 2) both simile
F5
Bb5
C
F5
love.
real sur-prise.
When she's
Here she comes a - gain.
hold

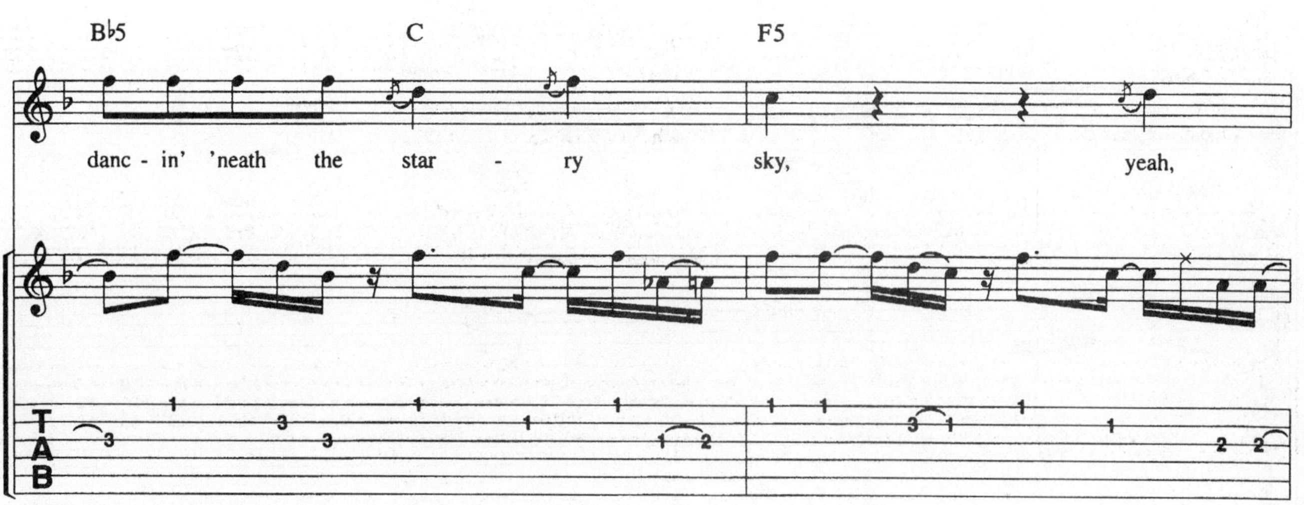
Bb5
C
F5
danc - in' 'neath the star - ry sky,
yeah,

Bb5
C
F5
I think you'll flip.
Here she comes a - gain.
When she's
Bb5
C
F5
danc - in' 'neath the star - ry sky,
Here she comes a - gain.
I kind - a
hold
Chorus:
w/Rhy. Figs. 3 (Gtr. 1)
& 3A (Gtr. 2) both simile
Bb5
C
Bb5
C5
Bb5
like the way, I like the way she dips.
She's my best friend's
T
A
B

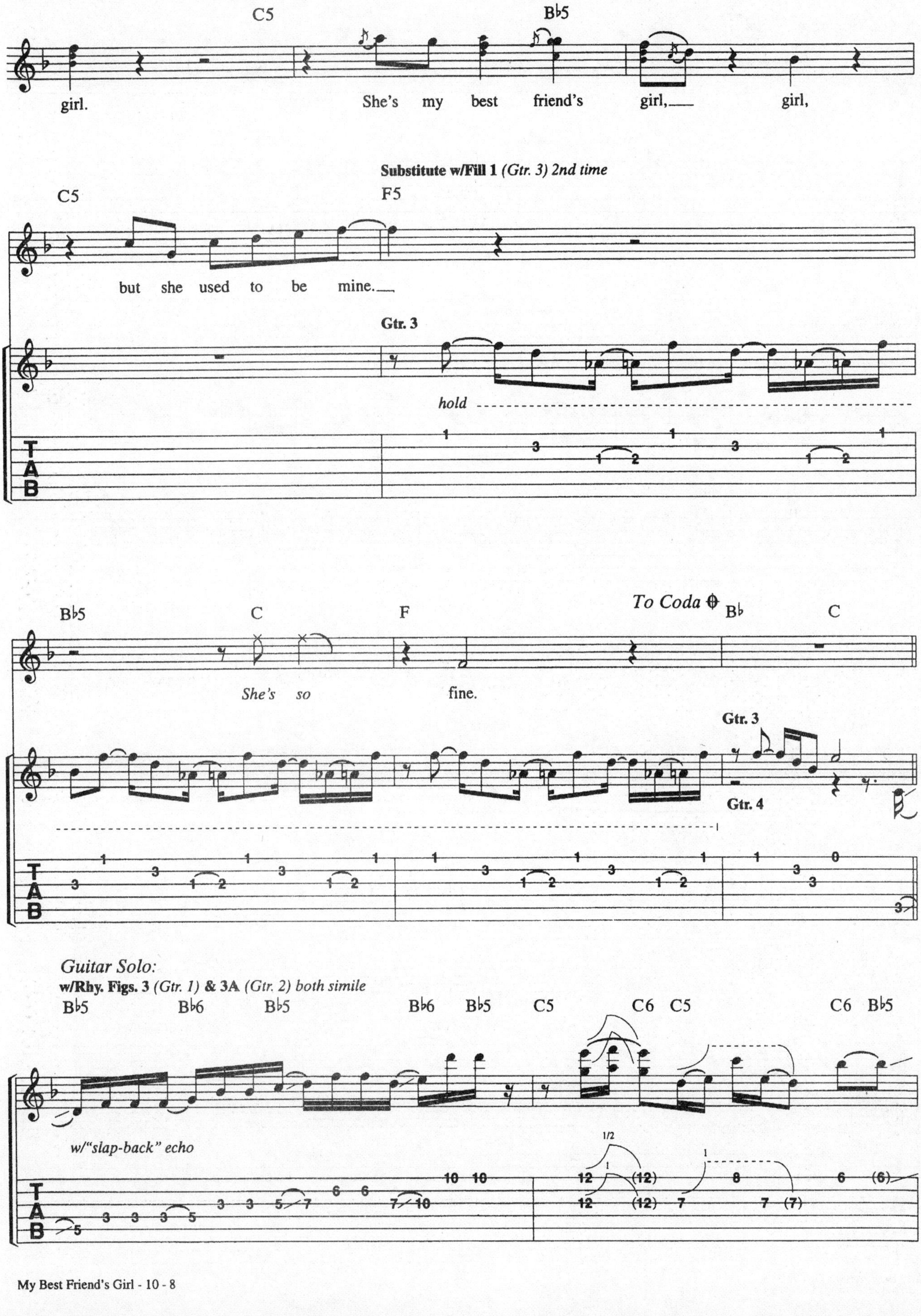

C5 B♭5

girl. She's my best friend's girl,___ girl,

Substitute w/Fill 1 *(Gtr. 3) 2nd time*

C5 F5

but she used to be mine.___

Gtr. 3

hold

B♭5 C F *To Coda* ⊕ B♭ C

She's so fine.

Gtr. 3

Gtr. 4

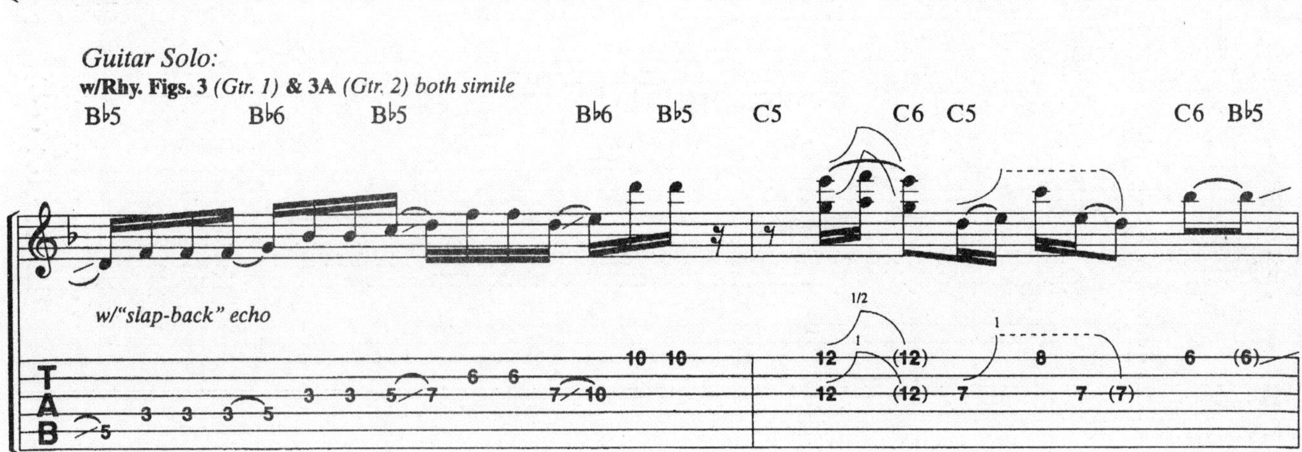

B♭6
B♭5
B♭6
C5
C6
C5
C6
B♭5
rake

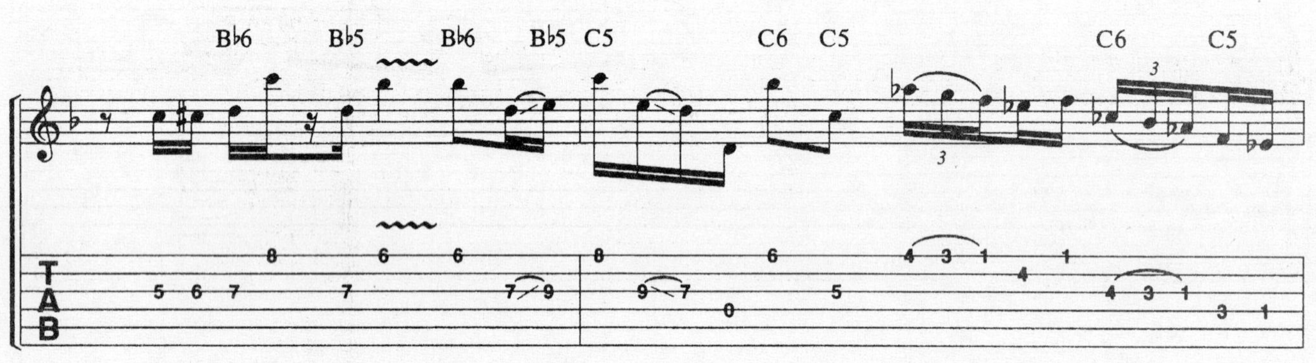
B♭6
B♭5
B♭6
B♭5
C5
C6
C5
C6
C5

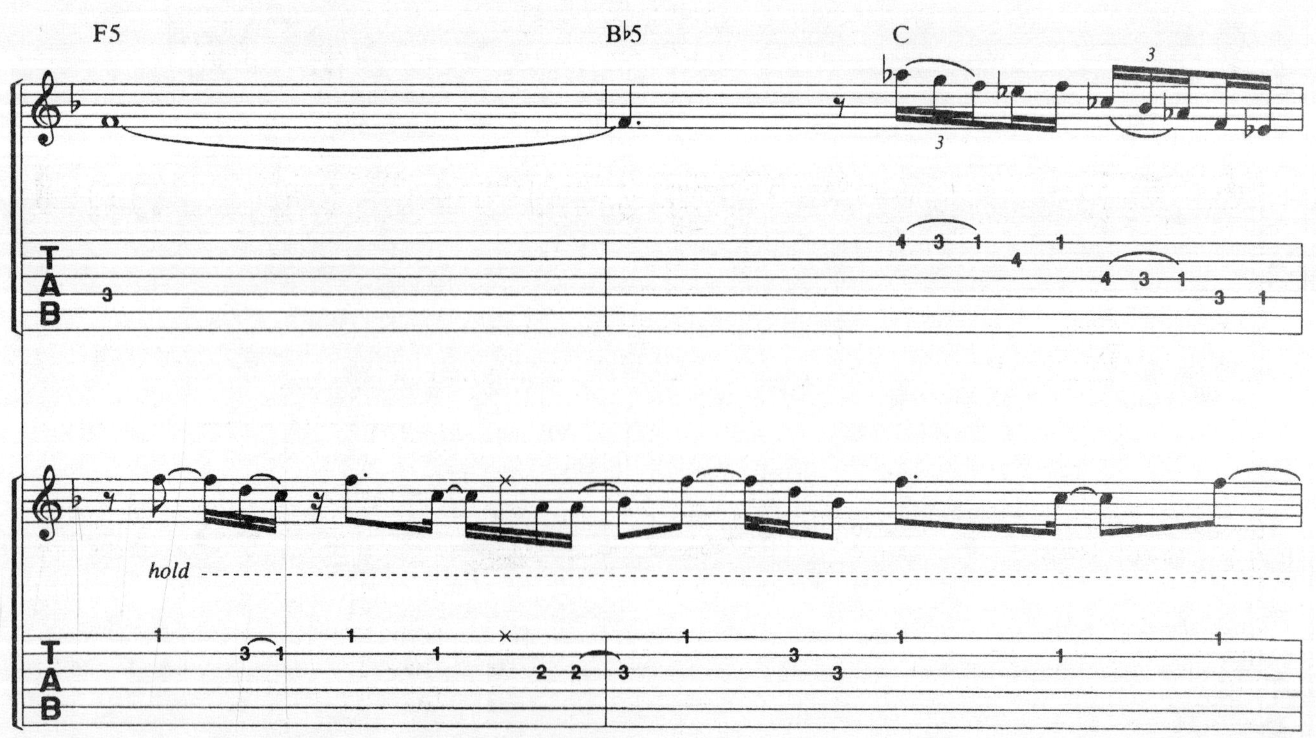
F5
B♭5
C
hold

D.S. 𝄋 al Coda
F5
B♭5
C
3. Al - ways d -
Coda
B♭5
C
Outro:
F5
Repeat and fade
Gtr. 1
My best friend's girl - friend.
Gtr. 2
Gtr. 3
(Enter 5th time)
hold
*w/Lead vocal ad lib. on repeats.

MY SPECIAL ANGEL

Words and Music by
JIMMY DUNCAN

Bridge:
Dm
G7
C
Am
Elec. Gtr.
Cont. rhy. simile
smile from your lips brings the sum - mer sun - shine, the
Dm
G7
C
C7
Em
B7
tears from your eyes bring the rain. I feel your touch, your
Em
B7
D7
1.
G7
2.
G7
Ab7
warm em-brace. And I'm in heav - en a - gain. gain.
Verse 4:
Db6/9
Bbm
Fm
Gb
Ab7
Elec. Gtr.
Resume rhy. fig. simile
You are my spe - cial an - gel through e - ter - ni -
Db
Ddim7
Ebm
Ab7
Db
Bbm
ty. I'll have my spe-cial an - gel
Eb7
Ab7
F7
Bb7
Eb7
Ab7
here to watch o - ver me. Here to watch o - ver
Db
Bbm
Ebm
rit.
Freely
Ebm
Fm
Ebm
Db6/9
Elec. Gtr.
me.
(An - gel, an - gel. Whoa.)

N 2 GETHER NOW

Lyrics by C. Smith and Fred Durst
Music by C. Martin, Wes Borland, Sam Rivers,
John Otto and Leor Dimant

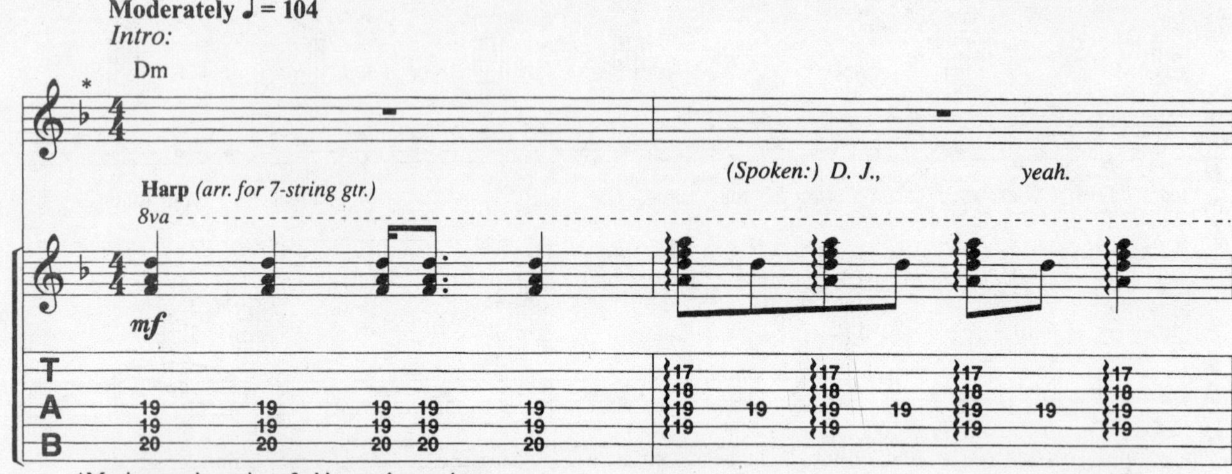

*Music sounds a minor 3rd lower than written.
There is no guitar on this recording. Some of the primary instrumental parts have been arranged to be played on 7-string guitar (tuned down a minor 3rd).

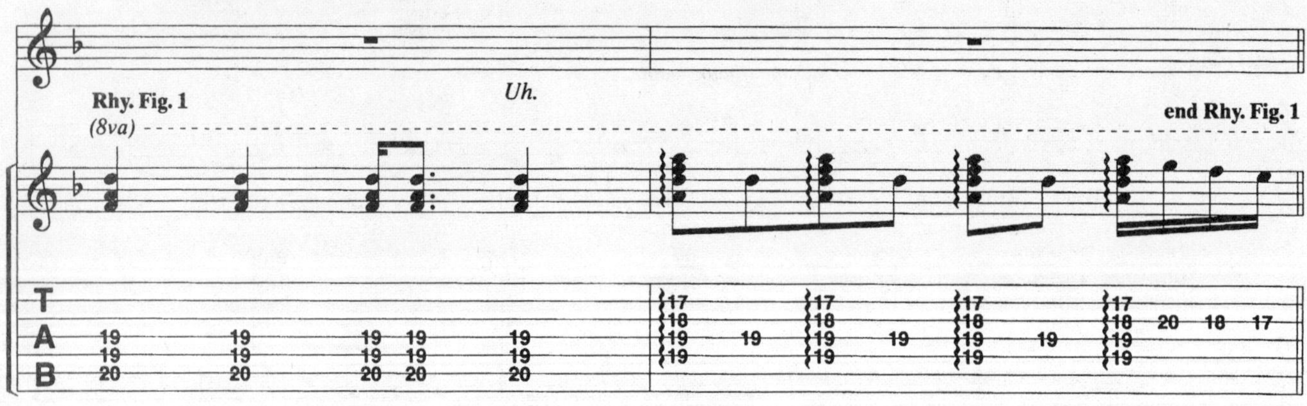

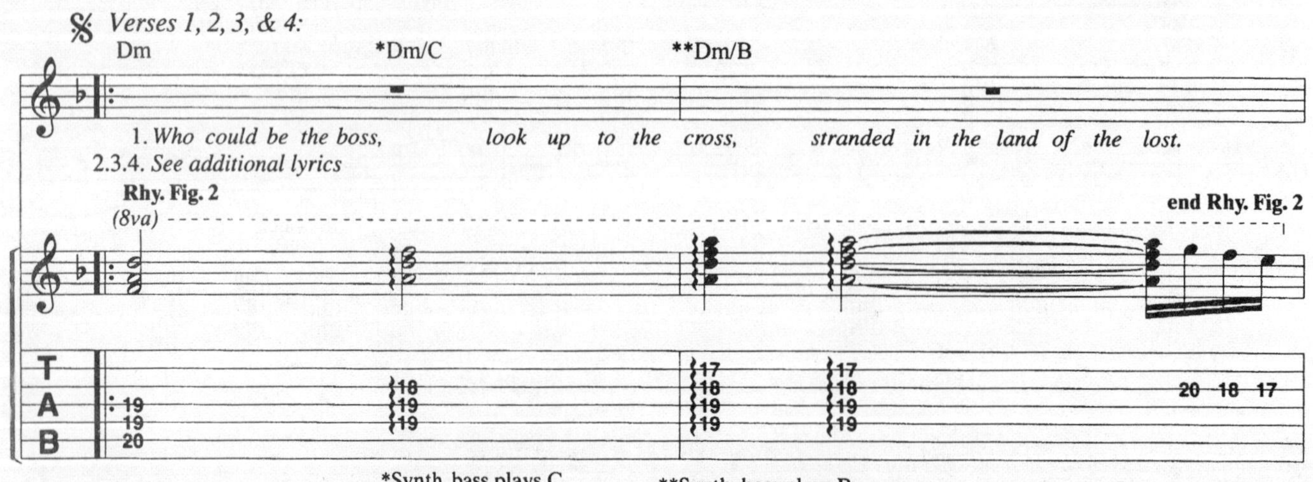

*Synth. bass plays C. **Synth. bass plays B.

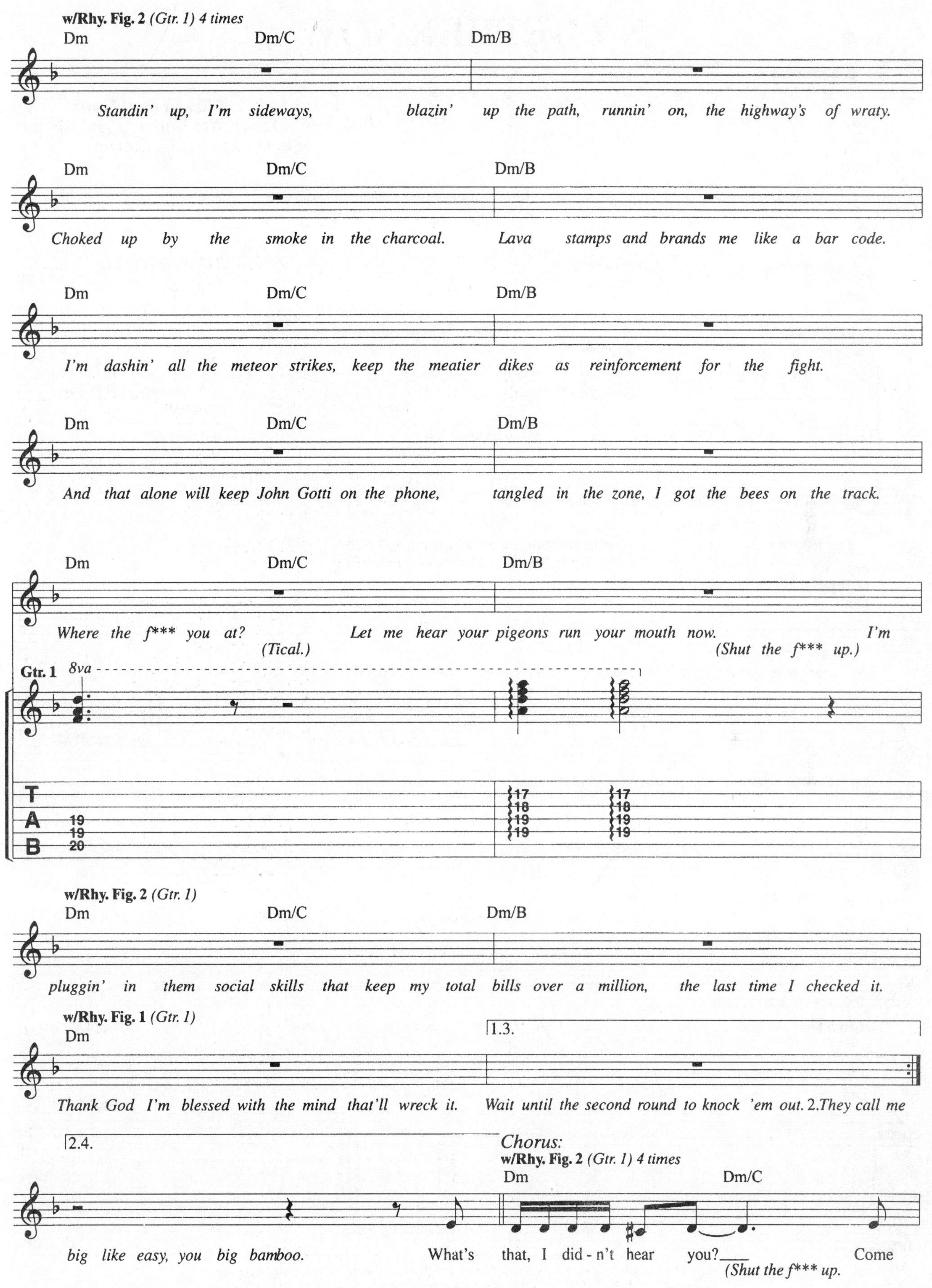
w/Rhy. Fig. 2 (Gtr. 1) 4 times
Dm Dm/C Dm/B
Standin' up, I'm sideways, blazin' up the path, runnin' on, the highway's of wraty.
Dm Dm/C Dm/B
Choked up by the smoke in the charcoal. Lava stamps and brands me like a bar code.
Dm Dm/C Dm/B
I'm dashin' all the meteor strikes, keep the meatier dikes as reinforcement for the fight.
Dm Dm/C Dm/B
And that alone will keep John Gotti on the phone, tangled in the zone, I got the bees on the track.
Dm Dm/C Dm/B
Where the f*** you at? Let me hear your pigeons run your mouth now. I'm
(Tical.) (Shut the f*** up.)
Gtr. 1 8va
T A B
19 19 20
17 18 19 19
17 18 19 19
w/Rhy. Fig. 2 (Gtr. 1)
Dm Dm/C Dm/B
pluggin' in them social skills that keep my total bills over a million, the last time I checked it.
w/Rhy. Fig. 1 (Gtr. 1)
Dm
1.3.
Thank God I'm blessed with the mind that'll wreck it. Wait until the second round to knock 'em out. 2.They call me
2.4.
Chorus:
w/Rhy. Fig. 2 (Gtr. 1) 4 times
Dm Dm/C
big like easy, you big bamboo. What's that, I did-n't hear you? Come
(Shut the f*** up.

Dm/B Dm Dm/C
on a lit - tle loud - er.___ Ev - 'ry - bod - y N 2 - geth - er now,___ what,__
Shut the f*** up. Shut the f*** up, just
Dm/B Dm Dm/C
__ uh.___ What's that, I did - n't hear you?___ Come
shut the f*** up, just shut the f*** up. Shut the f*** up.
Dm/B Dm Dm/C
on, a lit - tle loud - er.___ Ev - 'ry - bod - y N 2 - geth - er now,___ what,__
Shut the f*** up. Shut the f*** up, just
1.
Dm/B
D.S. 𝄋
2.
Dm/B
__ uh.___ __ uh.___
shut the f*** up, shut the f*** up.)
Verse 5:
w/Rhy. Fig. 2 (Gtr. 1) 4 times
Dm Dm/C Dm/B
It was over your head all day, every day. S I N Y one O three O
Dm Dm/C Dm/B
four. Wu Tang, Killer Bee and the Limp B I Z K I T.
Dm Dm/C Dm/B
Ya'll know the time, ya'll know the rhyme. It ain't easy being greasy in a world full of
w/Rhy. Fig. 1 (Gtr. 1)
Dm Dm/C Dm/B
cleanliness and... You know all that other madness we gone. Peace.
Outro:
w/Rhy. Fig. 2 (Gtr. 1) 3 times
Dm Dm/C Dm/B
Limp Bizkit. Method Man.
Dm Dm/C Dm/B
Ro - ro - rock the house, ya'll. Bring it on.

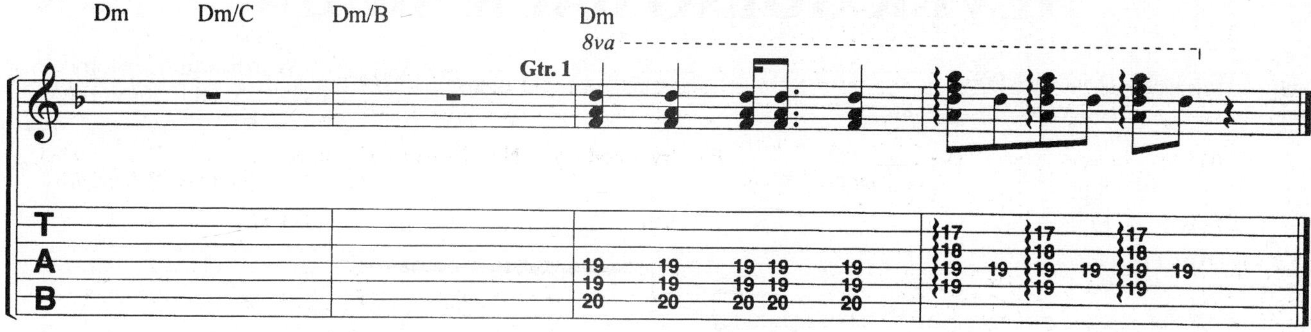

Verse 2:
They call me Big John Stud, my middle name Mudd
Dirty water flow too much for you thugs
Can't stand the flood. What up, Doc?
Hold big gun like Elmer Fudd, the sure shot.
Mister Meth, I'm unplugged, learn.
Temperature's too hot for sun block, burn.
Playing with minds, they get you state time
Lock behind twelve bars from a great mine.
Killer Bee's in the club with his lady bug,
Brought a sword to the dance floor to cut a rug.
Love is love all day till they throw slug
And take another life in cold blood.
Can't feel me till it's your blood.
Murder rate's tremendous, crime is endless.
*Same s***, different day.*
Father forgive us, they know not what they do.
All praises due, I'm big like easy, you big bamboo.
(To Chorus:)

Verse 3:
Head strong dead calm, dead by dawn.
Dead weight, they dead wrong, let's get it on.
Twelve rounds of throw down, who hold crown.
Protect the land with four pound, Limp Bizkit.
Get around like merry go, bust the scenario,
Comin' through your stereo, why risk it?
Lifestyles of the prolific and gifted,
Eight essential vitamins and minerals, delicious.
Word on the street is they bit my thesis,
Knocked out they front teethes, tryin' to taste mine.
Acting like they heard through the grapevine.
Dope feenin for the baseline, two for five by me.
Pharmaceuticals, hard as nails to the cuticles.
Where'd you find that monster? She's beautiful.
Wu Tang and Limp Bizkit roll on the set,
Kick a hole in the speaker, pull the plug and inject.

Verse 4:
My check. So what's it all about, where we gonna run?
Maybe we can meet upon the sun.
Discretion is advised for the blood of virgin eyes,
When limping on the track with the Method.
So get the sun block, you're gettin' one shot,
Until you dissolve I revolve around everything you got.
From out of nowhere, prepare, you'll be blinded by the glare.
I told you not to stare.
Now you're turned into stone
Without a microphone, but don't forget you're in a zone.
*So, shut the f*** up and take that s*** back*
*'Cause all your s***'s wacked, dodo with dodo, when it's weighed out like that.*
Burnin' up your brain like a piston, so all those who didn't listen,
Now they even knew what they're missin'.
And now they even knew that the sky was fallin' down.
Wu Tang Clan for the crown.
(To Chorus:)

NEVER GOING BACK AGAIN

Words and Music by
LINDSEY BUCKINGHAM

A13(♭9)
3141
D
312
made me see
Come down and
where I've been.
see me a - gain.
A13(♭9)
3141
D
312
Chorus:
D
7fr.
1114
A7
7fr.
1(3)24
D
7fr.
1144
Been down one
Rhy. Fig. 2
A7
7fr.
1(3)24
D
7fr.
1144
A7
7fr.
1(3)24
time.
Been down two times.

D
7fr.
1144
Bm
13 2
F♯m7
3 111
Bm
13 2
A
1114
I'm nev - er go - ing back a -
D
312
gain.
Mm,
A13(♭9)
3141
mm.

Interlude:
w/Rhy. Fig. 1 (Gtr. 1) 2 times, simile
Vocals tacet
To Coda
D
A7
D
D
A13(♭9)
D
A7
D
A13(♭9)
D
A7
w/Rhy. Fig. 2 (Gtr. 1) simile
D
A
D
A7
D
A7
D.S. al Coda
Bm
F♯m7
Bm
A
Coda
D
Mm,
hmm.

NEW WORLD MAN

Words by
NEIL PEART

Music by
GEDDY LEE and ALEX LIFESON

w/Rhy. Fig. 2 (Gtr. 1) 3 1/2 times
Fsus2
He's got a prob- lem with his poi - sons, but you
know he'll find a cure. He's clean - ing up his sys - tems,
w/Rhy. Fill 1 (Gtr. 1)
D5
to keep his na - ture pure.
Bridges 1 & 2:
Rhy. Fig. 3
Gtr. 1
F
B♭5
F/A
Gm(9)
end Rhy. Fig. 3
P.M.
w/Rhy. Fig. 3 (Gtr. 1)
1. Learn- ing to match the beat of the Old World man.
2. See additional lyrics
Rhy. Fill 1
Gtr. 2

w/Rhy. Fill 2 (Gtr. 1)
w/Rhy. Fig. 3 (Gtr. 1) 1st 2 bars only
w/Rhy. Fill 3 (Gtr. 1)
F
B♭5
F/A
Gm(9)
Learn - ing to catch the___ heat_____ of the Third World man.
Interlude 1 & 2:
Gtr. 1
D5
1. He's got___ to make__ his own__
2. See additional lyrics
Rhy. Fill 2
Gtr. 1
P.M.
Rhy. Fill 3
Gtr. 1
P.M.

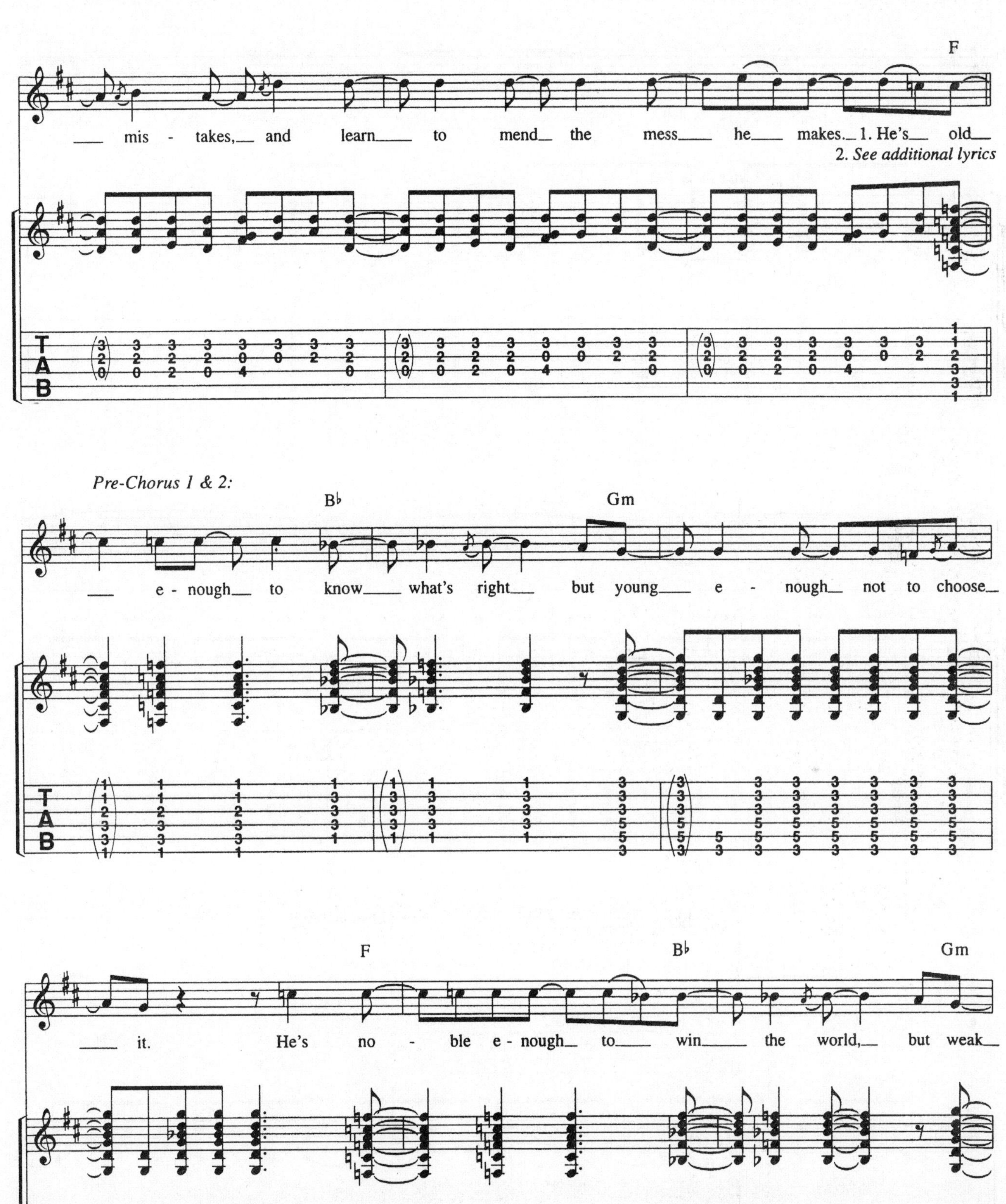
F
mis - takes, and learn to mend the mess he makes. 1. He's old
2. See additional lyrics
TAB
Pre-Chorus 1 & 2:
B♭
Gm
e - nough to know what's right but young e - nough not to choose
TAB
F
B♭
Gm
it. He's no - ble e - nough to win the world, but weak
TAB

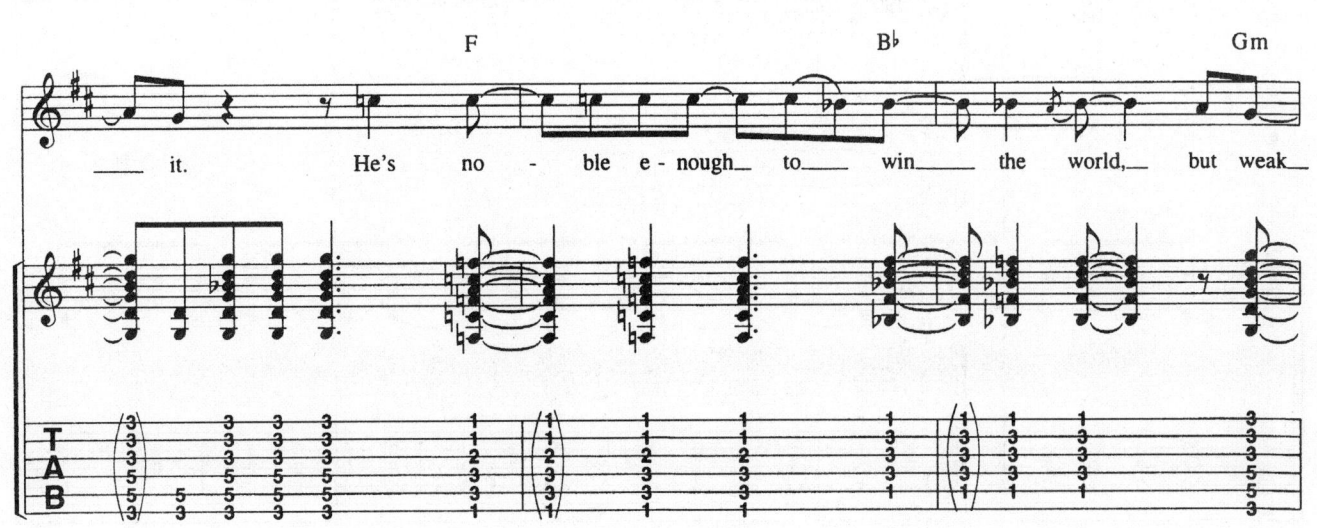

e - nough
to
lose
it.
He's
a
New
Chorus:
D5
World
Man.
1.
2. He's
a
T
A
B

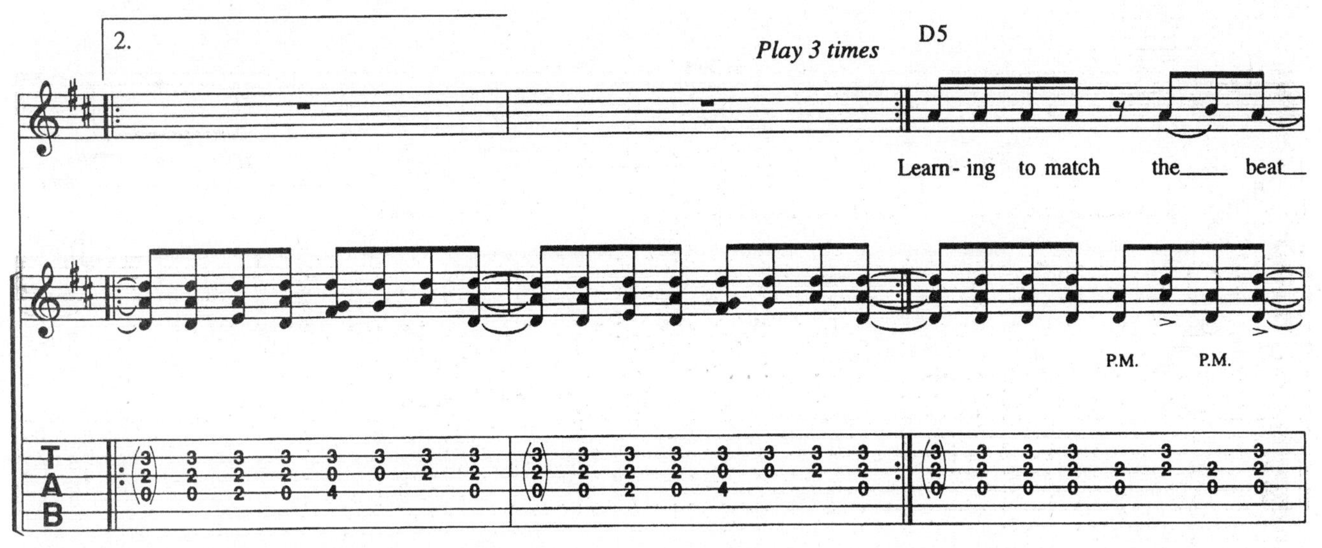
2.
Play 3 times
D5
Learn- ing to match the___ beat___
P.M. P.M.

___ of the Old World man.
He's learn-
P.M. P.M. P.M. P.M. P.M. P.M. P.M. P.M. P.M.

ing to catch the___ heat___ of the Third World man.
P.M. P.M. P.M. P.M. P.M. P.M. P.M. P.M.

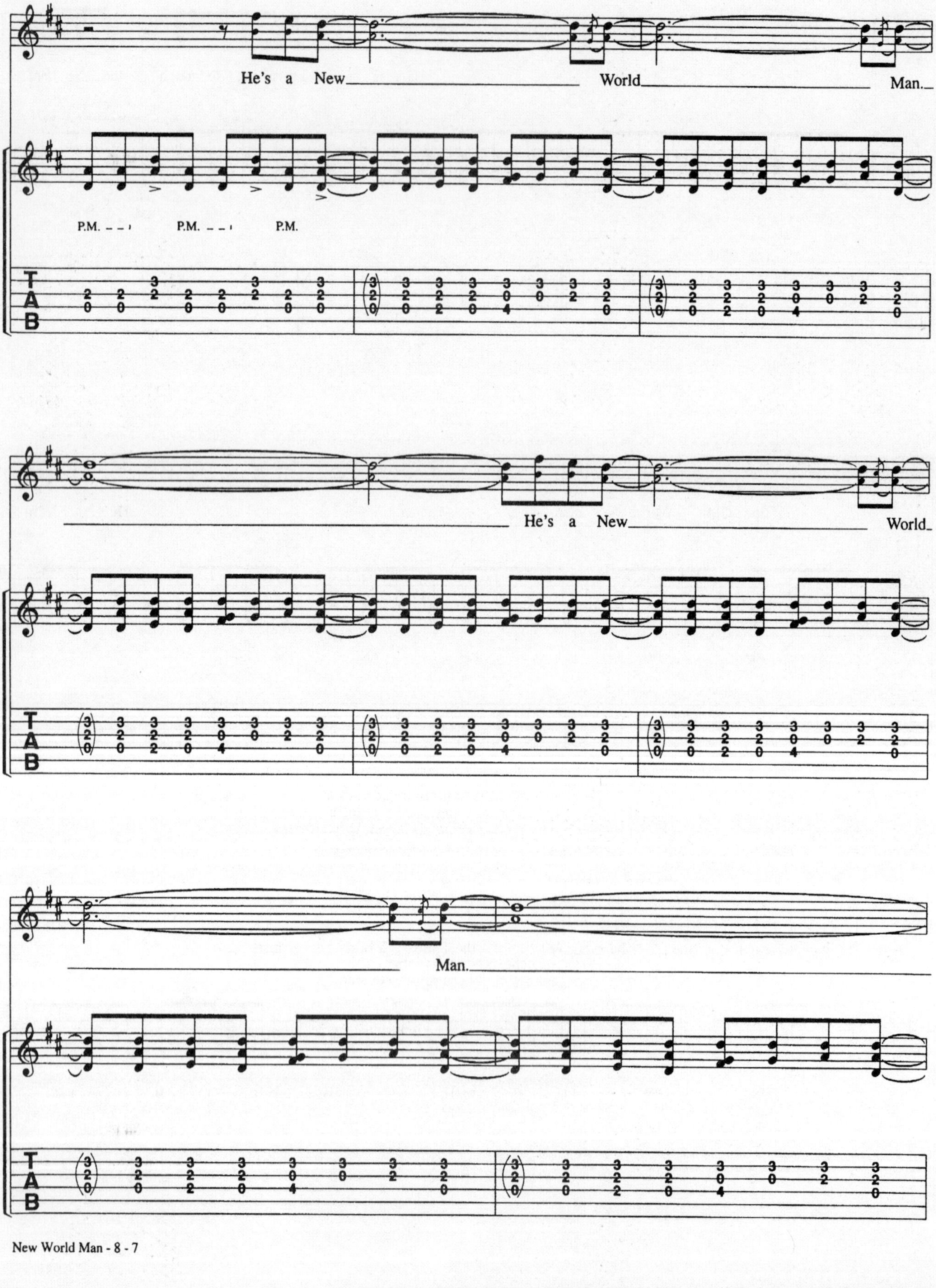

He's a New World Man.

P.M. P.M. P.M.

He's a New World

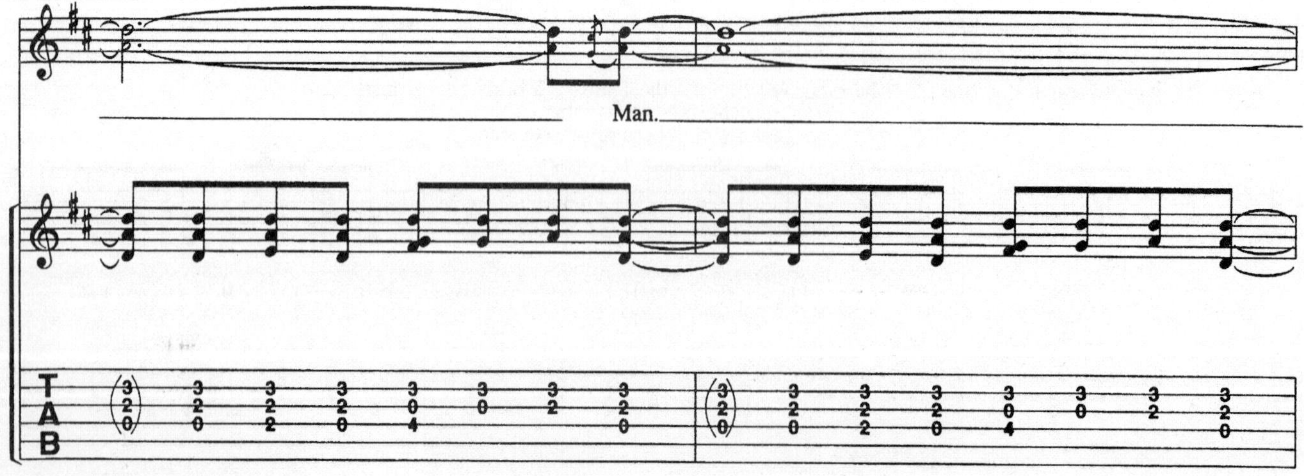

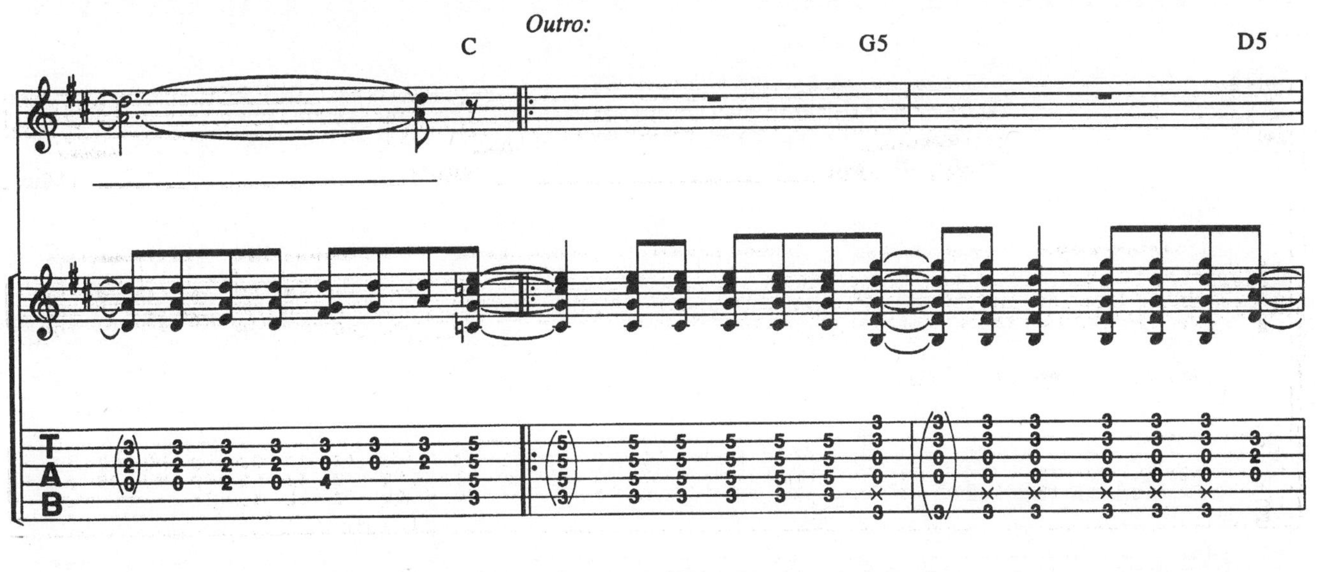

Verse 2:
He's a radio receiver, tuned to factories and farms.
He's a writer and arranger and a young boy bearing arms.
He's got a problem with his power, with weapons on patrol.
He's got to walk a fine line and keep his self-control.

Bridge 2:
Trying to save the day for the Old World man.
Trying to pave the way for the Third World man.

Interlude 2:
He's not concerned with yesterday.
He knows constant change is here today.

Pre-Chorus 2:
He's noble enough to know what's right,
But weak enough not to choose it.
He's wise enough to win the world,
But fool enough to lose it.

THE NIGHT THEY DROVE OLD DIXIE DOWN

Robertson played fingerpicking-style backup acoustic guitar on this, the Band's most well-known song. It first appeared on "The Band" album, and was later a hit for Joan Baez. It has also been recorded by Merl Saunders, Tanya Tucker and others.

By
ROBBIE ROBERTSON

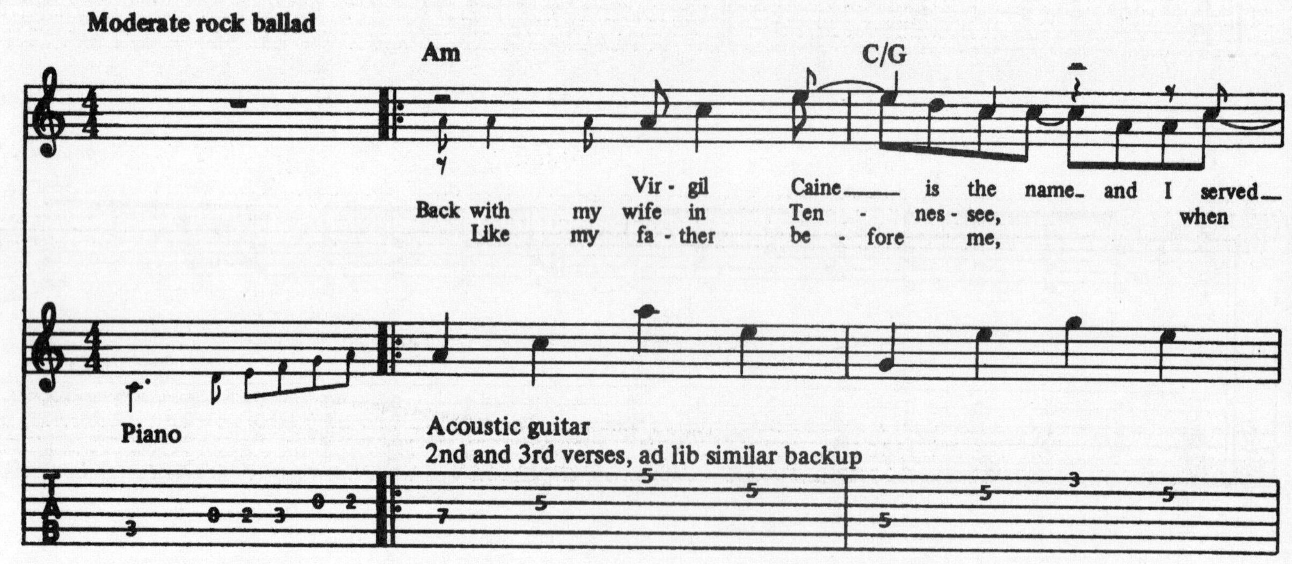

C/G
F
F/E
cav - al - ry came ___ and tore up the tracks a - gain. ___
quick, come see, there goes Rob - ert E.
bove me, who took a Reb - el stand; ___
Dm
Am/E
In the win - ter of
Lee." ___ Now, I don't mind
he was just eigh - teen,
F
C
'six - ty - five, we were hun - gry, just
chop - pin' wood, and I don't care if the
proud and brave, but a Yan - kee laid him

F
Am/E
bare - ly a - live.
mon - ey's no good.
in his grave.
By May the tenth,
Ya take what ya need and ya
I swear by the mud be - low
F
C
Rich - mond had fell; it's a time
leave the rest, but they should nev - er
my feet, ya can't raise a
I re -
have
Caine back
Dm
D
mem - ber, oh, so well:
tak - en the ver - y best.
up when he's in de - feat.
The

C/G
F
night they drove old Dix - ie down,
C/G
F
and the bells were ring - in'; the
C/G
F
night they drove old Dix - ie down,
C/G
F
and the peo - ple were sing - in', they went

C/G
Am
Gsus
"La la la la la, la la la la la la
F
la la la."
1.C/E
C
Fade on D.S.
Piano
2. C
F
C
Piano
D.S. 𝄋 play 1st ending and Fade
3. C
Bm
B♭
F/A
Fm6/A♭
C/G
G♭dim
The
Piano

NIGHTS IN WHITE SATIN

Words and Music by
JUSTIN HAYWARD

To Coda
1.
2.
Em
D
Em
D
Em
D
Em
love you,
oh.
Oh, how I love you.
Interlude 1:
Flute
loco
D
C
B7
Em
D
C
B7
Em
C
Em
C
Am
B7
Am
B7
Em
D
C
Em
D.S. 𝄋 al Coda
D
Em
D
Coda
Em
D
Em
A
Acous. Gtr.
Resume rhy. fig simile
Oh, how I love you.
Yes, I love you,
yes, I
C
Em
D
Em
D
love you,
oh,
how I
love you,
oh, how I love you.
Em
Interlude 2:
Strings

Spoken: Breathe deep, the gathering gloom,
Watched lights fade from every room.
Bedsitter pensive people look back and lament,
Another day's useless, energy spent.
Impassioned lovers, wrestle as one
Lonely man cries for love and has none.
New mother picks up and suckles her son,
Senior citizens wish they were young.
Cold hearted orb that rules the night,
Removes the colors from our sight.
Red is gray, and yellow white,
But we decide which is right,
And which is an illusion.

NOOKIE

*Tuning (all gtrs.):
⑥=F♯ ③=E
⑤=F♯ ②=omit
④=B ①=omit

Lyric by FRED DURST
Music by WES BORLAND, SAM RIVERS, JOHN OTTO and LEOR DIMANT

Moderately slow rock ♩ = 98
Intro:

Play 4 times
N.C.
8vb
loco
8vb
Play 4 times
loco
8vb
Riff A
8vb
loco
8vb
loco
8vb
Gtr. 1
**
mf
clean tone
f
dist. tone
T
A
B
15
13
3 0 0 0 3 0
15
13
0
3 0 0
15
13
0 3 0
15
13
0

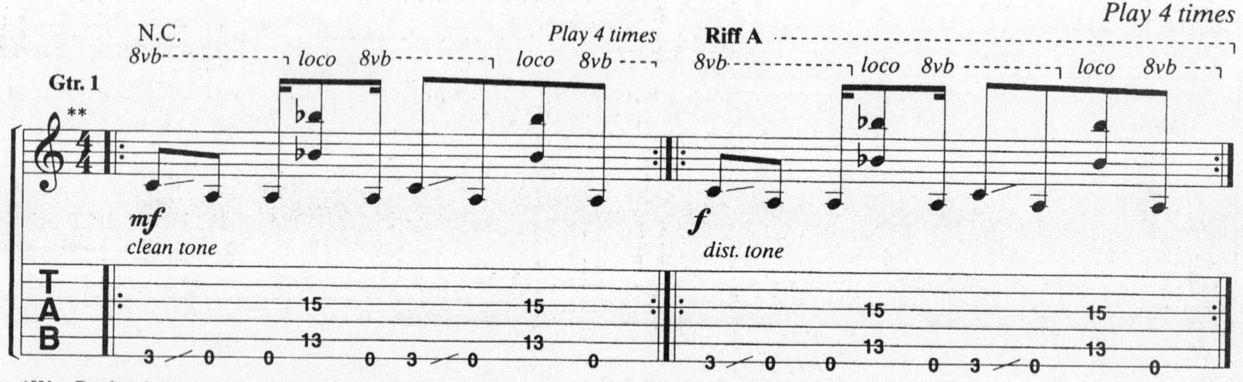

*Wes Borland uses a custom 4-string guitar. You can use a standard 6- or 7-string, remove the top strings, and tune the bottom 4 strings as indicated using heavy gauge strings (the 6th is a .65 bass string).
**Music sounds a minor 3rd lower than written.

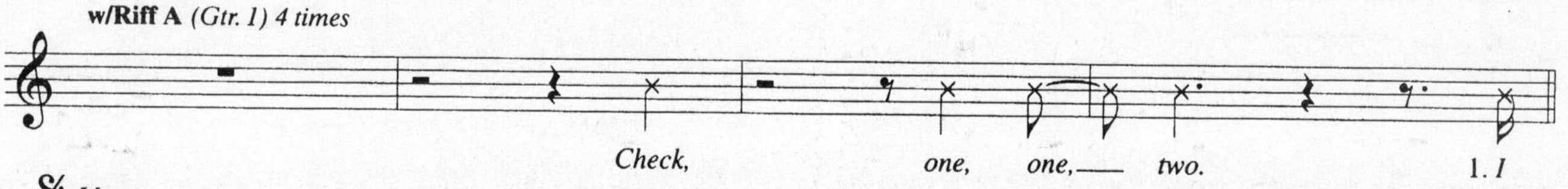

w/Riff A (Gtr. 1) 4 times
Check, one, one, two. 1. I

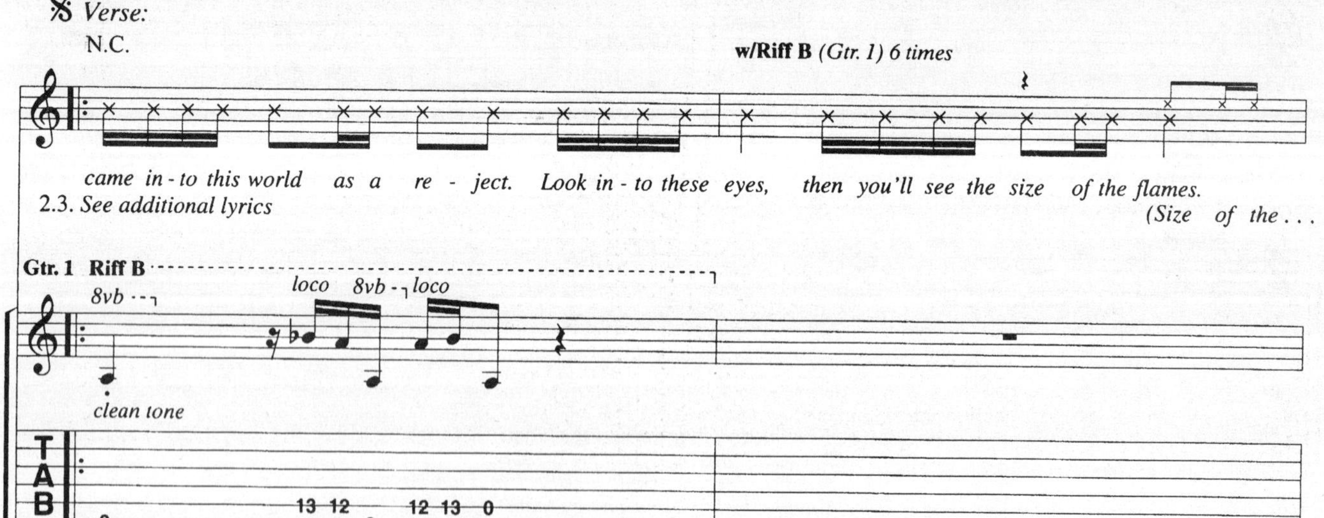

𝄋 Verse:
N.C.
w/Riff B (Gtr. 1) 6 times
came in - to this world as a re - ject. Look in - to these eyes, then you'll see the size of the flames.
2.3. See additional lyrics
(Size of the . . .
Gtr. 1 Riff B
8vb
loco
8vb
loco
clean tone
T
A
B
0
13 12
0
12 13 0

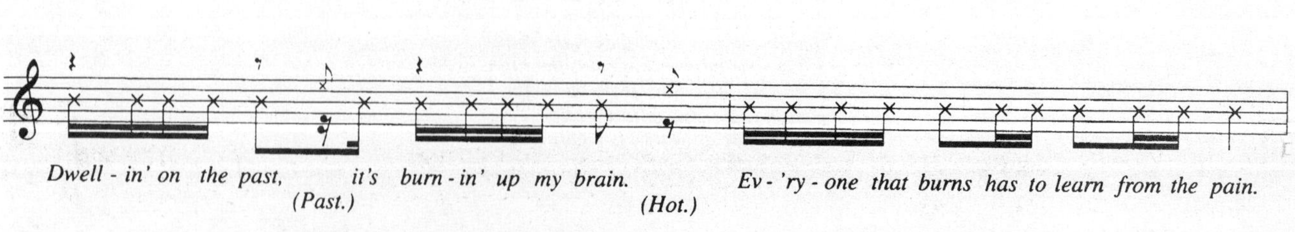

Dwell - in' on the past, it's burn - in' up my brain. Ev - 'ry - one that burns has to learn from the pain.
(Past.)
(Hot.)

Hey, — I think a - bout the day my girl-ie ran a-way with my pay when fel - las came to
(Days.)

w/Fill 1 (Gtr. 2)
1.
play. Now she's stuck with my hom - ies that she f***ed, and I'm just a suck-er with a lump in my
(Play.)
(Ooh.)
Gtr. 1
Rhy. Fill 1
8vb
loco
8vb
loco
T
A
B
0
13 12
0 12 13
0

w/Riff C (Gtr. 3) 3 times
throat like a chump, like a chump, like a chump, like a
(Hey. Hey. Hey. Hey.
Riff C
8vb loco 8vb loco 8vb loco 8vb loco 8vb loco
Gtr. 1
P.M. P.M. P.M. P.M. P.M.
T
A
B
0 14 12 0 0 14 12 0 0 14 12 0 0 14 12 0 0 14 12 15 13

chump, like a chump, like a chump, like a chump. 2. Should I be
Hey. Hey. Hey. Hey.)

2.
To Next Strain (To Chorus:)
3.
w/Riff B (Gtr. 1)
w/Rhy. Fill 1 (Gtr. 1)
w/Riff C (Gtr. 1) 4 times
I won't lie that I can't de-ny.
heart in a blend-er and still I sur-ren-dered
like a chump, like a
(Hey. Hey.
chump, like a chump, like a chump, like a chump, like a chump, like a chump.
Hey. Hey. Hey. Hey. Hey.)
Chorus:
w/Riff A (Gtr. 1) 8 times
I did it all for the nook-ie, come on, the nook-ie, come on. So you can take that cook-ie and
Gtr. 2
Fill 2
end Fill 2
dist. tone
1
1/2
w/Fill 2 (Gtr. 2) 4 times
stick it up your. . . Yeah! Stick it up your. . . Yeah! Stick it up your. . . Yeah! Stick it up your. . .
I did it all for the nook-ie, come on, the nook-ie, come on. So you can take that cook-ie and
To Coda
1.
D.S.
stick it up your. . . Yeah! Stick it up your. . . Yeah! Stick it up your. . . Yeah! Stick it up your. . .
2.
Bridge:
N.C.(A5)
Stick it up your. . . Yeah! Stick it up your. . .
I'm on - ly hu -
Riff D
8vb
Gtr. 1 (clean-tone)
mf

w/Bkgd. vcl. ad lib. (next 14 bars)
G5
C5
B♭5
man.
It's so eas - y for your friends
to give you their ad - vice.
end Riff D
8vb
loco
w/Riff D (Gtr. 1) 3 times
A5
They'll tell you just let it go.
It's
G5
C5
B♭5
A5
eas - i - er said than done.
I ap - pre - ci - ate it.
G5
C5
B♭5
I do, but just leave me a - lone.
G5
C5
B♭5
Leave me a - lone.
Just leave me a - lone,
A5
C5
Ain't noth - ing gon - na change,
'cause you can go a - way
a - lone,
a - lone,
Riff E
8vb loco
8vb loco
Gtr. 1
(w/dist)

D5
Bb5
A5
and I'm just gon - na stay here and al - ways be the same.
a - lone,
a - lone,
8vb loco
8vb loco
end Riff E
f
w/Riffs E (Gtr. 1) 2 times & E1 (Gtr. 2) 1 1/2 times
C5
Ain't noth - ing gon - na change,
'cause you can go a - way
a - lone,
a - lone,
D5
Bb5
A5
and I'm just gon - na stay here and al - ways be the same.
a - lone.
C5
Ain't noth - ing gon - na change,
'cause you can go a - way
Al - ways be the same,
al - ways be the same,
D5
E5
G5
D.S.S. al Coda
and I'm just gon - na stay here and al - ways be the same.
you'll al - ways be the same.
Gtr. 2
*Hold note into Chorus.

Coda
N.C.

Stick it up your. . . Yeah! Stick it up your. . .

Outro:
w/Fill 3 (Gtr. 2) 1st time

Gtr. 1 (clean tone)

8vb loco 8vb loco 8vb loco 8vb loco 8vb loco

mf

P.M. P.M. P.M. P.M. P.M.

| T A B | 14 12 0 | 14 12 0 0 0 | 14 12 0 0 | 14 12 0 0 | 14⁄15 12⁄13 |

8vb loco 8vb loco 8vb loco 8vb loco 8vb loco

Repeat and fade

P.M. P.M. P.M. P.M. P.M. P.M. P.M. P.M.

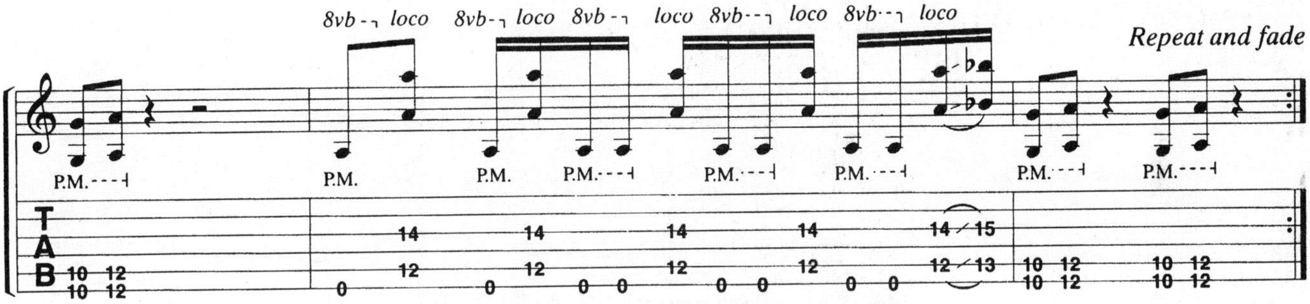

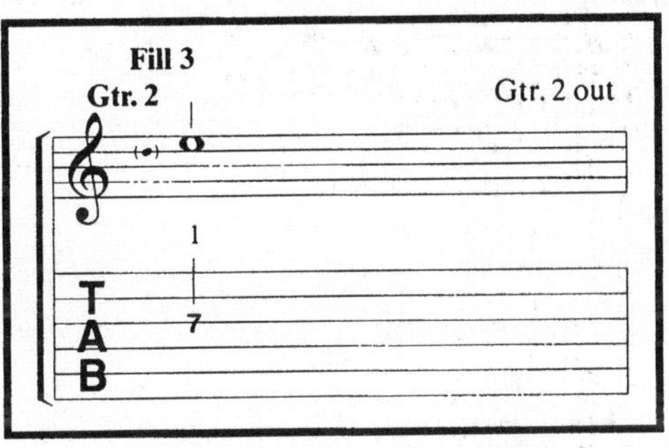

Verse 2:
Should I be feelin' bad? (No.) Should I be feelin' good? (No.)
It's kinda sad, I'm the laughin' stock of the neighborhood.
And you would think that I'd be movin' on, (Movin'.)
*But I'm a sucker like I said, f***-up in the head. (Not.)*
Maybe she just made a mistake and I should give her a break.
My heart'll ache either way.
Hey, what the hell. What you want me to say?
I won't lie that I can't deny.
(To Chorus:)

Verse 3:
Why did it take so long?
Why did I wait so long, huh, to figure it out?
But I didn't.
And I'm the only one underneath the sun who didn't get it.
I can't believe that I could be deceived (But you were.) by my so-called girl,
But in reality had a hidden agenda.
She put my tender heart in a blender,
And still I surrendered
(Hey.) like a chump, etc.
(To Chorus:)

OH, PRETTY WOMAN

Words and Music by
ROY ORBISON and BILL DEES

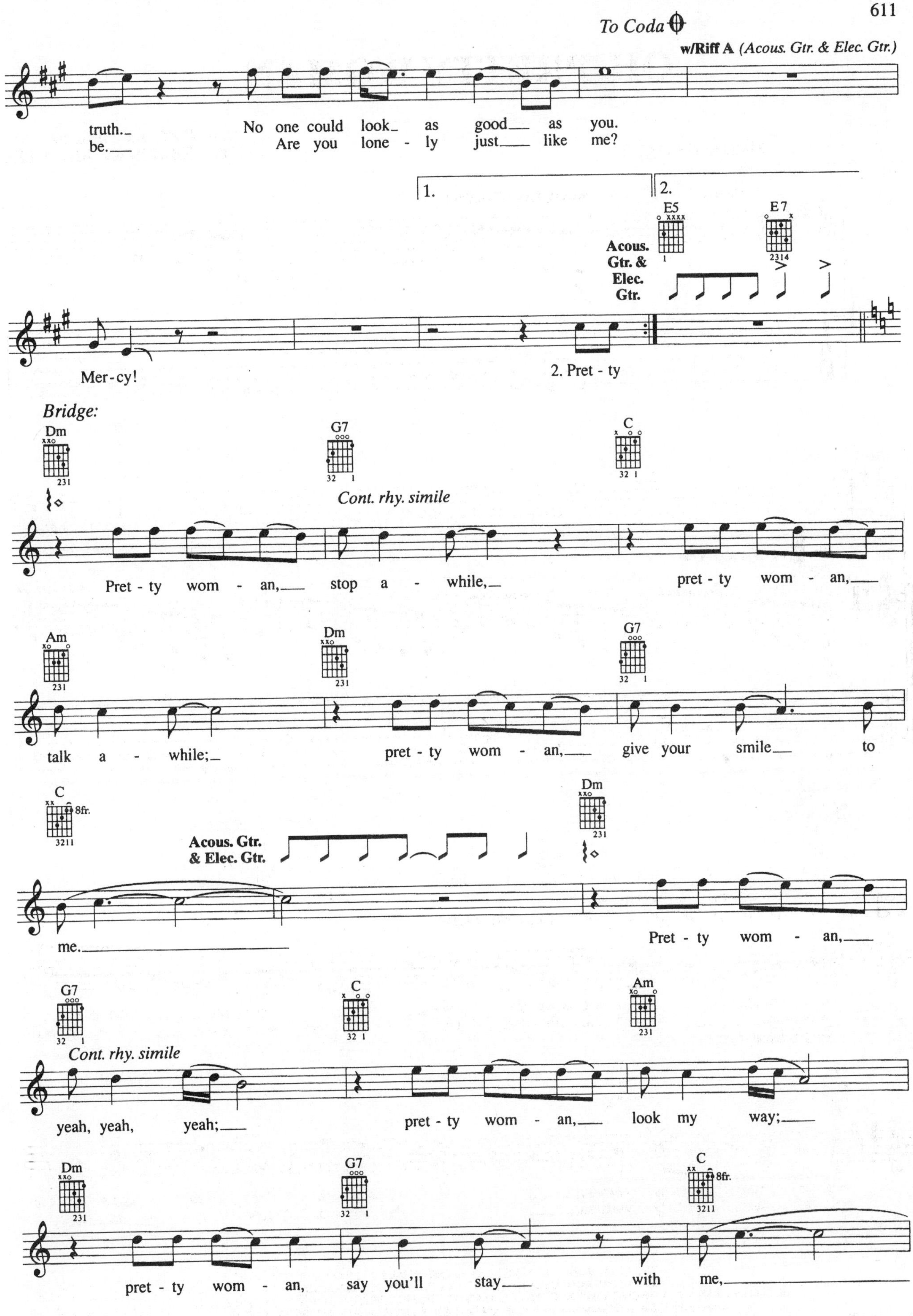

To Coda 

w/Riff A *(Acous. Gtr. & Elec. Gtr.)*

truth.__ No one could look__ as good__ as you.
be.__ Are you lone - ly just__ like me?

1. 2.

E5 E7

Acous. Gtr. & Elec. Gtr.

Mer-cy! 2. Pret - ty

Bridge:

Dm G7 C

Cont. rhy. simile

Pret - ty wom - an,__ stop a - while,__ pret - ty wom - an,__

Am Dm G7

talk a - while;__ pret - ty wom - an,__ give your smile__ to

C 8fr. Dm

Acous. Gtr. & Elec. Gtr.

me.__ Pret - ty wom - an,__

G7 C Am

Cont. rhy. simile

yeah, yeah, yeah;__ pret - ty wom - an,__ look my way;__

Dm G7 C 8fr.

pret - ty wom - an, say you'll stay__ with me,__

A7
F#m
Dm
Acous. Gtr. & Elec. Gtr.
Cont. rhy. simile
'cause I need you.
I'll treat you
E7
A7
F#m
Dm
right.
Come to me, baby,
be mine to-
w/Riff A (Elec. Gtr.)
E7
Acous. Gtr.
D.S. % al Coda
night.
3. Pret-ty
Coda
E7
Acous. Gtr. & Elec. Gtr.
If that's the way it must be, o-kay.
I guess I'll go on home, it's late.
There'll be to-
mor-row night, but wait!
What do I see?

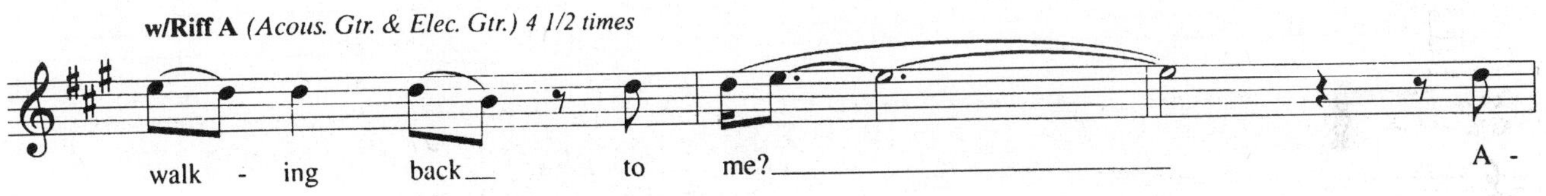

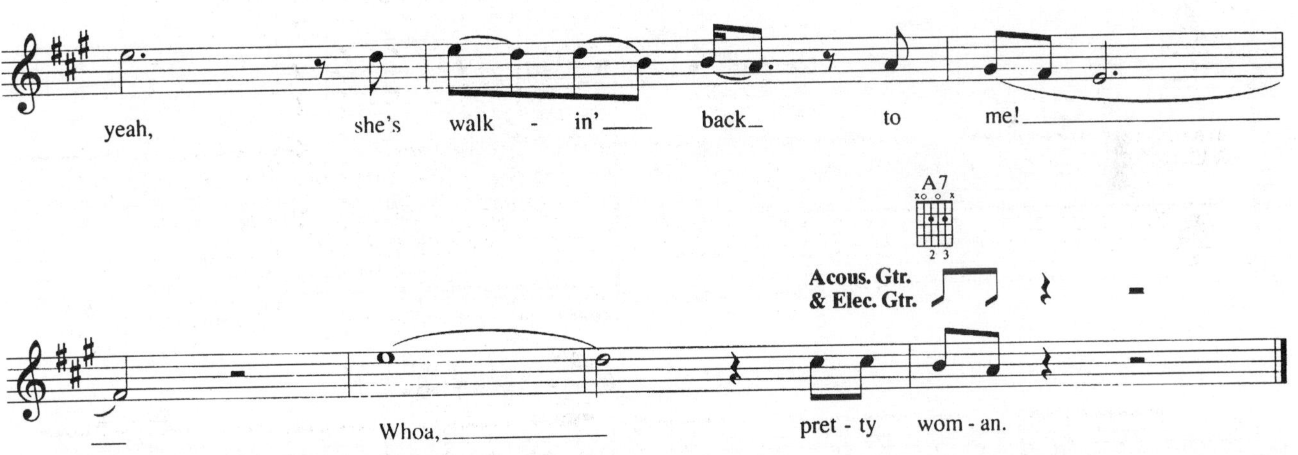

Verse 2:
Pretty woman, don't walk on by;
Pretty woman, don't make my cry;
Pretty woman, don't walk away.
(To Coda)

OLD MAN

Words and Music by
NEIL YOUNG

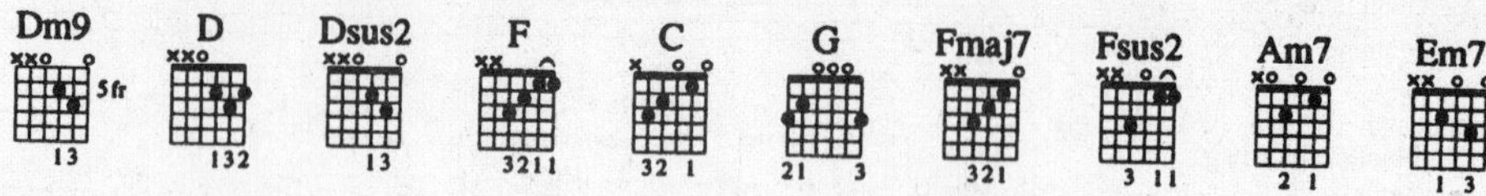

D
F
look at my life,
I'm a lot like you were.
Rhy. Fig. 1
To Coda
C
G
D
Fmaj7
Verse :
C
F Fsus2 F
D
F
1. Old man, look at my life,
2. See additional lyrics
end Rhy. Fig. 1
C
G
D
F Fsus2 F
twen-ty-four and there's so much more. Live a-lone in a par - a - dise that
let ring

C
F
Fsus2
F
D
F
Fsus2
F
makes me think _ of two. ______
Love lost,
such a cost, _
C
G
D
give me things
that
don't _
get
lost,
like a coin
that
C
F
C
G
won't
get
tossed,
roll - in' home _ to you. ______
D
Dsus
D
Dsus2
Am7
Em7
G
Rhy. Fig. 2
end Rhy. Fig. 2
TAB

Verse 2:
Lullabies look in your eyes, run around the same old town.
Doesn't mean that much to me to mean that much to you.
I've been first and last, look at how the time goes past.
But I'm all alone at last, rolling home to you.
(To Chorus:)

ONE HEADLIGHT

Words and Music by
JAKOB DYLAN

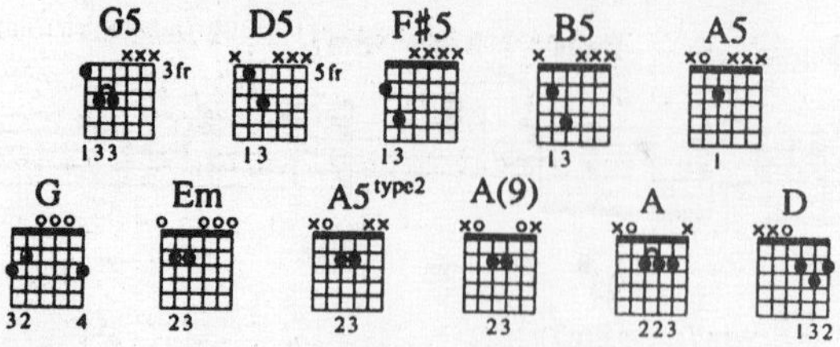

G5 D5 F#5 B5 A5
G Em A5 type2 A(9) A D

Gtr. 1 tuned:
⑥-D ③-G
⑤-A ②-B
④-D ①-E

Gtr. 3 (Dobro) tuned:
⑥-D ③-G
⑤-G ②-B
④-D ①-D

Moderately ♩ = 106

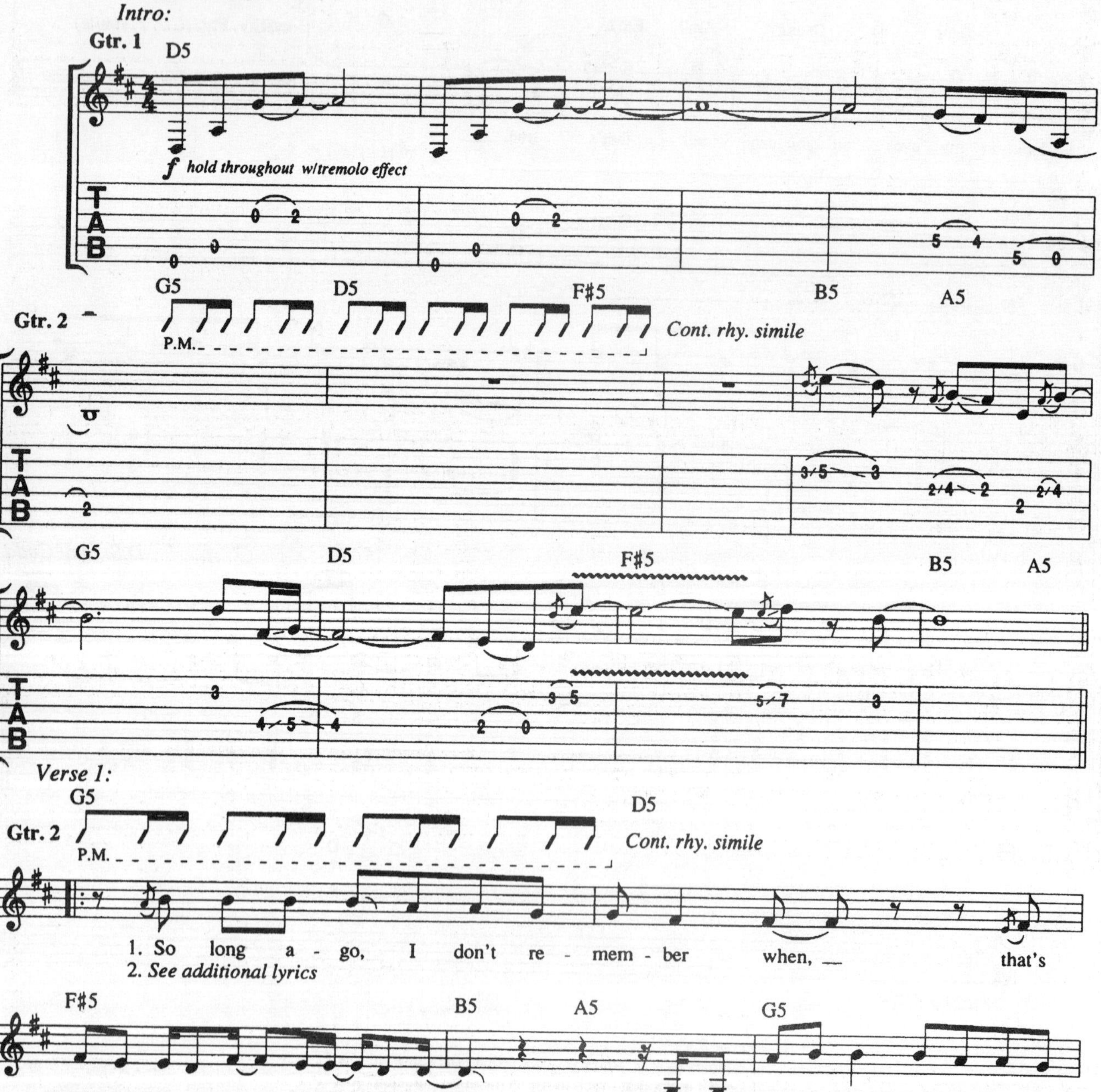

Intro:

Gtr. 1
D5

f *hold throughout w/tremolo effect*

G5 D5 F#5 B5 A5
Gtr. 2
P.M.
Cont. rhy. simile

G5 D5 F#5 B5 A5

Verse 1:
G5

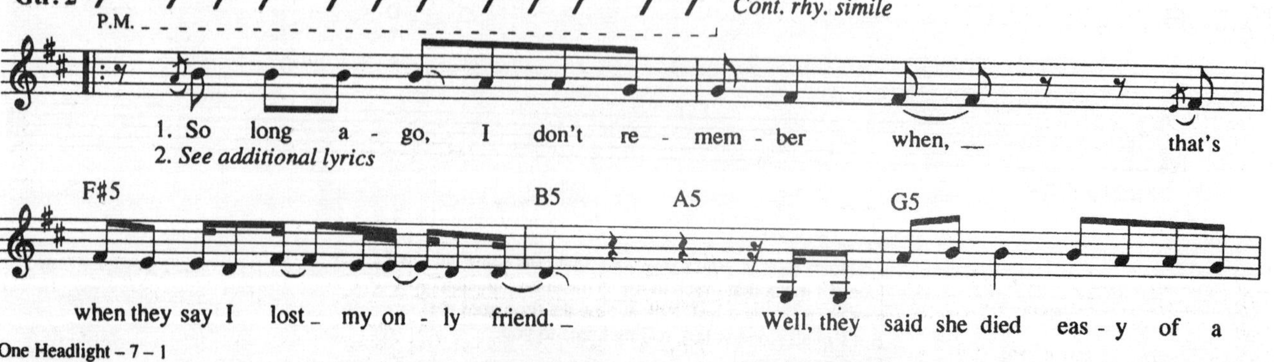

*2 gtrs. arr. for 1.

A5 type2
A(9)
G
D5
F♯
A
D5
bet - ter than in the mid - dle. But me and Cin - der - el - la, we put it all _ to - geth - er,
Em
A
A(9)
end Rhy. Fig. 2
Cont. in notation
we can drive it home with one _ head -
G5
D5
F♯5
B5
A5
Gtr. 2
Cont. rhy. simile
light.
3. She said, "It's
Gtr. 1
Verses 3 & 5:
G5
D5
F♯5
Gtr. 2
Cont. rhy. simile
P.M.
cold. _ An' it feels like In - de - pend-ence Day, _ and I can't _ break a - way from this pa -
5. See additional lyrics
*Gtr. 1
*Gtrs. 1 & 3 ad lib. simile on Verse 4.

B5
A5
G5
D5
rade. _
But there's got to be an o - pen - ing _
some-where here in front of me, _
harm.
F#5
B5
A5
G5
through this maze of ug - li - ness and greed." _
I seen the sign _ up a - head ___ at the
D5
F#5
B5
A5
Coun-ty Line Bridge,
say-in', "All is good and noth-ing-ness is dead." _
4. Run -
1/2
1/2
Verses 4 & 6:
G5
D5
- ning till she's out of breath. She ran un - til there's noth - ing left. She
6. See additional lyrics

F♯5
B5
A5
hit the end, it's just her win - dow ledge.
1/2
w/Rhy. Fig. 1 (Gtr. 1) simile
G5
F♯5
Hey,
Chorus:
w/Rhy. Fig. 2 (Gtr. 1) simile
G
D5
Em
come on, try a lit - tle, noth-in' is for - ev - er. There's got to be some-thin'
A5type2
A(9)
G
D5
bet - ter than in the mid - dle. But me and Cin - der - el - la, we put it all to - geth - er,
To Coda
Em
A
A(9)
we can drive it home
with one head -
Guitar Solo:
G5
D5
F♯5
Gtr. 2
Cont. rhy. simile
P.M.
light.
Gtr. 1 (w/slide)
8va throughout section

D.S.𝄋 al Coda
B5
A5
5. This place is
Coda
Guitar Solo:
G
D
Gtr. 2
Cont. rhy. simile
with one head - light.
Gtr. 1
hold bend
1/2
Em
A
G
hold bend
1/2
1/2
1/2
D
Em
A
Gtr. 3 (Dobro w/slide)

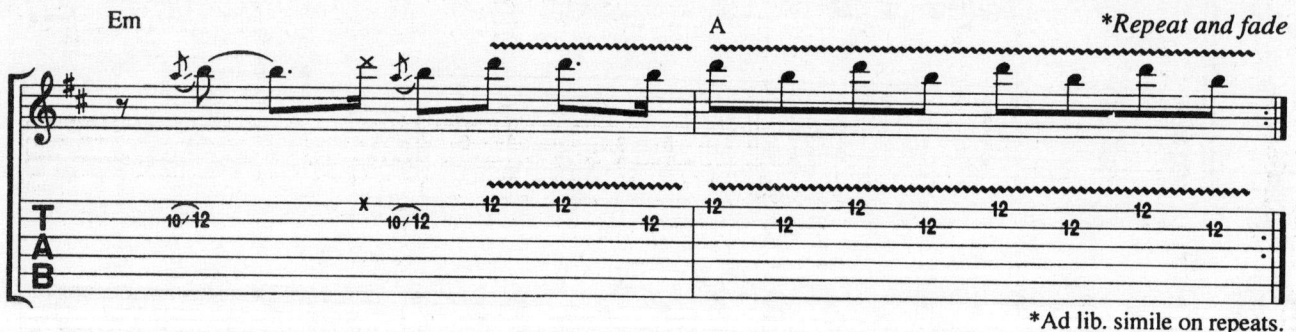

*Ad lib. simile on repeats.

Verse 2:
I seen the sun comin' up at the funeral at dawn,
Of the long broken arm of human law.
Now, it always seemed such a waste,
She always had a pretty face;
I wondered why she hung around this place.
(To Chorus:)

Verse 5:
This place is old, and it feels just like a beat-up truck.
I turn the engine, but the engine doesn't turn.
It smells of cheap wine and cigarettes,
This place is always such a mess;
Sometimes I think I'd like to watch it burn.

Verse 6:
Now I sit alone, and I feel just like somebody else.
Man, I ain't changed, but I know I ain't the same.
But somewhere here, in between these city walls of dying dreams,
I think her death, it must be killing me.
(To Chorus:)

ONE OF US

Words and Music by
ERIC BAZILIAN

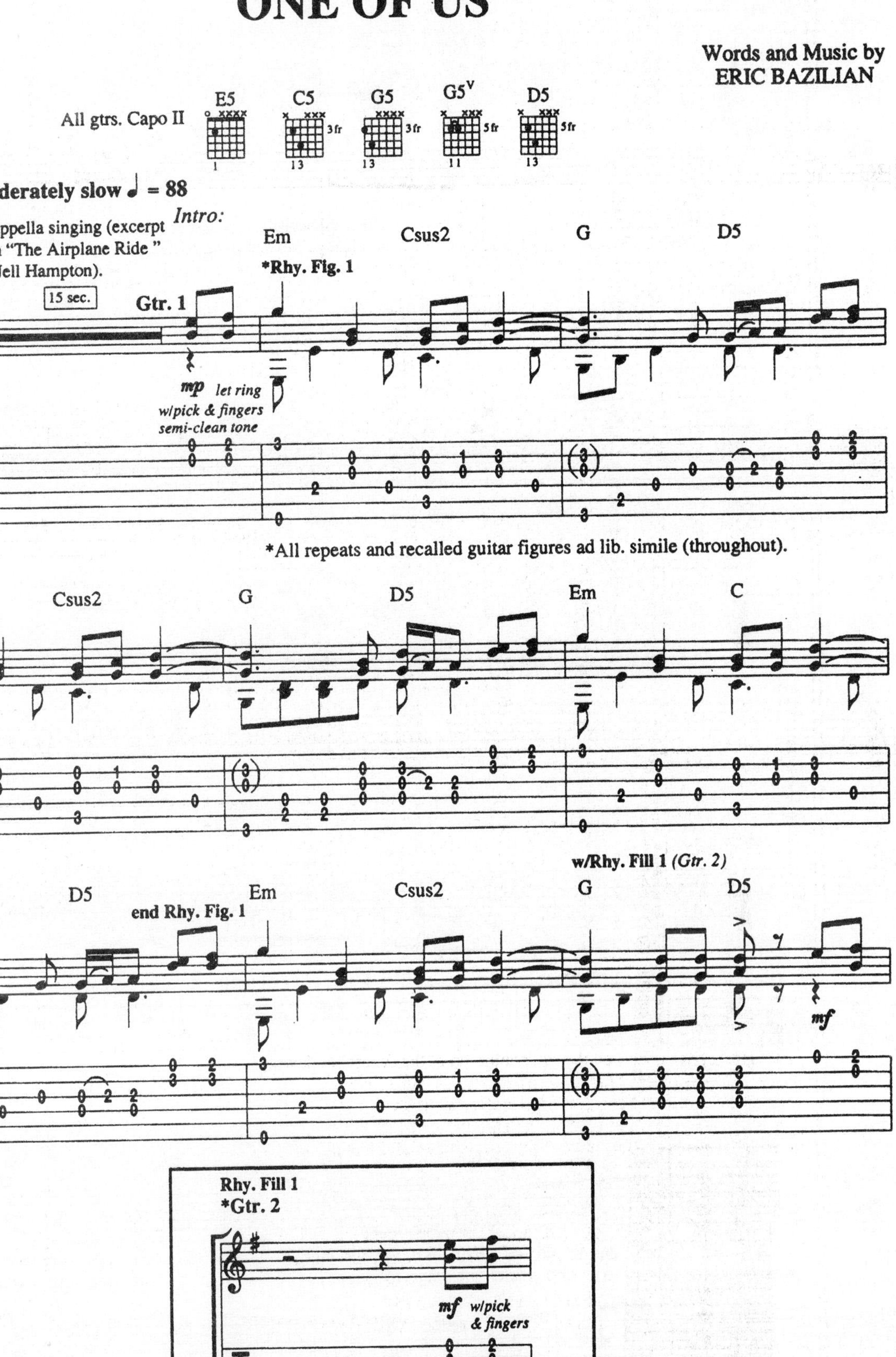

w/Rhy. Fig. 1 (Gtrs. 1 & 2)
E5 C5 G5 G5ᵛ D5 E5 C5
Rhy. Fig. 1A
Gtr. 3
w/distortion
*Throughout Rhy. Fig. 2A & Rhy. Fill 2A, when H is indicated don't strike chord. Hammer on ④ while letting ⑤ ring.
Hey, yeah,
G5 G5ᵛ D5 E5 C5 G5 G5ᵛ D end Rhy. Fig. 1A
yeah, yeah, yeah, yeah.
(Gtr. 3 out) Verses 1 & 2:
E5 C5 G5 G5ᵛ D5 Em C
Rhy. Fill 2A
end Rhy. Fill 2A
sl.
1. If God had a name,
God had a face,
Gtrs. 1 & 2
Rhy. Fill 2
(Gtr. 2 out)
end Rhy. Fill 2
Gtr. 1
mp
P.M.
G D5 Em C G D5
what would it be and would you call it to his face if you were faced with him in
what would it look like and would you want to see, if see - ing meant that you would

Em
C
G
D5
Em
C
all his ___ glo - ry?
have to be - lieve ___
What would you ask if you had just one ques-tion?
in things like heav - en and in Je - sus and the saints and
Pre-Chorus:
2nd time w/Riff A (Gtr. 3)
G
D5
C
Csus2
D
Dsus
D
all the proph - ets?
And
And
yeah, yeah, God is ___ great.
Rhy. Fig. 2
w/Rhy. Fill 1 (Gtr. 2)
C
Csus2
D5
C
Csus2
Dsus
D
Yeah, yeah, God is ___ good. ___ Yeah, yeah, yeah, yeah, yeah. What if
end Rhy. Fig. 2
H
mf
Riff A
Gtr. 3
1.
2.

Chorus:
w/Rhy. Figs. 1 (Gtrs. 1 & 2) & 1A (Gtr. 3)
w/Bkgd. Voc. Fig. 1 3rd time only
E5 C5 G5 G5 D5 E5 C5 G5 G5 D5
God was one of us, just a slob like one of us, just a
E5 C5 G5 G5 D5
stran - ger on the bus try'n' to make his way home?
1.
w/Rhy. Fills 2 (Gtrs. 1 & 2) & 2A (Gtr. 3)
E5 C5 G5 G5 D5
2. If
2.
w/Rhy. Fill 3 (Gtrs. 1 & 2)
w/Rhy. Fig. 1A (Gtr. 3) 1st 2 bars only
w/Rhy. Figs. 1 (Gtrs. 1 & 2) (1st 2 bars only)
& 1A (Gtr. 3) (complete)
E5 C5 G5 G5 D5 E5 C5 G5 G5 D5
home?
1. He's try'n' to make his way home, back up to heav-en all a -
2. Just try'n' to make his way home, like a ho - ly roll-in'
w/Rhy. Fill 3 (Gtrs. 1 & 2)
w/Rhy. Fill 2
To Coda
E5 C5 G5 G5 D5 E5 C5 G5 G5 D5
lone. No-bod - y call - ing on the phone, 'cept for the Pope, may-be, in
stone. Back up to heav-en all a - lone, just try'n' to make his way
Guitar Solo:
w/Rhy. Fig. 2 (Gtr. 2)
C5 D5 C5
Gtr. 3
Rome.
A.H.
(8va)
Gtr. 1
w/distortion
A.H.
1/2
1/2
Bkgd. Voc. Fig. 1
Sing 7 times
Oh.
Rhy. Fill 3
Gtrs. 1 & 2

D5
C5
w/Rhy. Figs. 1 (Gtr. 2) & 1A (Gtr. 3)
D5
E5
C5
G5
G5
D5
E5
C5
G5
G5
D5
E5
C5
Yeah,
yeah,

w/Rhy. Fills 2 (Gtr. 2) & 2A (Gtr. 3)
G5
G5
D5
E5
C5
yeah,
yeah.
Pre-Chorus:
G5
G5
D5
Csus2
And
yeah,
yeah,
mp semi-clean tone
D5
C
Csus2
D5
God
is
great.
Yeah,
yeah,
God
is
good.
D.S. (take 2nd ending) al Coda
w/Rhy. Fill 1 (Gtrs. 1 & 2)
C
Csus2
Dsus
D
Yeah,
yeah,
yeah,
yeah,
yeah.
What
if

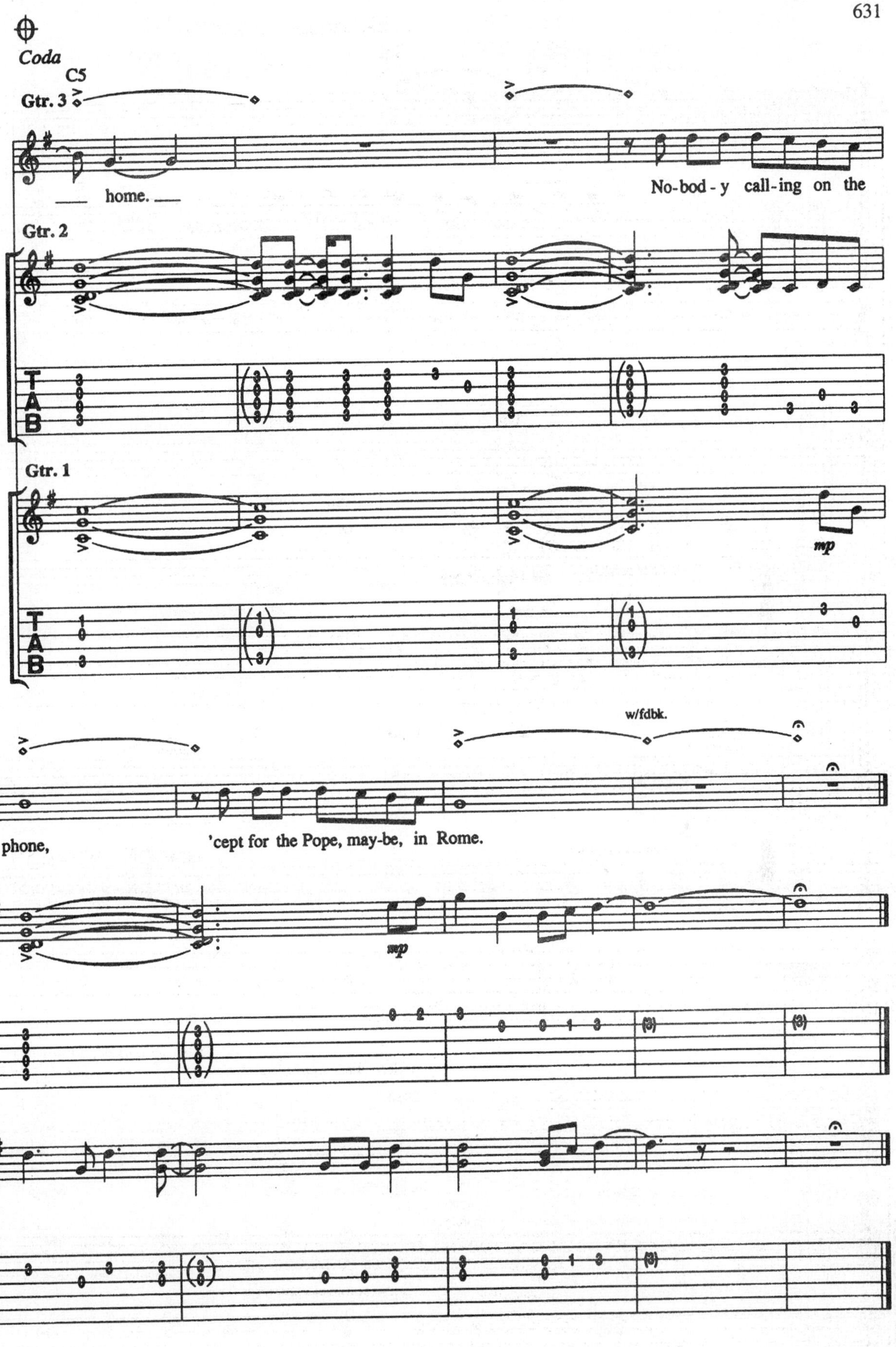

Coda

C5

Gr. 3

Gtr. 2

Gtr. 1

home.

No-bod-y call-ing on the

phone, 'cept for the Pope, may-be, in Rome.

w/fdbk.

mp

ONE WAY OR ANOTHER
Elec. Gtr. 1 tuned to Drop D:
⑥ = D ③ = G
⑤ = A ② = B
④ = D ① = E
Words and Music by
DEBORAH HARRY and
NIGEL HARRISON
Fast ♩ = 164
Intro:
D5
C♯5 C5 B5
Rhy. Fig. 1
Elec. Gtr. 1
P.M.
*Elec. Gtr. 2
Rhy. Fig. 1A
mf hold throughout
*2nd time only.
1. 2.
C5 C♯5 D5
end Rhy. Fig. 1
end Rhy. Fig. 1A
Verse:
w/Rhy. Figs. 1 (Elec. Gtr. 1) & 1A (Elec. Gtr. 2) 2 times, simile
D5
1. One way or an - oth - er, I'm gon - na find ya. I'm gon - na
2. One way or an - oth - er, I'm gon - na find ya. I'm gon - na
3. One way or an - oth - er, I'm gon - na lose ya. I'm gon - na
*Elec. Gtr. 3
f hold throughout
*1st 2 measures during Verse 3 only.

w/Fill 1 (Elec. Gtr. 3) Verses 2 & 3 only, simile
C♯5 C5 B5
4fr. 3fr.
134 134 134
get ya, get ya, get ya, get ya, One way or an - oth - er, I'm gon - na
get ya, get ya, get ya, get ya. One way or an - oth - er, I'm gon - na
give you the slip. A slip o' the hip or an - oth - er, I'm gon - na
C5 C♯5 D5
3fr. 4fr. 5fr.
134 134 134
win ya. I'm gon - na get ya, get ya, get ya, get ya. One way or an -
win ya. I'll get ya, I'll get ya. One way or an -
lose ya. I'm gon - na trick ya. I'll trick ya. One way or an -
C♯5 C5 B5
4fr. 3fr.
134 134 134
oth - er, I'm gon - na see ya. I wan - na meet ya, meet ya, meet ya, meet ya.
oth - er, I'm gon - na see ya. 1.How 'bout I meet ya, meet ya, meet ya, meet ya.
oth - er, I'm gon - na lose ya. 3. I'm gon - na trick ya, trick ya, trick ya, trick ya.
Fill 1
Elec. Gtr. 3
TAB
2 4 3 5 7 5 7
To Coda
One day, may-be next week, I'm gon-na meet ya. I'm gon-na meet ya. I'll meet ya.
One day, may-be next week, I'm gon-na meet ya, I'll meet ya, ah.
One way or an - oth - er, I'm gon-na lose ya. I'm gon-na
Fill 2
TAB
2 4 2 4 2 0 2 4 2 4 2 0 2

Bridge:
G5
5fr.
111
B5
134
A5
23
F♯5
4fr.
111
G5
5fr.
111
B5
134
A5
23
1. I will drive past_ your house. And if the lights are_ all
2. And if the lights are_ all out, I'll fol - low your bus_down-
Elec. Gtr. 3
F♯5
4fr.
111
G5
5fr.
111
E5
111
F♯5
4fr.
111
1.
2.
down, I'll see who's_ a - round.
town; see who's hang - ing out.
Guitar Solo:
F♯5
4fr.
111
A
223
C♯m
4fr.
1432
F♯5
4fr.
111
Elec. Gtr. 1
Cont. rhy. simile
Elec. Gtr. 3

A
C♯m
B5
E5
Elec. Gtr. 1
F♯5
G5
G♯5
A5
D.S. 𝄋 al Coda
A♯5
C5
C♯5
D5

*Vocal 2nd and 3rd times only.

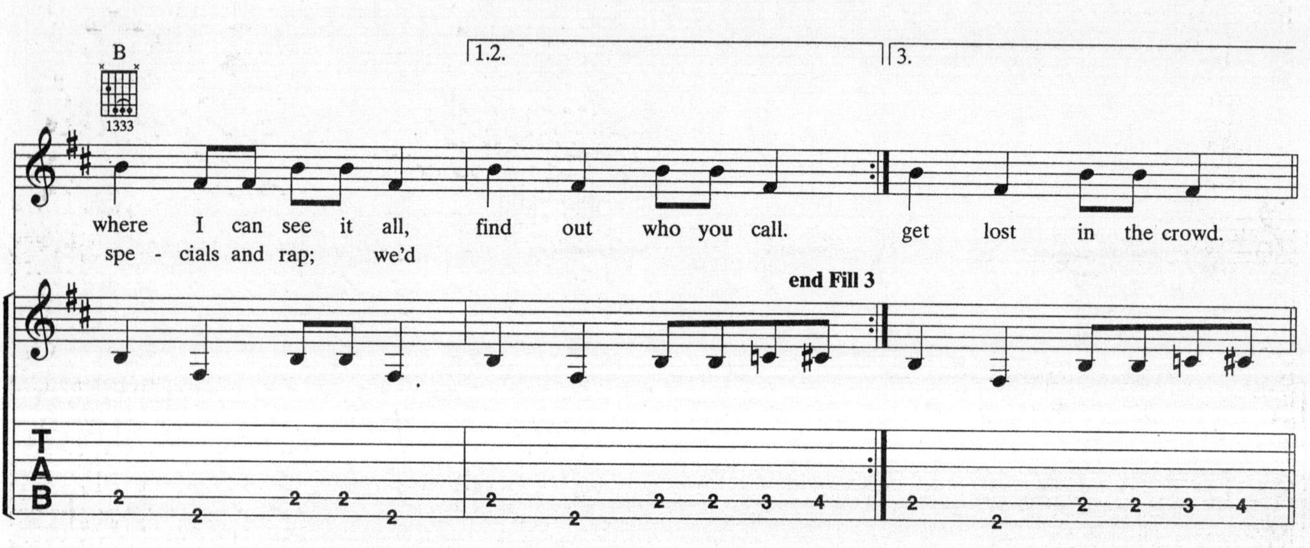

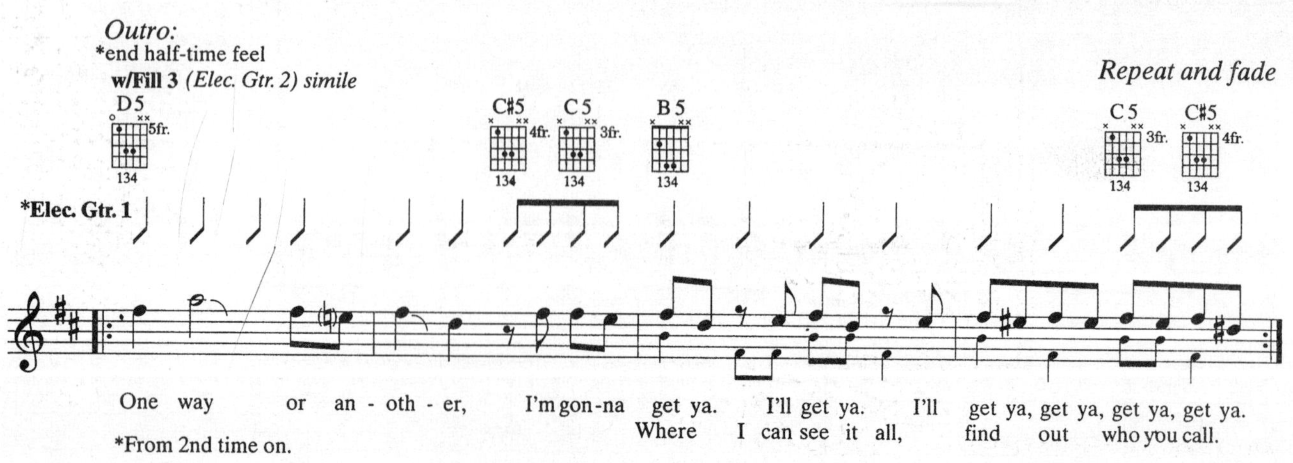

*From 2nd time on.

ONLY THE LONELY (Know The Way I Feel)

Words and Music by
ROY ORBISON and JOE MELSON

F
C7
F
134211
3241
lone - ly,
on - ly the lone - ly.
1. On - ly the
2. On - ly the
Cont. rhy. simile
T
A
B
Verses 1 & 2:
Acous. & Elec. Gtrs./Keybd. resume intro figures simile
lone - ly
lone - ly
know the way I feel to -
know the heart - aches I've been
Bkgd. Vcl.: Dum, dum, dum, dum - by, doo, wah.
Gm
134111
night.
through.
Oo, yay, yay, yay, yeah.
On - ly the lone - ly
On - ly the lone - ly
Dum,
B♭
1333
know this feel - ing ain't right.
know I cry for you.
dum, dum, dum - by, doo, wah.
Dum, dum, dum,
Chorus:
Acous. & Elec.
Gtrs./Keybd.
There goes my ba - by;
May - be to - mor - row,
there goes my
a new ro -
dum - by, doo, wah.

F7
131241
B♭
1333
heart.
mance;
They're gone for - ev - er,
no___ more sor - row
so far a -
but that's the
To Coda
G
32 4
G7
32 1
C7
3241
F
134211
part.___
chance___
But on - ly the lone - ly
know_ why_ I,__
B♭
1333
C7
3241
F
134211
Cont. rhy. simile
D.S. % al Coda
I,
I___ cry.__
On - ly the lone - ly.
Dum, dum, dum,
Outro:
C7
3241
Freely
N.C.
B♭
1333
Acous. Gtr.
Coda
you've___ got_______ to take___
if your_ lone - ly heart -
C7
3241
F
134211
Cont. rhy. simile
Acous. Gtr.
breaks.
On - ly the lone - ly.
Dum, dum, dum, dum - by, doo, wah._

ONLY GOD KNOWS WHY

Words and Music by
ROBERT "KID ROCK" RITCHIE,
MATTHEW SHAFER and JOHN TRAVIS

Verses 1, 2, 4, & 5:
E
B
Acous. Gtr.
Cont. rhy. simile on repeats
sit-tin' here _ try'n'_ to find my - self, _ I get be - hind _
num-ber one _ and yet I'm last in line. _ I watch my young -
4.5. See additional lyrics
Elec. Gtr. 1
Elec. Gtr. 2 & Acous. Gtr. (composite arrangement 1st time only)
dim.
*(D)
A
(A)
E
_ my - self. _ I need to re - wind _ my - self. Look-in' for the
- est son _ and it helps to pass _ the time. I take too
Cont. in slashes
*Play parenthetic chords on 4th verse only.

Elec. Gtr. 2 & Acous. Gtr.
B
pay back, lis-ten for the play - back. They say that
man-y pills, it helps to ease the pain. I made a cou-ple
A
To Coda
1.3.
E
ev-'ry man bleeds just like me. 2. And I feel like
dol-lar bills but still I feel
hold
2.
E
Verse 3:
B
the same. Ev-'ry-bod-y knows my name, they say it way out loud. A lot of folks
A
E
f*** with me. It's hard to hang out in crowds. I guess that's the
hold
hold

D
price you pay to be some big shot like I am. Out-
A
stretched hands and one night stands.
Bridge: take D.S. on repeat
E
*Elec. Gtr. 2 & Acous. Gtr. dbld. by Elec. Gtr. 3 (w/dist.)
C#m
Still I can't find love. And when the
hold
F#
C#m
walls come tum-bling down I will

D.S. 𝄋 al Coda
Guitar Solo:
F♯
A
E
Elec. Gtr. 2
Acous. Gtr.
Cont. rhy. simile
al - ways be __ a - round. ___
Yeah, ___
mm, _
B
D
A
__ hmm. __
E
P.M.

Coda
E
Verse 6:
peo-ple get what they de - serve. Still I ain't seen mine. No, I ain't
Elec. Gtr. 1
D
A
seen mine. I've been giv-in', I just ain't been get - tin'. Been
E
walk - ing down that line. So I think I'll keep a - walk - in' with my
hold
B
A
head held high. I'll keep mov - in' on and on - ly God

Chorus:
E
knows why. On - ly God, on - ly God,
B
A
E
on - ly God knows why. On - ly God
D
knows why, why, why. On - ly God knows
E
D
A
E
why. Take me to the riv-er. Oh, Take me to the
TAB

Outro:

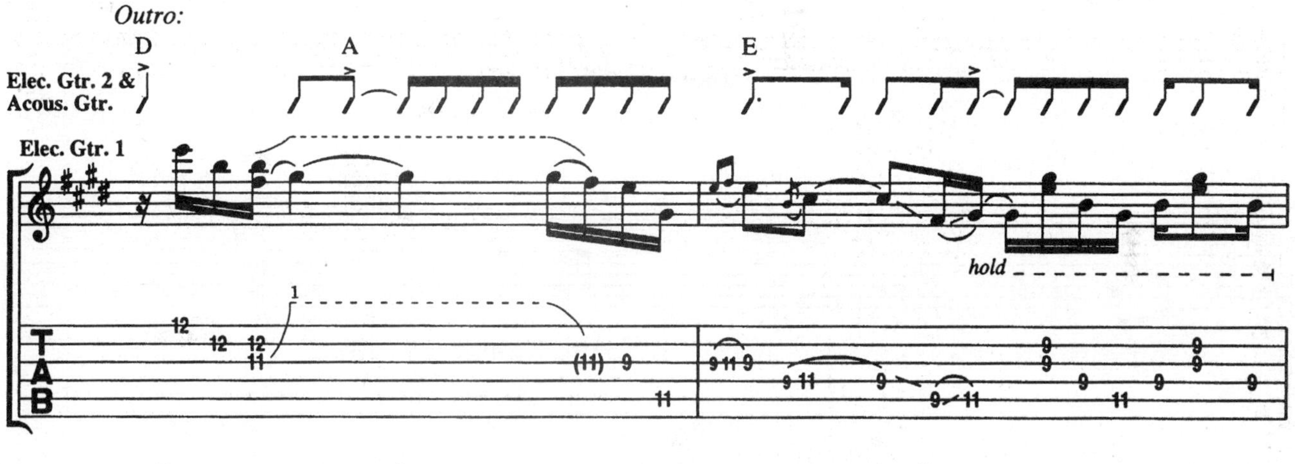

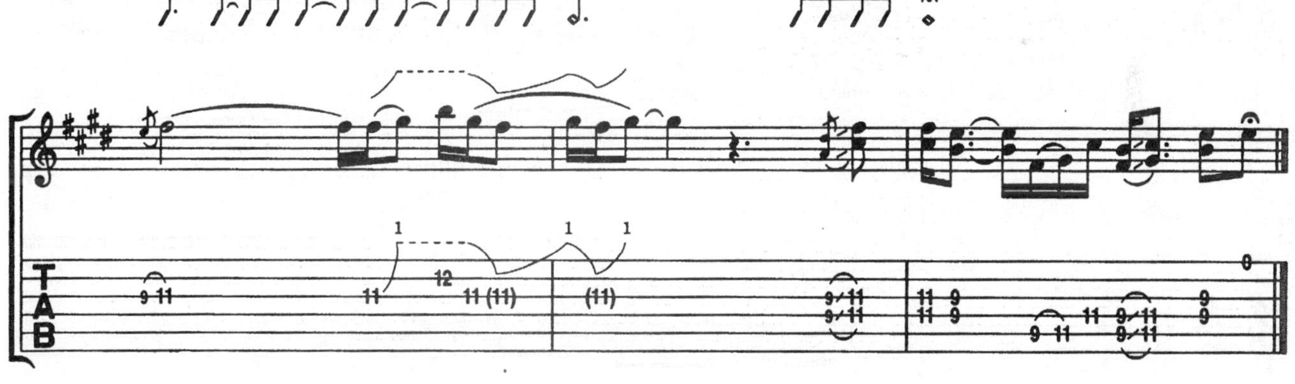

Verse 4:
People don't know about the things I say and do.
They don't understand about the s*** that I've been through.
It's been so long since I've been home.
I've been gone. . . I've been gone for way too long.

Verse 5:
Maybe I forgot all things I miss.
Oh, somehow, I know there's more to life than this.
I said it too many times
And I still stand firm:
You get what you put in
And people get what they deserve.

PAPA'S GOT A BRAND NEW BAG

Words and Music by
JAMES BROWN

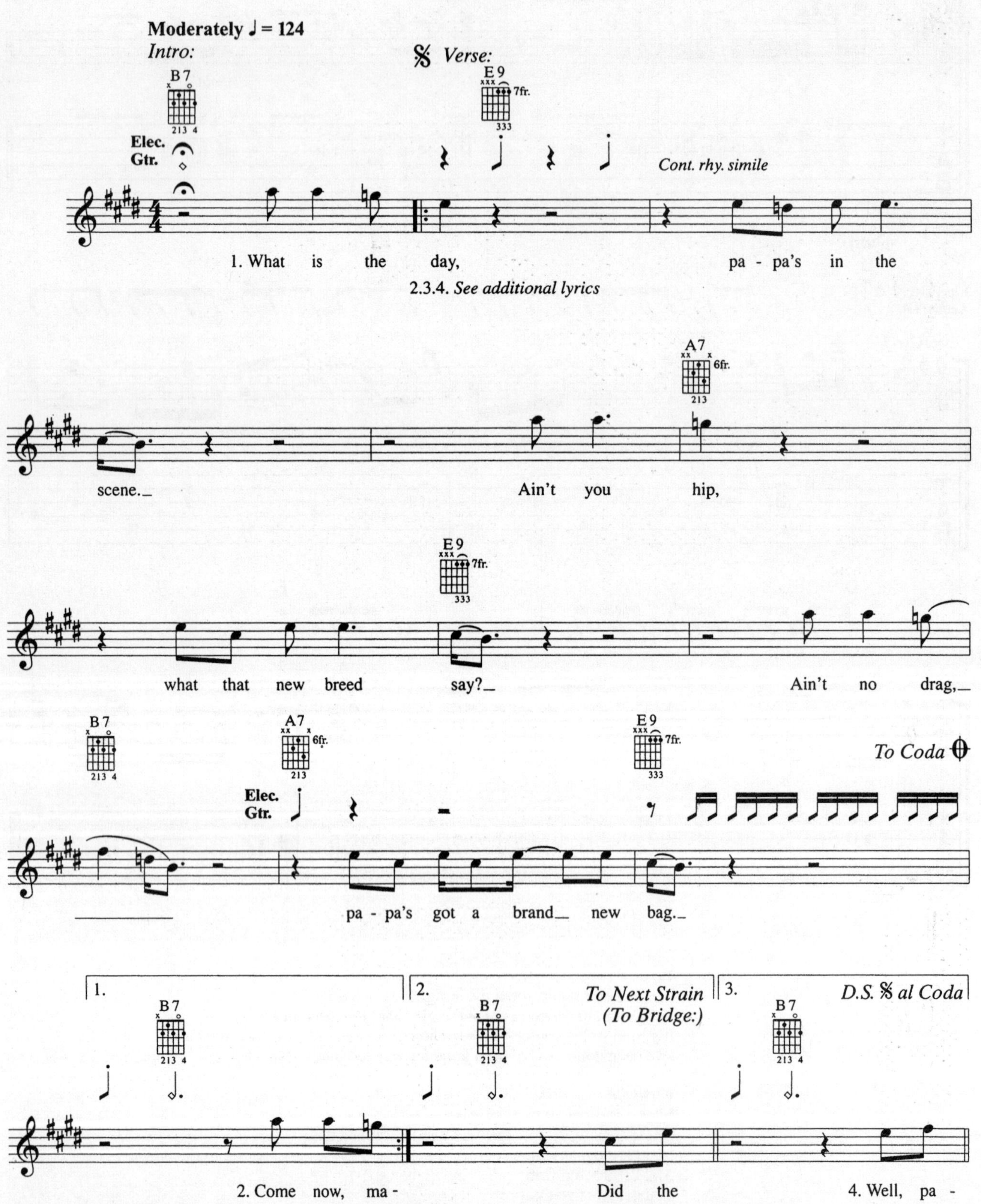

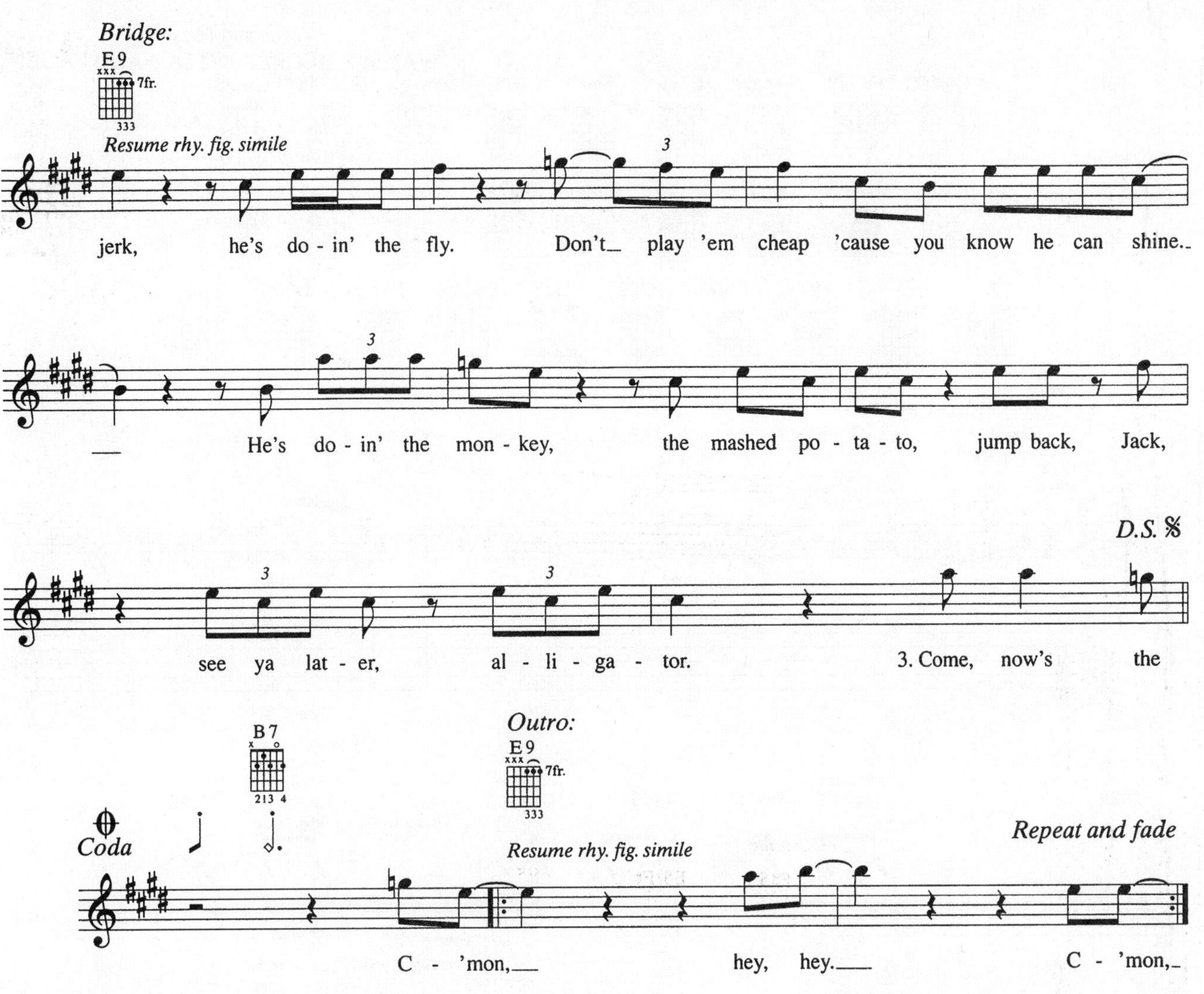

Verse 2:
Come now, mama,
And if it's plain to see.
Not too fancy,
But his line is pretty clean.
Ain't no drag,
Papa's got a brand new bag.
(To Bridge:)

Verse 3:
Come, now's the time,
Papa's on the street.
Ain't you hip now,
But I can dig the new breed.
Ain't no drag,
He's got a brand new bag.

Verse 4:
Well, papa, he's doin' the jerk,
Papa, he's doin' the jerk.
He's doin' the twist, just like this,
He's doin' the fight every day and every night.
The thing,
Like a boomerang.
(To Outro:)

PEG

Words and Music by
WALTER BECKER and DONALD FAGEN

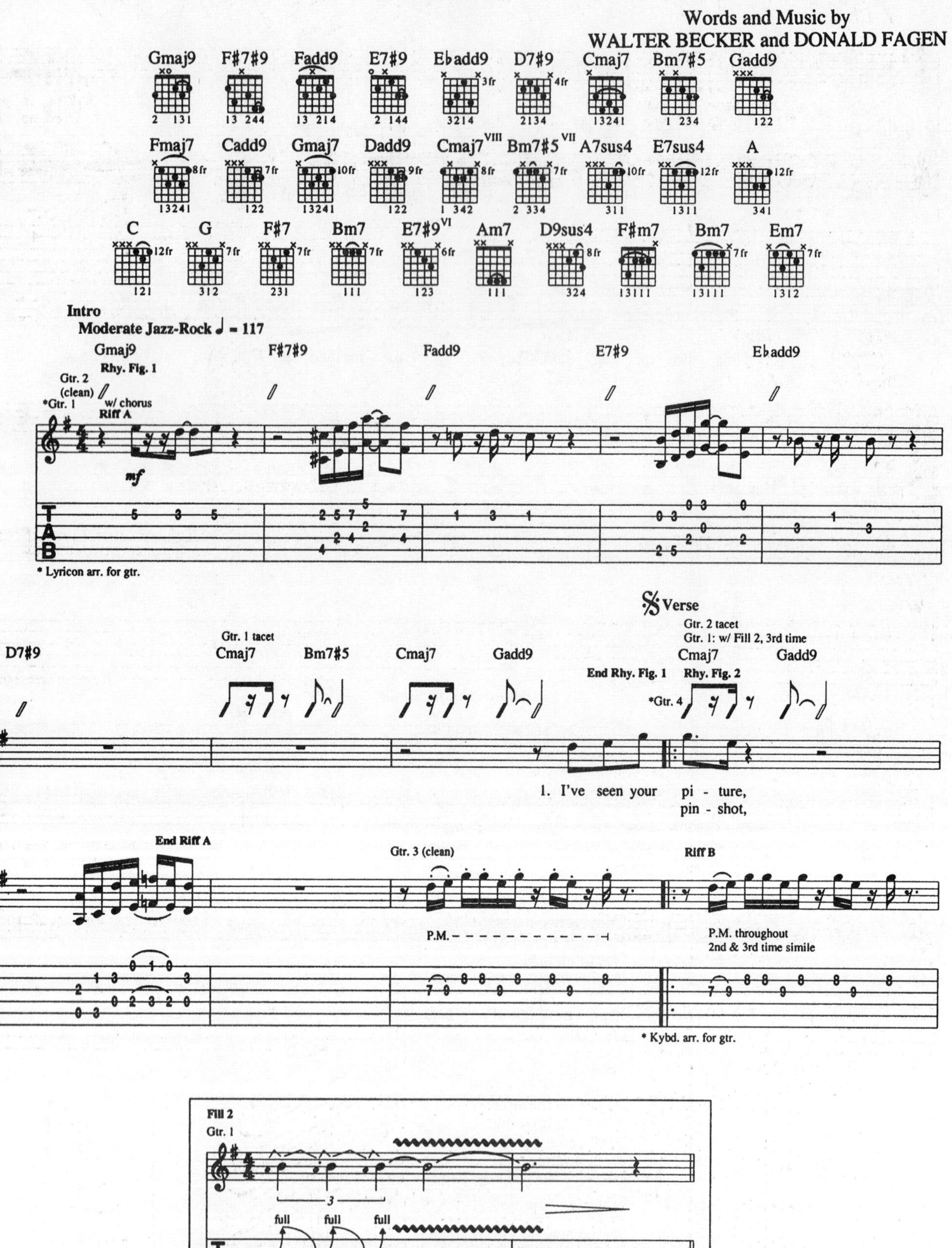

Gtr. 1: w/ Fill 1, 2nd & 3rd time
Cmaj7
Gadd9
your name in lights a - bove it.
I keep it with your let - ter.
This is your
Done up in
Fmaj7
Cadd9
big de - but,
blue - print - blue,
it's like a dream come true.
it sure looks good on you,
Gmaj7
Dadd9
So won't you smile for the cam - 'ra?
and when you smile for the cam - 'ra,
I know they're gon - na
I know I'll love you
Fill 1
Gtr. 1
T
A
B

1.
2.
End Rhy. Fig. 2
Gtr. 3: w/ Fill 3, 2nd time
Cmaj7
Gadd9
love it,
bet - ter.
Peg.
2. I like your
End Riff B
(cont. in slash)
Chorus
Gtr. 4 tacet
Cmaj7 VIII Bm7#5 VII
A7sus4
E7sus4
Rhy. Fig. 3
Gtr. 3
Peg, it will come back to you.
(Peg. Back to you.
To Coda
Gtr. 1: w/ Fill 4, 2nd time
A
C
G
F#7
Bm7
E7#9 VI
Am7
D9sus4
End Rhy. Fig. 3
(cont. in notatoion)
Then the shut - ter falls, you see it all in three D. It's your fav - 'rite for - eign
Ah, shut - ter falls all in three D. for - eign mo - vie.)
Gtr. 3 tacet
F#m7
Em7
Gtr. 2
mo - vie.
P.M.
Fill 3
Gtr. 3
Fill 4
Gtr. 1
T
A
B

Interlude

Guitar Solo (Jay Graydon)

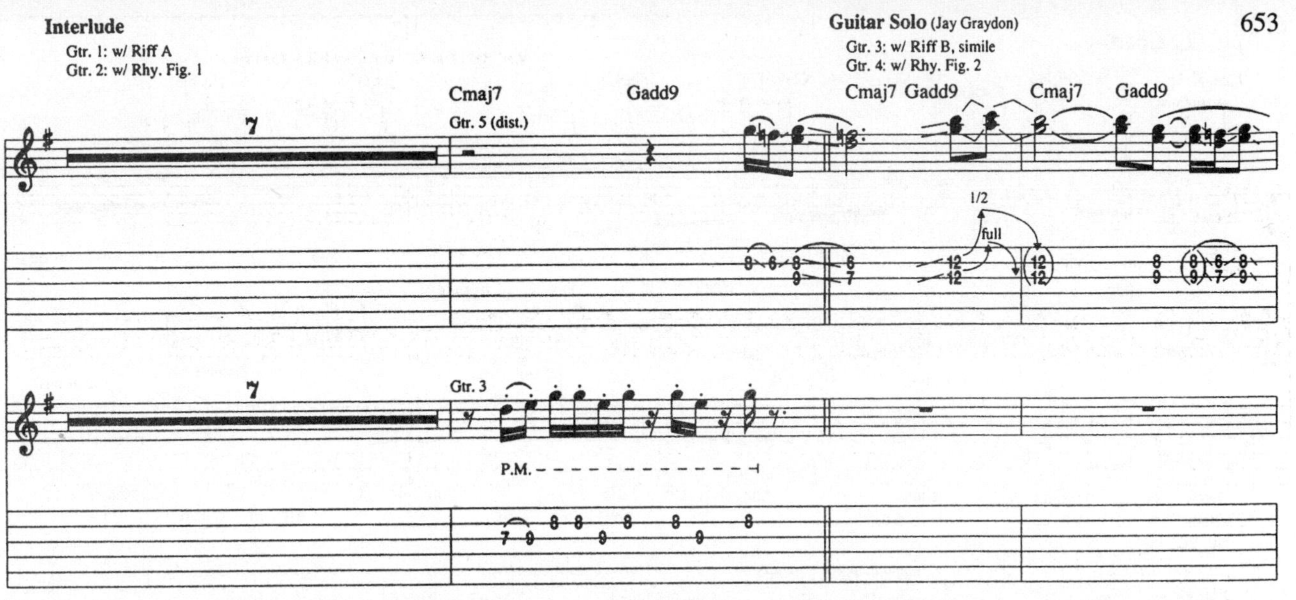

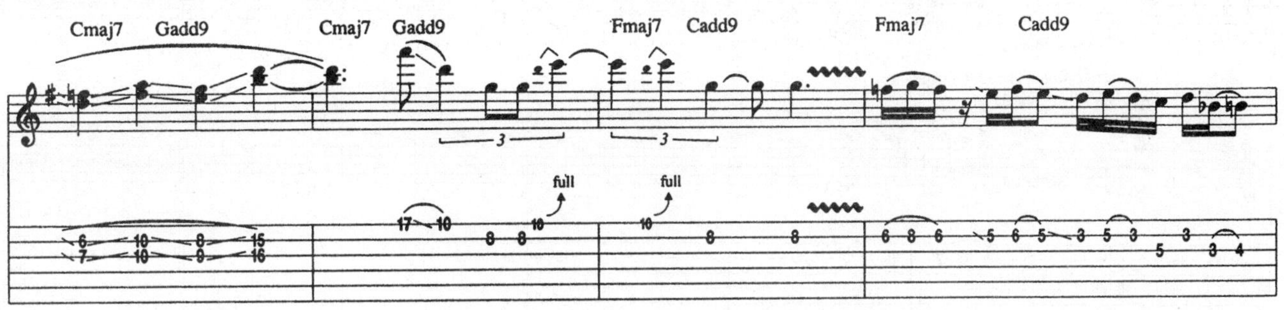

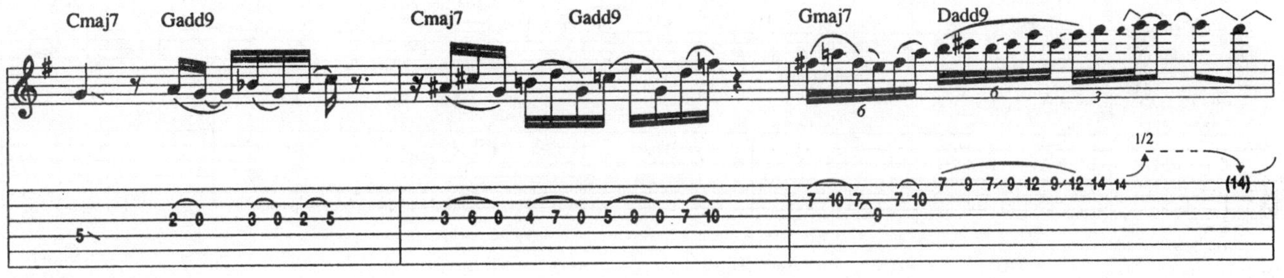

D.S. al Coda
(take 2nd lyrics/2nd ending)

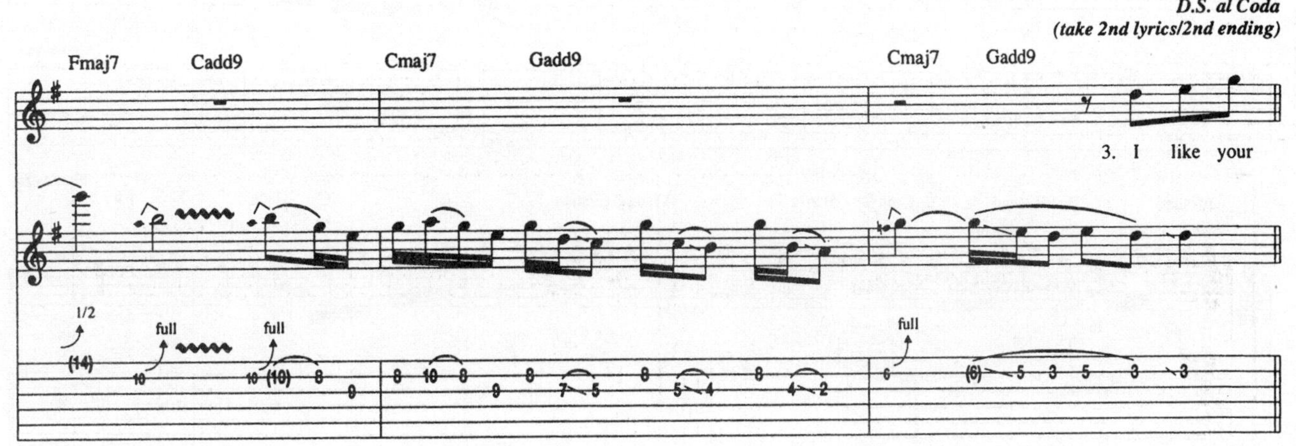

Coda
Outro
Gtr. 3: w/ Rhy. Fig. 3, 4 times & fade
Cmaj7 Bm7#5 A7sus4 E7sus4 Cmaj7 Bm7#5
Voc. Fig. 1
mo - vie it will come back to __ you. ____ Peg, ________ it will come
(Peg. Back to __ you. ____ Peg.
A7sus4 E7sus4 A C G F#7 Bm7 E7#9
back to __ you. __ then the shut - ter falls you see it all in three _ D. __
Back to __ you. __ Ah, ______ shut - ter falls __ all in three _ D.
w/ Voc. Fig. 1, 3 times
Am7 D9sus4 Cmaj7 Bm7#5 Asus4 E7sus4 Cmaj7 Bm7#5 Asus4 E7sus4
End Voc. Fig. 1
It's your fav 'rite for - eign
for - eign mo - vie.)
Gtr. 5 (dist.)
Bm7 E7#9 Am7 D9sus4 Cmaj7 Bm7#5 A7sus4 E7sus4 Cmaj7 Bm7#5 A7sus4 E7sus4
full full full
Begin Fade
A C G F#7 Bm7 E7#9 Am7 D9sus4 Cmaj7 Bm#5
A7sus4 E7sus4 Cmaj7 Bm7#5 A7sus4 E7sus4 A C G F#7
Fade Out
8va
loco
full full full full full full full

PERFECT

Words and Music by
BILLY CORGAN

Gtr. 1 tuning:
⑥ = E ③ = G
⑤ = B ② = B
④ = D ① = E
All other gtrs. in standard tuning

Moderate rock ♩ = 112

Intro:

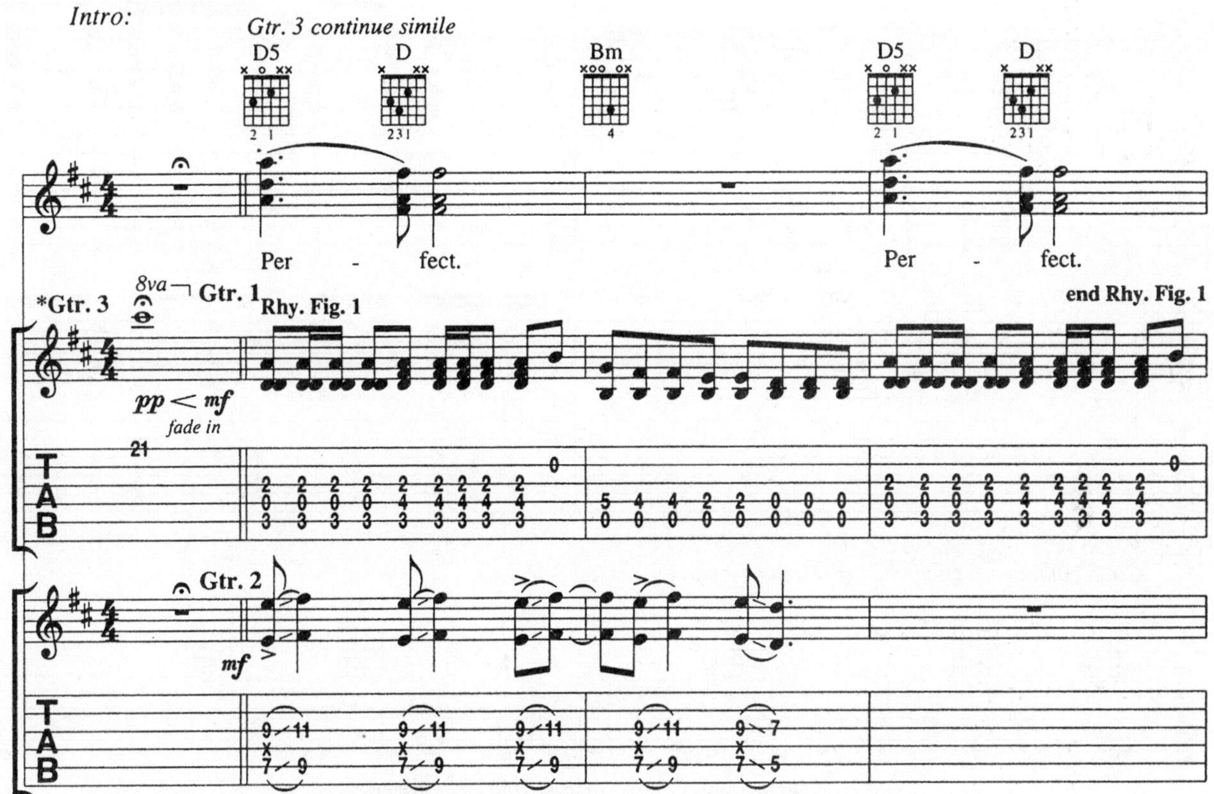

* On recording, this note is played one octave lower and sounds an octave higher (as written) due to the use of an octave shifting device, such as a whammy pedal.

D/A
Em
Ah.
I know
Verse 1:
Gtr. 3 continues high-pitched effects (next 3 bars)
D5
D
Bm
we're just like old friends, we
Rhy. Fig. 2
just can't pre - tend that lov-ers make a - mends.

D/A
Em
2. We are
end Rhy. Fig. 2
Verses 2, 3, & 4:
w/Rhy. Fig. 2 (Gtr. 1) simile
D5
D
Bm
rea - sons so un - real. We
3.4. See additional lyrics
can't help but feel that some-thing has been lost.
1. But please,
Chorus:
w/additional high-pitched gtr. effects (Gtr. 3)
G(9)
D6
Gtr. 1
you know you're just like me.
2.3. See additional lyrics
Gtr. 2
hold throughout

1.
G(9)
Em
Next time, _
Time, _
I prom-ise we'll _ be
w/Rhy. Fig. 1 (Gtr. 1) 2 times
D5
D
Bm
per - fect.
Per - fect.
2.
Interlude:
w/additional high-pitched gtr. effects (Gtr. 3)
won-der who _ I was. _
Per - fect.
Gtr. 1

B5
D
B5
3.
w/Rhy. Fig. 1 (Gtr. 1)
Em
D5
D
Bm
Gtr. 1
prom - ise we'll be per - fect.
Gtr. 2
Verse 5:
w/Rhy. Fig. 2 (Gtr. 1)
D5
D
Bm
D5
D
Bm
Per - fect stran-gers when we meet.
Stran-gers on the street.
D5
D
Bm
D/A
Em
Lov - ers when we sleep.

Outro:
w/additional high-pitched gtr. effects (Gtr. 3) until end
w/Rhy. Fig. 1 (Gtr. 1) 3 times
w/Fill 1 (Gtr. 4) 3 times
D5
D
Bm
Per - fect. You know this has to be.
We al - ways were so free.
We prom - ised that we'd be
Fill 1
Gtr. 4
fdbk.

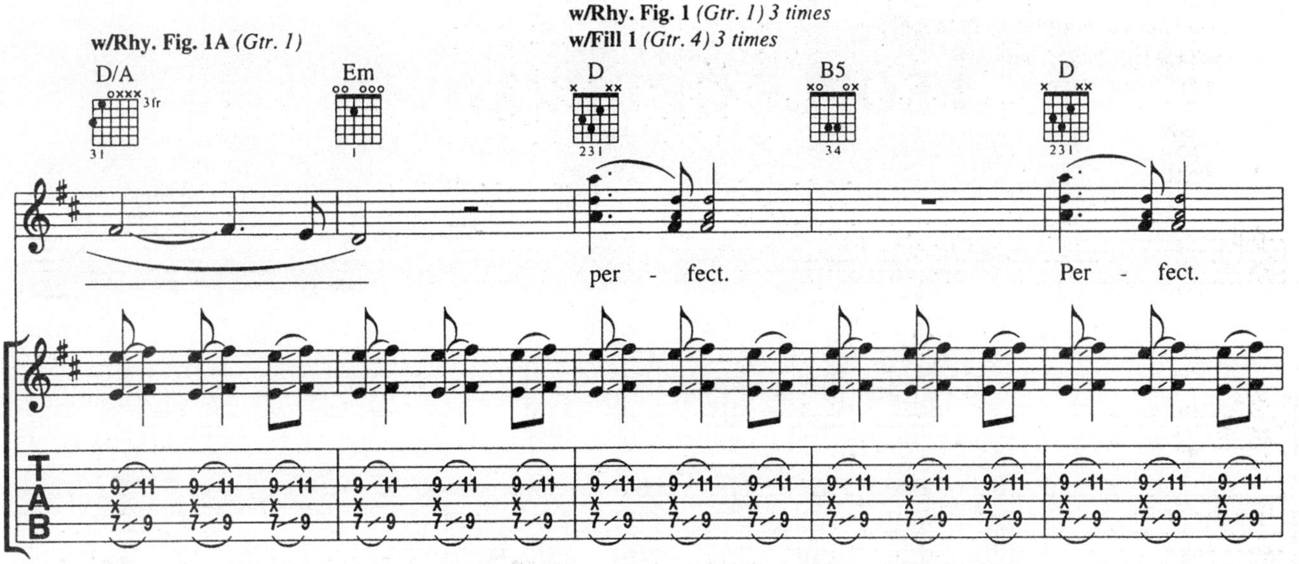

w/Rhy. Fig. 1A *(Gtr. 1)*

w/Rhy. Fig. 1 *(Gtr. 1) 3 times*
w/Fill 1 *(Gtr. 4) 3 times*

D/A Em D B5 D

per - fect. Per - fect.

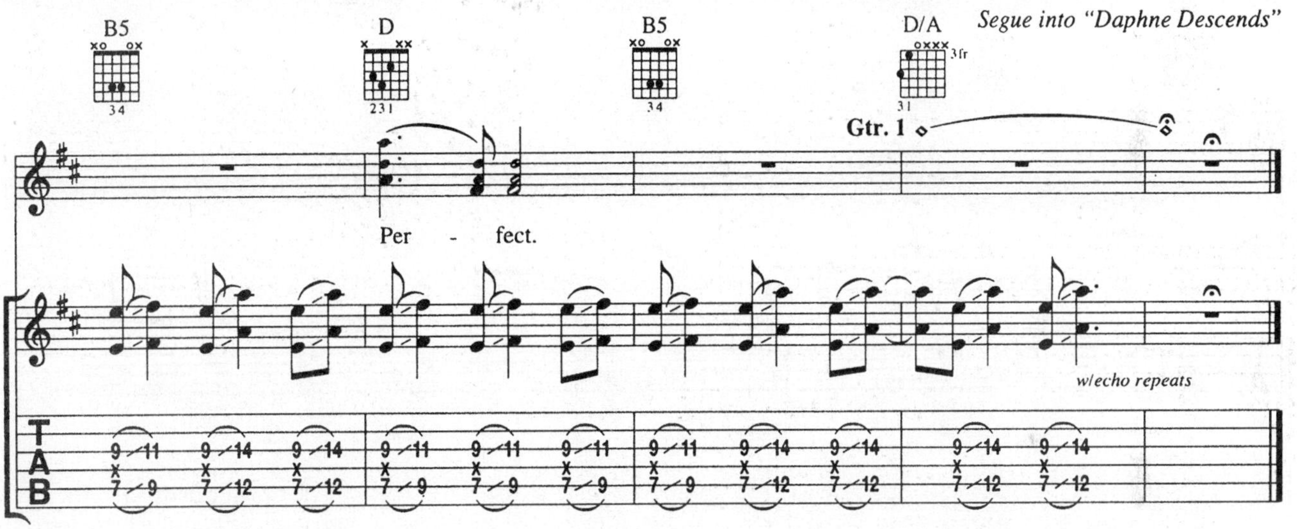

B5 D B5 D/A *Segue into "Daphne Descends"*

Gtr. 1

Per - fect.

w/echo repeats

Verse 3:
Perfect strangers down the line,
Lovers out of time.
Memories unwind.

Chorus 2:
So far, I still know who you are.
But now, now I wonder who I was.
(To Interlude:)

Verse 4:
Angel, you know that's not the end.
We'll always be good friends.
But the letters have been sent on.

Chorus 3:
So please, you always were so free.
You'll see, I promise we'll be perfect.
(To Verse 5:)

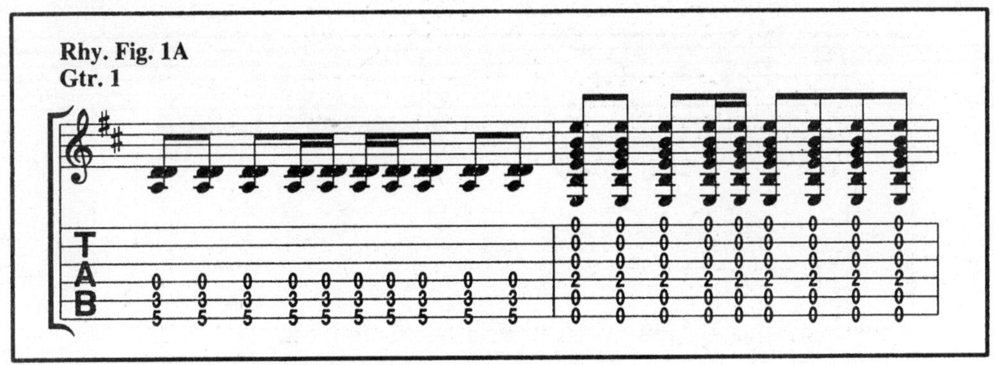

PEOPLE GET READY

Words and Music by
CURTIS MAYFIELD

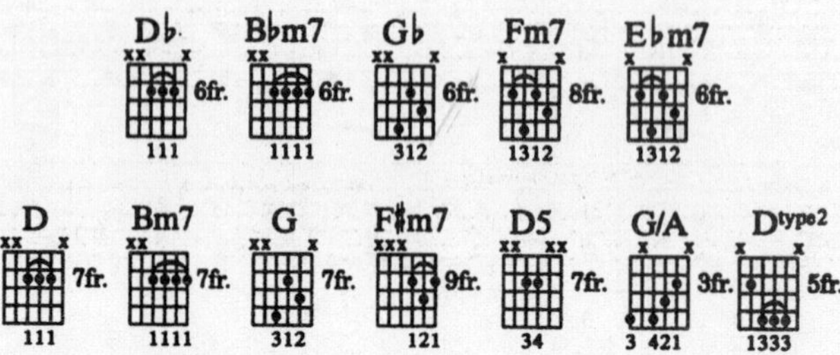

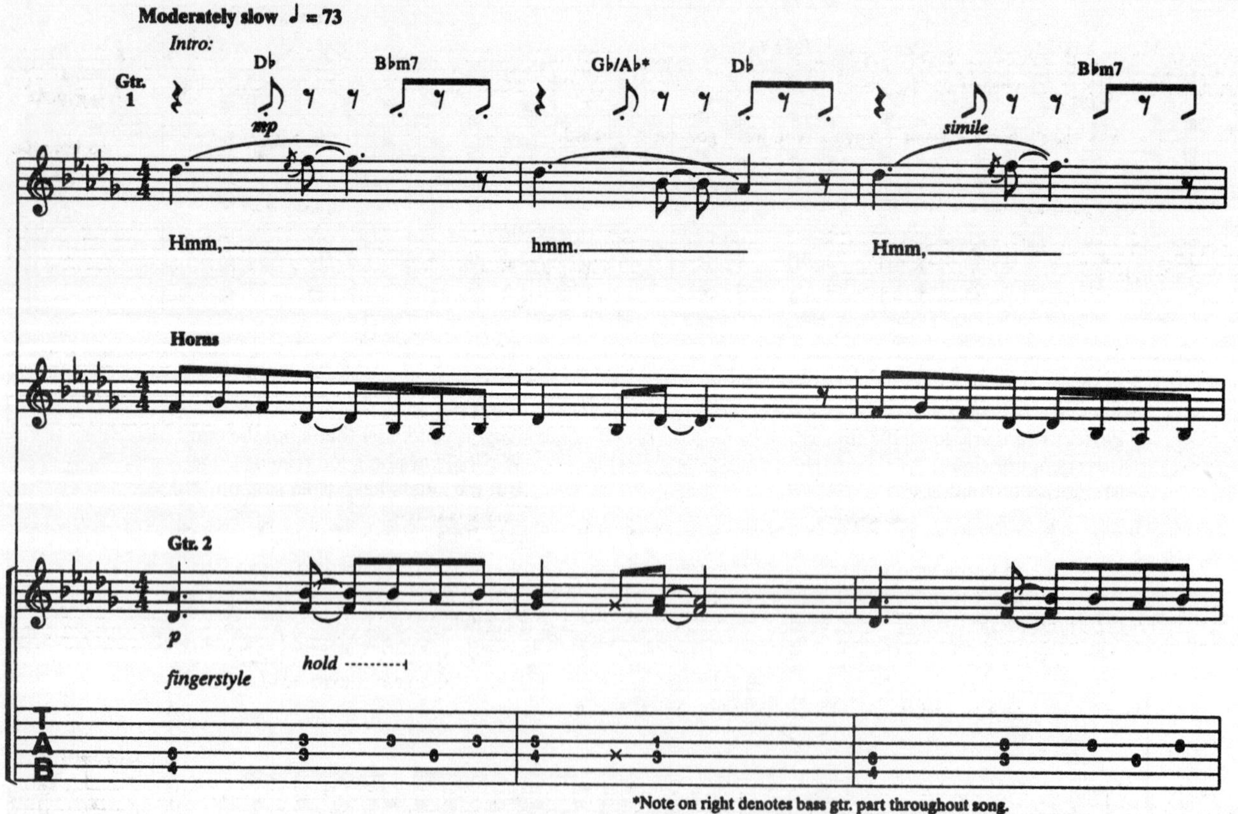

*Note on right denotes bass gtr. part throughout song.

Gb/Ab
Db
Verse:
Bbm7
Gb/Ab
Db
hmm.
1. Peo - ple, get read - y,
2. See additional lyrics
there's a train a - com - ing.
Bbm7
Gb/Ab
Db
Bbm7
You don't need no bag - gage, you just get on board.
All you need is faith to hear the
Gb/Ab
Db
Fm7
Ebm7
(Gb/Db)
(Db)
die - sels hum - ming.
Don't need no tick - et,
you just thank the Lord.
hold
hold
hold
*Play note in parentheses on Verse 2.

1.
*Interlude:
D♭
B♭m7
G♭/A♭
D♭6
2.
D♭
B♭m
hold
hold
hold
hold
*Gtr. 1 tacet.
G♭(2)
D♭
D
Bm
G/D
D
hold
Verse 3:
Gtr. 1
D
Bm7
G/A
D
Bm7
There ain't no room for the hope - less sin - ner who would hurt all man - kind,
Hmm, hmm. Hmm, just to
hold

G/A
D
Bm7
G/A
D
be - lieve me, now.
Have pit - y on those — whose
chanc- es grow thin - ner, for there's
save his own.
hold
hold
F♯m7/D
Em7
(G/D)
(D)
D
Bm7
no hid - ing place —— a - gainst the King - dom's throne.
So peo - ple, get read - y, there's a
King - dom's throne.
Peo - ple, get read - y, there's a
hold
hold

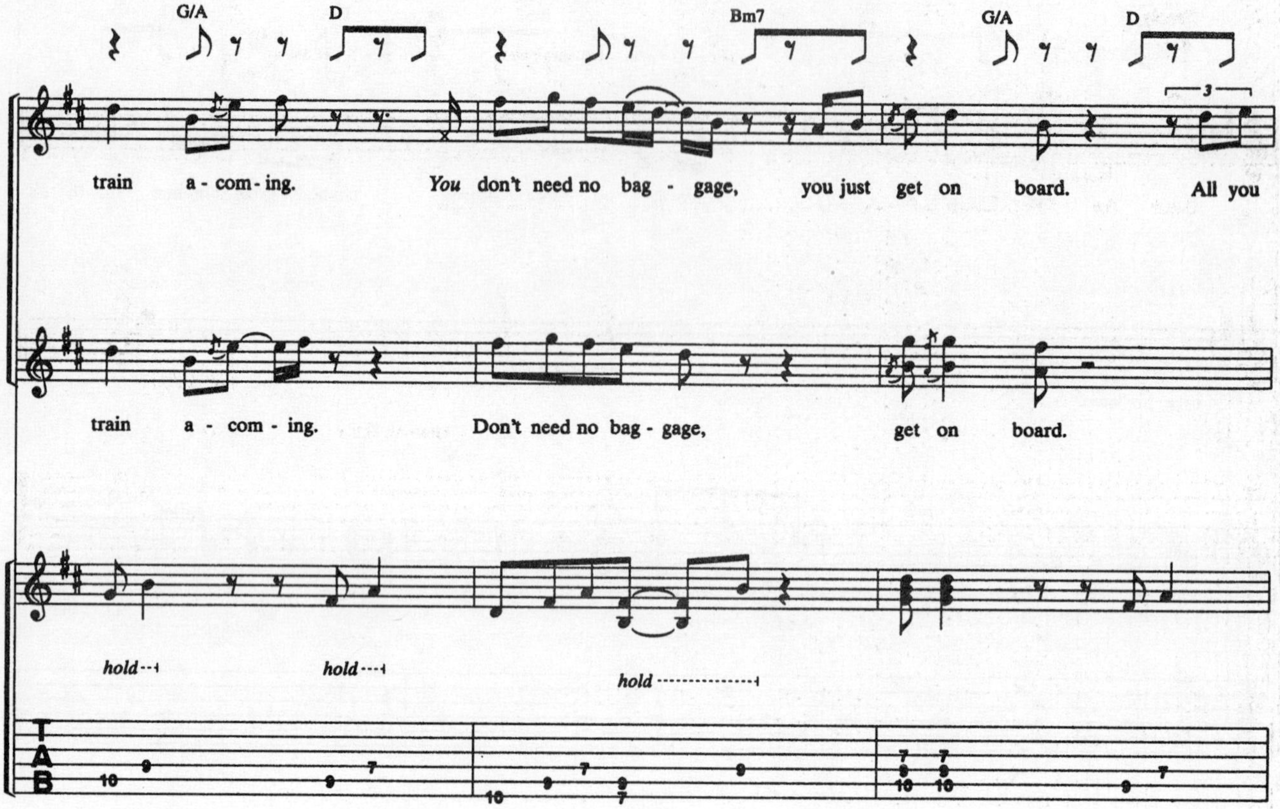

G/A D Bm7 G/A D
train a - com - ing. You don't need no bag - gage, you just get on board. All you
train a - com - ing. Don't need no bag - gage, get on board.
hold hold hold

Bm7 G/A D F♯m7 (Em7)
need is faith to hear the die - sels hum - ming. Don't need no tick - et, you just
Need is faith, die - sels hum - ming. Tick - et.
hold hold

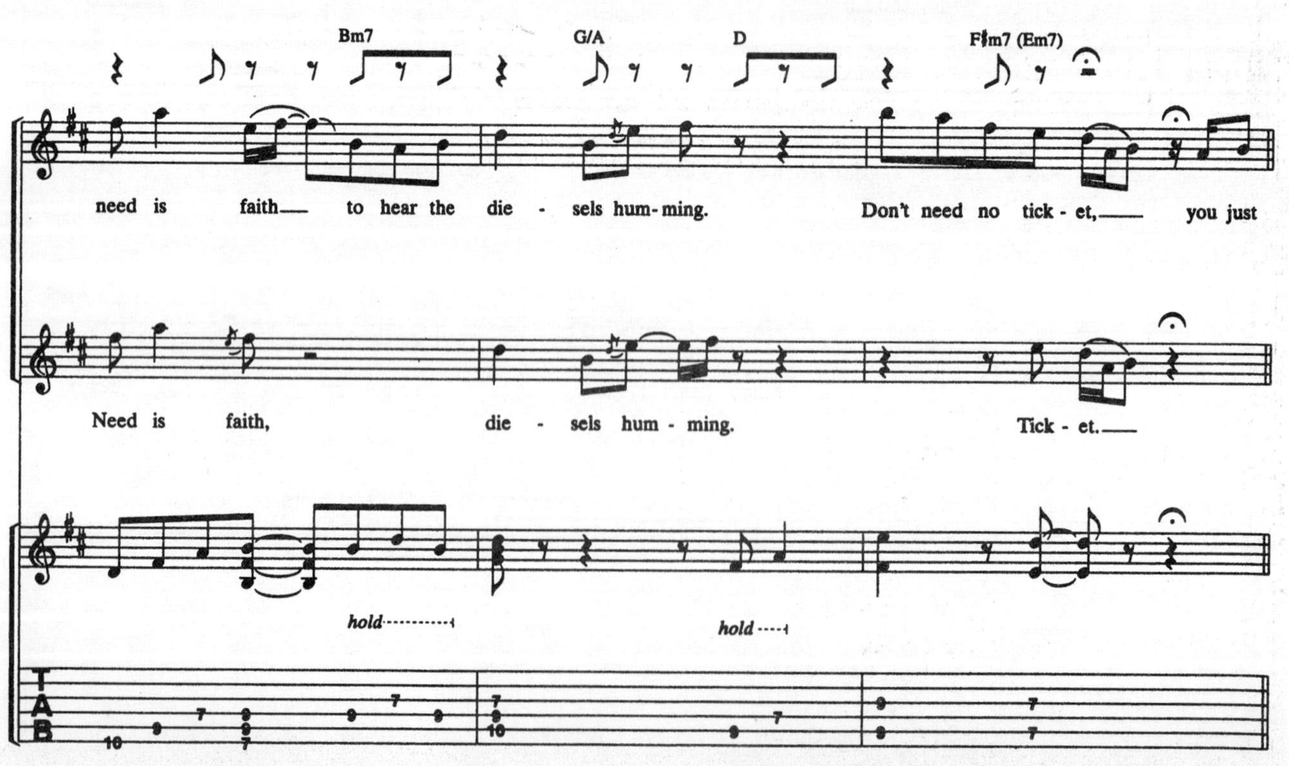

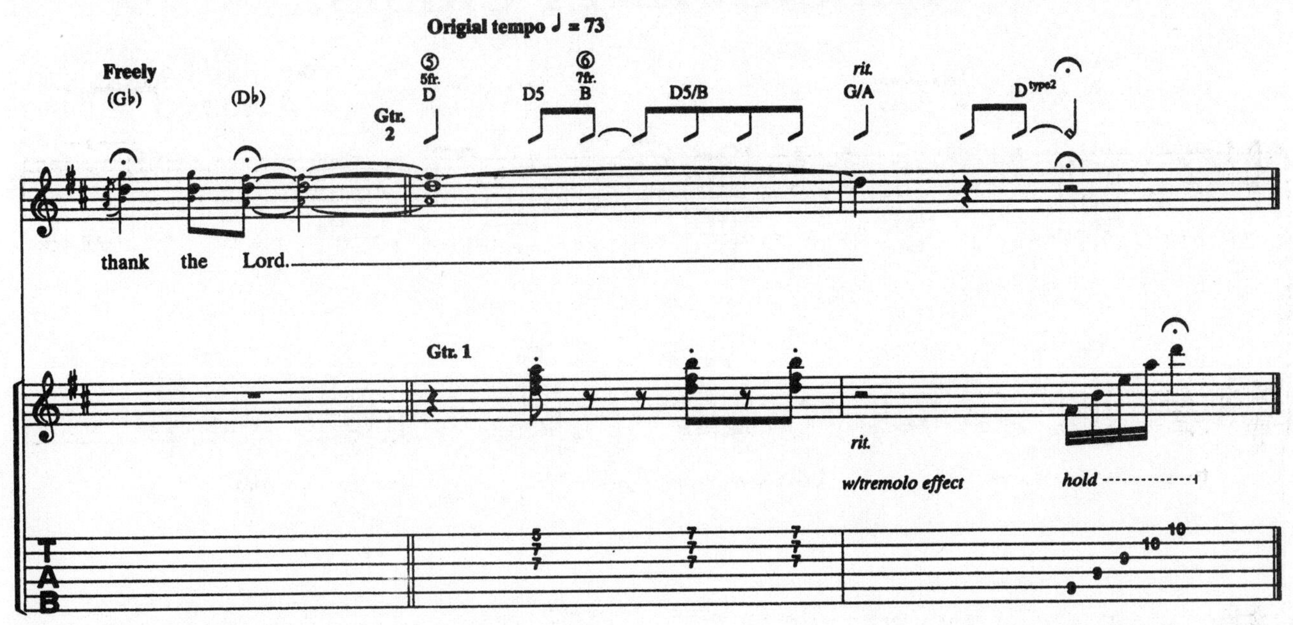

Verse 2:
So people, get ready for the train to Jordan,
Picking up passengers coast to coast.
Faith is the key; open the doors and board them.
There's hope for all among those loved the most.

PERSONALITY CRISIS

Words and Music by
DAVID JOHANSEN and
JOHNNY THUNDERS

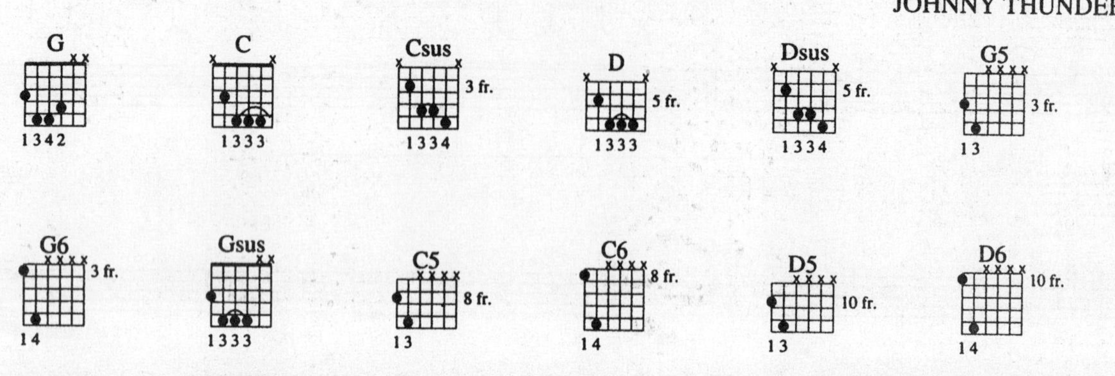

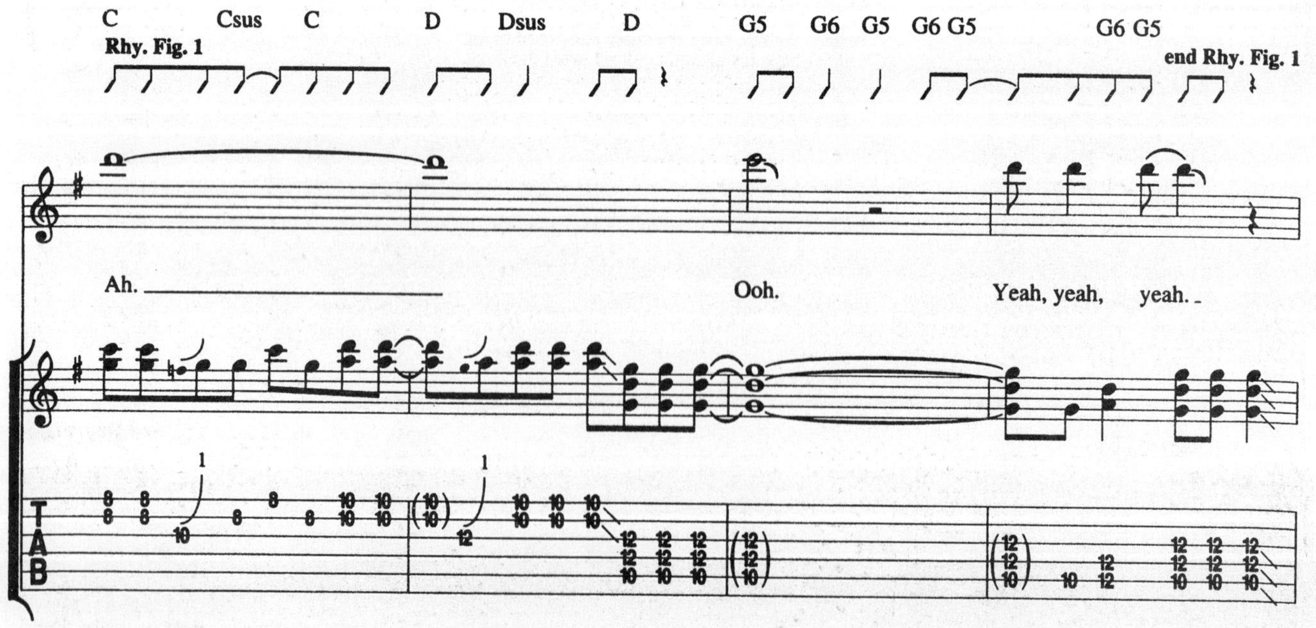

C Csus C D Dsus D G5 G6 G5 G6 G5 Gsus G
No, no, no, no, no, no, no, no.
Rhy. Fig. 2
C Csus C D Dsus D G5 E G5 E G5 E G5 E G5 E
⑥ open
end Rhy. Fig. 2
1. Well, we
Verse 1:
Rhy. Fig. 3A
G5 E G5 E G5 E G5 E G5 E G5 E G5 E G Gsus G
end Rhy. Fig. 3A
can't take her this week. And her friends all want an-oth-er splash.
Rhy. Fig. 3
end Rhy. Fig. 3

w/Rhy. Fig. 1 (Gtr. 2) simile
C Csus C D Dsus D G
Hop-ing for a bet-ter day __ to hear what she's got to say. All a-bout that
Gtr.1 Rhy. Fig. 4
end Rhy. Fig. 4
Chorus:
w/Rhy. Fig. 1 (Gtr. 2) 3 times, simile
C Csus C D Dsus D G5
per - son-al - i-ty cri - sis, you got it while it was hot. But now
Gtr. 1
C Csus C D Dsus D G5
frus - tra - tion and heart-ache is what you got. __ It's time we talk a-bout the

C Csus C D Dsus D G5
per - son - al - i - ty, per-son - al - i - ty.
w/Rhy. Fig. 2 (Gtr. 2)
C Csus C D Dsus D G5
2. Well,
Verses 2 & 4:
w/Rhy. Figs. 3 (Gtr. 1) & 3A (Gtr. 2)
G5
now you try'n' to be some-thin', now you got - ta do some-thin'. Wan-na be some - one who
4. See additional lyrics
w/Rhy. Fig. 1 (Gtr. 1) 3 times, simile
w/Rhy. Fig. 4 (Gtr. 2) 3 times
C Csus C D Dsus D G
cares, but you're think-in' 'bout the times you did, they take ev-'ry ounce.
C Csus C D Dsus D G
Well, it sure got to be a shame when you start to scream and shout. You got to
To Coda
C Csus C D Dsus D G
con - tra-dict all these times, you but-ter - flied a-bout. You was but-ter-flied. Got a

Chorus:
w/Rhy. Fig. 1 (Gtr. 2) 4 1/2 times, simile
C Csus C D Dsus D G5
per - son - al - i - ty cri - sis, you got it while it was hot.
Gtr. 1 Rhy. Fig. 5
C Csus C D Dsus D
It's al - ways hot. You know it's frus - tra - tion and heart-ache is what you got.
G5 C Csus C
Ow! I'm try'n' to talk a - bout per - son - al - i - ty,

D
Dsus
D
G
yeah, yeah,
yeah.
Ow!
C
Csus
C
D
Dsus
D
G
end Rhy. Fig. 5
C
Csus
C
D
Dsus
D
Freely
G
A tempo ♩ = 155
Gtr. 2
3. And you're a
Gtr. 1
rit.

Verse 3:
w/Rhy. Fig 3 (Gtr. 1) 2 times, simile
w/Rhy. Fig. 1 (Gtr. 2) 2 times, simile
C Csus C D Dsus D G
prim - a bal - le - ri - na on a spring af - ter - noon.

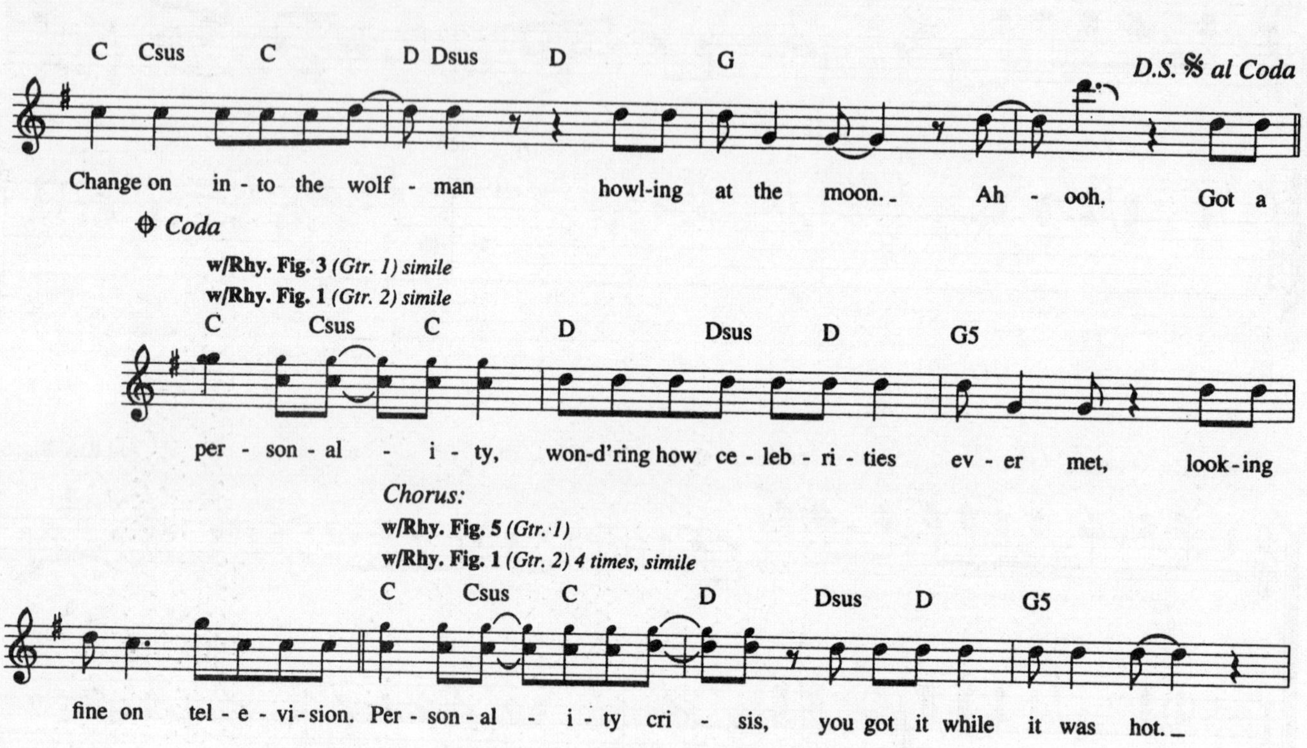
C Csus C D Dsus D G
D.S. % al Coda
Change on in - to the wolf - man howl-ing at the moon. Ah - ooh. Got a
Coda
w/Rhy. Fig. 3 (Gtr. 1) simile
w/Rhy. Fig. 1 (Gtr. 2) simile
C Csus C D Dsus D G5
per - son - al - i - ty, won-d'ring how ce - leb - ri - ties ev - er met, look - ing
Chorus:
w/Rhy. Fig. 5 (Gtr. 1)
w/Rhy. Fig. 1 (Gtr. 2) 4 times, simile
C Csus C D Dsus D G5
fine on tel - e - vi - sion. Per - son - al - i - ty cri - sis, you got it while it was hot.

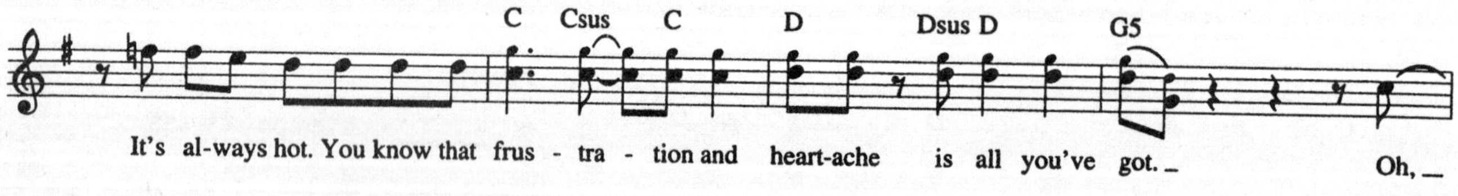
C Csus C D Dsus D G5
It's al-ways hot. You know that frus - tra - tion and heart-ache is all you've got. Oh,

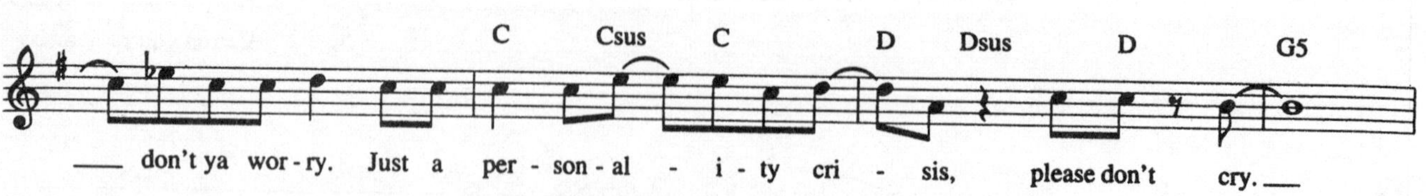
C Csus C D Dsus D G5
don't ya wor - ry. Just a per - son - al - i - ty cri - sis, please don't cry.

C Csus C D Dsus D
It's just a per - son - al - i - ty cri - sis, please don't

Verse 4:
Now, with all the trust and faith that Mother Nature sends,
Your mirror's getting jammed up with all your friends.
That's personality, everything is starting to blend. (You thought you'd won.)
Personality, when your mind starts to blend.
Got so much personality, passion of a friend of a friend of a friend of a friend.
(To Coda)

PETER GUNN

By HENRY MANCINI

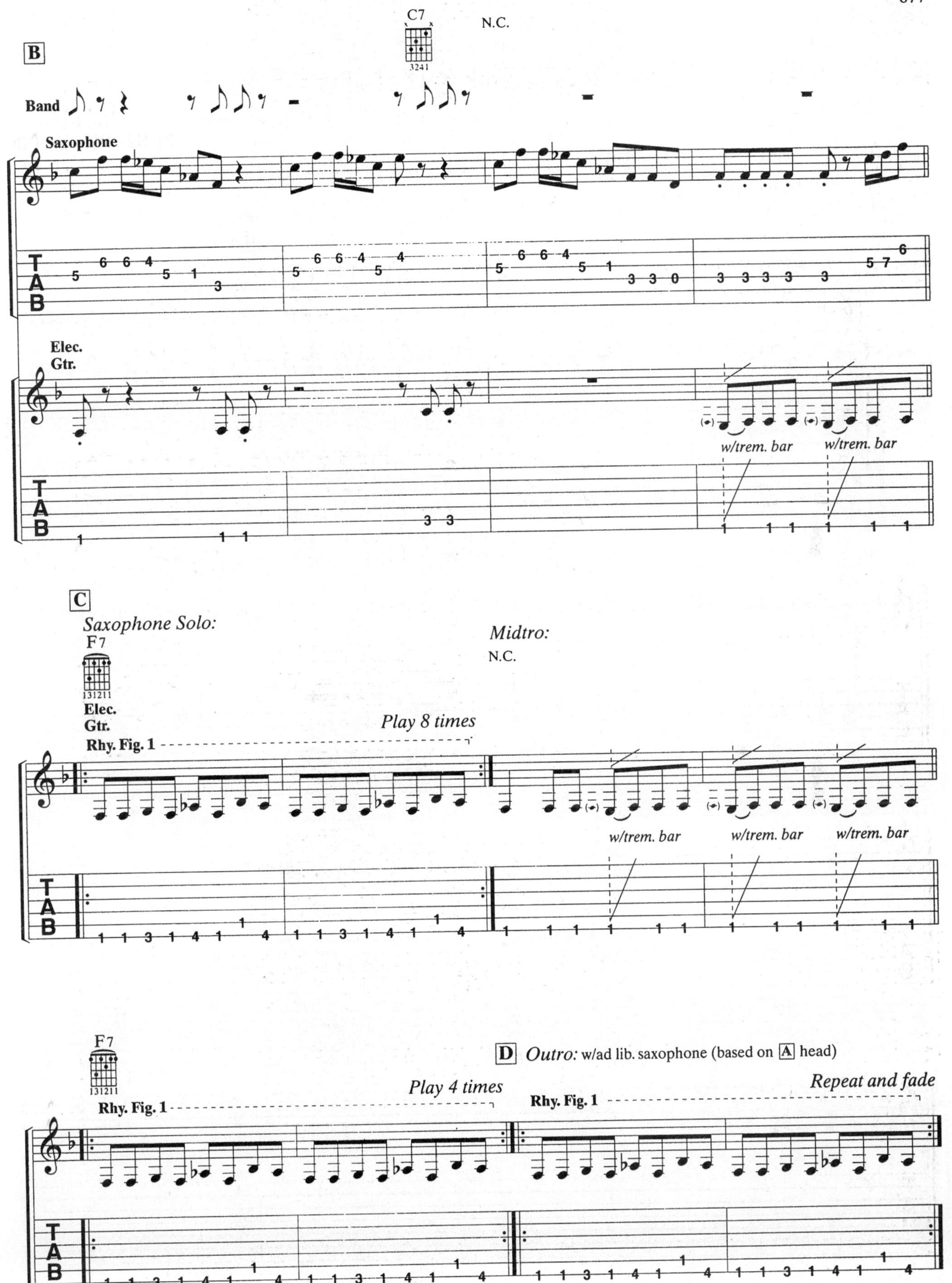
B
C7
N.C.
Band
Saxophone
Elec. Gtr.
w/trem. bar
C
Saxophone Solo:
F7
Elec. Gtr.
Rhy. Fig. 1
Play 8 times
Midtro:
N.C.
F7
Rhy. Fig. 1
Play 4 times
D Outro: w/ad lib. saxophone (based on A head)
Rhy. Fig. 1
Repeat and fade

PHOTOGRAPH

Words and Music by
STEVE CLARK, JOE ELLIOTT, R.J. LANGE,
RICK SAVAGE and PETE WILLIS

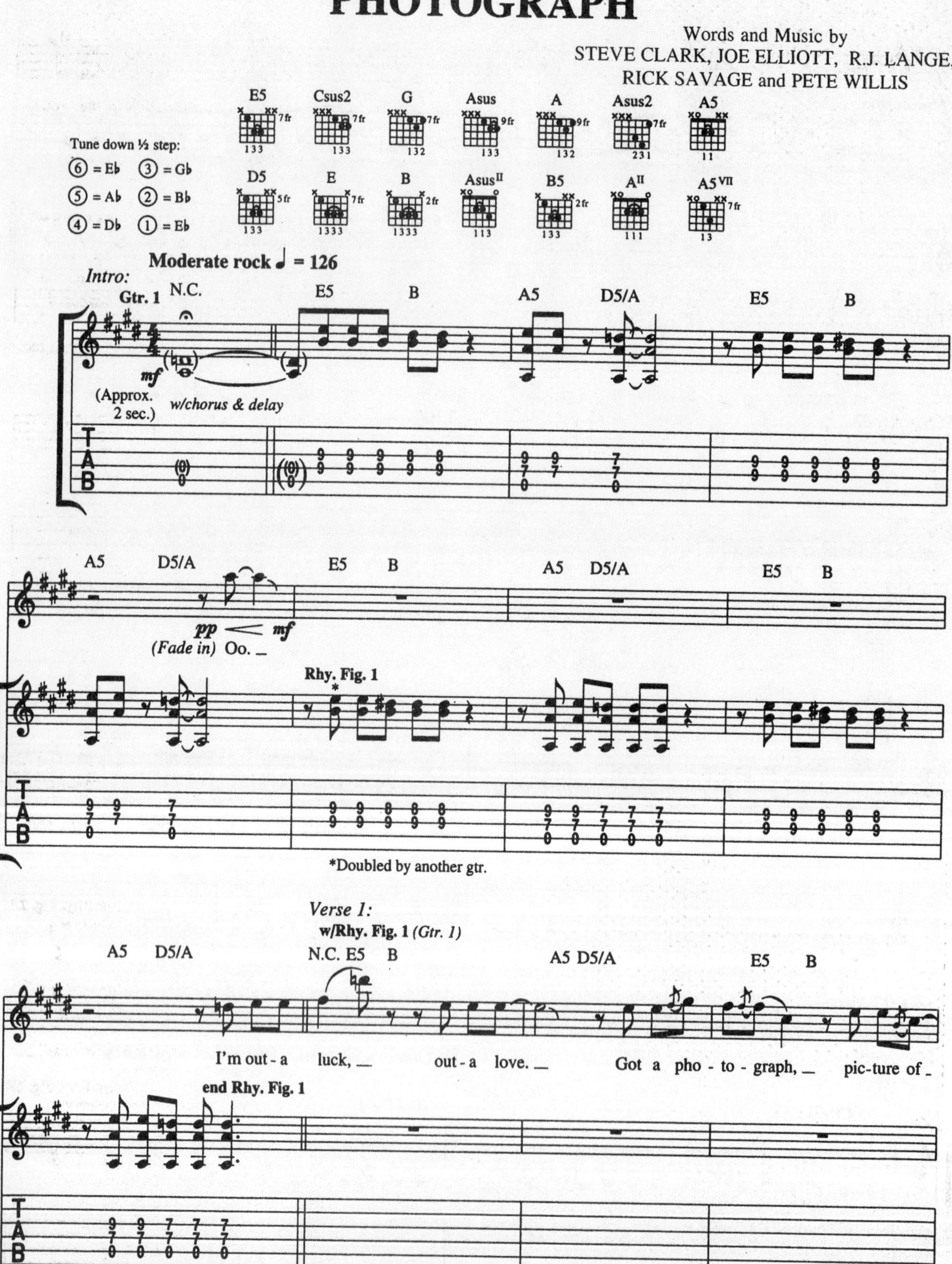

w/Rhy. Fig. 1 (Gtr. 1) 1st 2 bars only
A5
D5/A
E5
B
A5
D5/A
uh, pas - sion kill - er,
you're too
much.
You're the on -
w/Rhy. Fig. 1 (Gtr. 1)
E5
B
A
*Gtr. 2
Asus
E5
Rhy. Fig. 2
open
E
P.M.
ly one
I wan - na
touch.
I see your
face ev - 'ry - time
Rhy. Fig. 1A
*Doubled by another gtr.
end Rhy. Fig. 2
E5
open
E
E5
(P.M.)
w/Rhy. Fig. 2 (Gtr. 2)
I dream.
On ev - 'ry
page, ev - 'ry
mag - a - zine.
So wild,
Rhy. Fig. 2A
open
E
P.M.
E5
end Rhy. Fig. 2A
so
free,
so
far
from
me.
You're
all
end Rhy. Fig. 1B
Rhy. Fig. 1B

E
B
A
A5
I want, my fan - ta - sy, yeah!
Gtrs. 1 & 2
Rhy. Fig. 2B
Pre-Chorus:
Rhy. Fig. 3A
Csus2
*Gtr. 3
G
Asus
A
Oh, look what you've done to this rock 'n' roll
Gtrs 1 & 2
Rhy. Fig. 3
*Keybd. arr. for gtr.
end Rhy. Fig. 3A
w/Rhy. Fig. 3 (Gtrs. 1 & 2) 1st 3 bars only
& Rhy. Fig. 3A (Gtr. 3)
Asus
A
Asus2
A
Csus2
G
clown. Oh, oh, look what you've
end Rhy. Fig. 3
1/2

Chorus:
Asus A Asus A Asus2 A G/B C
done.
(Bkgd. voc.) Pho - to - graph.
Rhy. Fig. 4
hold throughout
D(11) Em(9) G/B C Em(9) D(11)
I don't want your... Pho - to - graph. I don't need your...
end Rhy. Fig. 4
2nd time To Coda I
3rd time To Coda II
G/B C D(11) Em(9) G/B C
Pho - to - graph. All I've got is a pho - to - graph.
Pho - to - graph.
N.C.
But it's not e - nough! I'd be your

Verse 2:
⑥ w/Rhy. Fig. 1 (Gtr. 1)
open
E
Gtr. 2
P.M.
lov - er, (if) you were there. Put your hurt on me, if you dare.
w/Rhy. Fig. 1 (Gtr. 1) 1st 2 bars only
Such a wom - an, you got style. You make ev -
w/Rhy. Fig. 1A (Gtr. 1)
A5
E5
w/Rhy. Fig. 1 (Gtr. 1)
& Rhy. Fig. 2 (Gtr. 2) 2 times
'ry man feel like a child, oh! You got some kind a hold
E5
on me. You're all wrapped up in mys - ter - y. So wild
w/Rhy. Figs. 1B (Gtr. 1) & 2A (Gtr. 2)
w/Rhy. Fig. 2B (Gtrs. 1& 2)
D.S. al Coda I
E5 E B A A5
an' free, so far from me. You're all I want, my fan - ta - sy.
G/B C E5 D5
Coda I
to - graph. You've gone straight to my
Pho - to - graph.
Gtrs. 1 & 2
Gtr. 1
hold

Interlude:
w/Rhy. Fig. 5 (Gtrs. 1 & 2) 2 times
N.C. E5
B
A5
D5/A
E5
B
A5
D5/A
head!
Gtrs. 1 & 2
Rhy. Fig. 5
Gtr. 3
trem. bar
(15ma)
fdbk.
E5
B
E
B
A
Asus²
Gtrs. 1 & 2
Gtr. 3
(8va)
hold bend
fdbk.
grad. release
Gtr. 4

Guitar Solo:
E5
open
A B5
open
A
A5
A II
open
A
E5
B5
open
A
Gtrs. 1 & 2
Gtr. 3
grad. release
A
A5 VII
E5
open
A B5
open
A
A
open
A E5
trem. bar
B5
A
A5 VII
D.S. al Coda II
Coda II
G/B
C
N.C.
C5
C
D
E
- to - graph.
Pho - to - graph.
I wan-na touch you!
Ah!
mf
cresc.
f
P.M.

Out-Chorus:
w/Rhy. Fig. 4 (Gtrs. 1 & 2) till fade
G/B
C
D(11)
Em(9)
Oh,
oh.
Yeah,
pho - to - graph.
(Bkgd. voc.) Pho - to - graph.
Pho-to - graph.
w/4-bar Bkgd. vocal figure & lead vocal ad lib. (both till fade)
Gtr. 3
(15ma)
A.H.
8va
Begin fade
hold bend
Fade

PLEASE PLEASE ME

Words and Music by
JOHN LENNON and PAUL McCARTNEY

*High octave is doubled by harmonica.

A
E
E
A
Elec. Gtr. 1
try, girl.
say, love.
C - 'mon.
(C - 'mon.)
C -
F#m
C#m
A
Cont. rhy. simile
'mon
(C - 'mon.)
C - 'mon
(C - 'mon.)
C - 'mon
(C - 'mon.)
Please
To Coda
E
A
B
E
Elec. Gtr. 2
Cont. rhy. simile
please me, whoa yeah, like I please you.

1.
2.
Bridge:
A 5fr. 134211
B 7fr. 134211
E 231
Elec. Gtr. 2
*Elec. Gtrs. 1 & 2
I don't wan - na sound com - plain - in',
(Ah.
Cont. in slashes
*Two gtrs. arr. for one.
Cont. rhy. simile
but you know there's al - ways rain in my heart. In my heart.
I do all the pleas - in' with you, it's so hard to rea - son with you. Whoa
w/Riff A (Elec. Gtr. 1)
D.S. al Coda
Elec. Gtr. 2 cont. rhy. simile
yeah, why do you make me blue?
Coda
w/Riff A (Elec. Gtr. 1) 2 times
you. (Please me, whoa yeah, like I please you.) Please me, whoa
G 3fr.
C 8fr.
Elec. Gtrs. 1 & 2
yeah, like I please you.

PROUD MARY

Words and Music by
J.C. FOGERTY

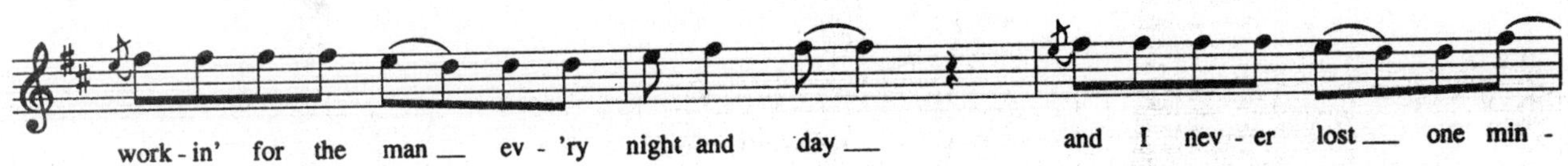

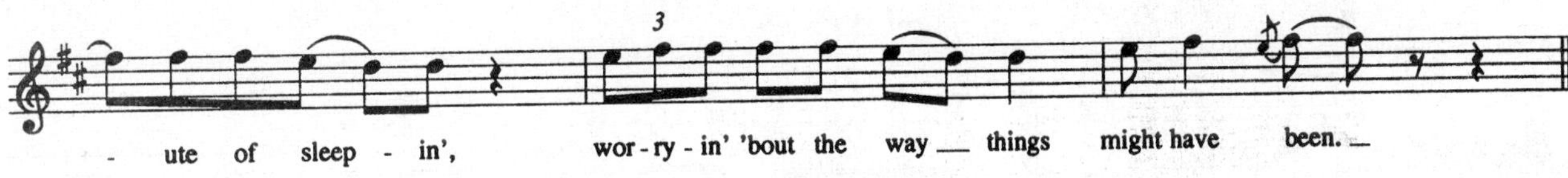

To Coda
D
- in', roll - in', roll - in' on the riv - er.
Riff A
C A G C A G C A G F
F6 F D
Guitar Solo :
Cont. rhy. simile

Verse 2:
Cleaned a lot of plates in Memphis,
Pumped a lot of pain down in New Orleans.
But I never saw the good side of the city
Till I hitched a ride on a river boat queen.
(To Chorus:)

Verse 3:
If you come down to the river,
Bet you're gonna find some people who live.
You don't have to worry
'Cause you have no money,
People on the river are happy to give.
(To Chorus:)

PROWLER

Words and Music by
STEVE HARRIS

Em D A F E G C Em-I B open chord

Fast Four

Em

(Lay right hand palm across all strings for staccato effect on chord)

D Em

trill. . . continue

Guitar Strum - I

Em

Walk - ing through the cit - y
See the la - dies flash - ing

D
look - ing— oh so pret - ty—
All their— legs and lash - es—
I've—— just—
B
B
1.3.
2.4.
Em
G A
got to find— my way.——
F
B B B
Well—— you see me crawl - ing through— the bush - es
E G A G O.C.
with it o - pen wide.
What you

E
Guitar Lick: A
see - ing girl.
10 8 7 8 7
10 8 7 8 7
F
Can't you be - lieve that feel - ing,
can't you be - lieve it,
can't you be - lieve your eyes.
E
G A G O.C. E
Guitar Lick: A
It's the real thing girl.
C D
Got me feel - ing my - self and reel - ing a - round.
(Let chord ring)
3 2 0 3 0 3 2 0 3 0
0 2 3 3 2 0

Guitar Strum - I
Em
Guitar Lick: B
C
D
To Coda
Got me talk - ing but feel like walk - ing a - round.
Em
Em
Em
F♯
A
1. Em
2. Em-I

Em
D
Em
D
Em-I
Em-I
D
2 0 3 2 0 3 2 0 3 2 0 3 2 0
Em
D
Guitar Strum - II
Em
B
B
D
B
B
C
B
C
D
Em
Got me feel - ing my - self and
reel - ing a
C
Got me talk - ing but
B
noth - ing's with
C
D
me
Em
Got me
feel - ing my
D
- self and reel - ing a -

Slow & freely
C
D
round.
tr
Guitar Strum - I
a tempo
Em
Slow & freely
D.S. al Coda (a tempo)
C
D
tr
Coda
Em
(Strum ⊓ V as fast as you can)

PSYCHO KILLER

Words and Music by
DAVID BYRNE, CHRIS FRANTZ
and MARTINA WEYMOUTH

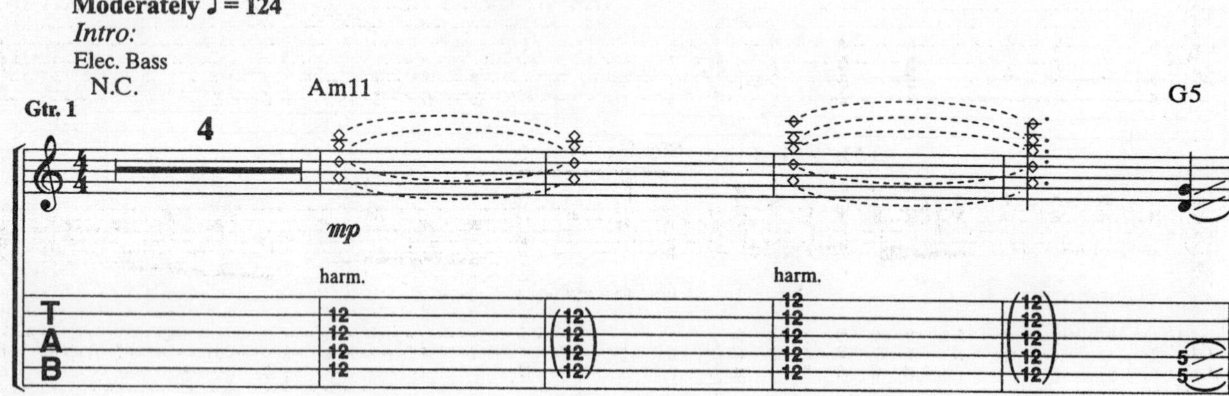

Verse:

A G

1. I can't seem to face up to the facts.__
2. *See additional lyrics*

end Rhy. Fig. 1 Rhy. Fig. 2

P.M.

end Rhy. Fig. 1A Rhy. Fig. 2A

hold throughout

w/Rhy. Figs. 2 *(Gtr. 1)* & 2A *(Gtr. 2)*

A G A

I'm tense and nerv - ous, and I can't re - lax.__ I can't sleep 'cause my

end Rhy. Fig. 2

P.M.

end Rhy. Fig. 2A

G
A
w/Fills 1 (Gtr. 1) & 1A (Gtr. 2)
bed's on fire.
Don't touch me, I'm a real live wire.
Chorus:
F
G
Am
Rhy. Fig. 3
Gtr. 1
Rhy. Fig. 3A
Gtr. 2
Psy - cho kil - ler.
Qu'est que c'est?
Fa, fa, fa, fa, fa, fa,
F
G
Gtr. 1
Gtr. 2
fa, fa, fa, fa. Bet - ter run, run, run, run, run, run, run a -
w/Rhy. Figs. 3 (Gtr. 1) & 3A (Gtr. 2) simile
C
end Rhy. Fig. 3
end Rhy. Fig. 3A
F
way.
Oh.
Psy - cho kil - ler.
Fill 1
Gtr. 1
Cont. in slashes
P.M.
T
A
B
7 5
7 5
7 5
7 5
7 5
Fill 1A
Gtr. 2
Cont. in slashes
T
A
B
0
2
0
0
0 0

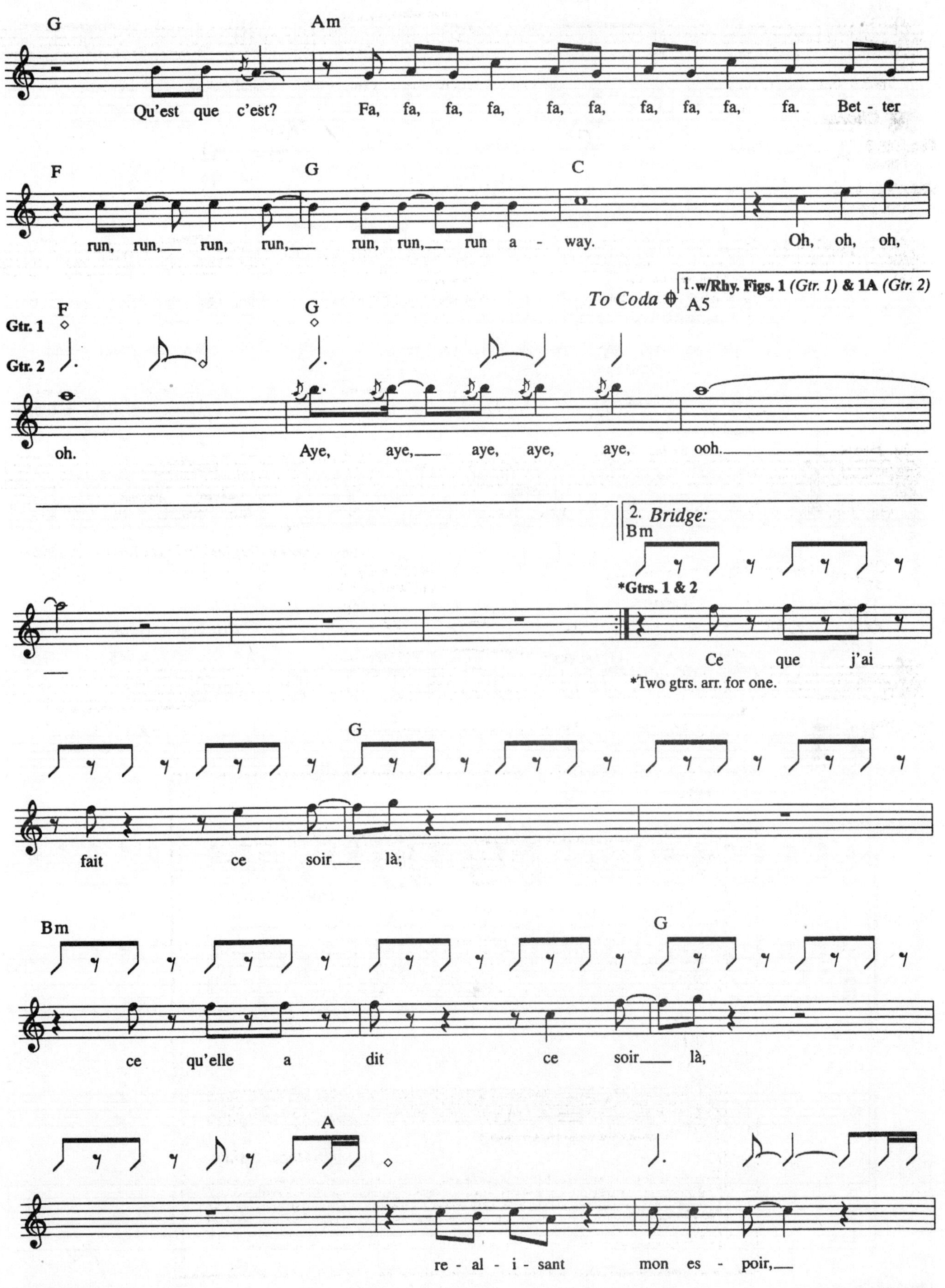
G
Am
Qu'est que c'est? Fa, fa, fa, fa, fa, fa, fa, fa, fa, fa. Bet - ter
F
G
C
run, run, run, run, run, run, run a - way. Oh, oh, oh,
To Coda
1. w/Rhy. Figs. 1 (Gtr. 1) & 1A (Gtr. 2)
A5
Gtr. 1
Gtr. 2
oh. Aye, aye, aye, aye, aye, ooh.
2. Bridge:
Bm
*Gtrs. 1 & 2
Ce que j'ai
*Two gtrs. arr. for one.
fait ce soir là;
ce qu'elle a dit ce soir là,
re - al - i - sant mon es - poir,

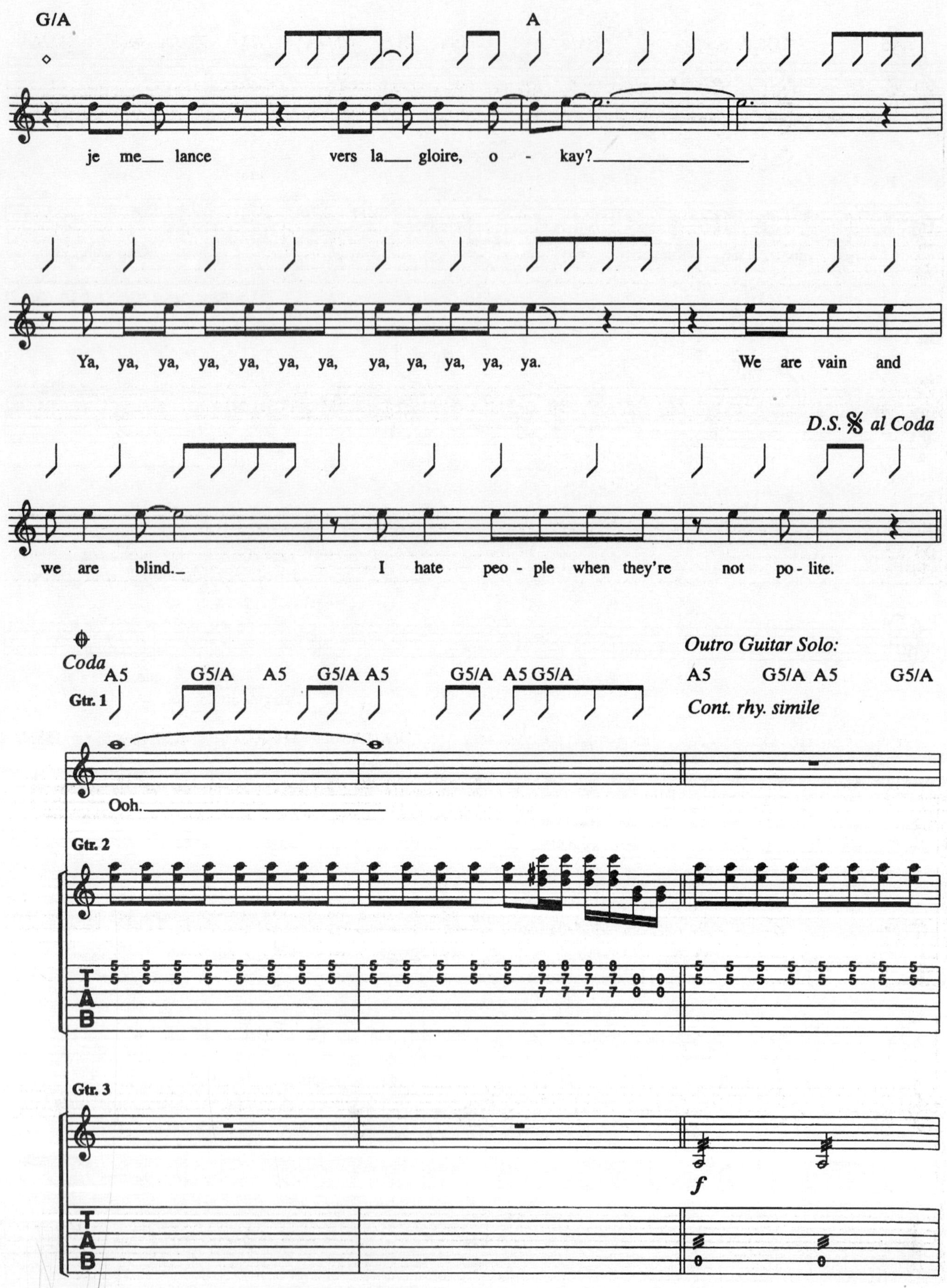
G/A
A
je me lance vers la gloire, o - kay?
Ya, ya, ya, ya, ya, ya, ya, ya, ya, ya, ya, ya.
We are vain and
D.S. al Coda
we are blind.
I hate peo - ple when they're not po - lite.
Coda
Outro Guitar Solo:
A5
G5/A
A5
G5/A
A5
G5/A
A5
G5/A
A5
G5/A
A5
G5/A
Gtr. 1
Cont. rhy. simile
Ooh.
Gtr. 2
Gtr. 3
f

A5
G5/A A5
G5/A A5
G5/A A5
G5/A A5
G5/A A5
G5/A
hold bend
1/2
1/2
f

A5 G5/A A5 G5/A
A5
G5/A A5
G5/A A5
G5/A A5
G5/A A5
G5/A A5
G5/A
1/2
1/2
1/2

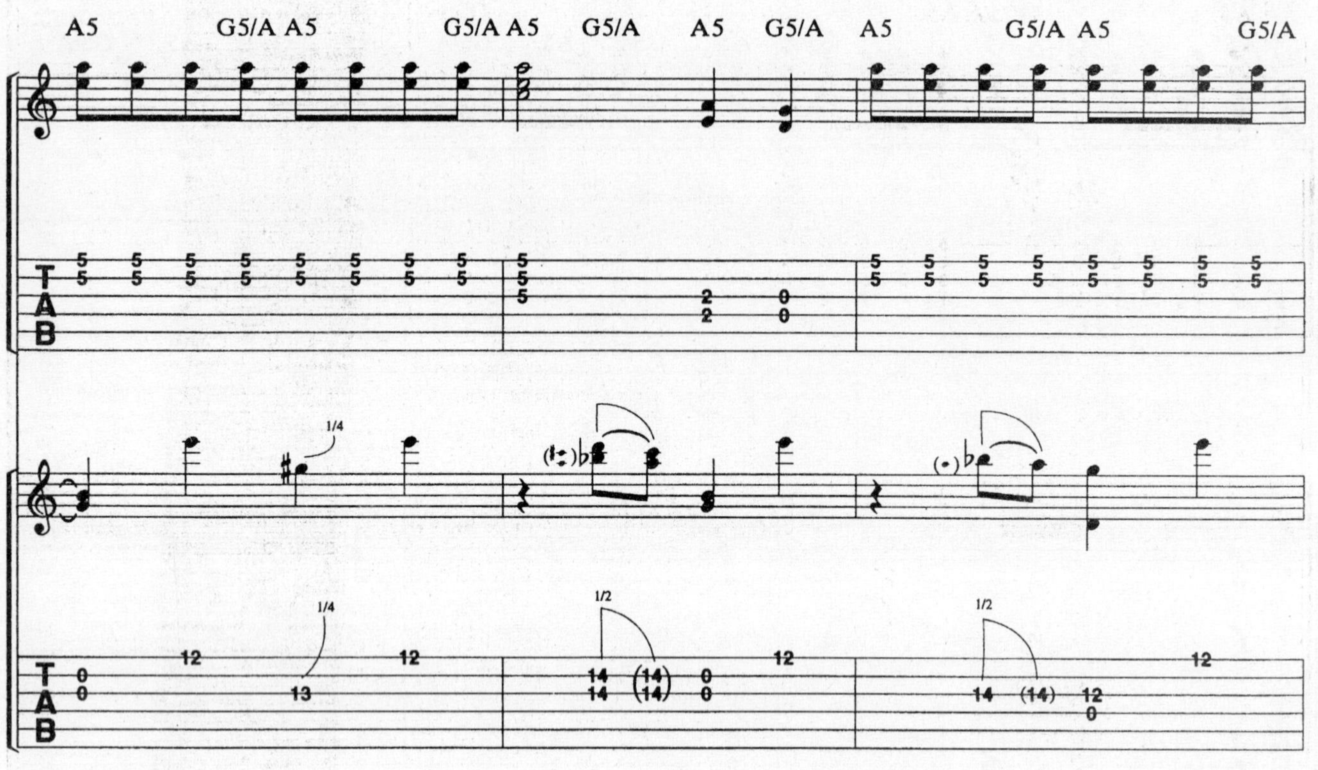
A5
G5/A A5
G5/A A5
G5/A
A5
G5/A
A5
G5/A A5
G5/A
1/4
1/2

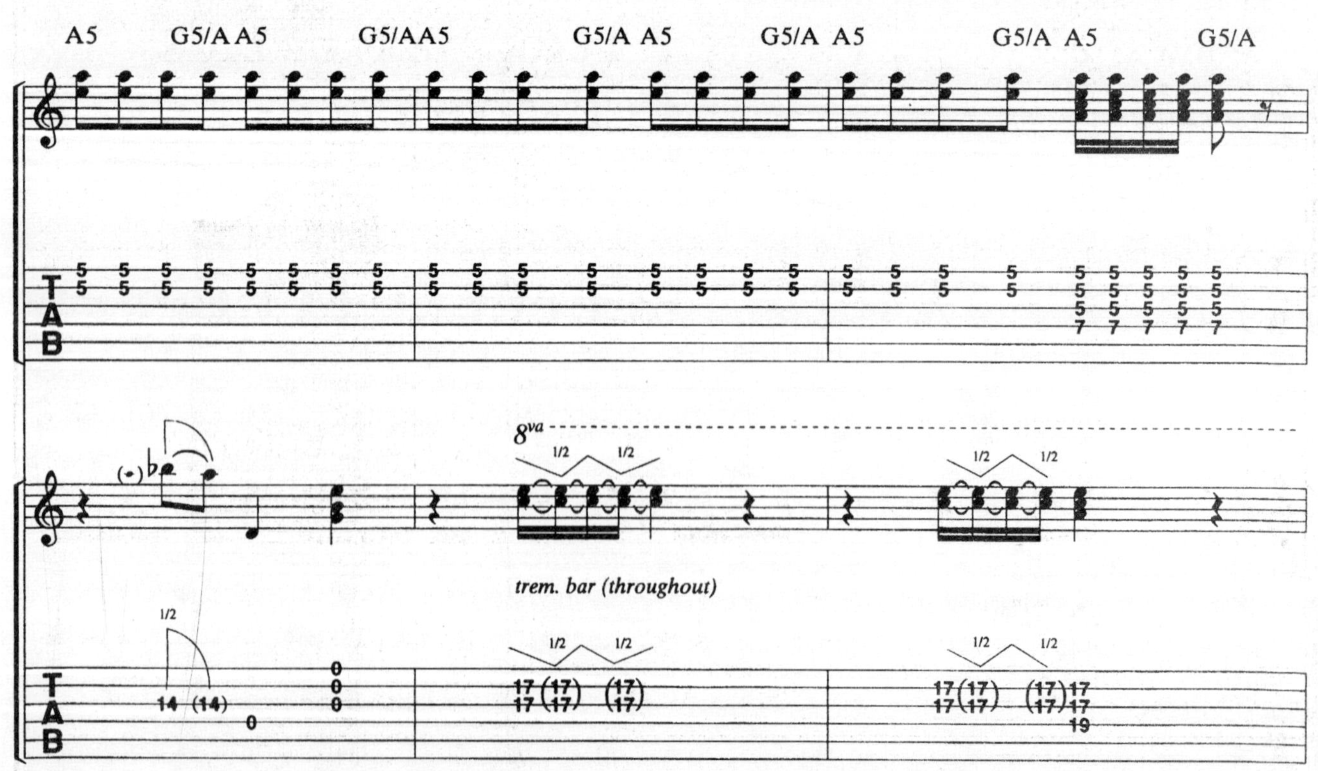
A5
G5/A A5
G5/AA5
G5/A A5
G5/A A5
G5/A A5
G5/A
8va
1/2
trem. bar (throughout)

Riff A
A5 G5/A A5 G5/A A5 G5/A A5 G5/A
8va
1/2

A5 G5/A A5 G5/A A5 G5/A A5 G5/A
end Riff A
1/2

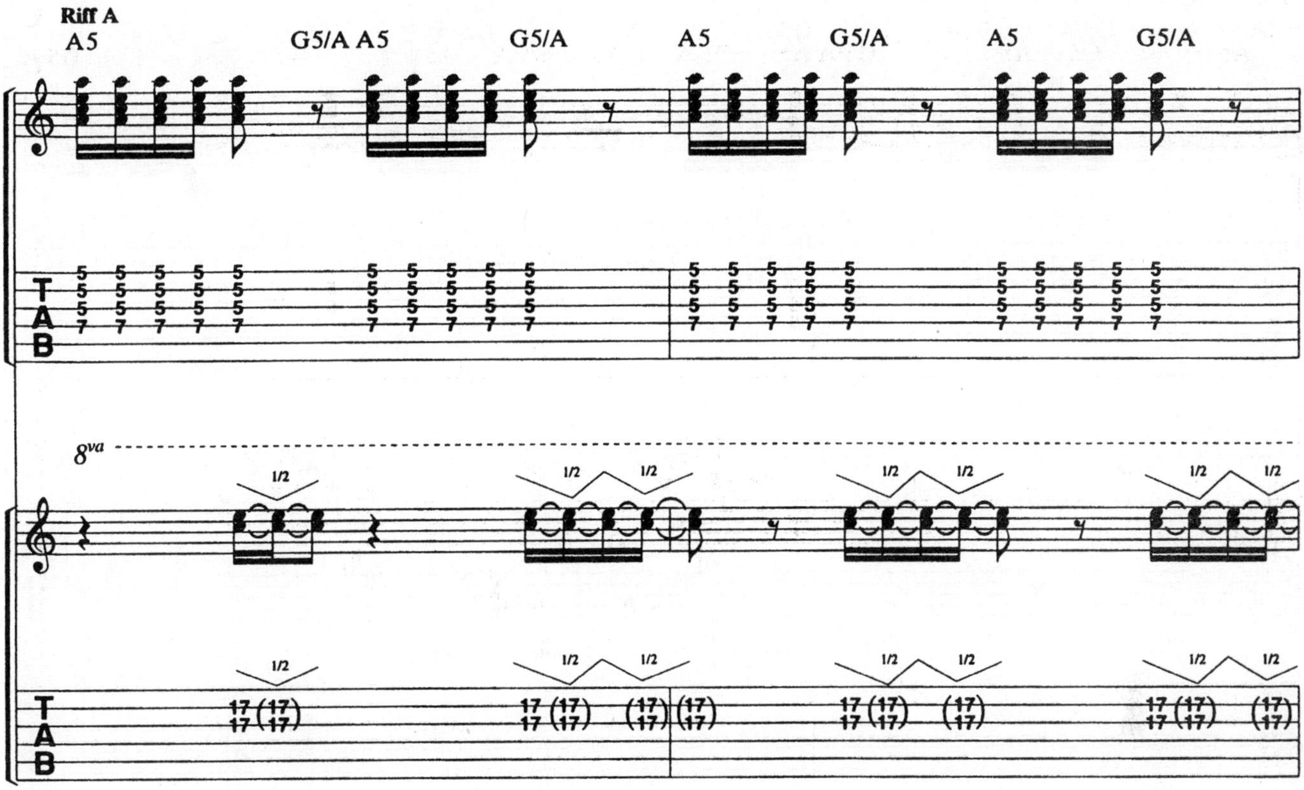

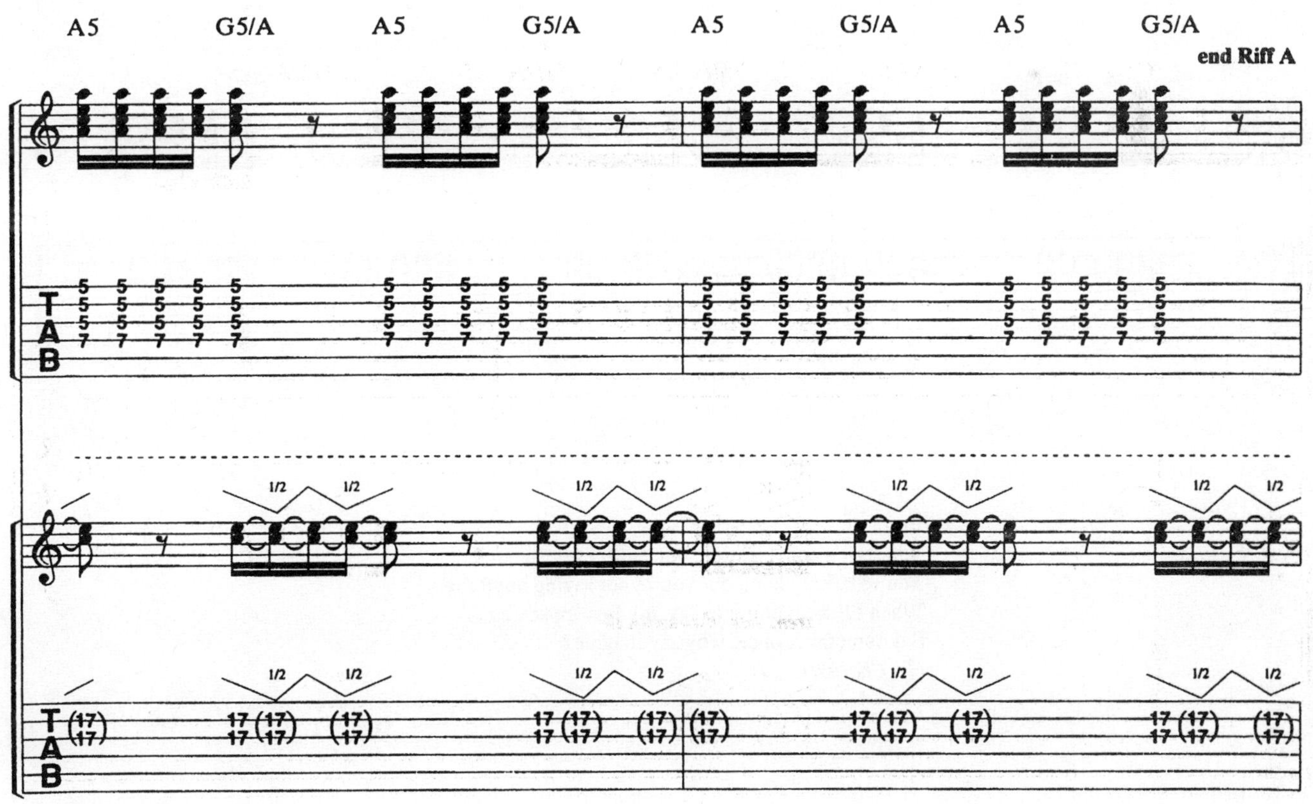

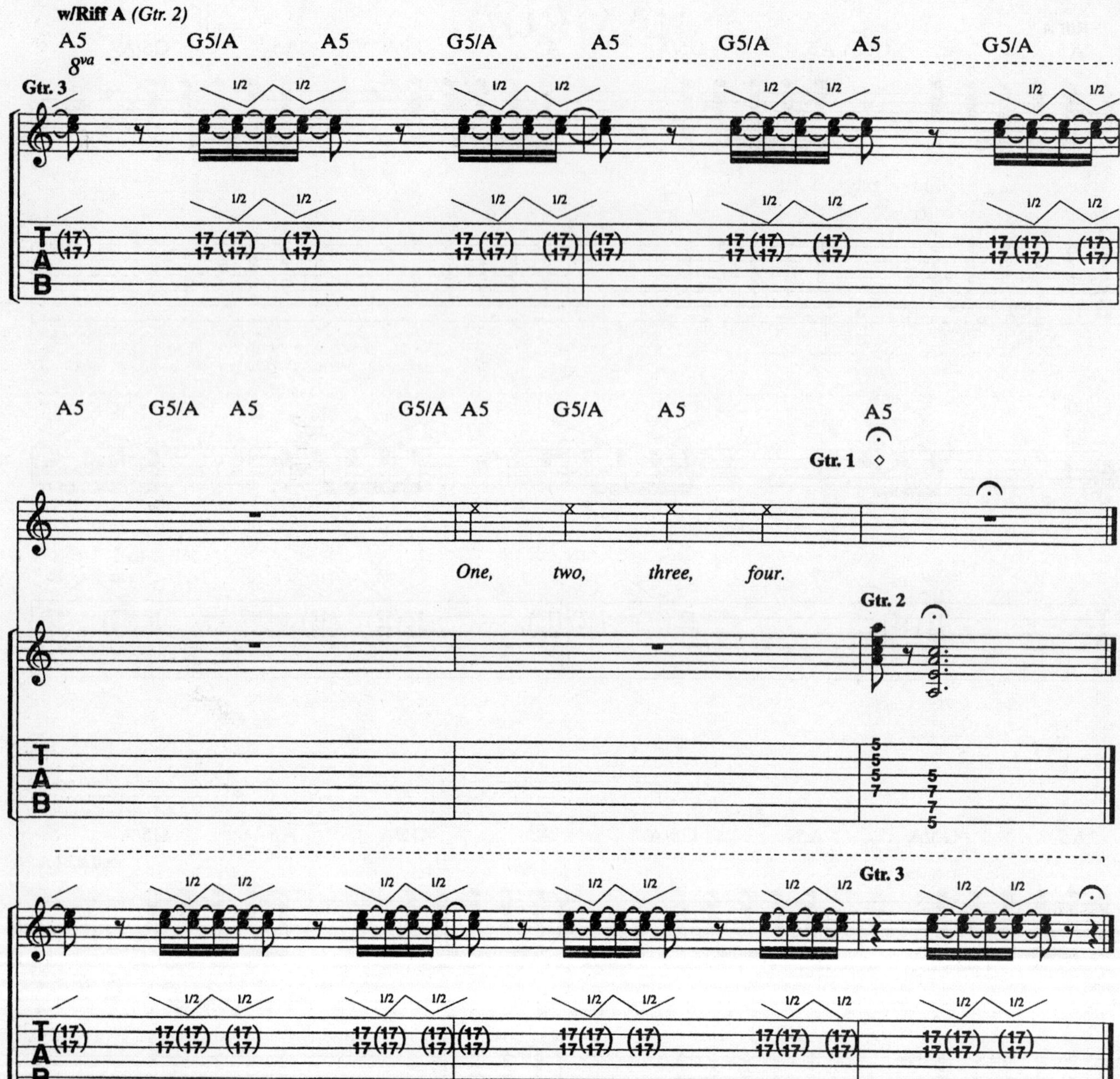

Verse 2:
You start a conversation, you can't even finish it.
You're talking a lot, but you're not saying anything.
When I have nothing to say, my lips are sealed.
Say something once, why say it again?
(To Chorus:)

RAMROD

By AL CASEY

E7
B
F♯7
To Coda
1.
end Rhy. Fig. 1
2.
To Next Strain
(To B)
3.
D.S. al Coda

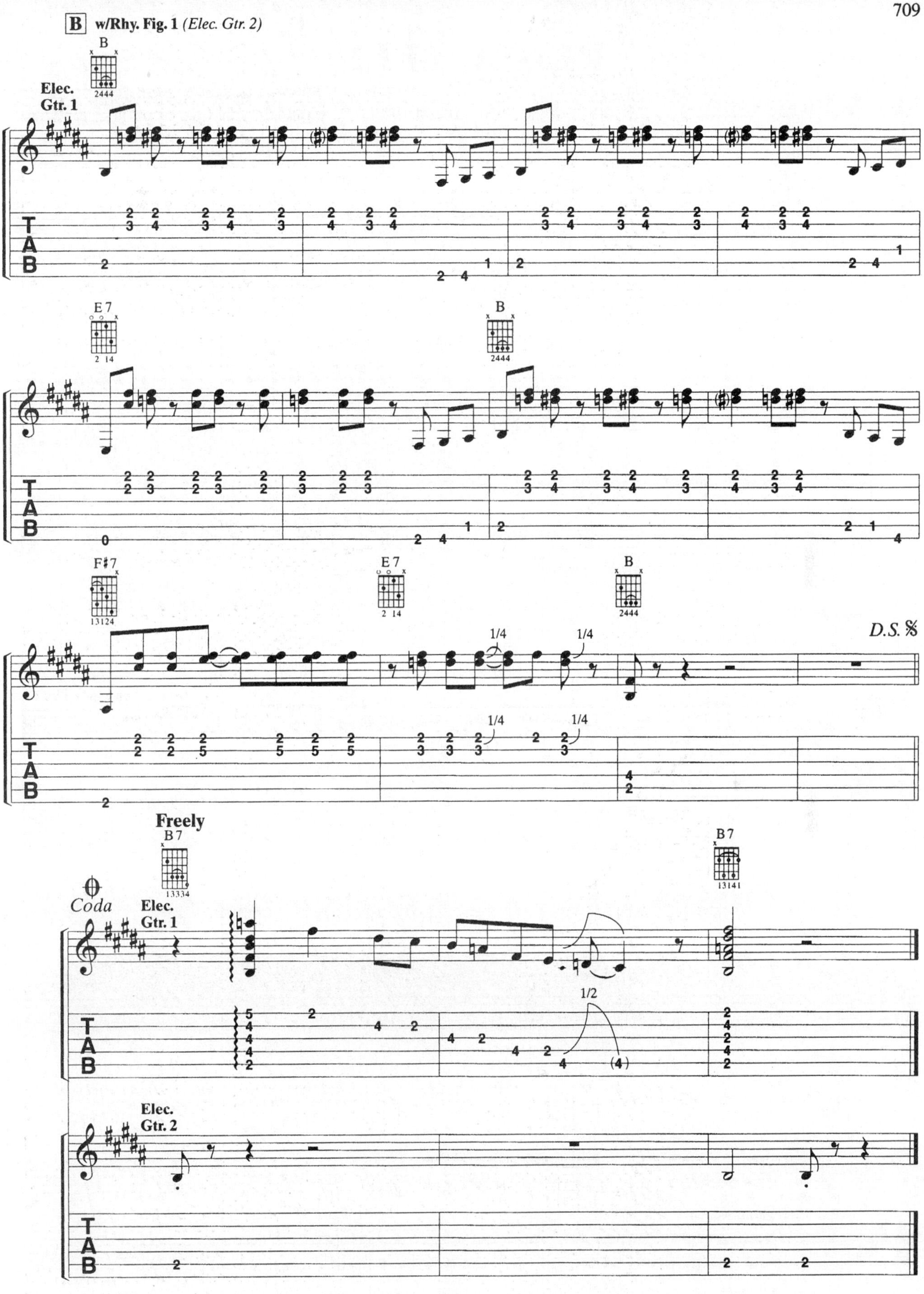

B **w/Rhy. Fig. 1** *(Elec. Gtr. 2)*

B

Elec. Gtr. 1

E7 B

F♯7 E7 B

1/4 1/4

D.S. 𝄋

Freely

Coda

B7 B7

Elec. Gtr. 1

1/2

Elec. Gtr. 2

REBEL YELL

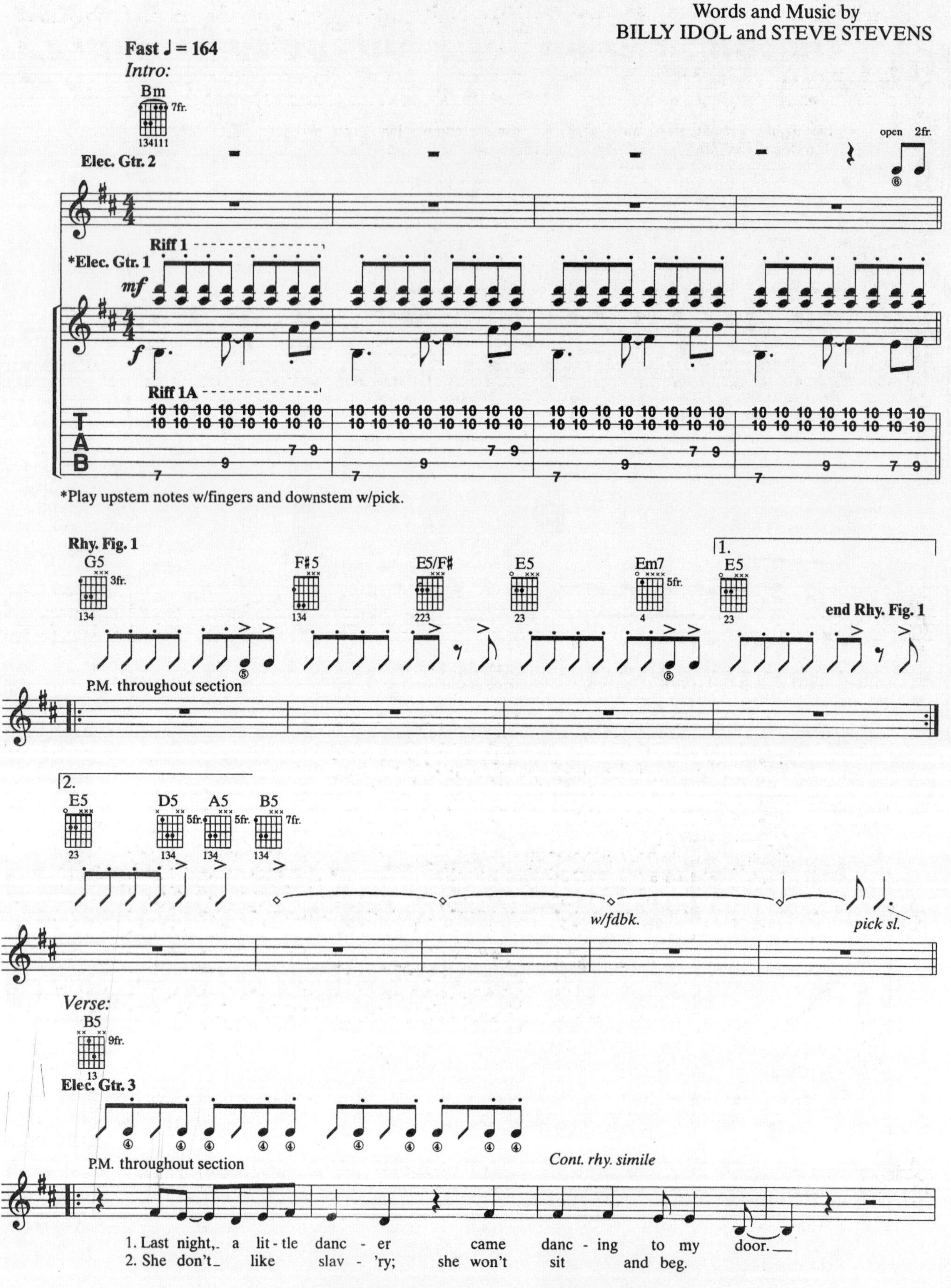
Words and Music by
BILLY IDOL and STEVE STEVENS
Fast ♩ = 164
Intro:
Bm
7fr.
134111
Elec. Gtr. 2
open 2fr.
Riff 1
*Elec. Gtr. 1
mf
f
Riff 1A
*Play upstem notes w/fingers and downstem w/pick.
Rhy. Fig. 1
G5
3fr.
F♯5
E5/F♯
E5
Em7
5fr.
1.
end Rhy. Fig. 1
P.M. throughout section
2.
E5
D5
5fr.
A5
5fr.
B5
7fr.
w/fdbk.
pick sl.
Verse:
B5
9fr.
Elec. Gtr. 3
P.M. throughout section
Cont. rhy. simile
1. Last night, a lit - tle danc - er came danc - ing to my door.
2. She don't like slav - 'ry; she won't sit and beg.

D/A
7fr.
111
D/G
5fr.
133
Elec. Gtr. 3
5fr.
5fr.
Last night a lit-tle an-gel came pump-ing on my floor.
But when I'm tired and lone-ly, she sees me to bed.
B5
9fr.
13
Cont. rhy. simile
She said, "I can't, ba-by, with-out a li-cense for love.
What set you free and brought you to me, babe?
D5
A5
134
And if it ex-pi-res, rain hell from a-bove."
What set you free? I need you here by me.
Be-cause
Chorus:
Bm
134111
Rhy. Fig. 2
P.M.
7fr.
in the mid-night hour, she cried, "More, more, more."
end Rhy. Fig. 2
With a reb-el yell, she cried, "More, more, more, wow!"

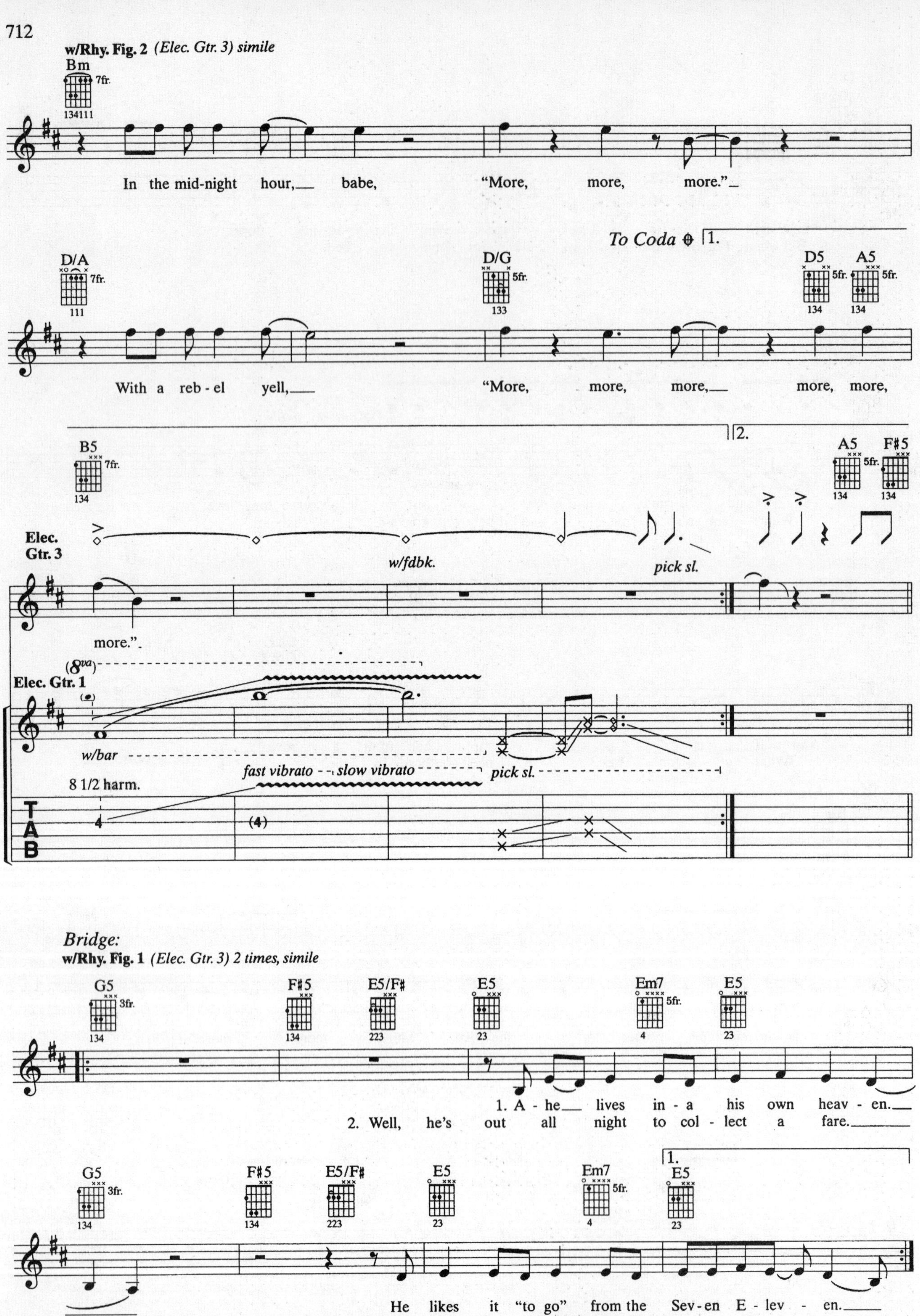
w/Rhy. Fig. 2 (Elec. Gtr. 3) simile
Bm
7fr.
134111
In the mid-night hour, babe, "More, more, more."
To Coda ⊕ 1.
D/A
7fr.
111
D/G
5fr.
133
D5
5fr.
134
A5
5fr.
134
With a reb-el yell, "More, more, more, more, more,
B5
7fr.
134
2.
A5
5fr.
134
F#5
134
Elec. Gtr. 3
w/fdbk.
pick sl.
more."
(8va)
Elec. Gtr. 1
w/bar
fast vibrato slow vibrato
pick sl.
8 1/2 harm.
T
A
B
4
(4)
Bridge:
w/Rhy. Fig. 1 (Elec. Gtr. 3) 2 times, simile
G5
3fr.
134
F#5
134
E5/F#
223
E5
23
Em7
5fr.
4
E5
23
1. A - he lives in - a his own heav - en.
2. Well, he's out all night to col - lect a fare.
G5
3fr.
134
F#5
134
E5/F#
223
E5
23
Em7
5fr.
4
1.
E5
23
He likes it "to go" from the Sev-en E-lev - en.
Just as long, just as long's it don't mess

2.
w/Riffs 1 (Elec. Gtr. 1) & 1A (Elec. Gtr. 2) 3 times, simile
E5
D5
A5
B5
Elec. Gtr. 3
w/fdbk.
up his hair.
Guitar Solo:
w/Rhy. Fig. 2 (Elec. Gtr. 3) 2 times, simile
Bm
Ow!
Ah!
Elec. Gtr. 4
hold throughout
grad. release & slide
w/bar
D/A
w/bar
D/G
D5
A5
Bm
grad. bend
w/sound effect from "echoplex"

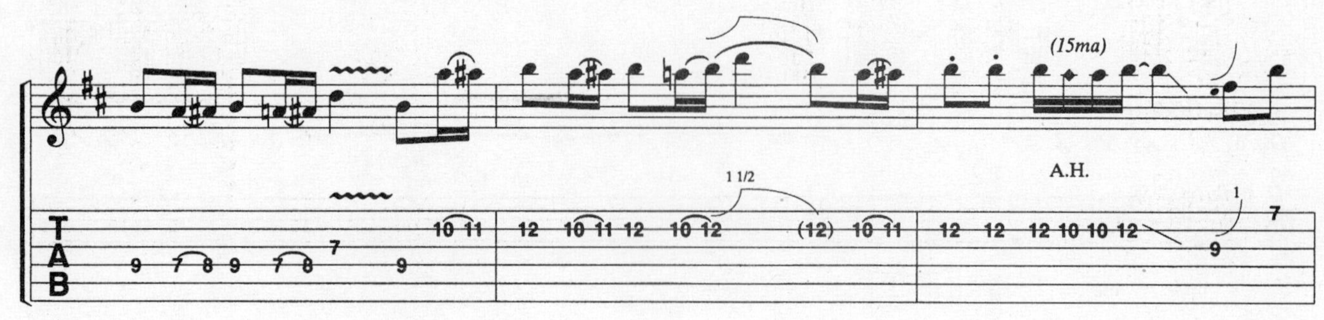

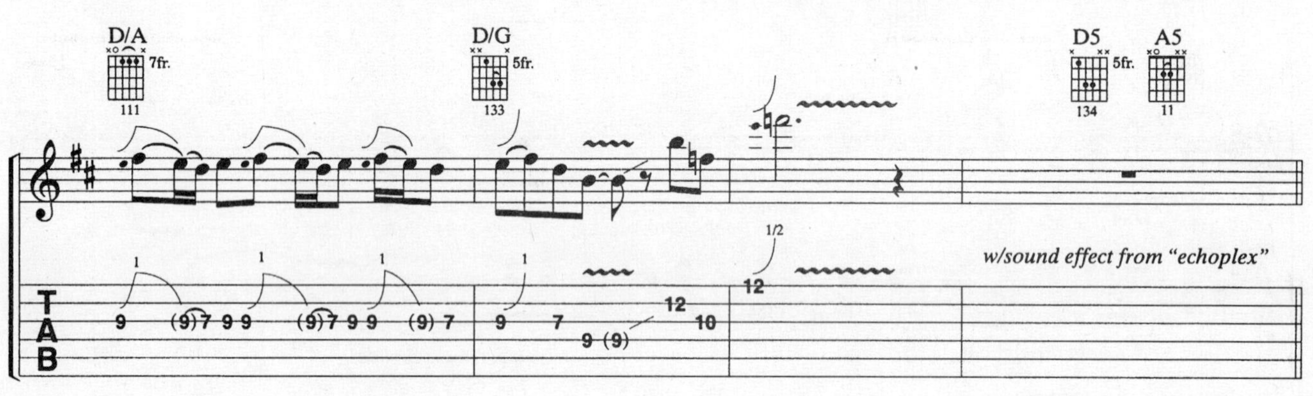

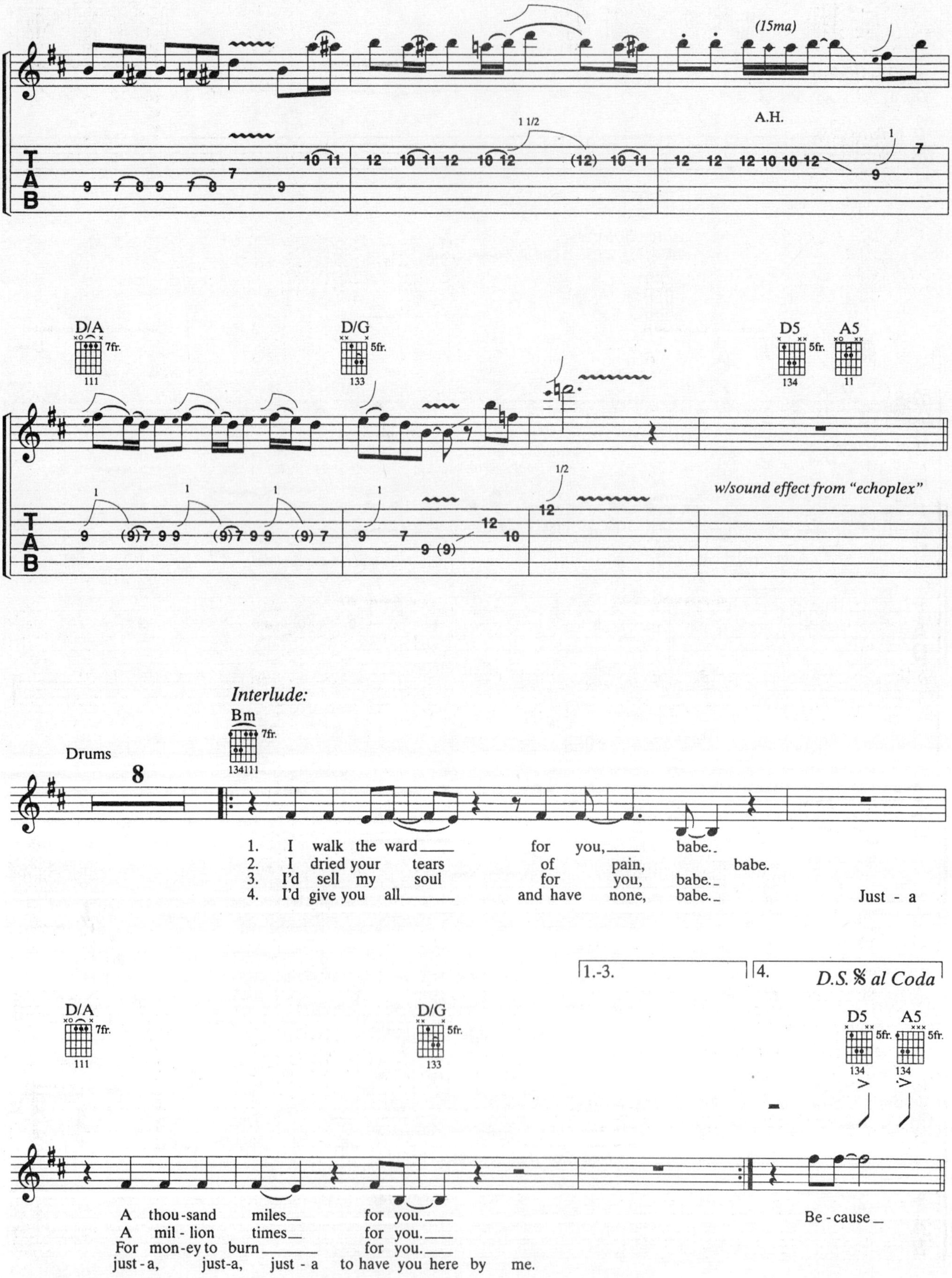

Interlude:

Drums 8

Bm 7fr. 134111

1. I walk the ward___ for you,___ babe._
2. I dried your tears of pain, babe.
3. I'd sell my soul for you, babe._
4. I'd give you all_____ and have none, babe._ Just - a

D/A 7fr. 111 — D/G 5fr. 133 — 1.-3. — 4. *D.S. 𝄋 al Coda* — D5 5fr. 134 — A5 5fr. 134

A thou-sand miles__ for you.___ Be - cause_
A mil - lion times__ for you.___
For mon-ey to burn______ for you.___
just-a, just-a, just - a to have you here by me.

Coda

Outro:

D/G D5 A5 Bm A5 B5 C♯5 C5

Elec. Gtr. 3

P.M.

more, more, more." ___

B5 Bm B5 C5 C♯5 D/A

P.M. P.M.

{Ooh yeah, ___ lit - tle ba - by.}
{Ooh yeah, ___ lit - tle an - gel.}

A5 B5 C♯5 C5 Gmaj7

1. D5 A5

P.M.

She want more. ___ More, more, more, more,

2. w/Riffs 1 *(Elec. Gtr. 1)* & 1A *(Elec. Gtr. 2)* 4 times, simile

D5 A5 B5 A5 B5

w/fdbk.

More, more, more, more, more. _

fdbk. *(8va)*

trem. bar

T	4 4 4 2	(4)	(4) (4) (4)	(4) (4) (4) (4) (4)	2 2 0	4 4 2

REMEMBER TOMORROW

Words and Music by
STEVE HARRIS and PAUL DI'ANNO

Guitar Pattern - A

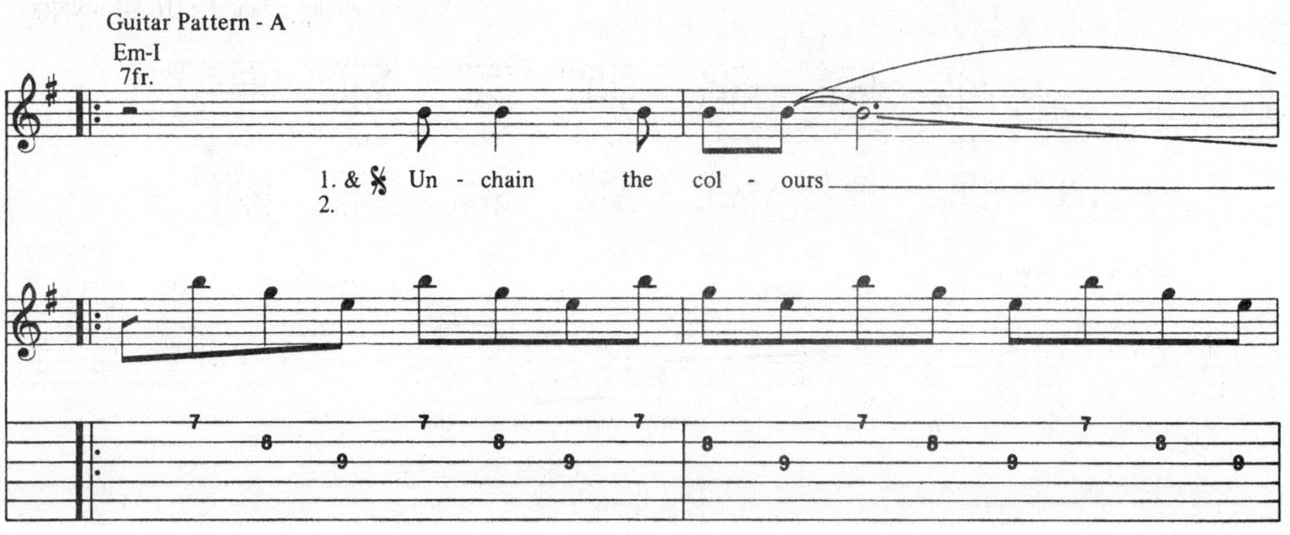

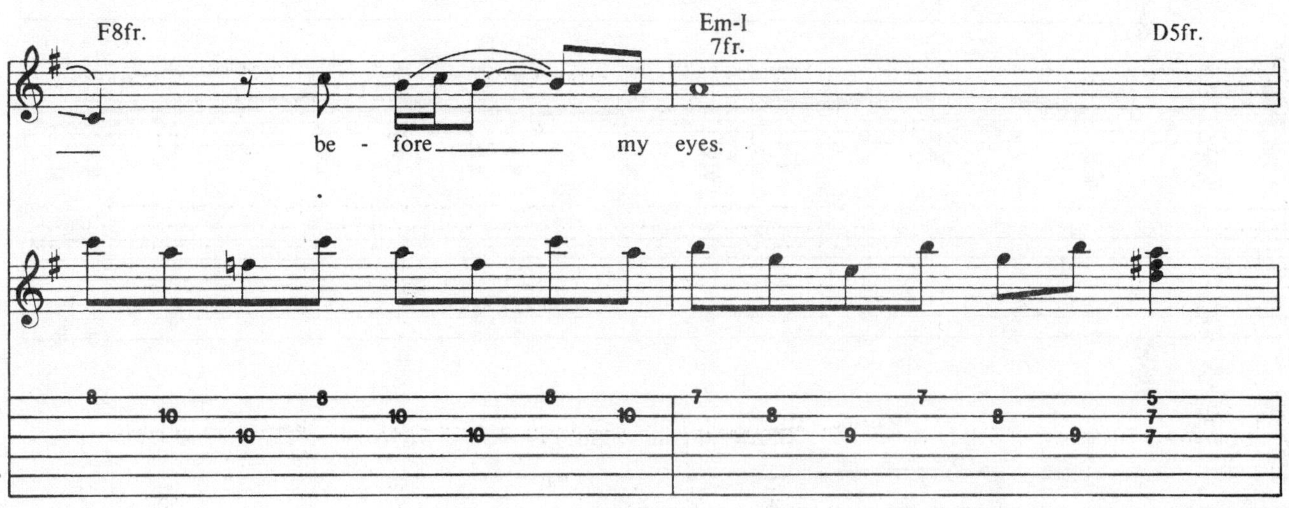

Guitar Pattern - A

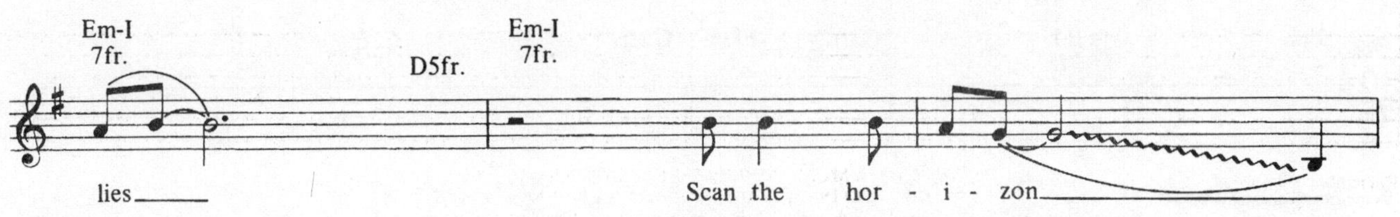

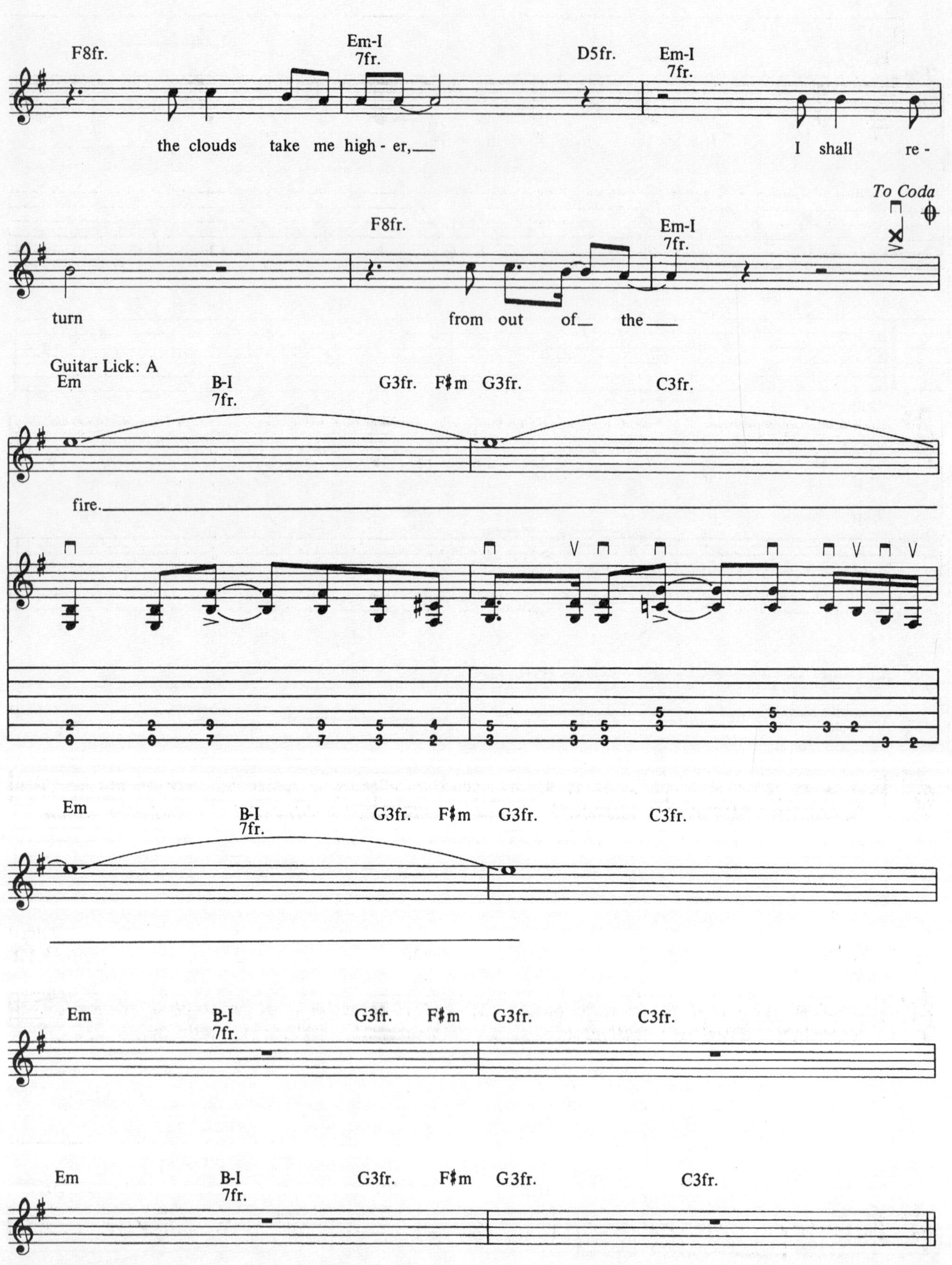

F8fr.
Em-I 7fr.
D5fr.
Em-I 7fr.
the clouds take me high - er,
I shall re -
To Coda
F8fr.
Em-I 7fr.
turn
from out of the
Guitar Lick: A
Em
B-I 7fr.
G3fr.
F♯m
G3fr.
C3fr.
fire.
Em
B-I 7fr.
G3fr.
F♯m
G3fr.
C3fr.
Em
B-I 7fr.
G3fr.
F♯m
G3fr.
C3fr.
Em
B-I 7fr.
G3fr.
F♯m
G3fr.
C3fr.

1.
Em
Em
2.
Moderately
D10fr.
C8fr.
D10fr.
C8fr.
3 times
B
Em7fr.
G10fr.
Em7fr.
G10fr.
A 12fr.
3 times
C8fr.
D10fr.
B 7fr.
C 8fr.
C 8fr.
D 10fr.
1.
2 times
2.

2. Tears for rememberance
and tears for joy,
Tears for somebody
and this lonely boy,
Out in the madness
the all seeing eye,
Flickers above us
to light up the sky.

RIKKI DON'T LOSE THAT NUMBER

Words and Music by
WALTER BECKER and
DONALD FAGEN

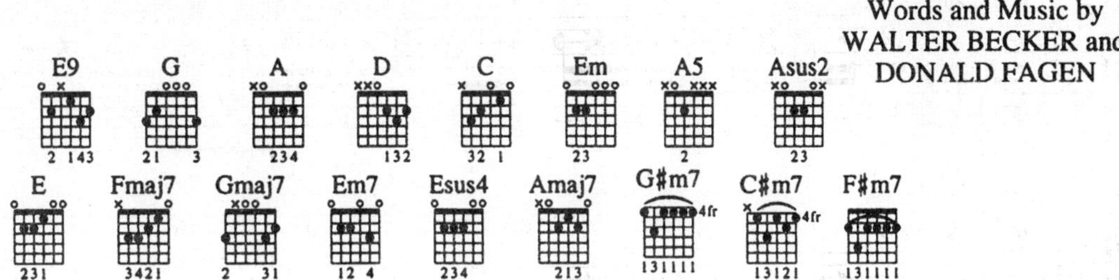

E
F#m11
A
B7#9
and run.
But if you have a change of heart,
End Rhy. Fig. 2
(cont. in slash)
Chorus
E9
Gtr. 1
G
Rik - ki, don't lose that num - ber, you don't want to call no - bod - y else.
A
G
Send it off in a let - ter to your - self.
Gtr. 2: w/ Fill 1, 2nd time
Gtr. 2: w/ Fill 3, 3rd time
D
C
Rik - ki don't lose that num - ber, it's the
Gtr. 2 (dist.)
mf
full
let ring
mp
2nd & 3rd time simile
Fill 1
Gtr. 2
let ring
full
hold bend
Fill 3
Gtr. 2
full

Em
Gtr. 2 w/ Fill 4, 3rd time
C
on - ly one you own.
You might use it if you feel
A5
Asus2
A
Gtrs. 1 & 2 tacet
To Coda 2
To Coda 1
Gtr. 2: w/ Fill 2, 2nd time
bet - ter, when you get home.
mf
Verse
Gtr. 1: w/ Rhy. Fig. 2, simile
D
Asus2
E
D
2. I have a friend in town, he's heard your name.
We can go out
Asus2
E
C#5
B5
D
A
driv - ing on Slow Hand - Row.
We could stay in - side and play games, I don't
D.S. al Coda 1
E
F#m
A
B7#9
know.
And you could have a change of heart.
Fill 2
Gtr. 2
full
Fill 4
Gtr. 2

Coda 1
Guitar Solo (Jeff "Skunk" Baxter)
D A D E
open 2fr 3fr open
A E A B
open 2fr 2fr open
E
Gtr. 1
let ring
Gtr. 2
full
1/2
hold bend
A
G
Fmaj7
Gmaj7
Em7
D

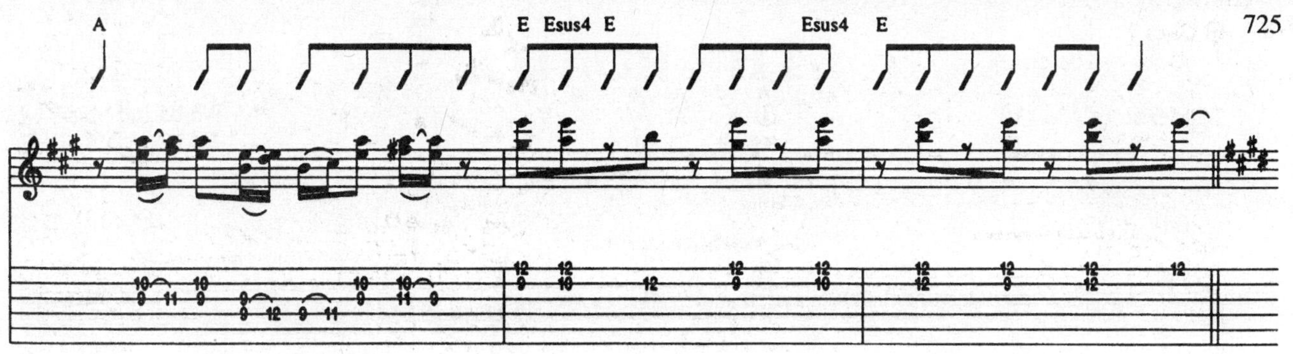
A
E Esus4 E
Esus4 E

Bridge
Amaj7
G#m7
Amaj7
You tell your-self you're not my kind,
but you don't e-ven
mf

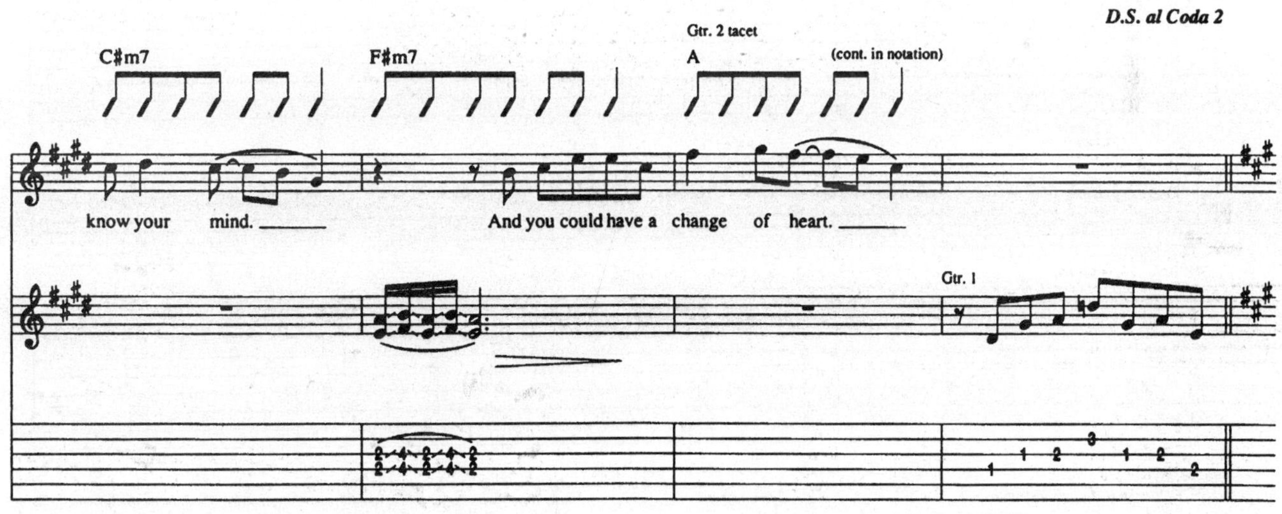
D.S. al Coda 2
Gtr. 2 tacet
C#m7
F#m7
A
(cont. in notation)
know your mind.
And you could have a change of heart.
Gtr. 1

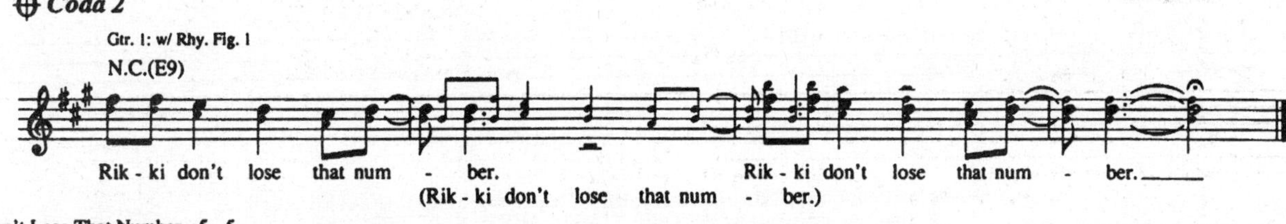
Coda 2
Gtr. 1: w/ Rhy. Fig. 1
N.C.(E9)
Rik-ki don't lose that num-ber.
Rik-ki don't lose that num-ber.
(Rik-ki don't lose that num-ber.)

THE ROAD

Moderately ♩ = 128
(in "2")

Words and Music by
DANNY O'KEEFE

G G+

G G+

Verses 1&2:

G G+ G

1. High - ways___ and dance___ halls;___ a good song takes you far.___
2. *See additional lyrics*

Rhy. Fig. 1

G+ G Gmaj7/F♯ Em7

___ You write a - bout the moon,________ and you

Csus2
G/B
Am9
G
dream_ a - bout_ the stars._
Blues_ in old_ mo - tel_
G+
G
G+
_ rooms;_
girls_ in Dad - dy's cars._
G
Gmaj7/F♯
Em7
Csus2
G/B
You sing a - bout the nights,_
and you laugh a - bout_ the scars._
1.
Am9
end Rhy. Fig. 1

2.
Am9
Chorus:
Em
But when you stop
Rhy. Fig 2
Am7
C♯m7(♭5)
Cmaj7
to let 'em know you got it down it's
Csus2
Em/B
A7
D11/F♯
G
just an - oth - er town a - long the road.
G+
G
G+
end Rhy. Fig. 2

G
G+
G
G+
TAB
Verses 3&4:
w/Rhy. Fig. 1
G
G+
G
3. Lad - ies come to see___ you if your name still rings a bell.__
4. See additional lyrics
G+
G
Gmaj7/F♯
Em7
They give you damn near noth - ing and they'll
Csus2
G/B
Am9
G
say__ they knew you well.____ So you tell 'em you'll__ re - mem-
G+
G
G+
G
Gmaj7/F♯
- ber, but they know it's just a game.____ And a - long the way__ their__
Em7
Csus2
G/B
Am9
fac - es all__ be - gin__ to look__ the same.__
Chorus:
w/Rhy. Fig.2
Em
Am7
C♯m7(♭5)
Cmaj7
And when you stop to let 'em know__ you got it down,______ it's

Csus2 Em/B A7(♯9) D11/F♯ 1. G G+

just an - oth - er town___ a - long___ the road.________

G G+ 2. G G+ G G+

4. Well, it ____

Violin Solo:

G G+ G

TAB

G+ G Gmaj7/F♯ Em7

TAB

Csus2 G/B Am9

TAB

Em Am7 C♯m7(♭5) Cmaj7 Csus2 Em/B A7(♯9) D11/F♯

G G+ G G+ *rit.* G

Verse: 2
Coffee in the morning, cocaine afternoon
You talk about the weather and you grin about the ruin
Phone calls long distance, to tell you how you've been
You forget about the losses; you exagerate the wins.
(To Chorus:)

Verse 4:
Well, it isn't for the money, and it's only for a while
You stalk about the rooms and you roll away the miles
Gamblers in the neon clinging to guitars
You're right about the moon but you're wrong about the stars.
(To Chorus:)

ROCK & ROLL BAND

Words and Music by
TOM SCHOLZ

Pre - Chorus
Gtr. 1: w/ Rhy. Fill 3, 3rd time
N.C. A5 N.C. E5 N.C. A5 N.C. E5
we did-n't have much mon - ey. We bare - ly made e-nough to sur-vive. But when we
Gtr. 1
N.C. F#5 N.C. A5
Gtrs. 2 & 3: w/ Riff A
B5
(w/ crowd noise)
got up on stage and got rea - dy to play peo-ple came a - live.
(cont. in slash)
Chorus
C#5 A5 B5 C#5 A5 B5
Gtr. 1
Rock 'n' roll band, ev-'ry bod-y's wait - ing, get-tin' cra - zy, an - tic - i - pat - ing
E5 E6 E5 E6 F#5
1.
G5 G#5 A5 B5 E5
love and mu - sic, play, play, play,
Rhy. Fill 3
Gtr. 1
Riff A
Gr. 2
Gtr. 3 (dist.)
divisi

Gtr. 1: w/ Rhy. Fill 2
N.C.
E5
2.
F#5
G5 G#5 A5
B5
E5
To Coda
— yeah, yeah, — yeah, yeah. —
2. Danc - — sic, —
play, — play, — play, —
Guitar Solo
F#5 E5 F#5 E5 F#5
E5
F#5
E5 F#5 E5 F#5
— yeah, yeah. —
Aah! —
Gtr. 2
steady gliss.
grad. release
semi - harm.
full
full full
3/4
1/2
1/2
B5
F#5
E5 F#5 E5 F#5
Gtr. 2
Gtr. 3
Rhy. Fill 2
Gtr. 1

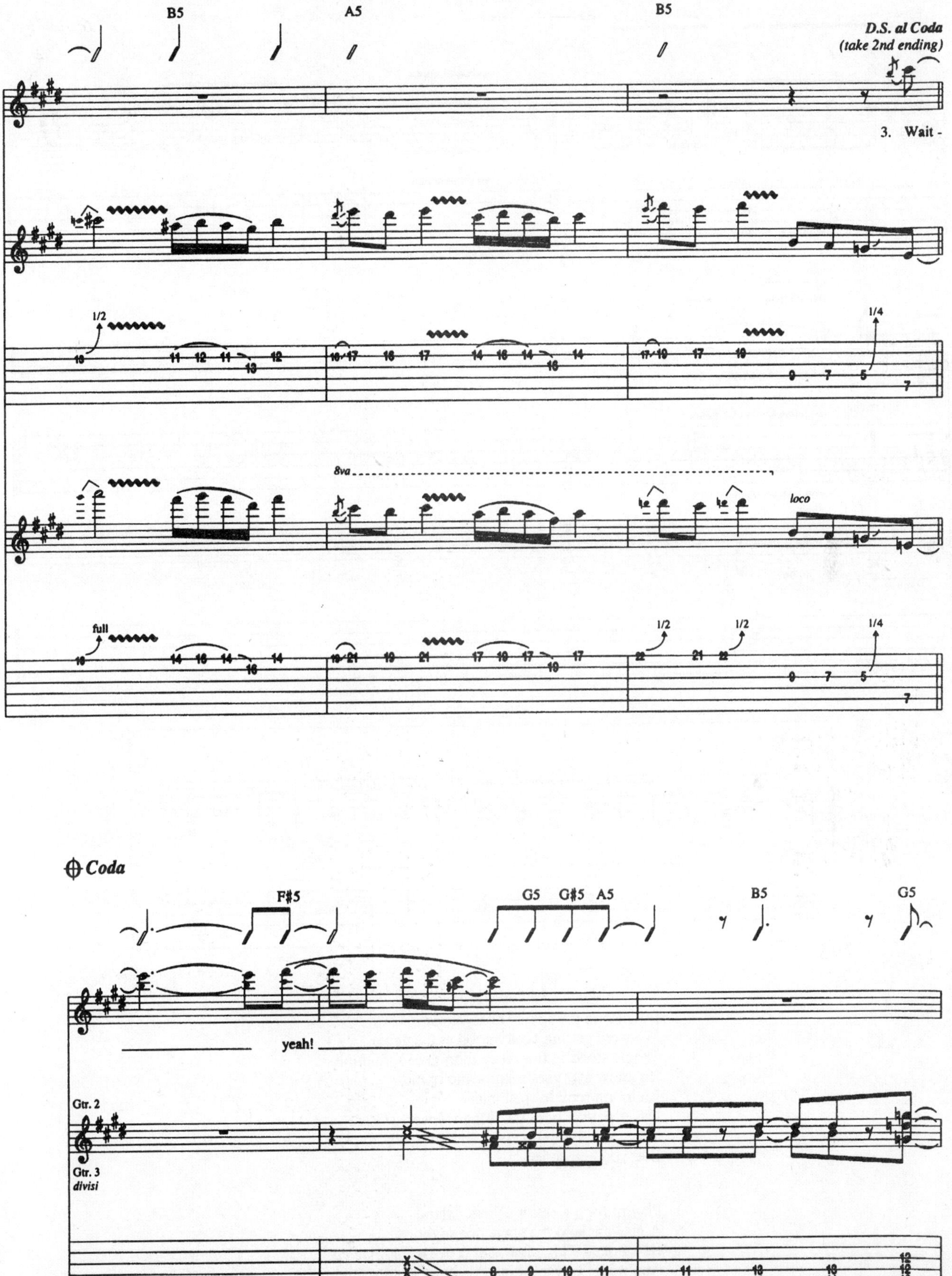

B5 A5 B5

D.S. al Coda (take 2nd ending)

3. Wait -

1/2 full 1/2 1/2 1/4 1/4

8va loco

Coda

Additional Lyrics

2. Dancin' in the streets of Hyannis,
We were getting pretty good at the game.
People stood in line, they didn't seem to mind,
Ya know everybody knew our name.
Livin' on rock 'n' roll music,
Never worry 'bout the thing we were missin'.
When we got up on stage and got ready to play
Everybody listened.

3. Playin' for a week in Rhode Island
A man came to the stage one night.
He smoked a big cigar and drove a Cadillac car
And said, "Boys, I think this band's outta' sight."
Signed a record company contract,
You know I've got great expectations.
When I hear you on the car radio
You're gonna be a sensation.

ROCK AND ROLL ALL NITE

Words and Music by
PAUL STANLEY and
GENE SIMMONS

Tune Down 1/2 Step
①-E♭ ④-D♭
②-B♭ ⑤-A♭
③-G♭ ⑥-E♭

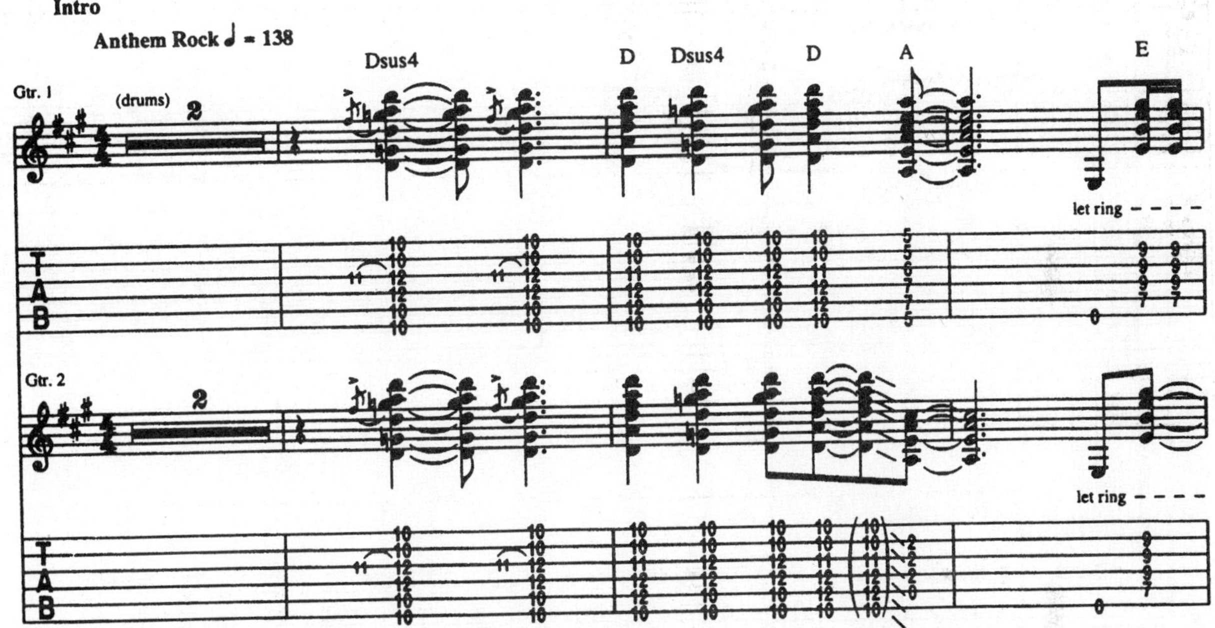

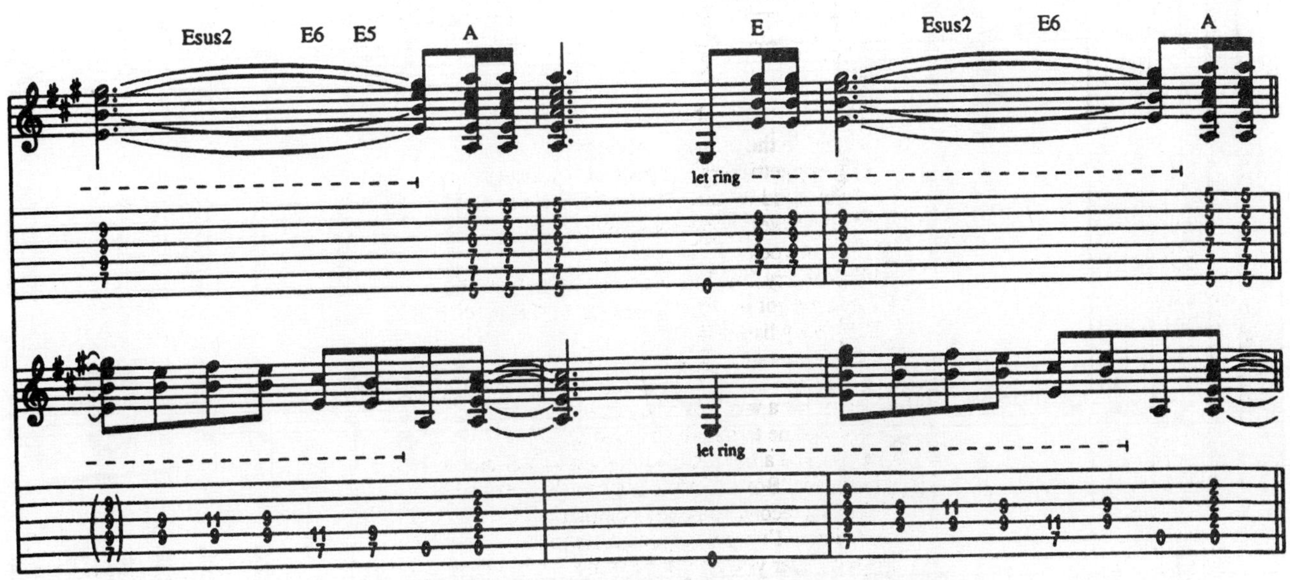

Verse

E Esus2 E6 A E Esus2 E6 D

1. You show us ev - ery - thing you've got. ___ You keep on danc-ing and the room gets hot.
2. You keep on say-in' you'll be mine for a - while. _ You're look-ing fan - cy and I like your style.

let ring
let ring
let ring
let ring
let ring

Dsus2 D6 E Esus2 E6 Dsus4 D Dsus4 D A

You drive us wild; ___ we'll drive you cra - zy. ___
And you drive us wild; ___ we'll drive you cra - zy. ___

let ring

E Esus2 E6 A E Esus2 E6 D

And you say you wan-na go for a spin. ___ The par-ty's just be-gun; we'll let you in.
And you show us ev - ery - thing you've got. ___ Oh ba-by, ba-by, that's quite a - lot.

let ring

let ring

let ring

let ring

let ring

Dsus2 D6 E Esus2 E6 Dsus4 D Dsus4 D E F

You drive us wild; ___ we'll drive you cra - zy.
And you drive us wild; ___ we'll drive you cra - zy.

let ring

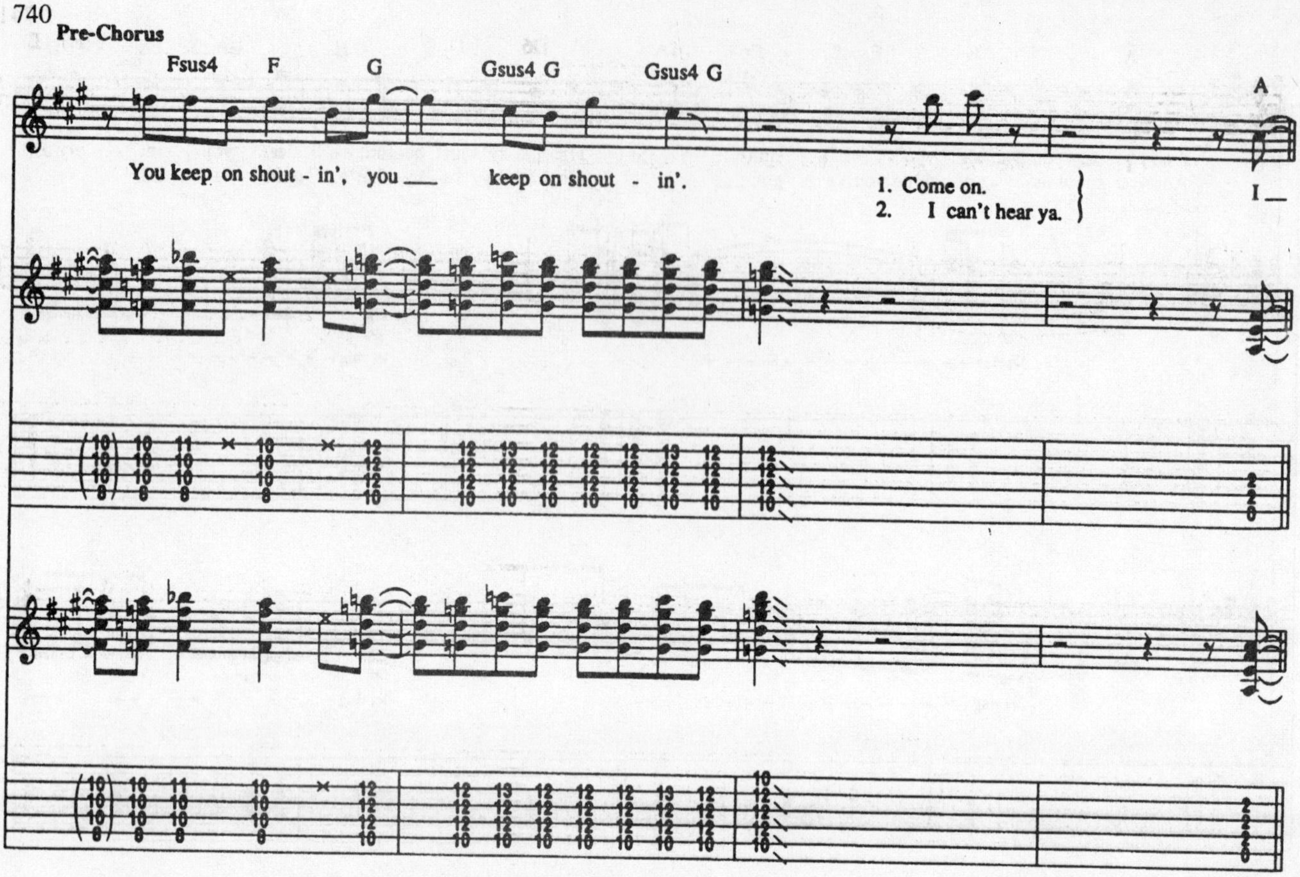

Pre-Chorus

Fsus4 F G Gsus4 G Gsus4 G A

You keep on shout - in', you ___ keep on shout - in'.

1. Come on.
2. I can't hear ya.

I ___

Chorus

D D6 D E E6 E E6 E

___ wan-na rock and roll ___ all night, ___ and par - ty ev - ery day.

P.M.

A D D6 D E E6 E E6 E

I wan-na rock and roll __ all night ______ and par-ty ev - ery day.

P.M.

A N.C.

I wan-na rock and roll __ all night ______ and par-ty ev - ery day.

(Drums & Vocals)
I wan-na rock and roll all night
and par-ty ev-ery day.
Guitar solo
Dsus4
D
Dsus4
D
A
A6
A5
A6
E
full
P.M.
E6
E5
E6
A
A6
A5
E
E6
E5
E6
D
D6
D5
D6
E
E6
E5
E6
E
Dsus4
D
Dsus4
D
Dsus4
A
1/2
full

A6 A5 A6 E E6 E5 E6 A A6 A5 E E6 E5 E6 D
8va
full
P.M.
D6 D5 D6 E E6 E5 E Dsus4 D Dsus4 D F
(8va)
loco
Fsus4 F G Gsus4 G Gsus4 G N.C. A
You keep on shout - in'. You keep on shout - in'.
What?
I

Chorus

D D6 D E E6 E E6 E

wan-na rock and roll ___ all night ___ and par-ty ev - ery day.

P.M.

A D D6 D E E6 E E6 E

I wan-na rock and roll ___ all night ___ and par-ty ev - ery day.

P.M.

(both gtrs. tacet 2nd time)
A
N.C.
I wan-na rock and roll all night
and par-ty ev - ery day.
Outro
Dsus4
D Dsus4
D (E) F
Fsus4 F
G
Gsus4 G
Gsus4
P.M.
N.C.
A
1/2
full
1/4

ROCK AROUND THE CLOCK

Words and Music by
MAX C. FREEDMAN and JIMMY DE KNIGHT

Guitar Solo:
A
D9
1/2
E9
D.S. 𝄋 al Coda
Instrumental:
Coda
D9(♭)IX

E9
A
When the
Verse 5:
clock strikes twelve, we'll cool off, then— start a - rock - in' 'round the
D9
clock a - gain.— We're gon - na rock a - round the clock to - night. We're gon - na
A
E9
rock, rock, rock 'til broad day - light. We're gon - na rock, gon - na rock a - round—
TAB

Verse 2:
When clock strikes two, three and four,
If the band slows down, we'll yell for more.
We're gonna rock around the clock tonight,
We're gonna rock, rock, rock 'til broad daylight.
Gonna rock, gonna rock around the clock tonight.
(To Guitar Solo:)

Verse 3:
When the chimes ring five, six and seven,
We'll be rockin' up in seventh heaven.
Were gonna rock around the clock tonight,
We're gonna rock, rock, rock 'til broad daylight.
Gonna rock, gonna rock around the clock tonight.

Verse 4:
When it's eight, nine, ten, eleven, too,
We'll be going strong and so will you.
We're gonna rock around the clock tonight,
We're gonna rock, rock, rock 'til broad daylight.
Gonna rock, gonna rock around the clock tonight.
(To Coda)

ROCKET MAN
(I Think It's Gonna Be A Long Long Time)

Words and Music by
ELTON JOHN and BERNIE TAUPIN

Elec. Gtr. tuned:
⑥ = E ③ = G
⑤ = A ② = B
④ = D ① = D
Slowly ♩ = 69
*Verse:
F♯m7
131111
B9
21333
1. She packed_ my bags__ last night pre - flight._
2. Mars ain't the kind__ of place____ to raise your kids.___
*To match key of recording, capo 1st fret.
F♯m7
131111
B9
21333
A/C♯
3111
Ze - ro hour,_____ nine A. M.___________
In fact,__ it's cold___ as hell.___________
*Elec. Gtr.
8va
mf
w/slide throughout; grad. slide
20
D
132
A/C♯
3111
Bm
13421
Bm7/A
3421
E/G♯
2 13
And I'm gon-na be high_______________ as a kite by__ then._______
And there's no one there__ to__ raise__ them_______ if you did.______________
16
F♯m7
131111
Bm11
11111
I miss__ the earth_ so much. I miss my wife.___
And all___ this sci - ence__ I un - der-stand.

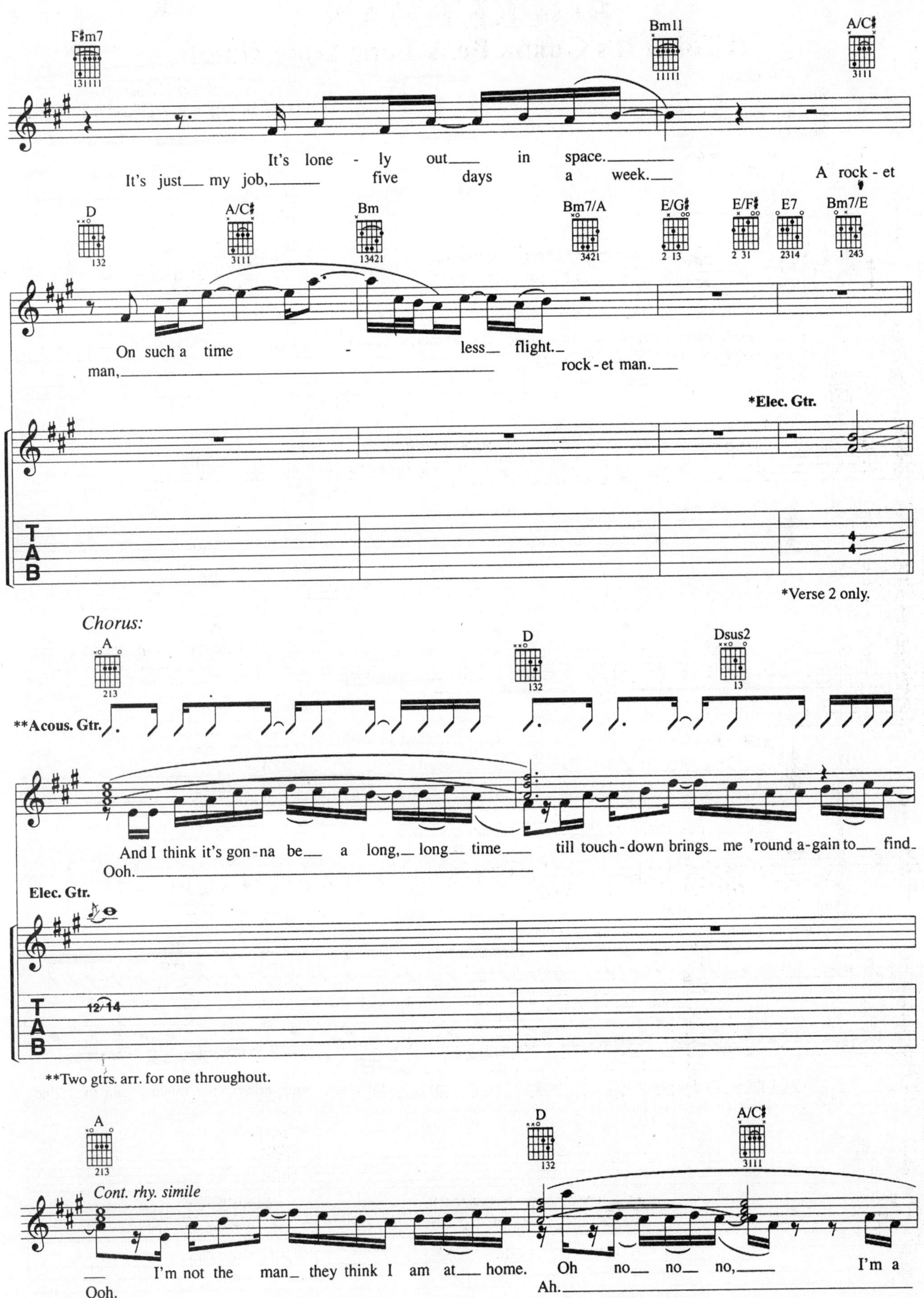
F♯m7
Bm11
A/C♯
It's lone - ly out in space.
It's just my job, five days a week.
A rock - et
D
A/C♯
Bm
Bm7/A
E/G♯
E/F♯
E7
Bm7/E
On such a time - less flight.
man, rock - et man.
*Elec. Gtr.
*Verse 2 only.
Chorus:
A
D
Dsus2
**Acous. Gtr.
And I think it's gon - na be a long, long time till touch - down brings me 'round a - gain to find
Ooh.
Elec. Gtr.
**Two gtrs. arr. for one throughout.
A
D
A/C♯
Cont. rhy. simile
I'm not the man they think I am at home. Oh no no no, I'm a
Ooh.
Ah.

B7
213 4
A/C♯
3111
D
132
Cont. in notation
rock-et man.
Rock-et man
burn - ing out his fuse up here
Rock-et man.
grad. slide
A
111
D/A
312
A
111
D
132
Dsus2
13
a - lone.
8va
*Elec. Gtr.
Acous. Gtr.
mf Rhy. Fig. 1
Elec. Gtr.
Cont. in slashes
*2nd time only.
A
213
D
132
Dsus2
13
And I think it's gon-na be a long, long time till touch-down brings me 'round a-gain to find
Ooh.

A
D
A/C♯
Cont. rhy. simile
I'm not the man they think I am at home. Oh no no no, I'm a
Ooh.
Ah.
1. w/Rhy. Fig. 1 (Acous. Gtr.) simile
B7
A/C♯
D
A
D/A
A
rock-et man.
Rock-et man burn-ing out his fuse up here a-lone.
Rock-et man.
8va
Elec. Gtr.
grad. slide
grad. slide
D.C.
2. w/Rhy. Fig. 1 (Acous. Gtr.) simile
†Outro:
D
Dsus2
A
D/A
A
D
Acous. Gtr.
Cont. rhy. simile
a-lone.
And I think it's gon-na be a long,
†Vocal & Acous. Gtr. ad lib. simile on repeats;
Elec. Gtr. solo ad lib. throughout.
A
D
A
Repeat and fade
long time.
And I think it's gon-na be a long, long time.

ROCKY MOUNTAIN WAY

Words and Music by JOE WALSH,
JOE VITALE, KEN PASSARELLI and
ROCKE GRACE

Gtrs. 1 & 2: w/ Rhy. Fig. 1, 1st 3 meas. only
Gtrs. 1 & 2: w/ Rhy. Fill 1 (see next page)
E E6 E E5 E E6 E D5/E D5 E5 E6 E5 E6 D5/E D5 E5 A
open open open open
End Rhy. Fig. 1
Verse
E5
Gtr. 3 tacet
A5 E5
1. Spent the last year rock-y mountain way, could-n't get much high-er.
tell-in' us this and he's tell-in' us that, chang-es ev-'ry day; says it does-n't mat-ter.
Gtrs. 1 & 2
mf
1/2
A5 E5 A5
Out to pas-ture, think it's safe to say,
Bas-es are load-ed and Cas-ey's at bat, play-in' it play by play;
E5
Chorus
A5 A A6 A A5 A A6
Rhy. Fig. 2
Gtrs. 1 & 2
"Time to o-pen fire."
time to change the bat-ter.
And we don't need the la-dies
Gtr. 3
w/ slide
(cont. in slash)

Gtr. 3: w/ Fill 1, 2nd time
A5 A A6 A A5 A A6 E E5 E E6 E E5 E E6 E E5 E6 E E5 E G G#
open open open open open open open open open open 3fr 4fr
cry - in' 'cause the sto - ry's sad, 'cause the
A5 A A6 A A5 A A6 A A5 A A6 A A5 A A6 E B5
rock - y moun - tain way is bet - ter than the way we had.
1.
Interlude
Gtr. 3: w/ Fill 2, 2nd time
Gtrs. 1 & 2: w/ Rhy. Fig. 1, 1 3/4 times
B5 B B5 B5 B B5 B5 B B5 E D5/E E5 E6 E5 E6
type 2
2fr open
End Rhy. Fig. 2
Whoa.
Ooh, hoo.
Rhy. Fill 1
Gtrs. 1 & 2
1/2
Fill 1
Gtr. 3
Fill 2
Gtr. 3

D5/E D5 E5 E6 E5 E6 D5/E D5 E5
E6 E5 E6 D5/E D5 E5
Gtrs. 1 & 2: w/ Rhy. Fill 1
A
2. Well, he's
steady gliss.
2. Interlude
Gtrs. 1 & 2: w/ Rhy. Fig. 1
D5/E D5 E5 E6 E5 E6 D5/E D5 E5
steady gliss.
Gtrs. 1 & 2: w/ Rhy. Fig. 1, 1st 3 meas. only
E6 E5 E6 D5/E D5 E5 E6 E5 E6
let ring
Gtrs. 1 & 2: w/ Rhy. Fill 1
D5/E D5 E5 E6 E
Gtr. 3 tacet
*N.C.(E5)
*Chord Symbols implied by kybd.

Guitar Solo
N.C.
Gtr. 4
mf
w/ talk box
Gtr. 5 (talk box)
Gtr. 4
divisi
full
E
6
open
E5
Gtr. 1
P.M.
Gtrs. 4 & 5
8va
Gtr. 5
Gtr. 4
divisi
full
1/2

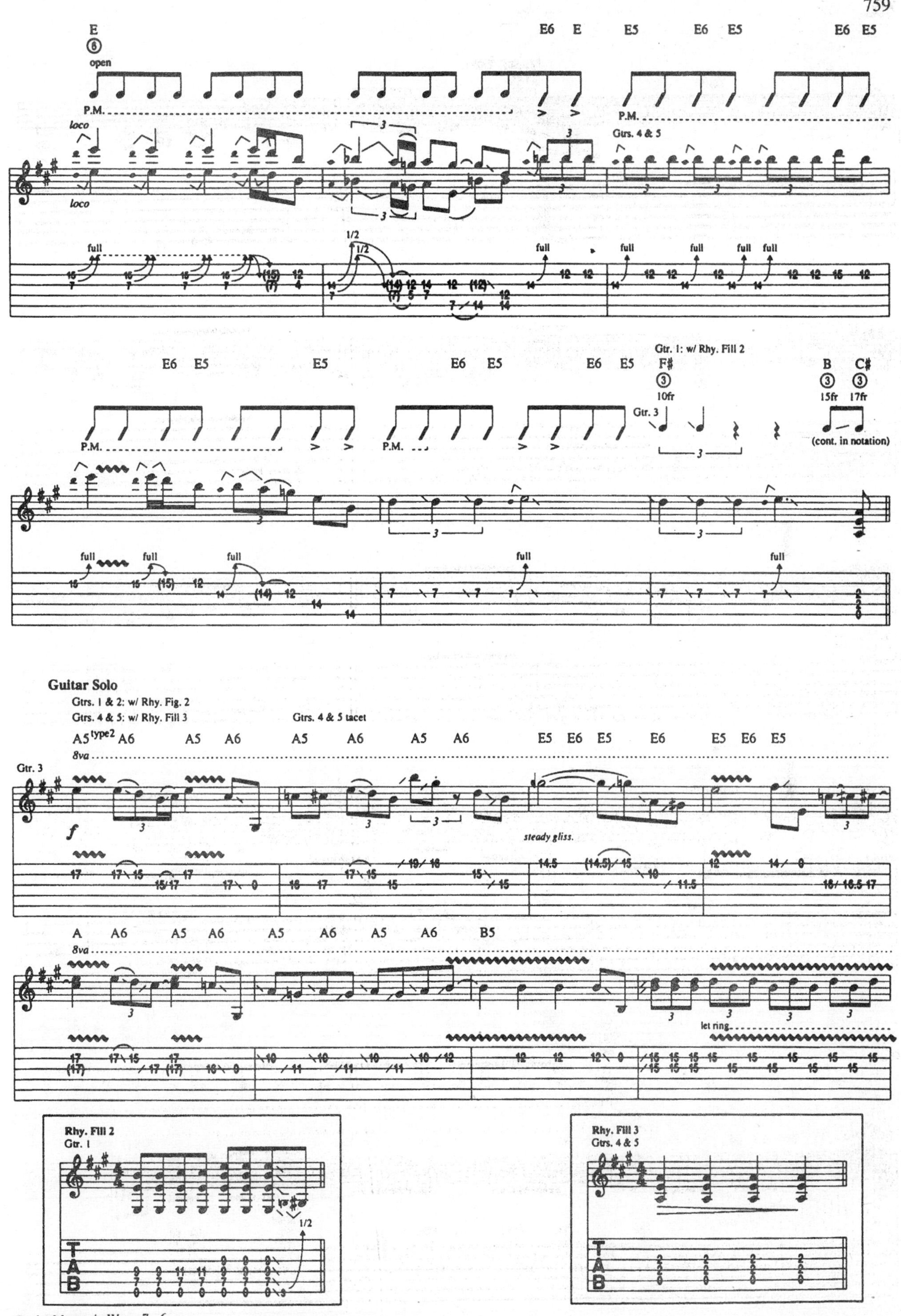
E
6
open
E6 E E5 E6 E5 E6 E5
P.M.
loco
Gtrs. 4 & 5
full
1/2
E6 E5 E5 E6 E5 E6 E5
Gtr. 1: w/ Rhy. Fill 2
F#
3
10fr
B C#
15fr 17fr
Gtr. 3
(cont. in notation)
Guitar Solo
Gtrs. 1 & 2: w/ Rhy. Fig. 2
Gtrs. 4 & 5: w/ Rhy. Fill 3
Gtrs. 4 & 5 tacet
A5type2 A6 A5 A6 A5 A6 A5 A6 E5 E6 E5 E6 E5 E6 E5
8va
steady gliss.
A A6 A5 A6 A5 A6 A5 A6 B5
let ring
Rhy. Fill 2
Gtr. 1
Rhy. Fill 3
Gtrs. 4 & 5

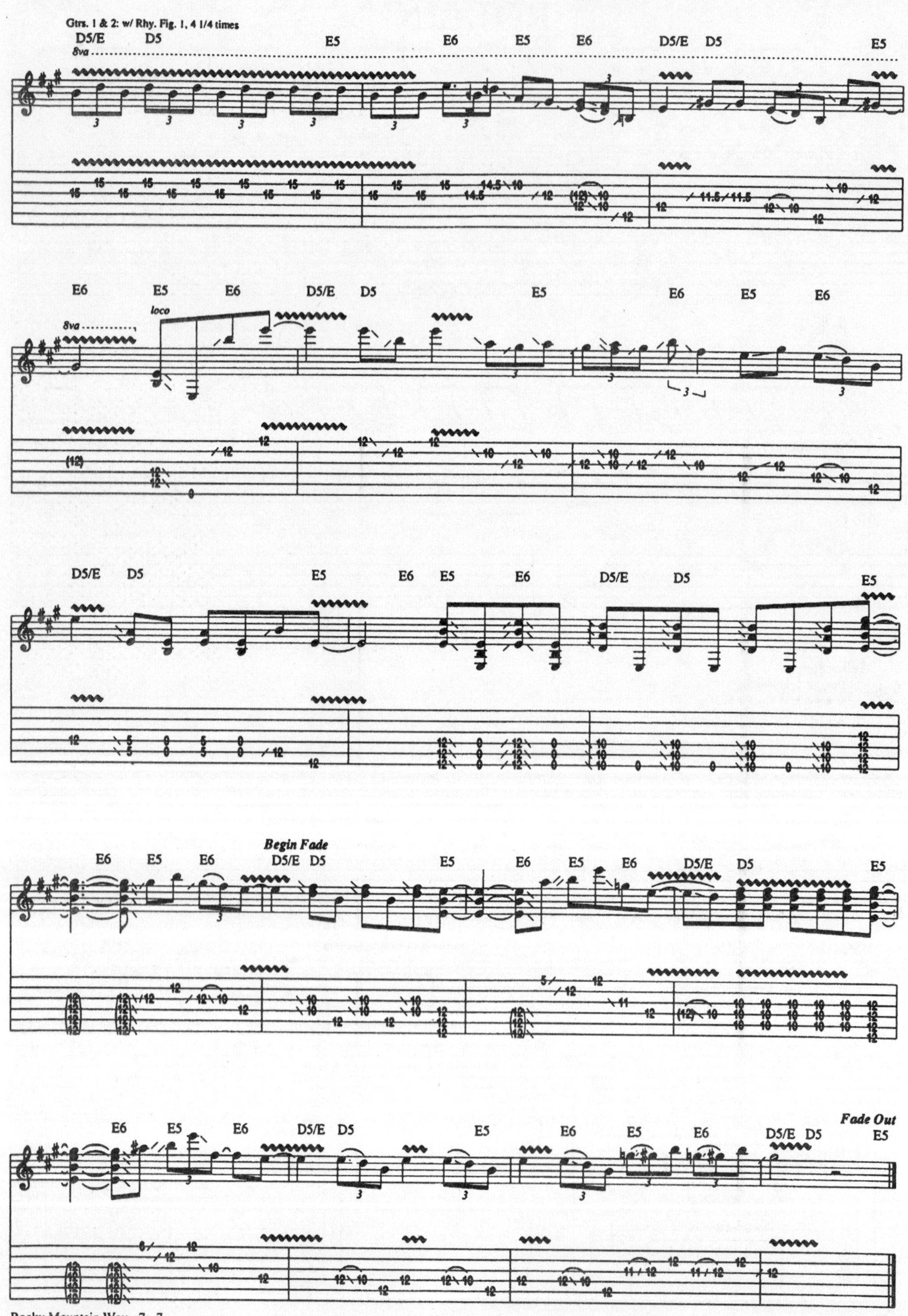
Gtrs. 1 & 2: w/ Rhy. Fig. 1, 4 1/4 times
D5/E
D5
E5
E6
8va
loco
Begin Fade
Fade Out

ROLLIN'
(Air Raid Vehicle)

Lyrics by FRED DURST
Music by WES BORLAND, SAM RIVERS, JOHN OTTO,
LEOR DIMANT and KASEEM DEAN

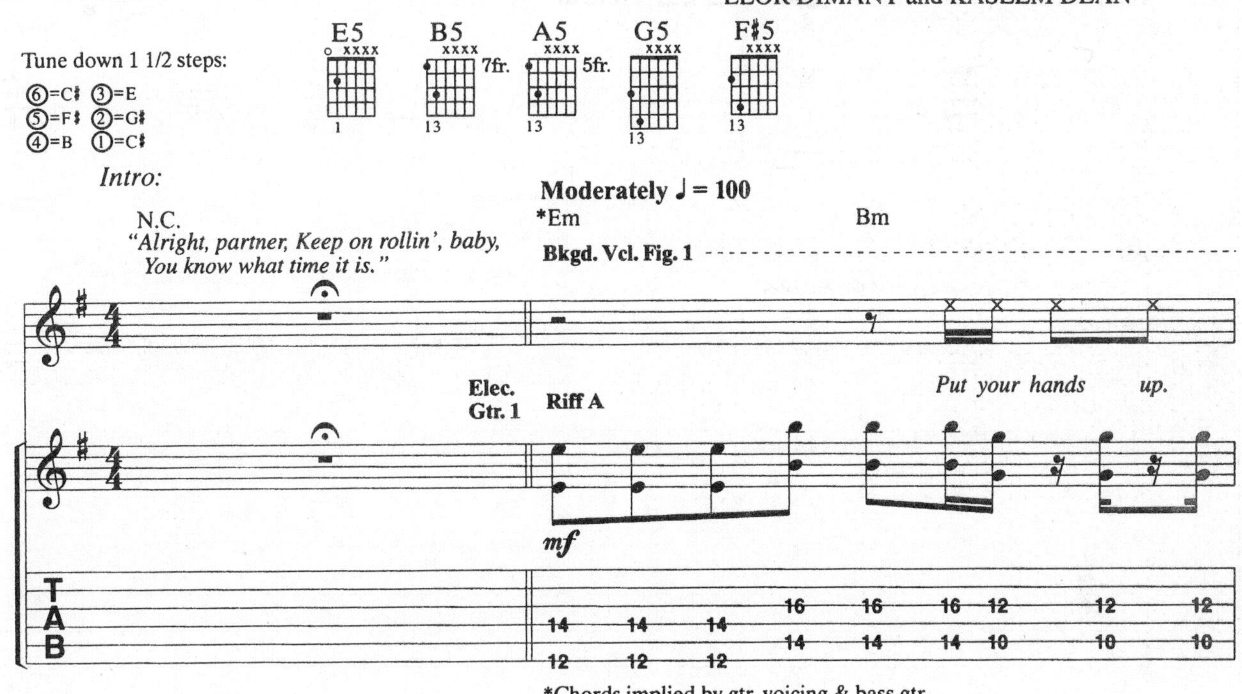

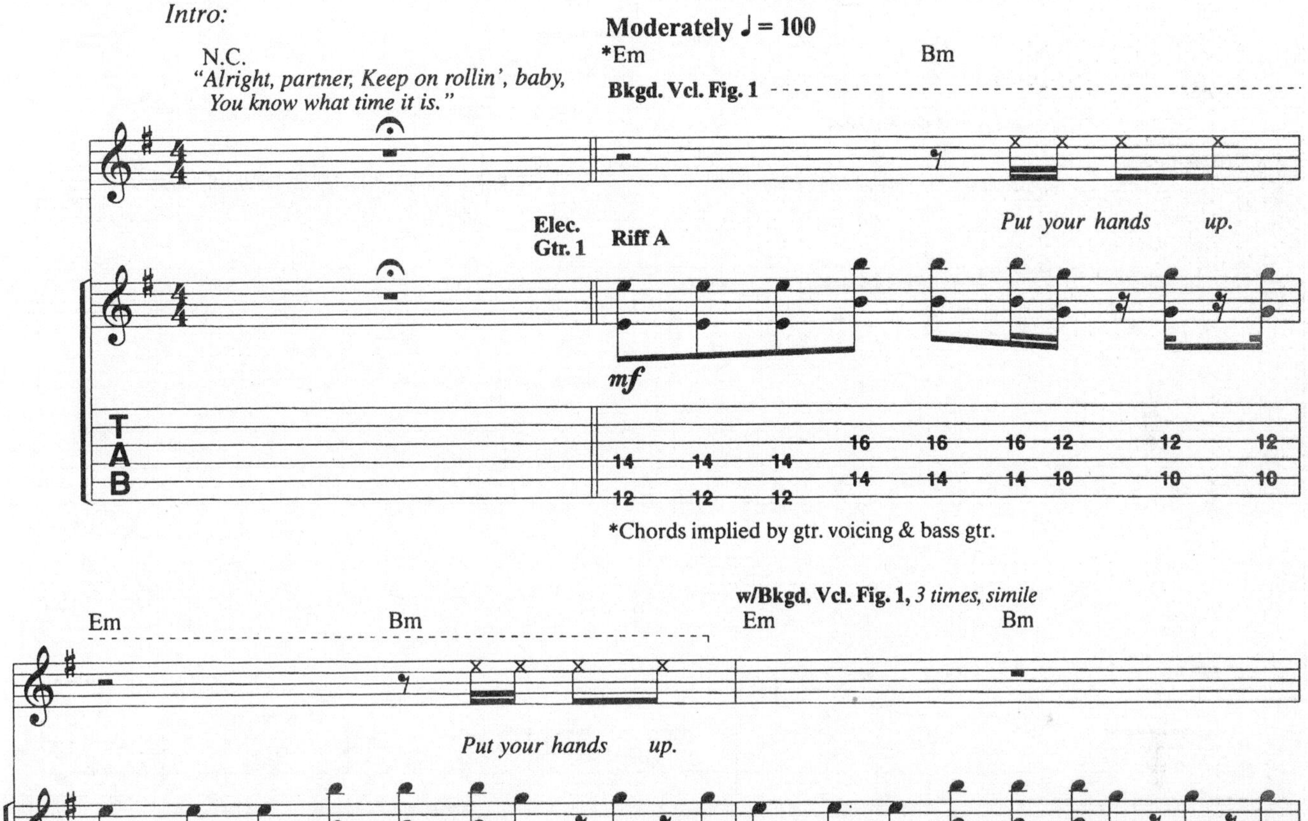

Tune down 1 1/2 steps:
⑥=C♯ ③=E
⑤=F♯ ②=G♯
④=B ①=C♯

E5
B5
7fr.
A5
5fr.
G5
F♯5

Intro:
N.C.
"Alright, partner, Keep on rollin', baby, You know what time it is."
Moderately ♩ = 100
*Em
Bm
Bkgd. Vcl. Fig. 1
Put your hands up.
Elec. Gtr. 1
Riff A
mf
T A B
*Chords implied by gtr. voicing & bass gtr.
Em
Bm
Put your hands up.
w/Bkgd. Vcl. Fig. 1, 3 times, simile
Em
Bm
w/Riff A (Elec. Gtr. 1)
Em
Bm
Em
Bm
Em
Bm
end Riff A
Choc - 'late star - fish.

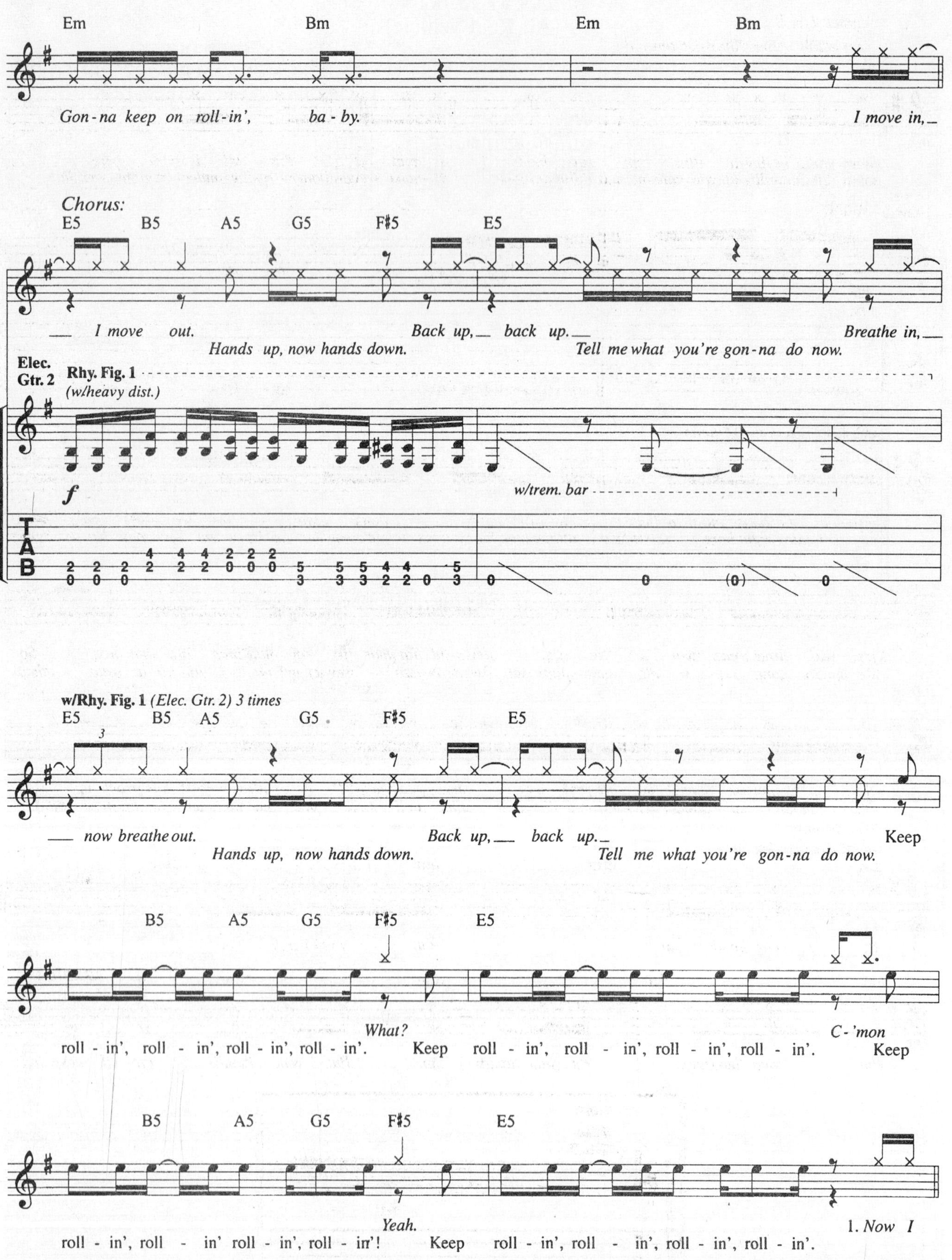
Em
Bm
Em
Bm
Gon-na keep on roll-in', ba-by.
I move in,
Chorus:
E5
B5
A5
G5
F♯5
E5
I move out.
Hands up, now hands down.
Back up, back up.
Tell me what you're gon-na do now.
Breathe in,
Elec. Gtr. 2
Rhy. Fig. 1
(w/heavy dist.)
f
w/trem. bar
T
A
B
w/Rhy. Fig. 1 (Elec. Gtr. 2) 3 times
E5
B5
A5
G5
F♯5
E5
now breathe out.
Hands up, now hands down.
Back up, back up.
Tell me what you're gon-na do now.
Keep
B5
A5
G5
F♯5
E5
What?
C-'mon
roll-in', roll-in', roll-in', roll-in'.
Keep
roll-in', roll-in', roll-in', roll-in'.
Keep
B5
A5
G5
F♯5
E5
Yeah.
1. Now I
roll-in', roll-in' roll-in', roll-in'!
Keep
roll-in', roll-in', roll-in', roll-in'.

Verses 1 & 2:
Sub. w/Fill 1 (Elec. Gtr. 3) 1st time only
Em
know you'll be lov-in' this shit right here, I. and P. Biz - kit is right here.
mess with Limp Biz-kit, you can't mess with Limp Biz-kit. Be-cause we get it on ev-'ry day and ev-'ry night. And this
Elec. Gtr. 3 Riff B
mf
P.M.
12 12 12 14 14 14 12 12 12 15 15 15 14 14 12 15 12 12 (12) 12
w/Riff B (Elec. Gtr. 3) 3 times
Peo-ple in the house put them hands in the air 'cause if you don't care, then we don't care. Yeah!
plat-i-num thing right here, yo, we're doin' it all the time. So you bet-ter get some bet - ter beats and get some bet -ter rhymes.
One, two, three times two, to the six, Jones-in' for your fix of that Limp Biz - kit mix. So
We got the gang set, so don't com - plain yet. Twen - ty-four - sev-en nev-er beg - gin' for a rain check.
where the f*** you at, punk? Shut the f*** up, and pack the f*** up while we f*** this track up.
Old school sol - diers blast - in' out the hot shit, that rock shit put - tin bounce in the mosh pit.
Pre-chorus:
w/Riff A (Elec. Gtr. 1)
Em Bm Em Bm
Put your hands up. Put your hands up.
Em Bm Em Bm
Put your hands up. Put your hands up. Put your hands up. I move in,
Fill 1
Elec. Gtr. 3
P.M.
10 10 7 10

Chorus:
w/Rhy. Fig. 1 (Elec. Gtr. 2) 4 times
E5 B5 A5 G5 F#5
I move out. Back up, back up. Breathe in,
Hands up, now hands down. Tell me what you're gon-na do now.
B5 A5 G5 F#5 E5
now breathe out. Back up, back up. Keep
Hands up, now hands down. Tell me what you're gon-na do now.
B5 A5 G5 F#5 E5
What? C-'mon.
roll-in', roll-in', roll-in', roll-in'. Keep roll-in', roll-in', roll-in', roll-in'. Keep
1.
B5 A5 G5 F#5 E5
Yeah. 2. You won't
roll-in', roll-in', roll-in', roll-in'. Keep roll-in', roll-in', roll-in', roll-in'.
2.
E5
Verse 3:
N.C.
roll-in', roll-in', roll-in', roll-in'. Hey, la-dies, hey, fel-las, and the
Elec. Gtr. 3 Riff C
TAB
w/Riff C (Elec. Gtr. 3) 3 times
peo-ple that don't give a f***. All the lov-ers, all the hat-ers, and all the
TAB
12 12 (12)

peo - ple that call them - selves play - ers. Hot ma - mas, pimp dad - dys, and the
peo - ple roll - in' up in Cad - dies. Hey, rock - ers, hip hop - pers, and
Chorus:
w/Rhy. Fig. 1 (Elec. Gtr. 2) 4 times
E5 B5 A5 G5 F♯5
ev - 'ry - bod - y all a - round the world. Move in, now move out. Back up,
Hands up, now hands down.
E5 B5 A5 G5 F♯5
back up. Breathe in, now breathe out. Back up,
Tell me what you're gon - na do now. Hands up, now hands down.
Sub. w/Rhy. Fill 1 (Elec. Gtr. 2) 1st time only.
E5 B5 A5 G5 F♯5
back up. Keep What?
Tell me what you're gon - na do now. roll - in', roll - in', roll - in', roll - in'. Keep
E5 B5 A5 G5 F♯5
C - 'mon. Yeah.
roll - in', roll - in', roll - in', roll - in'. Keep roll - in', roll - in', roll - in', roll - in'. Keep
1. E5
2. E5
Move in,
roll - in', roll - in', roll - in', roll - in'. roll - in', roll - in', roll - in', roll - in'.
Rhy. Fill 1
Elec. Gtr. 2
8va
fdbk.
w/trem. bar
T
A
B
0
0
0
17
17

ROUNDABOUT

Words and Music by
JON ANDERSON and STEVE HOWE

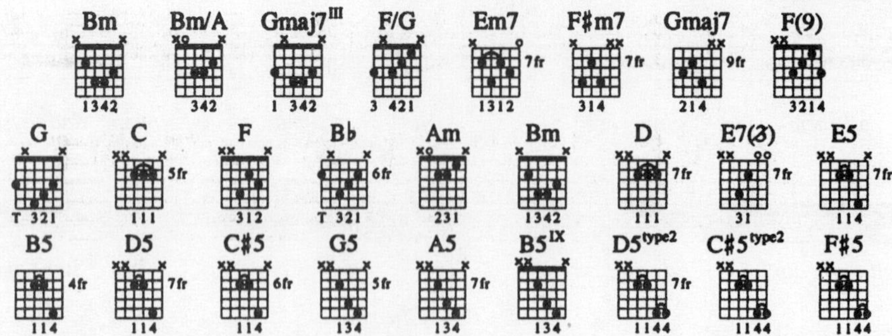

Kybd. chords arr. for gtr.

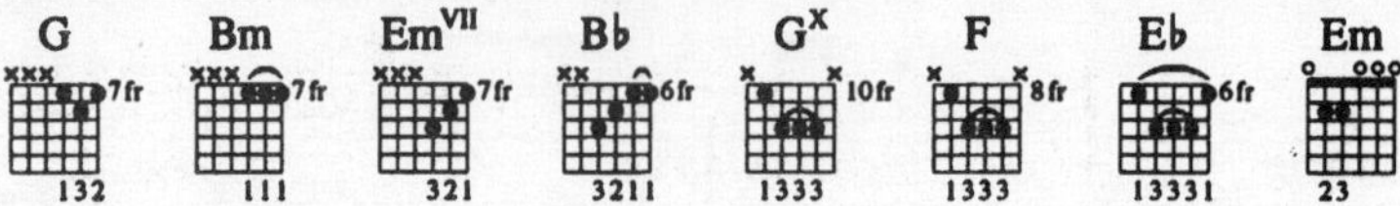

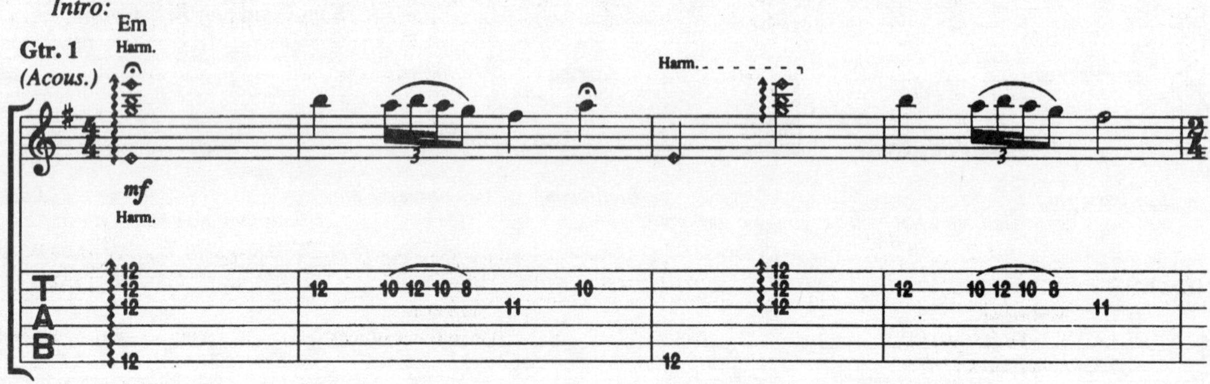

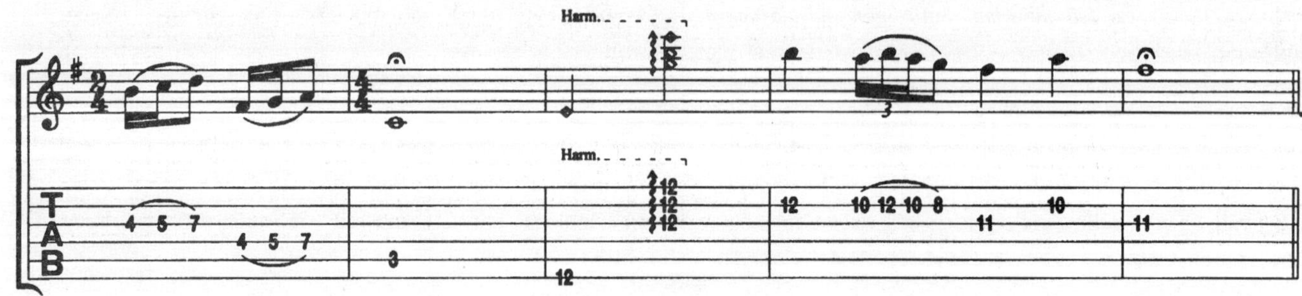

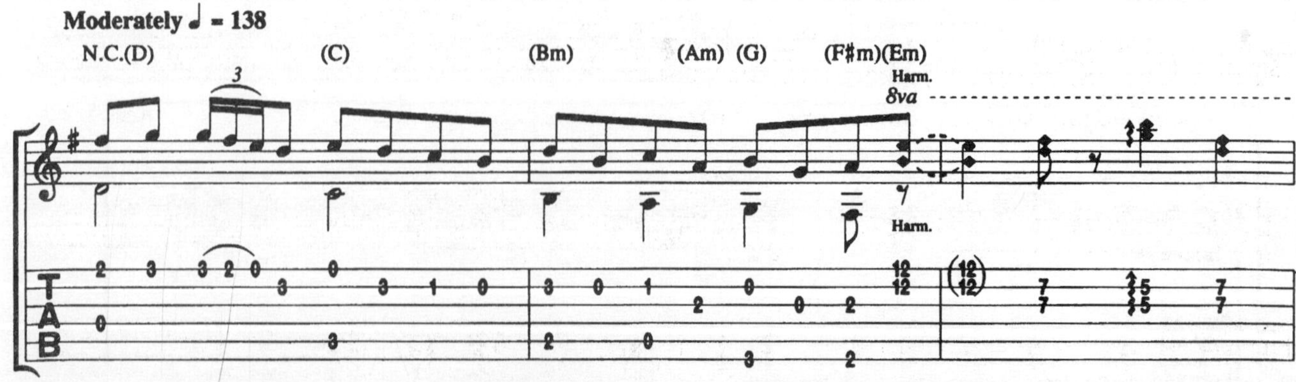

8va
8va
Verse:
N.C.
1.4. I'll be the round - a - bout; the words will make you out and out,
2.3. See additional lyrics
Harm.
8va
Am7
I'll spend the day your way. Call it
8va
loco

Bm
Bm/A
Gmaj7 III
1.
F/G
morn - ing driv - ing through the sun and in and out the val - ley.
Em7
F#m7 Gmaj7
2.-4.
F(9)
val - ley.
In and a - round
hold
Chorus:
G C F C F C G C F C Bb
the lake, mount - tains come out of the sky, and they stand
w/ Rhy. Fig. 1 (2 times)
end Rhy. Fig. 1
C F C F C G C F C Bb
there. One mile o - ver we'll be there and

G C F C G C F C B♭
we'll see you. Ten true sum-mers we'll be there, and
w/ Rhy. Fig. 1 (1st 3 bars only)
G C F C F C G C F C B♭
laugh-ing too. Twen - ty - four be - fore my love, you'll
To Coda 1
To Coda 2
Am Bm C D Em7 Em7
see, I'll be there with you.
Interlude:
F♯m7 Gmaj7 F♯m7 Gmaj7 F♯m7 Em7 F♯m7 Gmaj7 F♯m E7(♯9)
Em7 F♯m7 Gmaj7 F♯m Gmaj7 F♯m7 Em7
N.C.
Riff A
D.S. al Coda 1

Coda 1
(Em7)
w/ Riff A
N.C.
Riff B
N.C.(Em)
Both gtrs.
end Riff B
w/ Riff B (3 times)
Play 3 times
1. A - long the drift-ing cloud, _ the ea - gle search-ing down _ on the land.
2. Catch-ing the swirl-ing wind, _ the sail - or sees the rim _ of the land.
3. The ea-gle's danc-ing wings _ cre - ate as weath - er spins _ out of hand.
E5 B5 D5 B5 C#5 G5 A5 B5IX D5type2 C#5type2 F#5
Gtr. 2
w/ Riff B (Gtr. 1) & Rhy. Fig. 1 (Gtr. 2)
Play 3 times
E5 B5 D5 B5 C#5 G5 A5 B5 D5 C#5 F#5
1. Go clos - er, hold the land, _ feel part - ly no more than _ grains of sand.
2. We stand to lose all time, _ a thou - sand an - swers lie _ in our hands.
3. Next to your deep - er fears, _ we stand sur - round - ed by (a) mil - lion years.
Chorus:
w/Riff B (Gtr. 1) & Rhy. Fig. 1 (Gtr. 2)
I'll be the round - a - bout, _ the words will make _
1.
2.
(Gtrs. out)
_ you out _ and out. _ you out _ and out. _

Freely, slowly
N.C.(Em)
Harm.
Gtr. 1
mf
Harm.
In and a - round
Bridge:
a tempo
(Kybd. arr. for gtr.)
G
Bm
Em
Bb
the lake,
mount - tains come out
of the sky,
they stand there.
G
F
Bb
Eb
Twen - ty - four be - fore my love and I'll be there.

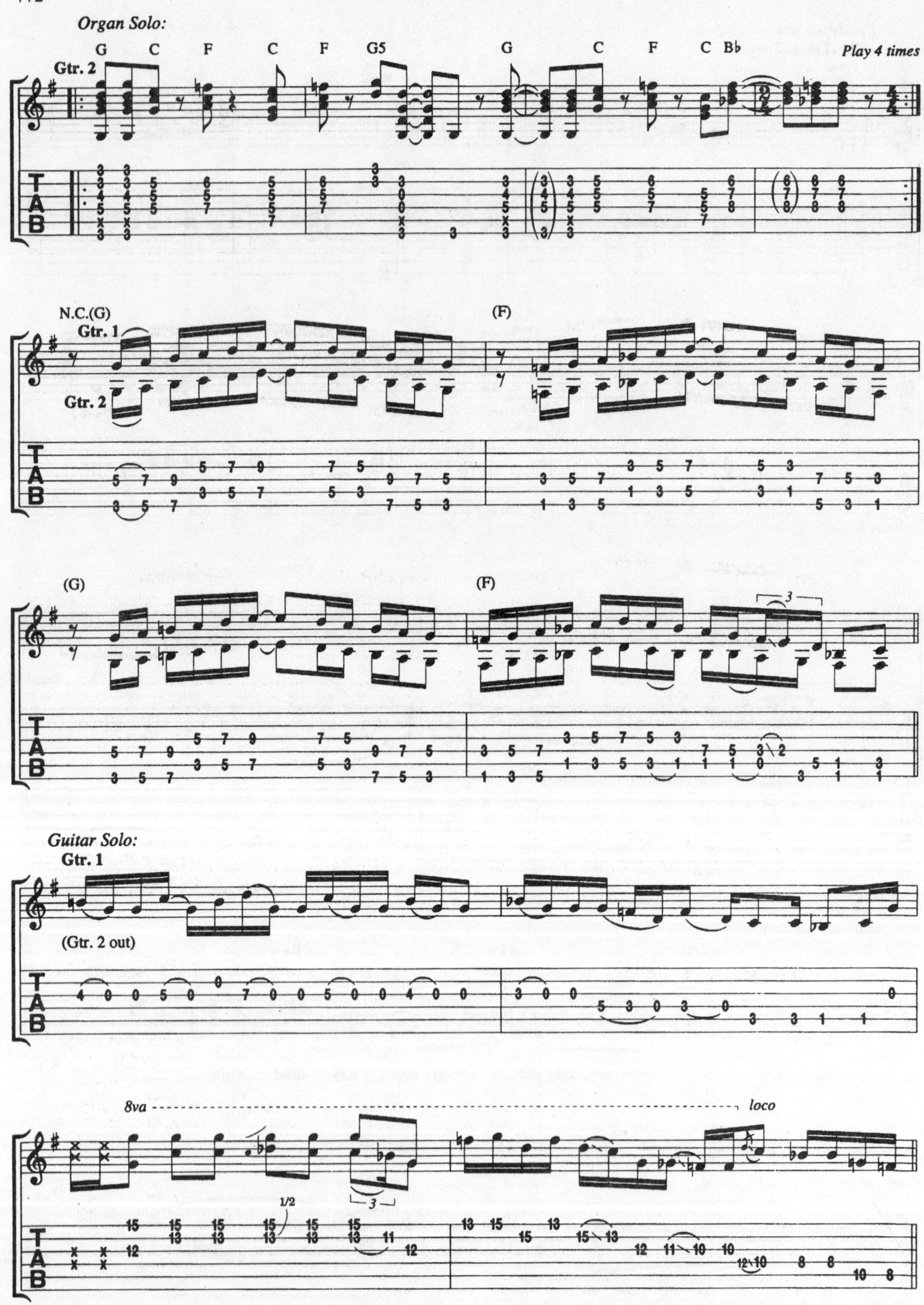
Organ Solo:
G C F C F G5 G C F C B♭
Play 4 times
Gtr. 2
N.C.(G)
Gtr. 1
Gtr. 2
(F)
(G)
(F)
Guitar Solo:
Gtr. 1
(Gtr. 2 out)
8va
loco
1/2

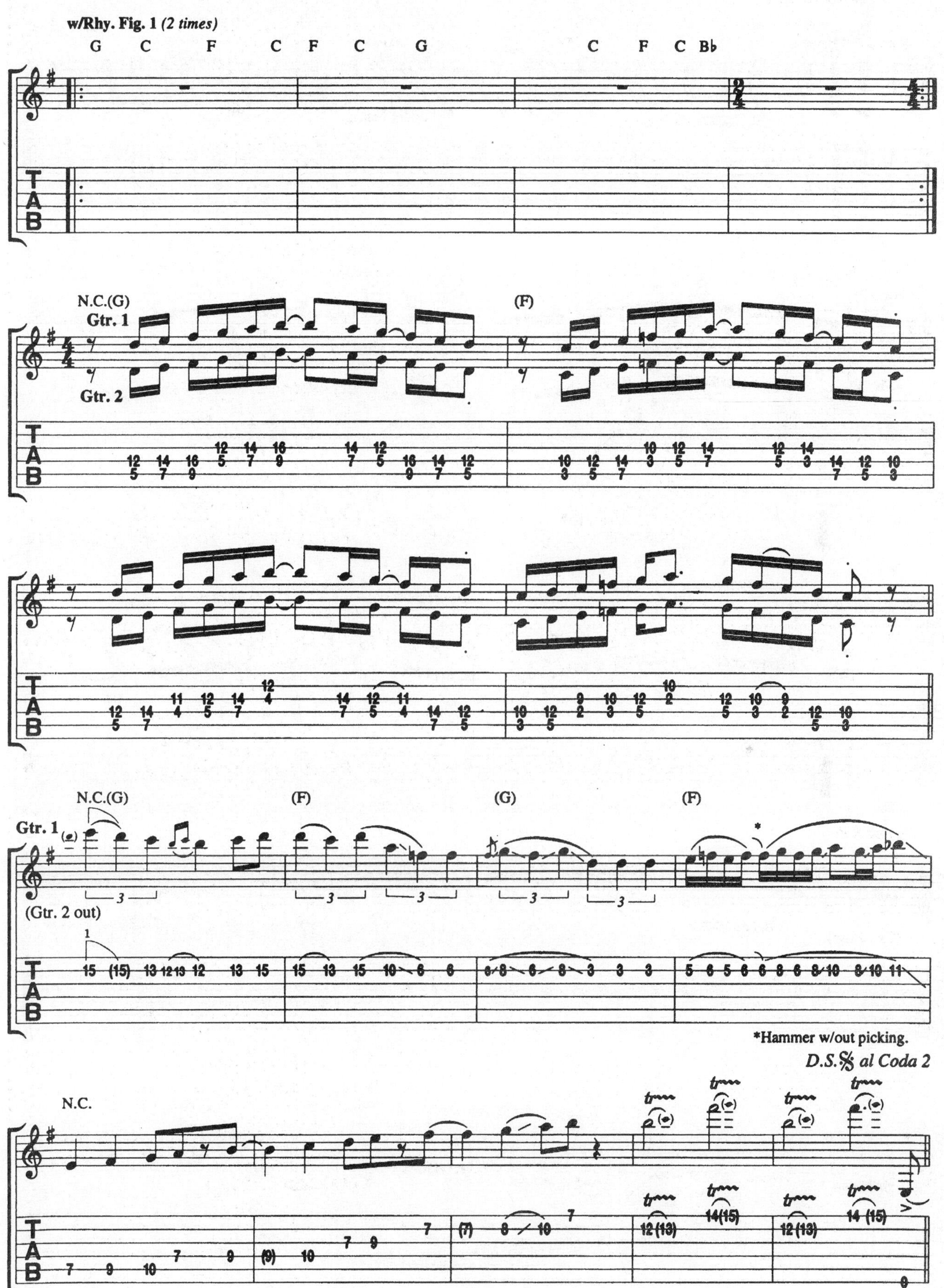
w/Rhy. Fig. 1 (2 times)
G C F C F C G C F C B♭
N.C.(G)
Gtr. 1
Gtr. 2
(F)
N.C.(G)
(F)
(G)
(F)
Gtr. 1
(Gtr. 2 out)
*Hammer w/out picking.
D.S.𝄋 al Coda 2
N.C.

Verse 2:
The music dance and sing.
They make the children really ring.
I spend the day your way.
Call it morning driving through the sun
And in and out the valley.

Verse 3:
I will remember you.
Your silhouette will charge the view
Of distant atmosphere.
Call it morning driving in the sun
And even in the valley.

RUNAWAY

Words and Music by
DEL SHANNON and
MAX CROOK

Am
G
F
E7
A
F#m
D
134111
134211
134211
2314
123
134111
132

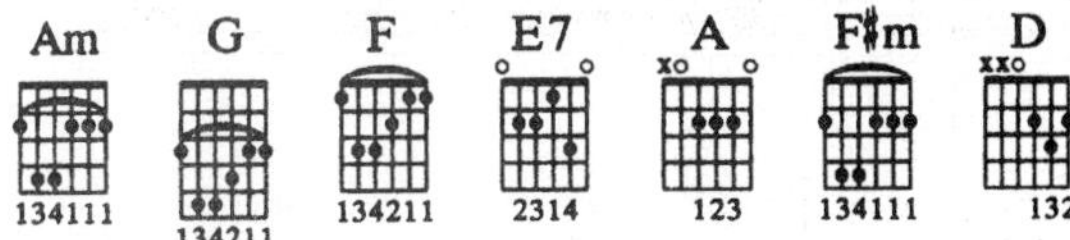

Moderately fast ♩ = 152

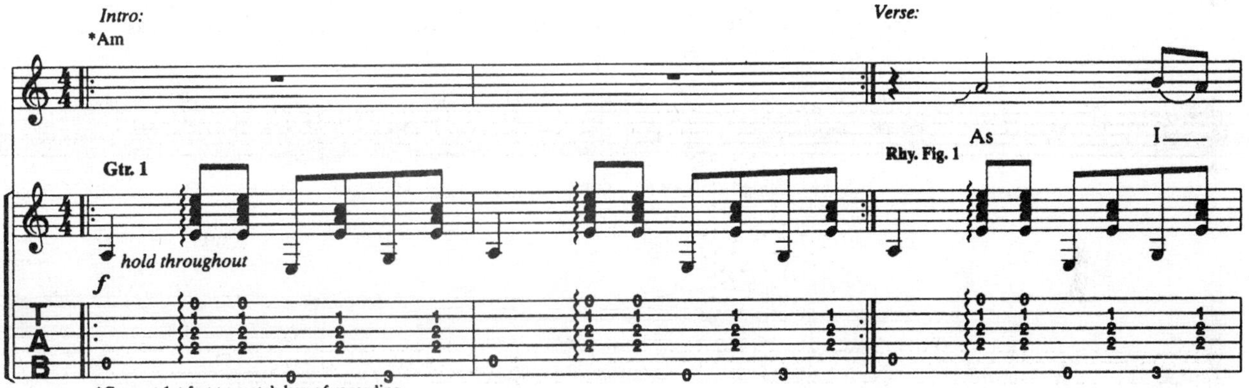

Intro:
*Am
Verse:
As I
Gtr. 1
Rhy. Fig. 1
hold throughout
f

*Capo at 1st fret to match key of recording.

G
walk a - long, I won - der a - what went wrong with our

F
E7
love, a love that was so strong.

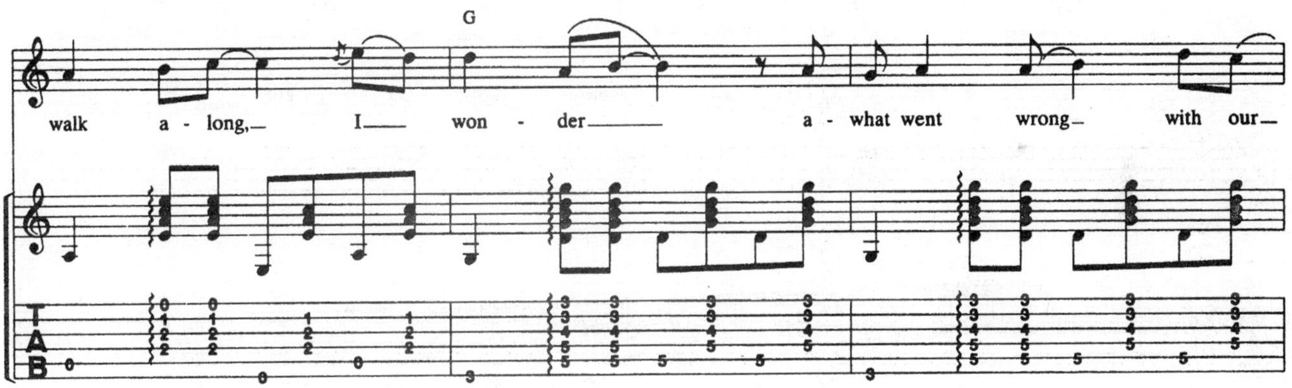

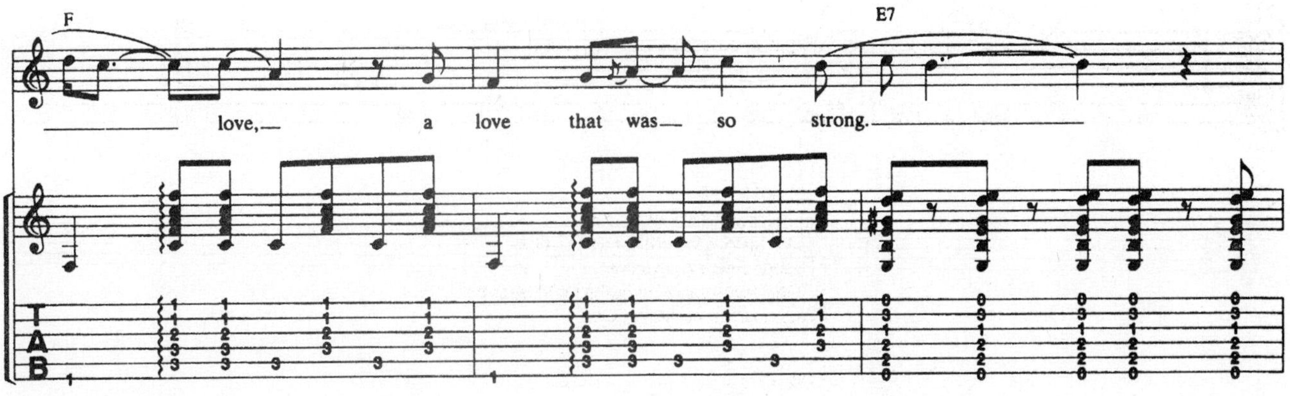

w/Rhy. Fig. 1
Am
And as I still walk on, I
end Rhy. Fig. 1
G
F
think of the things we've done to-geth - er a-
E7
while our hearts were young.
Pre-Chorus:
A
Cont. rhy. simile
F♯m
I'm a-walk - ing in the rain, tears are fall - ing and I
A
feel a pain. A-wish-ing you were here by me
F♯m
Chorus:
A
to end this mis-er - y, and I won - der. I
F♯m
wah, wah, wah, wah, won - der
A
F♯m
why, a - why, why, why, why, why she ran a - way

D
and I wonder where she will stay-
E7
To Coda
A
yay, my lit - tle run-a - way, a-
D
A
E7
Synth.
(8va throughout)
run, run, run, run, run-a - way.
Instrumental:
Am
G
*Ad lib. on 2nd time a la 1st time.
F
E7
D.S. al Coda (2nd time)
Repeat & fade
A
D
Coda
my lit - tle run-a - way. A - run, run, run, run,

RUNAROUND SUE

Words and Music by
DION DI MUCCI and ERNIE MARESCA

A
D
La la la la.
Whoa,
Bm
G
A
Gtr. 1
whoa.
Verse:
Gtr. 2 continue simile throughout
D
1. Yeah, I should - 've known it from the ver - y start,
Bm
Cont. rhy. simile
G
this girl would leave me with a bro - ken heart.
A - lis - ten peo - ple, what I'm

A
tell - in' you, a - keep a - way from a - Run - a - round Sue.
D
Bm
2. I miss her lips and that girl's warm em - brace. The touch of her hand and the smile
3.4. See additional lyrics
G
on her face. So, if you don't want to cry like I do,
A
Chorus:
D
a - keep a - way from a - Run - a - round Sue. Whoa,
Bm
oh, whoa,
G
A
To Coda
whoa. 1. She'll
Bridge:
G
D
Cont. rhy. simile
give you the run - a - round, yeah, she'll love you and she'll put you down.
2. See additional lyrics
Gtr. 2
T
A
B

Verses 3 & 4:
Here's the moral of the story from the guy who knows.
I fell in love and my love still grows.
Ask any fool that she ever knew,
They'll say keep away from Runaround Sue.

Bridge 2:
She likes to travel 'round, yeah,
She'll love you and she'll put you down.
Now, people let me put you wise;
Sue goes out with other guys.
(To Verse 4:)

RUNNIN' WITH THE DEVIL

Words and Music by
EDWARD VAN HALEN, ALEX VAN HALEN,
MICHAEL ANTHONY and DAVID LEE ROTH

1st Verse
C/ED/E
G/EA/E E
A5
G/A
F♯m/A
Em/A
I live my life like there's no to-mor-row,
(end Rhy. Fig. 1)
Rhy. Fig. 2
mf
sl.
*Lightly palm mute staccatoed notes
A5
G/A
F♯m Em
and all I've got I had to steal.
Least I don't need to
Harm.
(8va)
let ring
**Open G stg. sounds with harmonic.
F♯m/A
Em/A
beg or bor-row.
Yes, I'm liv-in' at a pace that kills.
(end Rhy. Fig. 2)
*Strum backwards from high to low.
*Chorus
w/Rhy. Fig. 1
C/E D/E
G/E A/E E
Run-nin' with the dev-il.
*w/lead voc. ad lib
Run-nin' with the dev-

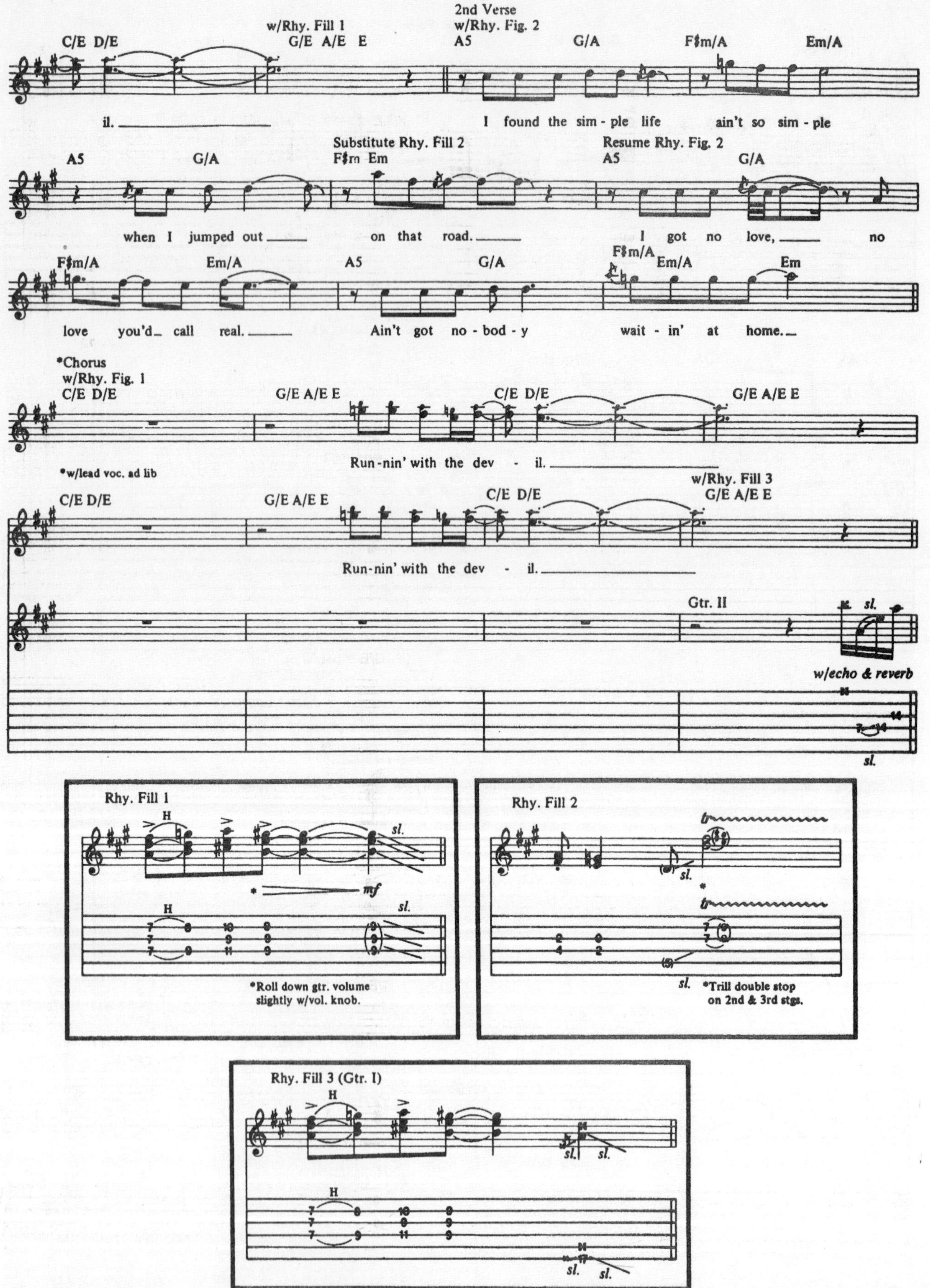
2nd Verse
w/Rhy. Fill 1
w/Rhy. Fig. 2
C/E D/E
G/E A/E E
A5
G/A
F♯m/A
Em/A
il.
I found the sim - ple life
ain't so sim - ple
Substitute Rhy. Fill 2
Resume Rhy. Fig. 2
A5
G/A
F♯m Em
when I jumped out
on that road.
I got no love,
no
F♯m/A
Em/A
Em
love you'd call real.
Ain't got no - bod - y
wait - in' at home.
*Chorus
w/Rhy. Fig. 1
Run-nin' with the dev - il.
*w/lead voc. ad lib
w/Rhy. Fill 3
Run-nin' with the dev - il.
Gtr. II
sl.
w/echo & reverb
Rhy. Fill 1
H
*Roll down gtr. volume slightly w/vol. knob.
Rhy. Fill 2
*Trill double stop on 2nd & 3rd stgs.
Rhy. Fill 3 (Gtr. I)

Guitar solo I
A5
Gtr. I
Gtr. II
pick slides
G5
⑥12fr.
E
P.M.
A5
pick slide
Full
G5
E5
⑥17fr
A
1/2Full
C/E
D/E
G/E
A/E
E
Whoo!
Rhy. Fig. 3
C/E
D/E
G/E
A/E
E
You know, I,

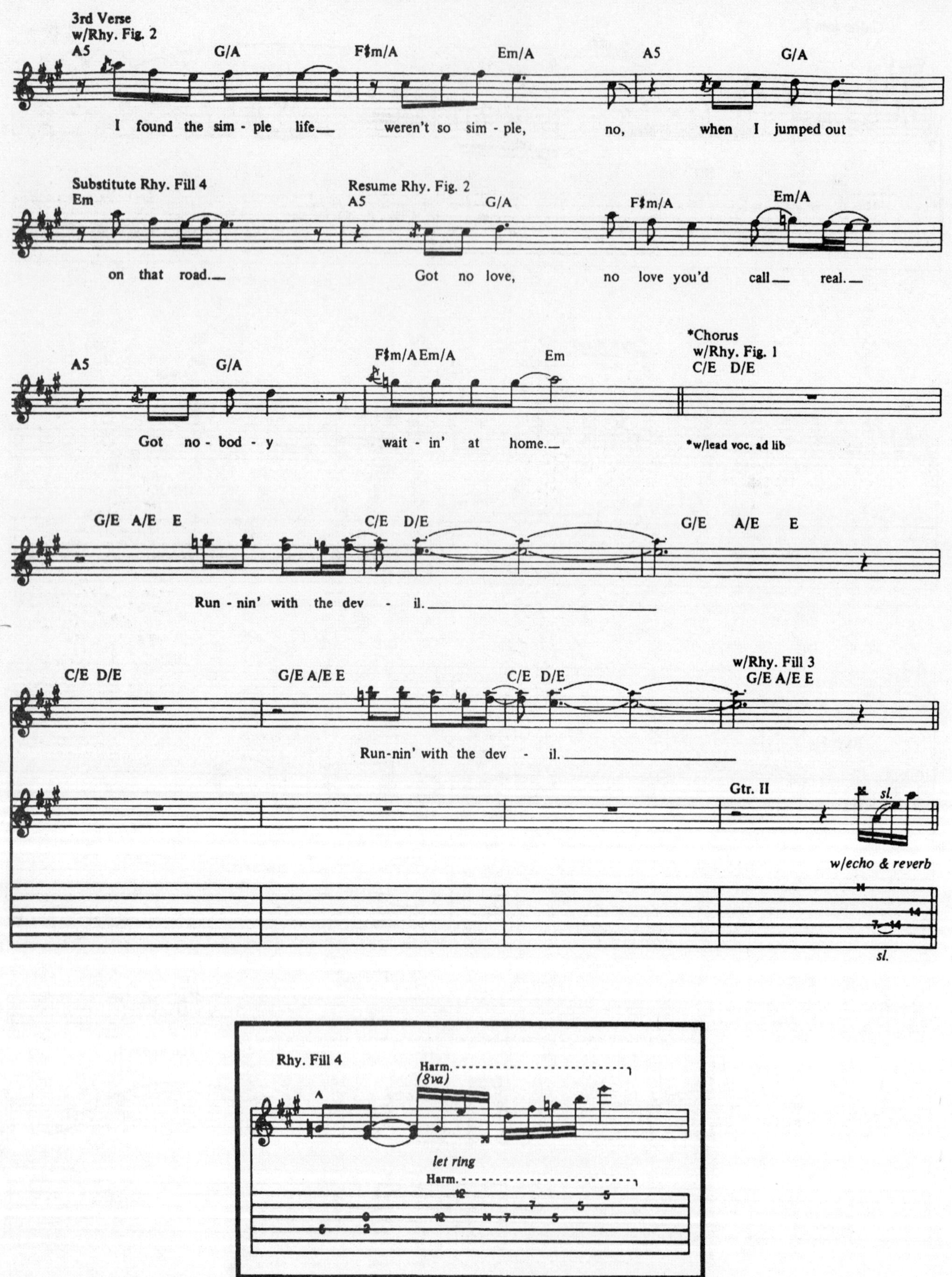
3rd Verse
w/Rhy. Fig. 2
A5 G/A F♯m/A Em/A A5 G/A
I found the sim - ple life___ weren't so sim - ple, no, when I jumped out
Substitute Rhy. Fill 4
Em
Resume Rhy. Fig. 2
A5 G/A F♯m/A Em/A
on that road.___ Got no love, no love you'd call___ real.___
A5 G/A F♯m/A Em/A Em
Got no - bod - y wait - in' at home.___
*Chorus
w/Rhy. Fig. 1
C/E D/E
*w/lead voc. ad lib
G/E A/E E C/E D/E G/E A/E E
Run - nin' with the dev - il.
C/E D/E G/E A/E E C/E D/E
w/Rhy. Fill 3
G/E A/E E
Run-nin' with the dev - il.
Gtr. II
sl.
w/echo & reverb
sl.
Rhy. Fill 4
Harm.
(8va)
let ring
Harm.

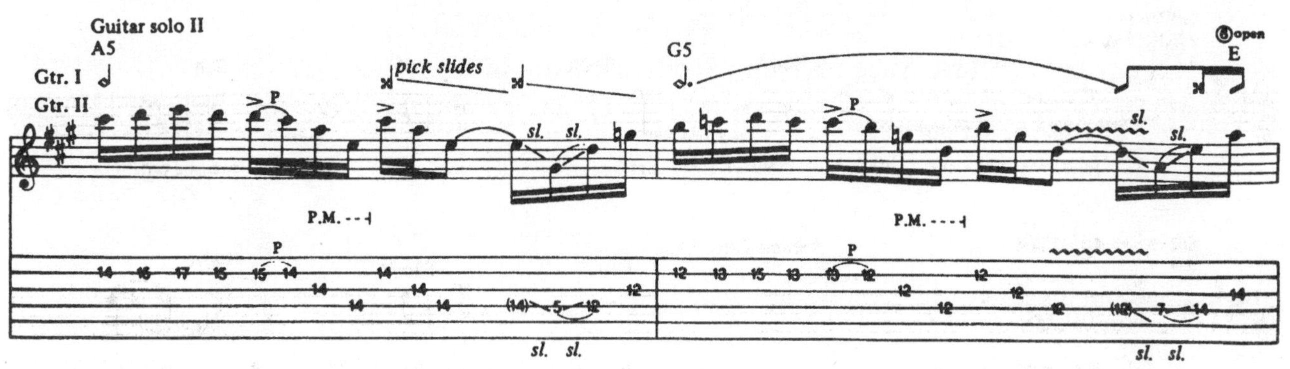
Guitar solo II
A5
Gtr. I
Gtr. II
pick slides
G5
⑥open
E
sl.
P.M.
P

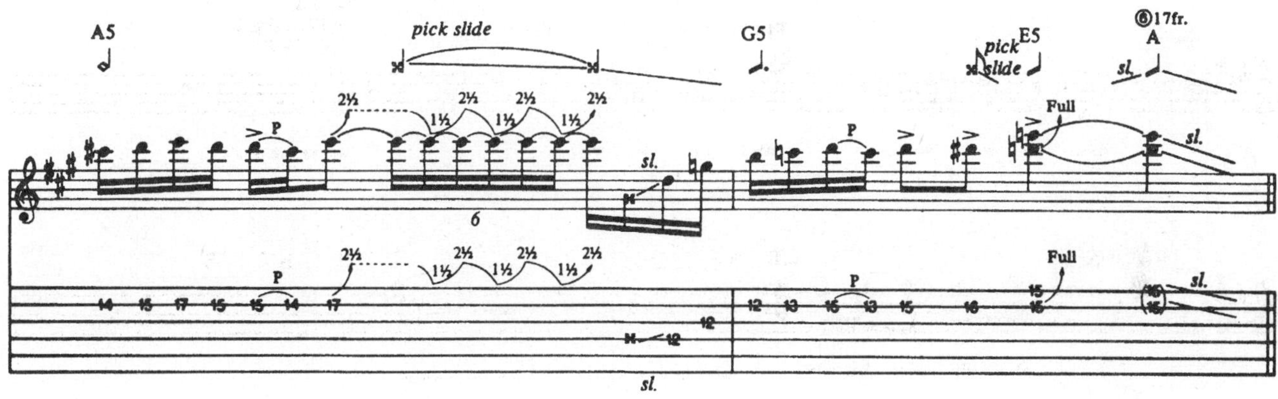
A5
pick slide
G5
pick slide
E5
⑥17fr.
A
Full
sl.
6
P

*Out-chorus
w/Rhy. Fig. 3 (4½ times)
C/E D/E
G/E A/E E
C/E D/E
Run - nin' with the dev - il.
*w/lead voc. ad lib till end

G/E A/E E
Play 3 times
C/E D/E
w/Rhy. Fill 5
G/E A/E E
Run - nin' with the dev - il.
poco rit.

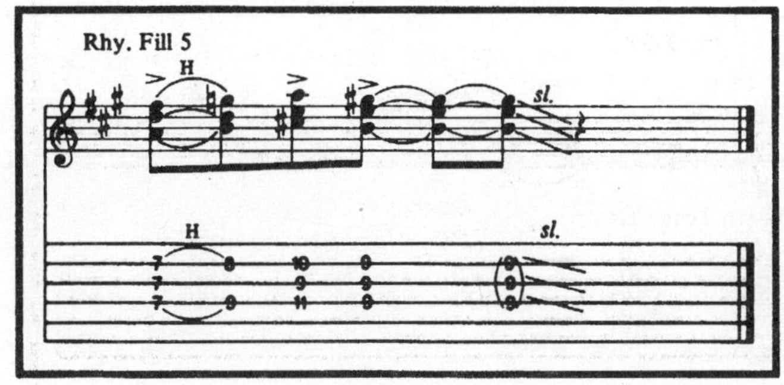
Rhy. Fill 5
H
sl.

SAN FRANCISCO

(Be Sure to Wear Some Flowers in Your Hair)

Bridge:
F
134211
12-str. Acous. Gtr.
Cont. rhy. simile
All a - cross_ the na - tion,_ such a strange_ vi - bra - tion._ Mm,_
G
32 1
F
134211
_ peo - ple in mo - tion._ There's a whole gen - er - a -
- tion with a new ex - pla - na - tion._
G
32 1
D7
213
D.S. 𝄋 al Coda
_ Peo - ple in mo - tion,_ peo - ple in mo - tion.
Coda
G
32 1
Em
23
Outro:
F♯m
134111
12-str. Acous. Gtr.
there._ If you
A
234
D
132
A
234
come to San Fran - cis - co,_ sum - mer -
C♯m
4fr.
13421
F♯m
134111
A
234
Cont. rhy. simile
time_ will be a love - in_ there._
F♯m
134111
Begin fade
A
234
D
132
A
234
Fade

SANCTUARY
Words and Music by
STEVE HARRIS, PAUL DI'ANNO
and DAVE MURRAY
D(add9) Dno3rd F G A
5fr. 024 3fr. 5fr.
D E C C Am D
5fr. 7fr. 3fr
Moderately fast
Guitar Lick: A
Dno3rd
T
A
B
Guitar Lick: B
Dno3rd
Guitar Lick: B
Dno3rd
1. Out of the win - ter came_ a war horse_of steel._ I've
nev - er killed a wo - man be - fore,_ but I know_how it feels._
F
G
3fr.
Guitar Lick: B
Dno3rd
I know_you'd have gone_ in - sane_ if you saw_ what I saw_
F
G
3fr.
so now I've got_ to_ look for_______
(to 2nd end on D.S.)

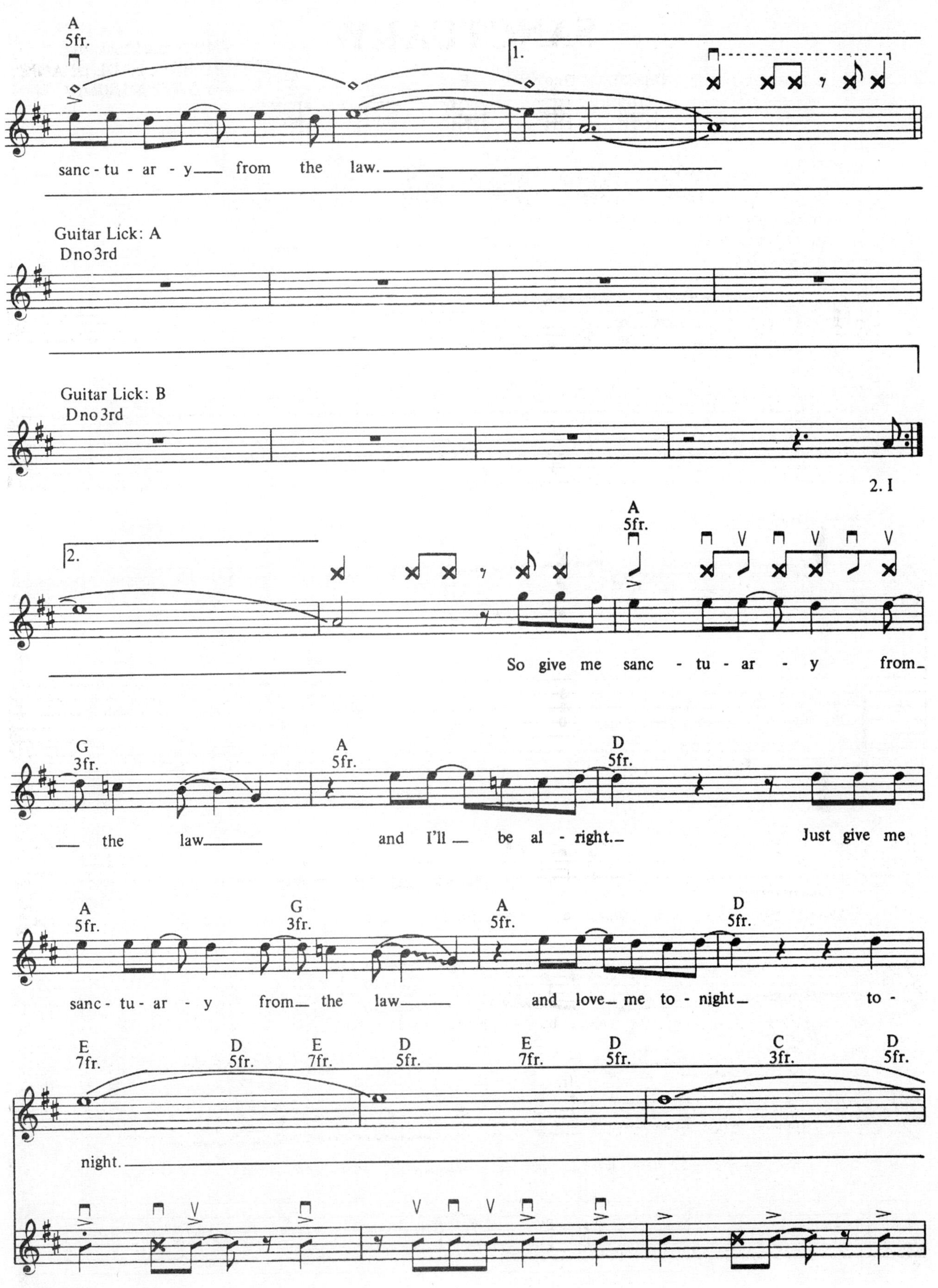
A
5fr.
1.
sanc - tu - ar - y from the law.
Guitar Lick: A
D no 3rd
Guitar Lick: B
D no 3rd
2. I
2.
A
5fr.
So give me sanc - tu - ar - y from
G
3fr.
A
5fr.
D
5fr.
the law
and I'll be al - right.
Just give me
A
5fr.
G
3fr.
A
5fr.
D
5fr.
sanc - tu - ar - y from the law
and love me to - night
to -
E
7fr.
D
5fr.
E
7fr.
D
5fr.
E
7fr.
D
5fr.
C
3fr.
D
5fr.
night.

C
3fr.
D
5fr.
Bm
7fr.
A
5fr.
To Coda
(Let first chord ring through measure)
B
Guitar Lick: B
D no 3rd
This is rhythm underneath improvised solo.
If used as the solo break, then cut all playing
in half.
Play eight times
F
G
3fr.
Guitar Lick: B
D no 3rd
F
G
3fr.
Guitar Lick: B
D no 3rd
Play three times
D no 3rd
C
Guitar Lick: B
D no 3rd
Play four times
Am
B
D
B

2. I met up with a 'slinger last night to keep me alive.
He spends all his money on gambling and guns to survive.

3. I can laugh at the wind, I can howl at the rain.
Down in the Canyon or out in the plain.

SATURDAY NIGHT SPECIAL

Words and Music by
EDWARD KING and RONNIE VAN ZANT

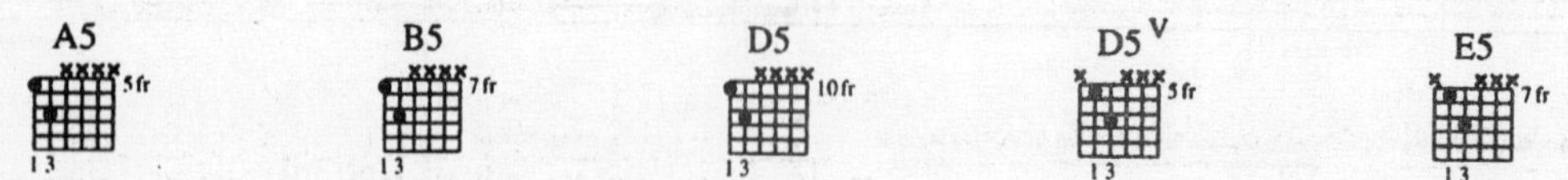

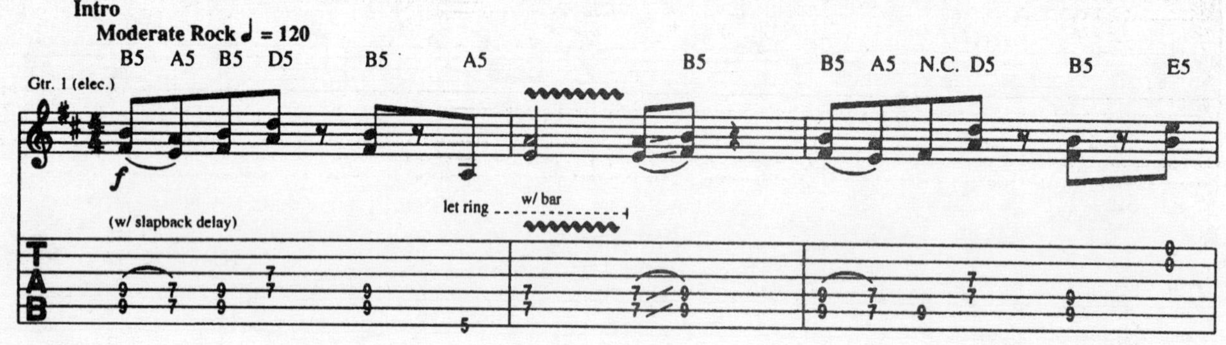

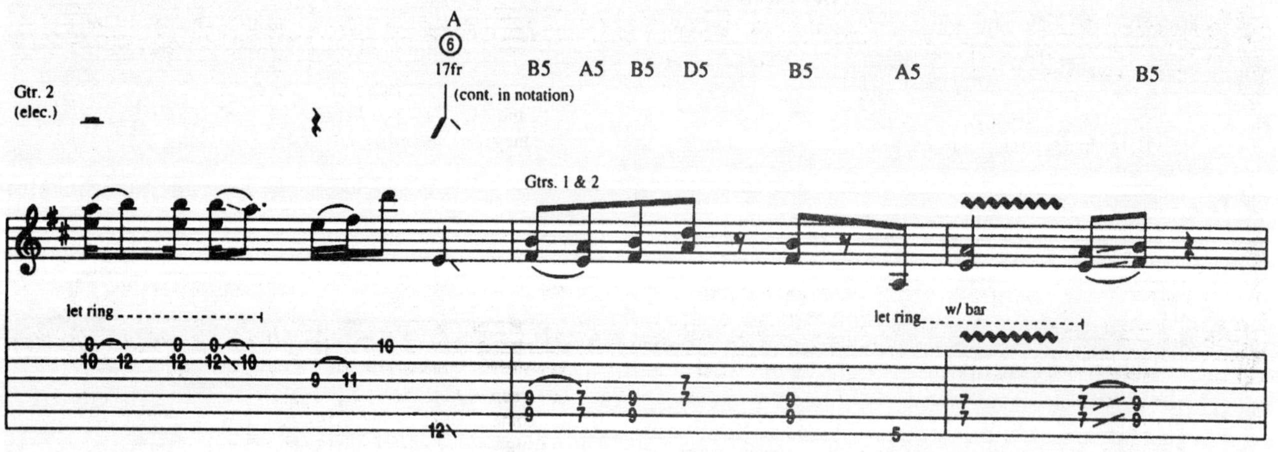

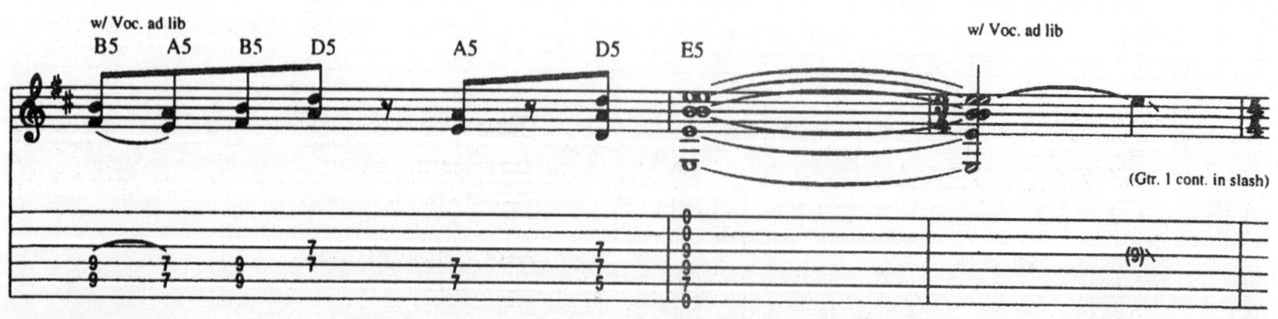

A B D B
⑥ ⑥ ⑤ ⑥
5fr 7fr 5fr 7fr

Gtr. 1 (cont. in notation)

D5 B5 N.C. A5 B5 D5 B5 D5 E5 N.C. D5 E5

Gtr. 3 (elec)

full let ring full full full

(cont. in Fill 1)

Gtr. 2 Rhy. Fig. 1 Gtrs. 1 & 2 End Rhy. Fig. 1

Verse

Gtrs. 1 & 2: w/ Rhy. Fig. 1, 2 times
Gtr. 3: w/ Fill 1, 1st & 3rd times; w/Fill 2, 2nd time

A5 B5 D5 B5 D5 B5 N.C. A5 B5 A5 B5 D5 B5 D5 E5 N.C. D5 E5

1. A - two feets _ they come _ a _ creep - in', like a black cat do. ___
2. Big Jim's . been drink - in' a whisk - ey, and play - in' po - ker on a los - in' night.
3. A hand - guns _ are made _ for _ kill - in', they ain't no good for noth - in' else.

A5 B5 D5 B5 D5 B5 N.C A5 B5 A5 B5 D5 B5 D5 E5 N.C D5 E5

And two bod - ies are lay - in' a na - ked, a creep-er think he got a - noth-in' to lose. ___
And pret - ty soon ol' Jim starts a think - in', a some - bod - y been cheat - in' and a ly - in'. ___
And if you like to drink _ ol' whisk - ey, you might e - ven a shoot your - self. ___

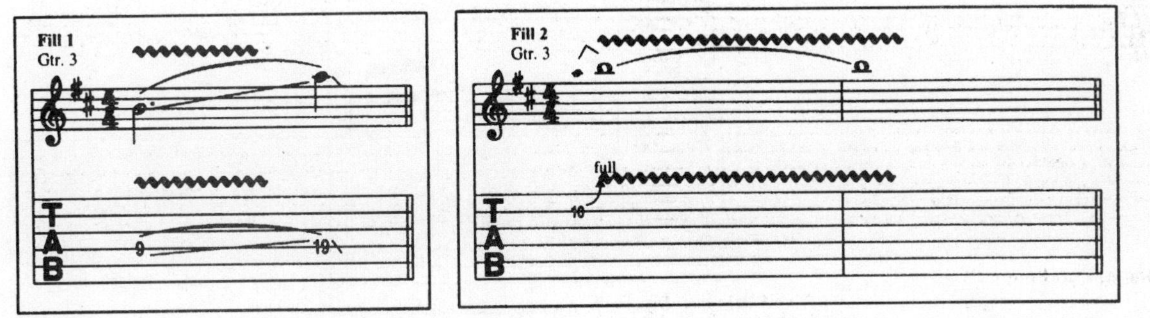

Gtrs. 1 & 2: w/ Rhy. Fig. 2, 2nd time
** N.C. (A5) (B5) (D5) (B5) (D5) (B5) (A5) (B5) (A5) (B5) (D5) (B5)
So he creeps in - to this a house, yeah, and un - locks the door.
So Big Jim com - menced to fight - in', I would - n't tell ya no lies,
So why don't we dump 'em peo - ple, to the bot - tom of a sea?
* Gtr. 1
* Gtr. 2
divisi
* Gtr. 1 to right of slash in TAB
** Rhy. Fig. 1 chords in parentheses
Gtr. 3: w/Fill 3, 2nd time
Gtrs. 1 & 2: w/ Rhy. Fig. 1, 1st 3 meas. only, 2nd time
(D5) (E5) D5 E5 (A5) (B5) (D5) (B5) (D5) (B5) (A5) (B5)
And as a man's reach - in' for his a - trou - sers,
Big Jim done a pulled his a pis - tol,
Be - fore some ol' fool come a - round here
8va
loco
P.H.
(Gtr. 1) pitch: F♯ * w/ slapback delay
Chorus
(A5) (B5) (D5) (B5) E5 D5 N.C. E5 N.C. N.C.
a shoots him full of a thir - ty eight holes.
shot his friend a right be - tween the eyes.
wan - na shoot ei - ther you or me.
Mis - ter Sat - ur - day Night
Gtrs. 1 & 2
P.M.
Fill 3
Gtr. 3
let ring
T
A
B

A5
E5
N.C.
Spe - cial, got a bar - rel that's a blue and cold.
15ma
loco
P.M.
P.H.
P.M
pitch: D♯
To Coda
D5
They ain't good for noth - in', but put a man six a
Interlude
Gtrs. 1 & 2: w/ Rhy. Fig. 1
B5
feet in a hole.
Gtr. 3
w/ bar
full
let ring
Gtrs 1 & 2
Gtr. 1

Interlude
w/ Voc. ad libs
Gtrs. 1 & 2
B5 A5 B5 D5 B5 A5 B5 A5 B5 D5 B5 N.C.
let ring
w/ bar
let ring
B5 A5 B5 D5 B5 A5 B5 A5
let ring
w/ bar
B5 A5 B5 D5 B5 E5
Gtr. 3: w/ Fill 4, 2nd time
N.C.
B5 A5 B5 D5 A5
let ring
let ring
B5 B5 A5 B5 D5 B5 N.C.
w/ bar
let ring
1.
let ring
full
1/4
2.
w/ Voc. ad lib
full
Guitar Solo
Gtrs. 1 & 2: w/Rhy. Fig. 1. 2 times
A5 B5 D5 B5 D5 B5 N.C. A5 B5
Gtr. 3
full
let ring
full
let ring
let ring
full
Fill 4
Gtr. 3
let ring

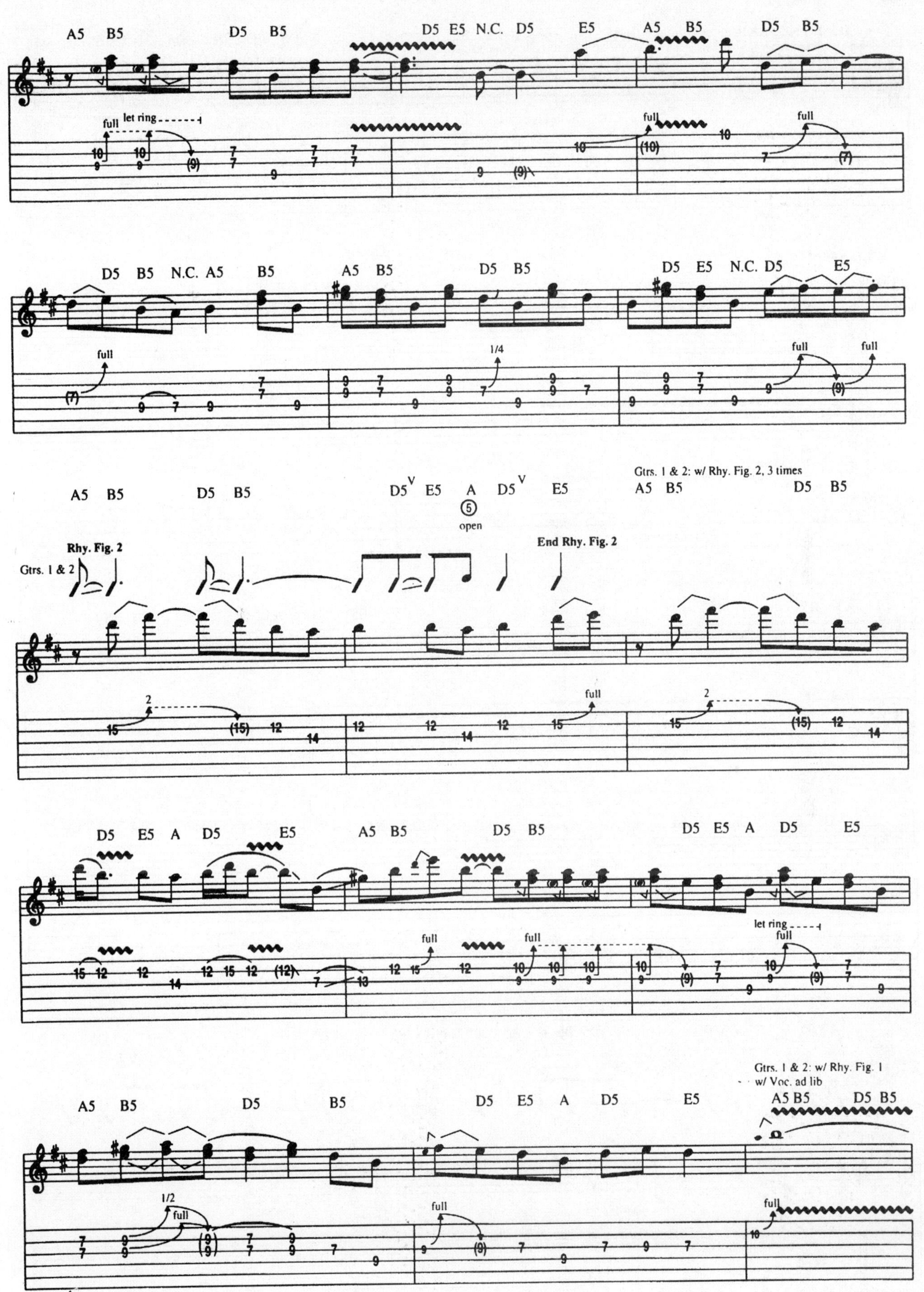
A5 B5 D5 B5 D5 E5 N.C. D5 E5 A5 B5 D5 B5
full
let ring
full
full
D5 B5 N.C. A5 B5 A5 B5 D5 B5 D5 E5 N.C. D5 E5
full
1/4
full
full
Gtrs. 1 & 2: w/ Rhy. Fig. 2, 3 times
A5 B5 D5 B5 D5 E5 A D5 E5 A5 B5 D5 B5
5
open
Rhy. Fig. 2
Gtrs. 1 & 2
End Rhy. Fig. 2
2
full
2
D5 E5 A D5 E5 A5 B5 D5 B5 D5 E5 A D5 E5
full
full
let ring
full
Gtrs. 1 & 2: w/ Rhy. Fig. 1
w/ Voc. ad lib
A5 B5 D5 B5 D5 E5 A D5 E5 A5 B5 D5 B5
1/2
full
full
full

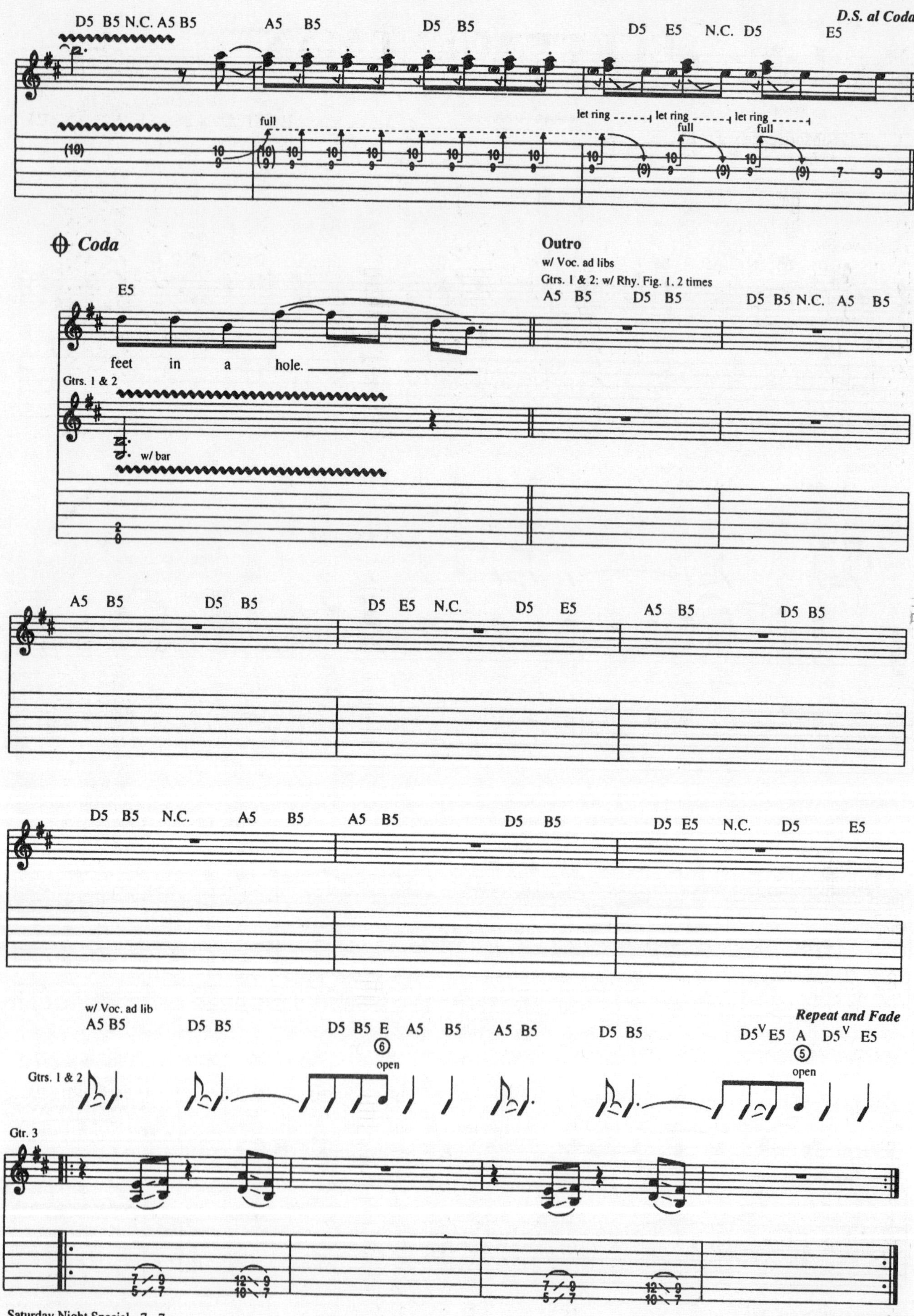
D.S. al Coda
D5 B5 N.C. A5 B5
A5 B5
D5 B5
D5 E5 N.C. D5
E5
full
let ring
full
Coda
E5
feet in a hole.
Gtrs. 1 & 2
w/ bar
Outro
w/ Voc. ad libs
Gtrs. 1 & 2: w/ Rhy. Fig. 1, 2 times
A5 B5
D5 B5
D5 B5 N.C. A5 B5
A5 B5
D5 B5
D5 E5 N.C.
D5 E5
A5 B5
D5 B5
D5 B5 N.C.
A5 B5
A5 B5
D5 B5
D5 E5 N.C.
D5 E5
w/ Voc. ad lib
Repeat and Fade
A5 B5
D5 B5
D5 B5 E
open
A5 B5
A5 B5
D5 B5
D5 E5 A
D5 E5
Gtrs. 1 & 2
Gtr. 3

SECRET AGENT MAN

Words and Music by
P.F. SLOAN and STEVE BARRI

Moderately ♩ = 148
Intro:

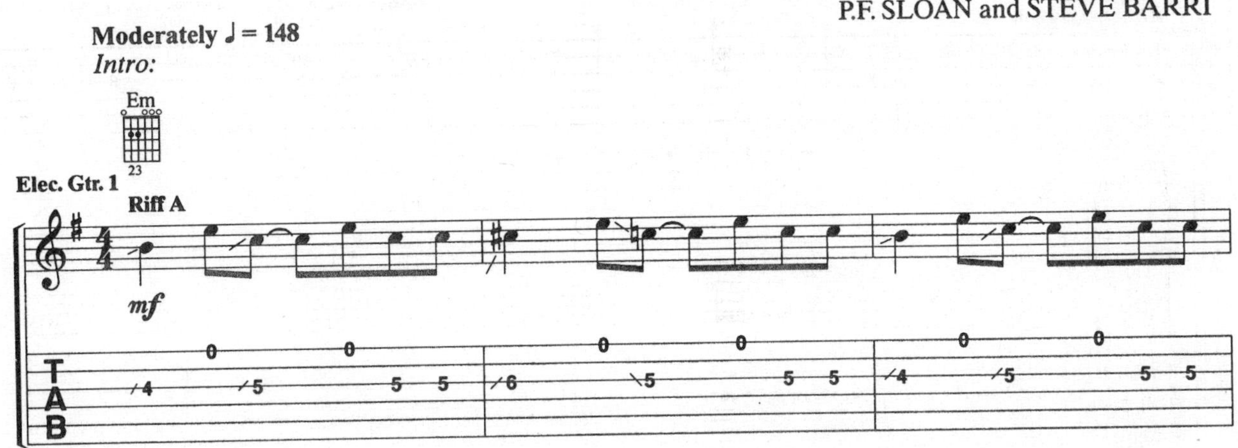

*Elec. Gtr. 1 fills simile on repeats.

To ev - 'ry - one he meets he stays a
A pret - ty face can hide an e - vil
And then lay - in' in a Bom - bay al - ley
B7
213 4
Em
23
strang - er.
mind.
the next day.
With ev - 'ry move he makes,
Ah, be care - ful what you say,
Ah, no, you let the wrong word slip,
hold
Am
231
an - oth - er chance he takes.
you'll give your - self a - way.
by kiss - ing per - sua - sive lips. The
Em
23
Am
231
Odds are he won't live to see to - mor - row.
Odds are you won't live to see to - mor - row.
odds are you won't live to see to - mor - row.
TAB

Chorus:
Em
Bm
Em
Elec. Gtr. 2
Resume rhy. simile
Se - cret a - gent man. Se - cret
Elec. Gtr. 1
hold
Bm
Em
C7
a - gent man. They've giv - en you a num-
hold
hold
To Coda w/Riff A (Elec. Gtr. 1) meas. 3-6 only
Bm
Em
Elec. Gtr. 2 tacet
- ber and tak - en 'way your name.
end Rhy. Fig. 1
hold
hold

1.
2.
2. Be -
Guitar Solo:
Em
Am
Elec. Gtr. 1
Elec. Gtr. 2 resume rhy. fig. simile
B7
hold
Em
Am
Em
Am
Em

Chorus:
w/Rhy. Fig. 1 (Elec. Gtr. 1)
Bm
Em
Bm
Elec. Gtr. 2
Resume rhy. fig. simile
Se - cret a - gent man. Se - cret a - gent man.
Em
C7
B7
They've giv - en you a num - ber and
w/Riff A (Elec. Gtr. 1) meas. 3-6 only
D.S. al Coda
Em
Elec. Gtr. 2 tacet
tak - en 'way your name.
w/Riff A (Elec. Gtr. 1)
Coda
Em
Elec. Gtr. 2 tacet
Freely
Elec. Gtr. 2
Se - cret a - gent man.
Elec. Gtr. 1

SEND HER MY LOVE

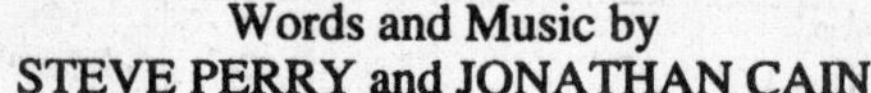

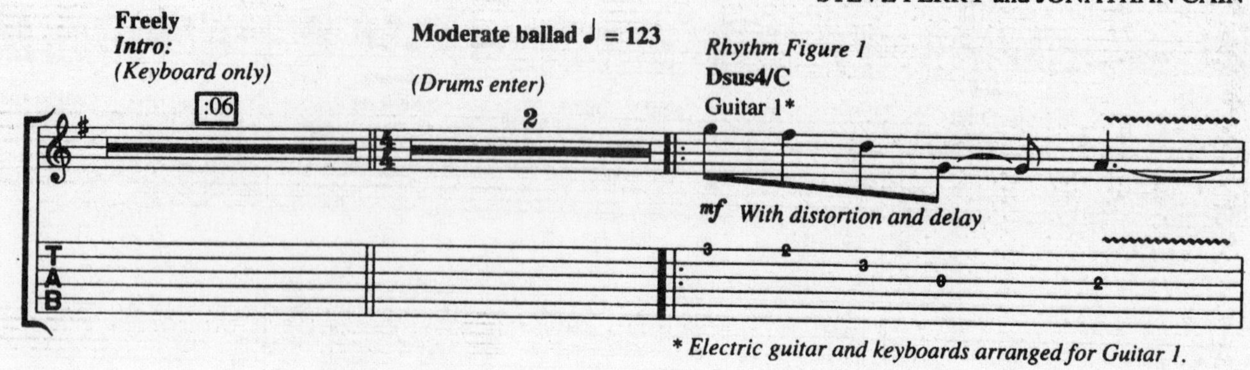

Verses 1 & 2:
Substitute Rhythm Figure 1 on Verse 2 (Guitar 1), 3 times

Dsus4/C
Em9
I still re - call a sad ca - fe;
Let ring
Let ring
Pre-Chorus:
C
Em9(no 5)
Bm
C
how it hurt so bad to see her cry.
Simile on repeat
Let ring
Let ring
Let ring
Let ring
Em9
Bm7
I did - n't want to say good - bye.
Let ring
Let ring
Chorus:
Em7
D(add E)/F#
Cmaj9(no 5)
Em7/A
Send her my love; mem - o - ries re - main. Send her my
Guitar 1
Rhythm Figure 2
End Rhythm Figure 2
Let ring
Let ring
Let ring
Let ring

Em7(no 5)
D/F#
C(add D)(no 5)
Em7(no 3)/A
love;
ros - es' nev - er fade.
Let ring
Let ring
Let ring
Let ring
Em7
D(add E)/F#
1.
Csus2
Send her my love.
Let ring
Let ring
2. Bridge:
C5
E5
Call - in' out her name. I'm dream - in' re - flec - tions of a face I'm see - in'.
C5
Bm7
It's her voice that keeps on haunt - ing me.

Guitar Solo:
With Rhythm Figure 2, 7 times with ad lib variations (Guitar 1)

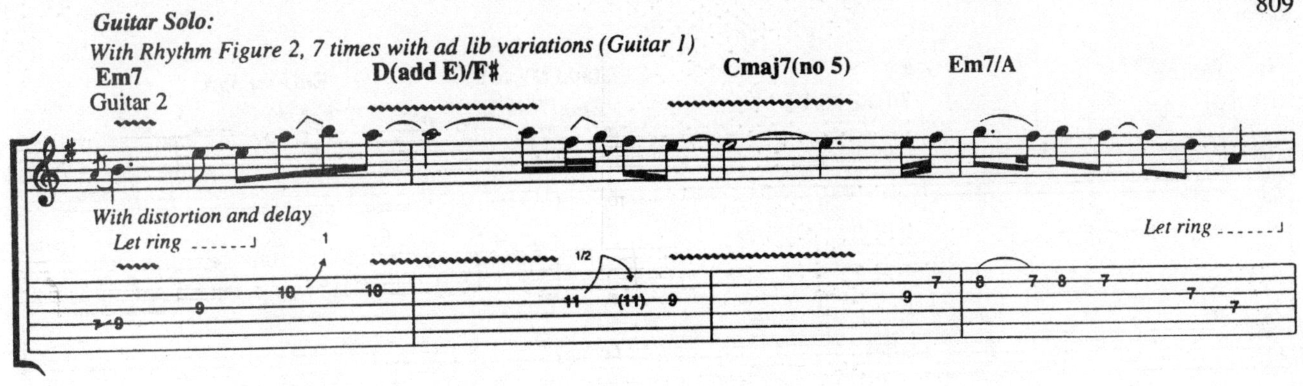

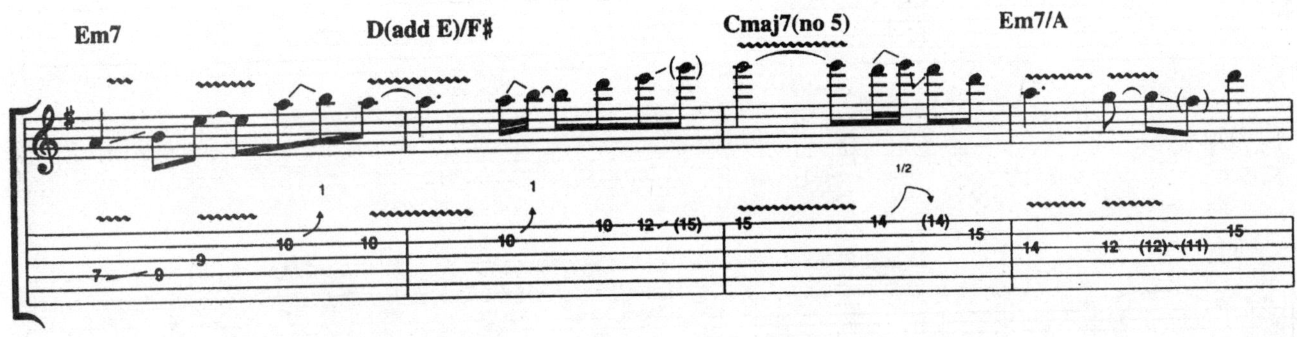

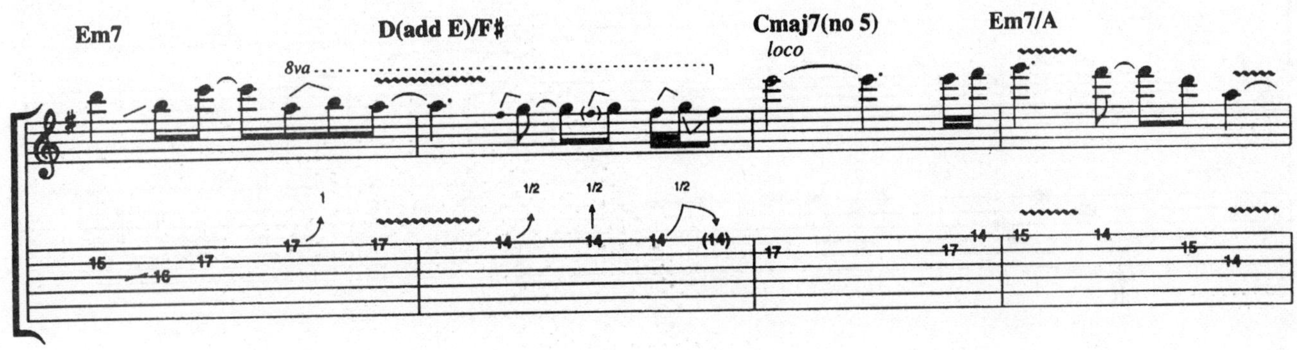

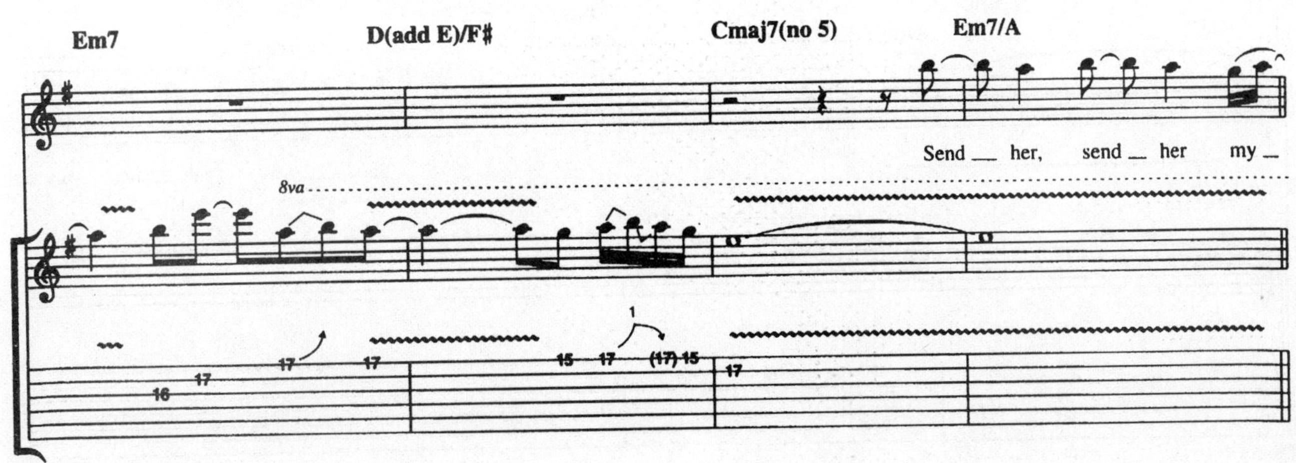

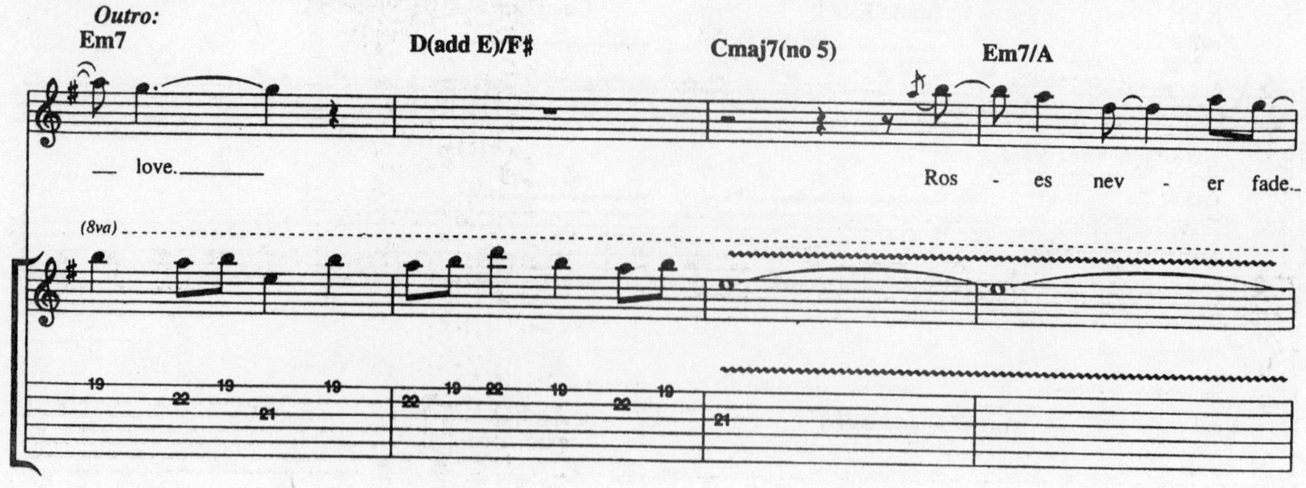
Outro:
Em7
D(add E)/F♯
Cmaj7(no 5)
Em7/A
love.
Ros - es nev - er fade.
(8va)
19 22 19 21 19
22 19 22 19 22 19
21

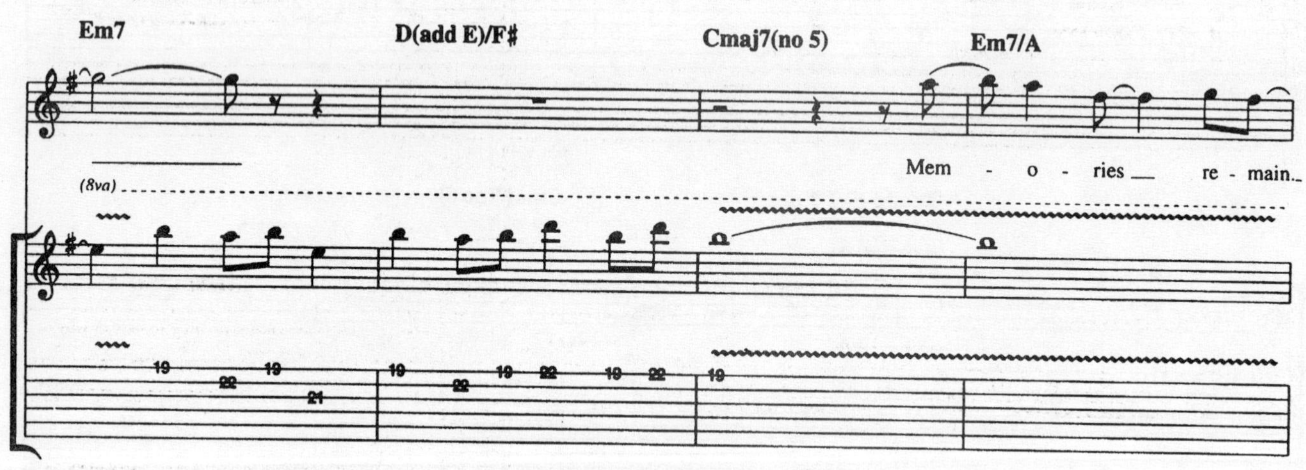
Em7
D(add E)/F♯
Cmaj7(no 5)
Em7/A
Mem - o - ries re - main.
(8va)
19 22 19 21
19 22 19 22 19 22
19

Em7
D(add E)/F♯
Cmaj7(no 5)
Em7/A
Send her, send her my
(8va)
19 22 19 21 19
22 19 22 19 22 19
21

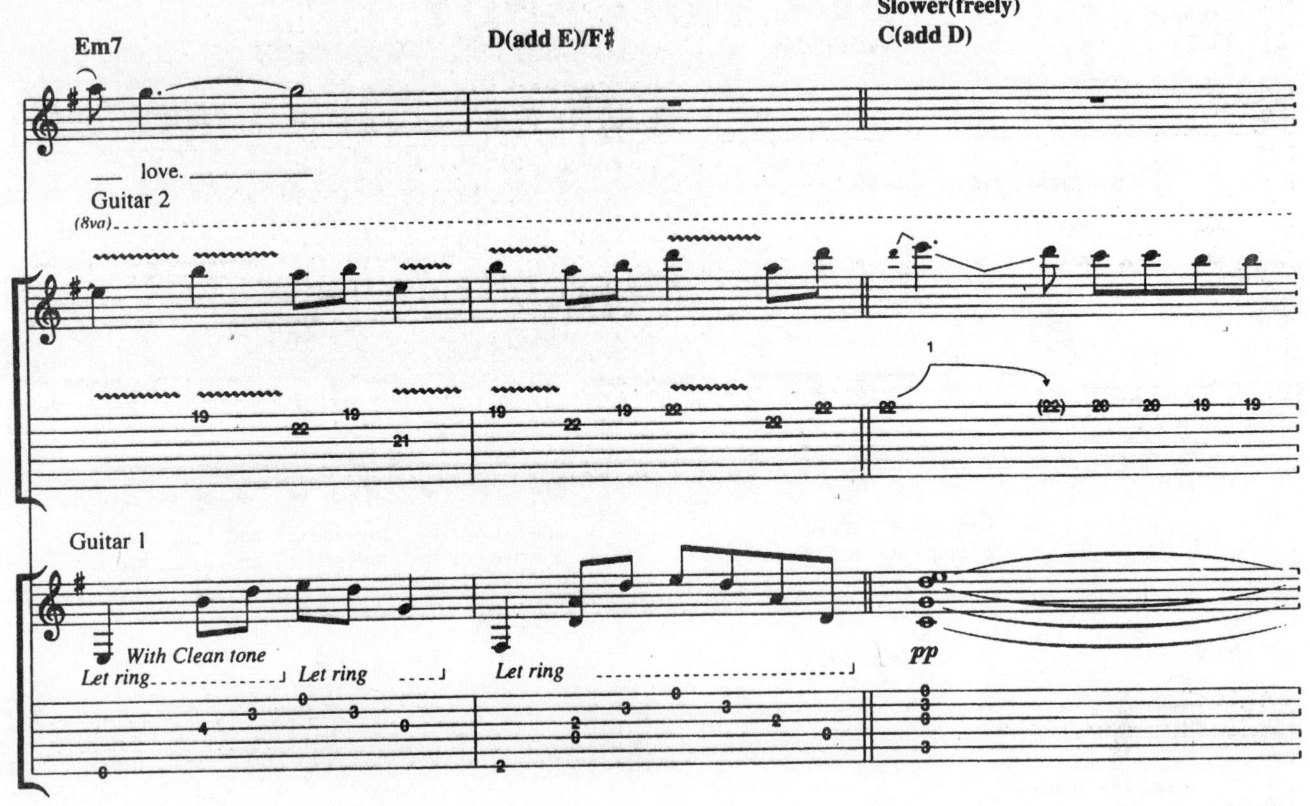

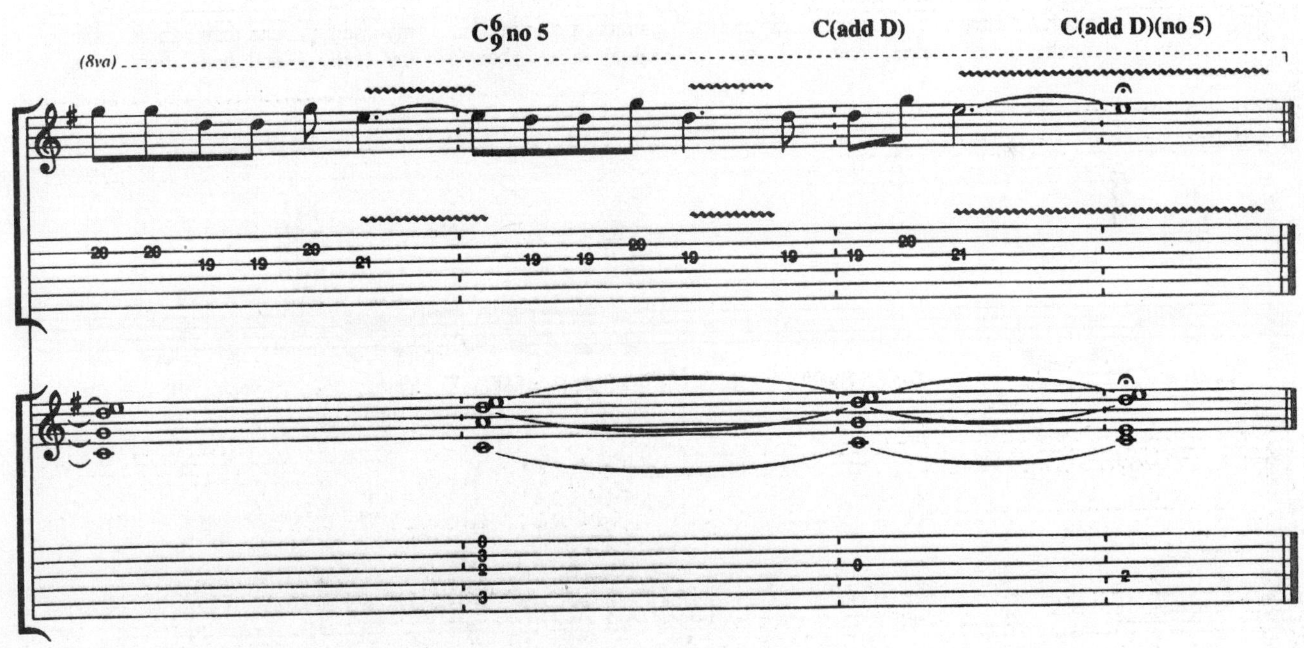

Additional Lyrics

Verse 2: The same hotel, the same old room;
I'm on the road again.
She needed so much more
Than I could give.
We knew our love could not pretend.
Broken hearts can always mend.

(To Chorus)

SEX AND CANDY

Words and Music by
JOHN WOZNIAK

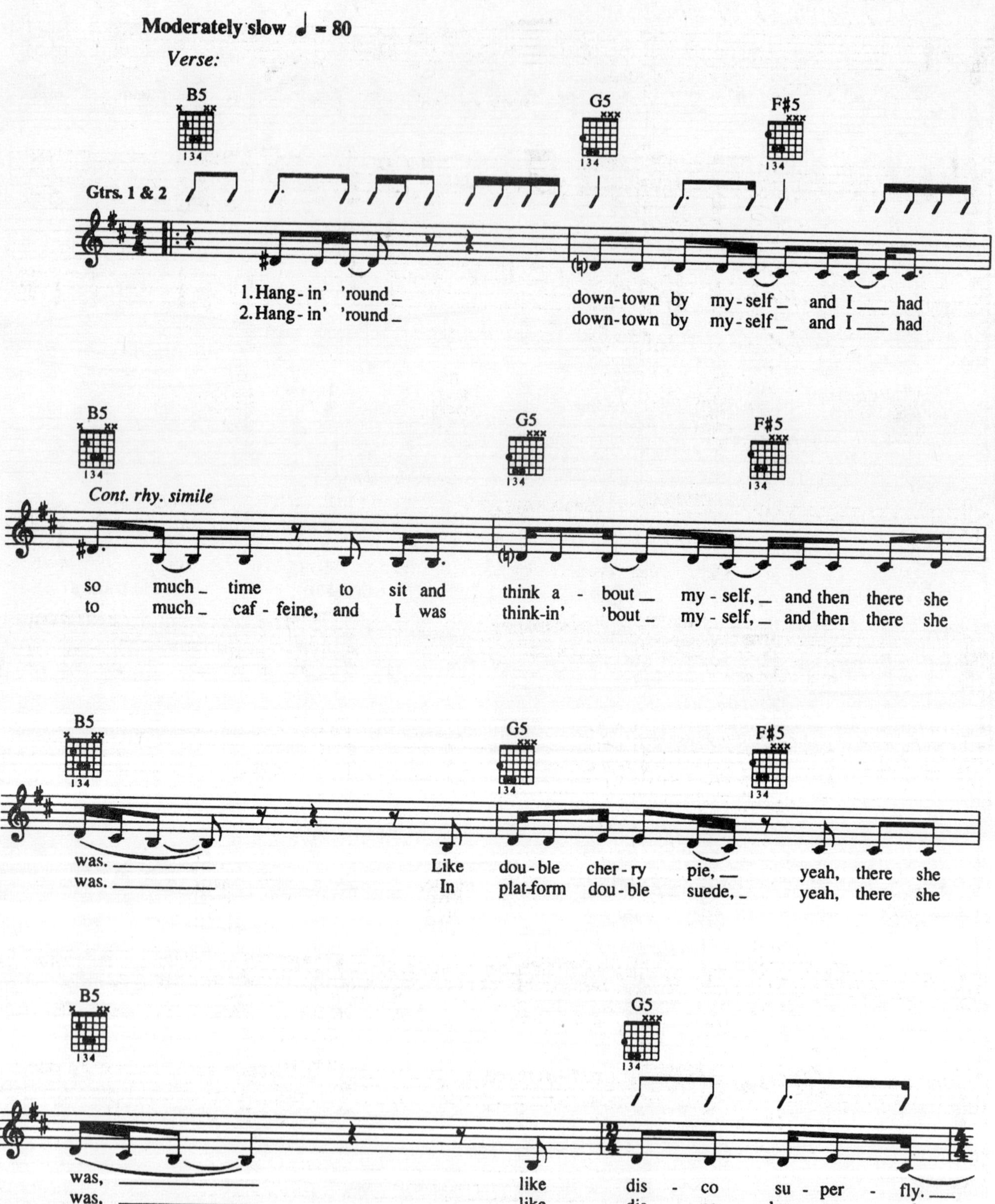
Moderately slow ♩ = 80
Verse:
B5
G5
F#5
Gtrs. 1 & 2
Cont. rhy. simile
1. Hang - in' 'round _ down - town by my - self _ and I ___ had so much _ time to sit and think a - bout _ my - self, _ and then there she was. ___ Like dou - ble cher - ry pie, _ yeah, there she was, ___ like dis - co su - per - fly. ___
2. Hang - in' 'round _ down - town by my - self _ and I ___ had to much _ caf - feine, and I was think-in' 'bout _ my - self, _ and then there she was. ___ In plat-form dou - ble suede, _ yeah, there she was, ___ like dis - co lem - on - ade. ___

Chorus:
F♯
D5
B5
G5
1342
134
Gtr. 2
I smell sex and can - dy here, mm.
Gtr. 1
A
Cont. rhy. simile
Who's that loung - ing in my chair, mm?
P.M.
Who's that cast - ing de - vi - ous stares in my di - rec -
111

A
D
A
*Gtr. 1
-tion? Ma - ma, this sure - ly is a dream, yeah.
*Two gtrs. arranged for one.
To Coda
1.
B5
G5
D
A
B5
G5
Cont. rhy. simile
Yeah, ma - ma, this sure - ly is a dream.
F#
2.
B5
G5
D
A
Gtr. 1
Yeah, ma - ma, this sure - ly is a dream, yeah.
D.S. al Coda
B5
G5
F#
D
Gtr. 1
I smell sex and
Coda
B5
G5
D
A
Gtr. 1
Yeah, ma - ma, this sure - ly is a dream, yeah.
B5
G5
D
Yeah, ma - ma, this must be my dream.

SHEENA IS A PUNK ROCKER

Words and Music by JEFFREY HYMAN, JOHN CUMMINGS, DOUGLAS COLVIN and THOMAS ERDELYI

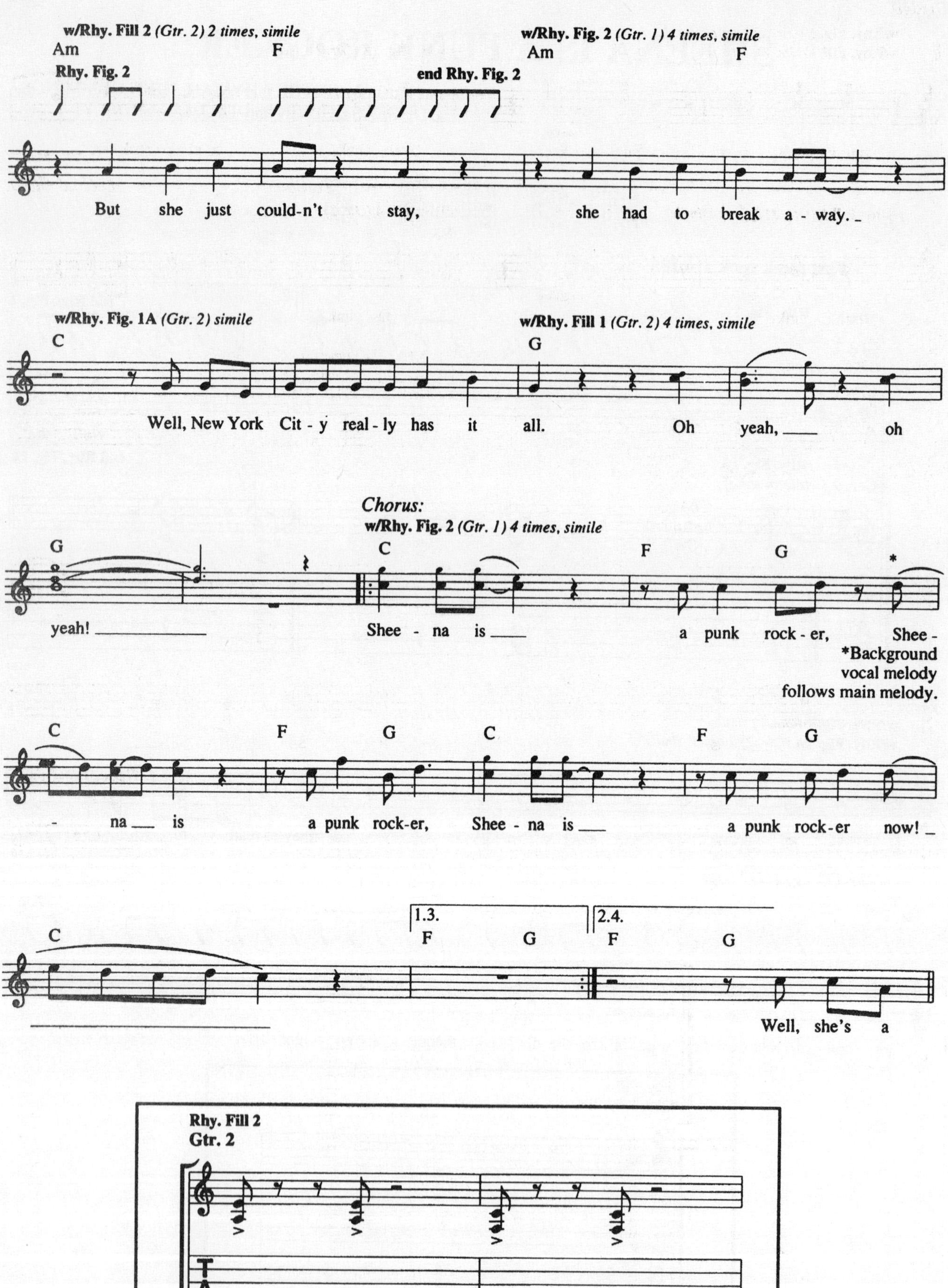
w/Rhy. Fill 2 (Gtr. 2) 2 times, simile
Am
F
Rhy. Fig. 2
end Rhy. Fig. 2
w/Rhy. Fig. 2 (Gtr. 1) 4 times, simile
Am
F
But she just could-n't stay, she had to break a - way. _
w/Rhy. Fig. 1A (Gtr. 2) simile
C
w/Rhy. Fill 1 (Gtr. 2) 4 times, simile
G
Well, New York Cit - y real - ly has it all. Oh yeah, ___ oh
Chorus:
w/Rhy. Fig. 2 (Gtr. 1) 4 times, simile
G
C
F
G
yeah! ___ Shee - na is ___ a punk rock - er, Shee -
*Background vocal melody follows main melody.
C
F
G
C
F
G
- na ___ is a punk rock-er, Shee - na is ___ a punk rock-er now! _
1.3.
2.4.
C
F
G
F
G
Well, she's a
Rhy. Fill 2
Gtr. 2
T
A
B
7
5
7
5
3
1
3
1

Bridge:

w/Rhy. Fig. 1 *(Gtr. 1) 4 times, simile*
w/Rhy. Fill 3 *(Gtr. 2) 2 times*
w/Rhy. Fig. 1A *(Gtr. 2) simile*

F C

punk, punk, a punk rock-er, punk, punk, a punk rock-er, ______

To Coda ⊕ *D.C. al Coda*

w/Rhy. Fill 1 *(Gtr. 2) 2 times, simile*
w/Rhy. Fill 4 *(Gtr. 2) 2 times, simile*

G B♭

__ punk, punk, a punk rock-er, punk, punk, a punk rock-er!

⊕ *Coda*

w/Rhy. Fig. 1 *(Gtr. 1) 2 times, simile*
w/Rhy. Fig. 1A *(Gtr. 2) 2 times, simile*

C

a punk rock - er!

Chorus:

w/Rhy. Fig. 2 *(Gtr. 1) 4 times, simile*

C F G

Shee - na is a punk rock - er, Shee -

C F G C

- na ____ is a punk rock - er, Shee - na is ____

Repeat and fade

F G C F G

a punk rock - er now! ____________________

Rhy. Fill 3
Gtr. 2

T
A
B
3 3
1 1

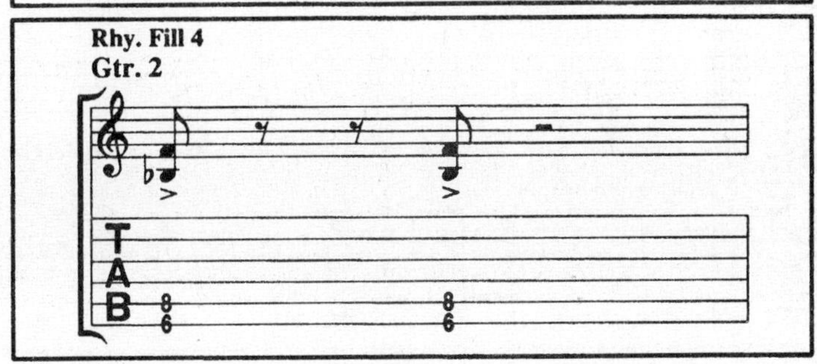

SHE'S NOT THERE

Words and Music by
ROD ARGENT

Moderately ♩ = 126
Intro:
Am
D
Elec. Gtr.
mf
Elec. Piano (arr. for gtr.)
Bass. Gtr.
Verse:
F
A
Cont. rhy. simile
1. Well, no one told me a - bout her, the way she lied.
2. Well, no one told me a - bout her; what could I do?
Well, no one told me a - bout her, how man-y peo - ple cried.
Well, no one told me a - bout her, though they all knew.
But it's too
Pre-chorus:
Dm
Em
C
E
late to say you're sor - ry. How would I know, why should I care?
Please don't both - er try'n' to find her, she's not there.

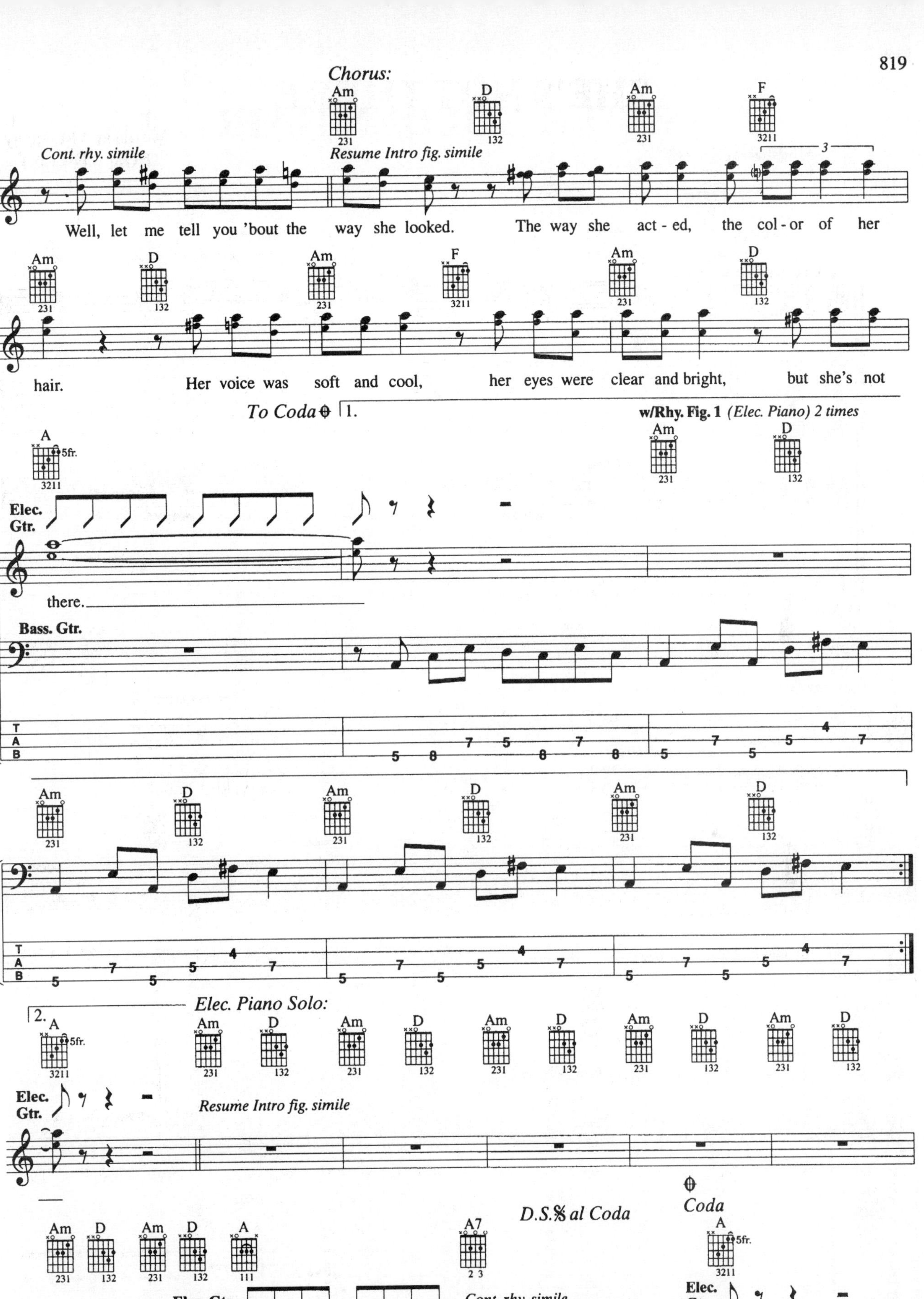
Chorus:
Cont. rhy. simile
Resume Intro fig. simile
Well, let me tell you 'bout the way she looked. The way she act - ed, the col - or of her
hair. Her voice was soft and cool, her eyes were clear and bright, but she's not
To Coda
w/Rhy. Fig. 1 (Elec. Piano) 2 times
Elec. Gtr.
there.
Bass. Gtr.
Elec. Piano Solo:
Resume Intro fig. simile
D.S. al Coda
Coda
Cont. rhy. simile
But it's too

SISTER GOLDEN HAIR

Words and Music by
GERRY BECKLEY

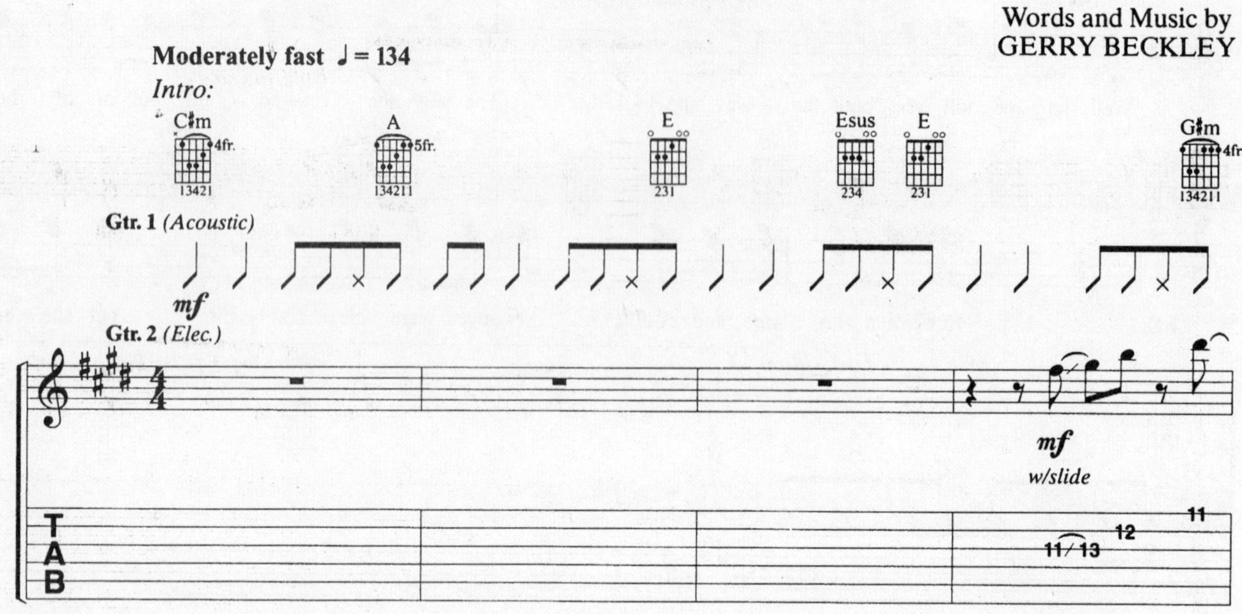

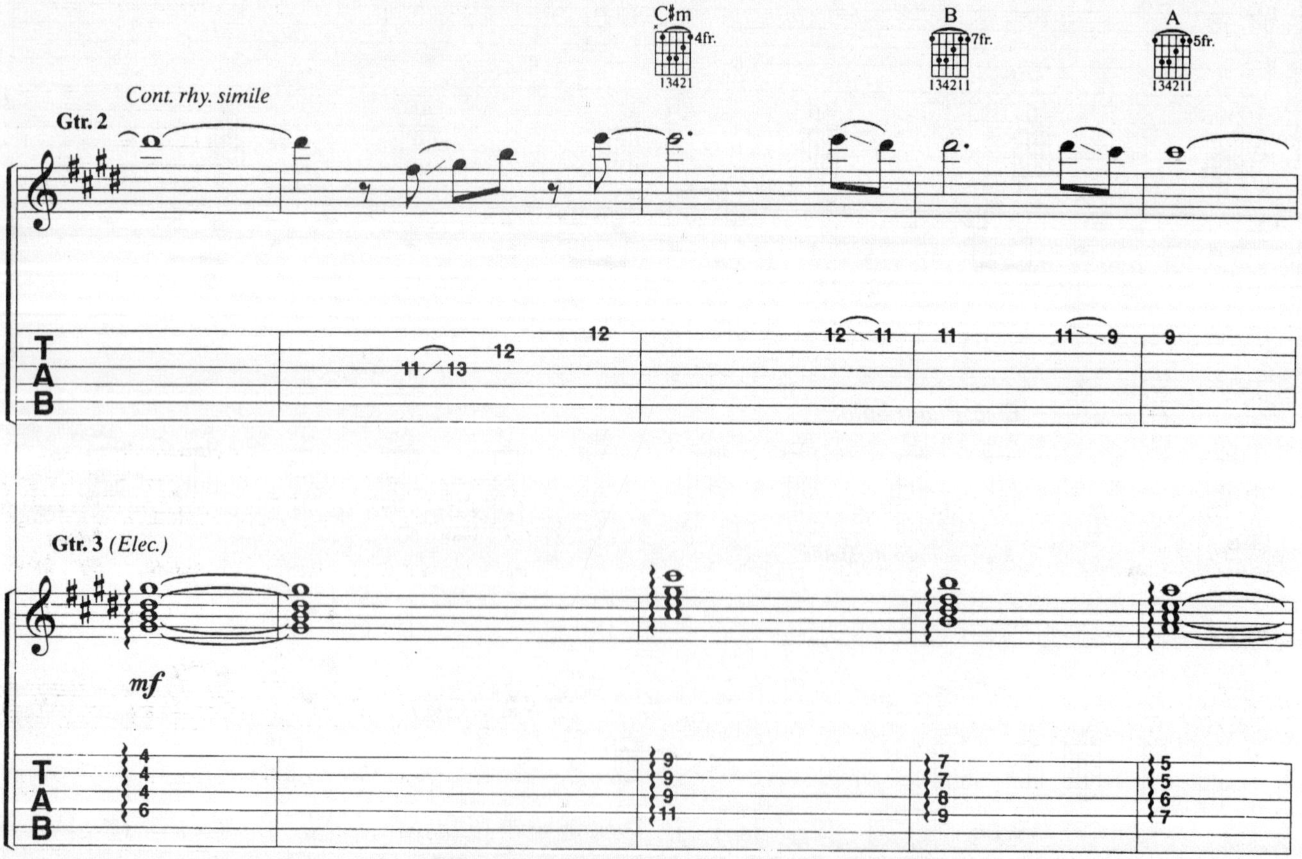

Cont. rhy. simile

Gtr. 2

C♯m B A

Gtr. 3 (Elec.)

mf

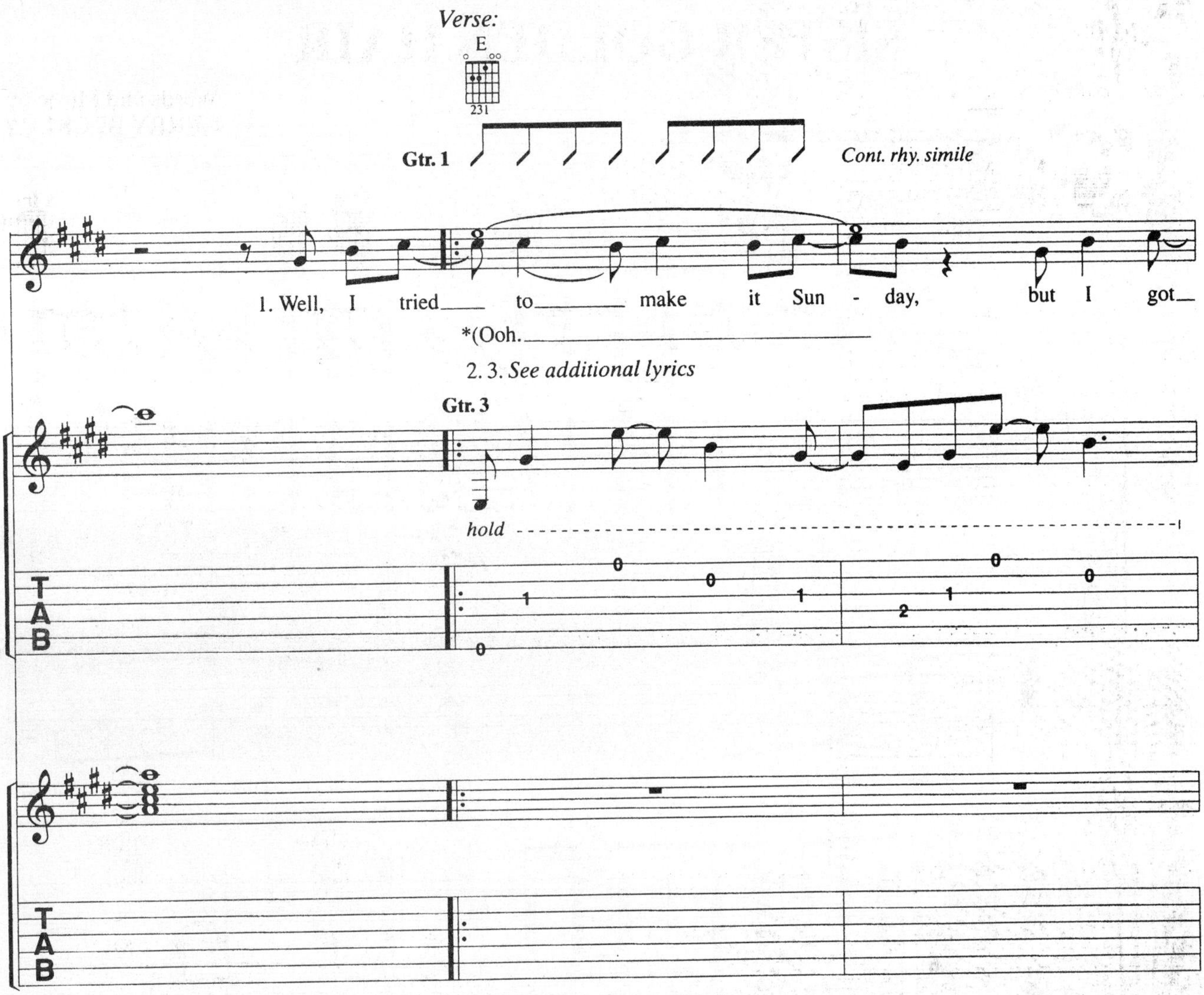

Verse:
E
231
Gtr. 1
Cont. rhy. simile
1. Well, I tried to make it Sun - day, but I got
*(Ooh.
2. 3. See additional lyrics
Gtr. 3
hold
TAB

*Background vocals tacet first time.

G♯m
4fr.
134211
A
5fr.
134211
so damned de - pressed that I set my sights on Mon-
Ooh.
Oh.
hold
hold
TAB

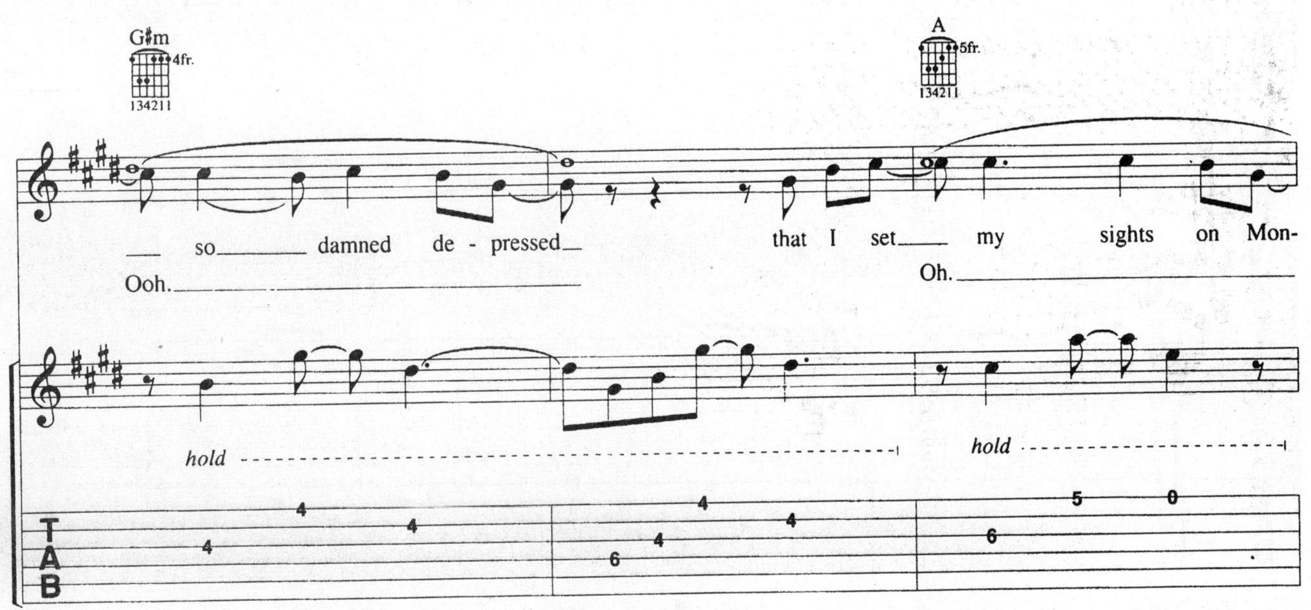

E
G♯m
4fr.
- day and I got my - self un - dressed. I ain't read-
Ooh.
hold
A
5fr.
F♯m
C♯m
4fr.
G♯m
4fr.
- y for the al - ter, but I do a - gree there's times
Ah.
Ah.
A
5fr.
F♯m
A
5fr.
when a wom - an sure can be a friend of mine.
hold
hold
hold

1.
2. 3.
E
231
Gtr. 1
2. Well, I keep
Will you meet
Gtr. 3
Gtr. 4 (Elec.)
w/slide
Chorus:
B
7fr.
134211
A
5fr.
134211
Cont. rhy. simile
me in the mid - dle? Will you meet me in the air?
(Ah. Ah.
Rhy. Fig. 1
Rhy. Fig. 1A

w/Rhy. Fig. 1 (Gtr. 3) & 1A (Gtr. 4) simile
E
B
7fr.
Will you love me just a lit - tle, just e - nough
Ah.
end Rhy. Fig. 1
Gtr. 2
end Rhy. Fig. 1A
A
5fr.
E
F♯m
Gtr. 1
to show you care?
Well, I tried to fake it, I
Ah.)
Gtr. 3

Outro:
w/Rhy. Figs. 1 (Gtr. 3) & 1A (Gtr. 4) simile
w/Ad lib. slide solo (Gtr. 2)
G♯m
4fr.
134211
Asus2
23
1. D.C.
2.
B
7fr.
134211
don't mind say - ing, I just can't make_ it.
Doo wop, doo wop, doo_
Cont. rhy. simile
A
5fr.
134211
E
231
Play 3 times
B
7fr.
134211
_ wop, doo wop, doo_ wop, doo wop, doo_ wop, doo wop. Doo_ _ wop, doo wop, doo_
Gtr. 3
Gtr. 4

Verses 2 & 3:
Well, I keep on thinkin' 'bout you,
Sister Golden Hair surprise.
And I just can't live without you;
Can't you see it in my eyes?
I been one poor correspondent,
I been too, too hard to find.
But it doesn't mean you ain't been on my mind.
(To Chorus:)

SOCIETY'S CHILD

(a/k/a "Society's Child (Baby I've Been Thinking")

Words and Music by
JANIS IAN

All gtrs. capo III

Moderately fast ♩ = 106

Intro:

*Harpsichord arranged for two gtrs.

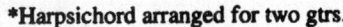

Verse:
accel. a tempo (on repeats)
a tempo ♩ = 106
Gtr. 1
(Acoustic)
Am7
D
1. Come to my door, ba - by
2.3. See additional lyrics
Face is clean and shin - ing
black as night
My moth - er went to an - swer, you know that you looked
so fine
G
Now, I could un - der - stand your
tears and your shame
B7
She called you boy in - stead of your name
Em
Em/D
C
When she would - n't let you in - side
When she turned and said
"But hon - ey, he's not our kind"
Dsus
Dsus2
poco rit.
She says,
They say,
I say,

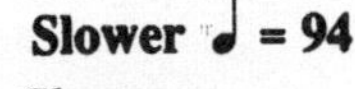

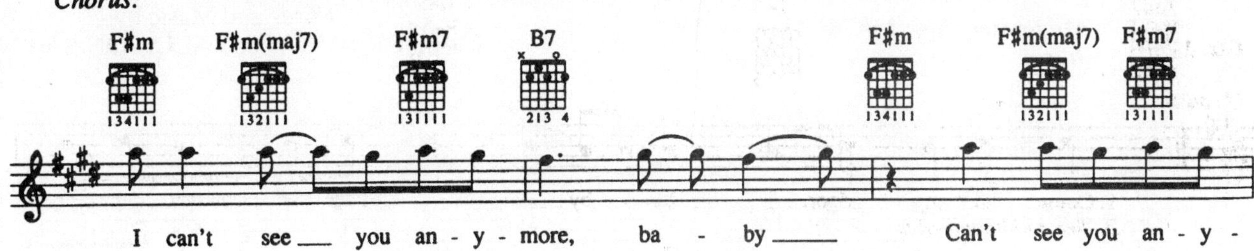

Verse 2:
Walk me down to school, baby
Everybody's acting deaf and blind
Until they turn and say
"Why don't you stick to your own kind?"
My teachers all laugh, their smirking stares
Cutting deep down in our affairs
Preachers of equality
Think they believe it
Then why won't they just let us be?
(To Chorus:)

Verse 3:
One of these days I'm gonna stop my listening
Gonna raise my head up high
One of these days I'm gonna
Raise up my glistening wings and fly.
But that day will have to wait for a while,
Baby, I'm only society's child
When we're older, things may change
But for now this is the way they must remain.
(To Chorus:)

SIXTEEN CANDLES

Words and Music by
LUTHER DIXON and ALLYSON KHENT

Verses 2, 3, & 4:
w/Rhy. Fig. 1 (Elec. Gtr.) simile
Bb Dm Bb7 Eb
can - dles,__ make your wish come true.
(3.4.) can - dles__ in my heart will glow
Ebm F7 C7 F7
To Coda
For__ I'll___ be__ wish - ing__ that you love___ me
for - ev - er__ and__ ev - er,__ for I love___ you
Bridge:
Bb Eb Bb Eb
Elec. Gtr.
too.
so.
(That you love me too.)
(For I love you so.)
You're_ on - ly six - teen,
Cont. rhy. simile
Bb
but you're my teen - age queen.___ You're_ the__
Gm Gb+ Bb/F C7
pret - ti - est, the love - li - est girl___ I've__ ev - er
Cm F7 F7
D.S. al Coda
Elec. Gtr.
seen. 3. Six - teen 4. Six - teen
(I've ev - er seen.) seen.)
Coda
Freely
Bb Eb Bb
Elec. Gtr.
so. For I love you so.

SOUR GIRL

Words and Music by
DEAN DELEO, ROBERT DELEO,
ERIC KRETZ and SCOTT WEILAND

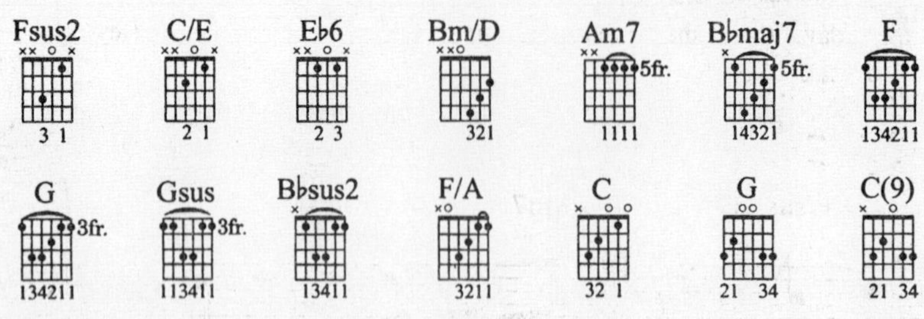

Moderately ♩ = 104
Half-time feel
Intro:

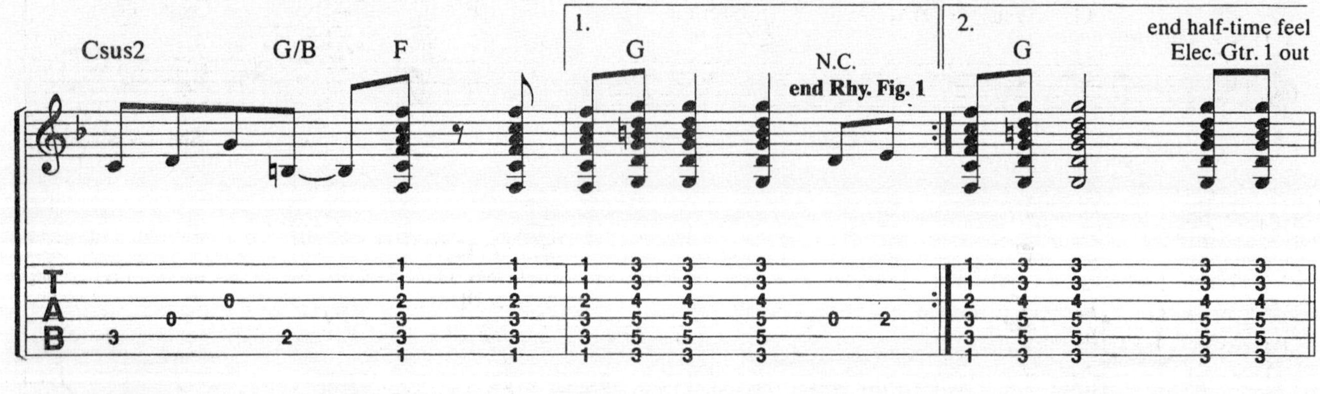

Verse:

w/Rhy. Fig. 2 (Acous. Gtr.) 7 times
Am7 Bbmaj7 F G Gsus G Am7 Bbmaj7
girl the day that she met me. Hey! What are you look-
F G Gsus G Am7 Bbmaj7 F G Gsus G
- ing at? She was a hap - py girl the day that she left me.
*Am7 Bbmaj7 F G Gsus G Am7 Bbmaj7
She turned a - way; what was she look - ing at? She was a sour girl the day that she met
*On repeat, Gtr. 2 plays Rhy. Fig. 2, 4 times.
F G Gsus G Am7 Bbmaj7 F G Gsus G
me. Hey! What are you look - ing at? She was a
Chorus:
Acous. Gtr. & Elec. Gtr. 1
Rhy. Fig. 3
Am7 Bbmaj7 F G Gsus G Bbsus2
hap - py girl when she left me. What would you do?
*Elec. Gtr. 2
T
A
B
*2nd time only.

F/A
C
G
What would you do___ if I fol - lowed you?_
Bbsus2
F/A
G
end Rhy. Fig. 3
What would you do___ (if) I fol - low?___
1.
w/Rhy. Fig. 2 (Acous. Gtr.) 2 times
Elec. Gtr. 1 out
Am7
Bbmaj7
F
G
Gsus G
Am7
Bbmaj7
Elec. Gtr. 3
w/E-bow & harmonizer

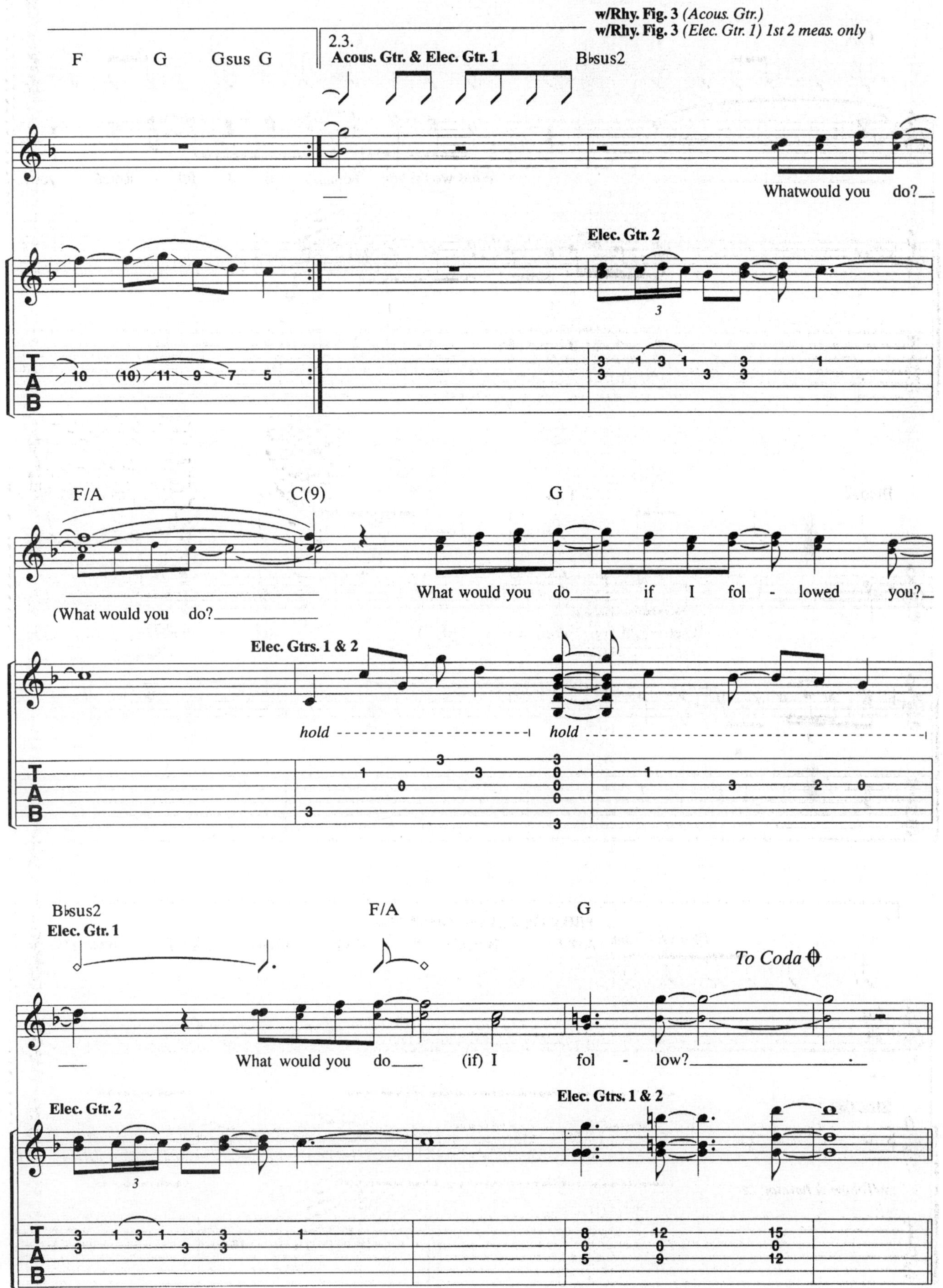

w/Rhy. Fig. 3 (Acous. Gtr.)
w/Rhy. Fig. 3 (Elec. Gtr. 1) 1st 2 meas. only
F G Gsus G
2.3.
Acous. Gtr. & Elec. Gtr. 1
B♭sus2
Whatwould you do?
Elec. Gtr. 2
F/A C(9) G
What would you do if I fol - lowed you?
(What would you do?
Elec. Gtrs. 1 & 2
hold
hold
B♭sus2 F/A G
Elec. Gtr. 1
To Coda
What would you do (if) I fol - low?
Elec. Gtr. 2
Elec. Gtrs. 1 & 2

w/Rhy. Fig. 1 (Acous. Gtr.)
Fsus2 C/E Eb6 Bm/D Csus2 G/B F G N.C.
Bridge:
Fsus2 C/E Eb6 Bm/D
The girl got rea - sons. They
Acous. Gtr.
hold
Csus2 G/B F G
D.S. % al Coda
all got rea - sons.
Coda
Acous. Gtr.
w/Rhy. Fig. 2 (Acous. Gtr.)
Am7 Bbmaj7 F G Gsus G
Elec. Gtrs. 1 & 2
Gtrs. 2 & 3 out

Outro:
w/Rhy. Fig. 2 *(Acous. Gtr.) till fade*

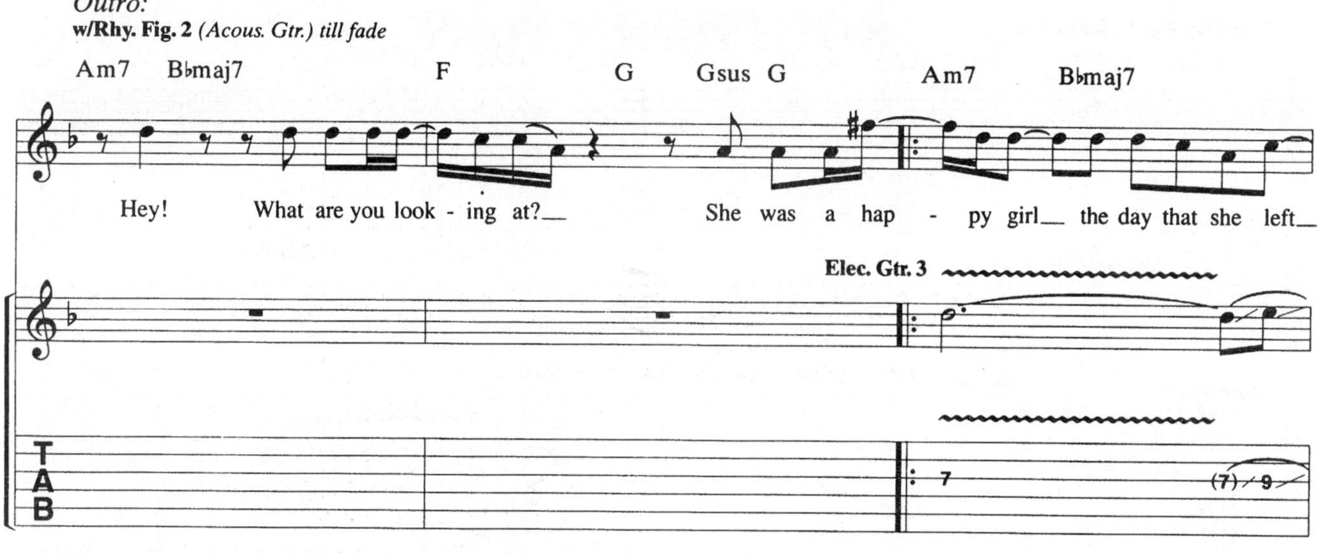

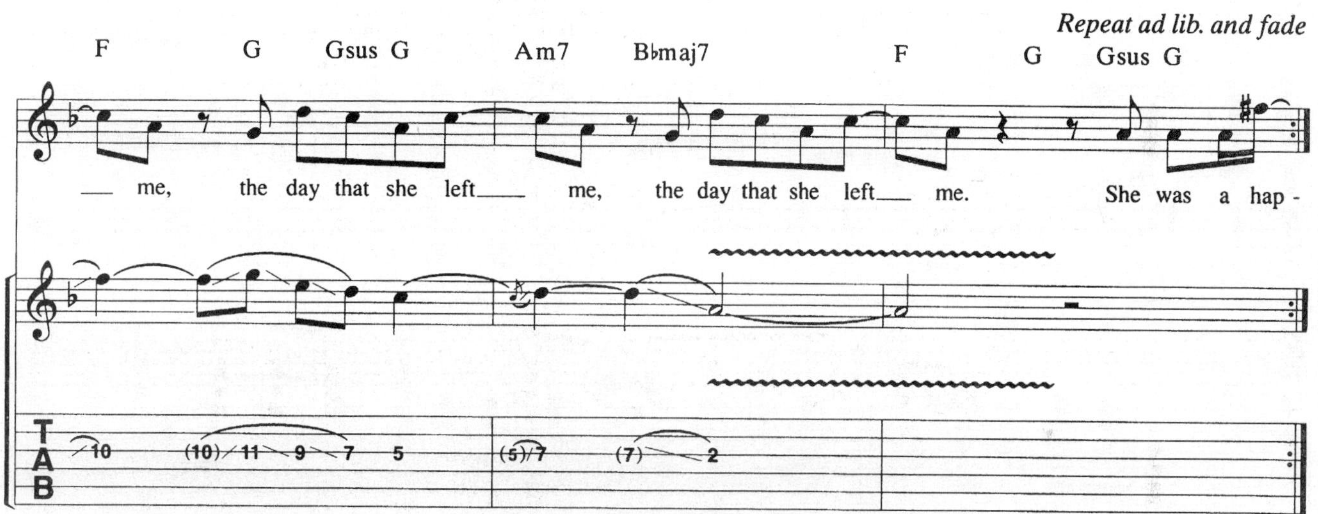

Verse 2:
Don't turn away; what are you looking at?
He was so happy on the day that he met her.
Say, what are you looking at?
I was a superman, but looks are deceiving.
The rollercoaster ride's a lonely one,
I'd pay a ransom note to stop it from steaming.
Hey! What are you looking at?
She was a teenage girl when she met me.
(To Chorus:)

SOUTHERN MAN

Words and Music by
NEIL YOUNG

Dm
Fmaj7/C
South-ern change gon-na come at last,
Bb
G
Dm/G
now your cross-es are burn-in' fast.
Dm
Bb
Gm
South-ern man.
hold
Dm
Bb
Gm
hold

Verse:
Dm
Bb
Gm
1. I saw cot - ton and I saw black,
Oo. Oo.
2. See additional lyrics
Dm
Cont. bkrd. vocal next 6 bars
Bb
Gm
tall white man - sions an' lit - tle shacks;
Dm
Bb
Gm
South-ern man when will you pay them back?
A
I heard scream - in' an' bull whips crack - in'.

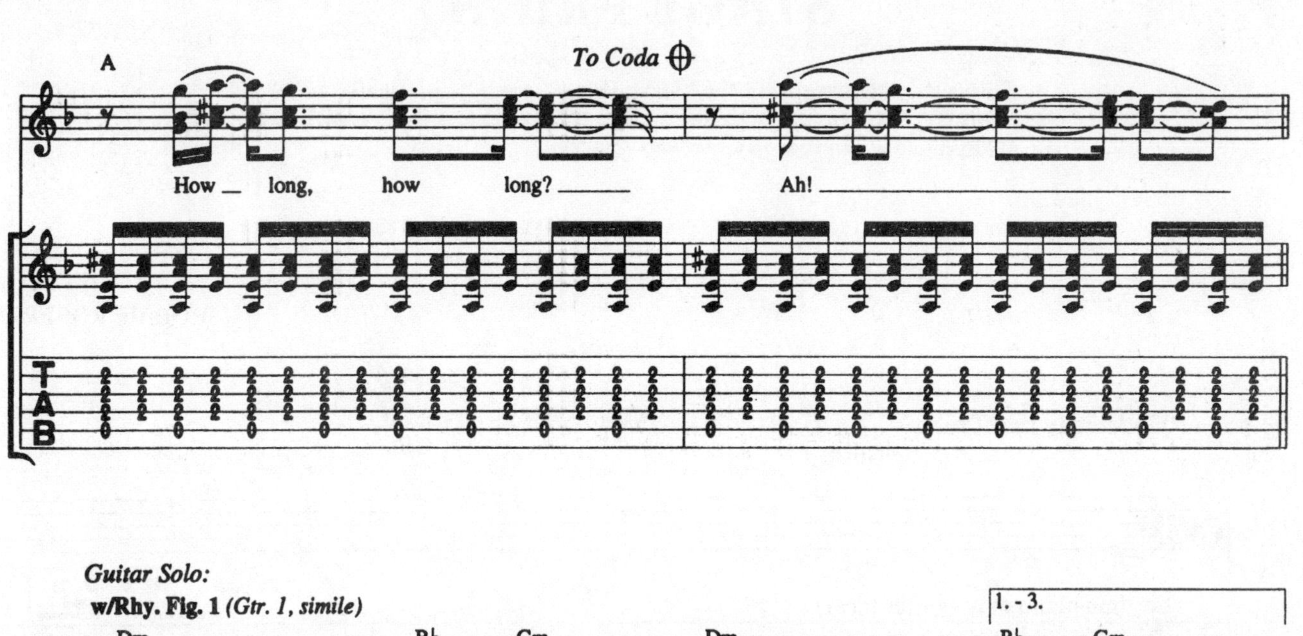

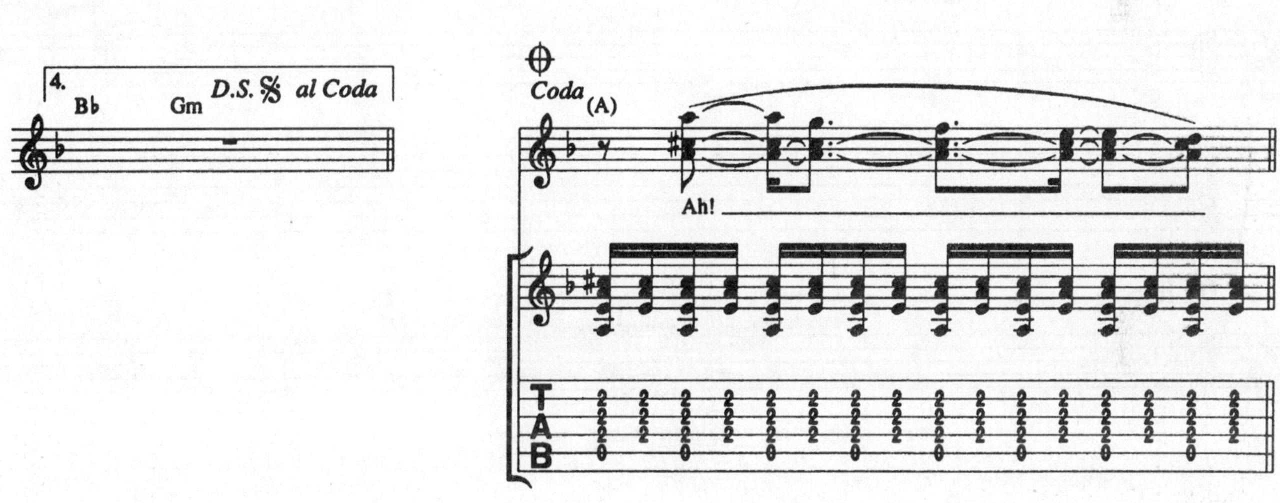

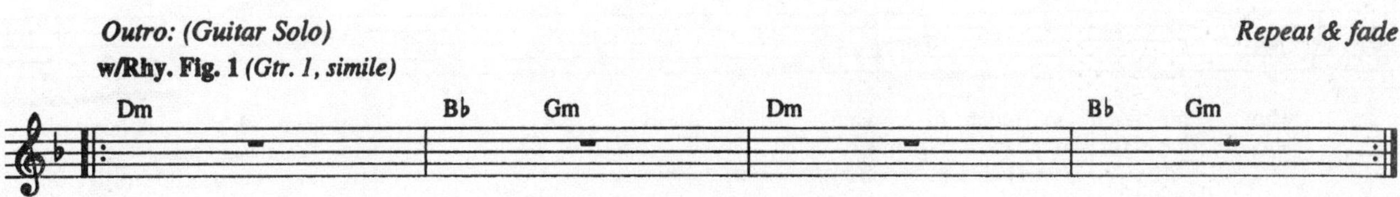

Verse 2:

Lilly - Belle, your hair is golden - brown.
I've seen your black man comin' 'round.
Swear by God I'm gonna cut him down.
I heard screamin' and
Bull whips crackin'.
How long, how long? Ah!
(To Chorus:)

STAGE FRIGHT

This is the title song from the "Stage Fright" recording, released in 1970. However, the frenetic, high-energy solo that concludes the transcription is from the 1976 "Last Waltz" concert recording.

By
ROBBIE ROBERTSON

G
Am
F
F/D
See the man with the stage - fright, just stand-in' up there t' give it
all his might, and he got / He got caught in the
Am
Am/G
F
F/E
spot - light. But when we get to the end
D
To Coda
G
he wants t' start all o - ver a - gain.
1.
2.
F♯m
Bm
C
D
Now if he says that he's a - fraid, take him at his word.

G
F♯m
Bm
C
C♯
And for the price that the poor boy has paid,
he gets to sing just like a
D
D♯
Em
C
Gm/B♭
F
3
bird. Oh, hoo oo oo.
(Organ solo)
G
C
Gm/B♭
F
1,2.
G
3.
D
D♯
Em
Am
Em
D.S.𝄋(3rd verse) al Coda
Full
3
2
(2)(2)(2)
2 0
CODA
G
F
D
C
G
again Mm, hmm, you wan-na try it once a-gain. Mm,
F
D
C
G
F
D
C
3
hmm, please don't make him stop. Mm, hmm, let him take it from
ritard
G
F
D
C
G
the top. Mm, hmm, let him start all o-ver a-gain.

Solo during vamp (live version)

STAY (I MISSED YOU)

Words and Music by
LISA LOEB

Am7
G
C2
Cm
G5
Am
Folk rock ♩ = 80
*All gtrs. Capo VI
Intro:
Rhy. Fig. 1
G(9)
Em7
Am7(♭3)
G/B
C2
(end Rhy. Fig. 1)
Gtr. 1
hold
Rhy. Fig. 1A
(end Rhy. Fig. 1A)
Gtr. 2
*On the recording, Gtr. 1 is Capo 6 (Key of G), Gtr. 2 is Capo 1 (Key of C).
For this arrangement both guitars are written Capo 6 to prevent having to indicate both parts in two different keys.
Verse 1:
w/Rhy. Figs. 1 & 1A (Gtrs. 1 & 2) 2 times
You say _ I on ly hear what I want to.
And you say _ I talk so all the time, — so _
w/Rhy. Fig. 2 (Gtrs. 1 & 2) 4 times sim.
Rhy. Fig. 2
(end Rhy. Fig. 2)
*Gtrs. 1 & 2
And I thought what I felt was sim - ple, and I thought that I don't be - long, _
*Arr. for one gtr.
and now _ that _ I am _ leav - ing, _ Now I know that I did some-thing wrong 'cause I

C2
Cm
missed you.
Yeah, ___ I
w/Rhy. Fig. 2 (Gtrs. 1 & 2)
Am7
G
Am7
G
Verse 2:
w/Rhy. Figs. 1 & 1A (Gtrs. 1 & 2) last 3 meas. sim.
G(9)
missed you.
And you say _
Em7
Am7(♭9)
G/B
I on - ly hear what I want to: I don't lis - ten hard, I don't pay at - ten - tion to the
C2
G
Am7(♭9)
G/B
dis - tance that you're run - ning to an - y - one, an - y - where, I don't un - der - stand _ if you real - ly care, I'm
Gtr. 1
hold
hold
hold
Gtr. 2
hold
hold
hold
C2
w/Fill 1
on - ly hear - ing neg - a - tive: no, no, no, bad. ___
So I

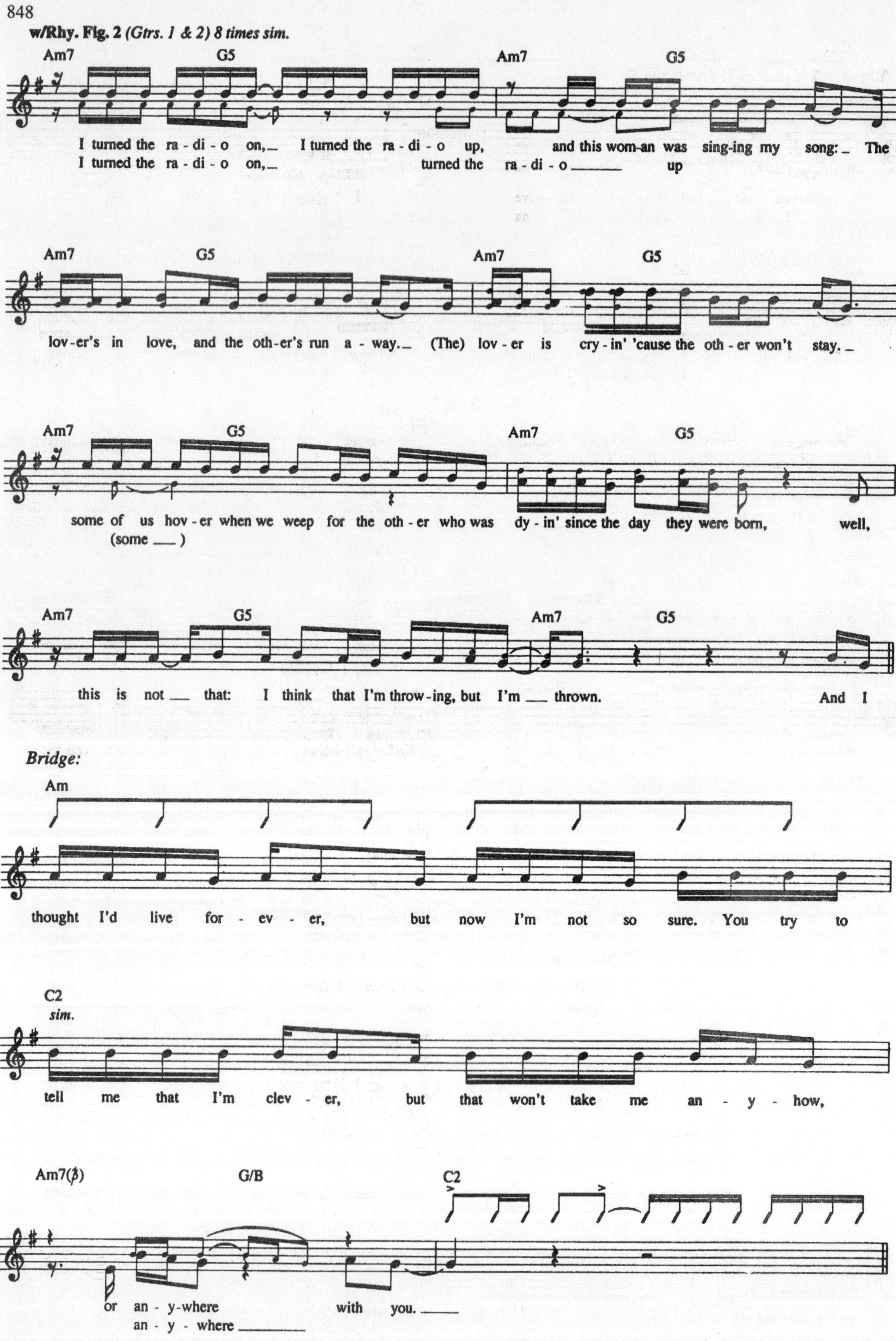
w/Rhy. Fig. 2 (Gtrs. 1 & 2) 8 times sim.
Am7
G5
I turned the ra - di - o on, I turned the ra - di - o up, and this wom-an was sing-ing my song: The
I turned the ra - di - o on, turned the ra - di - o up
lov - er's in love, and the oth - er's run a - way. (The) lov - er is cry - in' 'cause the oth - er won't stay.
some of us hov - er when we weep for the oth - er who was dy - in' since the day they were born, well,
(some)
this is not that: I think that I'm throw - ing, but I'm thrown. And I
Bridge:
Am
thought I'd live for - ev - er, but now I'm not so sure. You try to
C2
sim.
tell me that I'm clev - er, but that won't take me an - y - how,
Am7(♭)
G/B
or an - y-where with you.
an - y - where

Verse:
w/Rhy. Fig. 2 (Gtrs. 1 & 2) 4 times sim.
Am7 G5 Am7 G5
And you said __ that I was na - ive, and I thought _ that I was strong. ___
I ______ was na - ive ______
Am7 G5 Am7 G5
I thought _ "Hey, I can leave, _ I can leave." __ But now I know that I __ was wrong __ 'cause I
I can leave, _ I can leave." ______
C2 Cm
missed you. Yeah! ______
w/Rhy. Fig. 2 (Gtrs. 1 & 2) 2 times sim.
Am7 G5 Am7 G5
Verse:
Am
__ I missed you. You said, "You caught me 'cause you want me, and one day I'll let you go." You try to
C2
sim.
Am7(♭6) G/B
give a - way a keep - er, or keep me 'cause you know you're just __ scared __ to lose. __
w/Rhy. Figs. 1 & 1A (Gtrs. 1 & 2) sim. (2 times) sim.
C2 G(9) Em7 Am7(♭6) G/B C2
And you say, ___ "Stay." _
G(9) Em7 Am7(♭6) G/B C2
You say __ I on - ly hear what I want to.

STOP DRAGGIN' MY HEART AROUND

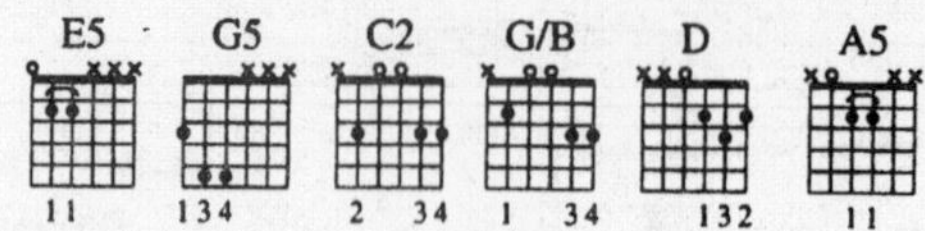

Moderate rock ♩ = 108

Words and Music by
TOM PETTY and MIKE CAMPBELL

Intro:

A5 C2 G/B C2

Rhy. Fig. 1
E5 *(Palm mute)* G5 A5 E5 G5 A5 (end Rhy. Fig. 1)

Fill 1 (end Fill 1)

w/Rhy. Fig. 1
E5 G5 A5 E5 G5 A5

1. Ba - by

Fill 2 (end Fill 2)

Verse 1:

E5 G5 A5 E5

you come knock - in' on my___ front door. Same old line you used to

G5 A5 E5 G5 A5
use be - fore. I said, yeah ___ well, ___ what am I s'pose to do?
E5 G5 A5
I did - n't know what I was get - ting in - to.
Chorus:
C D C D
So you had a lit - tle trou - ble in town. __ Now you're keep - in' some de - mon down. __
C D C2 G/B C2
Stop drag - gin' my, stop drag - gin' my, stop drag - gin' my heart a - round.
w/Rhy. Fig. 1
E5 G5 A5 E5 G5 A5
Verse 2:
w/Rhy. Fig. 1
E5 G5 A5 E5
2. It's hard to think a - bout what you want - ed. It's hard to think a - bout
3. See additional lyrics.
G5 A5 E5 G5 A5
what you've lost. This does - n't have to be the big "get e - ven."
E5 G5 A5 E5
This does - n't have to be ___ an - y - thing at all. ___ I know you real - ly want to
G5 A5 E5 G5 A5
tell me good - bye. I know you real - ly want to be your own girl.

Chorus:
C D
Baby you could never look me in the eye.
C D C
Yeah, you'd buckle with the weight of the world. Stop draggin' my,
D C2 G/B C2
stop draggin' my, stop draggin' my heart around.
To Coda
Interlude:
w/Rhy. Fig. 1 (1st 2 bars)
E5 G5 A5
Rhy. Fig. 3
D C2 G
(end Rhy. Fig. 3)
hold
w/Rhy. Fig. 3 (2 times)
D C2 G D C2 G
A5 C2 G/B C2
w/Rhy. Fig. 1
w/Fill 1 (see page 1)
E5 G5 A5 E5 G5 A5
D.S. al Coda
Ooh.
Coda
w/Rhy. Fig. 1
w/Fill 2 (see page 1)
E5 G5 A5 E5 G5 A5
Repeat and fade
Stop draggin' my heart around.
(vocal tacet 1st time)
Verse 3:
There's people runnin' 'round loose in the world.
Ain't got nothin' better to do
Than make a meal out of some bright-eyed kid.
You need someone looking after you.
I know you really want to tell me goodbye.
I know you really want to be your own girl.
(To Chorus:)

STRANGE WORLD

Words and Music by
STEVE HARRIS

Em
C
D
Em-I
7fr.
G
7fr.
D
5fr.
C
3fr.

Moderately slow
Em
T
A
B
Moderately slow
Em
To Coda

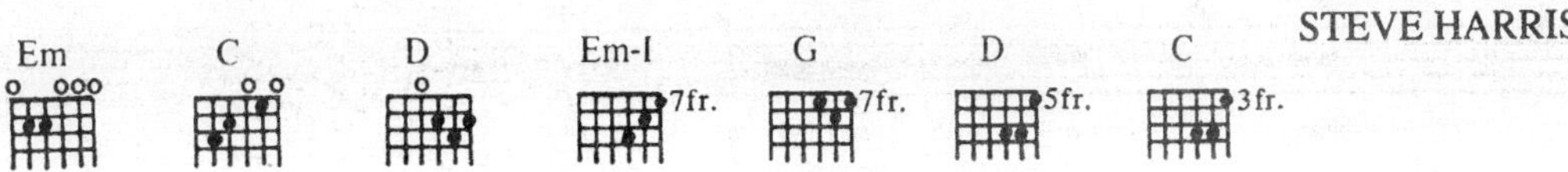

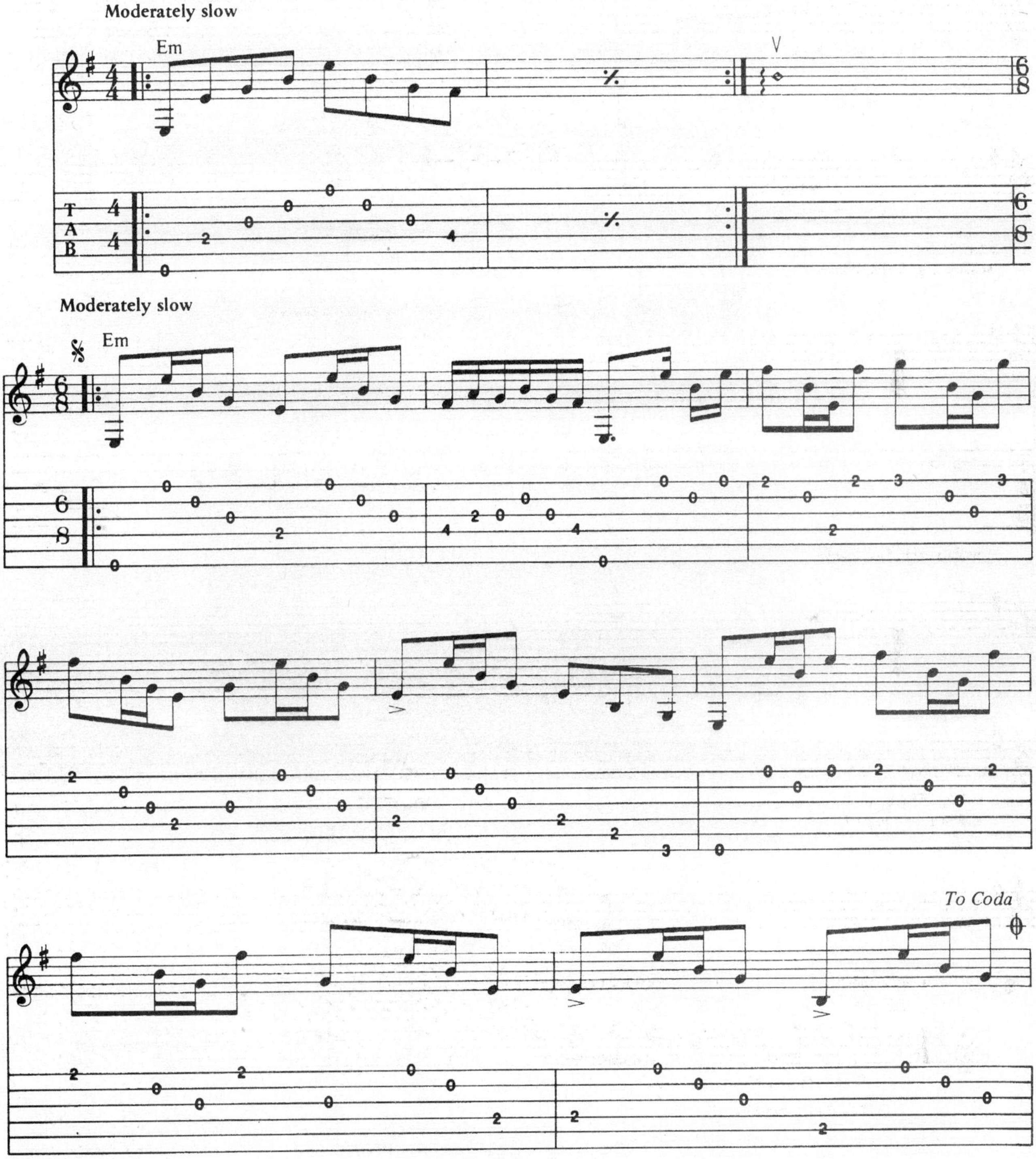

Solo
X pos.
XII pos.
C
XIV pos.
2nd Guitar
C
P.O.
B
B
B

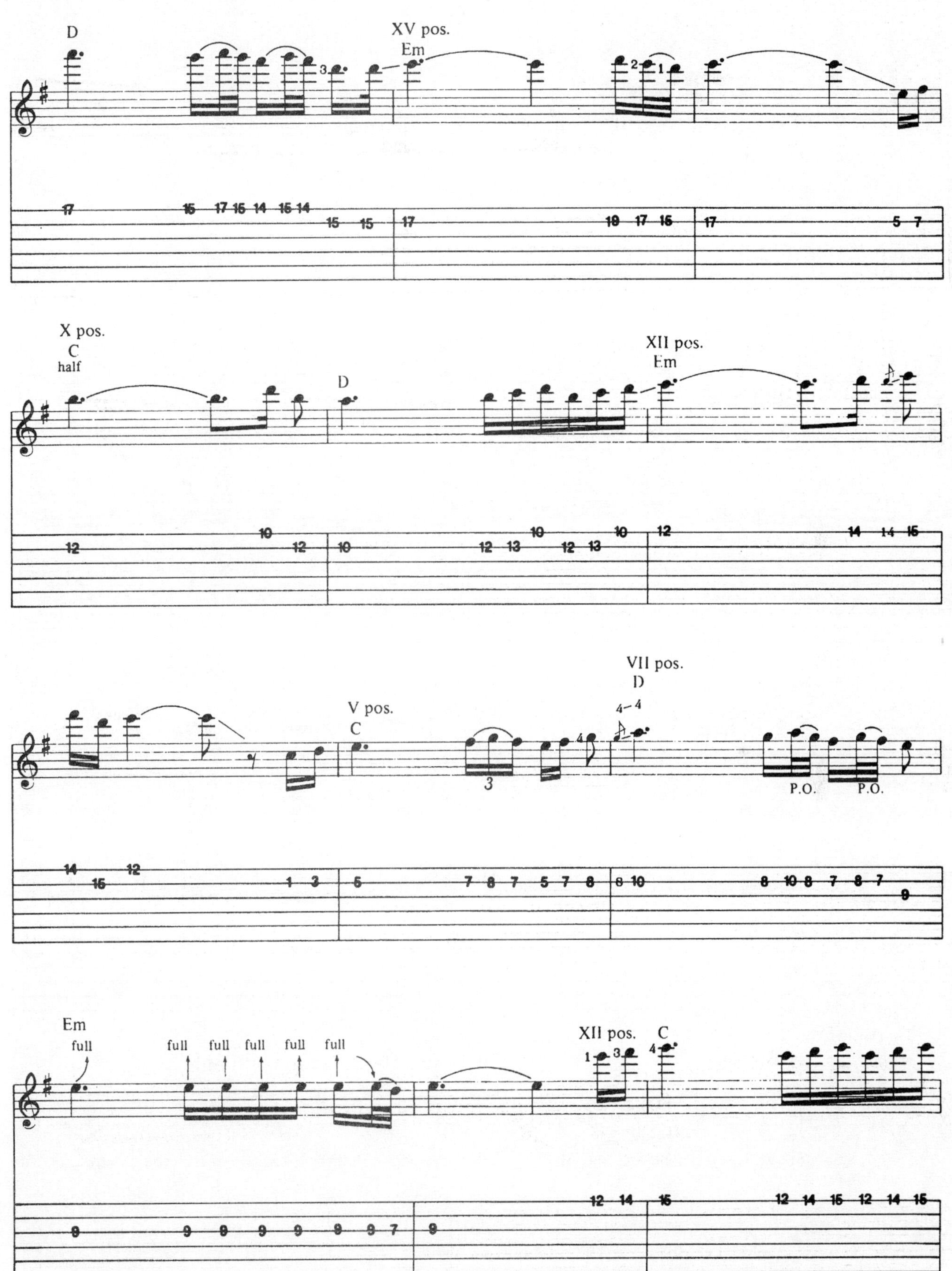
D
XV pos.
Em
17 15 17 16 14 16 14 15 15 17 19 17 15 17 5 7
X pos.
C
half
D
XII pos.
Em
12 10 12 10 12 13 10 12 13 10 12 14 14 15
VII pos.
D
V pos.
C
P.O.
P.O.
14 15 12 1 3 5 7 8 7 5 7 8 8 10 8 10 8 7 8 7 9
Em
full
full full full full full
XII pos.
C
9 9 9 9 9 9 9 7 9 12 14 15 12 14 15 12 14 15

D
full
full
full
full
15 17 14 15 12 14 10 12 8 7 8 10
10
Guitar Pattern - I
Em-I
7fr.
G
7fr.
The on - ly place where you can dream
8 9 7 8 9 7 8 9 7 8 9
8 7 7 8 7 7 8 7 7 8 7
D
5fr.
C
3fr.
liv - ing here is not what it seems.
7 7 5 7 7 5 7 7 5 7 7
5 5 3 5 5 3 5 5 3 5 5
Guitar Pattern - I
Em-I
7fr.
G
7fr.
D
5fr.
C
3fr.
1. Ship of white light in the sky no - bod - y there to reas - on why
2nd verse
Em-I
7fr.
G
7fr.
D
5fr.
here I am, I'm not real - ly there. smil - ing fa - ces

C
3fr.
Em-I
7fr.
G
7fr.
ev - er so rare
a - let's walk in deep - est space,
D
5fr.
C
3fr.
3
liv - ing here just is - n't the place
D.S. al Coda
Coda
Em
Don't you
hear me call?
Ooh
ritard.

2. Stalks of light come from the ground
When I cry there isn't a sound
All my feelings cannot be held
I'm happy in my new strange world.
Shades of green grasses twine,
girls drinking plasma wine.
A look at love, a dream unfolds
living here, you'll never grow old.

STRENGTH BEYOND STRENGTH

All gtrs. tune down 1/2 step:
⑥=E♭ ③=G♭
⑤=A♭ ②=B♭
④=D♭ ①=E♭

Words and Music by
VINCENT PAUL ABBOTT, DARRELL LANCE ABBOTT,
REX ROBERT BROWN and PHILIP HANSEN ANSELMO

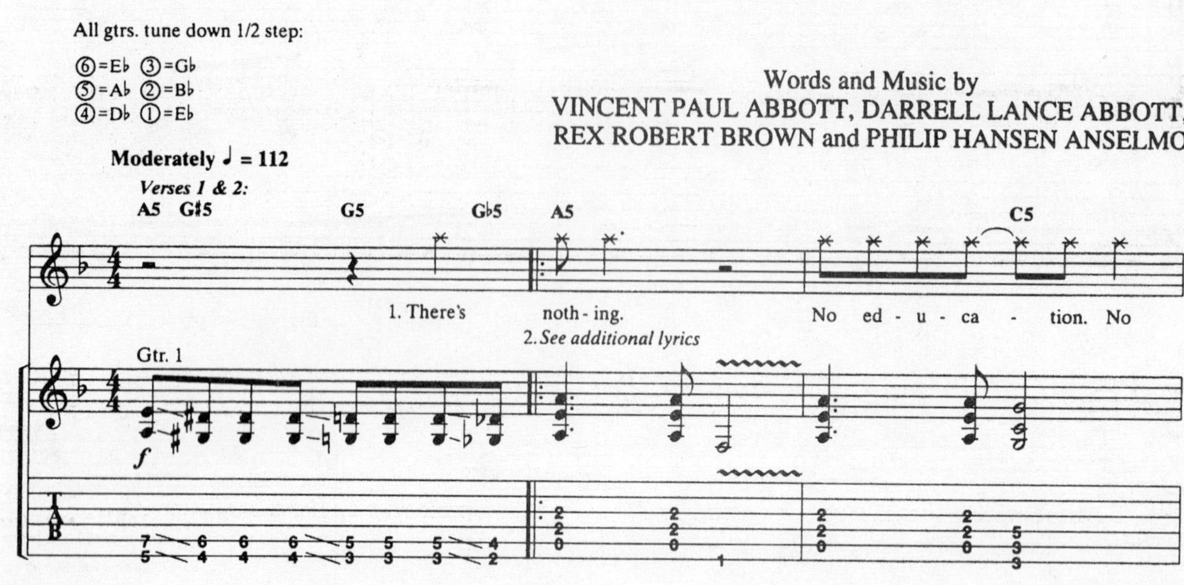

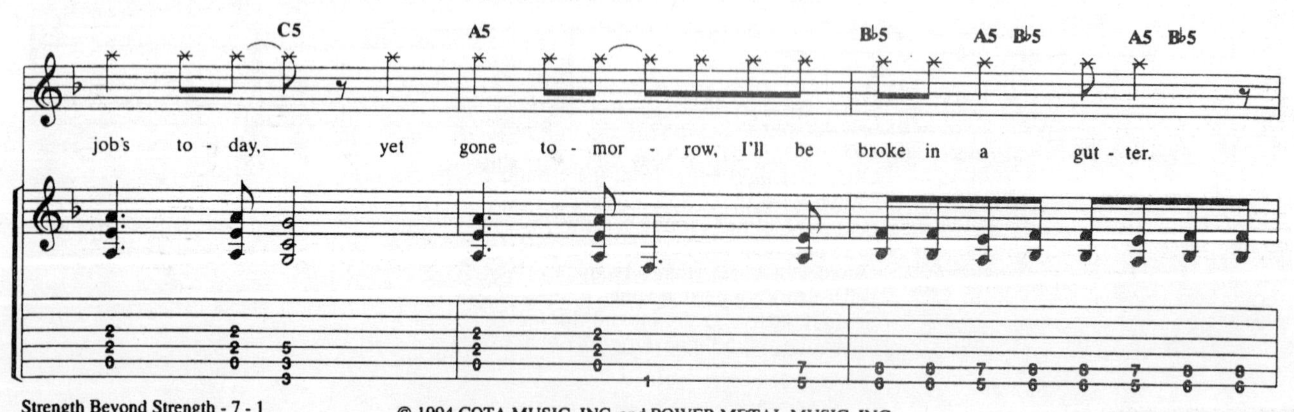

Gb5
F5
Ab5
F5
I know the op - in - ion. A
P.M.
No Chord
Gb5
F5
bro - ken rec - ord. Fuck
Ab5
F5
E5
you and your col- lege dream. Fact is, we're strong- er than all.
1.
A5 G♯5
G5
Gb5
2.
N.C.
2. You're

Play 3 times
Interlude I:
Half-time feel
Play 3 times
Verse 3:
A5 G♯5 G5 G♭5 G♭5 F5
Sad state of af - fairs.
P.M.
A♭5 F5 N.C. G♭5 F5
Crip - pled A - mer - i - ca. Pipe
P.M.
A♭5 F5 E5
dream butt - fucked Im - mune. Strong - er than all.
P.M.

w/Fill 1 (Gtr. 2, 2nd time)
Half-time
F5 C/E F5 G♭5 F5 C/E F5 G♭5 F5 C/E F5 G♭5 F5 C/E F5 G♭5
(2nd time)Rrrr!
We've
Rhy. Fig. 1
(end Rhy. Fig. 1)
Bridge I:
F5 C/E F5 G♭5 F5 C/E F5 G♭5 F5 C/E F5 G♭5
grown in - to a mon - ster. An ar - ro - gant, ex - plo - sive
See additional lyrics
1.- 3.
w/Fill 1 (Gtr. 2)
F5 C/E F5 G♭5
4.
Interlude II:
Play 3 times
F5 G♭5
moth - er - fuck.
Far too late!
A.H.
A.H.
With bar (dive)
F5 G♭5 F5 G♭5 F5
grad. dive
Fill 1
Gtr. 2
f

Guitar Solo:
w/Rhy. Fig. 1 (Gtr. 1, 4 times)
F5 C/E F5 G♭5
Gtr. 2
w/harmonizer effect
1/2
Gtr. 3
f w/harmonizer effect
8va
F5
w/trem. bar
-1/2

F5 C/E F5 G♭5
Gtr. 3
1/2
1/2
F5 C/E F5 G♭5
Bridge II:
F5 C/E F5 G♭5
Hail
kings.
The
new
kings.
P.M.
F5 C/E F5
Strong - er than all.
Double-time
N.C.
A5 G♯5 G5 G♭5
Verse 4:
G♭5 F5 A♭5 F5
A sim - ple pro - gress to
(See additional lyrics)
P.M.

Additional Lyrics

Verse 2:
You're working for perfect bodies, perfect minds and perfect neighbors.
But I'm helping to legalize dope on your pristine streets and I'm making a fortune.
You're muscle and gall. Naive at best. I'm bone, brain and cock.
Deep down stronger than all.
(To Interlude I)

Bridge I:
Hard as a rock. Shut like a lock.
Finally, the president in submission.
He holds out his hand on your television and draws back a stump.
It's too late for some.
(To Interlude II)

Verse 4:
Be there no question of certain strenghths.
Know this intention. Forever stronger than all.
(To End)

SMOKE GETS IN YOUR EYES

Words by
OTTO HARBACH
Music by
JEROME KERN

THE STROLL

Moderately ♩ = 98
Intro:
Words and Music by
CLYDE OTIS and NANCY LEE
F
Elec. Gtr.
Cont. rhy. simile
Drums
Stroll - in'. Stroll - in'.
Verse:
Cont. rhy. simile
1. Come let's stroll, stroll a-cross the floor.
feel so good, take me by my hand.
3. There's my love, stroll-in' in the door.
(Stroll - in'.)
I
B♭7
Come let's stroll, stroll a-cross the floor.
feel so good, take me by my hand.
There's my love, stroll-in' in the door.
(Stroll - in'.)
Now
And
Ba-by,
C7
3fr.
B♭7
F
1.
2.3.
turn a-round, ba-by, let's stroll once more.
let's go stroll-in' in won-der-land.
let's go stroll-in' by the can-dy store.
(Stroll - in'.)
2. I
Chorus:
Cont. rhy. simile
B♭7
1. Stroll - in' whoa, yeah. Stroll - in', ah, ha. Rock-'n'-roll -
2. Ad lib. whistling w/bkgd. vocals.
Fade out 2nd time
F
C7
B♭7
F
D.S.
in'. Stroll - in'. Well, rock-a-my soul, how I love to stroll. Stroll - in'.

STRONG ENOUGH

Words and Music by
SHERYL CROW, KEVIN GILBERT, BRIAN MacLEOD,
DAVID RICKETTS, BILL BOTTRELL and DAVID BAERWALD

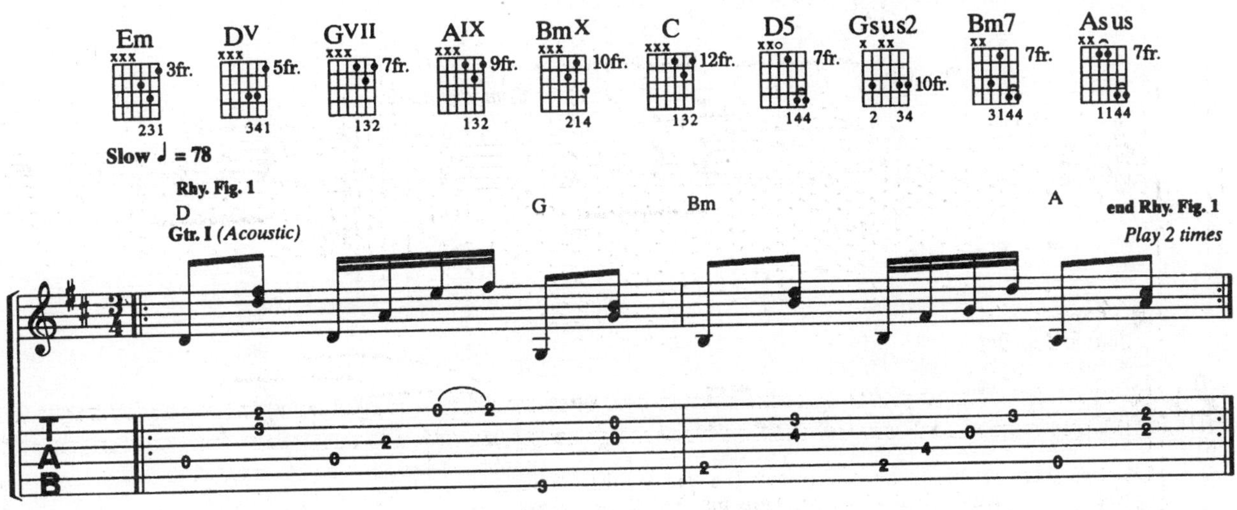

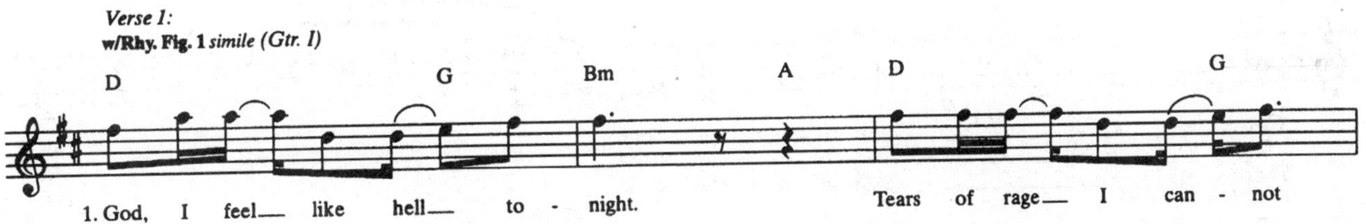

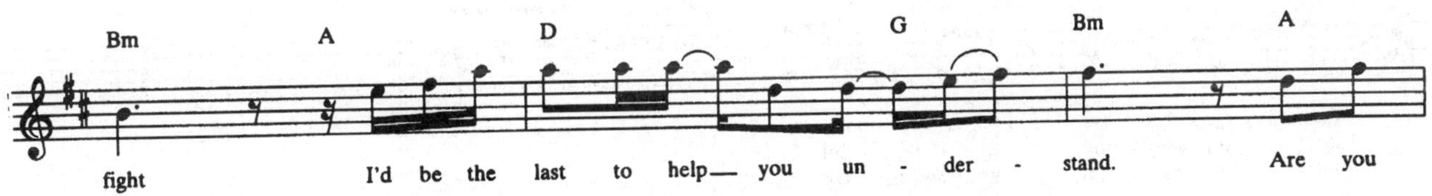

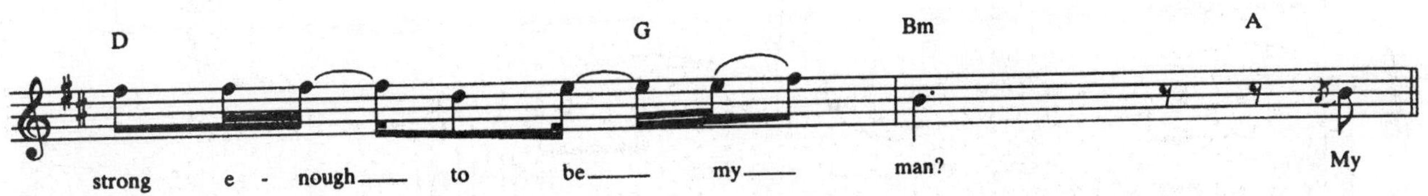

Interlude 1:
w/Rhy. Fig 1 simile (Gtr.I)
w/Gtr. II (12 string Acoustic), simile
D G Bm A D G Bm A
man.
D G Bm A D G Bm A
Verses 2, 3 & 4:
w/Rhy. Fig. 1 (Gtrs. I & II)
D G Bm A D G
1. Noth - ing's true and noth - ing's right. So let me be a - lone to -
2.3.See additional lyrics
Bm A D G Bm A
night. 'Cause you can't change the way I am. Are you
D G To Coda I Bm A
strong e - nought to be my man?
Chorus:
Rhy. Fig. 2
Em D G A
Gtr. II
Lie to me. I
Rhy. Fig. 3
Gtr. I
Bm C G A end Rhy. Fig. 2
prom - ise, I'll be - lieve.
end Rhy. Fig. 3

Verse 3:
I have a face I cannot show.
I make the rules up as I go.
It's try and love me if you can.
Are you strong enough to be my man?
My man.

Verse 4:
When I've shown you that I just don't care,
When I'm throwing punches in the air,
When I'm broken down and I can't stand,
Will you be man enough to be my man?

SUFFRAGETTE CITY

A
5fr.
B
7fr.
C♯5
9fr.
D5
10fr.
I've got to straight - en my face.___ The
'cause she's a to - tal blam blam.___ She
Dear droog - ie, don't crash here.___ There's
Hey man.___
1.
F5
G5
3fr.
smell of that chick___ just put my spine out of place.___
said she had to squeeze it but she,
on - ly room for one and here she
2.3.
F5
G5
3fr.
Chorus:
A
5fr.
Elec. Gtr. 1
Resume verse fig. simile
and then she.
comes, here she comes.
Oh,_ don't_ lean___ on me, man, 'cause you
Elec. Gtr. 2
Rhy. Fig. 1
mf
D
5fr.
F5
C5
3fr.
G5
3fr.
G♯5
4fr.
can't af - ford the tick - et___ back from Suf - fra - gette Cit - y.___ Oh, don't___
end Rhy. Fig. 1

*Two similar solo tracks arr. for one.

A
B
C♯5
D5
F5
G5
Cont. rhy. simile
Oh,_ don't_
A.H.
Chorus:
w/Rhy. Fig. 1 (Elec. Gtr. 2) 2 times, simile
D
C5
G♯5
Elec. Gtr. 1 cont. verse fig. simile
lean_ on me, man, 'cause you can't af-ford the tick-et_ back from Suf-fra-gette Cit - y._ Oh, don't_
lean_ on me, man, 'cause you ain't got time to check it._ No more Suf-fra-gette Cit - y._ Don't_
*Outro:
A5
G5/A
Elec. Gtr. 1 resume chorus fig. simile
y._ It's out of sight. Whoa,_ she's all right.
*Vocal ad lib. on repeats.
1.-3.5.-7.
4.8.
Oh, Suf - fra - gette Cit - y._ Well, Suf-fra-gette Cit - Suf-fra-gette.
E
N.C.
D.S.S.
pick sl.
grad. crescendo
Uh, whambamthankyou, ma'am!_ Suf-fra-gette!

SUGAR MAGNOLIA

Words by
ROBERT HUNTER and BOB WEIR

Music by
BOB WEIR

A
C#m
F#m
don't care.
Saw my ba - by down by the riv - er.
E
D
A
1. 3.
knew she'd have to come up soon for air.
end Rhy. Fig. 1
2. 4.
To Coda
Bridge:
D
G
D
A
1. She's got ev - 'ry - thing de - light - ful, she's got ev - 'ry - thing

D
G
D
I need. Takes the wheel when I'm seein' double,
I need. A breeze in the pines and the summer night moonlight,
E
A
pays my ticket when I speed.
crazy in the sunlight, yes, indeed.
Guitar Solo:
To Coda 2
A
D
A
E
A
D.S. al Coda 1

Coda 1
Chorus:
A G D A G D
Sug-ar Mag-no - lia, ring-in' that blue-bell,
Woo doo doo doo
A G D A
doo doo doo doo.
caught up in sun - light,
Doo doo doo doo doo doo doo doo.
E G D
go on out sing-in', I'll walk you in the sun - shine. Oo, come on hon-ey,
Doo doo doo doo doo doo doo doo.
D.S. 𝄋𝄋 al Coda 2
A E A
come a - long with me.
doo doo doo.

Coda 2
Verse 5:
A
D
A
D
Uh, some-times _ when the cuck - oo's cry - ing, when the moon _ is half -
A
B
E
B
- way _ down, _ some - times _ when the night is _ dy - ing,
Oo.
F#7
E
D
I take me out _ and I wan - der a - round.
A
E
B
A
E
I wan - der 'round. _
Ah.

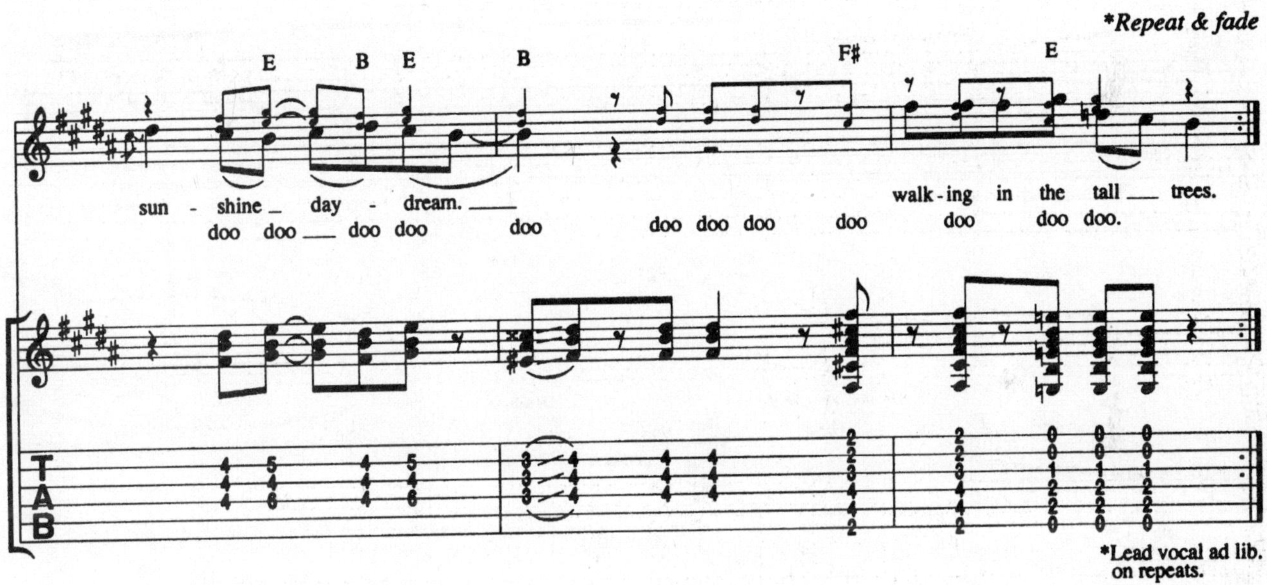

Verse 2:
Sweet blossom, come on under the willow,
We can have high times if you abide.
We can discover the wonders of nature,
Rolling in the rushes, down by the riverside.
(To Bridge:)

Verse 3:
Well, she comes skimmin' through rays of violet,
She can wade in a drop of dew.
She don't come and I don't follow,
Waits backstage while I sing to you.

Verse 4:
Well, she can dance a Cajun rhythm,
Jump like a Willys in four - wheel - drive.
She's a summer love in the spring, fall and winter.
She can make happy any man alive.
(To Chorus:)

Bridge 2:
She's got everything delightful,
She's got everything I need.
A breeze in the pines, and the summer moonlight,
Crazy in the sunlight, yes indeed.
(To Coda 2:)

SUNDAY WILL NEVER BE THE SAME

Words and Music by
TERRY CASHMAN and GENE PISTILLI

Moderately fast ♩ = 122
Intro:
C
A
Dm
G
Piano
Bkgd. Ba, da, da, ba, da, da,
Vcl.: Ba, da, ba, da, da, da, da, da, ba, da, da, da, da, da,
*Keybd. (arr. for gtr.)

*w/harpsichord sound.

C
F
Dm
G
ba, da, da, ba, da, ba.
ba, da, da, da, da, ba, da, ba.
Cont. simile

Verse:
C
A
Dm7
1. I re - mem - ber Sun - day morn - ing, I would meet him at
2. And now I wake up Sun - day morn - ing, walk a - cross the way
3.4. See additional lyrics
Elec. Gtr.
(clean-tone)
G
C
Am
the park. We'd walk to - geth - er hand in hand 'til
to find no - bod - y wait - ing for me. Sun - day's just
Dm
D7
1.3.
G
2.4.
G
it was al - most dark.
an - oth - er day.

Chorus:
C
F
C
Cont. rhy. simile
Sun - day will nev - er be the same.
Bkgd. Vcl.: Be the same. Sun - day will
F
C
F
nev - er be the same.
I lost my Sun - day song, he'll
Dm
1.
G7sus
G
D.S. 𝄋
not be back a - gain.
2.
G7sus
G
Bridge:
C
B♭6
I re - mem - ber chil - dren
Chil - dren
Elec. Gtr.
w/fast vibrato
C
B♭6
C
Elec. Gtr. cont. rhy. simile
feed - ing flocks of pi - geons.
pi - geons.
I re - mem - ber

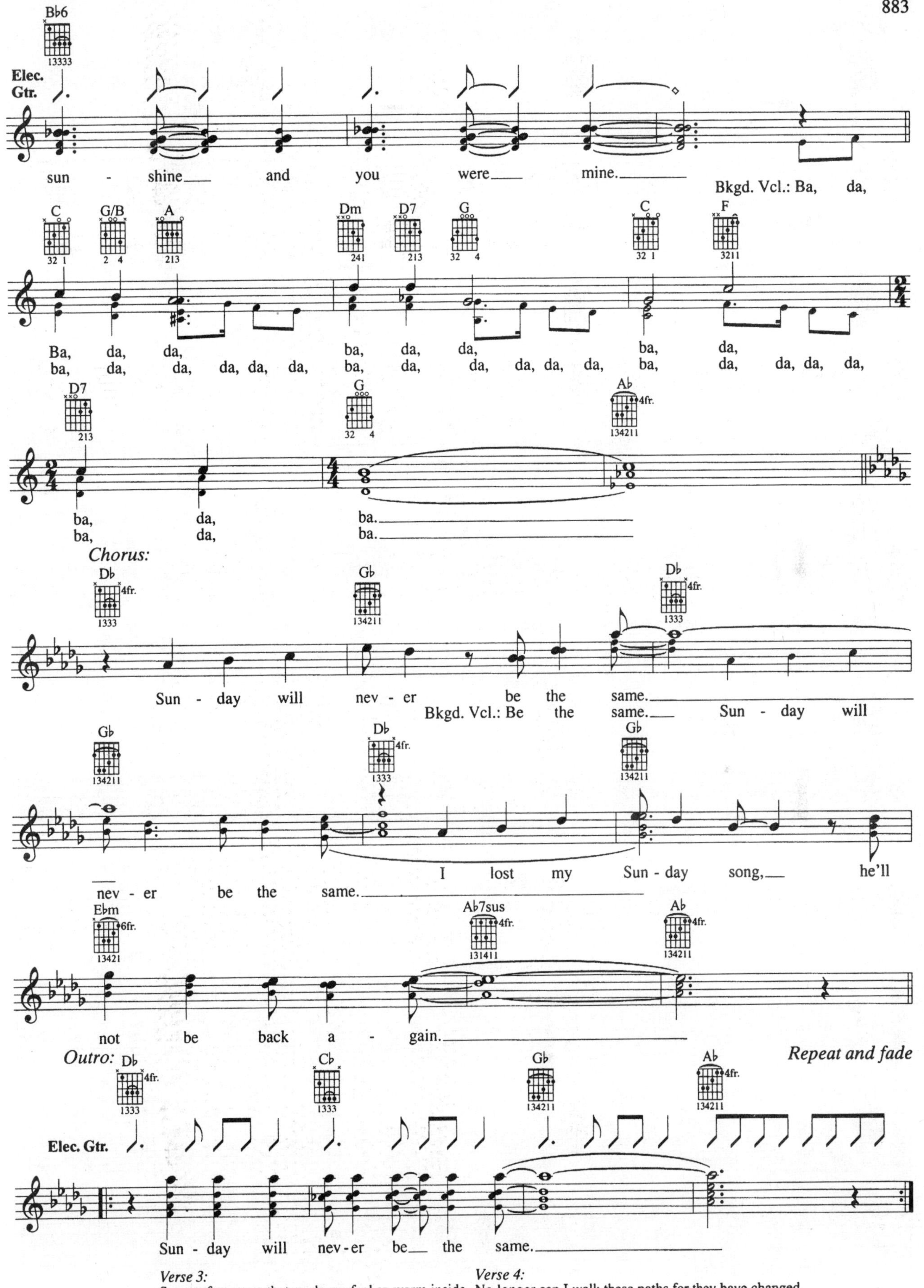

Verse 3:
Sunny afternoons that made me feel so warm inside
Have turned as cold and gray as ashes
As I feel the embers die.

Verse 4:
No longer can I walk these paths for they have changed.
I must be home, the sun is gone and I think it's gonna rain.
(To Chorus:)

SUNSHINE OF YOUR LOVE

Words and Music by
JACK BRUCE, PETE BROWN
and ERIC CLAPTON

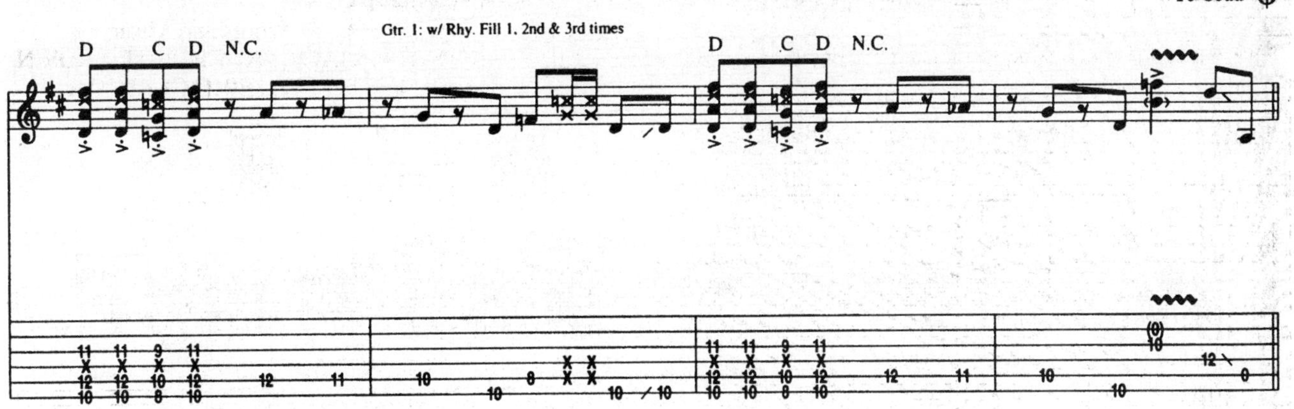
To Coda
Gtr. 1: w/ Rhy. Fill 1, 2nd & 3rd times
D C D N.C.
D C D N.C.

Chorus

A C G A C G
I've been wait - ing so long to be where I'm go - ing
Rhy. Fig. 2
End Rhy. Fig. 2

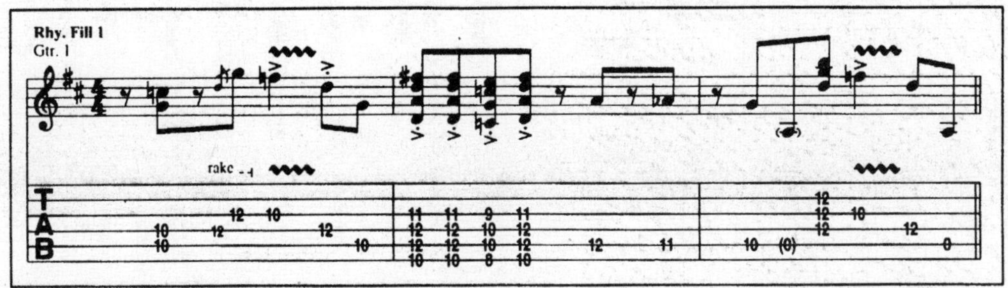
Rhy. Fill 1
Gtr. 1
rake

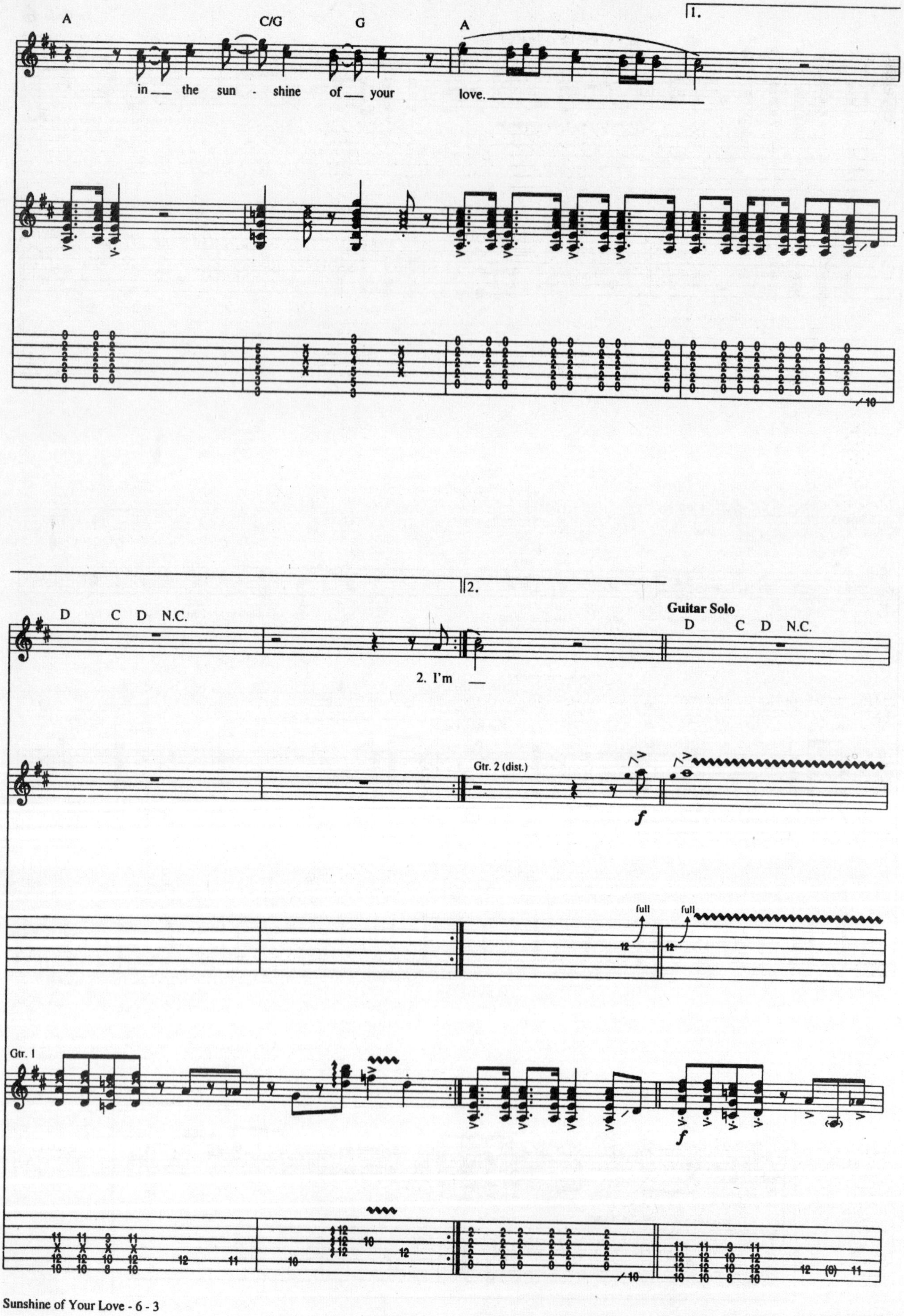

2.

D C D N.C.

2. I'm

Guitar Solo

D C D N.C.

Gtr. 2 (dist.)

f

full full

Gtr. 1

f

D C D N.C.
D C D N.C.
full
full
full
1/2
1/2 3/4
1/4
D C D N.C.
G F G N.C.
1/2
3/4
1/2 3/4
1/2 3/4
grad. bend
2
full
2
1 3/4
full
full
1/4
G F G N.C.
full
full
1/2
full
1 1/2
full
rake

D
C
D
N.C.
(cont. in slash)
G
F
10fr
8fr
A
C/G
Gtr. 1
Gtr. 2
full
1/2
C
P.M.
(cont. in notation)

D.S. al Coda (2nd lyrics)

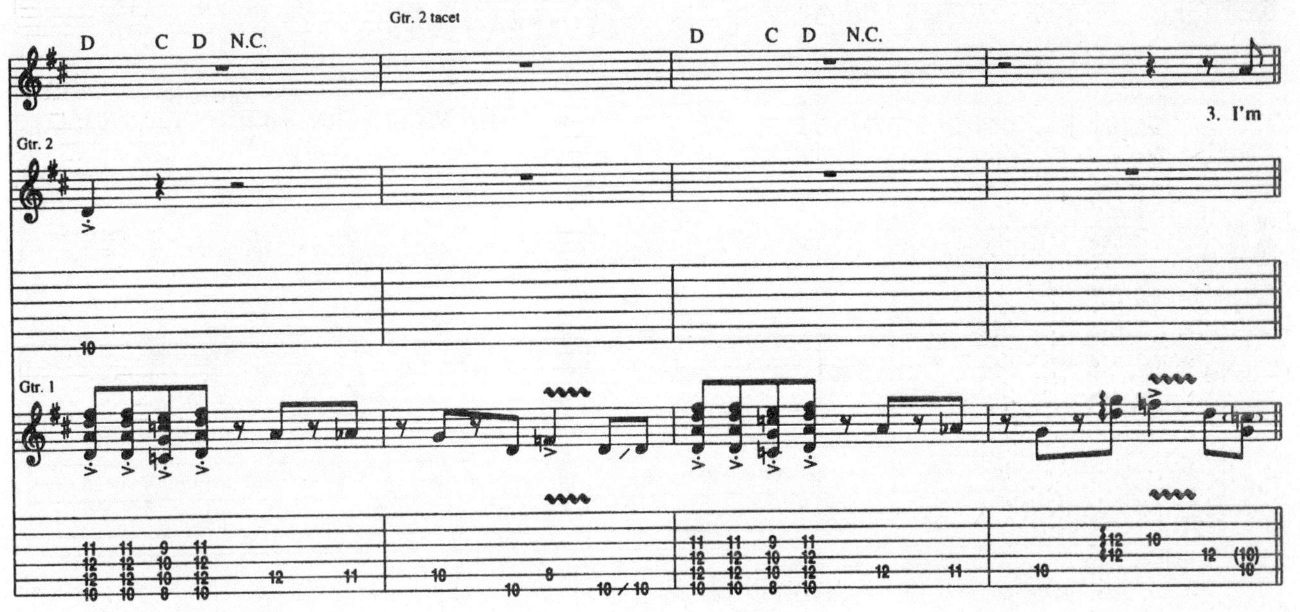

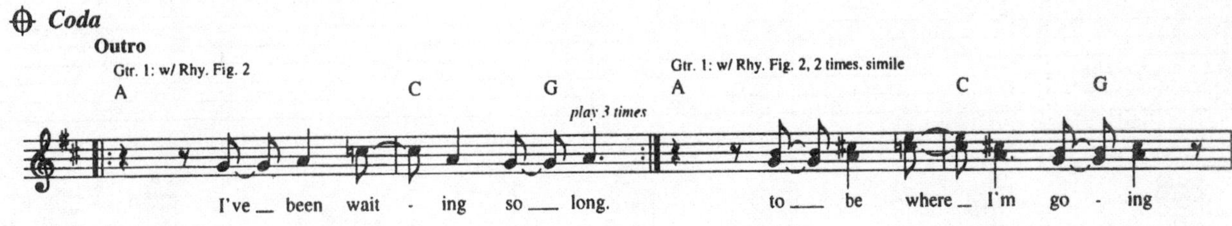

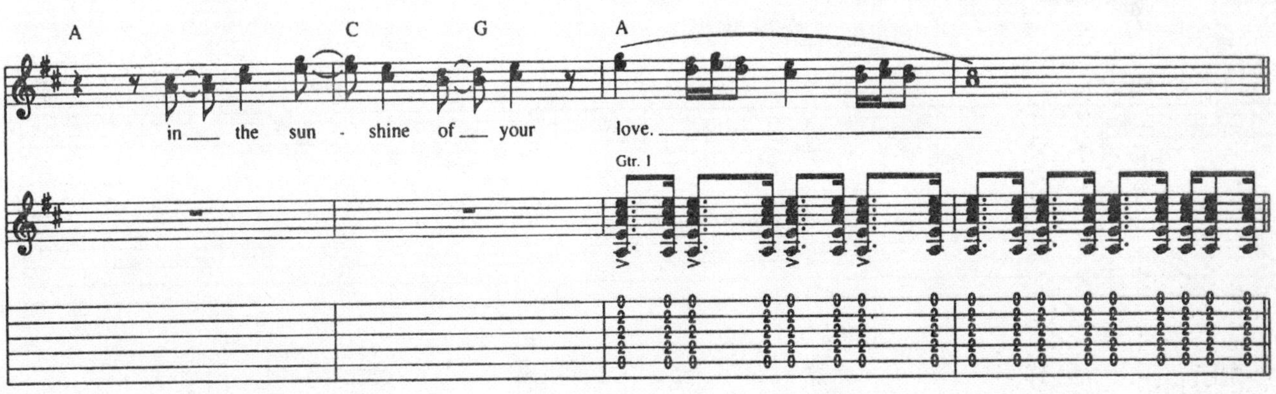

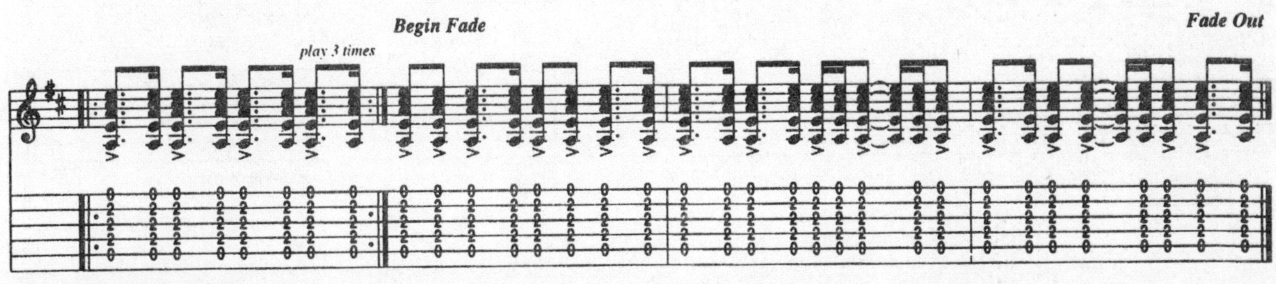

SUNNY CAME HOME

Words and Music by
SHAWN COLVIN and JOHN LEVENTHAL

Verse 1:
Am G F Em Am G
6-st. Acous. Gtr.
Cont. rhy. simile
Sun-ny came home to her fa-v'rite room. Sun-ny sat down in the
C G F#m7(b5) G F Em
kitch-en. She o-pened a book and a box of tools.
Dm Am F
Sun - ny came home with a mis - sion. She says, "Days
Chorus:
C G Dm11 Fsus2
6-st. Acous. Gtr.
Cont. rhy. simile
go by, I'm hyp - no - tized. I'm walk -
C G Dm C G
- ing on a wire. I close my eyes and fly
Dm11 Am D/F# G Fmaj7 G
6-st. Acous. Gtr.
out of my mind in-to the fire."

Interlude:
Am
G
F
Em
Am
G
6-st. Acous. Gtr.
Cont. rhy. simile
Mm, mm.
12-st. Acous. Gtr.
Verse 2:
C
G
Am
G
C
G
6-st. Acous. Gtr.
Cont. rhy. simile
Sun-ny came home with a list of names.
Am
G
C
Em
F
G
She did-n't be-lieve in tran - scend-ence. "And it's time for a few small re -

Am
G/B
Dm
Am
F
pairs," she said.
Sun-ny came home with a ven-geance. She says, "Days
Chorus:
C
G
Dm11
Fsus2
6-st. Acous. Gtr.
Cont. rhy. simile
go by, I don't know why. I'm walk-
C
G
Dm11
C
G
-ing on a wire. I close my eyes and fly
Dm11
Am
D/F#
G
Fmaj7
G
6-st. Acous. Gtr.
out of my mind in-to the fire." Get
Bridge:
G/B
Em
F
6-st. Acous. Gtr.
Cont. rhy. simile
the kids and bring a sweat - er. Dry

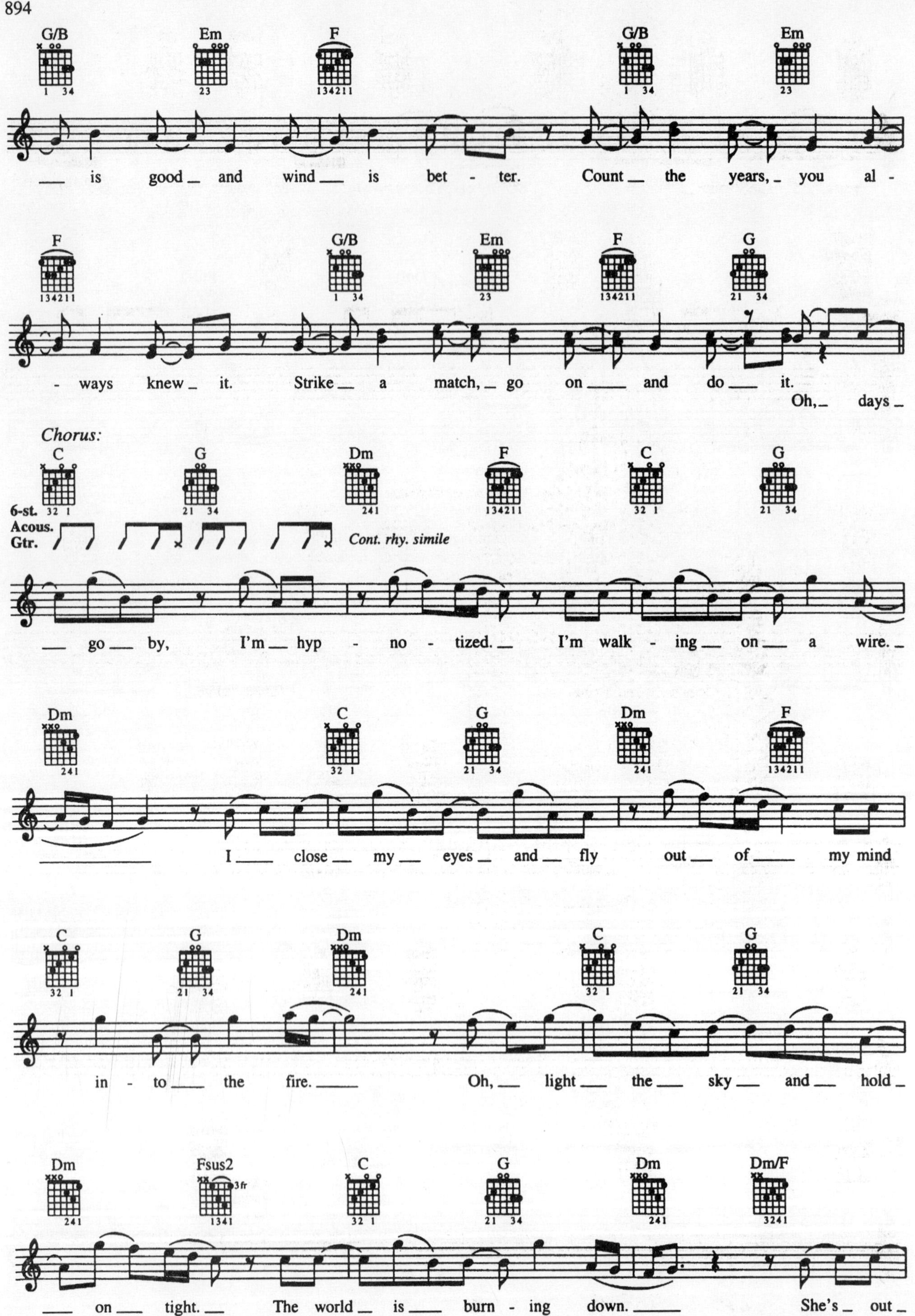
G/B
Em
F
G/B
Em
is good and wind is bet - ter. Count the years, you al -
F
G/B
Em
F
G
- ways knew it. Strike a match, go on and do it.
Oh, days
Chorus:
C
G
Dm
F
C
G
6-st. Acous. Gtr.
Cont. rhy. simile
go by, I'm hyp - no - tized. I'm walk - ing on a wire.
Dm
C
G
Dm
F
I close my eyes and fly out of my mind
C
G
Dm
C
G
in - to the fire. Oh, light the sky and hold
Dm
Fsus2
C
G
Dm
Dm/F
on tight. The world is burn - ing down. She's out

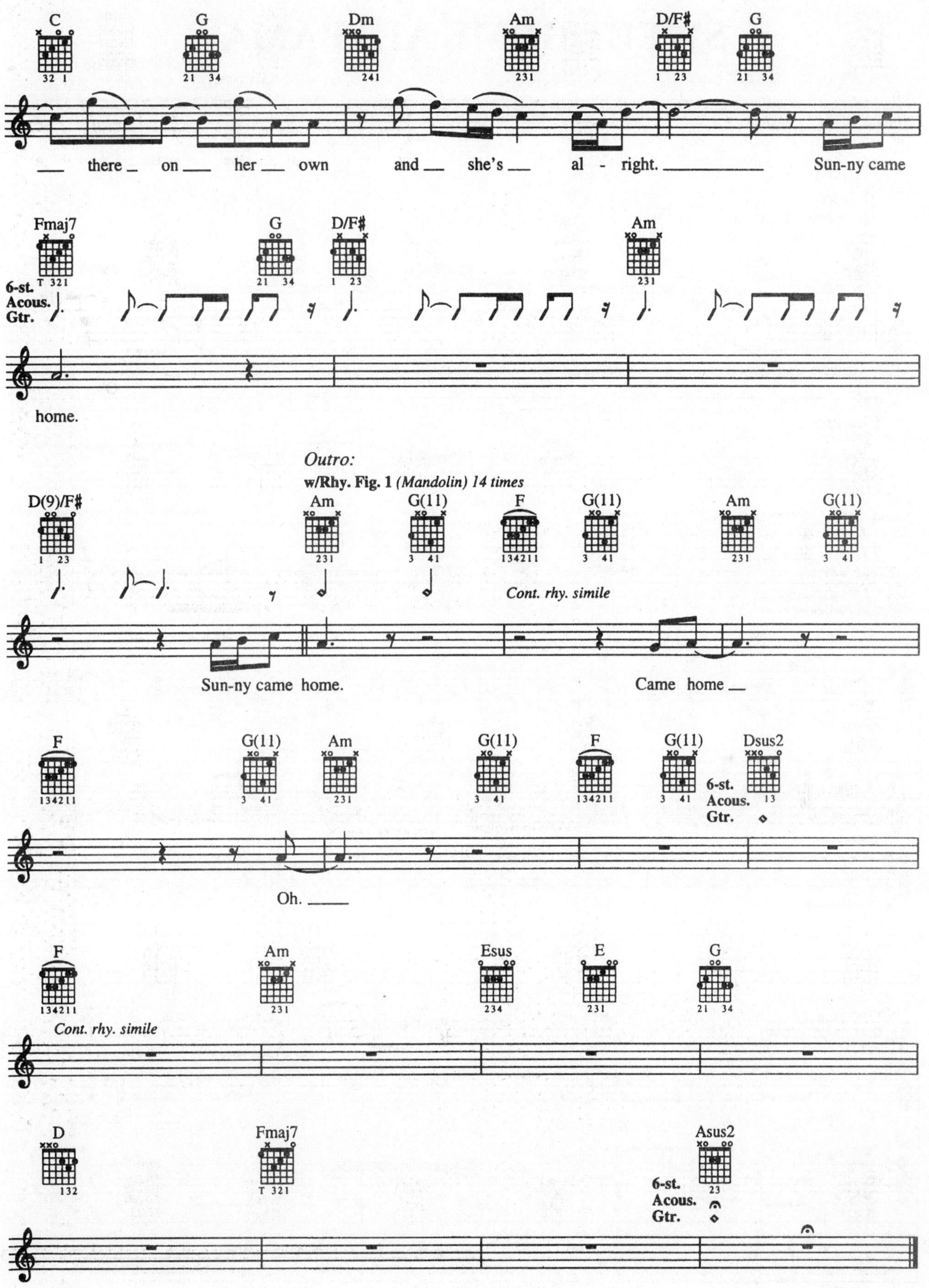
C
G
Dm
Am
D/F♯
G
there on her own and she's al - right. Sun-ny came
Fmaj7
G
D/F♯
Am
6-st. Acous. Gtr.
home.
Outro:
w/Rhy. Fig. 1 (Mandolin) 14 times
D(9)/F♯
Am
G(11)
F
G(11)
Am
G(11)
Cont. rhy. simile
Sun-ny came home. Came home
F
G(11)
Am
G(11)
F
G(11)
Dsus2
6-st. Acous. Gtr.
Oh.
F
Am
Esus
E
G
Cont. rhy. simile
D
Fmaj7
Asus2
6-st. Acous. Gtr.

SWEET HOME ALABAMA

Words and Music by
RONNIE VAN ZANT, ED KING
and GARY ROSSINGTON

G
D
Csus2
G
Sing-in' songs a - bout - the south - land.
D
Csus2
G
Interlude
N.C.(D)
(C)
I miss ole 'Bam - ee once a - gain - and I think it's a sin, - yes.
Gtr. 2
Riff A1
End Rhy. Fig. 1
Gtr. 1
(G)
End Riff A1
(D)
(C)
(G)
let ring
let ring
w/ bar
harm.
slight vib. w/ bar
Harm.
*Depress and release trem. bar at each beat indicated
Verse
Gtr. 1: w/ Rhy. Fig. 1
Gtr. 2: w/ Riff A, 1 3/4 times
D
Csus2
G
D
Csus2
2. Well, I heard Mist-er Young sing a - bout - her.
Well, I heard old Neil - put 'er down. -
(Ooh, ooh, ooh.
Ooh, ooh,

G
D
Csus2
G
D
Csus2
Well, I hope Neil Young will re-mem - ber,
a south- ern man _ don't need him a -
ooh.
Ooh,
ooh,
ooh.
South ern man don't need him a -
Gtr. 2: w/ Riff B
Chorus
Rhy. Fig. 2A
D5 D6 D5 C5 C6 C5 G5 G6 G5 Csus2
Gtr. 2
round, an-y-how.
round.)
Sweet _ home Al - a-bam - a,
Gtr. 1
Riff B1
End Riff B1
Rhy. Fig. 2
let ring
D5 D6D5 C5 C6C5 G5 C5 D5 D6 D5 C5 C6 C5
where the skies are so blue. _
Sweet _ home Al - a -
Riff B
Gtr. 2
let ring

Gtr. 2: w/ Fill 1

G5 G6 G5 Csus2 D5 D6 D5 C5 C6 C5 G5 F/C C

End Rhy. Fig. 2A

bam - a, Lord, I'm com-in' home to you.

End Rhy. Fig. 2

Guitar Solo

Gtr. 1: w/ Rhy. Fig. 3, 2 times

D Csus2 G D Csus2

Gtr. 2

P.H. P.H. full P.H. full full

Verse

Gtr. 2: w/ Riff A, 1st meas. only

Gtr. 2: w/ Riff C (see p. ?)

G D Csus2 G F/C C

3. In Bir-ming - ham they love the gov - 'nor, boo, boo,

let ring

Fill 1

Gtr. 2

mf *f* full

Rhy. Fig. 3

Gtr. 1

let ring

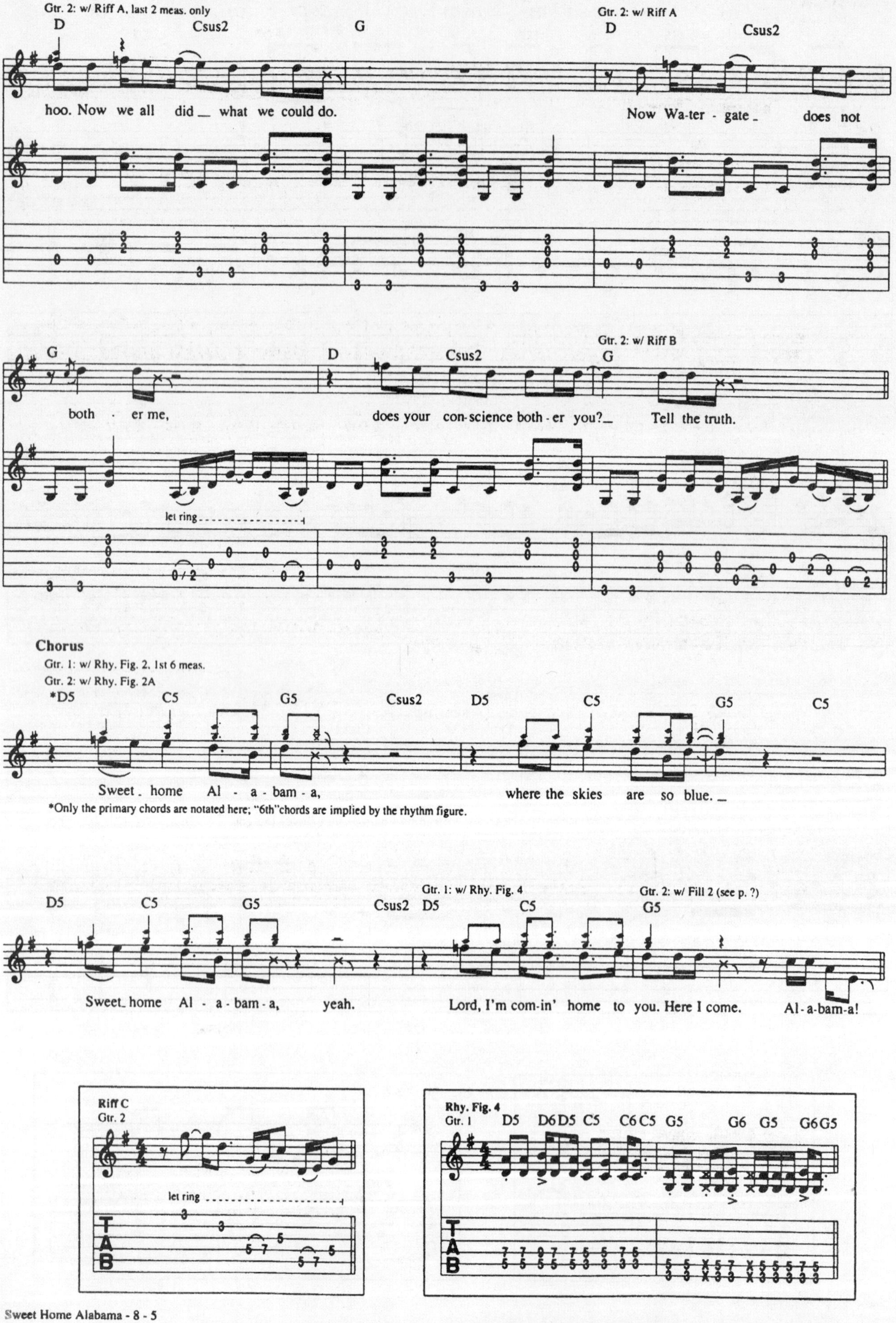

Gtr. 2: w/ Riff A, last 2 meas. only

D Csus2 G

hoo. Now we all did _ what we could do.

Gtr. 2: w/ Riff A

D Csus2

Now Wa-ter - gate _ does not

G D Csus2

both - er me, does your con-science both - er you?_

Gtr. 2: w/ Riff B

G

Tell the truth.

let ring

Chorus

Gtr. 1: w/ Rhy. Fig. 2, 1st 6 meas.

Gtr. 2: w/ Rhy. Fig. 2A

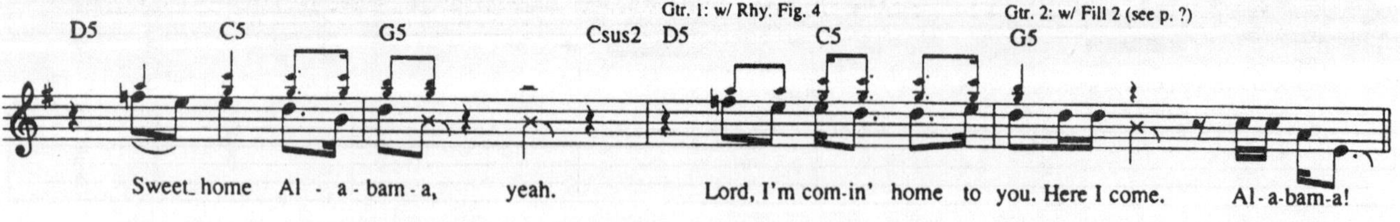

*Only the primary chords are notated here; "6th" chords are implied by the rhythm figure.

D5 C5 G5 Csus2

Sweet_ home Al - a - bam - a, yeah.

Gtr. 1: w/ Rhy. Fig. 4

D5 C5

Lord, I'm com-in' home to you.

Gtr. 2: w/ Fill 2 (see p. ?)

G5

Here I come. Al-a-bam-a!

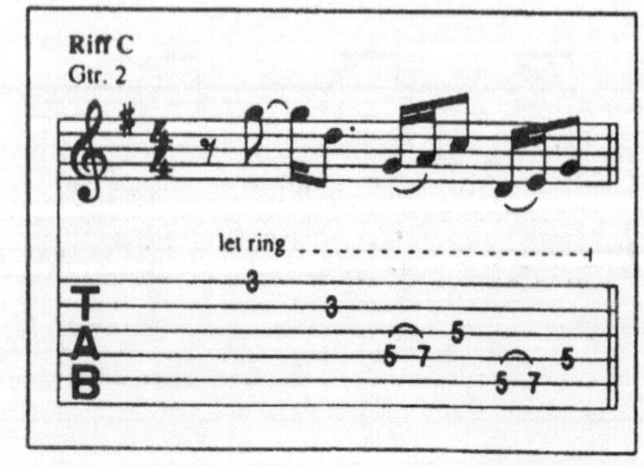

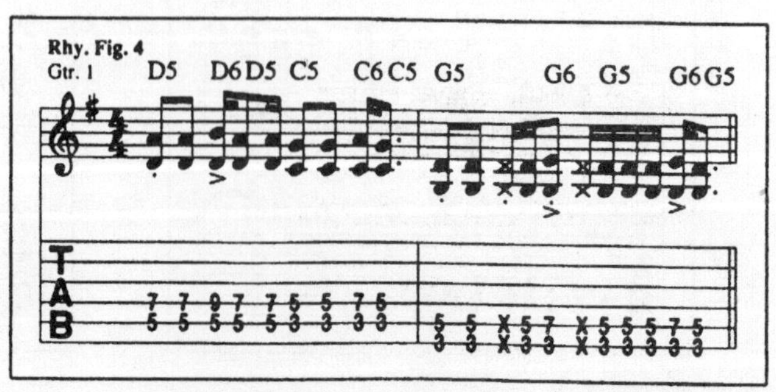

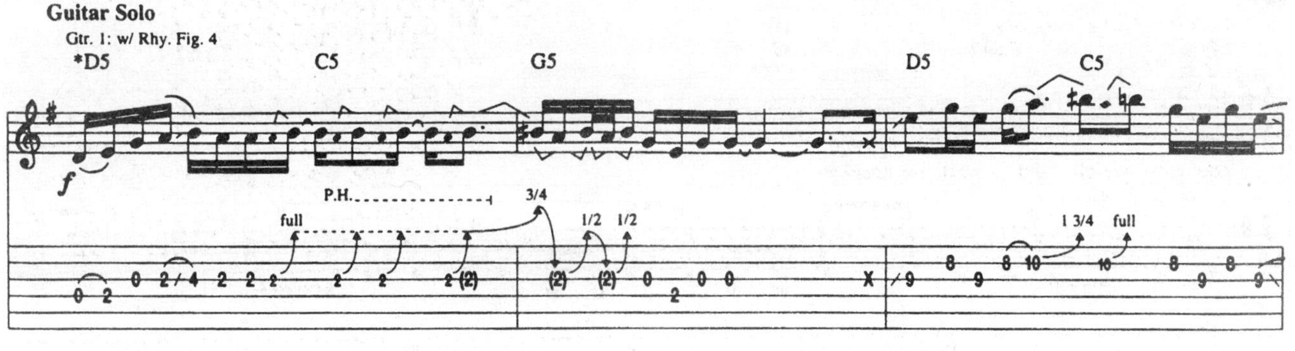
Guitar Solo
Gtr. 1: w/ Rhy. Fig. 4
*D5
C5
G5
D5
C5
f
P.H.
full
3/4
1/2
1/2
1 3/4
full

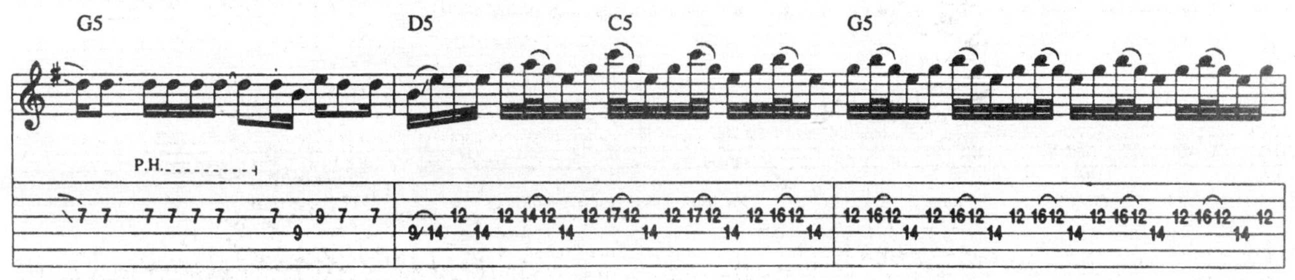
G5
D5
C5
G5
P.H.

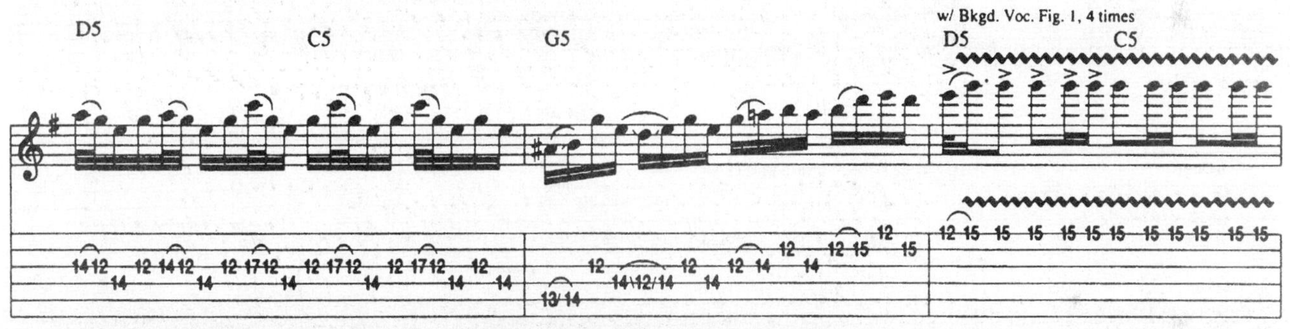
w/ Bkgd. Voc. Fig. 1, 4 times
D5
C5
G5
D5
C5

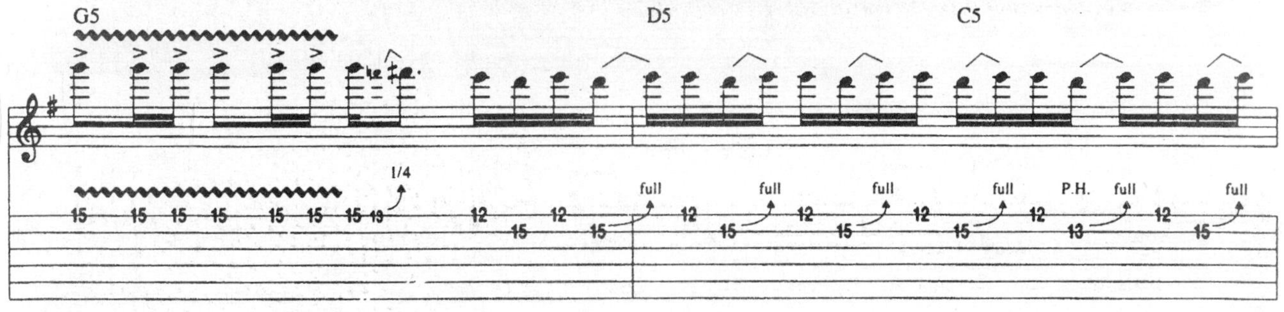
G5
D5
C5
1/4
full
full
full
full
P.H.
full
full

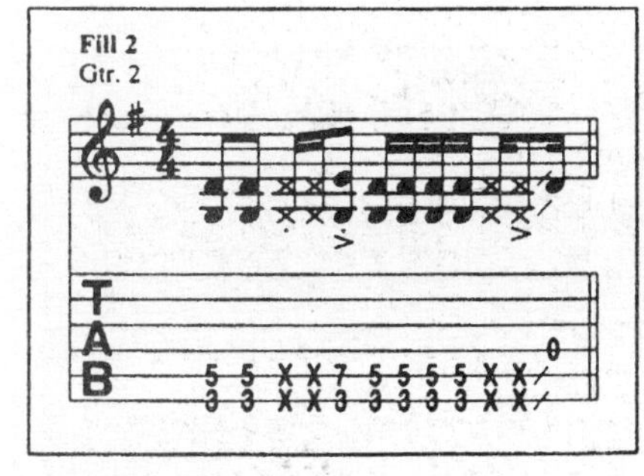
Fill 2
Gtr. 2
T
A
B

Bkgd. Voc. Fig. 1
Ah, ah, ah, Al-a-bam-a!

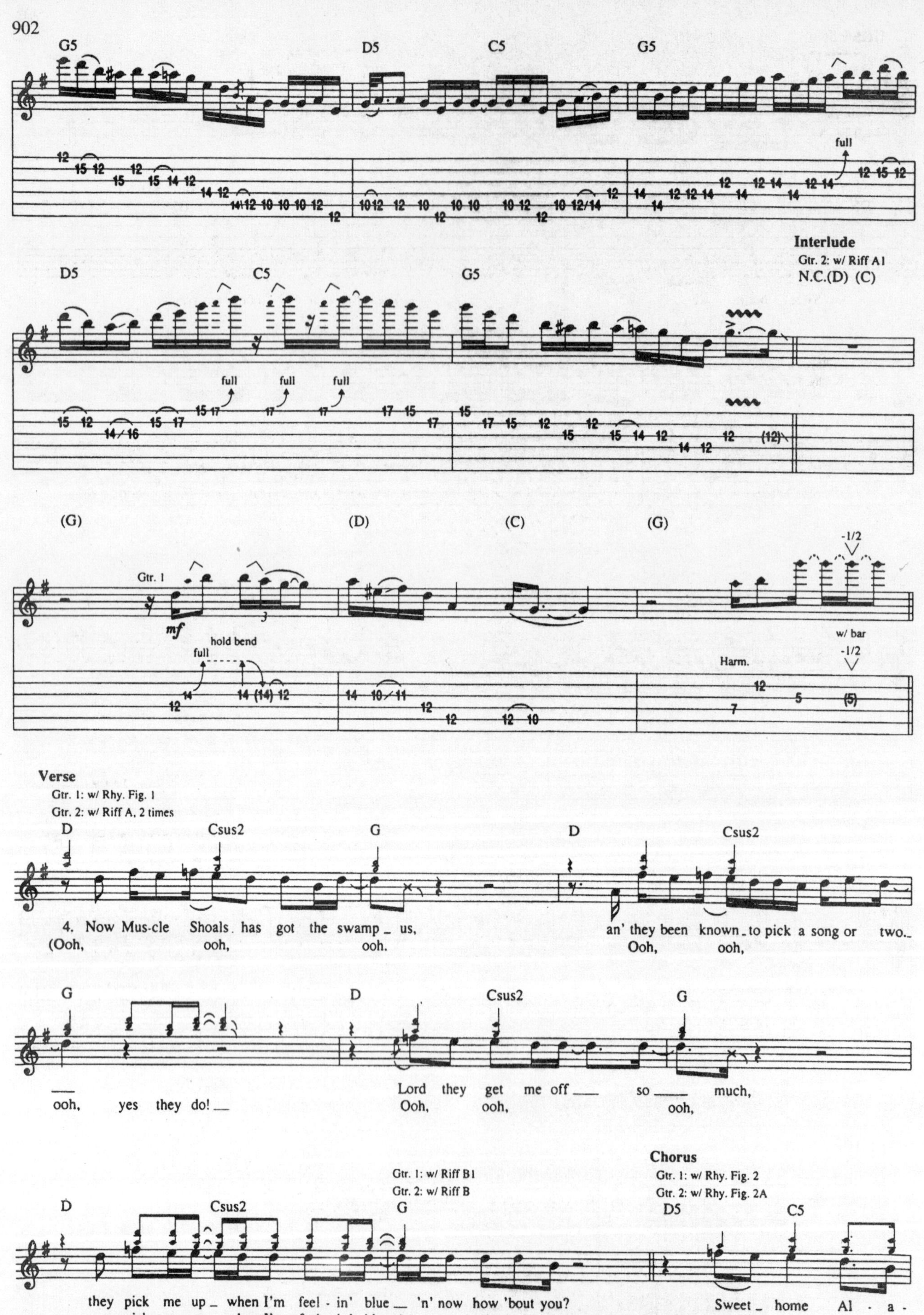
G5
D5
C5
G5
full
D5
C5
G5
full
full
full
Interlude
Gtr. 2: w/ Riff A1
N.C.(D) (C)
(G)
(D)
(C)
(G)
Gtr. 1
mf
hold bend
full
-1/2
w/ bar
-1/2
Harm.
Verse
Gtr. 1: w/ Rhy. Fig. 1
Gtr. 2: w/ Riff A, 2 times
D
Csus2
G
D
Csus2
4. Now Mus-cle Shoals has got the swamp _ us,
(Ooh, ooh, ooh.
an' they been known _ to pick a song or two._
Ooh, ooh,
G
D
Csus2
G
ooh, yes they do! _
Lord they get me off ___ so ___ much,
Ooh, ooh, ooh,
Gtr. 1: w/ Riff B1
Gtr. 2: w/ Riff B
Chorus
Gtr. 1: w/ Rhy. Fig. 2
Gtr. 2: w/ Rhy. Fig. 2A
D
Csus2
G
D5
C5
they pick me up _ when I'm feel - in' blue __ 'n' now how 'bout you?
pick me up _ when I'm feel - in' blue._)
Sweet _ home Al - a -

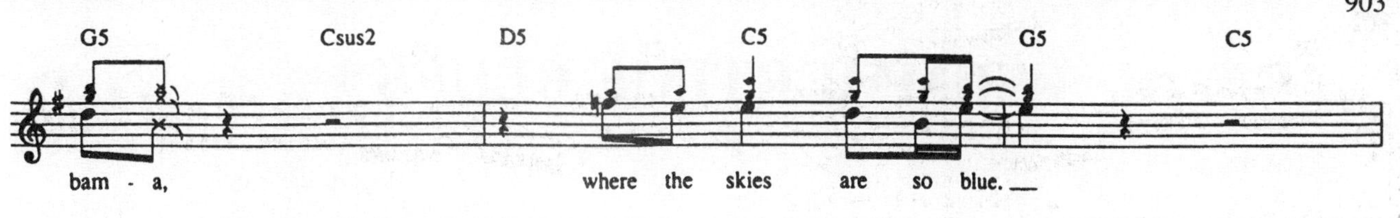
G5
Csus2
D5
C5
G5
C5
bam - a,
where the skies are so blue.

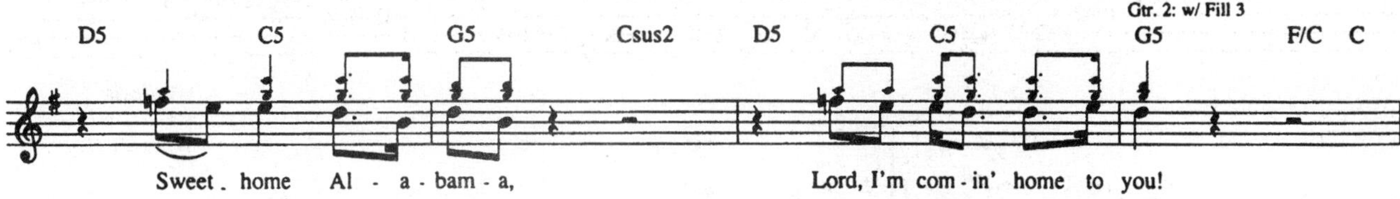
Gtr. 2: w/ Fill 3
D5
C5
G5
Csus2
D5
C5
G5
F/C
C
Sweet home Al - a - bam - a,
Lord, I'm com - in' home to you!

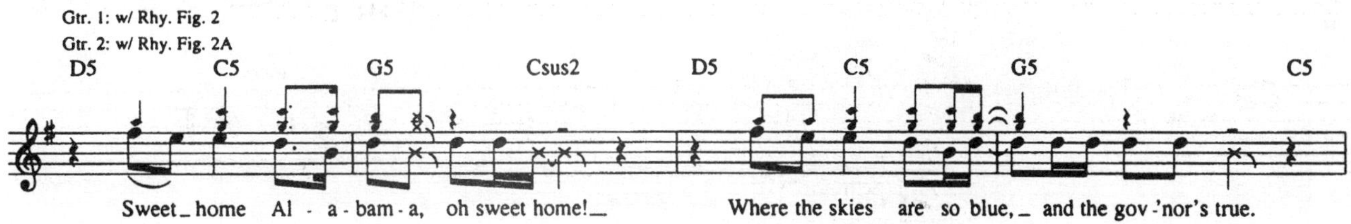
Gtr. 1: w/ Rhy. Fig. 2
Gtr. 2: w/ Rhy. Fig. 2A
D5
C5
G5
Csus2
D5
C5
G5
C5
Sweet home Al - a - bam - a, oh sweet home!
Where the skies are so blue, and the gov-'nor's true.

Gtrs. 1 & 2: w/ Rhy. Fig. 4
D5
C5
G5
Csus2
D5
C5
G5
Sweet home Al - a - bam - a, oh yeah.
Lord, I'm com in' - home to you.
Yeah.
(Oo! Oo! Oo!)

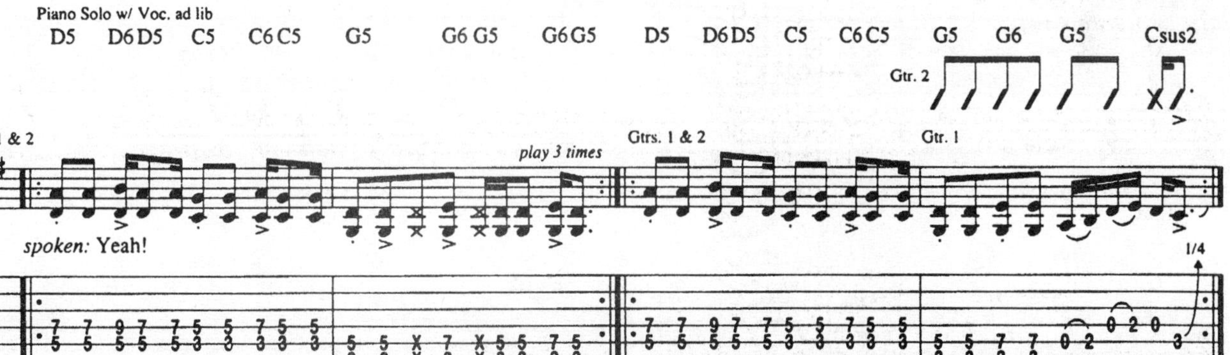
Play 6 times and Fade
Piano Solo w/ Voc. ad lib
D5 D6 D5 C5 C6 C5 G5 G6 G5 G6 G5 D5 D6 D5 C5 C6 C5 G5 G6 G5 Csus2
Gtr. 2
Gtrs. 1 & 2
play 3 times
Gtrs. 1 & 2
Gtr. 1
spoken: Yeah!
1/4

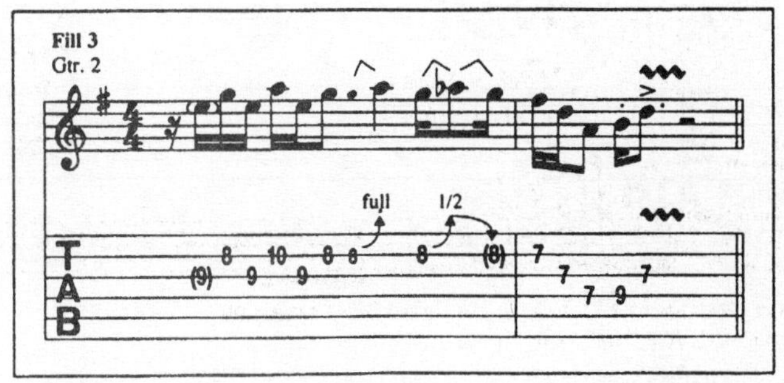
Fill 3
Gtr. 2
full
1/2
T
A
B

SUMMERTIME BLUES

Words and Music by
EDDIE COCHRAN and JERRY CAPEHART

B
E
Cont. rhy. simile
a - bout a - work - in' all sum - mer just to try to earn a dol - lar.
T
A
B
B
E
A
Ev - 'ry time I call my ba - by,
E
A5
try to get a date; my boss says, "No dice, son, you got - ta work late."
Chorus:
E
Some - times I won - der what I'm - a gon - na do, but there ain't no cure for the

Verse 2:
A-well, my mom and papa said,
"Son, you gotta make some money
If you wanna use the car to go ridin' next Sunday."
A-well, I didn't go to work, told the boss I was sick,
"Now you can't use the car, 'cause you didn't work a lick."
(To Chorus:)

Verse 3:
I'm gonna take two weeks, gonna have a fine vacation.
I'm gonna take my problem to the United Nations.
Well, I called my Congressman and he said, quote,
"I'd like to help you, son, but you're too young to vote."
(To Chorus:)

THESE DREAMS

Words and Music by
BERNIE TAUPIN and MARTIN PAGE

G♯7sus C♯m7 D♯m Esus2 G♯5 C♯m7(11) F♯/G♯ B/D♯
F♯5 B5 F♯/A♯ E/G♯ B/F♯ E/F♯ B B/D♯ C♯m

Moderately ♩ = 112

Intro:

G♯7sus C♯m7 D♯m Esus2

*Gtr. 1

*Synths. arr. for gtr. throughout.

G♯7sus C♯m7 D♯m Esus2

Verse 1:

G♯5 C♯m7(11) D♯m

Spare a lit - tle can - dle, save __ some light for me. __

G♯7sus C♯m7(11) D♯m Esus2

Fig-ures up __ a - head, __ mov - ing in the trees. White skin in lin-en, per-

F♯/G♯ Esus2 B/D♯

- fume on my wrist, __ and the full moon _ that hangs _ o - ver _

C♯m7 Esus2 F♯5 B5

these dreams _ in __ the mist. ______

𝄋 *Verses 2-4:*

G♯5 C♯m7(11) D♯m

Dark - ness on __ the edge, _____ shad - ows where I stand.

3.4. *See additional lyrics* Shad - ows where _ I stand. __

G#7sus
C#m7(11)
D#m
I search for the time on a watch with no hands. How I
Esus2
F#/G#
want to see you clear - ly. Come clos - er than this. But
All that I re - mem -
Esus2
B/D#
C#m7
all I re - mem - ber are the dreams in the mist.
ber.
Chorus:
G#5
B/D#
F#/A#
E/G#
These dreams go on when I close my
B/F#
C#m7
B/D#
F#/A#
E/G#
eyes. Ev - 'ry sec - ond of the night, I
B/F#
Esus2
B/D#
F#/A#
E/G#
live an - oth - er life. These dreams that sleep when it's cold out -
B/F#
C#m7
B/D#
F#/A#
E/G#
To Coda
side, ev - 'ry mo - ment I'm a - wake the

Verse 3:
Is it cloak and dagger?
Could it be spring or fall?
I walk without a cut through a stained glass wall.
Weaker in my eyesight, the candle in my grip.
And words that have no form
Are falling from my lips.
(To Chorus:)

Verse 4:
The sweetest song is silence that I've ever heard.
Funny how your feet in dreams never touch the earth.
In a wood full of princes, freedom is a kiss.
But the prince hides his face from the dreams in the mist.
(To Chorus:)

TAKE IT EASY

Words and Music by
JACKSON BROWNE and GLENN FREY

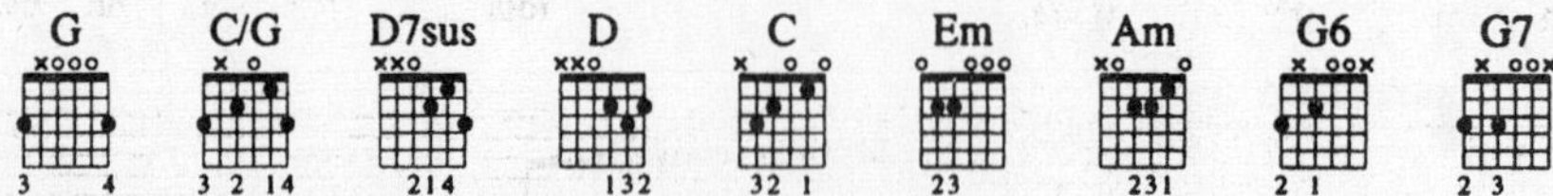

Moderate country feel ♩ = 138

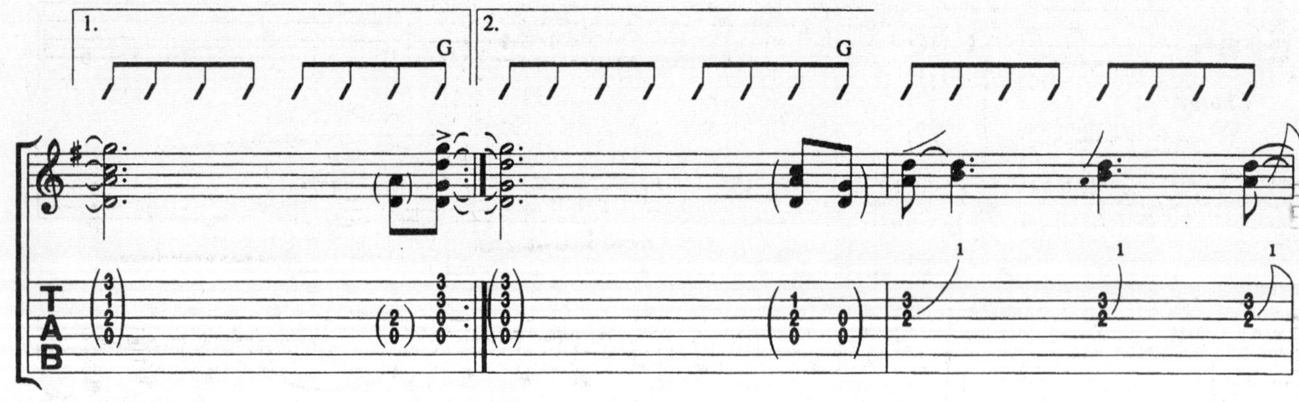

D
*C
G
- en wom - en on my ___ mind; four ___ that wan - na own me, ___ two ___
*Substitute w/Am, Verse 3 only.
D
C
G
___ that wan - na stone me, ___ one ___ says she's a friend _ of mine. ___ Take it ___ eas -
Chorus:
Em
C
- y, take it ___ eas
2. 3. See additional lyrics
G
Am
C
y, don't let the sound of your ___ own _ wheels ___ drive you cra -
Oo, ___ oo, ___

Em
end Rhy. Fig. 1
C
G
zy.
Light-en up
while you still can,
don't e-ven
To Coda
C
G
Am
C
try to un-der-stand,
just find a place to make your stand
an' take it eas-
hold
G G6 G7 G6 G
1.
G G6 G7 G6 G G6 G7 G6 G G6 G7 G6 G
y.
2. Well, I'm a

Verse 2:
Well, I'm a-standing on a corner in Winslow, Arizona,
And such a fine sight to see.
It's a girl, my lord, in a flatbed Ford
Slowing down to take a look at me.
(To Guitar Solo:)

Verse 3:
Well I'm a-running down the road,
Trying to loosen my load,
Gotta a world of trouble on my mind.
Looking for a lover who won't blow my cover,
She's so hard to find.
(To Chorus:)

Chorus 2:
Come on baby, don't say maybe.
I gotta know if your sweet love is gonna save me.
We may lose, and we may win.
Though we will never be here again.
So open up, I'm climbing in,
So take it easy.
(To Guitar Solo:)

Chorus 3:
Take it easy, take it easy.
Don't let the sound of your own wheels make you crazy.
Come on baby, don't say maybe.
I gotta know if your sweet love is gonna save me.
(To Coda)

TAKIN' IT TO THE STREETS

Words and Music by
MICHAEL McDONALD

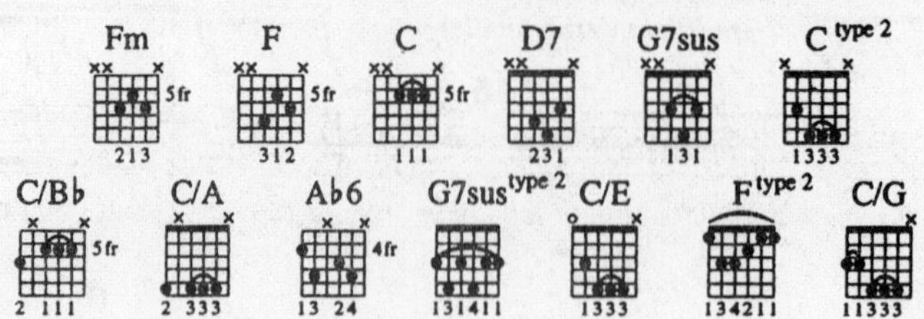

Moderately fast ♩ = 138

Intro:

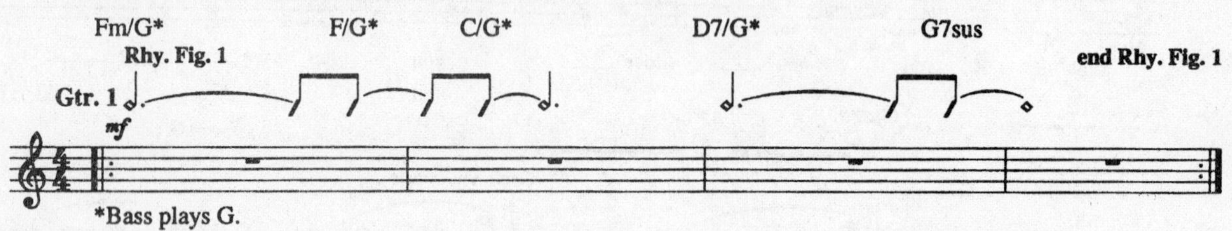

*Bass plays G.

Verse:

w/Rhy. Fig. 1 *(Gtr. 1) 4 times* **& Fill 1** *(Gtr. 2) 8 times, Verse 2 only*

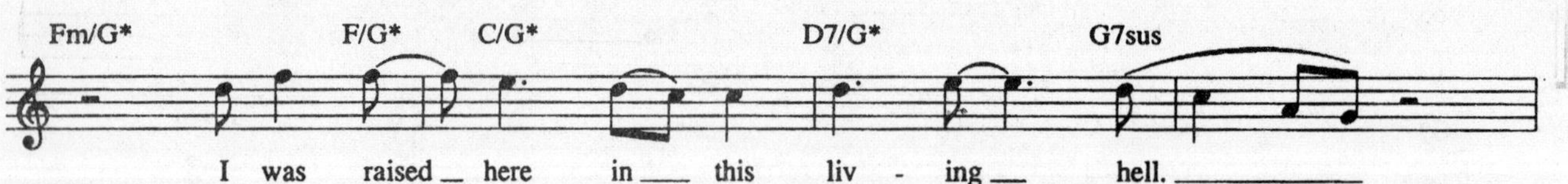

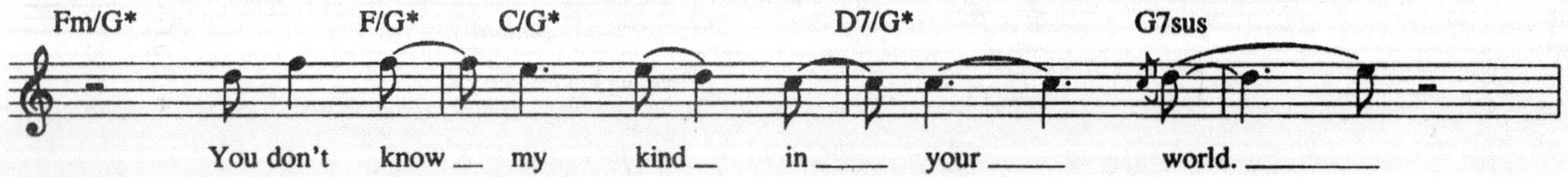

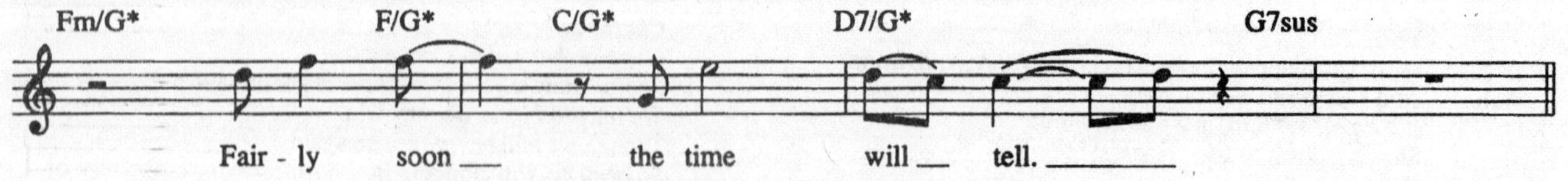

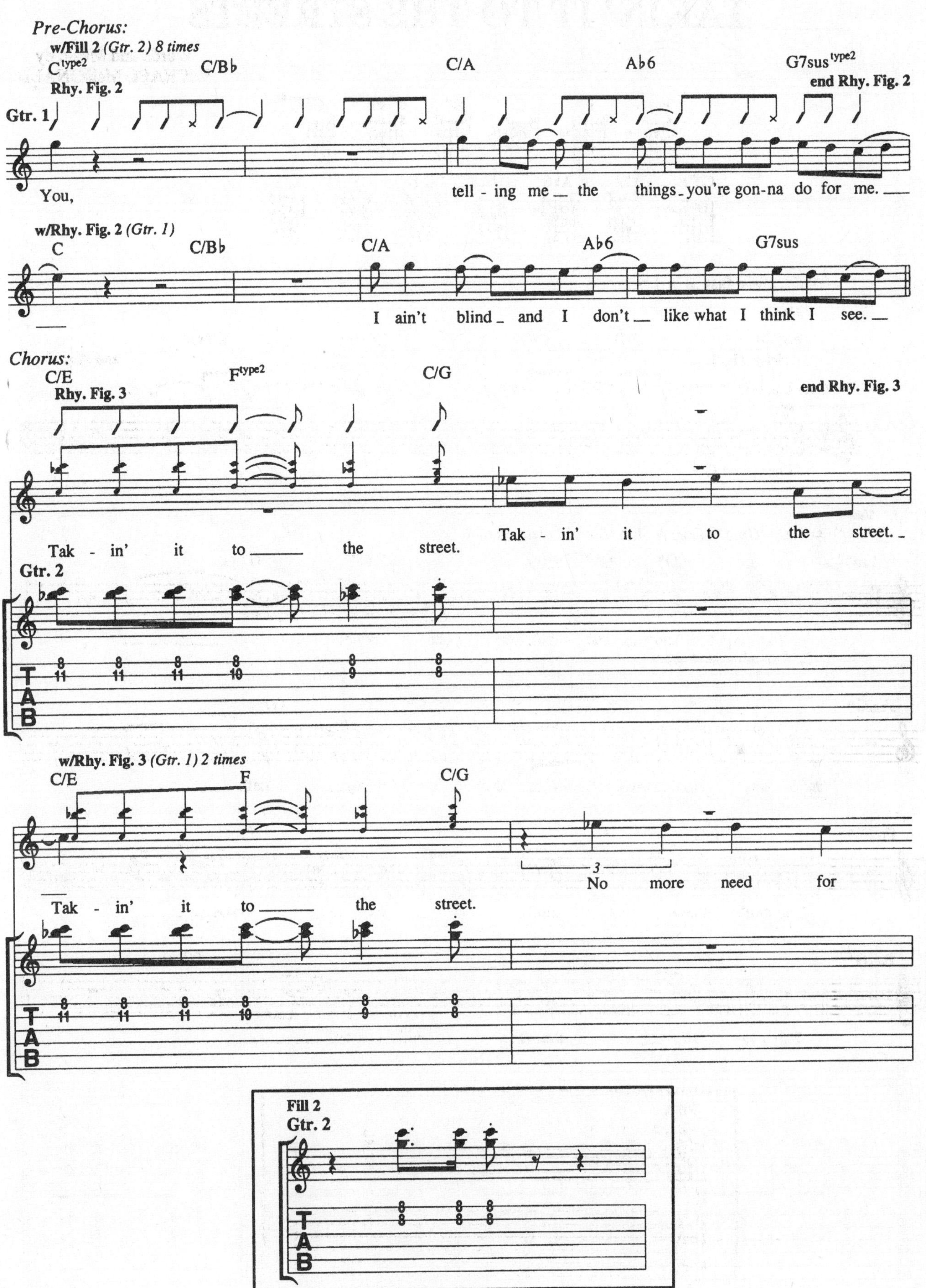
Pre-Chorus:
w/Fill 2 (Gtr. 2) 8 times
C type2 C/B♭ C/A A♭6 G7sus type2
Rhy. Fig. 2
end Rhy. Fig. 2
Gtr. 1
You, tell - ing me the things you're gon-na do for me.
w/Rhy. Fig. 2 (Gtr. 1)
C C/B♭ C/A A♭6 G7sus
I ain't blind and I don't like what I think I see.
Chorus:
C/E F type2 C/G
Rhy. Fig. 3
end Rhy. Fig. 3
Tak - in' it to the street. Tak - in' it to the street.
Gtr. 2
w/Rhy. Fig. 3 (Gtr. 1) 2 times
C/E F C/G
Tak - in' it to the street. No more need for
Fill 2
Gtr. 2

C/E F C/G

run - ning, oh.

Tak - in' it to ___ the streets.

1/4

1. 2.

C/E F C/G Fm/G* C/E F C/G Fm/G*

Gtr. 1

Tak - in' it to ___ the.

1/4

Sax Solo:

w/Rhy. Fig. 1 *(Gtr. 1)* **4 times**

Fm/G* F/G* C/G* D7/G* G7sus Fm/G* F/G*

P.M.

w/wah wah

1. 2.

C/G* D7/G* G7sus

Oh

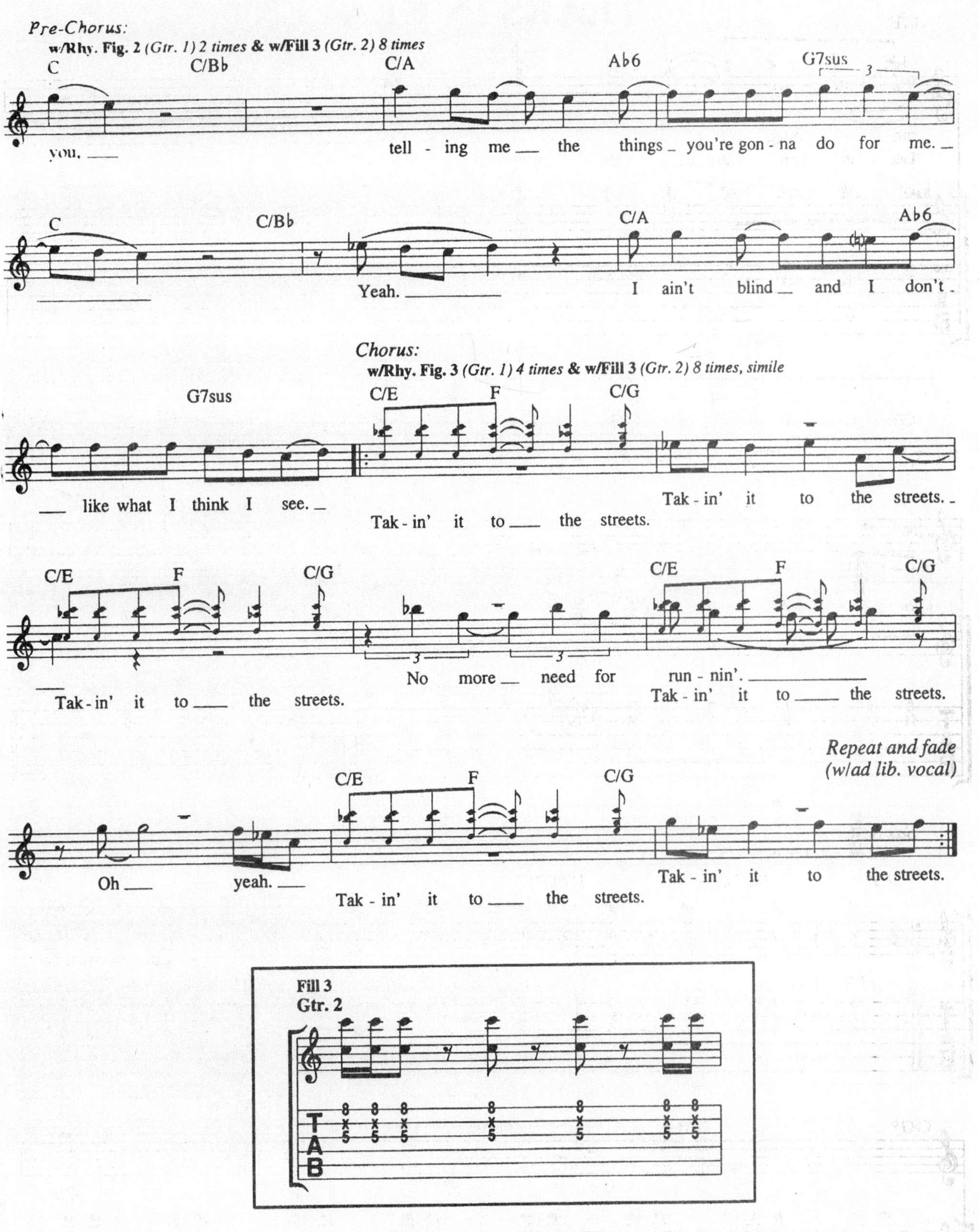

Verse 2:
Take this message to my brother.
You will find him everywhere.
Wherever people live together,
Tied in poverty's despair.
(To Pre-Chorus:)

TEARS IN HEAVEN

Words and Music by
WILL JENNINGS and ERIC CLAPTO

A
E/G♯
F♯m7
F♯m7/E
D/F♯
A/E
Would it be the same
Would ya help me stand
if I saw you in hea -
if I saw you in hea -
Ton ⑥
Ton ⑥
E
A/E
Chorus
F♯m7
C♯/E♯
ven?
ven?
I must be strong
I'll find my way
Ton ⑥
A7/E
F♯7
F♯7sus4
F♯/A♯
Bm7
and car - ry on,
through night and day
'cause I know
'cause I know
I don't be - long
I just can't stay
D/E
To Coda
N.C.
A
E/G♯
F♯m7
F♯m7/E
here in hea - ven.
here in hea - ven.
T on ⑥

1.
D/F#
E7sus4
E7
A
2.
T on 6
Bridge
C
G/B
Am
D/F#
Time can bring ya down, time can bend your knees.
G
Em
Time can break your heart
have ya beg - gin' please, beg - gin' please.
E
A/E
E7/5

Interlude
A
N.C. E/G# N.C. F#m7
F#m7/E
D/F#
A
T on ⑥
T on ⑥
E
A/E
E7 5
A
E/G#
F#m7
F#m7/E
T on ⑥
D/F#
A
E
A/E
E7 5
Chorus
F#m
Be - yond the door
T on ⑥
C#/E#
A7/E
F#7
G#m F#/A#
there's peace, I'm sure,
and I know
T on ⑥

Bm7 D/E N.C. A E/G♯ F♯m7
there'll be no more tears in hea - ven.
T on ⑥
F♯m7/E D/F♯ E7sus4 E7 A
3rd Verse
A E/G♯ F♯m7 F♯m7/E D/F♯ A
3. Would you know my name if I saw you in hea -
T on ⑥
T on ⑥
E A/E E7 5 A E/G♯ F♯m7 F♯m7/E
ven? Would you be the same
T on ⑥

D.S. 𝄋 al Coda ⊕
D/F♯
A/E
E
A/E
E^7_5
if I saw you in hea - ven?
T on ⑥
Coda
A
E/G♯
F♯m7
F♯m7/E
ven.
'Cause I
T on ⑥
Bm7
D/E
N.C.
A
E/G♯
F♯m
know I don't be - long here in hea - ven.
T on ⑥
Rubato
F♯m/E
D/F♯
E7sus4
E7
A
rit.
T on ⑥
let ring

THE BEAT GOES ON

Words and Music by
SONNY BONO

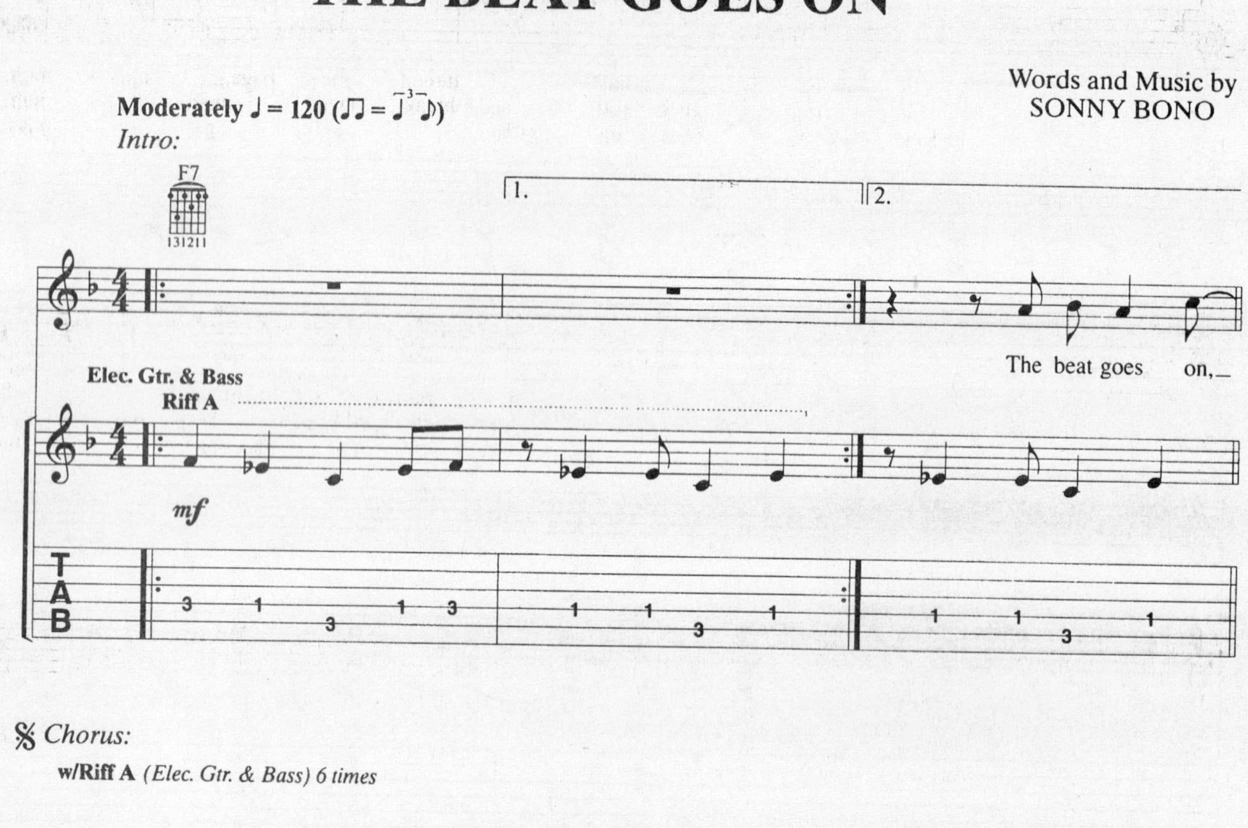
Moderately ♩= 120
Intro:
F7
131211
1.
2.
The beat goes on,
Elec. Gtr. & Bass
Riff A
mf
T
A
B
3 1 3 1 3
1 1 3 1
1 1 3 1

Chorus:
w/Riff A (Elec. Gtr. & Bass) 6 times
the beat goes on.

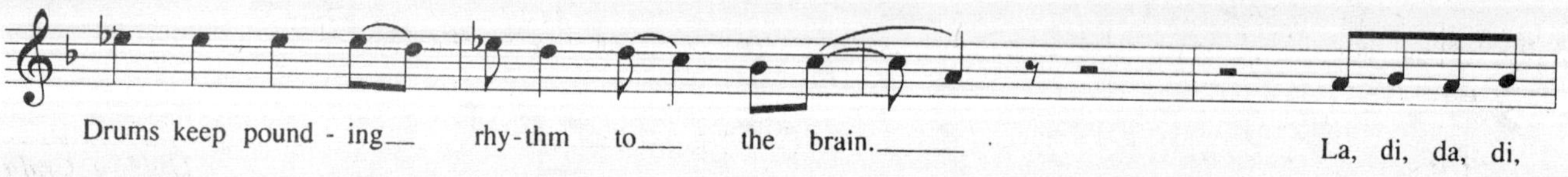
Drums keep pound - ing rhy-thm to the brain.
La, di, da, di,

To Coda
dee.
La, di, da, di, die.
2. The

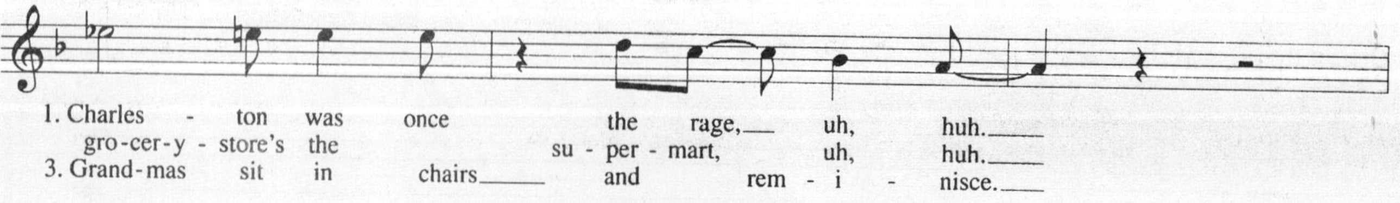
Verse:
w/Riff A (Elec. Gtr. & Bass) 8 times
1. Charles - ton was once the rage, uh, huh.
gro-cer-y - store's the su - per - mart, uh, huh.
3. Grand-mas sit in chairs and rem - i - nisce.

His - to - ry___ has turned the page,__ uh, huh.___
Lit - tle girls still break their hearts, uh, huh.___
Boys keep chas - ing girls to get a kiss.___

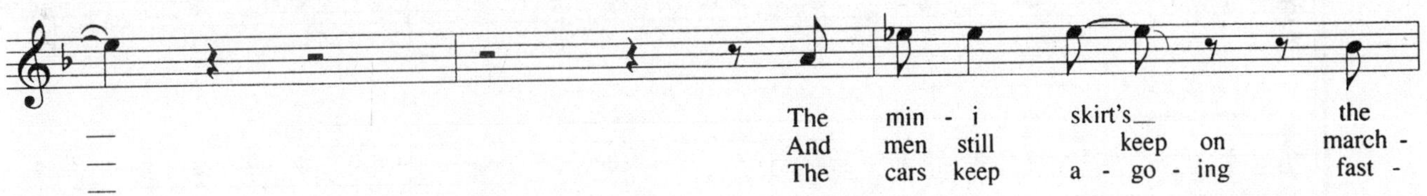
The min - i skirt's__ the
And men still keep on march -
The cars keep a - go - ing fast -

cur - rent thing,__ uh, huh,___
- ing off to war.___
- ter all___ the time.___
E -

Teen - y bop - per is our___ new - born king, uh, huh.___
lec - tri - c'lly they_ keep___ a base - ball score.
Bum still cries, "Hey, bud - dy, have you got a dime?"_

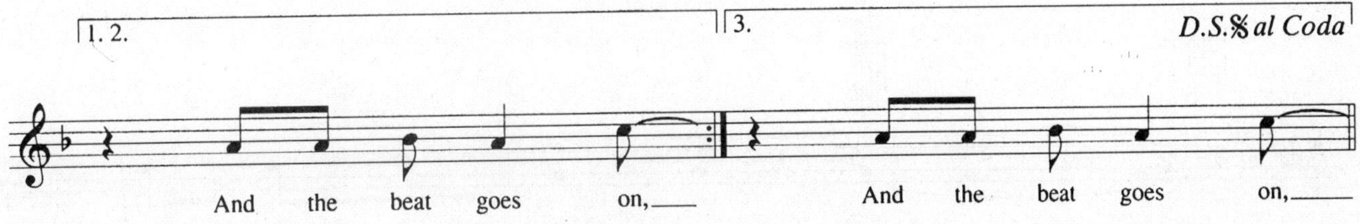
1. 2.
3.
D.S. al Coda
And the beat goes on,___
And the beat goes on,___

Coda
Outro:
w/Riff A (Elec. Gtr. & Bass)
Repeat and fade
And the beat goes on.___
Yes, the beat goes on.___
And the beat goes_ on._

THIS DIAMOND RING

Words and Music by
BOB BRASS, AL KOOPER
and IRWIN LEVINE

Chorus:
G♭
B♭m/F*
E♭m
6fr.
Rhy. Fig. 1
Elec. Gtr.
1. This dia - mond ring does - n't shine for me an - y - more. And this dia - mond ring does - n't
2.3. This dia - mond ring can be some - thing beau - ti - ful. And this dia - mond ring can be
*Bass plays F.
B♭m
mean what it did be - fore. So if you've got some - one whose love is
dreams that are com - ing true. And then your heart won't have to break like
A♭m
4fr.
To Coda
D♭7
end Rhy. Fig. 1
true, let it shine for you.
mine did, if there's love be - hind it.
G
Keyboard
1.
2.
Interlude:
Cm
Cm7
Elec. Gtr. resume Verse Fig. simile
Organ
12-string Elec. Gtr.
f w/tremolo
T
A
B

F/C
Cm
Cm7
F/C
Db7
D.S. % al Coda
Chorus:
w/Rhy. Fig. 1 (Elec. Gtr.)
Db7
Gb
Bbm/F*
Ebm
Coda
Elec. Gtr.
if there's love be - hind it.
(2nd time) you.
This dia-mond ring does-n't shine for me an-y-more. And
Gb
Bbm/F*
Ebm
Bbm
this dia-mond ring does-n't mean what it did be-fore. So if you're got some -
Ebm
Bbm
Abm
Db7
Repeat and fade
one whose love is true, let ot shine for

THREE MARLENAS

Words and Music by
JAKOB DYLAN

G5 Asus D Asus G5 Asus
went, it was - n't how she paid her rent.
1. A -
Chorus:
w/Rhy. Fig. 1 (Gtr. 1) 4 times, simile
*D Asus G5 Asus D Asus G5 Asus
one, two, three Mar - le - nas.
There's
Gtr. 2
(E) (A5) (E5) (A5)
Rhy. Fig. 2
mf hold throughout
*Chords derived from overall tonality.
To Coda 1.
D Asus G5 Asus G5 D Asus G5 Asus G5
got to be some-one we can trust out here a-mong us.
(E) (A5) (E) (A5)
end Rhy. Fig. 2
w/Rhy. Fig. 1 (Gtr. 1) 2 times, simile
D G D Dm/G
2.
G5 Asus G5 type2
Gtr. 1
2. Now
A -
(E) (A5) (E) (A5) (A5)
Gtr. 2
w/Rhy. Fig. 1 (Gtr. 1) 4 times, simile
w/Rhy. Fig. 2 (Gtr. 2) simile
D Asus G5 Asus G5 D Asus G5 Asus
one, two, three Mar - le - nas.
It's

Verse 2:
Now, lookin' out across the city lights,
She thought they'd be a good pair.
Well, he could make a livin' sellin' cars,
Maybe she could work there.
She's gonna pick a star in the night
And pray to make it all right.
She tried so hard not to pick a kite.
She always prayed to headlights.
(To Chorus:)

Verse 3:
Man, I think I'm gonna buy myself a Rolls,
Maybe a Chevrolet.
One where I can pull that top down,
Just let my radio play.
Now, I'm headin' out on that highway.
I'm goin' right out of state.
Now, I ain't lookin' back until I'm gone,
Right through heaven's gate.
(To Chorus:)

TIGHTEN UP

Words and Music by
BILLY BUTTIER and
ARCHIE BELL

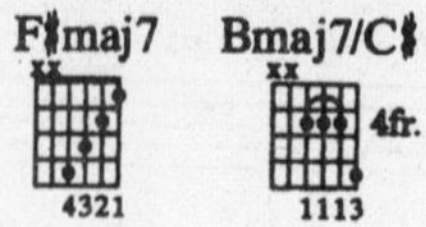

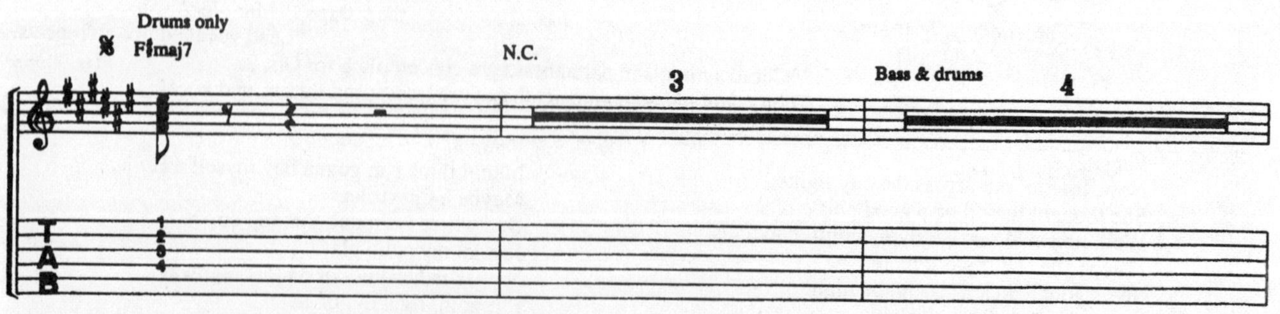

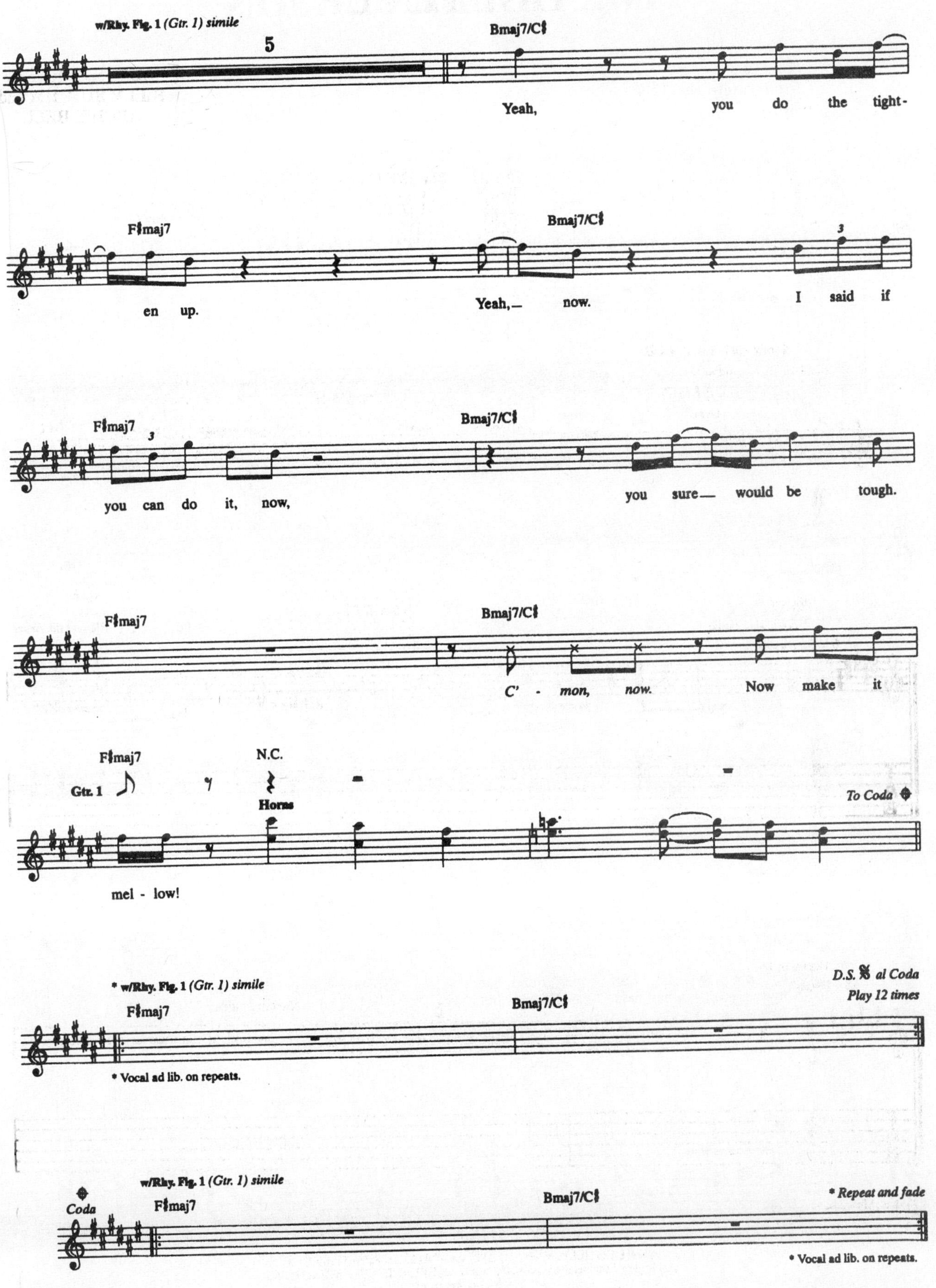
w/Rhy. Fig. 1 (Gtr. 1) simile
5
Bmaj7/C♯
Yeah, you do the tight-
F♯maj7
en up.
Bmaj7/C♯
Yeah,— now. I said if
F♯maj7
you can do it, now,
Bmaj7/C♯
you sure— would be tough.
F♯maj7
Bmaj7/C♯
C' - mon, now. Now make it
F♯maj7
N.C.
Gtr. 1
Horns
To Coda
mel - low!
* w/Rhy. Fig. 1 (Gtr. 1) simile
D.S. 𝄋 al Coda
Play 12 times
F♯maj7
Bmaj7/C♯
* Vocal ad lib. on repeats.
w/Rhy. Fig. 1 (Gtr. 1) simile
Coda
F♯maj7
Bmaj7/C♯
* Repeat and fade
* Vocal ad lib. on repeats.

TIME OF THE SEASON

1.
N.C.
Em
Ah! Ah! Ah! Ah! 2. What's your name,
Bass Gtr.
2.
Organ Solo:
Em7
C(9)
Elec. Gtr.
Cont. rhy. simile
G
Em
C
G/B
Interlude:
Am
E
D.S.% al Coda
Ah! Ah! Ah! Ah! 3. What's your name,
Coda
Outro/Organ Solo:
Repeat and fade

TOM SAWYER

Words by
NEIL PEART and PYE DUBOIS

Music by
GEDDY LEE and ALEX LIFESON

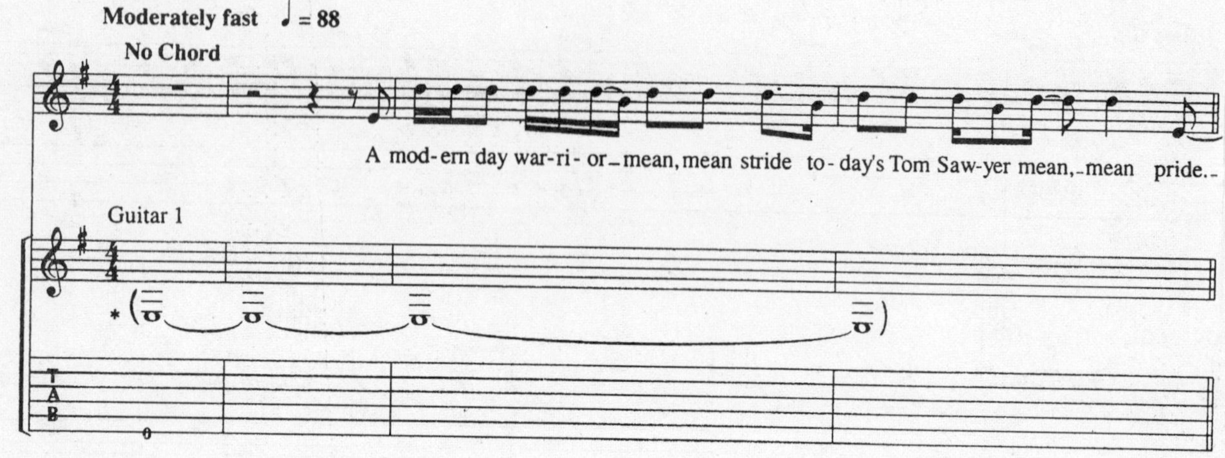
Moderately fast ♩ = 88
No Chord
A mod-ern day war-ri-or mean, mean stride to-day's Tom Saw-yer mean, mean pride.
Guitar 1
T
A
B

E5
D5
E5
A5
E5
Csus2

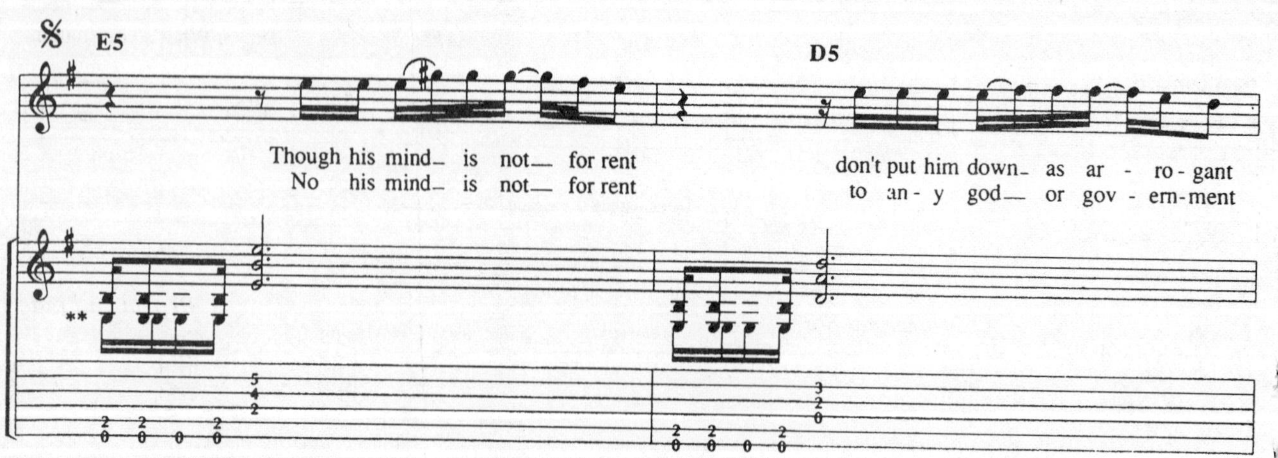
E5
D5
Though his mind is not for rent
No his mind is not for rent
don't put him down as ar-ro-gant
to an-y god or gov-ern-ment

* *Bass and flanged keyboard Intro.*
***Downstemmed figure on repeat.*

E5
A5
E5
Csus2
his re-serve a quiet_ de-fense_ rid-ing out the day's_ e-vents
al-ways hope-ful yet dis-con-tent_ he knows chan-ges are per-ma-nent
C5
B5
A5
C5
B5
A5
E5
D5
the_ riv-er.
the_chang-es.
E5
A5
Dsus4
D
Dsus2
G5
F♯5
Em
E5
What do you say_a-bout his com-pa-ny_ is what you say_a-bout so-ci-e-ty.
And what do you say_a-bout his com-pa-ny_ is what you say_a-bout so-ci-e-ty.

Catch the mist,— catch the myth,- catch the mys - t'ry, catch the drift.-
Catch the wit-ness, catch the wit,— catch the spir - it, catch the spit.-
Bsus2
A5
Bsus2
A5
Bsus2
A5
The world is the world– is—
The world is the world– is—
B5
A5
love and life are deep,— may - be as his skies are
love and life are deep,— may - be as his eyes are
To Coda
E5
wide.—
wide.—
To-day's Tom Saw-yer he gets high on you and the space he in-vades he gets by — on you.

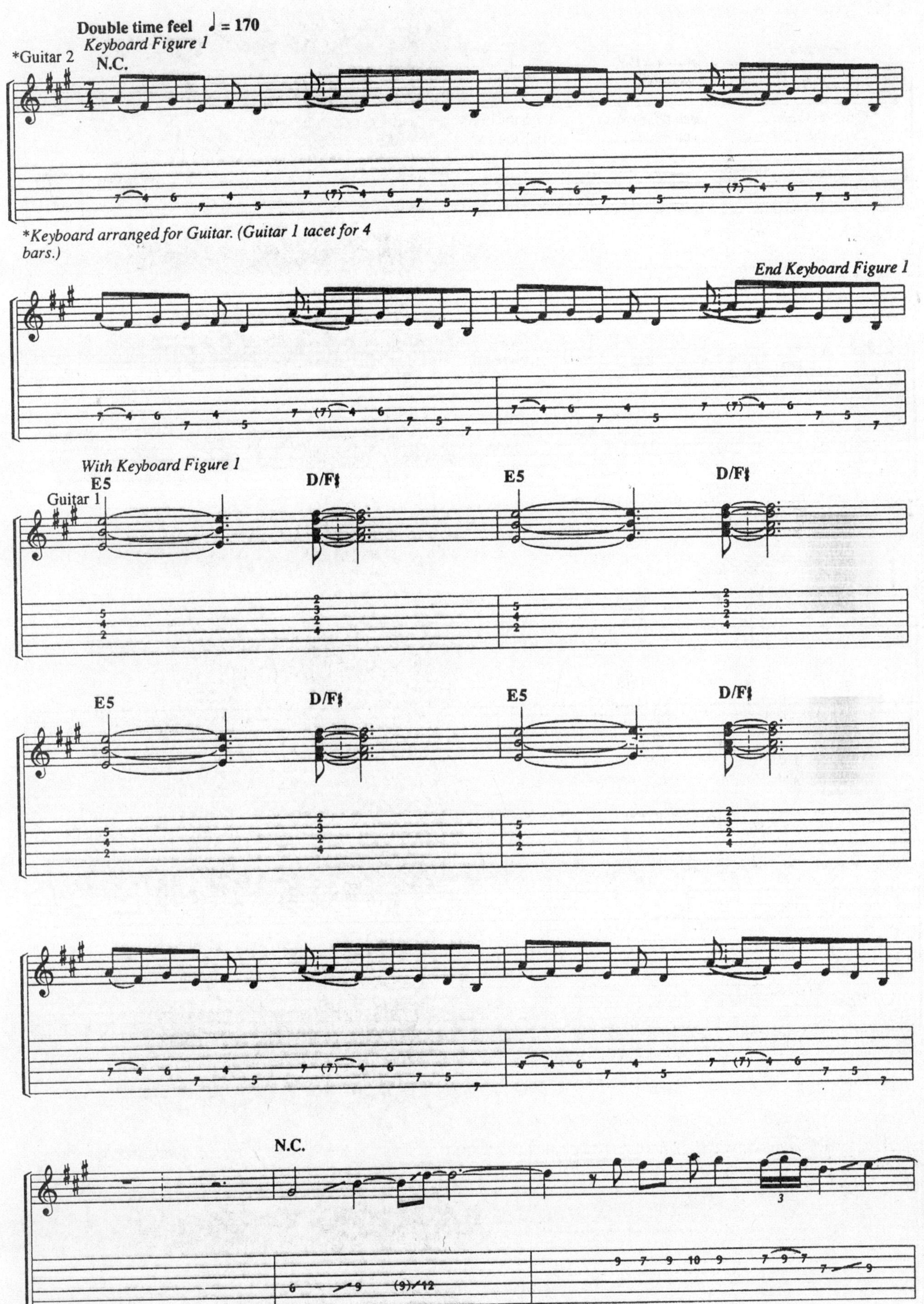
Double time feel ♩ = 170
Keyboard Figure 1
*Guitar 2
N.C.
*Keyboard arranged for Guitar. (Guitar 1 tacet for 4 bars.)
End Keyboard Figure 1
With Keyboard Figure 1
E5
D/F♯
Guitar 1
N.C.

A.H.

8va loco

A.H.

8va

8va

D.S. 𝄋 al Coda 𝄌
End double time feel ♩ = 88
E5
D5
A5
Csus2
Coda
N.C.
Ex- it the war-ri- or to-day's Tom Saw-yer he gets high on you___ and the en- er- gy you trade_ he gets
Double time feel ♩ = 170
Repeat and fade
right on to the fric - tion of the day.___
(Vocal 1st time only)
Let ring
Let ring
Let ring
Let ring

TONIGHT, TONIGHT

Tune down 1/2 step:
⑥ = E♭ ③ = G♭
⑤ = A♭ ② = B♭
④ = D♭ ① = E♭

Words and Music by
BILLY CORGAN

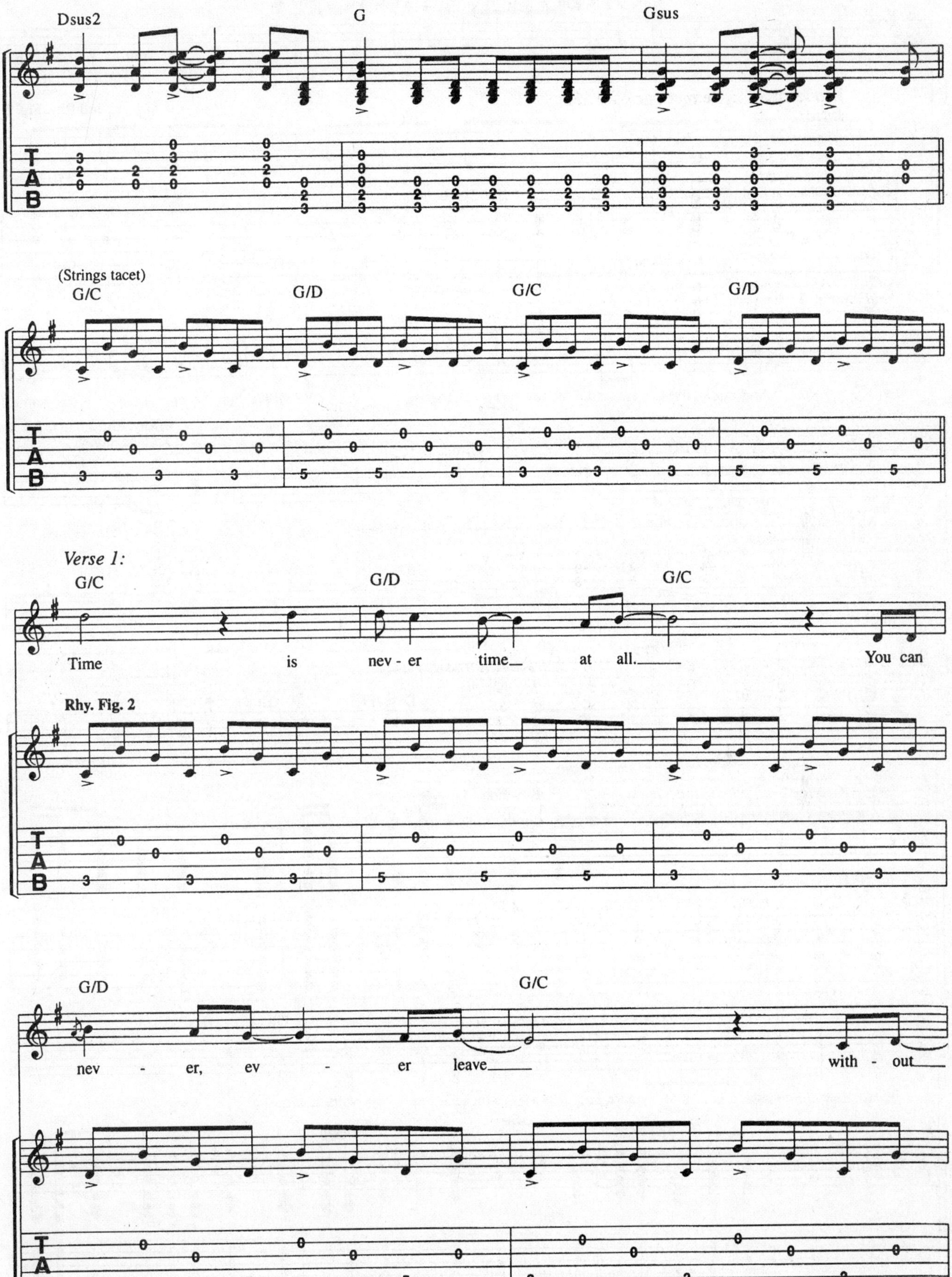

Dsus2 G Gsus

(Strings tacet)

G/C G/D G/C G/D

Verse 1:

G/C G/D G/C

Time is nev - er time at all. You can

Rhy. Fig. 2

G/D
Em
G
leav - ing a piece of youth.
end Rhy. Fig. 2
w/Rhy. Fig. 2 (Gtrs. 1 & 2)
G/C
G/D
G/C
G/D
And our lives are for - ev - er changed. We will nev - er be the same.
w/Rhy. Fig. 2 (Gtrs. 1 & 2)
1st 5 bars only
G/C
G/D
Em
G
G/C
The more you change, the less you feel. Be - lieve,
G/D
G/C
G/D
G/C
be - lieve in me, be - lieve,
Pre-Chorus 1:
(Strings in)
G/D
G
Dsus/F♯
Em
be - lieve that life
Gtrs. 1 & 2
Rhy. Fig. 3
cresc.
f
Am
C
G
Dsus/F♯
can change, that you're not stuck in vain.

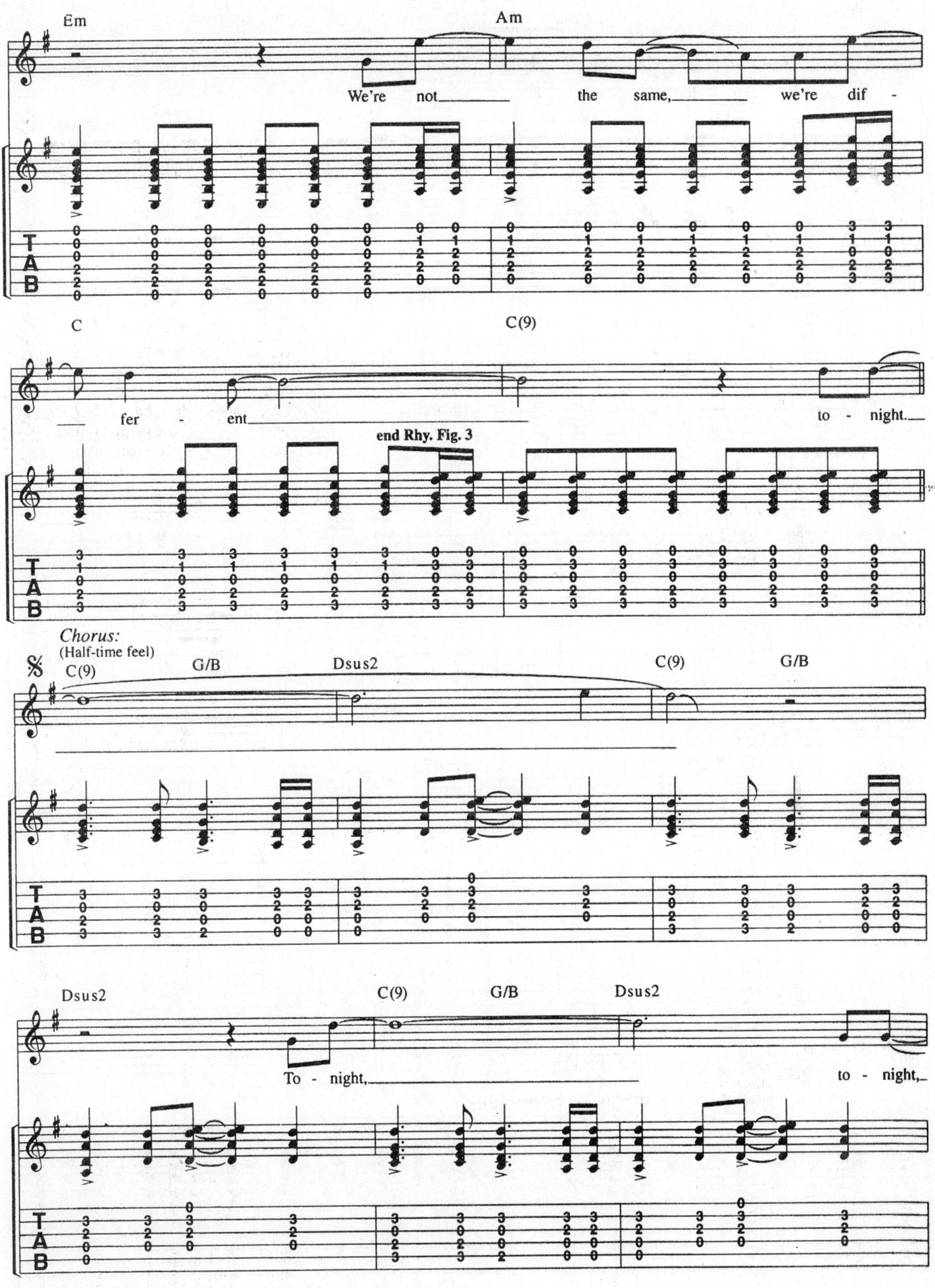
Em
Am
We're not the same, we're dif -
C
C(9)
fer - ent
to - night.
end Rhy. Fig. 3
Chorus:
(Half-time feel)
C(9)
G/B
Dsus2
C(9)
G/B
Dsus2
C(9)
G/B
Dsus2
To - night,
to - night,

To Coda
(Double-time feel)
Em
A(9)
(Half-time feel)
C(9)
G/B
so
bright.
To - night,
Slight P.M.
Dsus2
C(9)
G/B
Dsus2
to - night.
(Double-time feel)
G
Gsus
G
Gsus
Em

Em(♭6)
Em
Em(♭6)
Verse 2:
w/Rhy. Fig. 1 (Gtrs. 1 & 2)
G
Gsus
G
Though you know you're nev - er sure, but you're
Gsus
Em
Em(♭6)
sure you could be right if you held your - self up to
w/Rhy. Fig. 1 (Gtrs. 1 & 2) 1st 7 bars only
Em
Em(♭6)
G
Gsus
G
the light. And the em - bers nev - er fade in your
Gsus
Em
Em(♭6)
Em
cit - y by the lake, the place where you were born.
Em(♭6)
G/C
G/D
Be - lieve, be - lieve
G/C
G/D
in me, be - lieve.

G/C
G/D
Be - lieve
cresc.
Pre-Chorus 2:
w/Rhy. Fig. 3 (Gtrs. 1 & 2)
G Dsus/F♯ Em Am C
in the res - o - lute, the ur - gen - cy of now.
G Dsus/F♯ Em Am C
D.S. 𝄋 al Coda
And if you be - lieve there's not a chance to - night.
Coda
Dsus2 G Dsus/F♯
to - night.
Rhy. Fig. 4
Em Am C(9)
We'll cru - ci - fy the in - sin - cere to - night.
end Rhy. Fig. 4
w/Rhy. Fig. 4 (Gtrs. 1 & 2) 5 times
G Dsus/F♯ Em Am C(9)
To - night. We'll make things right, we'll feel it all to - night.

G Dsus/F♯ Em Am C(9) G Dsus/F♯
To - night. We'll find a way to of - fer up the night, to - night.
Em Am C(9) G Dsus/F♯ Em
The in - de - scrib - a - ble mo - ments of your life, to - night. The im - pos -
Am C(9) G Dsus/F♯ Em
si - ble is pos - si - ble, to - night. To - night. Be - lieve
Slower ♩ = ca. 120
(Strings tacet)
Asus2 C(9) G/C
in me as I be - lieve in you, to - night.
Gtr. 1
rit.
mp
freely
G/D G/C G/D
To - night, to - night. To - night,
G/C G/D G D/F♯ Em
to - night.
Gtrs. 1 & 2
f rit.

TOWN WITHOUT PITY

To Coda
1.
Em7
Gm
D/A
A7(♯5)
C/G
G7
F♯7sus
F♯7(♯5)
those in___ love would know what a town___ with - out pit - y can do. 2. If we
___ ti - gers___ in a cage. What a
___ a - ny - thing sur - vive when these
(8va)
10
2.
Bridge:
D/A
A7(♯5)
A7
A13
D
C/D
D7
G
G6
town_ with-out pit - y___ can do.___ Though_ young have__ prob - lems, man - y
8va
12/14 12 10 10
12/14 12 11
Gmaj7
G6
G
G7/B
F
Esus
E
prob - lems,_ we need an un - der - stand - ing heart.___ Why__ don't they__
8/10 12 9

A
A6
Amaj7
F♯m7
— help us, — try — to — help us — be - fore this
Bm(11)
E6
A7
F♯7(♯5 ♭9)
D.S. 𝄋 al Coda
plain gran - ite plan - et falls a - part? — 3. Take — these
Coda
D/A
A7(♯5)
C/G
G7
F♯7sus
F♯7
Gmaj7
G7
A7
A13
lit - tle minds tear you in two? What a town — with - out pit - y — can

Verse (Instrumental):
D
5fr.
1333
G7(♯5)
3fr.
1 234
Cm
3fr.
13421
do.
1/2
1/2
Fm
134111
How_ can
Db6
4fr.
13333
C7
3fr.
13141
Fm7
131141
Abm
4fr.
134111
Eb/Bb
6fr.
1 333
Bb7(♯5)
6fr.
1 234
Db/Ab
4fr.
1 333
Ab7
4fr.
1 243
we keep_ love a-live? How can_ a-ny-thing sur-vive when these lit - tle minds tear you in
8va
TAB

G7sus
G7
Abmaj7
Ab7
Ab6
Ab7
G7(#5)
G7
two? What a town_ with-out pit - y can do. No, it
Cm
G7/B
Gm/Bb
Am7(b5)
Ab7
G7 N.C.
Freely
Outro:
A tempo
is - n't ver - y pret - ty what a town with-out pit - y can_ do._
Cm
Fm
Cm(maj7)
Elec. Gtr.

TRASH

Words and Music by
DAVID JOHANSEN
and SYLVAIN SYLVAIN

D5
C5
knife a - way.
1. And
(Ooh, ooh, ooh, ooh.
Gtrs. 1 & 2

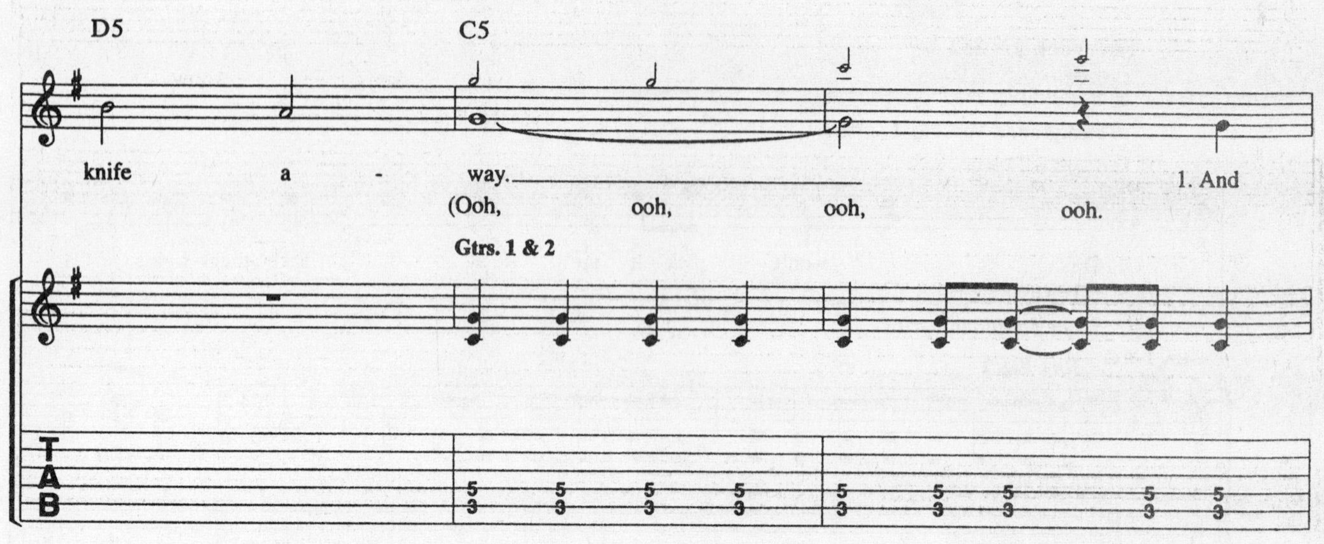

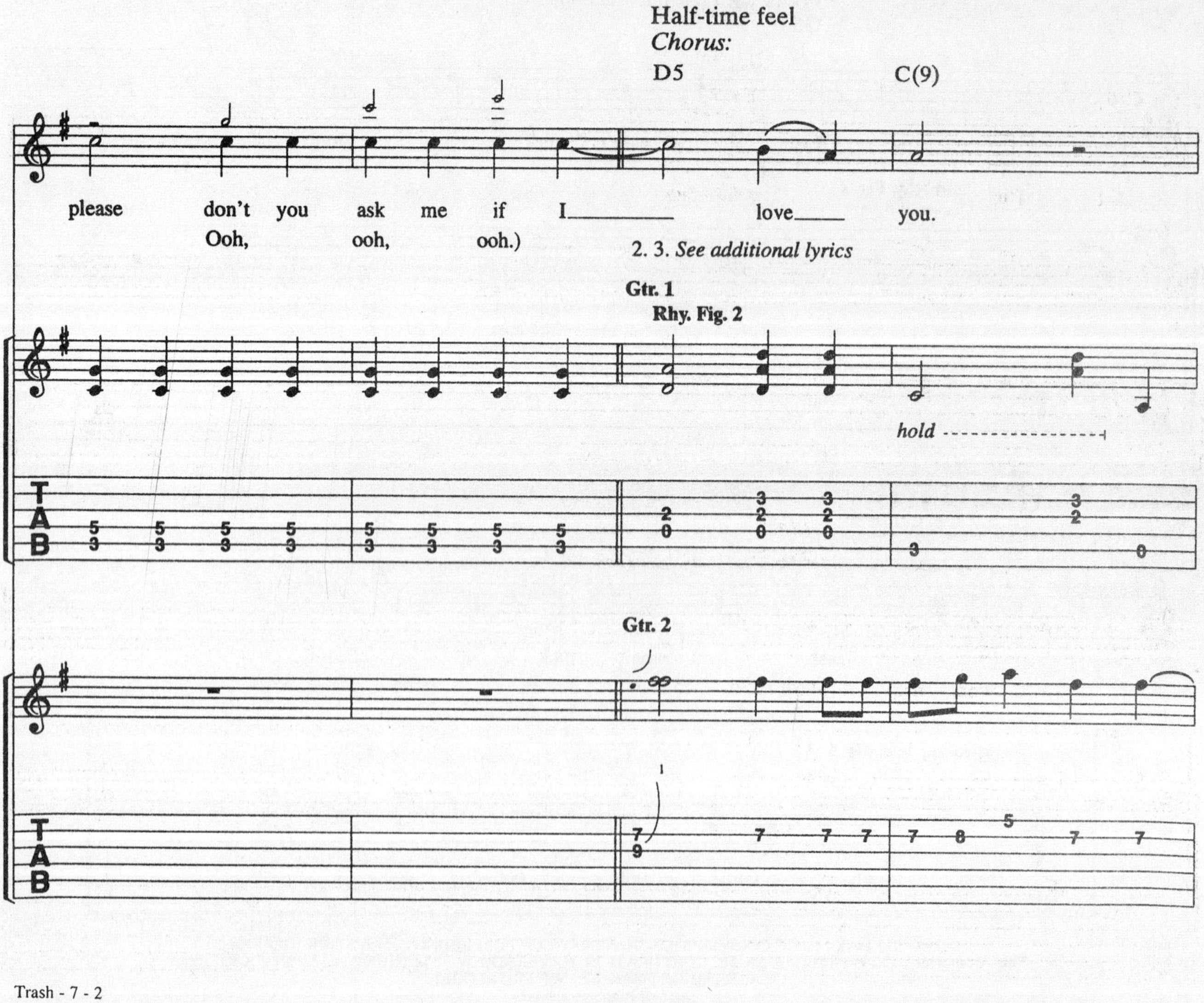

Half-time feel
Chorus:
D5
C(9)
please don't you ask me if I love you.
Ooh, ooh, ooh.)
2. 3. See additional lyrics
Gtr. 1
Rhy. Fig. 2
hold
Gtr. 2

Bm7
D5
w/Rhy. Fig. 2 (Gtr. 1) simile
If you don't know
end Rhy. Fig. 2
hold
C(9)
Bm7
1. 2.
D5
what I'm do - ing, what you know is...
Gtr. 2
Bridge:
3.
w/Rhy. Fig. 2 (Gtr. 1) 2 times, simile
D5
C(9)
Bm7
I won - der, what did I feel with you?
8va
hold bend

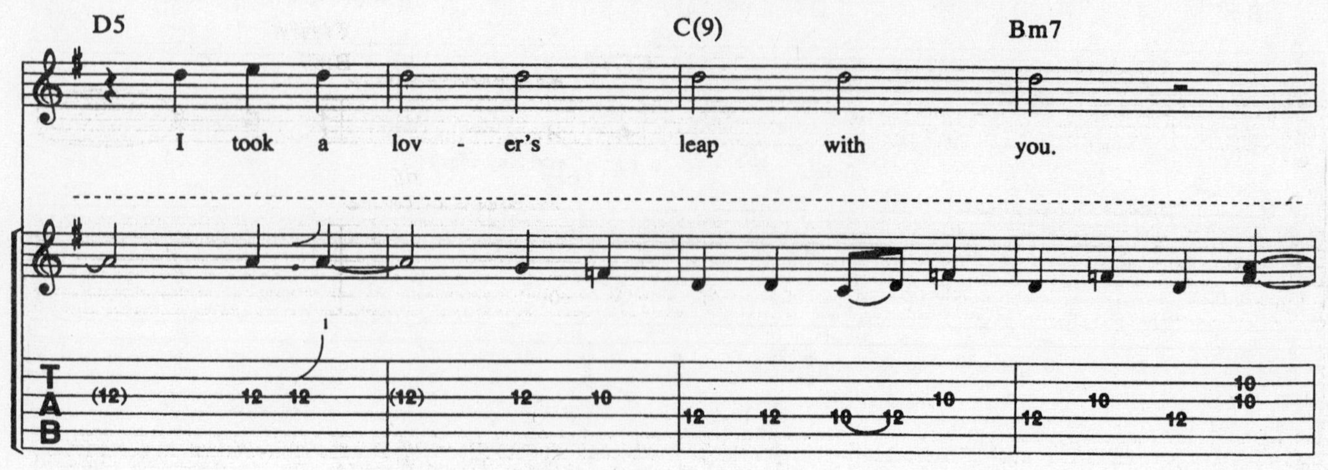
D5
C(9)
Bm7
I took a lov - er's leap with you.

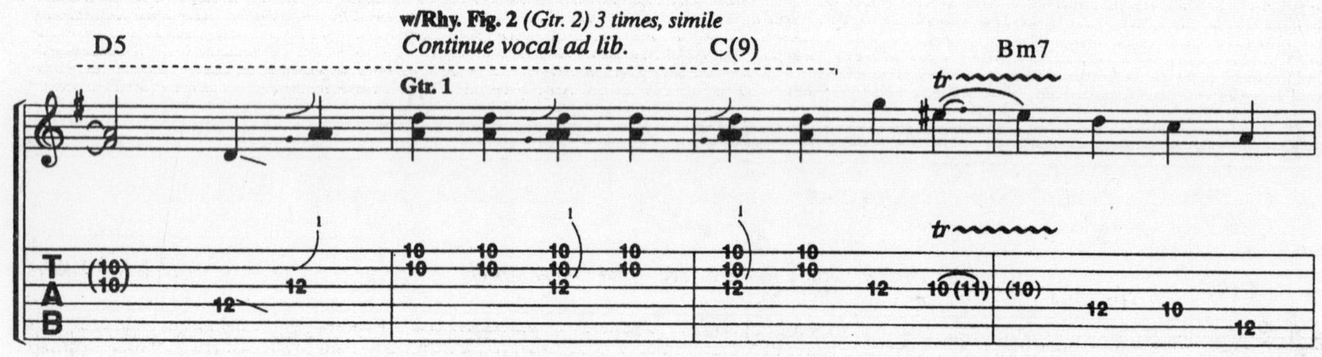
w/Rhy. Fig. 2 (Gtr. 2) 3 times, simile
Continue vocal ad lib.
D5
C(9)
Bm7
Gtr. 1

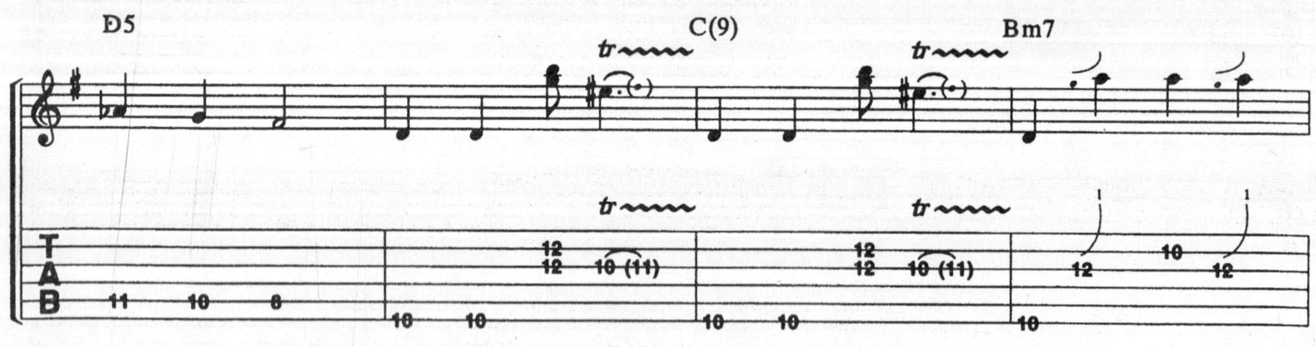
D5
C(9)
Bm7

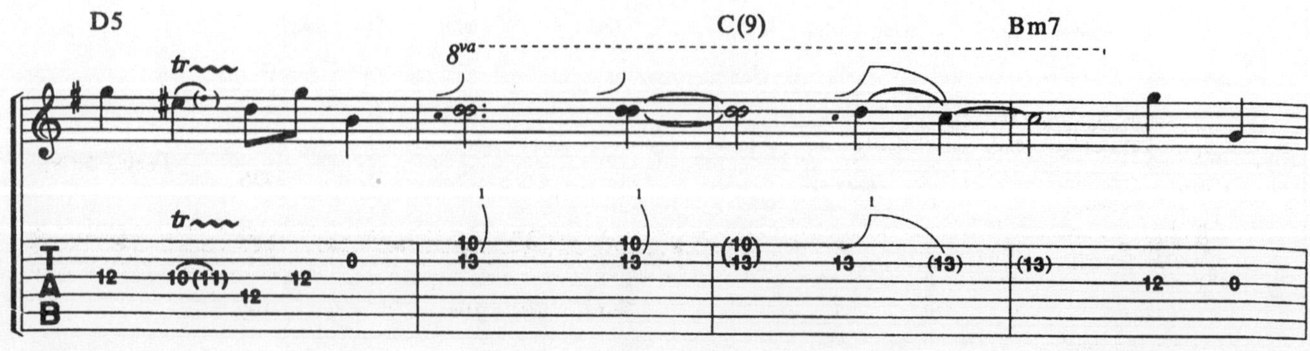
D5
C(9)
Bm7

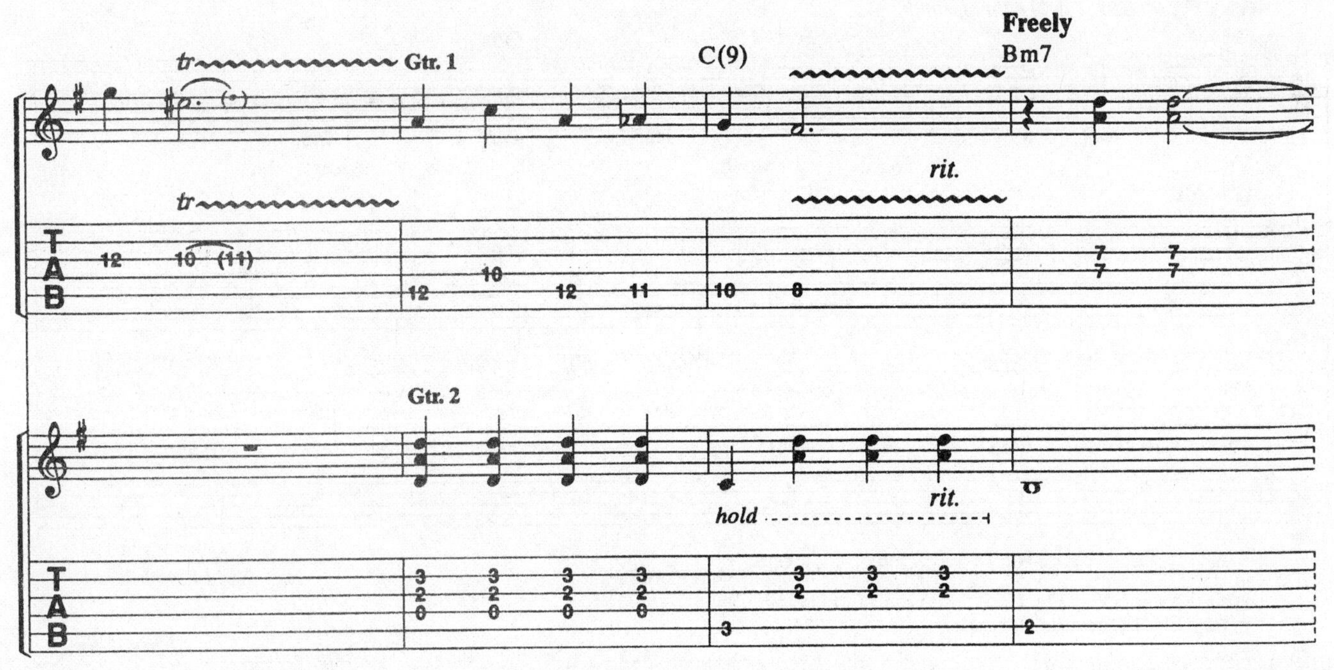
Freely
Gtr. 1
C(9)
Bm7
rit.
Gtr. 2
hold
rit.

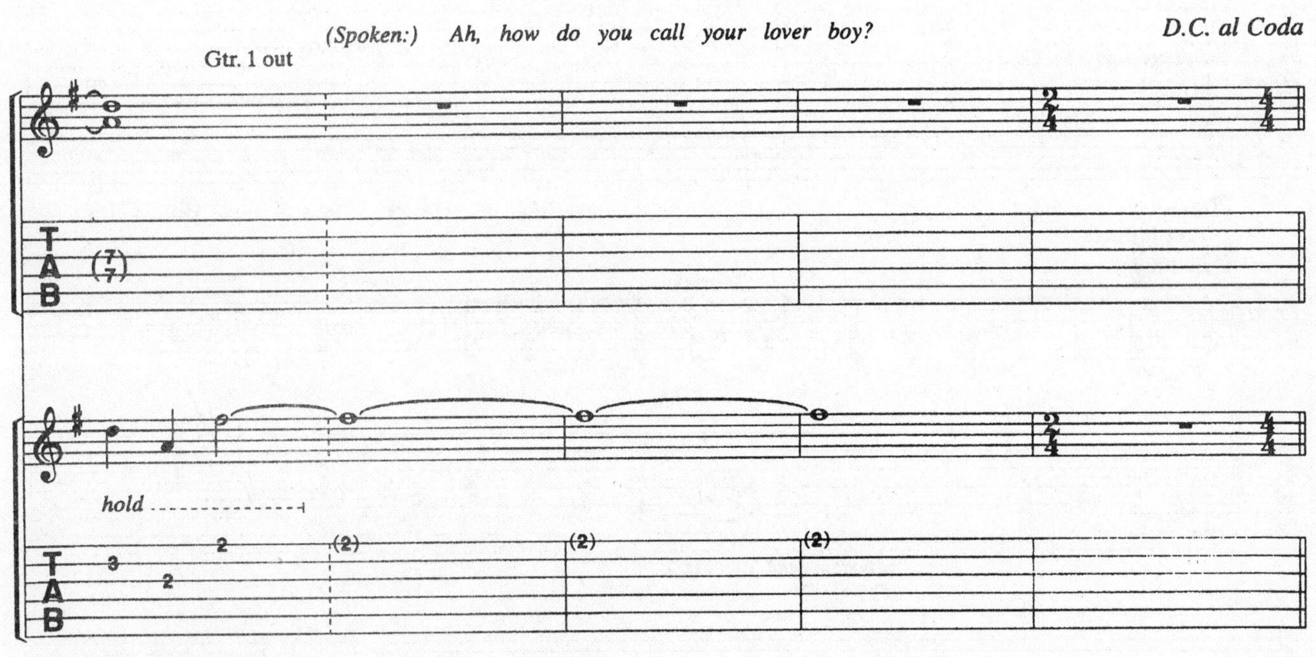
(Spoken:) Ah, how do you call your lover boy?
D.C. al Coda
Gtr. 1 out
hold

w/Background Voc. Fig. 1
w/Rhy. Fig. 1 (Gtrs. 1 & 2) simile
Coda
G5
C5
D5
Play 5 times
Trash, won't pick it up. Don't take your life a - way.
(Trash.)

w/Background Voc. Fig. 1 (4 times, simile)
w/Rhy. Fig. 1 (Gtrs. 1 & 2) 4 times, simile
G5
C5
D5
G5
Trash.
(Trash.)
Woah, woah.
My sweet ba - by.
Yeah, yeah.
C5
D5
G5
Oh, oh, trash.
Woah,
C5
D5
G5
C5
D5
woah, ba - by, you're the one.
w/Background Voc. Fig. 1
w/Rhy. Fig. 1 (Gtrs. 1 & 2) simile
G5
C5
D5
Play 4 times
Trash,
(Trash.)
pick it up.
Take them lights a - way.
w/Background Voc. Fig. 1
G5
C5
Trash.
(Trash.)
Don't take my knife a -
Gtrs. 1 & 2
D5
w/Background Voc. Fig. 1
G5
way. Oh,
trash.
(Trash.)
Don't

Verse 2:
Trash, won't pick it up.
Take them lights away.
Trash, won't get it up.
Don't throw your love away.
Trash, won't pick it up.
Don't try to take my knife away.

Chorus 2:
And please don't you ask me if I love you.
'Cause I don't know why I do up my nose.

Verse 3:
Trash, won't pick it up.
Take them lights away.
Trash, won't pick it up.
Don't take my knife away.
Trash, won't pick it up.
Forgot to take them all away.

Chorus 3:
And please don't you ask me if I love you.
'Cause I don't know if I do.

Verse 4:
Trash, won't pick it up.
Take them lights away.
Trash, don't pick it up.
Don't put that knife away.

TRUCKIN'

Words by ROBERT HUNTER
Music by JERRY GARCIA, BOB WEIR
and PHIL LESH

B
doo - dah man. To - geth - er, more or less in line.
Gtr. 1
A
A7
E
Just keep truck - in' on.
Gtr. 1
end Rhy. Fig. 1
Gtr. 2
Riff A
P.M.

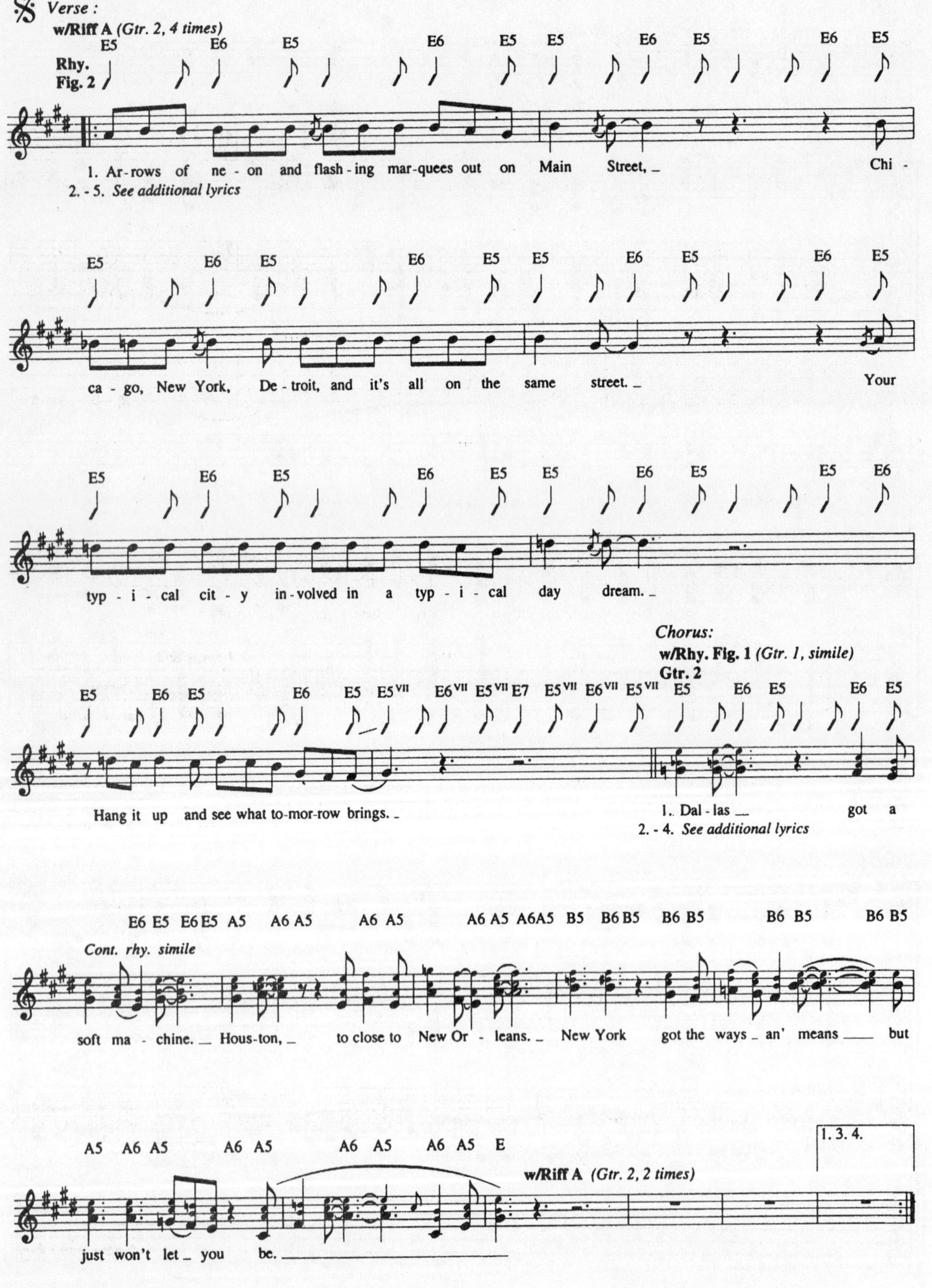
Verse:
w/Riff A (Gtr. 2, 4 times)
Rhy. Fig. 2
1. Ar-rows of ne-on and flash-ing mar-quees out on Main Street, _ Chi-
2.-5. See additional lyrics
ca-go, New York, De-troit, and it's all on the same street. _ Your
typ-i-cal cit-y in-volved in a typ-i-cal day dream. _
Chorus:
w/Rhy. Fig. 1 (Gtr. 1, simile)
Gtr. 2
Hang it up and see what to-mor-row brings. _
1. Dal-las _ got a
2.-4. See additional lyrics
Cont. rhy. simile
soft ma-chine. _ Hous-ton, _ to close to New Or-leans. _ New York got the ways _ an' means _ but
just won't let _ you be. _
w/Riff A (Gtr. 2, 2 times)
1. 3. 4.

2. 5.
Bridge:
E F# G# A N.C.
Gtr. 1
Some - times the light's all shin - in' on me.
Gtr. 2
Gtrs. 1 & 2
P.M.
A D N.C.
Oth - er times I can bare - ly see.
D Bm F#
Late - ly it oc - curs to me

To Coda
Bm
F♯
A5
A6
A5
A6
A5
A6
A5
A6
A5
E5
E6
E5
E6
E5
what a long, strange trip it's been.
8va
D.S. al Coda
Coda
E
D5
E
D5
E
A5
E
Gtr. 1

Verse 2:
Most of the cats that you meet on street speak of true love.
Most of the time they're sitting and crying at home.
One of these days they know they gotta get going
Out of the door and down to the street all alone.

Chorus 2:
Truckin' like the doo da man.
Once told me you got to play your hand.
Sometimes the cards ain't worth a dime
If you don't lay them down.
(To Bridge:)

Verse 3:
What in the world ever became of sweet Jane?
She lost her sparkle, you know, she isn't the same.
Living on reds, vitamin C and cocaine,
All a friend can say is ain't it a shame.

Chorus 3:
Truckin' up to Buffalo. Been thinkin' you got to mellow slow.
It takes time, you pick a place to go,
And just keep truckin' on.

Verse 4:
Sitting and staring out of the hotel window.
Got a tip they're gonna kick the door in again.
I'd like to get some sleep before I travel,
But if you've got a warrant, I guess you're gonna come in.

Chorus 4:
Busted down on Bourbon Street,
Set up like a bowling pin,
Knocked down, it gets to wearing thin,
They just won't let you be.

Verse 5:
You're sick of hangin' around and you'd like to travel.
Get tired of traveling, you want to settle down.
I guess they can't revoke your soul for trying.
Get out of the door, light out and look all around.
(To Bridge:)

UNCLE JOHN'S BAND

Words by
ROBERT HUNTER

Music by
JERRY GARCIA

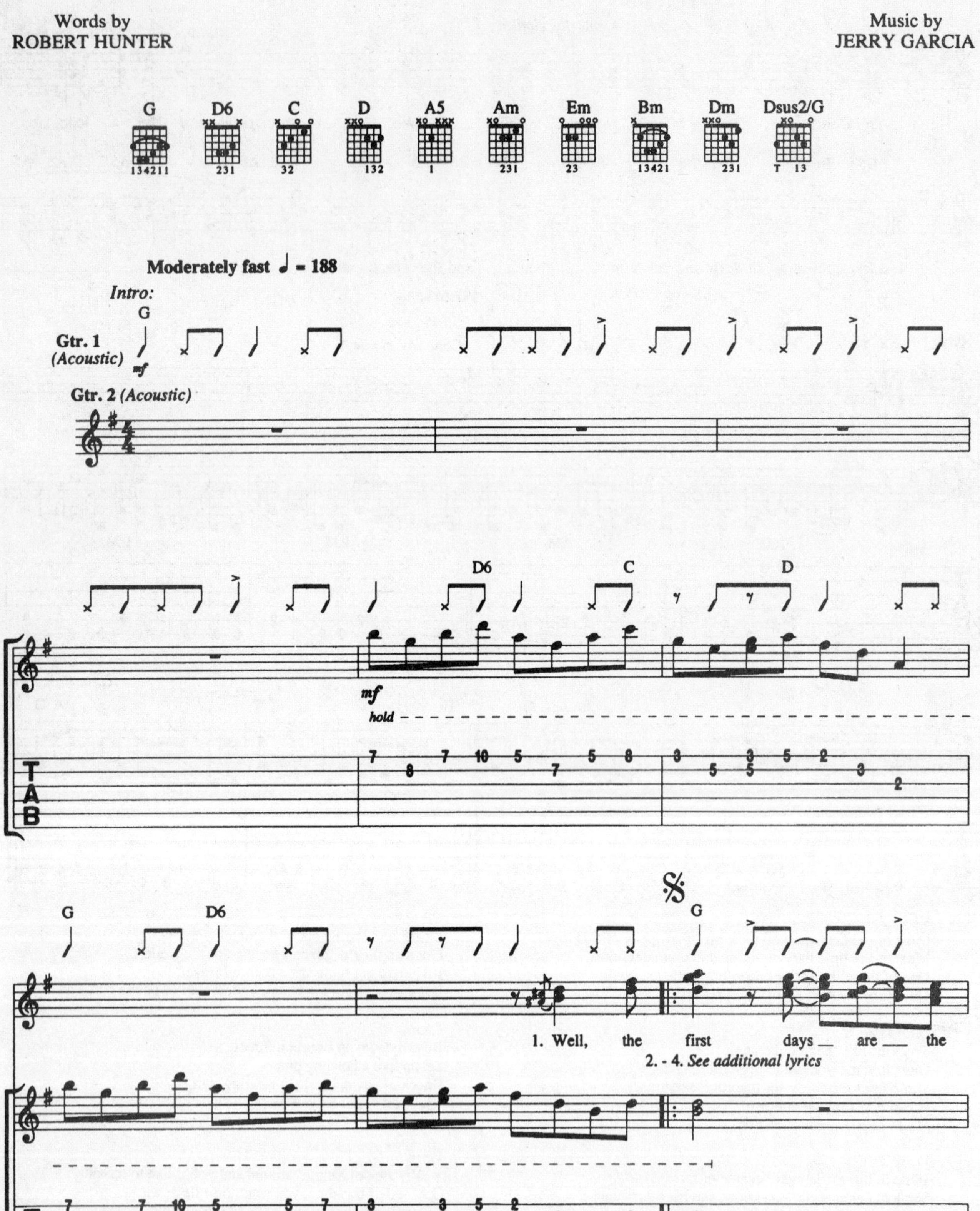

C
G
hard - est days, don't you wor - ry an - y more. 'Cause
C
G
when life looks like eas - y street, there is dan - ger at your door.
A5
Am
A5
Am
Em
C
D
Think this through with me; let me know your mind.
C
D
G
D
C
G
D
G
Woah - oh, what I want to know is, are you kind?
1. 3.
2. 4.
To Coda
G
2. It's a
C
Am
G
D
God damn, well I de - clare, have you seen the like? Their
C
G
D
C
D
walls are built of can - non balls; their mot-to is: "Don't tread on me."

Chorus:
G C A5 Am G D
Come hear Un - cle John's band play - ing to the tide.
C G D C D
Come with me or go a - lone, he's come to take his chil - dren home.
G D6 C D G Bm C D G
Gtr. 2
f
G Bm C D G Bm C D
D.S. al Coda
Coda 1
Chorus:
G C Am G
Come hear Un - cle John's Band by the ri - ver - side.

D
C
G
D
C
Got some things to talk a - bout here be-side the ris -
ing tide.
Come hear Un - cle John's Band
Am
playing to the tide.
Come on a - long or go
To Coda 2
a - lone, he's come to take his chil - dren home.
Dm
Play 7 times
Gtr. 1
Gtr. 2
hold
Wo oh, what I want to know:

Verse 2 :
It's a buck dancer's choice my friends;
Better take my advice.
You know all the rules by now
And the fire from the ice.
Will you come with me?
Won't you come with me?
Woah oh, what I want to know:
Will you come with me?
(To Guitar Solo:)

Verse 3 :
It's the same story the crow told me,
It's the only one he knows.
Like the morning sun you come
And like the wind you go.
Ain't no time to hate;
Barely time to wait
Woah oh, what I want to know:
Where does the time go?

Verse 4 :
I live in a silver mine
And I call it Beggars Tomb.
I got me a violin
And I beg you call the tune.
Anybody's choice,
I can hear your voice.
No oh, what I want to know:
How does the song go?
(To Chorus :)

UNSKINNY BOP

Words and Music by
B. MICHAELS, B. DALL,
C.C. DEVILLE and R. ROCKETT

A
G/A*
D/A
why can't you sit still?
Like
Gtr. 3
8va
Verse 2 only
Gtr. 1
Gtr. 2
A
G/A*
D/A
gas - o - line, you want to pump - me,
and leave -

A
G/A*
D/A
— me when you get your fill, — yeah.
Ev-'ry
Pre-Chorus:
(E)
(G)
(E)
(G)
time I touch you, you get hot, —
I wan-na make love, you nev - er stop, —
Gtr. 3
Gtr. 1

(E)
(G)
(E)
(G)
come up for air, you pull me to the floor. What's been go-ing on in that head of
Gtr. 2
8va
Gtr. 1
Chorus:
(A)
G5
D
yours?
Un - skin-ny bop
just blows me a - way, yeah.
Gtr. 2
(A)
G5
D
Un - skin-ny bop bop, all night and day.

(A)
G5
D
Un - skin-ny bop bop bop bop, she just love to play,
1/2
T
A
B
E
1.
2.
G5
G#5
un - skin-ny bop, no-thing more to say.
2. You
Bridge:
D5
A
(D)
(A)
You're say - in' my love won't do ya,
D5
A
D/A
A
that ain't love writ - ten on your face

D5
A
Well, hon - ey, I can see right through ya. We'll see
E5
who's rid - ing who at the end of the race?
Guitar Solo:
A5
G5
D
8va
Gtr. 1
Gtr. 2

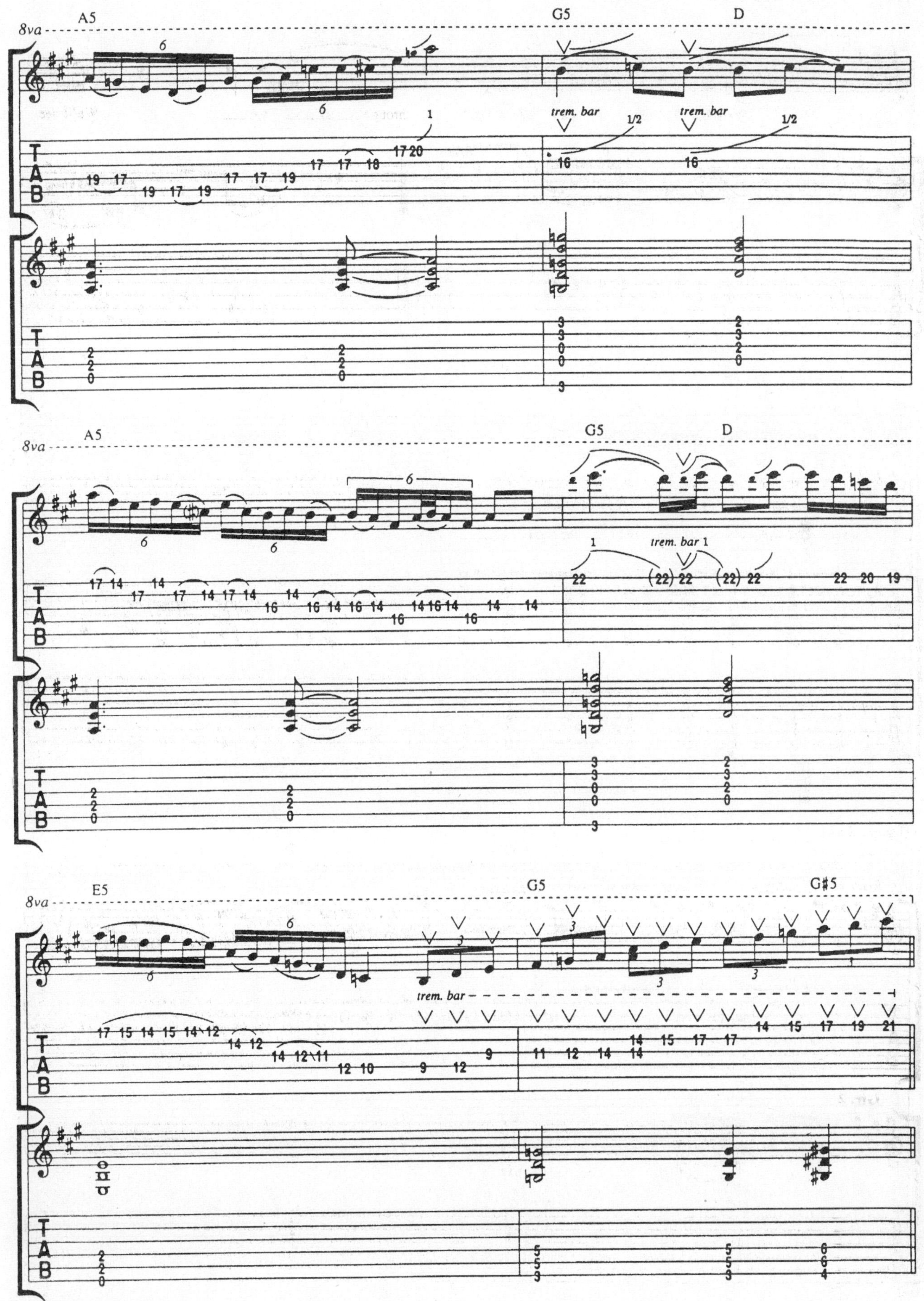
A5
G5
D
8va
trem. bar
1/2
E5
G#5
T
A
B

N.C.
What's right,
what's wrong, _
8va
loco
(D)
G5
G#
what's left,
what the hell is go - ing on?

Verse 2:

You look at me so funny,
Love bite got you acting oh so strange.
You got too many bees in your honey.
Am I just another word in your page?
Yeah, yeah.

(To Pre-Chorus:)

UNINVITED

Music and Lyrics by ALANIS MORISSETTE

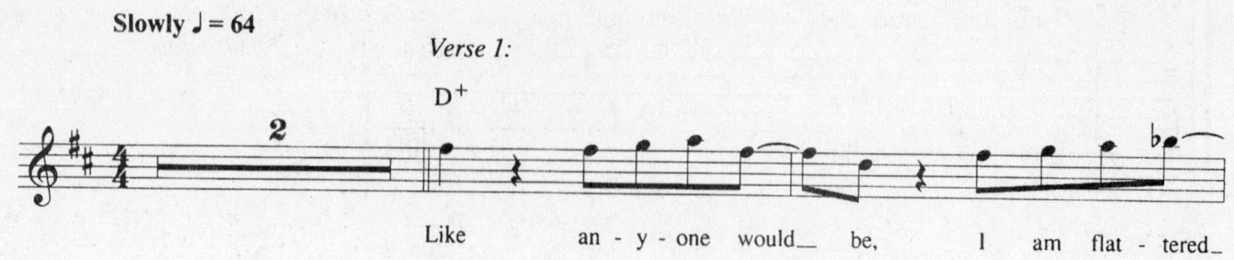
Slowly ♩ = 64
Verse 1:
D+
2
Like an - y - one would_ be, I am flat - tered_

Gm
D+
_ by your fas - ci - na - tion with_ me. Like an - y hot - blood - ed wom -

Gm
D+
- an, I have sim - ply___ want - ed an ob - ject to crave._ But

D7
G
D
you, you're not_ al - lowed; you're un - in - vit - ed: an un - for - tu -

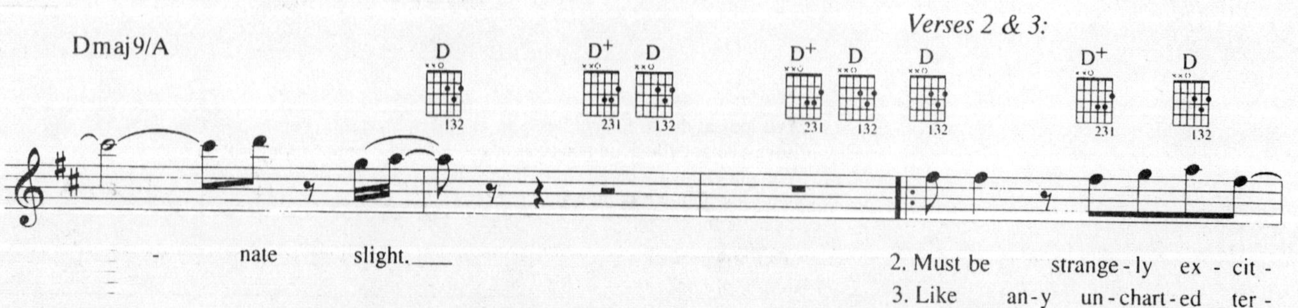
Dmaj9/A
D
D+
D
D+
D
D
Verses 2 & 3:
D+
D
132
231
132
231
132
132
231
132
- nate slight.___
2. Must be strange - ly ex - cit -
3. Like an - y un - chart - ed ter -

D+ D Gm D D+ D
- ing to___ watch the sto - ic squirm.___
- ri - tor - y, I must___ seem great - ly in - trigu - ing.
D+ D D+ D Gm
Must be some - what heart - en - ing to___ watch shep - herd___ meet shep - herd.___
You speak of my love___ like you___ have ex - per - i - enced love like mine be -
D D+ D D7 G
___ But you, you're not___ al - lowed; you're un - in - vit -
fore. But this is not___ al - lowed; you're un - in - vit -
D Dmaj9/A D D+ D D+ D
- ed: an un - for - tu - nate slight.___
- ed: an un - for - tu - nate slight.___
Outro:
D+ D D+ D D+
2
I don't think you un - wor - thy, I need a mo -
Play 4 times
Gm D D D+ D D+ D Dmaj9/A
- ment to de - lib - er - ate.___

VOODOO

Words and Music by
SALVATORE ERNA and ROB MERRILL

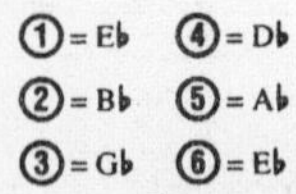

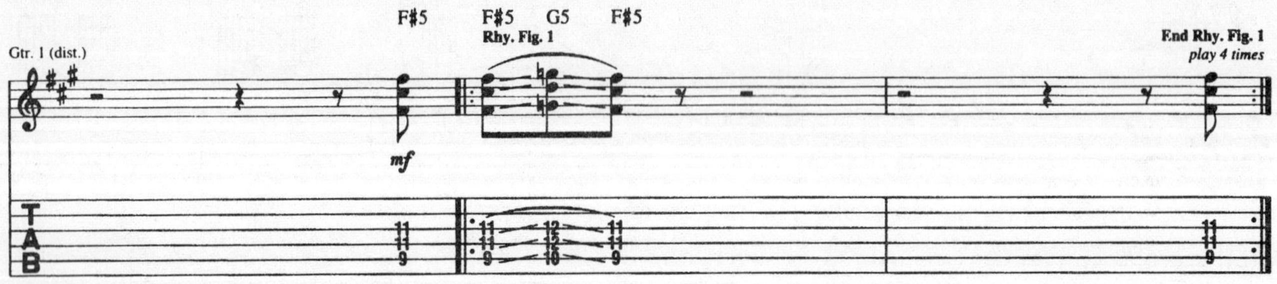

G5 F#5
G5 F#5
no more rea - son to stay.
why my thoughts aren't so clear.
Freez - ing feel -
De - mons dream -

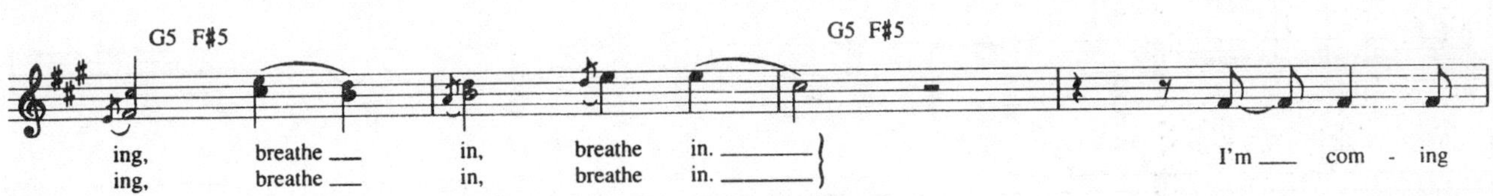
G5 F#5
G5 F#5
ing, breathe in, breathe in.
ing, breathe in, breathe in.
I'm com - ing

Chorus
E5
F#5 N.C.
F#5
E5
F#5
back a - gain.
I'm not the one who's so far a - way when I
Gtr. 1
Rhy. Fig. 2
P.M.

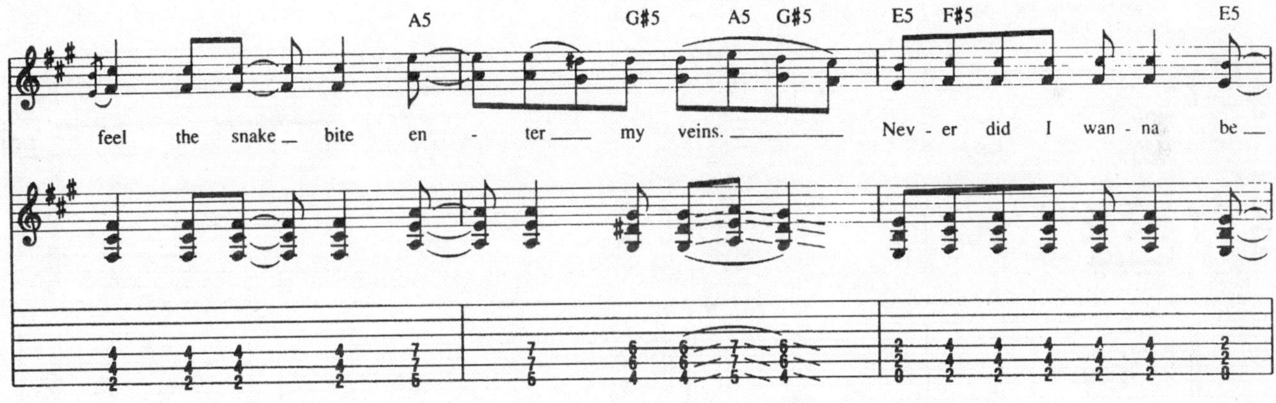
A5
G#5
A5 G#5
E5 F#5
E5
feel the snake bite en - ter my veins.
Nev - er did I wan - na be

1.
F#5
E5
F#5
here a - gain, and I don't re - mem - ber why I came.
End Rhy. Fig. 2

2.
Interlude
Gtr. 1: w/ Rhy. Fig. 1, 4 times
A5
N.C. (G#5) (A5) (G#5) (E5)
don't re - mem - ber why I came.
Gtr. 1: w/ Rhy. Fig. 2
F#5 E5 F#5 A5 G#5 A5 G#5
I'm not the one who's so far a - way when I feel the snake bite en - ter my veins.
To Coda
E5 F#5 E5 F#5 E5 F#5
Nev - er did I wan - na be here a - gain, and I don't re - mem - ber why I came.
Interlude
w/ Lead Voc. ad lib. 2nd & 3rd times
F#5 G5 F#5
play 3 times
Yeah,
Gtr. 1
w/ Lead Voc. ad lib. next 4 meas.
E5
Voc. Fig. 1
F#5 G5 F#5
End Voc. Fig. 1
Bkgd. Voc.: w/ Voc. Fig. 1
E5
yeah, yeah, yeah, yeah, yeah, oh, yeah.
(Yeah, yeah.)
Voo - doo, voo -

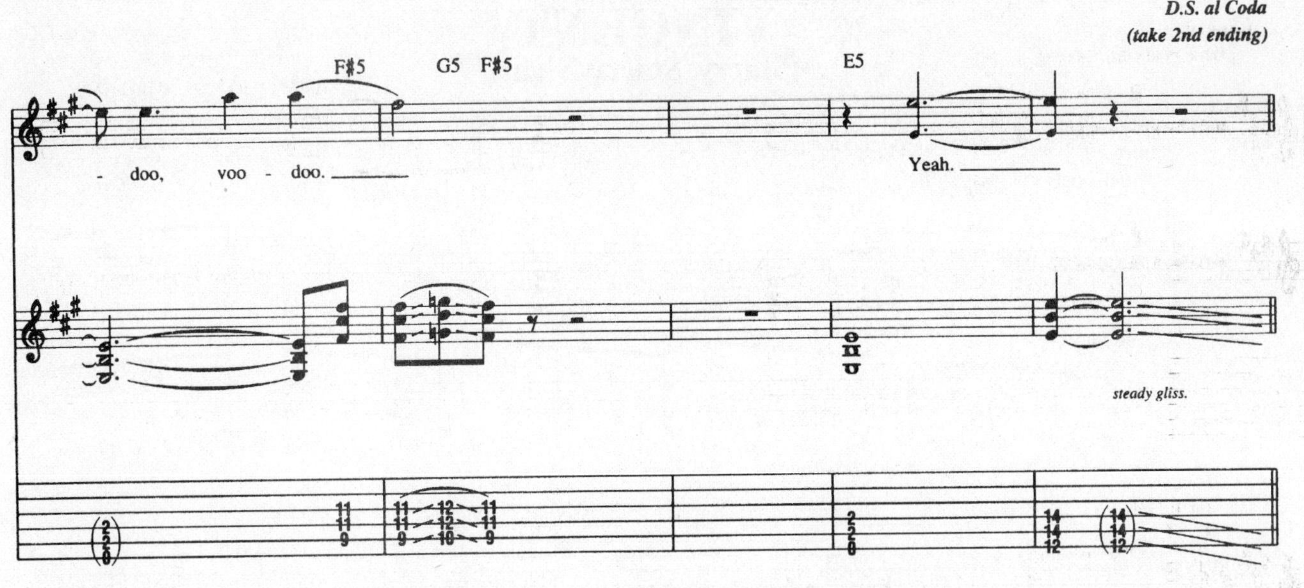
D.S. al Coda
(take 2nd ending)
F#5
G5 F#5
E5
- doo, voo - doo.
Yeah.
steady gliss.

Coda
Outro
Gtr. 1: w/ Rhy. Fig. 1, 7 1/2 times
F#5 G5 F#5
G5 F#5
Voo - doo, voo - doo. Voo - doo, voo -

G5 F#5
G5 F#5
doo. Voo - doo, voo - doo. Voo - doo, voo - doo.

G5 F#5
G5 F#5
Voo - doo, voo - doo. Voo - doo, voo -
So far a - way. I'm not the one who's so far a - way.

G5 F#5
G5 F#5
doo. Voo - doo, voo - doo.
I'm not the one who's so far a - way. I'm not the one who's so far a - way.

VINCENT
(Starry, Starry Night)

Words and Music by
DON McLEAN

C
Cmaj7
D7
G
an' the win-ter chills _ in _ col-ors on the snow-y lin-en land. _
End Rhy. Fig. 1
Chorus
Am
D7
Now I un - der - stand what you tried
Rhy. Fig. 2
G
G/F#
Em
Em7
Am7
to say to me. _ An' how you suf-fered for your _ san - i - ty. _
D7
Em
A7
An' how you tried _ to set them free. They would not list - en, _ they did not know _ how.

Am7 D7 G Gmaj7 G6 G G6 N.C.
Per-haps they'll list - en now. 2. Star-ry, star-ry
Verse
Gtr. 1: w/ Rhy. Fig. 1, simile
G6 Gsus4 G Am
night, flam - ing flow - ers that bright - ly blaze. Swirl - ing clouds
night, por - traits hung in emp - ty halls. Frame-less heads
C Cmaj7 D7 G
To Coda
in vio - let haze re - flect in Vin - cent's eyes of Chi - na blue. Col - ors chang - ing
on name - less walls with eyes that watch the world and can't for - get. Like stran-gers that you've
Gsus4 G Am
hue, morn - ing fields of am - ber grow. Weath - ered fac - es
C Cmaj7 D7
Gtr. 1: w/ Rhy. Fill 1
G
lined in pain are soothed be - neath the art - ist's lov - ing hand. Now I un - der -
Chorus
Gtr. 1: w/ Rhy. Fig. 2, simile
Am D7 G G/F# Em Em7
stand what you tried to say to me. An' how you suf - fered for your
Am7 D7 Em
san - i - ty. An' how you tried to set them free. They would not list - en, they did
A7 Am7 D7
Gtr. 1: w/ Rhy. Fill 2
G Am G/B
not know how. Per-haps they'll list - en now. For they could not love
Rhy. Fill 1
Gtr. 1
mf
T
A
B
Rhy. Fill 2
Gtr. 1
poco rit.
poco accel.
T
A
B

Bridge
Am
Asus4
Am
D7
D7/A
G
G/F#
Em
you
but still your love was true.
And when no hope
Gtr. 1
Free Time
Am
Cm
G
F
was left in sight on that starry, starry night,
you took your life as lover's often do.
E7
Am7
C
Cmaj7
But I could have told you, Vincent,
this world was never meant for one as
A Tempo
D.S. al Coda
D7
G
C
G
N.C.
beautiful as you.
3. Starry, starry

Coda
G
Gsus4
G6
Am
met, the rag-ged men in rag-ged clothes. The sil-ver-thorn, a
C
Cmaj7
D9
D7
G
N.C.
blood-y rose lie crushed and brok-en on the vir-gin snow. Now I think I
Outro-Chorus
Gtr. 1: w/ Rhy. Fig. 2, simile
Am
D7
G
G/F#
know what you tried to say to me.
Em
Em7
Am7
D7
An' how you suf-fered for your san-i-ty. An' how you tried to set them
Em
A7
Am7
D7
free. They would not list-en, they're not list-'ning still. Per-haps they nev-er
G
Gmaj7
G
G6
Gsus4
N.C.
G
will.
Gtr. 1
mf
rit.

WANTED DEAD OR ALIVE

Words and Music by
JON BON JOVI and RICHIE SAMBORA

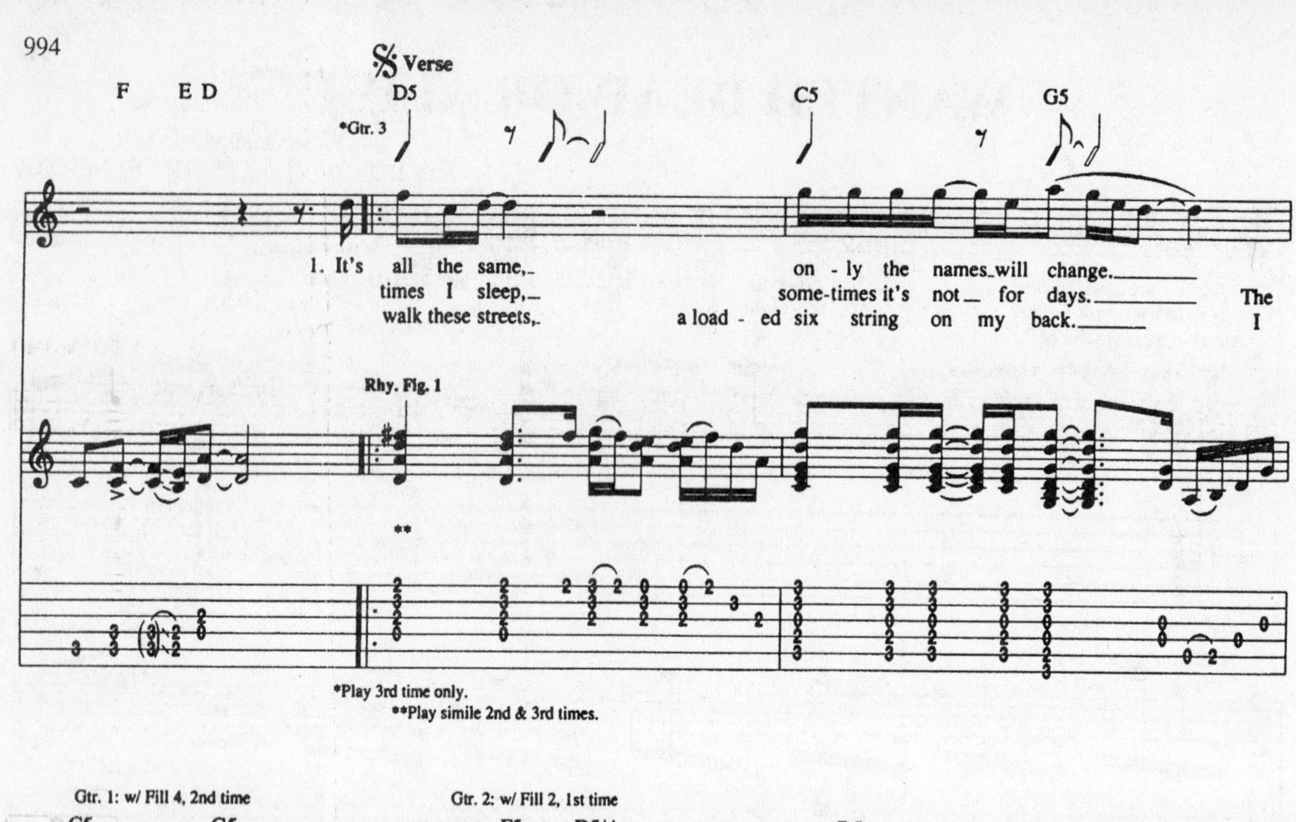
Verse
F
E D
D5
C5
G5
*Gtr. 3
1. It's all the same, on - ly the names will change.
times I sleep, some-times it's not for days. The
walk these streets, a load - ed six string on my back. I
Rhy. Fig. 1
*Play 3rd time only.
**Play simile 2nd & 3rd times.

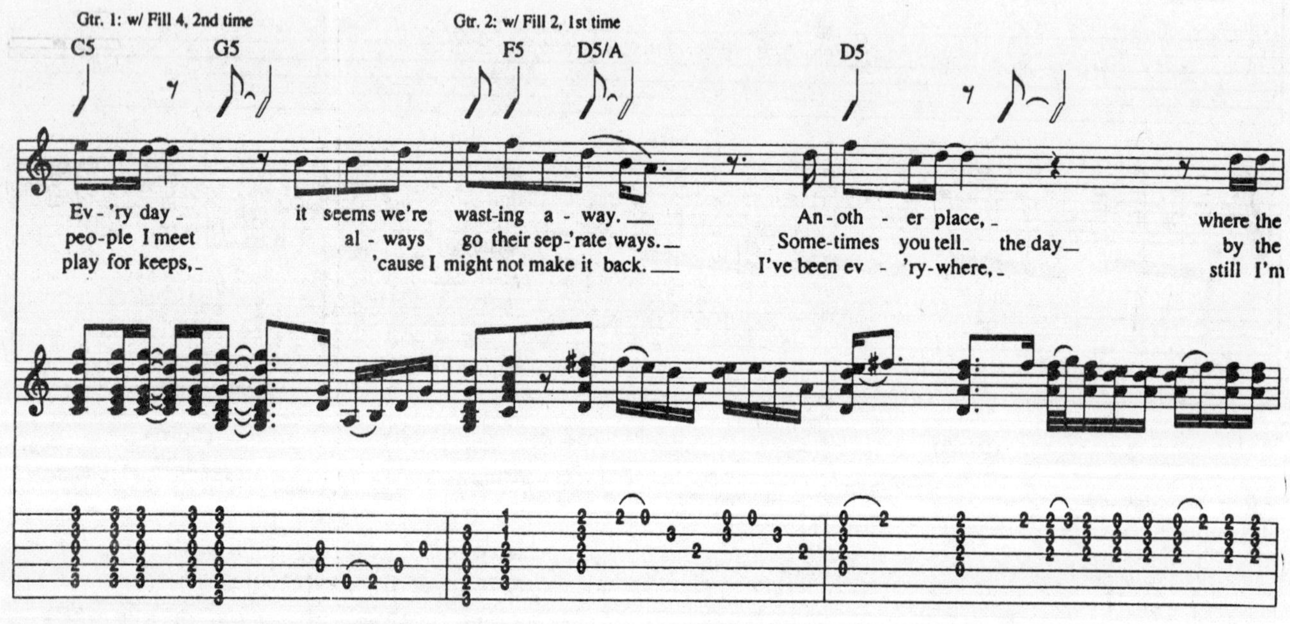
Gtr. 1: w/ Fill 4, 2nd time
Gtr. 2: w/ Fill 2, 1st time
C5
G5
F5
D5/A
D5
Ev - 'ry day it seems we're wast-ing a - way. An - oth - er place, where the
peo-ple I meet al - ways go their sep-'rate ways. Some-times you tell the day by the
play for keeps, 'cause I might not make it back. I've been ev - 'ry-where, still I'm

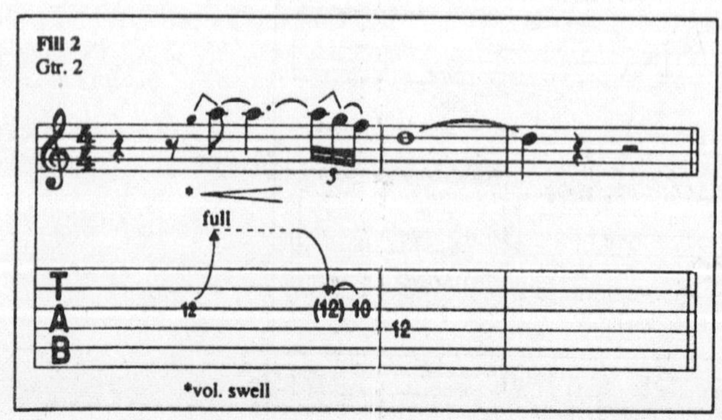
Fill 2
Gtr. 2
full
*vol. swell

Fill 4
Gtr. 1

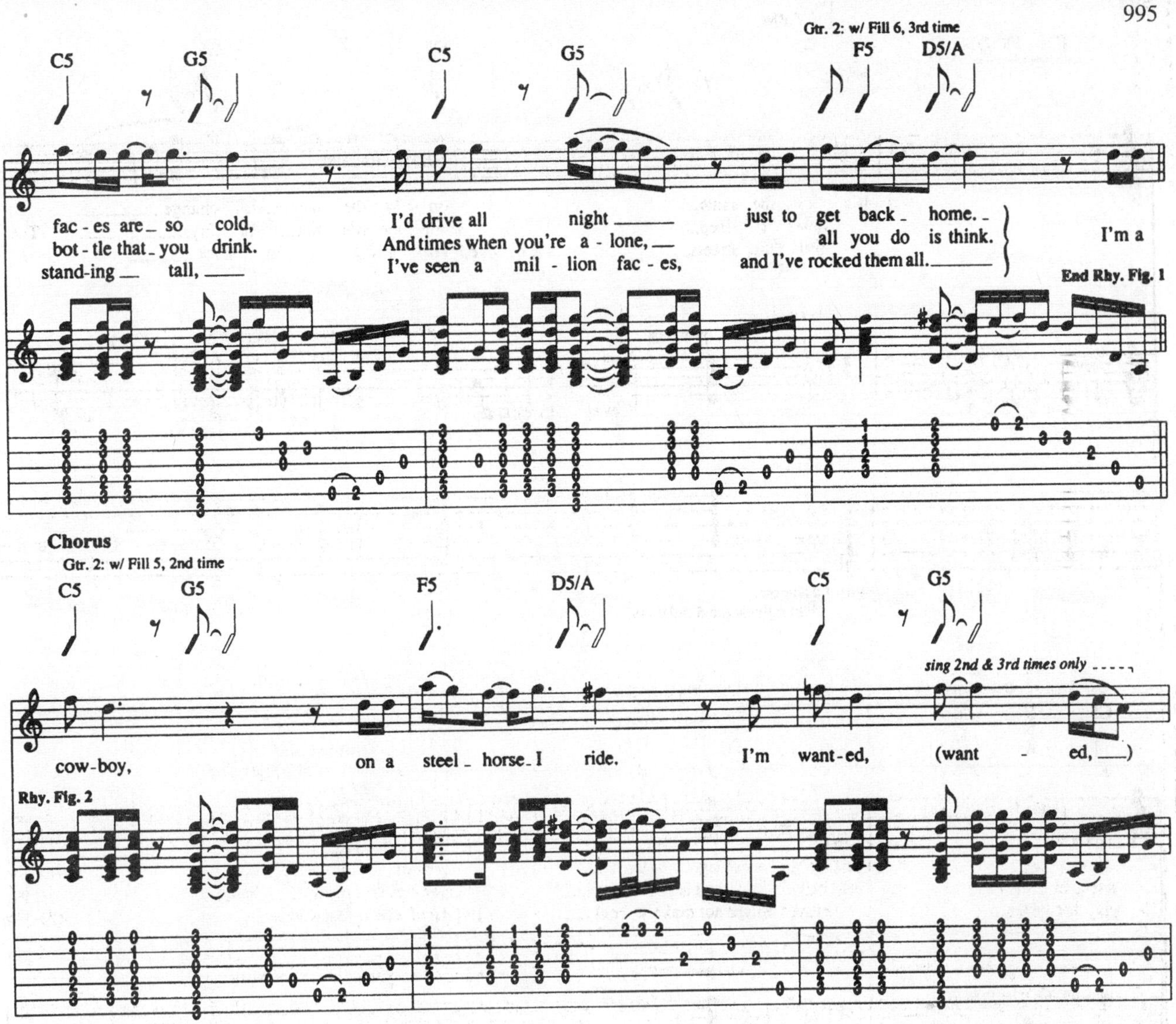

Gtr. 2: w/ Fill 6, 3rd time

C5 G5 C5 G5 F5 D5/A

fac - es are _ so cold, I'd drive all night ____ just to get back _ home. _
bot - tle that _ you drink. And times when you're a - lone, __ all you do is think. I'm a
stand-ing __ tall, ____ I've seen a mil - lion fac - es, and I've rocked them all. ______

End Rhy. Fig. 1

Chorus

Gtr. 2: w/ Fill 5, 2nd time

C5 G5 F5 D5/A C5 G5

sing 2nd & 3rd times only

cow-boy, on a steel _ horse _ I ride. I'm want - ed, (want - ed, __)

Rhy. Fig. 2

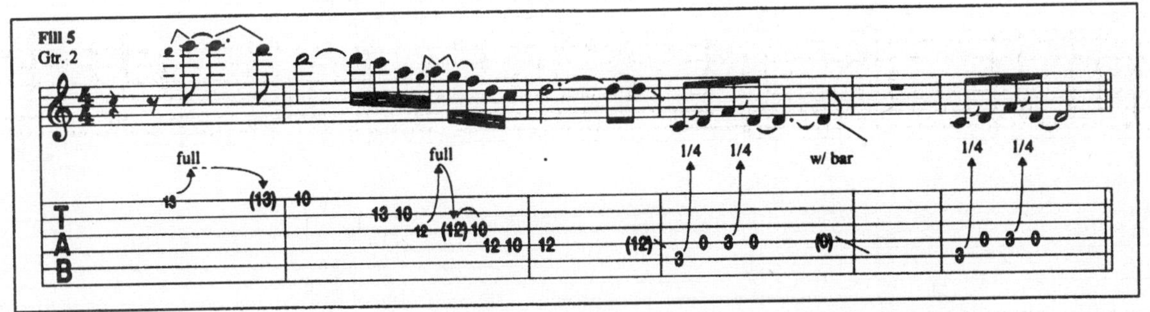

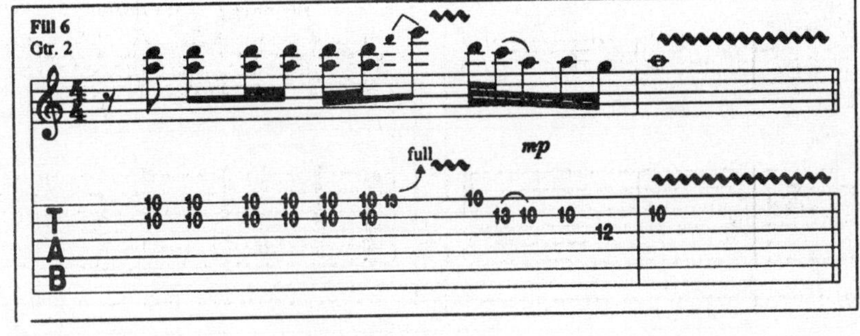

C5 D5 F5VIII D5
To Coda C
G5
N.C.
D
(cont. in notation)
sing 2nd time only
dead or a - live. ('Cause I'm a) Want-ed, (want - ed.) dead or a - live.
End Rhy. Fig. 2
1/4
*Upper harmony tacet 1st time.
**Sing 3rd time only.
Gtr. 2: w/ Fill 3, 1st time
1.
2.
Guitar Solo
Gtr. 1: w/ Rhy. Fig. 1, simile
D5
2. Some - Al - right.
Gtr. 1
Gtr. 3 (dist.)
mf
Gtr. 2
Fill 3
Gtr. 2
full
T
A
B

C5
G5
C5
G5
F5
D5
P.H.
full
pitch: C♯ D C♯
pitch: A
8va
loco
P.M.
1/4
pitch: E♭
pitch: D D E D C
pitch: D E D C
pitch: D E D F
Chorus
Gtr. 1: w/ Rhy. Fig. 2, 1st 3 meas., simile
Gtr. 2 tacet
Oh, I'm a cow-boy, on a steel_ horse_ I ride. I'm

C5 G N.C. D5 *D.S. al Coda*

wanted, wanted, dead or alive. 3. And I

Gtrs. 1 & 3

1/4 1/4

Coda

Gtr. 1: w/ Rhy. Fig. 2, simile
Gtr. 2: w/ Fill 7

C5 G5 F5 D5 C5 G5

cowboy, I got the night on my side. And I'm wanted, wanted,

Gtr. 3

Gtr. 1: w/ Rhy. Fig. 2, last 2 meas., simile

N.C. D5 C5 G5 N.C. D5

dead or alive, dead or alive, dead or alive, dead or alive. I still

1/4 1/4 1/4 1/4

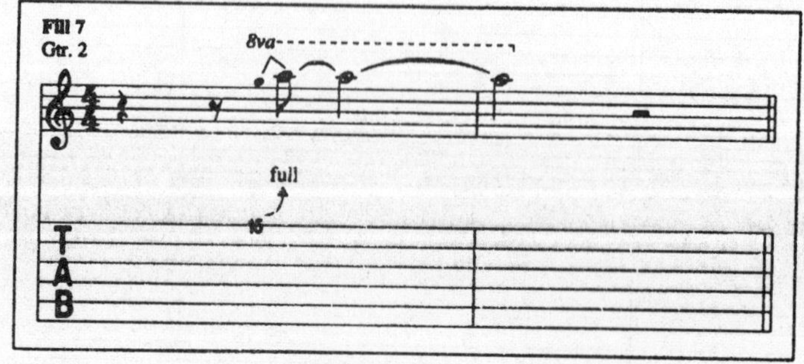

Gtr. 1: w/ Rhy. Fig. 2, last 2 meas., simile
C5 G5
drive, I still drive,

N.C. D5
dead or a - live,

Gtr. 1: w/ Rhy. Fig. 2, last 2 meas., simile
N.C. G5
dead or a - live,

1/4 1/4 1/4 1/4

N.C. D5
dead or a - live,

N.C. G5
dead or a - live,

Gtrs. 1 & 3

N.C. D5
dead or a - live.

1/4 1/4 1/4 1/4 1/4 1/4

Outro

Gtr. 3 tacet
N.C.
Gtr. 1

WALKING TO NEW ORLEANS

Words and Music by
ANTOINE DOMINO, DAVE BARTHOLOMEW
and ROBERT GUIDRY

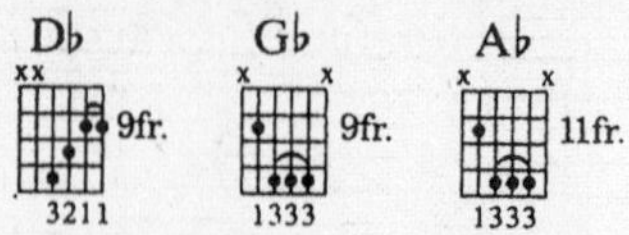

Verse 2:
I've got my suitcase in my hand.
Now, ain't that a shame?
I'm leaving here today,
Yes, I'm going back home to stay,
Yes, I'm walkin' to New Orleans.

Verse 3:
You used to be my honey 'til I lost all my money.
No use for me to cry,
I'll see you by and by
When I get back to New Orleans.

Verse 4:
And I got no time for talkin';
I've got to keep walkin'.
'Cause New Orleans is my home,
That's the reason why I'm goin', 'cause I'm walkin' to New Orleans.
(To Outro:)

THE WANDERER

Words and Music by
ERNEST MARESCA

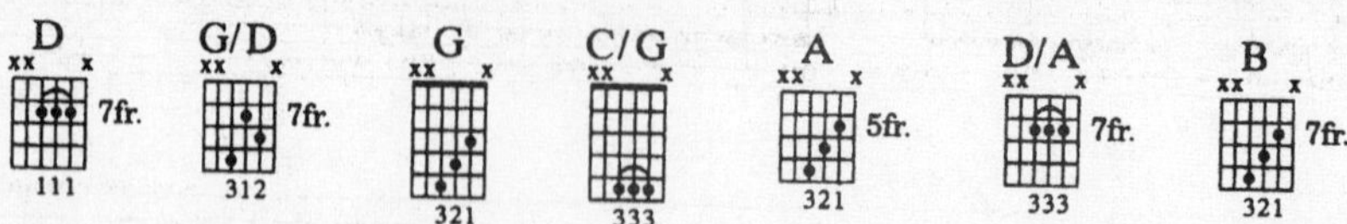

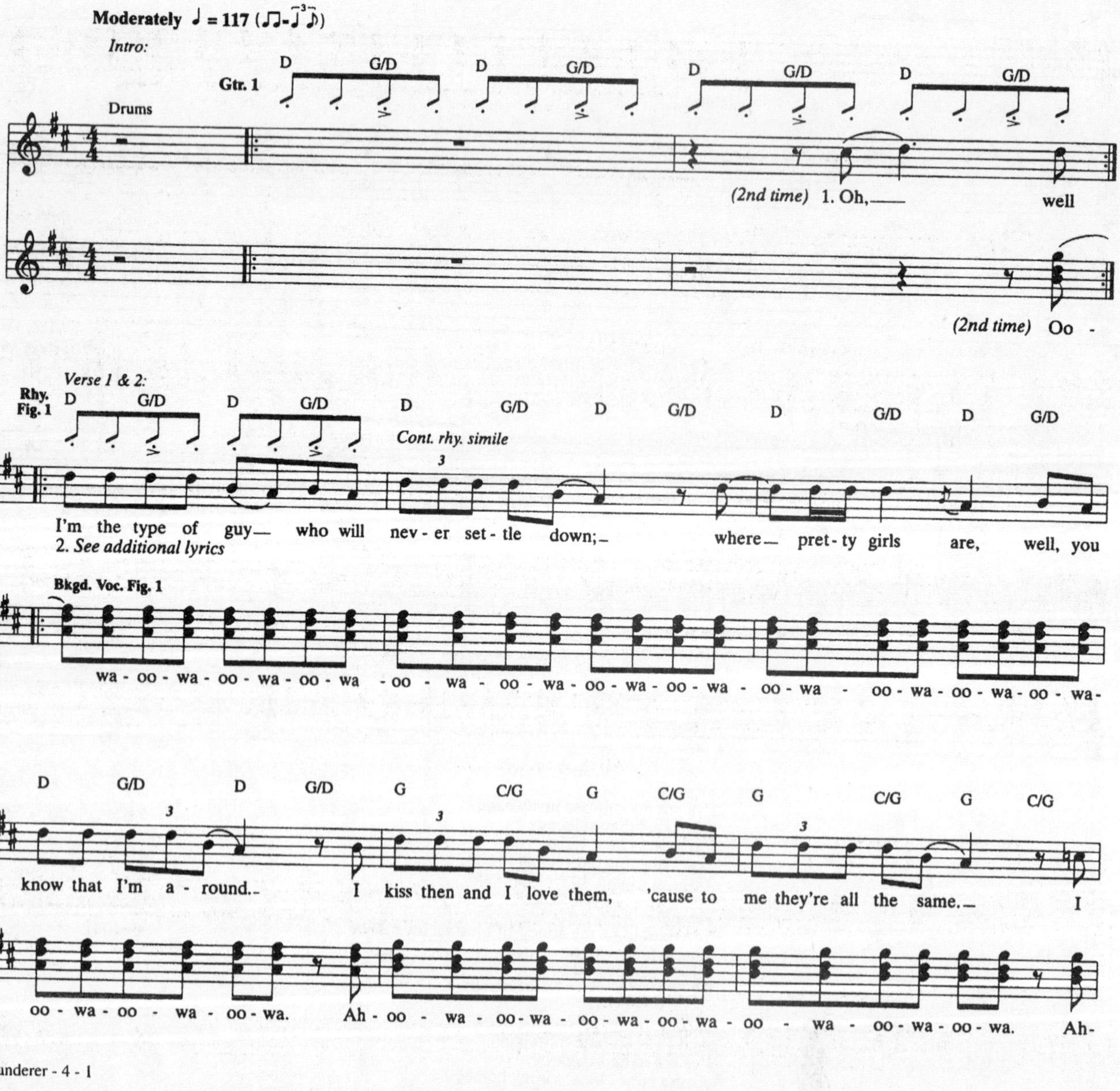

Moderately ♩ = 117

Intro:

Gtr. 1

Drums

D G/D D G/D D G/D D G/D

(2nd time) 1. Oh, well

(2nd time) Oo -

Verse 1 & 2:

Rhy. Fig. 1

Cont. rhy. simile

D G/D D G/D D G/D D G/D D G/D D G/D

I'm the type of guy who will nev- er set- tle down; where pret- ty girls are, well, you

2. *See additional lyrics*

Bkgd. Voc. Fig. 1

wa - oo - wa - oo - wa - oo - wa - oo - wa - oo - wa - oo - wa - oo - wa - oo - wa - oo - wa - oo - wa - oo - wa-

D G/D D G/D G C/G G C/G G C/G G C/G

know that I'm a - round. I kiss then and I love them, 'cause to me they're all the same. I

oo - wa - oo - wa - oo - wa. Ah - oo - wa - oo - wa - oo - wa - oo - wa - oo - wa - oo - wa - oo - wa. Ah-

D G/D D G/D D G/D D G/D A D/A A D/A
hug them and I squeeze them; they don't e - ven know my name. They call me the wan - der - er, yeah, the
end Bkgd. Voc. Fig. 1
Bkgd. Voc. Fig. 2
oo - wa - oo - wa - oo - wa - oo - wa - oo - wa - oo - wa - oo - wa. Ah.
1.
A
end Rhy. Fig. 1
G C/G G C/G D G/D D G/D
wan - der - er. I roam a - round, a - round, a - round, a - round. 2. Oh, well, there's
Uh oo - wa - oo - wa - oo - wa - oo - wa - oo - wa - oo - wa - oo - wa. Oo -
2.
Bridge:
A
a. Oh, well, I roam - a from town to town, I go through
end Bkgd. Voc. Fig. 2
oo - wa - oo - wa - oo - wa - oo. Ah.
life with - out a care, and I'm as hap - py as a clown.
Ah.
B
I'm with my two fists of iron but I'm go - ing no - where, no. 3.5. Yeah,
Ah.
Oo -

Verses 3-5:
w/Bkgd. Voc. Fig. 1 (Verses 3 & 5)
w/Rhy. Fig. 1 (Verses 3 & 4)
w/Rhy. Fig. 1 (1st 8 bars only, Verse 5)
D G/D D G/D D G/D D G/D D D/G D D/G
I'm the type of guy that likes to roam a - round; I'm nev - er in one place, I
4. Sax solo
ah.
*For Sax solo (lead vocal tacet).
D D/G D D/G G C/G G C/G G C/G G C/G
roam from town to town. And when I find my - self a - fall - ing for some girl, yeah, I
Wop, ah. Ah.
To Coda
w/Bkgd. Voc. Fig. 2 (Verse 3)
D G/D D G/D D G/D D G/D A D/A A D/A
hop right in - to that car of mine; I drive a - round the world. Yeah, I'm a wan - der - er, yeah, the
Wop, ah. Ah,
G C/G G C/G D G/D D G/D
wan - der - er. I roam a - round, a - round, a - round, a - round, eh,
Ah.
1. 2.
D.S. al Coda
A A
a - let's roam, let's go! Ooh, whoa, uh, yeah.
Wop, ah. Ma -

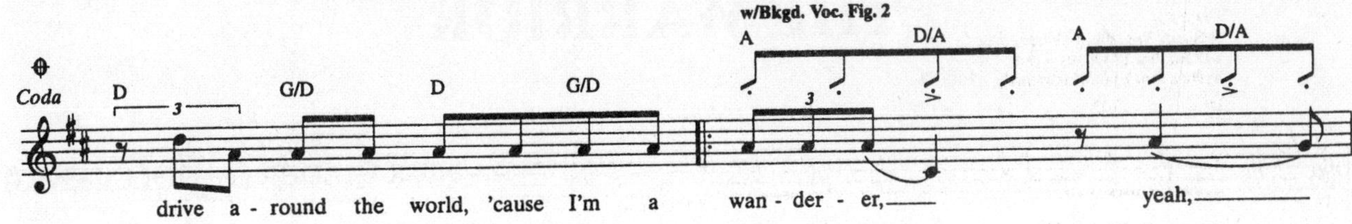

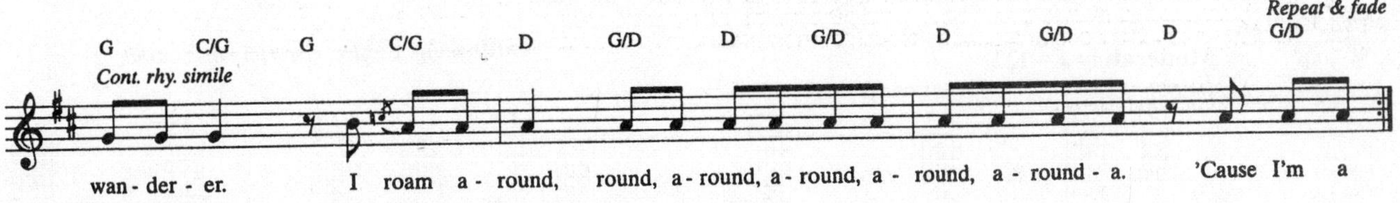

Verse 2:
Oh, well, it's Flo on my left arm
And there's Mary on my right-a,
And Janie is the girl, well,
That I'll be with tonight-a.
And when she ask me which one I love the best-a.
I tear open my shirt and I show her Rosie on my chest
'Cause I'm a wanderer, yeah, wanderer.
I roam around, around, around, around, around-a.
(To Bridge:)

THE WARRIOR

Words and Music by
NICK GILDER and HOLLY KNIGHT

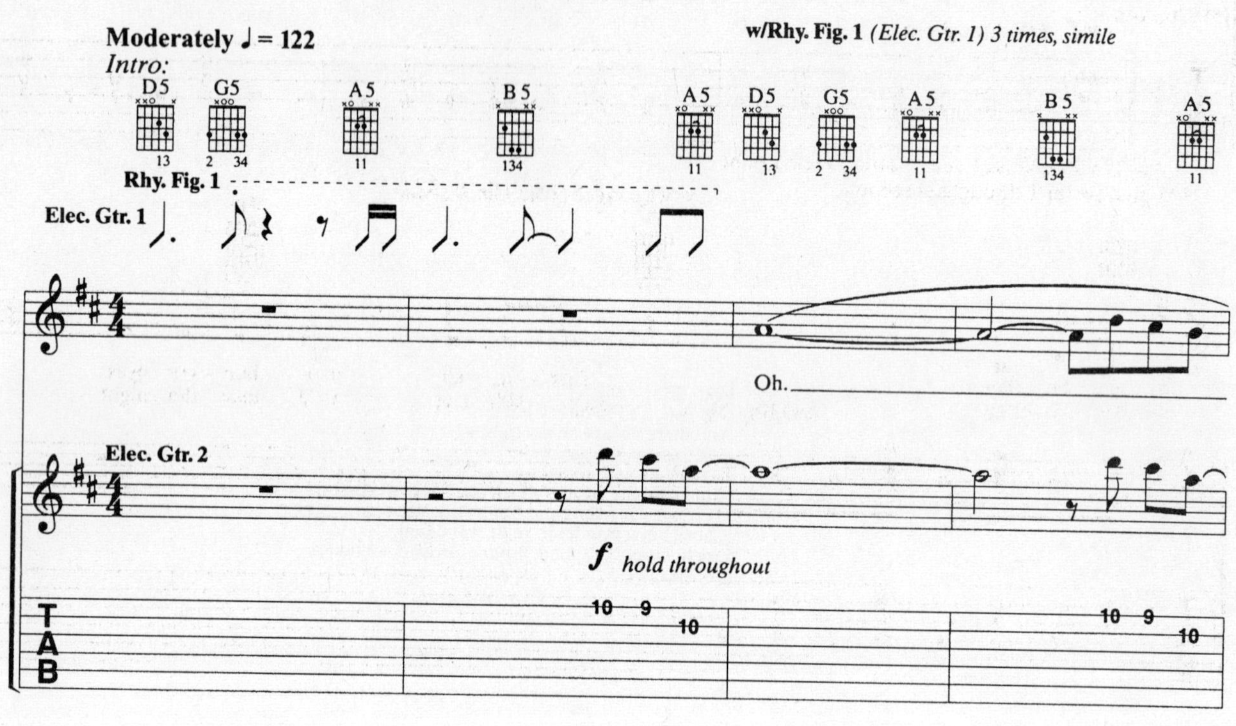

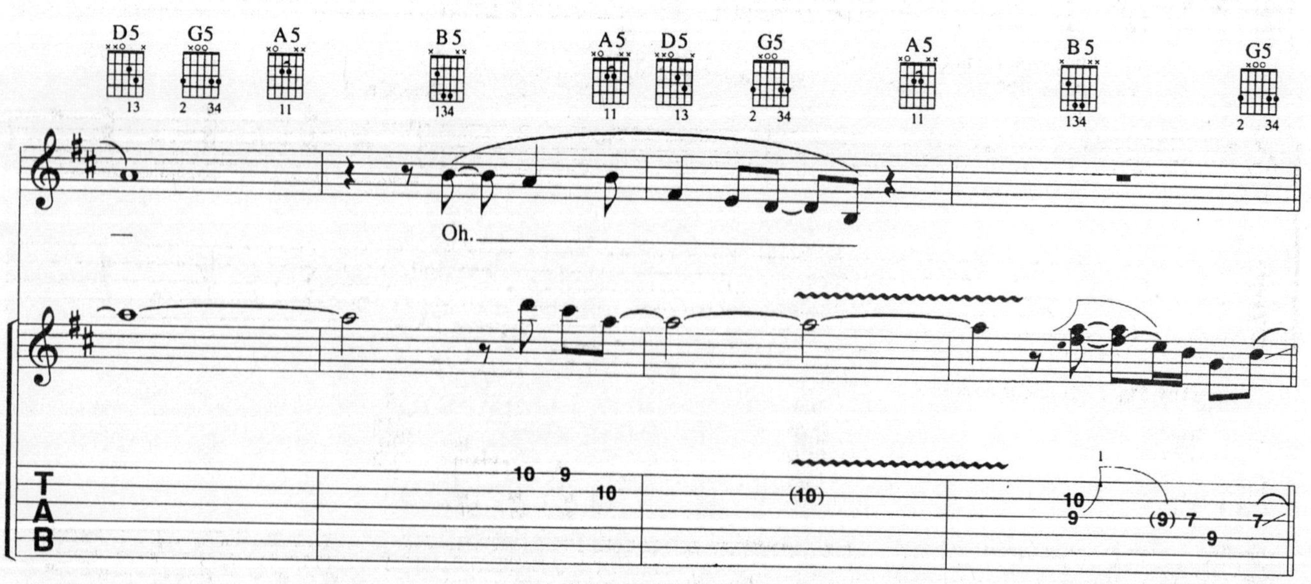

Verse:
A
Bm
A
1. You run, run, run a - way.
2. You talk tall talk to me.
It's your heart that
Your eyes touch me
Elec. Gtr. 2
Elec. Gtr. 2 out
Rhy. Fig. 2
**Elec. Gtr. 3
mf P.M. throughout
* Play E during Verse 1 and A during Verse 2 only.
**2 gtrs. arr for 1 throughout section.
w/Rhy. Fig. 2 (Elec. Gtr. 3) simile
G
A
Bm
you be - tray.
phys - i - c'lly.
Feed - ing all your hun - gry eyes,
Stay with me; we'll take the night
end Rhy. Fig. 2
A
G
I bet you're not so civ - i - lized.
as pas - sion takes an - oth - er bite.
Elec. Gtr. 3
w/Rhy. Fig. 2 (Elec. Gtr. 3) simile
A
Bm
A
Elec. Gtr. 1
5fr.
Well, is - n't love prim - i - tive?
Who's the hunt - er? Who's the game?
A wild gift that you
I feel the beat,

G
A
Bm
wan - na give.
call your name.
Break out of cap - tiv - i - ty.
I'll hold you close in vic - to - ry.
1. If
Elec. Gtr. 3
T
A
B
Pre-chorus:
G5
A5
G5
Elec. Gtr. 1
I know me a ste - re - o jun - gle child.
2. I don't wan - na tame your an - i - mal style.
Love is the kill; your heart's still wild.
You won't be caged from the call of the wild.
Chorus:
D5
G5
A5
B5
A5
Shoot - ing at the walls of heart - ache, bang bang!
D5
G5
A5
B5
A5
D5
G5
A5
Cont. rhy. simile
I am the war - ri - or.
Well, I am the war - ri - or.
To Coda
B5
A5
Asus
A
D/F#
G5
And heart to heart you'll win if you sur - vive.

w/Rhy. Fig. 1 (Elec. Gtr. 1) 2 times, simile
D5
G5
A5
B5
The war - ri - or.
The war - ri - or.
2. w/Rhy. Fig. 1 (Elec. Gtr. 1) 2 times, simile
The war - ri - or.
I am the war - ri - or.
Guitar Solo:
G5
3fr.
Elec. Gtr. 1
P.M. throughout section
Elec. Gtr. 2
Elec. Gtr. 3
Rhy. Fig. 3
hold

w/Rhy. Fig. 3 (Elec. Gtr. 3) 7 times, simile
Cont. rhy. simile
(15ma)
fdbk.
P.M.
P.M.

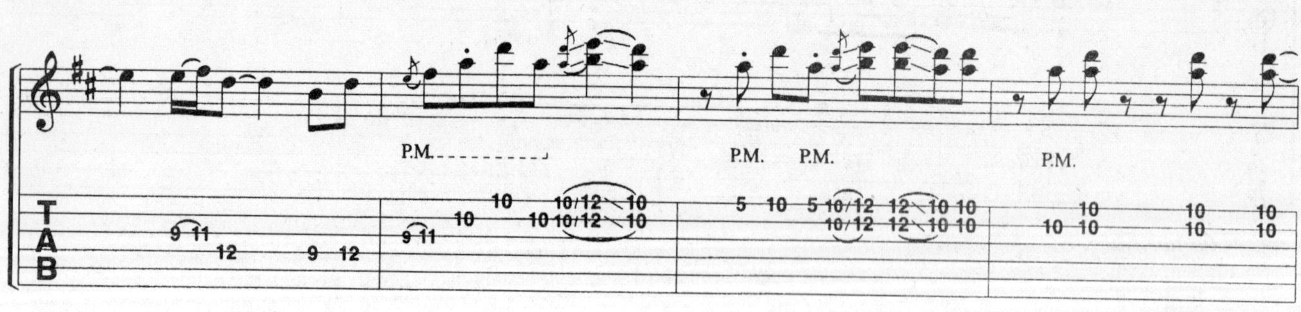
P.M.
P.M.
P.M.
P.M.

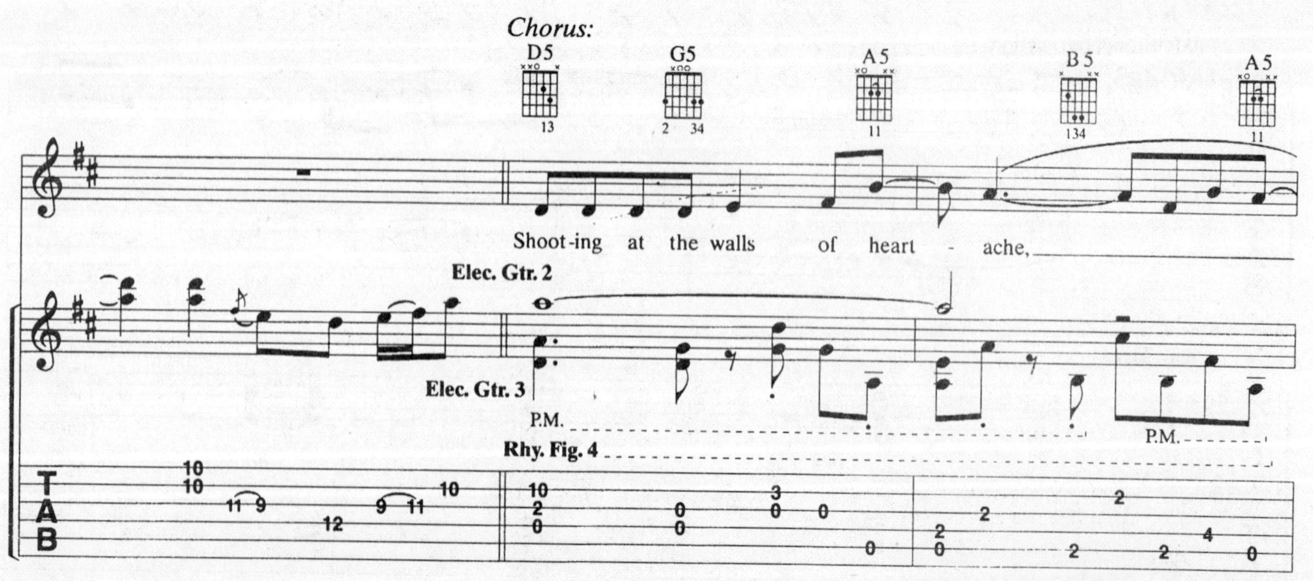
Chorus:
D5
G5
A5
B5
A5
Shoot-ing at the walls of heart - ache,
Elec. Gtr. 2
Elec. Gtr. 3
P.M.
Rhy. Fig. 4
P.M.

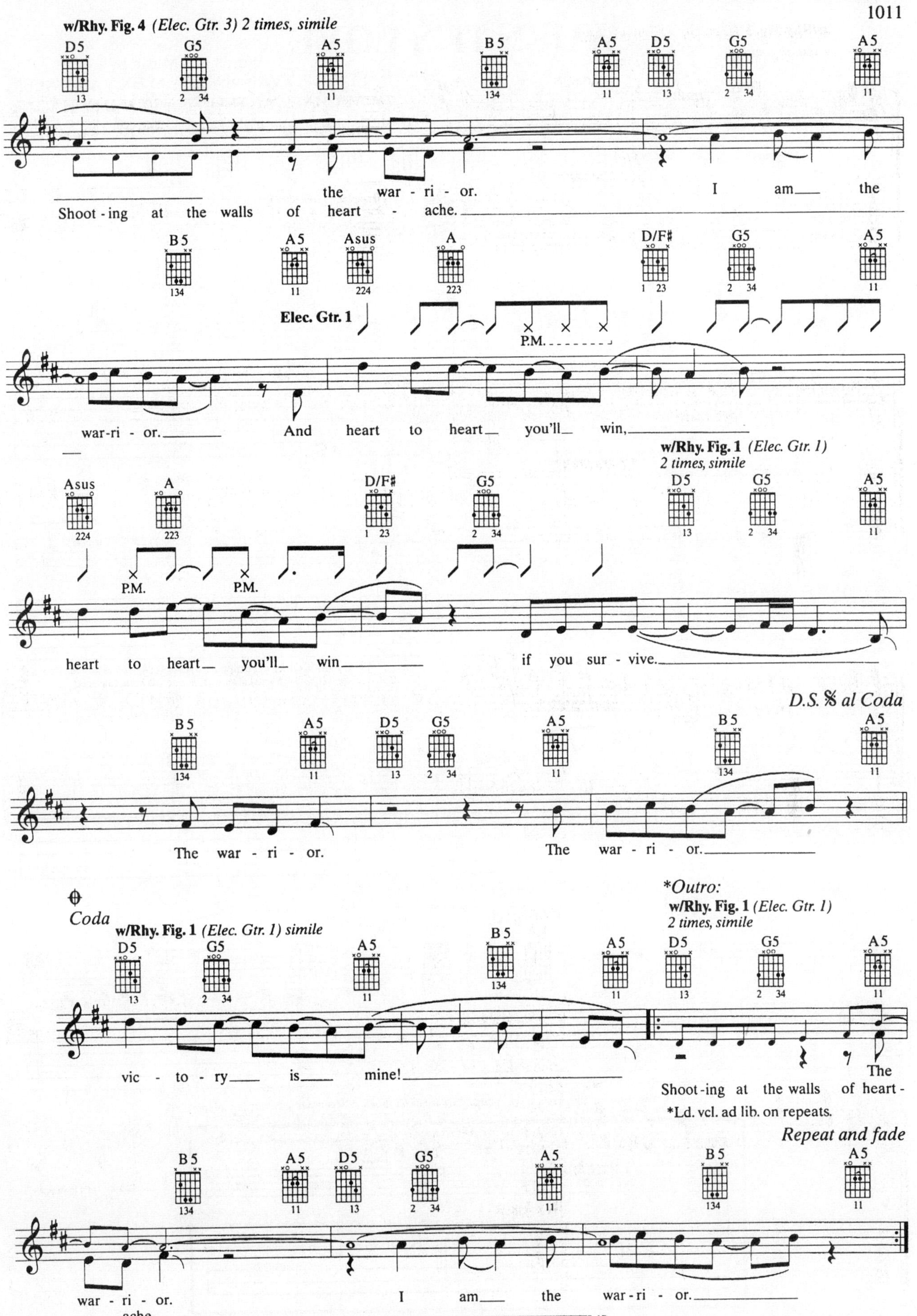
w/Rhy. Fig. 4 (Elec. Gtr. 3) 2 times, simile
D5 G5 A5 B5 A5 D5 G5 A5
the war-ri - or. I am the
Shoot - ing at the walls of heart - ache.
B5 A5 Asus A D/F# G5 A5
Elec. Gtr. 1
P.M.
war-ri - or. And heart to heart you'll win,
w/Rhy. Fig. 1 (Elec. Gtr. 1)
2 times, simile
Asus A D/F# G5 D5 G5 A5
P.M.
P.M.
heart to heart you'll win if you sur - vive.
D.S. 𝄋 al Coda
B5 A5 D5 G5 A5 B5 A5
The war - ri - or. The war - ri - or.
*Outro:
w/Rhy. Fig. 1 (Elec. Gtr. 1)
2 times, simile
Coda
w/Rhy. Fig. 1 (Elec. Gtr. 1) simile
D5 G5 A5 B5 A5 D5 G5 A5
vic - to - ry is mine!
The
Shoot-ing at the walls of heart -
*Ld. vcl. ad lib. on repeats.
Repeat and fade
B5 A5 D5 G5 A5 B5 A5
war - ri - or. I am the war - ri - or.
- ache.

WHEN IT'S LOVE

Words and Music by
EDWARD VAN HALEN, ALEX VAN HALEN,
MICHAEL ANTHONY and SAMMY HAGAR

D5
(Voc.: Hey!)
Riff A
C5/F
D5/G
Am
D5
C5/F
D5/G
B♭maj7
C5
(end Riff A)
*Combined gtr. & synth. riff (Gtr. I), Gtr. III in upstems. Bass in steady 8ths.
Riff B
(end Riff B)
1st Verse
w/Riff A
Ev - 'ry-bod - y's look - in' for some-thin',
some-thin' to fill in the holes.
w/Riff C
We think a lot but don't talk much a - bout it
till things get out of con - trol.
Oh!
Chorus
How do I know when it's love?
I can't tell you but it lasts for - ev - er.
Oh.
Rhy. Fig. 2
Gtr. I
let ring
*Synth. chords arr. for gtr.
**Synth. bass arr. for gtr.
How does it feel when it's love?
It's just some - thing you feel to - geth - er.
when it's love.
(end Rhy. Fig. 2)

w/Riff B
D5
C5/F
D5/G
Am
D5
C5/F
D5/G
F5
w/vol.
2nd Verse
w/Riff A
D5
sl.
C5/F
D5/G
Am
You look at ev - 'ry face in the crowd.
⑤1fr.
B♭
C5
P.M.
w/Riff C
D5
C5/F
D5/G
Some shine and some keep you guess - in'.
Wait - ing for some - one to
Am
D5
C5/F
C
C/A
come in - to fo - cus.
Teach you your fi - nal love les - son.
Ugh!
Chorus
w/Rhy. Fig. 2 (1st 6 bars only)
⑥open
D
⑤open
A
⑤2fr.
B
⑥2fr.
E
How do I know when it's love?
I can't tell you but it lasts for - ev -
④4fr.
F♯
⑤open
A
⑥open
D
⑤open
A
er.
Oh.
How does it feel when it's love?
It's just some -
⑥2fr.
B
⑥3fr.
F
⑥5fr.
G
Bridge
F5(type 2)
Gtr:
P.M.
thing you feel to - geth - er.
(Ah ah.)
Rhy. Fig. 3
let ring
*Synth. chords upstems.
Synth. bass downstems.
Riff C
sl.

G5(type 2)
sim.
F5(type 2)
G5(type 2)
Oh, when it's love.
(Ah ah.)
You can feel it, yeah.
F5(type 2)
*G5(type 2)
w/Rhy. Fill 1
(Ah ah.)
(end Rhy. Fig. 3)
Gtr. IV
Noth - ing's miss - ing.
Yeah.
Harm.
trem. bar
slow bend
*Doubled by synth. bass on root.
*Pull up on bar.
Guitar solo
w/Riff A
D5
C5/A
D5/G
Am
D5
C5/F
D5/G
hold bend
w/Riff C
B♭maj7
C5
D5
C5/F
D5/G
Am
hold bend
Rhy. Fill 1
*Synth. arr. for gtr.

D5
C5/F
C
C/A
Full
P
H
1/2
*Full
sl.
Bridge
w/Rhy. Fig. 3
*Sustain to beat 3 of next measure.
F5(type 3)
G5(type 3)
P.M.
(Ah ah.)
Yeah, you can feel it.
Oh, when it's love.
w/Fill 2
*Doubled by synth. bass on root.
w/Rhy. Fill 1
⑥7fr.
(When) Noth - ing's miss - ing.
⑥2fr. ⑥5fr. ⑥7fr.
E G A
Ow!
Chorus
w/Rhy. Fig. 2 (1st 7 bars only)
D5
A5
How do I know when it's love?
I can't tell
B5
⑥2fr.
E
D
A
you but it lasts for - ev - er.
Ooh.
How does it feel when it's love?
It's just some - thing you feel to - geth - er.
Hey.
Fill 2
semi-harm.
pick slide

⑥2fr.
w/Rhy. Fig. 2 (1st 3 bars only)
D5
A5
B5
E
How do I know when it's love?
I can't tell you but it lasts for - ev-
D Asus4 A
w/Rhy. Fig. 1
D
A
D/F♯
er. When it's love.
G5
D
A
D/F♯
Ooh, when it's love.
*Bass plays steady quarters. Hey!
G5
w/Rhy. Fig. 1 (3 times)
D5
Bkgd. Voc. Fig. 1
A5
D/F♯
It - 'll last for - ev - er.
When it's love.
(Na na na na na. Na na na
w/Bkgd. Voc. Fig. 1 (5 times)
G5
pick sl.
Rhy. Fig. 4
D5(type 2)
A5
D/F♯
na na.)
You and I,
G5
(end Rhy. Fig. 4)
w/Rhy. Fig. 4 (4 times)
D5
A5
we're gon - na feel this thing to - geth - er.
When it's love.
D/F♯
G5
D5
A5
Ooh. When it's love, ba - by.
D/F♯
G5
D5
A5
D/F♯
You can feed it, yeah!
G5
D5
A5
D/F♯
G5
We'll make it last for - ev - er.
Ooh, when it's love.
w/Rhy. Fig. 1A (2 times)
F5(type 2)
C5
F5(type 2)
C5
D5(type 2)

WHITE WEDDING (Part 1)

Words and Music by
BILLY IDOL

Verse:
B5
A5
E5
Elec. Gtr. 1
Cont. rhy. simile
1. Hey, lit-tle sis - ter, what_ have you_ done?
2. Hey, lit-tle sis - ter, who_ is it you're with?
3. Hey, lit-tle sis - ter, what_ have you_ done?
*Elec. Gtr. 2
Rhy. Fig. 1
end Rhy. Fig. 1
*Verses 2 & 3 only.
w/Rhy. Fig. 1 (Elec. Gtr. 2) Verses 2 & 3 only, simile
Hey, lit - tle sis - ter, who's_ the on - ly one?
Hey, lit - tle sis - ter, what's_ your vice_ a wish?
Hey, lit - tle sis - ter, who's_ the on - ly one?
Pre-chorus:
w/Rhy. Fig. 2 (Elec. Gtr. 2)
Pre-choruses 2 & 3 only, 2 times, simile
Cont. rhy. simile
Hey, lit - tle sis - ter, who's your su - per - man? Hey, lit - tle sis - ter, who's_
Hey, lit - tle sis - ter, shot - gun, oh_ yeah. Hey, lit - tle sis - ter, who's_
I've been a - way for so_ long. (So_ long.) I've been a - way for so_
Rhy. Fig. 2
*Pre-choruses 2 & 3 only.
_ the one_ you want? Hey, lit - tle sis - ter, shot - gun.
_ your su - per - man? Hey, lit - tle sis - ter, shot - gun.
_ long. (So_ long._) I let you go for so_ long.
It's a

Chorus:
w/Rhy. Fig. 2 (Elec. Gtr. 2) Chorus 2 & 3 only, 4 times, simile
A5
E5
B5
E5
Elec. Gtr. 1
pick sl.
nice day to start_ a - gain._ It's a nice day for a
To Coda
1.
D5
B5
E5
D
white wed - ding._ It's a nice day to start_ a - gain._
2.
B5
E5
D
nice day to start_ a - gain,_
Elec. Gtr. 2
B5
Cont. rhy. simile
ow!

Interlude:
Bm
E
D
D5
Bm
D
E7
Bm7
E9
6fr.
Bm7
D
E
B5
Pickit up!
A5
E5
B5
D.S. 𝄋 al Coda
Take me back home, yeah!

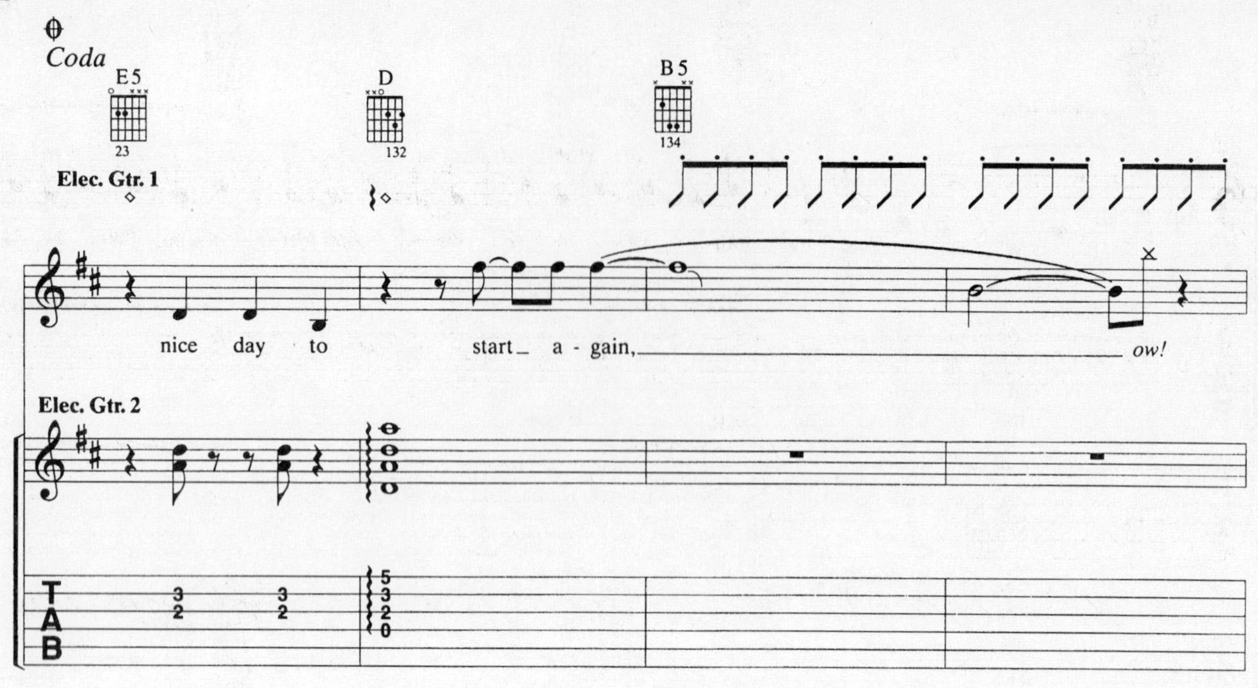
Coda
E5
D
B5
Elec. Gtr. 1
nice day to start_ a - gain,
ow!
Elec. Gtr. 2
TAB

Outro:

B5
Cont. simile until chorus
There is noth - ing fair_ in this world,_ world._

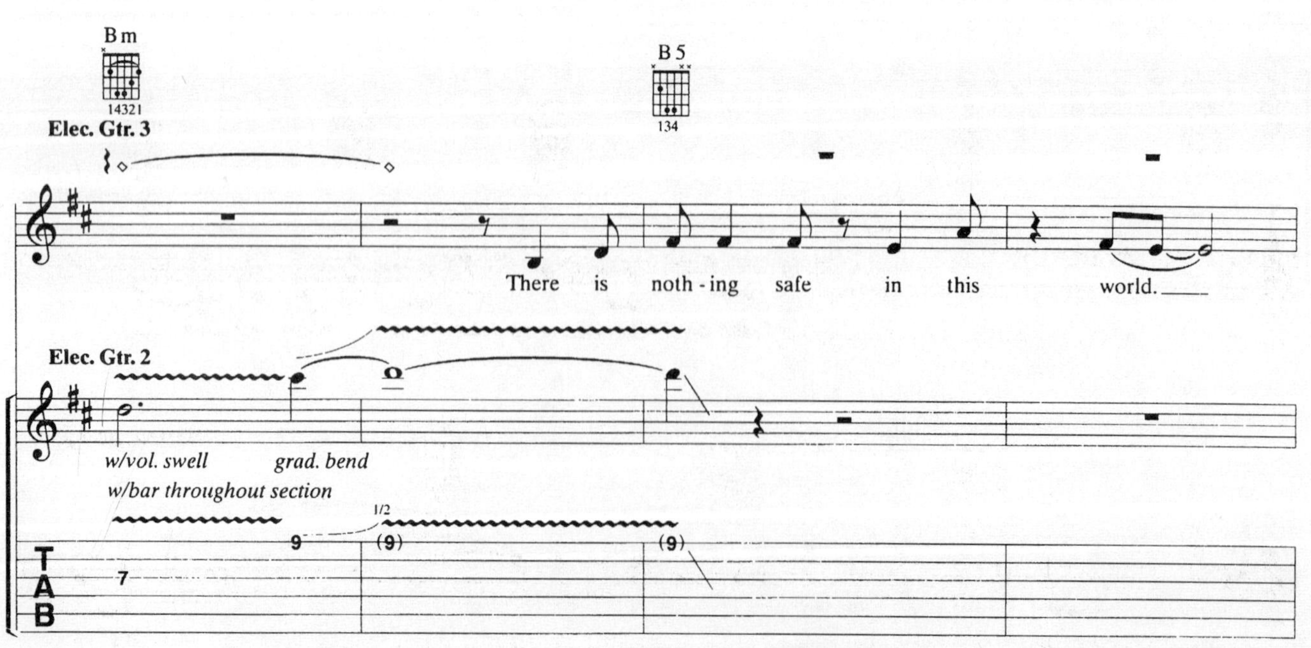
Bm
B5
Elec. Gtr. 3
There is noth - ing safe in this world.____
Elec. Gtr. 2
w/vol. swell
grad. bend
w/bar throughout section
TAB

Bm
14321
B5
134
Bm
14321
And there's noth-ing sure in this world. And there's noth-ing pure in this
A.H.
10
10
11
Chorus:
w/Rhy. Fig. 2 (Elec. Gtr. 3)
4 times, simile
E5
23
Elec. Gtr. 1
world. Look for some-thing left in this world.
1/2
1 1/2
2 1/2
9
(9)
10
10
D5
13
B5
134
D5
13
E5
23
B5
134
Start a-gain! Come on, it's a nice day for a white wed-ding.
Outro:
E5
23
D5
13
B5
134
Repeat and fade
Woah, it's a nice day to start a-gain. It's a

WHO WILL SAVE YOUR SOUL

Words and Music by
JEWEL KILCHER

Chorus:
w/Rhy. Fig. 1 (Gtr. 1) 4 times, simile
Am C(9) G Dsus D
who will save your soul, when it comes to the flow-ers, now?
Am C(9) G Dsus D
Oh, who will save your soul after all those lies that you told, boy?
Am C(9) G Dsus D
And who will save your souls if you won't save your own?
To Coda I
Am C(9) G Dsus D
La da da da di da da la da da ya die.
Verses 2 & 3:
Am C(9) G
1. We try to hus-tle them, try to bus-tle them, try to cuss them. The cops want some-one to bust down on Or-
2. See additional lyrics
Rhy. Fig. 2
Dsus D Am C(9)
leans Av-e-nue. An-oth-er day, an-oth-er dol-lar, an-oth-er war, an-oth-er

w/Rhy. Fig. 2 (Gtr. 1) simile
G
Dsus
D
Am
tow - er went up where the home - less had their homes. So we pray_ to as man - y
end Rhy. Fig. 2
C(9)
G
Dsus
D
dif - f'rent__ gods_ as there are flow - ers, but we call re - li - gion our friend._
To Coda II
Am
C(9)
G
We're so wor - ried a - bout_ sav - ing our souls,_ a - fraid that God will take his toll that we for -
D.S. al Coda I
Coda I
Dsus
D
G
Bass gtr.
get to be - gin. But
Interlude:
N.C.(Em)
D.S. al Coda II

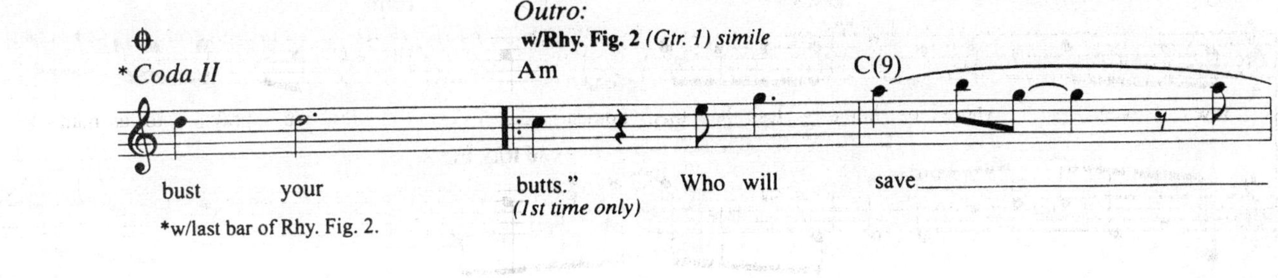

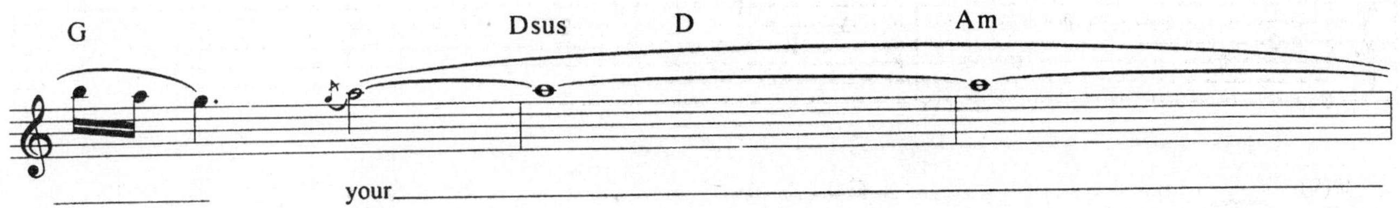

Verse 3:
Some are walking, some are talking, some are stalking their kill.
Got social security, but that don't pay your bills.
There are addictions to feed and there are mouths to pay,
So you bargain with the devil, but you're O. K. for today.
Say that you love them, take their money and run.
Say, "It's been swell, sweetheart, but it was just one of those things,
Those flings, those strings you got to cut,
So get out on the streets, girls, and bust your butts."
(To Chorus:)

WHO'S CRYING NOW

Words and Music by
STEVE PERRY, NEAL SCHON and JONATHAN CAIN

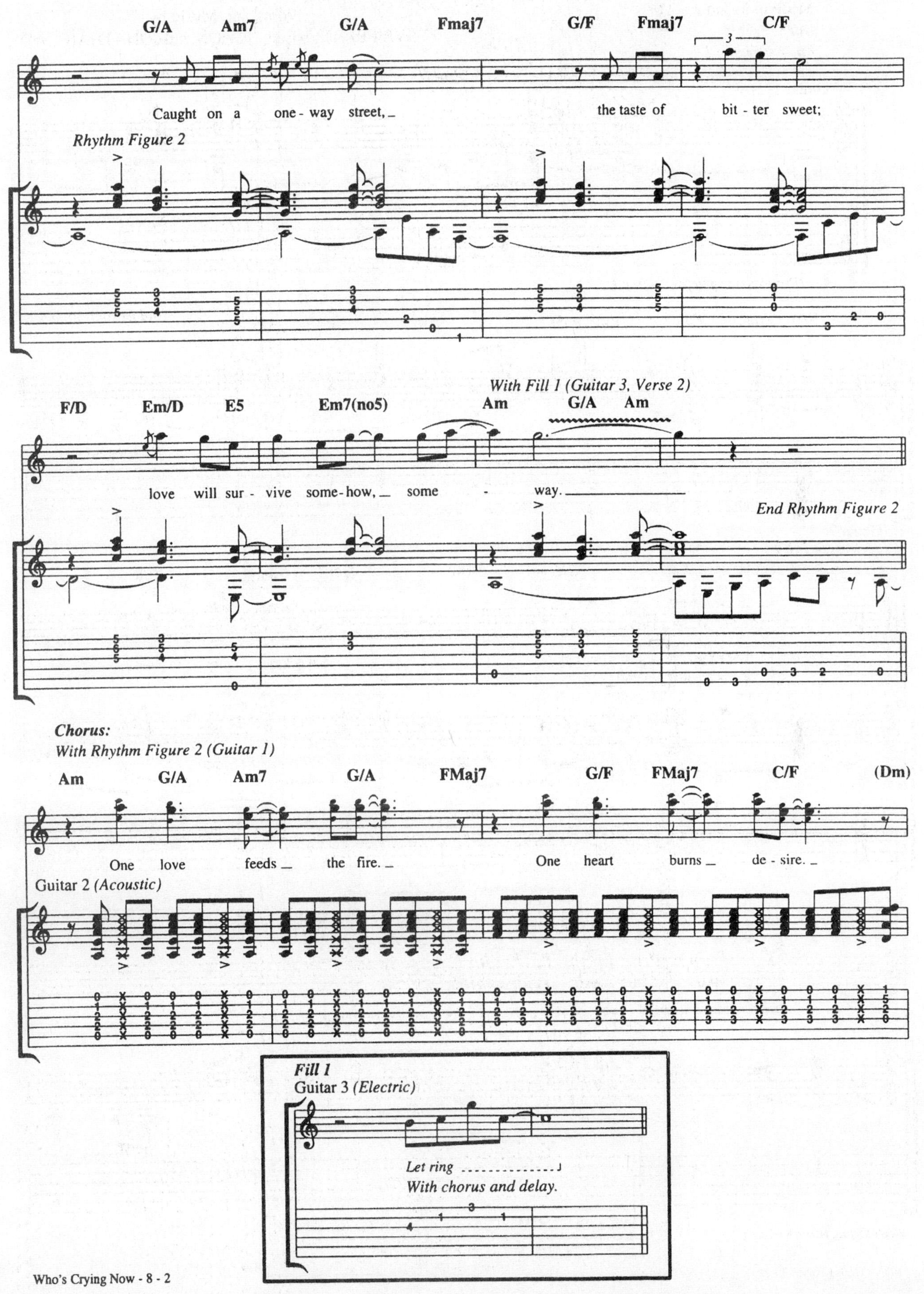
G/A Am7 G/A Fmaj7 G/F Fmaj7 C/F
Caught on a one - way street, _ the taste of bit - ter sweet;
Rhythm Figure 2
F/D Em/D E5 Em7(no5)
With Fill 1 (Guitar 3, Verse 2)
Am G/A Am
love will sur - vive some-how, _ some - way.
End Rhythm Figure 2
Chorus:
With Rhythm Figure 2 (Guitar 1)
Am G/A Am7 G/A FMaj7 G/F FMaj7 C/F (Dm)
One love feeds _ the fire. _ One heart burns _ de - sire. _
Guitar 2 (Acoustic)
Fill 1
Guitar 3 (Electric)
Let ring
With chorus and delay.

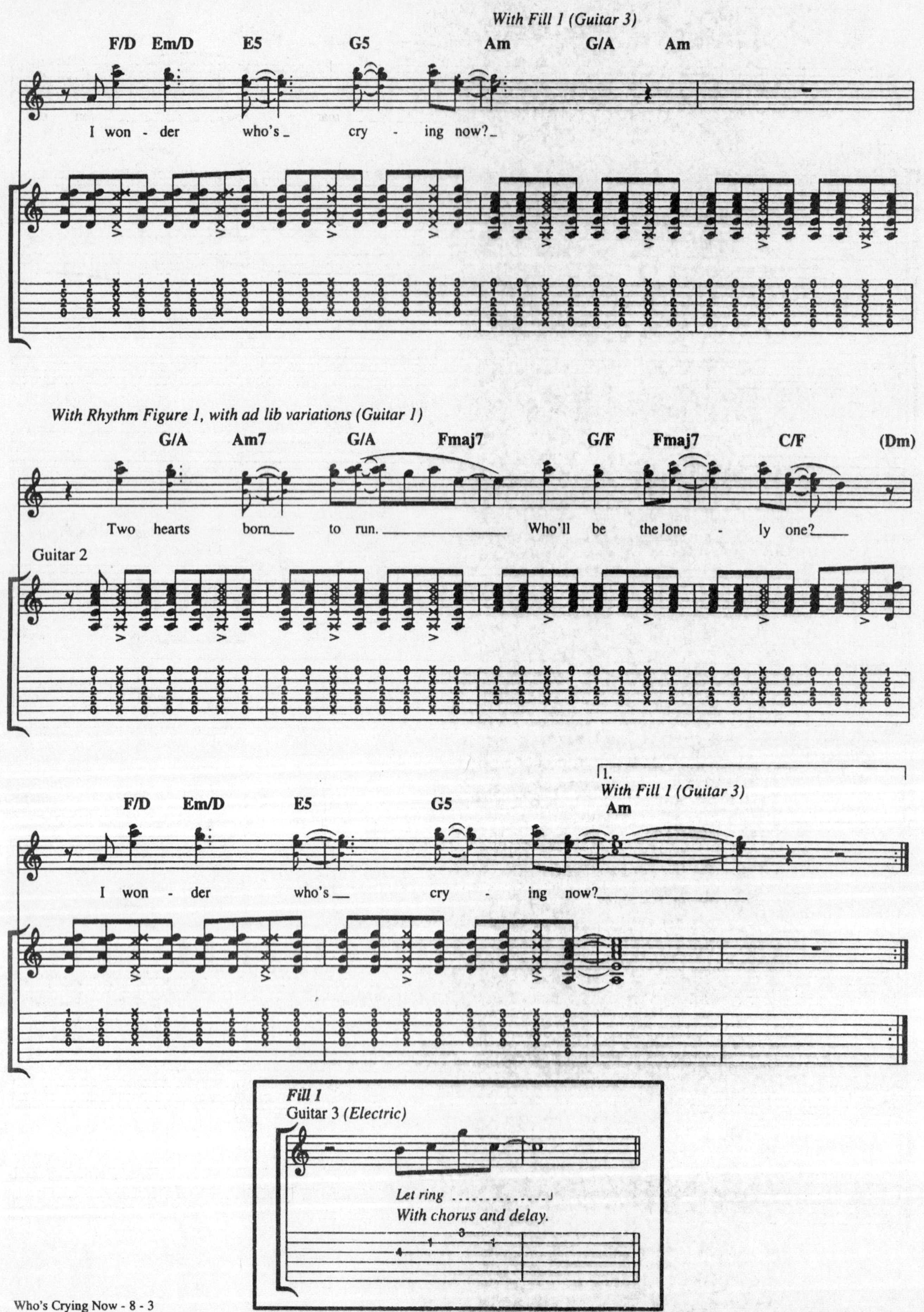
With Fill 1 (Guitar 3)
F/D Em/D E5 G5 Am G/A Am
I won - der who's _ cry - ing now? _
With Rhythm Figure 1, with ad lib variations (Guitar 1)
G/A Am7 G/A Fmaj7 G/F Fmaj7 C/F (Dm)
Two hearts born ___ to run. ___ Who'll be the lone - ly one? ___
Guitar 2
1.
With Fill 1 (Guitar 3)
F/D Em/D E5 G5 Am
I won - der who's ___ cry - ing now? ___
Fill 1
Guitar 3 (Electric)
Let ring
With chorus and delay.

2.
Bridge:
Am
Fmaj7
Dm
On - ly so many - y tears you can
Guitar 1
Let ring
Guitar 2
Am G/A Am G/A Am Fmaj7 Dm
cry 'til the heart - ache is o - ver, and
Let ring
C G B♭(add C) B♭
now you can say your love will nev - er die.
Let ring

With Rhythm Figure 1 (Guitar 1)
Am G/A Am7 G/A Fmaj7 G/F Fmaj7 C/F
Wo,
With Fill 1 (Guitar 3)
F/D Em/D E5 Em7(no 5) Am G/A Am
ooh wo ooh wo.
Chorus: With Rhythm Figure 2, with ad lib variations 2 times (Guitar 1)
Am G/A Am7 G/A Fmaj7 G/F Fmaj7 C/F
One love feeds the fire. One heart burns de - sire.
With Fill 1 (Guitar 3)
F/D Em/D E5 G5 Am G/A Am
Won - der who's cry - ing now?
G/A Am7 G/A Fmaj7 G/F Fmaj7 C/F
Two hearts born to run. Who'll be the lone - ly one?
With Fill 1 (Guitar 3)
F/D Em/D E5 G5 Am G/A Am
I won - der who's cry - ing now?
Outro Guitar Solo:
With Rhythm Figure 2 with ad lib variations until fade (Guitar 1)
Am G/A Am7 G/A Fmaj7 G/F Fmaj7
8va
With distortion and sustain
Fill 1
Guitar 3 (Electric)
Let ring
With chorus and delay.

C/F
F/D
Em/D
E5
G5
(8va)
With Fill 1 (Guitar 3)
Am
G/A
Am
G/A
Am7
G/A
Fmaj7
G/F
Fmaj7
C/F
F/D
Em/D
E5
G5
With Fill 1 (Guitar 3)
Am
G/A
Am
G/A
Am7
G/A
Fmaj7
G/F
Fmaj7
loco

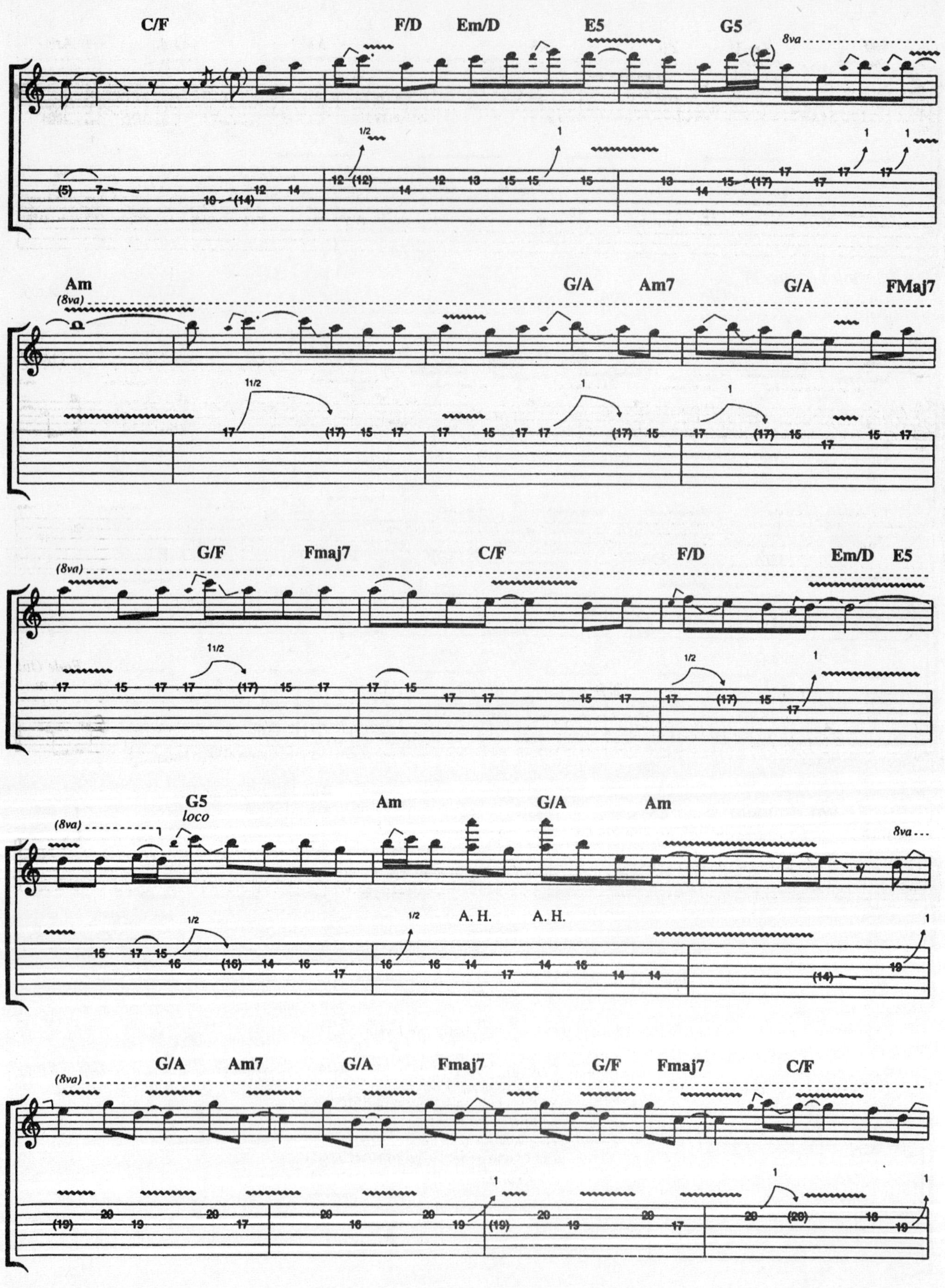
C/F
F/D
Em/D
E5
G5
8va
1/2
1
Am
(8va)
G/A
Am7
G/A
FMaj7
11/2
1
1
G/F
Fmaj7
C/F
F/D
Em/D
E5
(8va)
11/2
1/2
1
G5
loco
Am
G/A
Am
(8va)
8va
1/2
1/2
A. H.
A. H.
1
G/A
Am7
G/A
Fmaj7
G/F
Fmaj7
C/F
(8va)
1
1
1

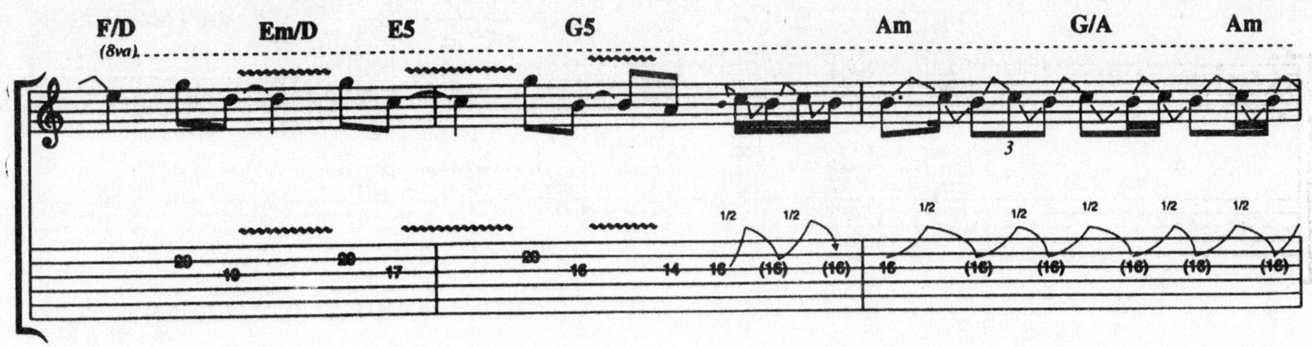

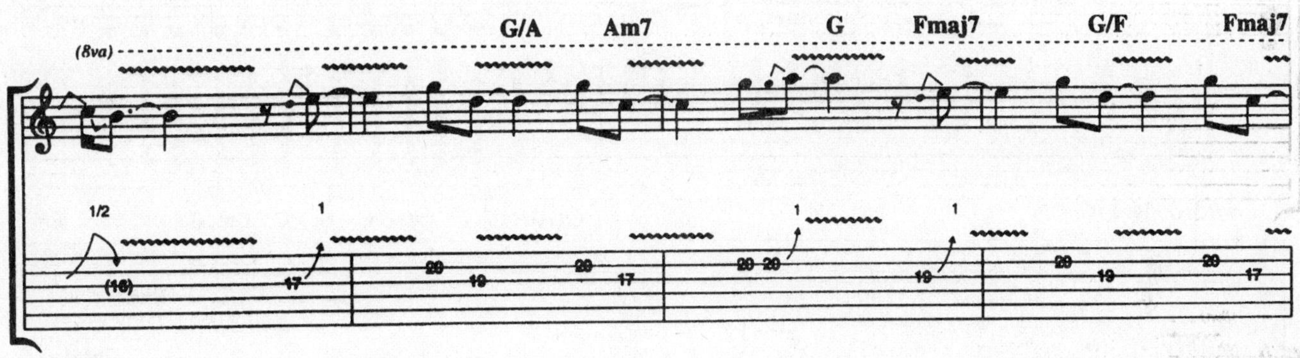

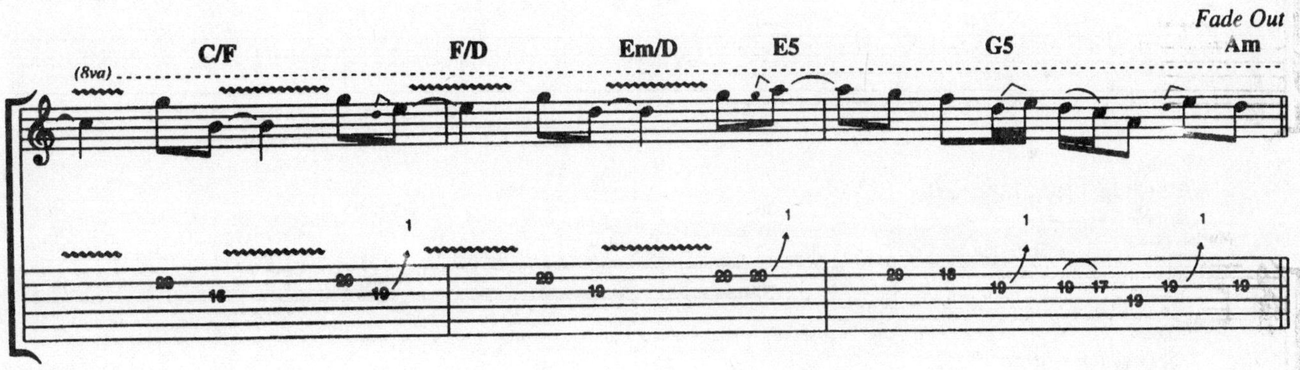

Additional Lyrics

Verse 2: So many stormy nights,
So many wrong or rights.
Neither could change their headstrong ways.
And in a lover's rage,
They tore another page.
The fightin' is worth the love they save...
(To Chorus)

WILD NIGHT

Words and Music by
VAN MORRISON

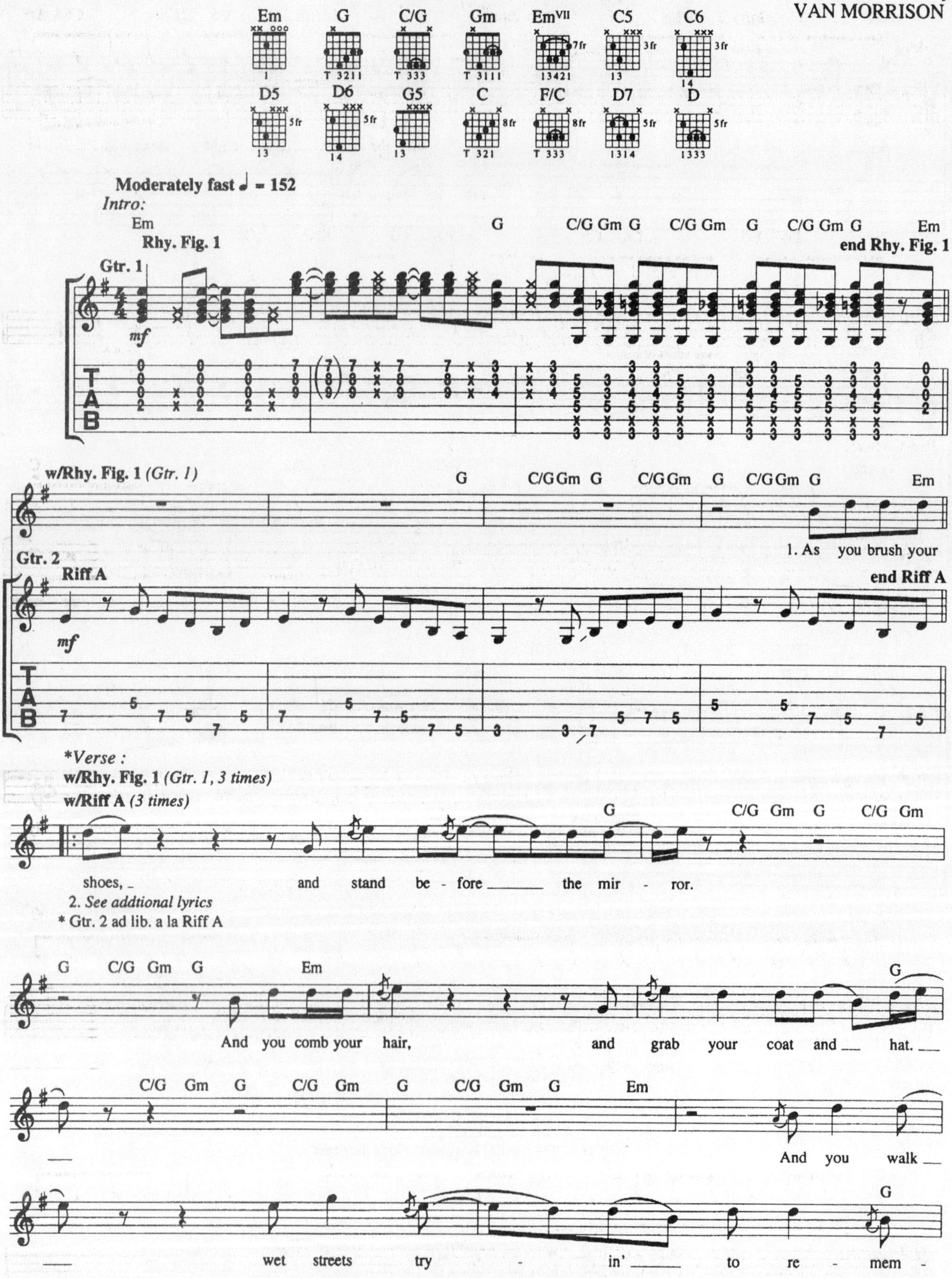

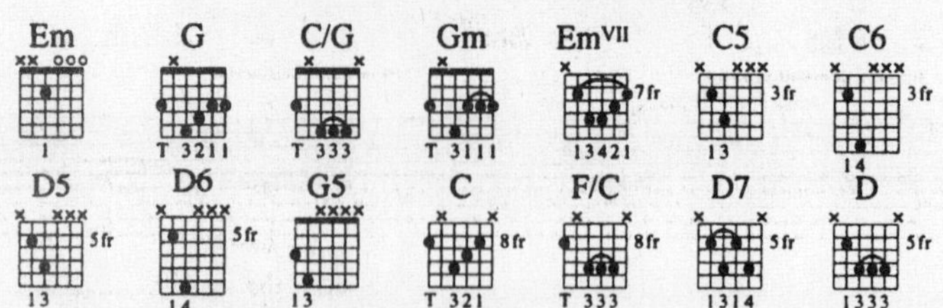

Em G C/G Gm Em VII C5 C6
D5 D6 G5 C F/C D7 D
Moderately fast ♩ = 152
Intro:
Em G C/G Gm G C/G Gm G C/G Gm G Em
Rhy. Fig. 1
end Rhy. Fig. 1
Gtr. 1
mf
w/Rhy. Fig. 1 (Gtr. 1)
G C/G Gm G C/G Gm G C/G Gm G Em
1. As you brush your
Gtr. 2
Riff A
end Riff A
mf
*Verse:
w/Rhy. Fig. 1 (Gtr. 1, 3 times)
w/Riff A (3 times)
G C/G Gm G C/G Gm
shoes, _ and stand be - fore _ the mir - ror.
2. See addtional lyrics
* Gtr. 2 ad lib. a la Riff A
G C/G Gm G Em G
And you comb your hair, and grab your coat and _ hat. _
C/G Gm G C/G Gm G C/G Gm G Em
_ And you walk _
G
_ wet streets try - in' _ to re - mem -

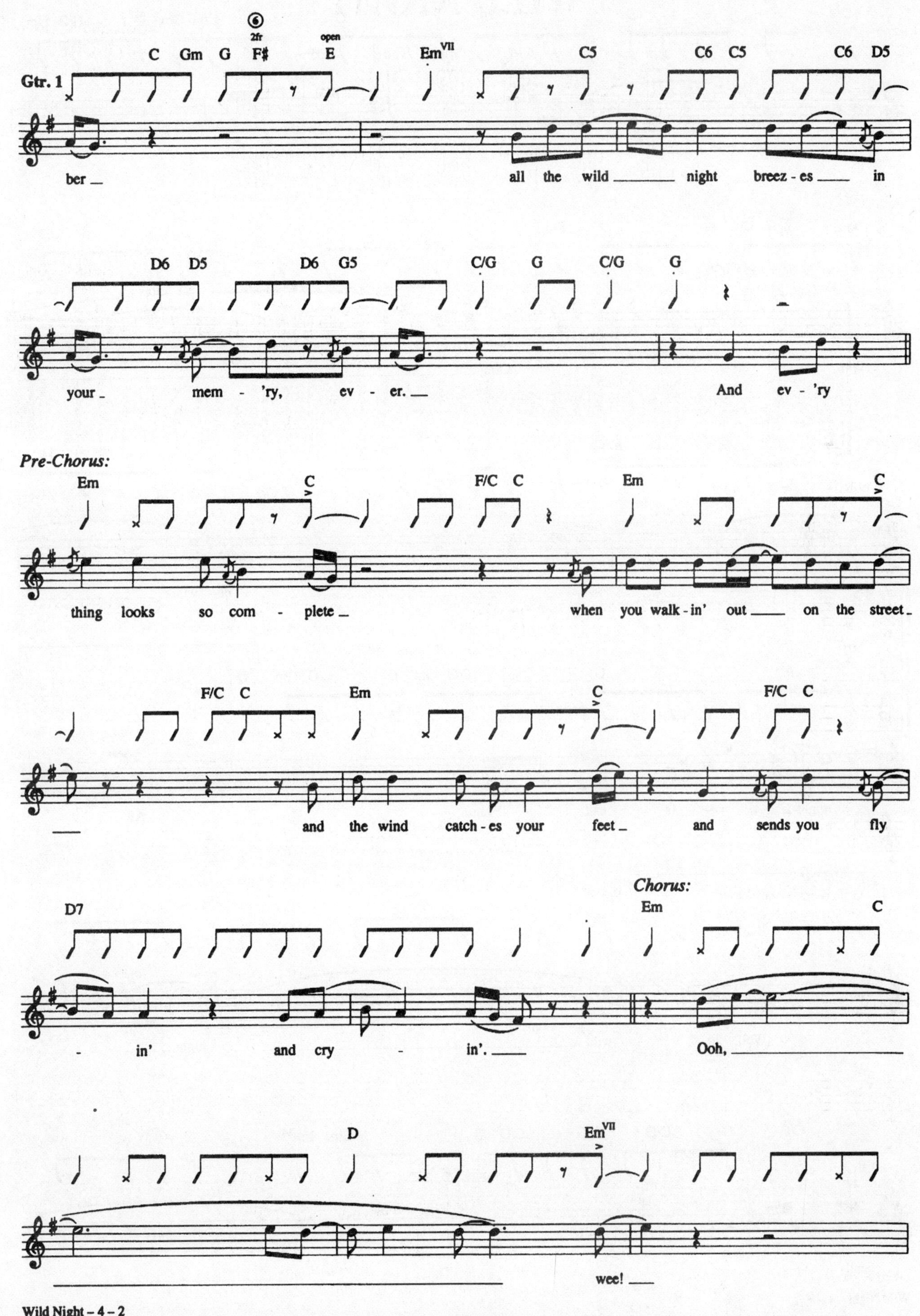
Gtr. 1
C Gm G F# E Em VII C5 C6 C5 C6 D5
6 2fr open
ber _ all the wild _ night breez - es _ in
D6 D5 D6 G5 C/G G C/G G
your _ mem - 'ry, ev - er. _ And ev - 'ry
Pre-Chorus:
Em C F/C C Em C
thing looks so com - plete _ when you walk - in' out _ on the street _
F/C C Em C F/C C
and the wind catch - es your feet _ and sends you fly
Chorus:
D7 Em C
- in' and cry - in'. _ Ooh, _
D Em VII
wee! _

D G C/G Gm G C/G Gm
The wild night is call - ing. Al -
G C/G Gm G Em C D
right. Ooh,
Em VII D
wee! The wild
G C/G Gm G C/G Gm
1. G
night is call - ing. All the
2. G
Em VII
Well, the wild night is
C/G G C/G G C/G G Em Em VII
call - ing. The wild

Verse 2:
And all the girls walk by, dressed up for each other.
And the boys do the boogie-woogie on the corner of the street.
And the people passin' by just stare in wild wonder.
And the inside juke-box roars out just like thunder.
(To Pre-chorus)

WHEN A MAN LOVES A WOMAN

Words and Music by
CALVIN LEWIS and ANDREW WRIGHT

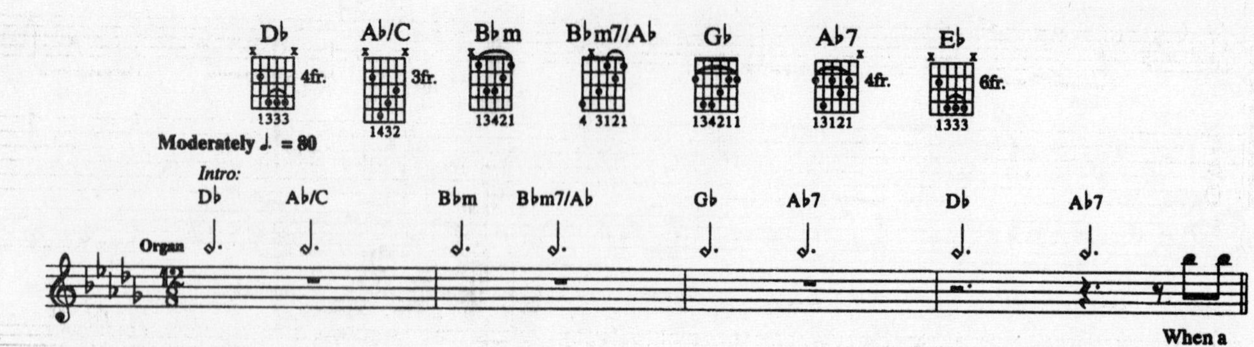

Db
Ab/C
Bbm
Bbm7/Ab
bad, he can't see it, she can do no wrong;
Gb
Ab7
1.3.
Db
Ab
turn his back on his best friend he put her down. 2. When a
*After Verse 3, repeat and fade ad lib. vocal.
2.
To Next Strain
4.
Repeat and fade
Db
Db7
Db
Ab
world.
Bridge:
Gb
Db
Well, this man loves you, wom-an,

Verse 2:
When a man loves a woman,
Spend his very last dime
Tryin' to hold on to what he needs.
He'd give up all of his comforts
And sleep out in the rain
If she said that's the way it ought to be.
(To Bridge:)

Verse 3:
When a man loves a woman
Down deep in his soul,
She can bring him such misery.
If she plays him for a fool,
He's the last one to know;
Loving eyes can never see.

Verse 4:
When a man loves a woman,
He could never do her wrong.
He'd never want some other girl.
Yes, when a man loves a woman,
I know exactly how he feels.
'Cause baby, baby, baby, you're my world.

WIPEOUT

By THE SURFARIS

B
C
8fr.
134211
F
8fr.
1333
C
8fr.
134211
G
10fr.
1333
F
8fr.
1333
C
8fr.
134211
To Coda
1.
2.
C Guitar Solo:
C
8fr.
134211
Elec. Gtr. 2 resume rhy. fig. A simile
1/4
1/4
F
8fr.
1333
C
8fr.
134211
1/4
1/4

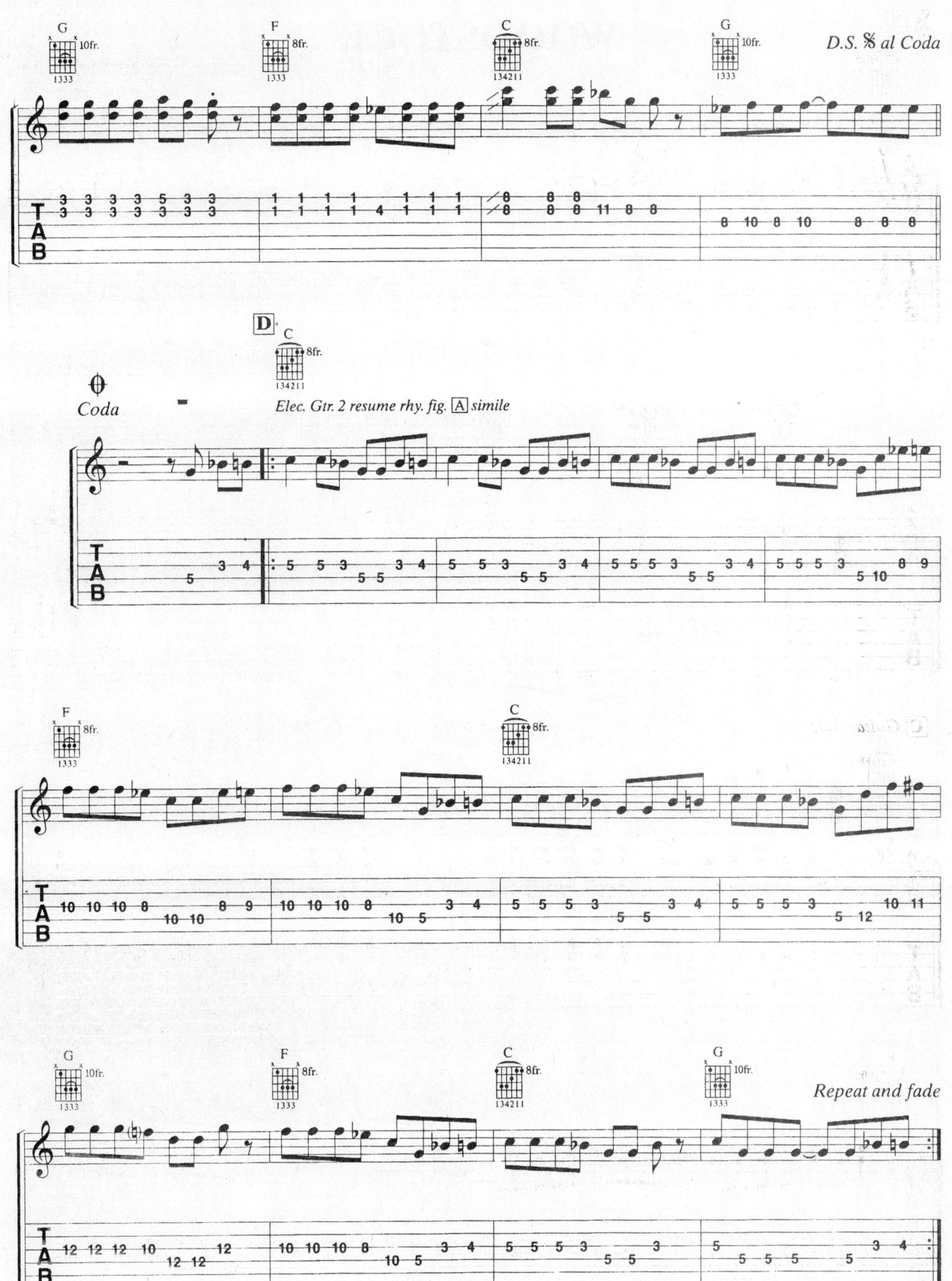

G
10fr.
1333
F
8fr.
1333
C
8fr.
134211
G
10fr.
1333
D.S. 𝄋 al Coda
D
C
8fr.
134211
Coda
Elec. Gtr. 2 resume rhy. fig. A simile
F
8fr.
1333
C
8fr.
134211
G
10fr.
1333
F
8fr.
1333
C
8fr.
134211
G
10fr.
1333
Repeat and fade

WOODSTOCK

Words and Music by
JONI MITCHELL

Gtr. in Drop D, down 1/2 step:

⑥ = D♭ ③ = G♭
⑤ = A♭ ② = B♭
④ = D♭ ① = E♭

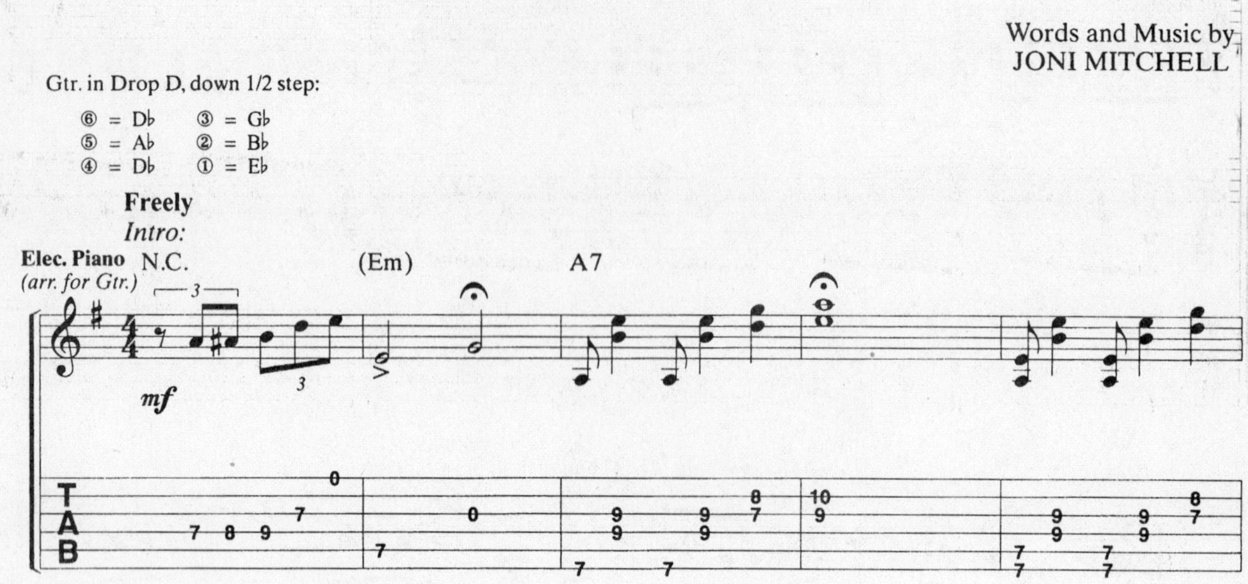

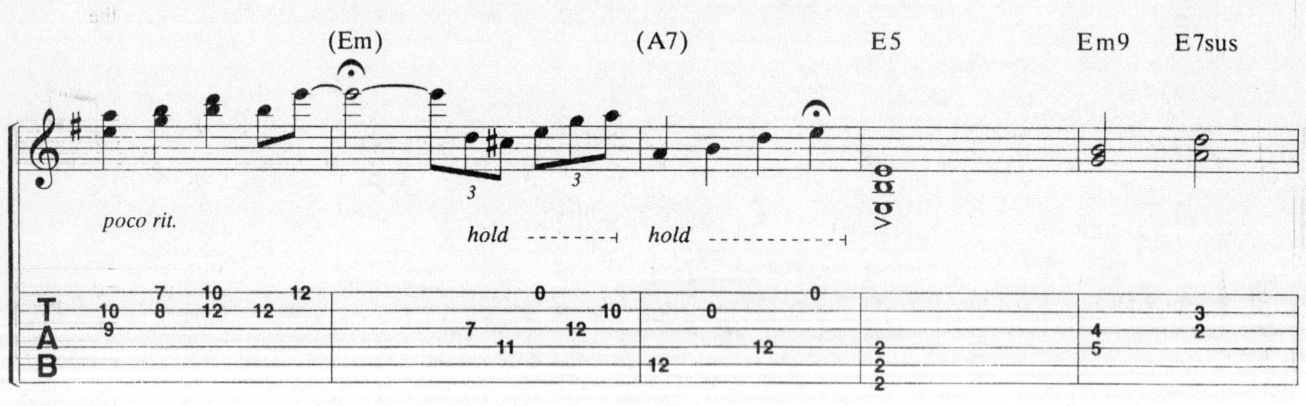

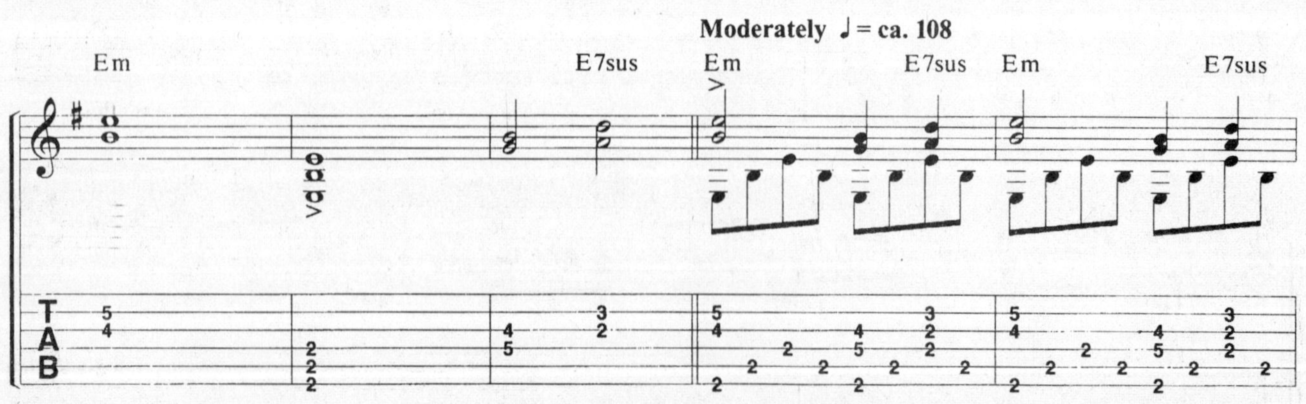

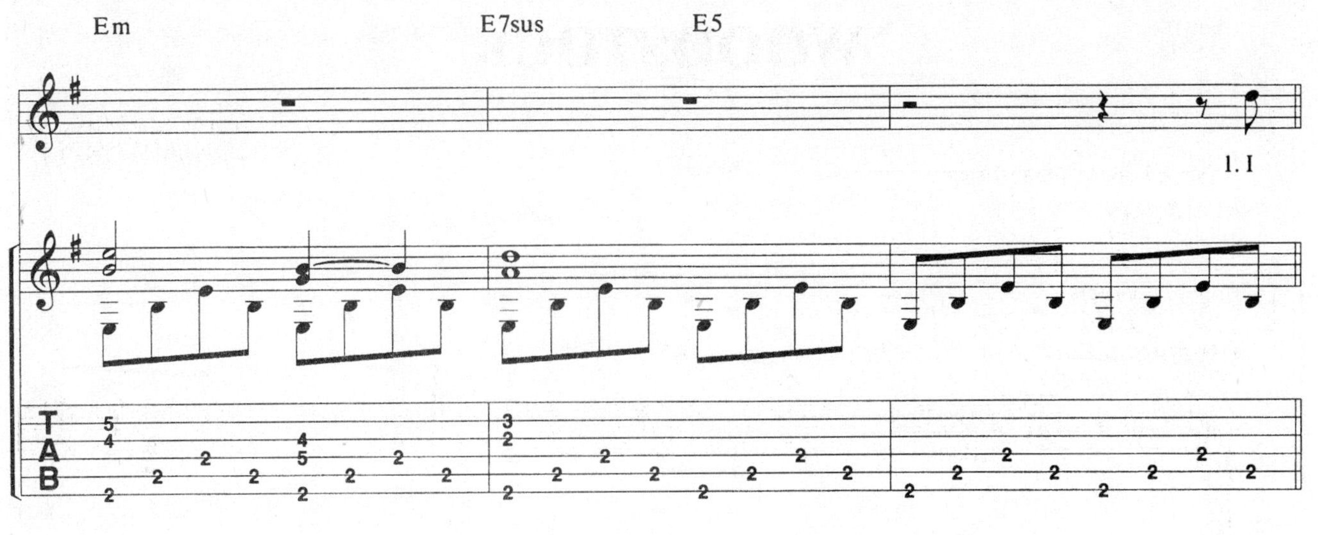
Em
E7sus
E5
1. I
T
A
B

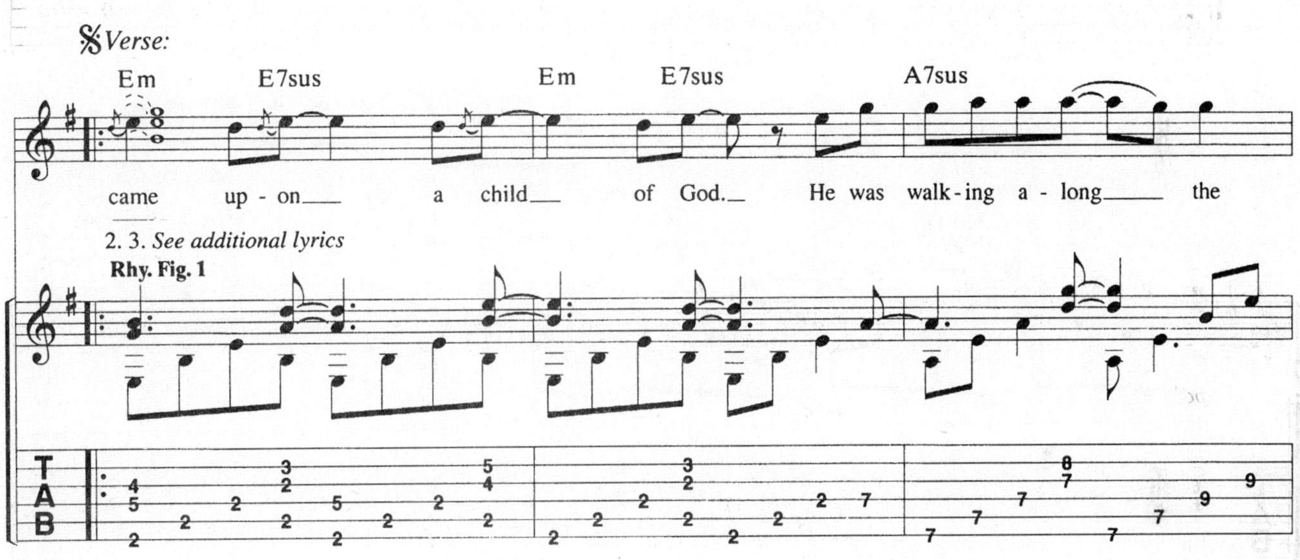
Verse:
Em
E7sus
Em
E7sus
A7sus
came up - on a child of God. He was walk - ing a - long the
2. 3. See additional lyrics
Rhy. Fig. 1
T
A
B

road and I asked him, "Where are you go - ing?" and this
T
A
B

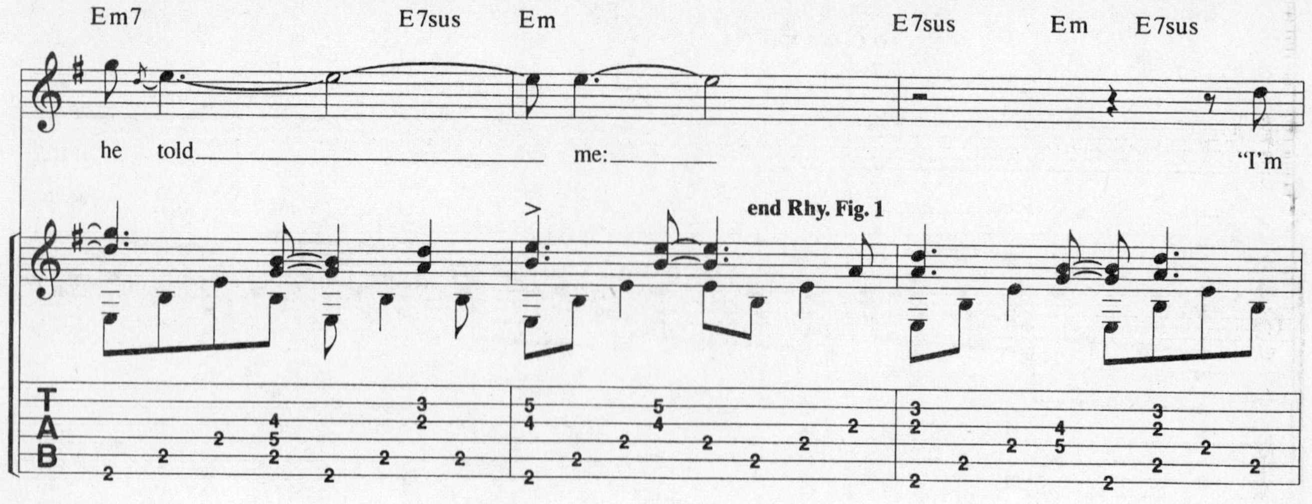
Em7
E7sus
Em
E7sus
Em
E7sus
he told
me:
"I'm
end Rhy. Fig. 1
TAB

Em
E7sus
Em
E7sus
A7sus
go-in' on down to Yas - gur's Farm. I'm gon-na join in a rock - 'n-roll
TAB

band; I'm gon-na camp out on the land; I'm gon-na try and get my
TAB

To Coda
Em7
E7sus
Em
E7sus
soul
free."
We are

Chorus:
A7sus
star - dust, we are gold -

Em
E7sus
Dsus2
en, and we've got to get our - selves back to the

G/B
A
Asus
Em
E7sus
gar - den.
Bkgd. vcl.: Doo, doo, doo, doo, doo, doo, doo,

Em
E7sus
E5
D.S. 𝄋 al Coda
2. Then
3. By the
doo, doo, doo, doo, doo, doo, doo, doo, doo, doo, doo, doo, doo, doo, doo, doo, doo.

Coda
Em
E7sus
E5
E7sus
Em
bove_ our na - tion. We are

Chorus:
A7sus
A7sus
star - dust,
bil - lion year old car -
TAB

A7
A9
- bon. We are gold - en,
TAB

A7sus
Em
E7sus
caught in the dev - il's bar - gain, and we got to get our -
TAB

Dsus2
A7sus
G(6)
selves back to the gar -
T
A
B

E7sus
Em7
- den.
rit. poco a poco
T
A
B

Em7/B
A9
Em
dim.
T
A
B

Slower
Outro:

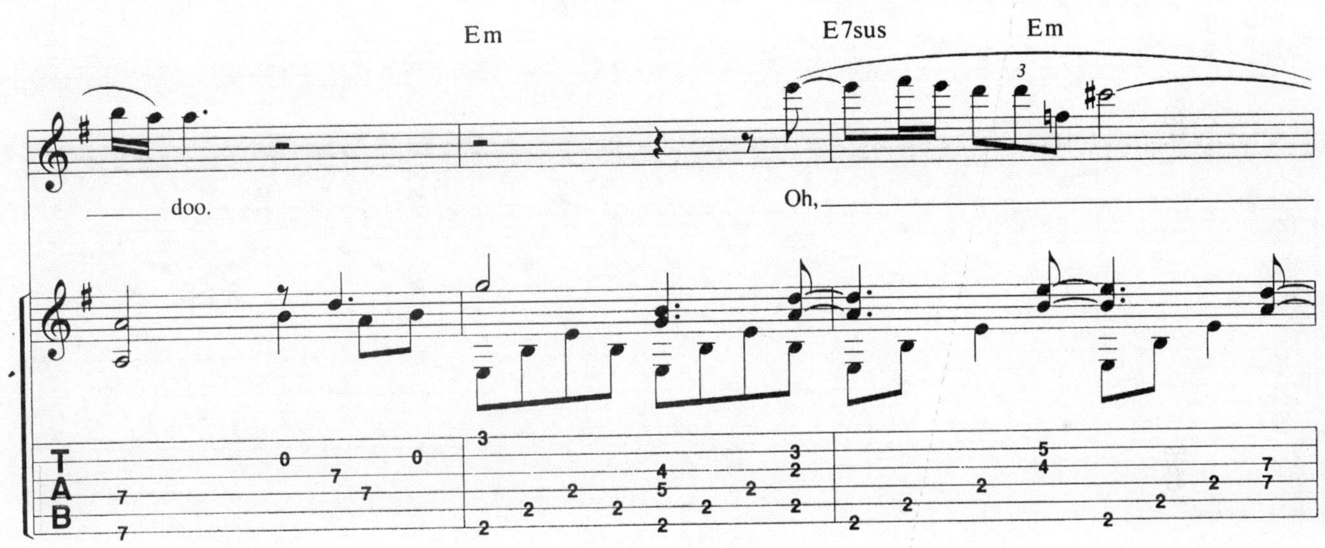

Freely

*Left-hand tap.
**Right-hand tap.

Verse 2:
Then can I walk beside you?
I have come here to lose the smog.
And I feel to be a cog
In something turning.
Well, maybe it is just the time of year,
Or maybe it's the time of man.
I don't know who I am,
But, you know, life is for learning.
(To Chorus:)

Verse 3:
By the time we got to Woodstock,
We were half a million strong,
And everywhere was song and celebration.
And I dreamed I saw the bombers
Riding shotgun in the sky,
And they were turning into butterflies
Above our nation.
(To Chorus:)

WORDS OF LOVE

Words and Music by
JOHN PHILLIPS

Moderately ♩ = 112 (♫ = ♩♪ triplet)

Intro:

E 12fr. 3211 — Abm/Eb 11fr. 3421 — Dbm 9fr. 3111 — Eb 11fr. 3211 — Ab 4fr. 3211 — Eb7 4fr. 3241

Elec. Gtr.

Drums — Piano enters

𝄋 *Verse:* **1st time** (♫ = ♩♪ triplet)
2nd time (♫ = ♫)

Ab7 4fr. 131211 — Gb7 131211 — Cb7 7fr. 131211 — Bb7 6fr. 131211 — Eb7 4fr. 3241

Cont. rhy. simile

Words of love, so soft and tender, won't win a girl's heart anymore.
2nd time (now.)

Ab7 — Gb7 — Cb7

If you love her, then you must send her somewhere where she's never

Bb7 — Ab7 — Gb7

been before. Worn out phrases and longing gazes won't
(Ooh, ooh,

Cb7 — *To Coda* ⊕ — Bb7 — A7 5fr. — Ab7

Elec. Gtr. — *Resume rhy. fig. simile*

get you where you want to go. Words of love,
ooh, ooh.) (Ooh,

Gb7 — E7 5fr. 3241 — Eb7 4fr. 3241

soft and tender, won't win her.
ooh, ooh.)

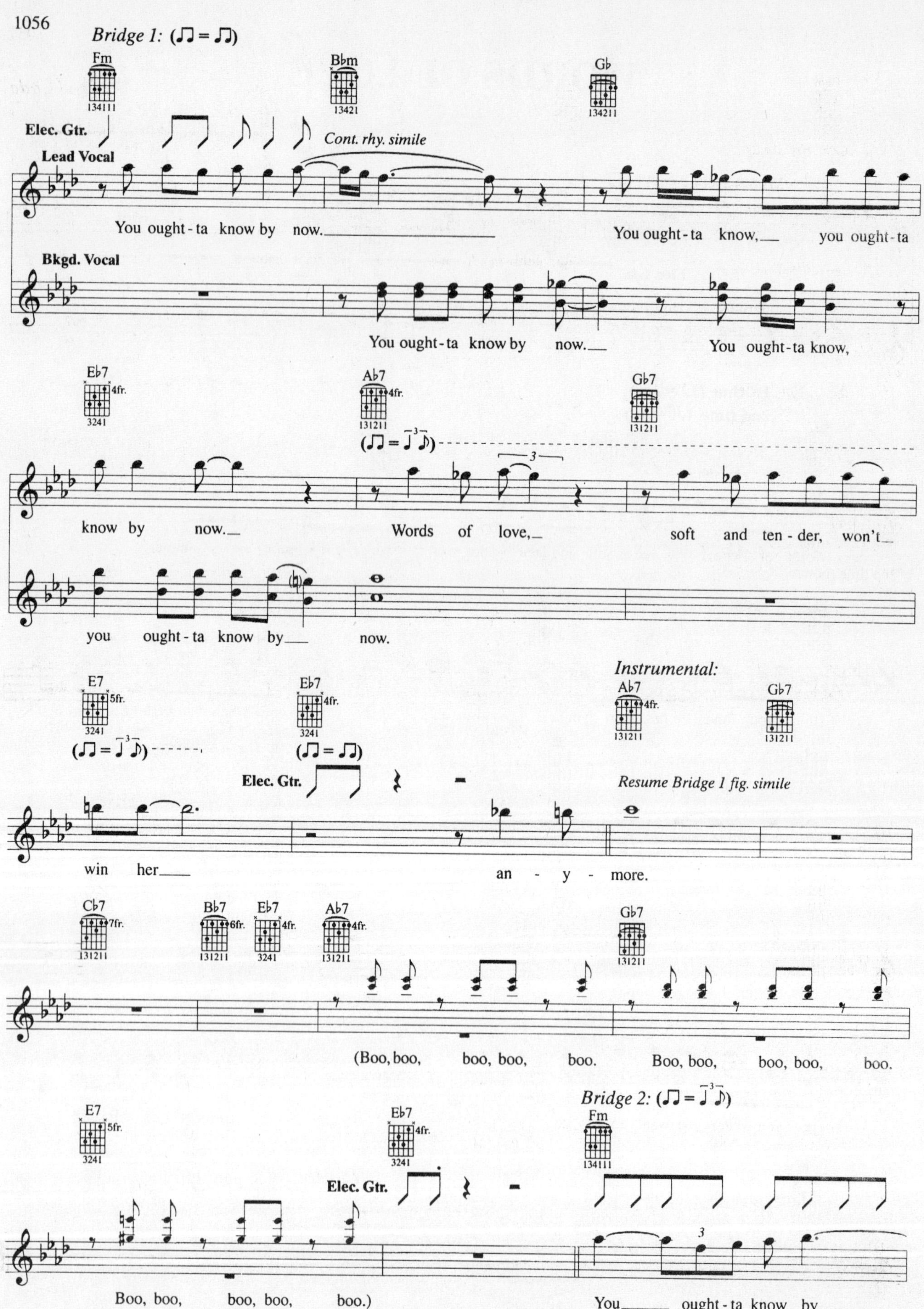
Bridge 1: (♫ = ♫)
Fm
134111
Bbm
13421
Gb
134211
Elec. Gtr.
Cont. rhy. simile
Lead Vocal
You ought - ta know by now.
You ought - ta know,
you ought - ta
Bkgd. Vocal
You ought - ta know by now.
You ought - ta know,
Eb7
4fr.
3241
Ab7
4fr.
131211
Gb7
131211
know by now.
Words of love,
soft and ten - der, won't
you ought - ta know by now.
Instrumental:
E7
5fr.
3241
Eb7
4fr.
3241
Ab7
4fr.
131211
Gb7
131211
Elec. Gtr.
Resume Bridge 1 fig. simile
win her an - y - more.
Cb7
7fr.
131211
Bb7
6fr.
131211
Eb7
4fr.
3241
Ab7
4fr.
131211
Gb7
131211
(Boo, boo, boo, boo, boo. Boo, boo, boo, boo, boo.
E7
5fr.
3241
Eb7
4fr.
3241
Bridge 2:
Fm
134111
Elec. Gtr.
Boo, boo, boo, boo, boo.)
You ought - ta know by

Bbm
13421
Gb
134211
Eb7
4fr.
3241
D.S. al Coda
Cont. rhy. simile
Elec. Gtr.
now.
You outht - ta know, you ought - ta know by now.
You ought - ta know by now. You ought - ta know, you ought - ta know by

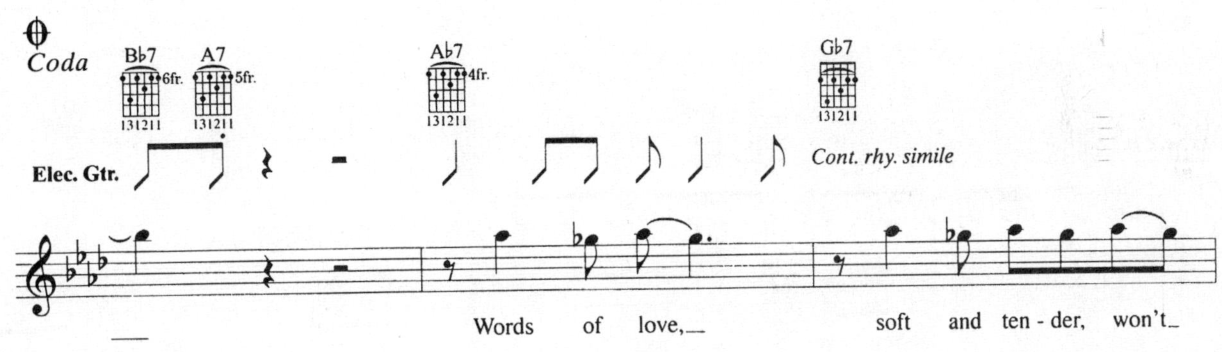
Coda
Bb7
6fr.
131211
A7
5fr.
131211
Ab7
4fr.
131211
Gb7
131211
Elec. Gtr.
Cont. rhy. simile
Words of love, soft and ten - der, won't

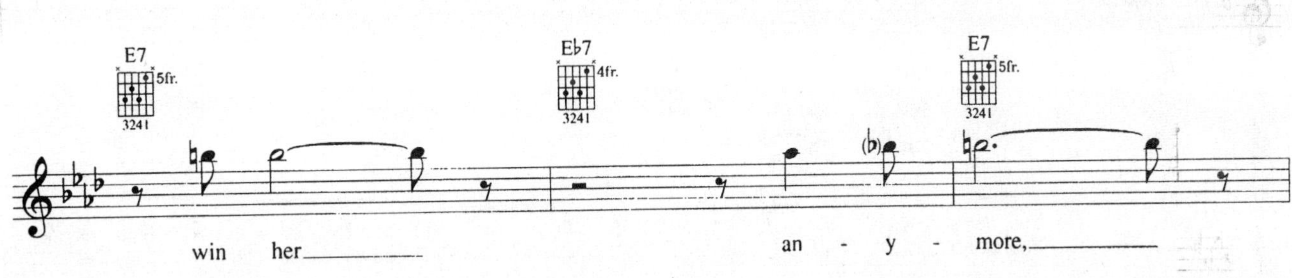
E7
5fr.
3241
Eb7
4fr.
3241
E7
5fr.
3241
win her an - y - more,

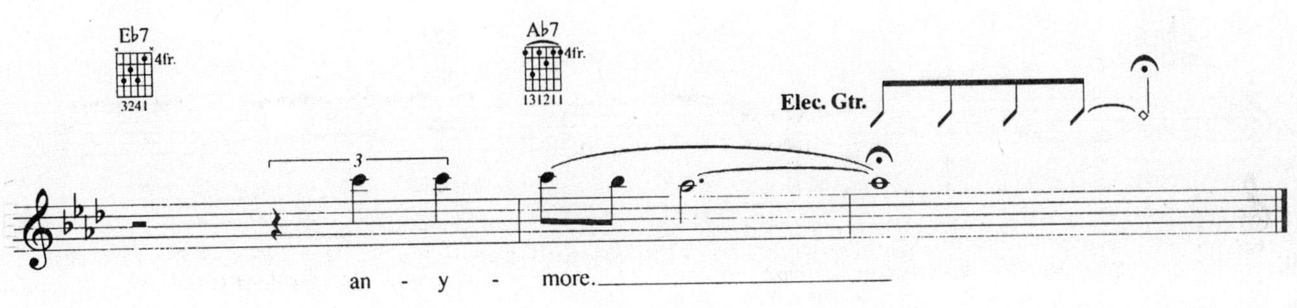
Eb7
4fr.
3241
Ab7
4fr.
131211
Elec. Gtr.
an - y - more.

YOU DON'T OWN ME

Words and Music by
JOHN MADARA and DAVE WHITE

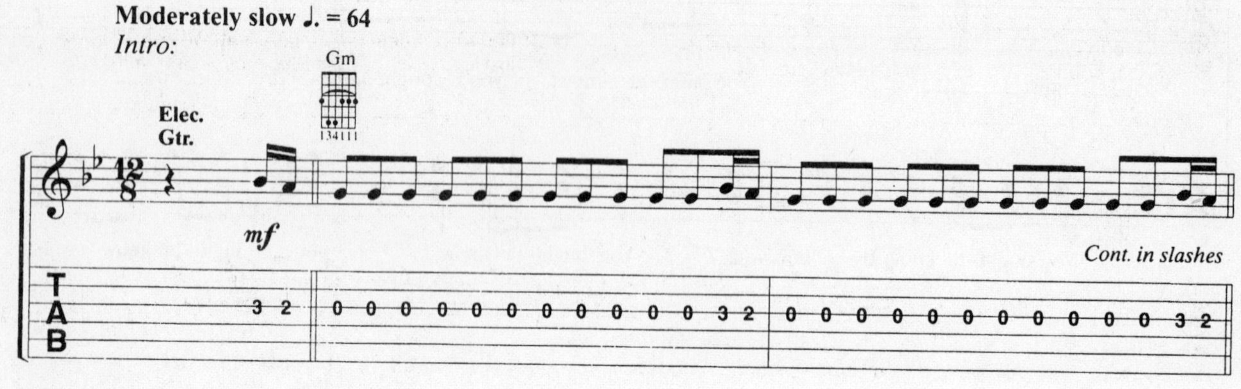
Moderately slow ♩. = 64
Intro:
Gm
Elec. Gtr.
mf
Cont. in slashes

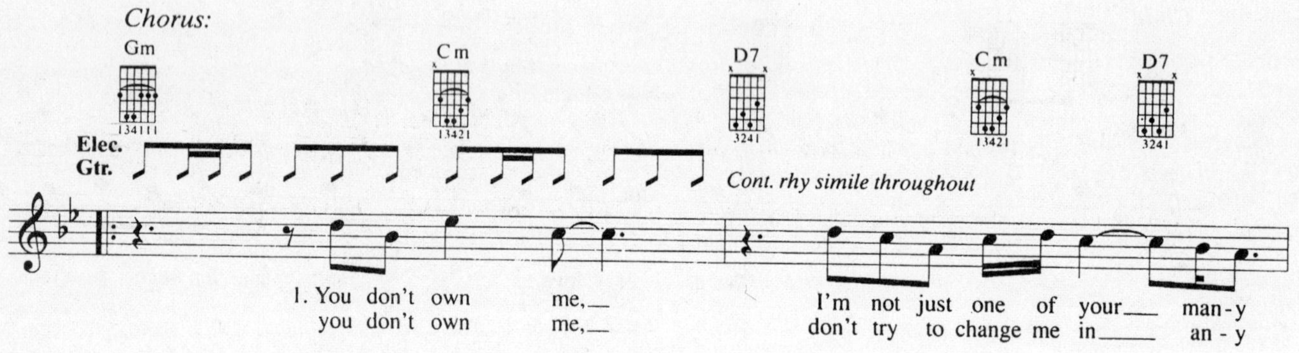
Chorus:
Gm
Cm
D7
Cm
D7
Elec. Gtr.
Cont. rhy simile throughout
1. You don't own me, I'm not just one of your man-y
you don't own me, don't try to change me in an-y

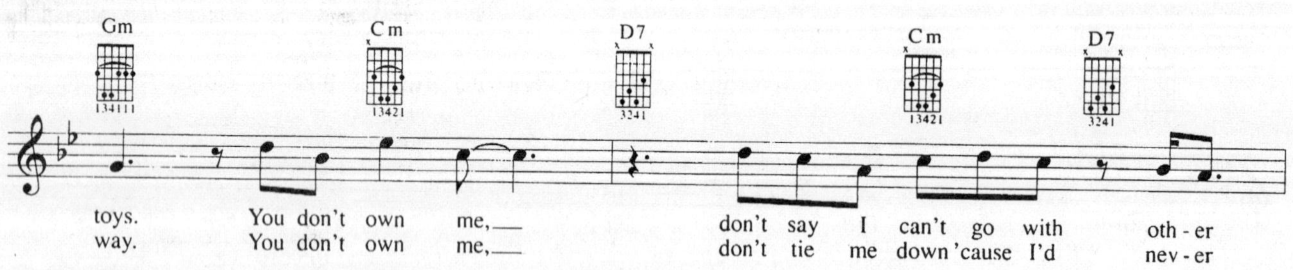
Gm
Cm
D7
Cm
D7
toys. You don't own me, don't say I can't go with oth-er
way. You don't own me, don't tie me down 'cause I'd nev-er

G
Verses 1 & 2:
boys. 1. And don't tell me what to do,
stay. 2. I don't tell you what to say,

Em
C
don't tell me what to say. Please when I go out with you
I don't tell you what to do. So just let me be my-self,
1.
D7
2.
D7
don't put me on dis-play. 2.'Cause that's all I ask of you. I'm
Verse 3:
Ab
Fm
young and I love to be young, I'm free and I love to be free to
Db
Eb7
live my life the way I want. To say and do what-ev-er I please.
Interlude:
G#m
C#m
D#7
C#m
D#7
Strings
G#m
C#m
D#7
C#m
D#7
G#
And

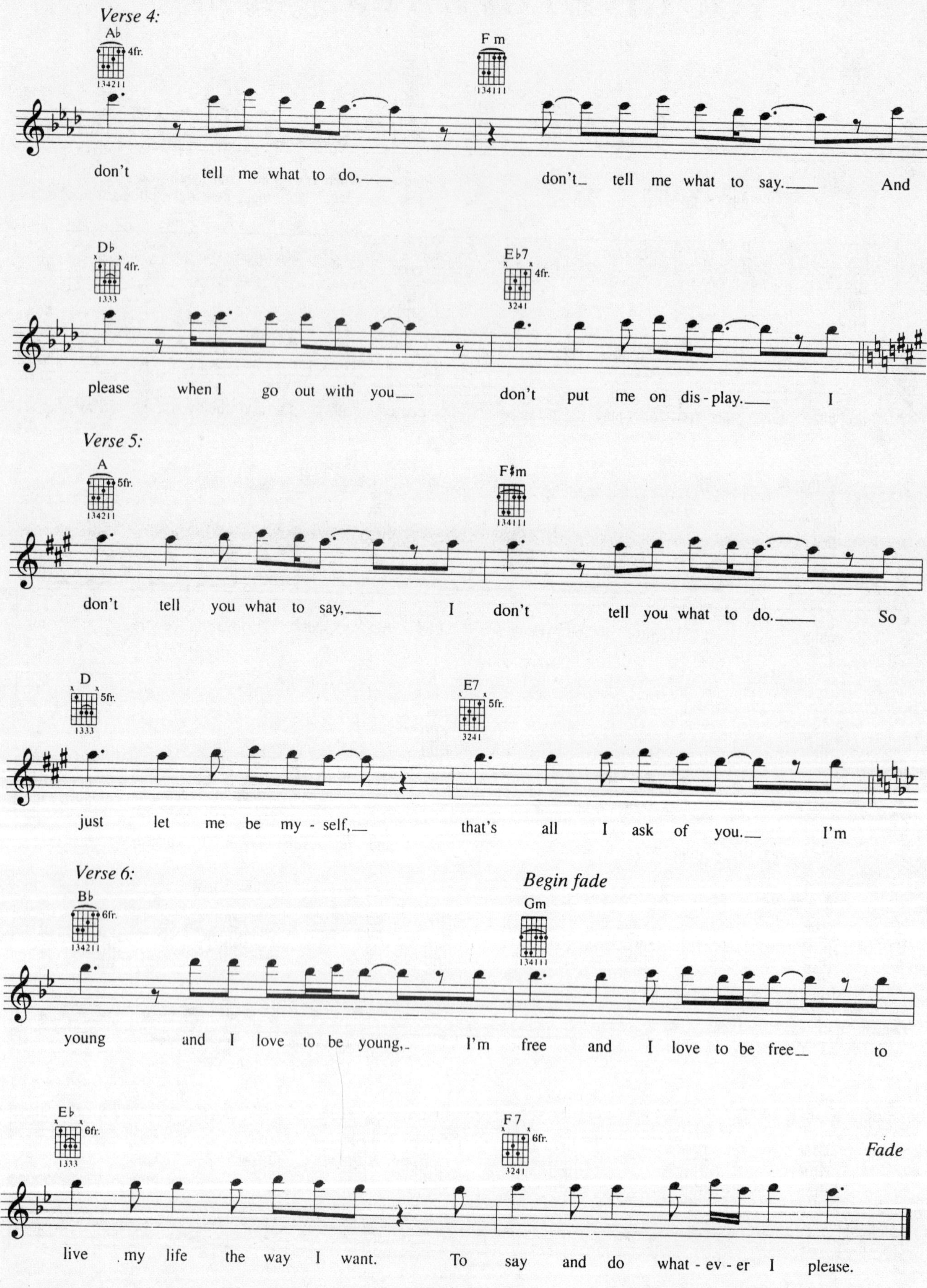
Verse 4:
A♭
4fr.
134211
F m
134111
don't tell me what to do, don't tell me what to say. And
D♭
4fr.
1333
E♭7
4fr.
3241
please when I go out with you don't put me on dis-play. I
Verse 5:
A
5fr.
134211
F♯m
134111
don't tell you what to say, I don't tell you what to do. So
D
5fr.
1333
E7
5fr.
3241
just let me be my-self, that's all I ask of you. I'm
Verse 6:
Begin fade
B♭
6fr.
134211
Gm
134111
young and I love to be young, I'm free and I love to be free to
E♭
6fr.
1333
F7
6fr.
3241
Fade
live my life the way I want. To say and do what-ev-er I please.

YOU GIVE LOVE A BAD NAME

Words and Music by
JON BON JOVI, RICHIE SAMBORA
and DESMOND CHILD

Gtr. 2 tacet
N.C. (Cm)
Gtr. 1: w/ Fill 1, 2nd time
Eb5
1. An
2. You
Gtr. 1
Rhy. Fig. 1
End Rhy. Fig. 1
P.M.
w/ bar
-1/2
Verse
Gtr. 1: w/ Rhy. Fig. 1, 4 times
N.C. (Cm)
an - gel's smile is what you sell. You prom - ised me heav - en, then put me through hell.
paint your smile on your lips, blood - red nails on your fin - ger tips. A
Chains of love got a hold on me. When pas - sion's a pris - on you can't break free.
school boy's dream, you act so shy. Your ver - y first kiss was your first kiss good - bye.
Pre-Chorus
F5
Eb5
Whoa, you're a load - ed gun. Yeah.
Fill 1
Gtr. 1

Bb5
N.C.(Bb)
Oh, there's no - where to run. No one can save me, the dam - age is done.
8va
loco
P.H.
w/ bar
P.H.
w/ bar
pitch: D
Chorus
C5
Ab5
C5
Bb5
C5
Ab5
Bb5
Eb5
C5
Shot through the heart, and you're to blame. You give love a bad name, bad name. I
Rhy. Fig. 2
End Rhy. Fig. 2
Ab5
C5
Bb5
C5
Ab5
Bb5
Eb5
C5
play my part, and you play your game. You give love a bad name, bad name. And
1.
2.
Ab5
Bb5
you give love a bad name.
* Gtr. 2
Harm.
* w/ harmonizer

Guitar Solo
Gtr. 1: w/ Rhy. Fig. 2, 3 times
C5 Ab5 C5 Bb5
C5
Ab5
C5 Bb5
C5
Gtr. 2
w/ bar
w/ bar
Ab5
C5 Bb5
C5
C5
Ab5
Gtr. 1
w/ bar
full
P.M.
G5
Chorus
Gtrs. 1 & 2 tacet
N.C.
Oh.
Shot through the heart, and
w/ bar
you're to blame. You give love a bad name. I play my part, and you
play your game. You give love a bad name, bad name.

C5 Ab5 C5 Bb5 C5 Ab5 Bb5 Eb5 C5
Shot through the heart, _ and you're to _ blame. You give love ___ a bad name, bad name. I
Gtr. 1
Ab5 C5 Bb5 C5 Ab5 Bb5 Eb5 C5
play my part, _ and you play your _ game. You give love ___ a bad name, bad name.
Outro
Play 3 Times and Fade
Ab5 Bb5 Eb5 C5 Ab5 Bb5 Eb5 C5
You give love. ___ You give love. ___ Bad name.
(Whoa. ___ Whoa. ___ Whoa. ___ Whoa. ___)
Gtr. 1
P.M.
*Gtr. 2
full
full
full
full
*w/ harmonizer

YOU GOT LUCKY

Words and Music by
TOM PETTY and MIKE CAMPBELL

w/Fill 2 (2nd time)
Am11
F
Yeah go,
but re - mem - ber:
w/trem. bar
f
pp
*3rd time only
Chorus:
C
Am11
Good love is hard to find.
Good love is hard to find. You got
To Coda
F
G
luck - y babe,
you got luck - y babe,
when I found you.
1. w/Rhy. Figs. 1 & 2
Am9
Am
Dm9
Dm
G7sus
G
G(9)
Fill 2
hold

Guitar Solo:
2. w/Rhy. Figs. 1 & 2 (2 times)
Am9
Am
Dm9
Dm
G7sus
G
G (9)
G7sus
w/trem. bar
D.S. 𝄋 al Coda
Yeah, go
⊕ Coda
w/Rhy. Figs. 1 & 2 (6 times)
8va
Am9
w/trem. bar

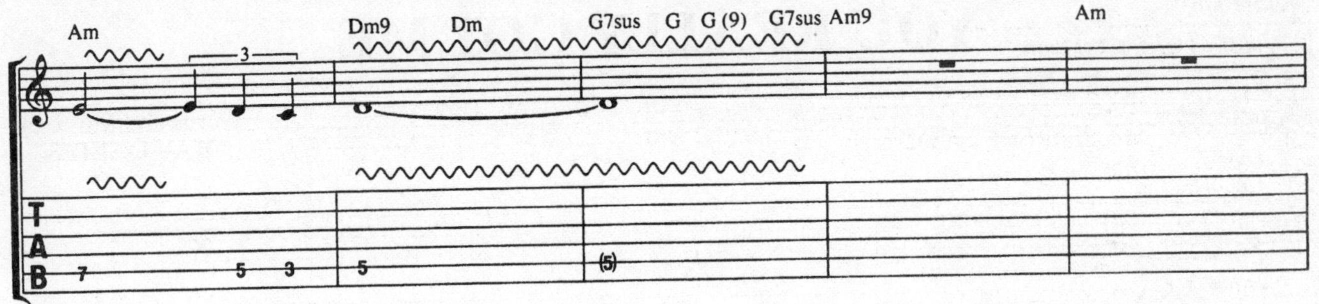

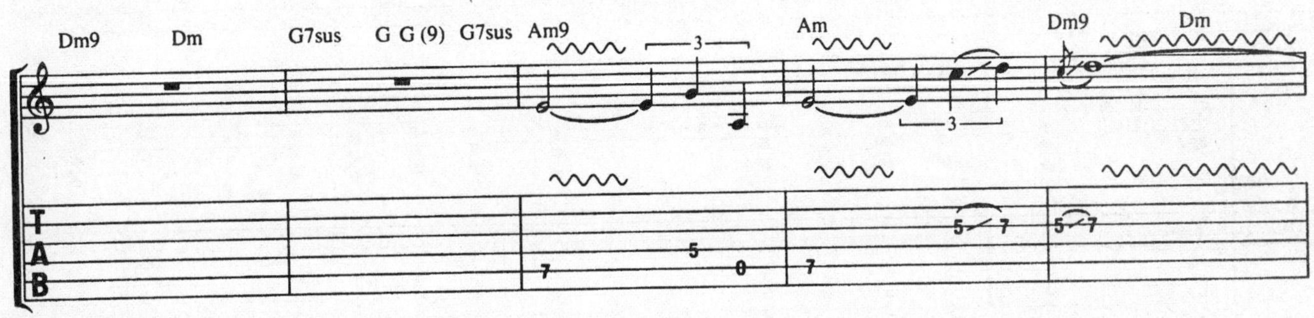

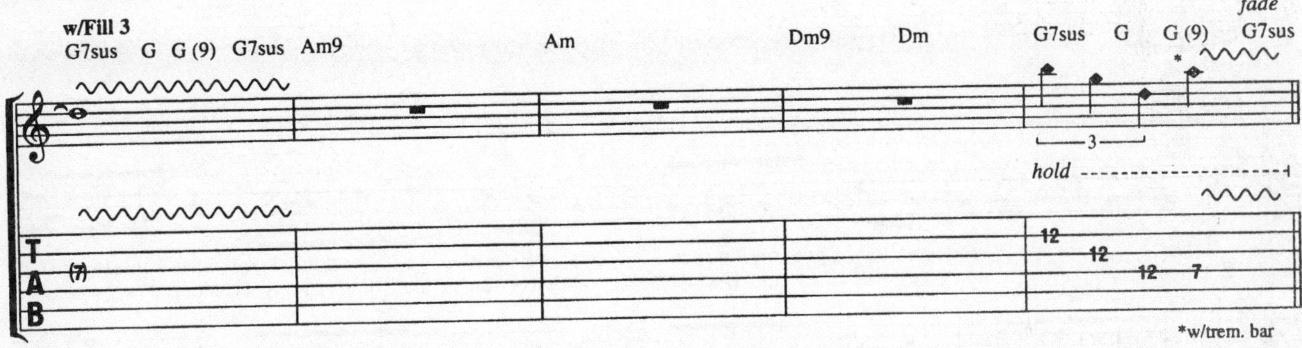

Verse2:
You put a hand on my cheek,
And then you turn your eyes away.
If you don't feel complete,
If I don't take you all of the way then go.
Yeah go, but remember:
(To Chorus:)

YOU REALLY GOT ME

Words and Music by
RAY DAVIES

A
5fr.
134211
so I can't sleep at night.
so I can't sleep at night.
Yeah, you real - ly
(Ah.
got me now, you got me so I don't know what I'm do - in', ah. Oh
)
D
10fr.
134211
yeah you real - ly got me now, you got me so I can't sleep at night. You
(Yeah.
)
TAB

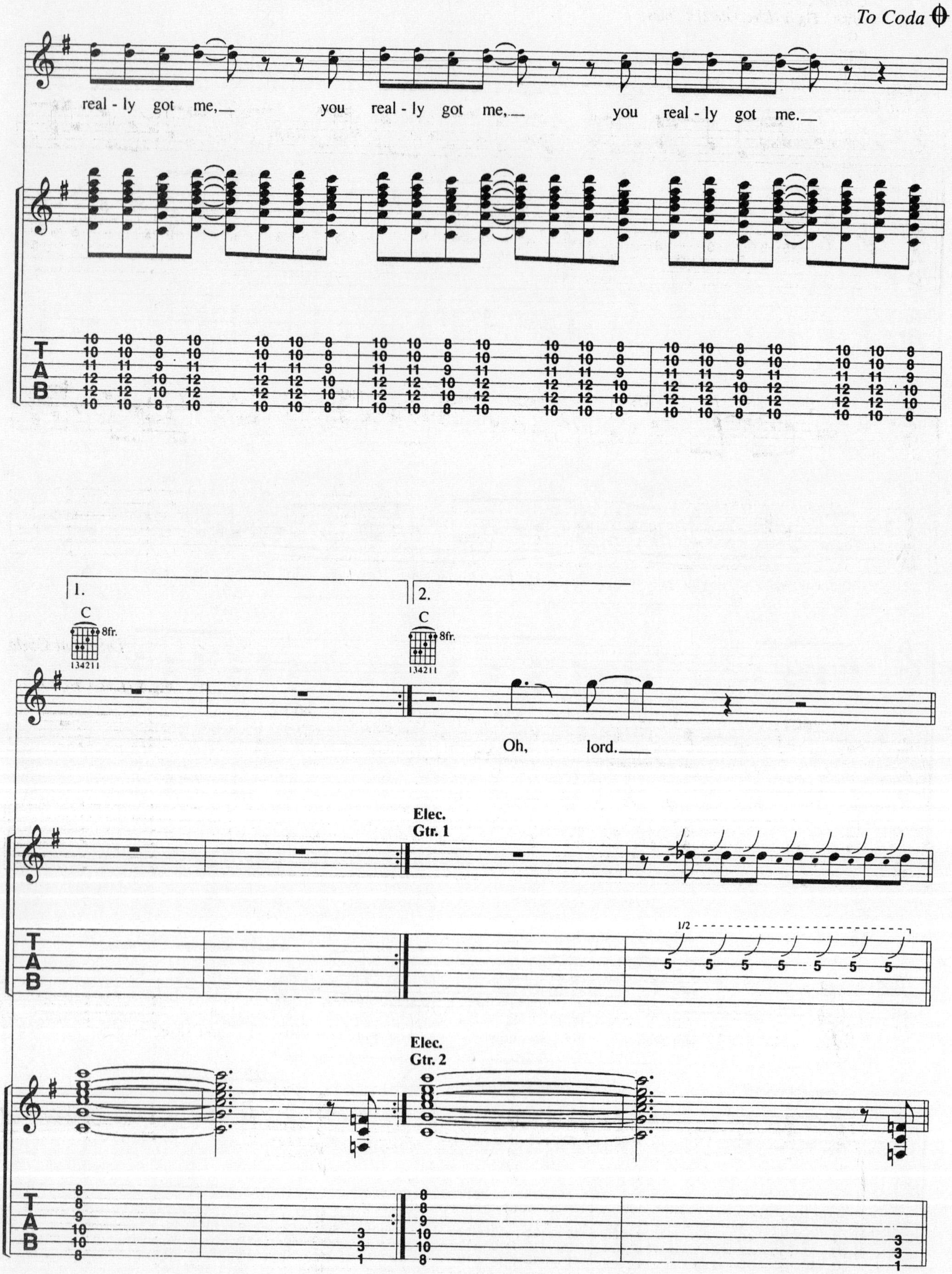

To Coda
real - ly got me,__ you real - ly got me,__ you real - ly got me.__

1. C 8fr. 134211

2. C 8fr. 134211

Oh, lord.___

Elec. Gtr. 1

1/2

Elec. Gtr. 2

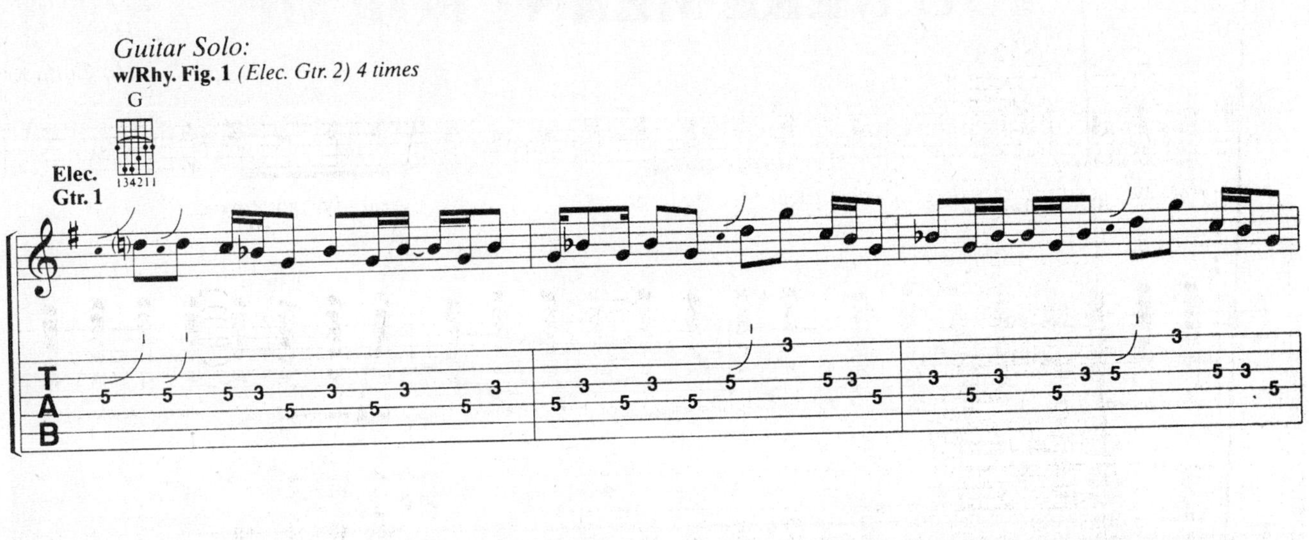
Guitar Solo:
w/Rhy. Fig. 1 (Elec. Gtr. 2) 4 times
G
134211
Elec.
Gtr. 1

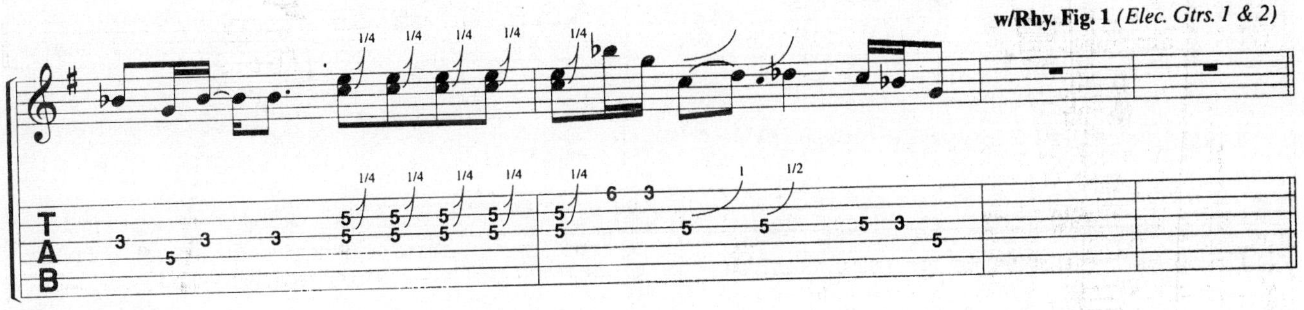
D.S. 𝄋 al Coda
w/Rhy. Fig. 1 (Elec. Gtrs. 1 & 2)

Coda

YOU WERE MEANT FOR ME

All gtrs. tune down 1/2 step:
⑥ = E♭ ③ = G♭
⑤ = A♭ ② = B♭
④ = D♭ ① = E♭

Words and Music by
JEWEL KILCHER and STEVE POLTZ

Moderately ♩ = 132

Intro:

C(9) G6/B C Em

Gtr. 1 (Acoustic)

mf

hold throughout

Verse:

C(9) G6/B C Em

1. I hear the clock, it's six A.__ M.,____ I feel so far__ from where I've__ been.__
2.3. *See additional lyrics*

Rhy. Fig. 1

C(9) G6/B C D

I got my eggs, I got my pan-cakes, too.____ *I got my ma-ple syr-up,* ev-'ry-thing but__ you.__

end Rhy. Fig. 1

w/Rhy. Fig. 1 (Gtr. 1)

C(9) G6/B

I break the yokes and make a smile - y____ face,________

C
Em
C(9)
I kind of like it in my brand-new place. Wipe the spots a-bove the mir-ror, don't leave my
G6/B
C
D
keys in the door. I never put wet tow-els on the floor an-y-more, 'cause
Chorus:
C
D
G
G5/F♯
Em
dreams last so long, e-ven af-ter you're gone.
C
D
G
G/F♯
Em
I know that you love me and soon you will see you were
To Coda
1.
C
D
Em
(D6)
meant for me, and I was meant for you.
8va
harm.

2.
Bridge:
Em
Am7
D
you.
I
go a- bout my bus- 'ness, I'm do- ing fine. Be- sides, a-
Bm
D
C
G/B
Am7
what would I say if I had you on the line?
Same old sto- ry not
D
Bm
E5
D.C. al Coda
much to say,
hearts are bro- ken ev- 'ry - day.
Coda
Em
C
you.
Yeah,
you were meant for me
and

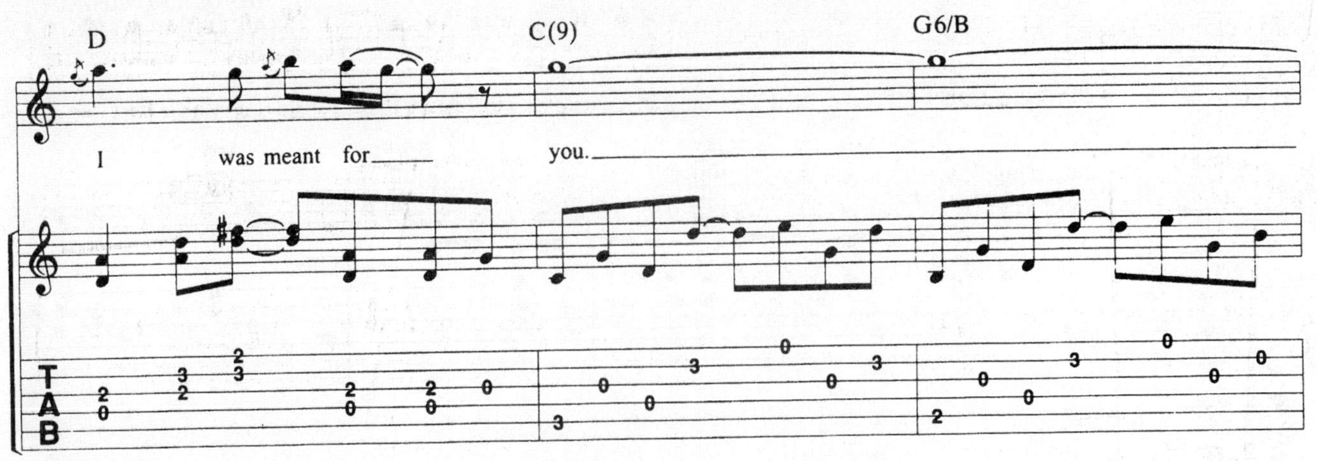

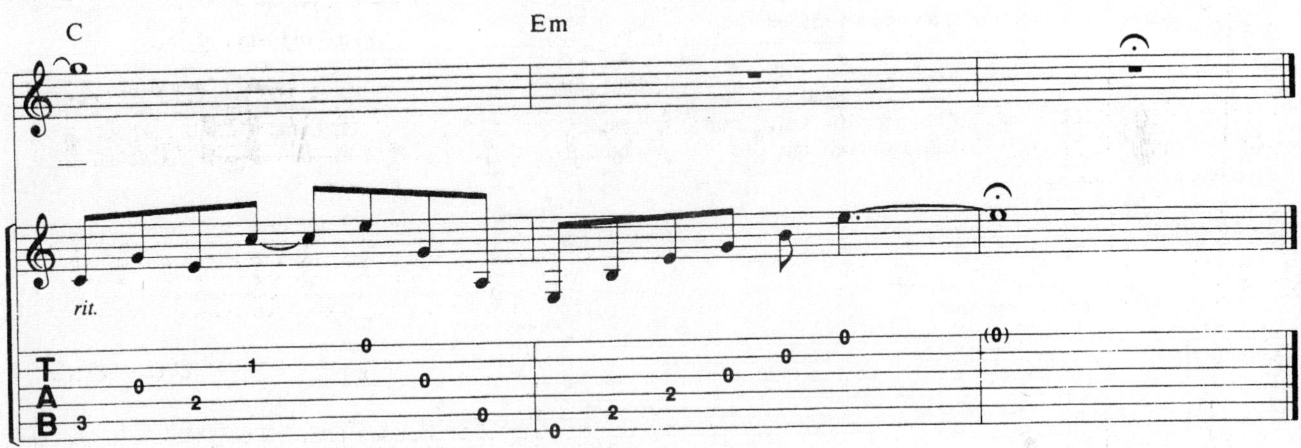

Verse 2:
I called my mama, she was out for a walk.
Consoled a cup of coffee, but it didn't wanna talk.
So I picked up a paper, it was more bad news.
More hearts being broken or people being used.
Put on my coat in the pouring rain.
I saw a movie, it just wasn't the same.
'Cause it was happy and I was sad
And it made me miss you, oh, so bad.
(To Chorus:)

Verse 3:
I brush my teeth and put the cap back on.
I know you hate it when I leave the light on.
I pick a book up and then I turn the sheets down,
And then I take a deep breath and a good look around.
Put on my pj's and hop into bed.
I'm half alive, but I feel mostly dead.
I try and tell myself it'll be all right,
I just shouldn't think anymore tonight.
(To Chorus:)

YOU'RE A GOD

All gtrs. tuned down 1/2 step:

⑥ = E♭ ③ = G♭
⑤ = A♭ ② = B♭
④ = D♭ ① = E♭

Words and Music by
MATTHEW SCANELL

Moderately slow ♩ = 98

Intro:

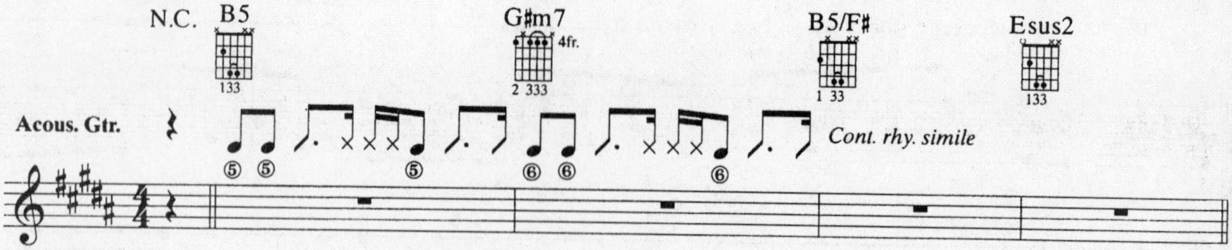

N.C.
B5
G♯m7
B5/F♯
Esus2
Acous. Gtr.
Cont. rhy. simile

𝄋 *Verse:*

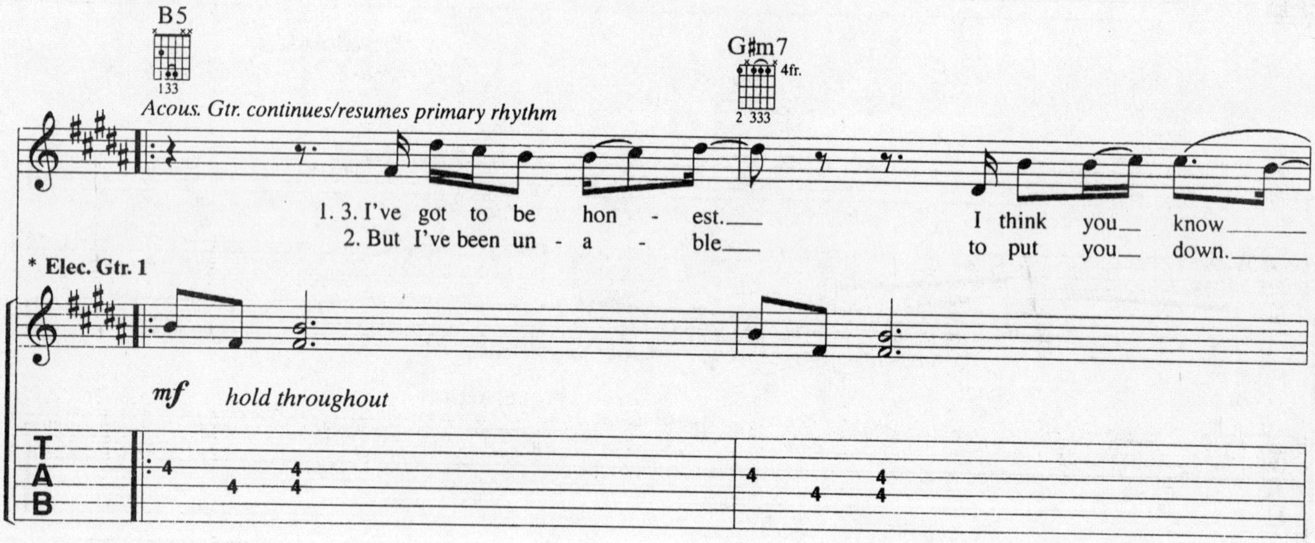

B5
G♯m7
Acous. Gtr. continues/resumes primary rhythm
1. 3. I've got to be hon - est. I think you know
2. But I've been un - a - ble to put you down.
* Elec. Gtr. 1
mf
hold throughout

*Verses 2 & 3 only.

B5/F♯
Esus2
we're cov-ered in lies and that's O K.
I'm still learn - ing things I ought to know by now.

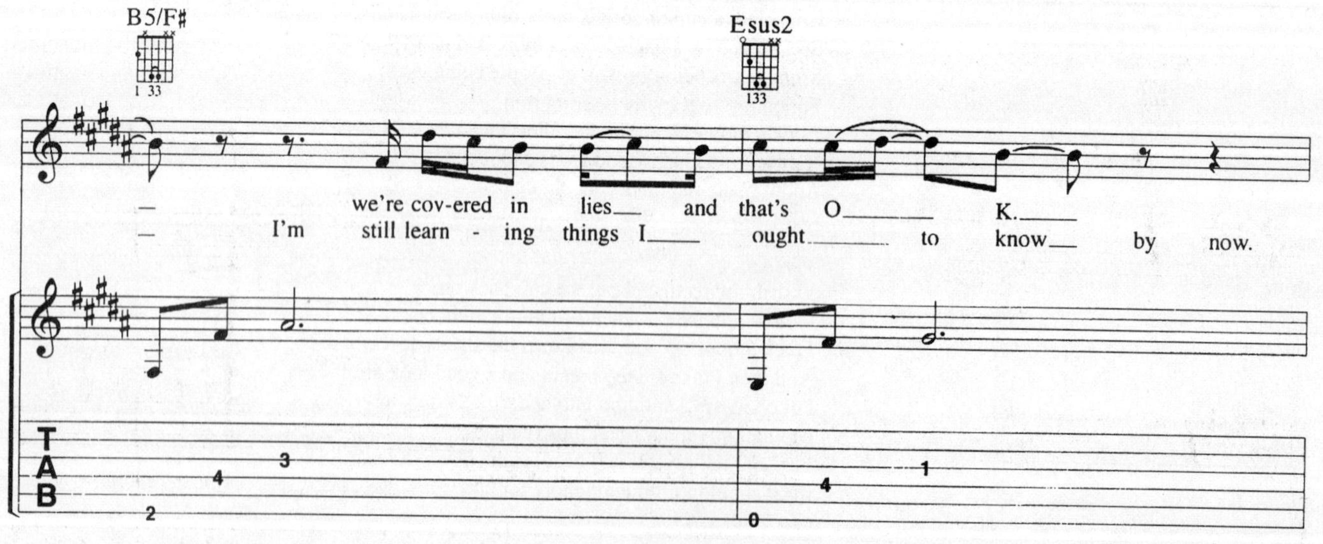

B5
G♯m7
There's some-where be - yond this, I know.
It's un - der the ta - ble, so
B5/F♯
Esus2
Pre-chorus:
Gsus2
Acous. Gtr. & Elec. Gtr. 2
But I hope I can find the words to say.
I need some-thing more to show some - how.
Nev - er a - gain,
*Elec. Gtr. 1
*Ad lib. simile on repeats.
Asus2
Gsus2
Asus2
no.
No, nev - er a - gain.
'Cause
**Elec. Gtr. 3
P.M. and harm.
Elec. Gtr. 1
**2nd & 3rd times only.

Chorus:
B5
G♯m7
B5/F♯
*Elec. Gtr. 2
Rhy. Fig. 1
you're a god and I am not. And I just thought that
* 2 gtrs. arr. for 1 throughout section.
w/Rhy. Fig. 1 (Elec. Gtr. 2)
E
end Rhy. Fig. 1
B5
G♯m7
you would know. You're a god and I am not. And
To Coda
1.
B5/F♯
E
Bsus
Elec. Gtr. 2
I just thought I'd let you go.
2.
E
Guitar Solo:
C♯m
A
Asus2
Elec. Gtr. 2
let you go.
Elec. Gtr. 1

B5
133
1.
2.
D.S. % al Coda
Coda
Chorus:
E
231
B5
133
G#m7
4fr.
2 333
*Elec. Gtr. 2
let you go.
You're a god.
Oh, and I am not.
* 2 guitars arr. for 1 throughout section.
B5/F#
1 33
Cont. rhy. simile
E
231
B5
133
Oh, I thought that you would know.
I just thought that you would know.
You're a god.
G#m7
4fr.
2 333
B5/F#
1 33
E
231
Oh, and I am not.
I'd let you go.
I just thought I'd let you go.
Outro:
Bsus
134
Repeat and fade
Acous. Gtr. resumes primary rhythm
**Elec. Gtr. 2
** 1st time only.

YOU LEARN

Lyrics by
ALANIS MORISSETTE

Music by
ALANIS MORISSETTE
and GLEN BALLARD

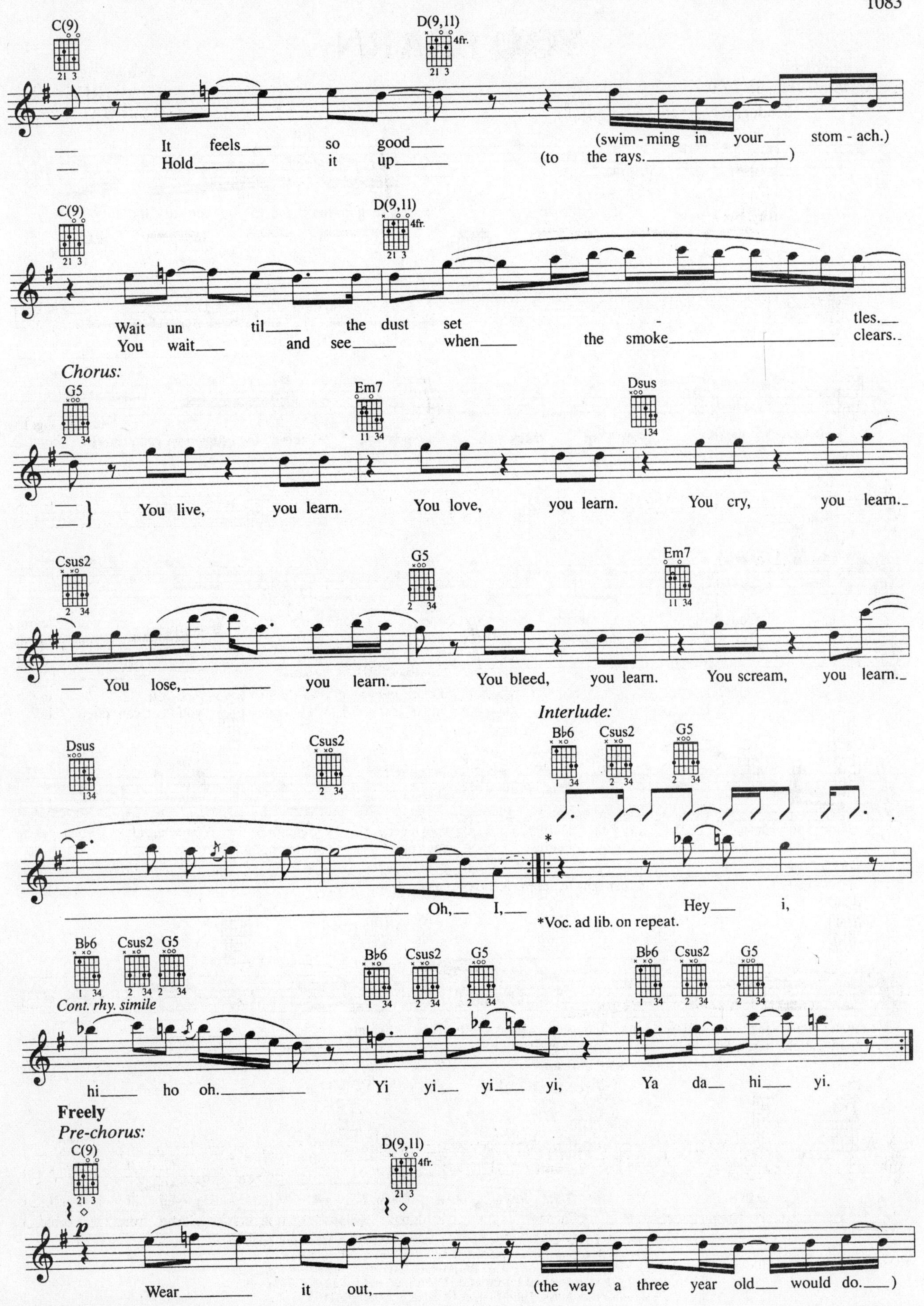
C(9)
D(9,11)
It feels so good (swim-ming in your stom-ach.)
Hold it up (to the rays.)
Wait un til the dust set - tles.
You wait and see when the smoke clears.
Chorus:
G5
Em7
Dsus
You live, you learn. You love, you learn. You cry, you learn.
Csus2
You lose, you learn. You bleed, you learn. You scream, you learn.
Interlude:
B♭6
Oh, I, Hey i,
*Voc. ad lib. on repeat.
Cont. rhy. simile
hi ho oh. Yi yi yi yi, Ya da hi yi.
Freely
Pre-chorus:
Wear it out, (the way a three year old would do.)

C(9)
D(9,11)
Melt it down, you're gon-na have to e-ven-tu-'lly an-y-way.
In time
cresc.
The fi-re trucks are com-ing up a-round the bend.
Chorus:
G5
Em7
Dsus
1. You live, you learn. You love, you learn. You cry, you learn.
2. You grieve, you learn. You choke, you learn. You laugh, you learn.
Csus2
You lose, you learn. You bleed, you learn. You scream, you learn.
You choose, you learn. You pray, you learn.
You ask, you learn.
Free time
You live, you learn.

YOUNG GIRL

Words and Music by
JERRY FULLER

A♭
A♭m
be - lieve you're old e - nough to give me love,
that it's wrong to be a - lone with me,
E♭
B♭
C♭
and now it hurts to know the truth.
that come on look is in your eyes.
Chorus:
E♭
A♭maj7
Gm
Whoa, young girl, get out of my mind,
A♭maj7
Gm
F7
my love for you is way out of line. Bet-ter run, girl,
B♭
D♭
C♭
1.
you're much too young, girl.
2.
Interlude:
E♭maj7
Horns
A♭maj7
E♭maj7
F♯m
B
Verse 3:
Emaj7
So hur - ry home

Amaj7
Emaj7
B
G♯7
A
Am
E
C
Chorus:
G♯m
F♯7
D
Repeat and fade
to your ma - ma,
I'm sure she
won - ders where you are.
Get out of here
be - fore I have the time to change my mind,
'cause I'm a - fraid we'll go too far
Whoa, young girl, get out of my mind,
my love for you is way out of line. Bet - ter run, girl,
you're much too young, girl.

YOUR SONG

Words and Music by
ELTON JOHN and BERNIE TAUPIN

*⑥ = D
Slowly ♩ = 66
Intro:
D
G/D
A/D
G/D
Piano (arr. for gtr.)
*To match key of recording, tune down a 1/2 step.
Verse:
D
Gmaj7
A♯/C♯
F♯m
1. It's a lit - tle bit fun - ny, this feel - ing in - side.
2. If I was a sculp - tor, but then a - gain, no, or a
3.4. See additional lyrics
Bm
Bm/A
Bm/G♯
G6
I'm not one of those who can eas - i - ly hide. I
man who makes po - tions in a trav - el - ing show. I
D/A
A
A♯dim
Bm
don't have much mon - ey, but boy, if I did,
know it's not much, but it's the best I can do.
D
Em7
1.3.
G
A
Asus
A
I'd buy a big house where we both could live.
My gift is my song and

2.4.
Pre-chorus:
G
D
Em7/D
D
A♯/C♯
Bm
Acous. Gtr.
this one's_ for you.___
And you_ can tell ev - 'ry - bod - y
Em7
G
A♯/C♯
Bm
Cont. rhy. simile
this is your song.___
It may_ be quite___ sim-ple, but___
Chorus:
Em7
G
Bm
Bm/A
Acous. Gtr.
now that it's done,___
I hope you don't mind,___ I hope you don't mind___
Bm/G♯
G6
D/F♯
G6
that I put down in words_ how_ won - der - ful life_ is_ while
1.
A
Asus
A
D.C.
2.
A
Asus
A
Acous. Gtr.
you're_ in_ the world.___

Verse 3:
I sat on the roof and kicked off the moss.
Well, a few of the verses, well, they've got me quite cross.
But the sun's been quite kind while I wrote this song.
It's for people like you that keep it turned on.

Verse 4:
So excuse me forgetting, but these things I do,
You see, I've forgotten if they're green or they're blue.
Anyway, the thing is, what I really mean . . .
Yours are the sweetest eyes I've ever seen.
(To Pre-chorus:)

GUITAR TAB GLOSSARY **

TABLATURE EXPLANATION

READING TABLATURE: Tablature illustrates the six strings of the guitar. Notes and chords are indicated by the placement of fret numbers on a given string(s).

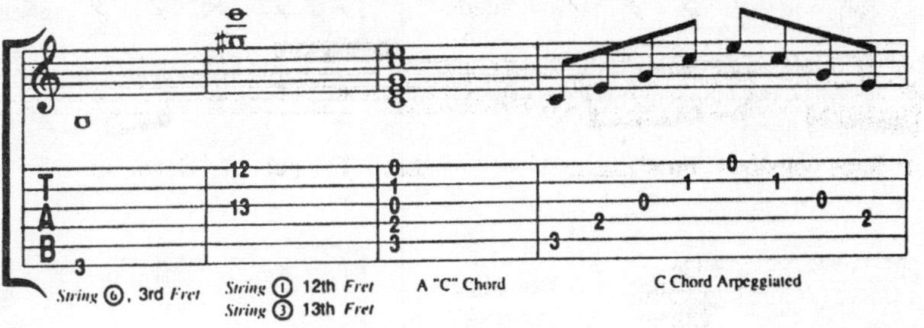

BENDING NOTES

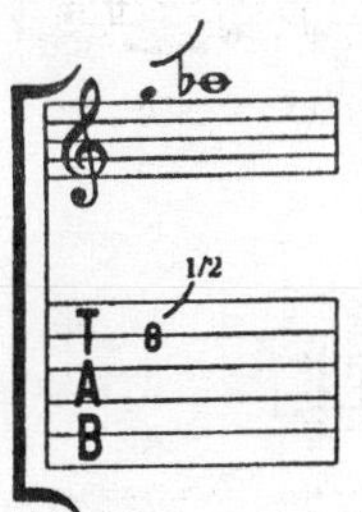

HALF STEP: Play the note and bend string one half step.*

SLIGHT BEND (Microtone): Play the note and bend string slightly to the equivalent of half a fret.

WHOLE STEP: Play the note and bend string one whole step.

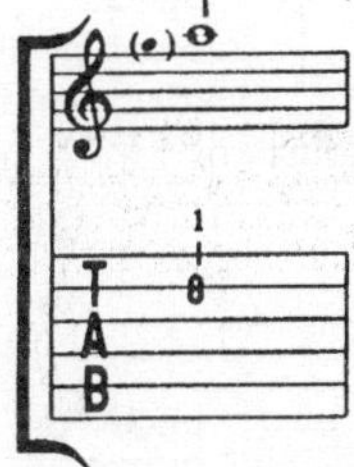

PREBEND (Ghost Bend): Bend to the specified note, before the string is picked.

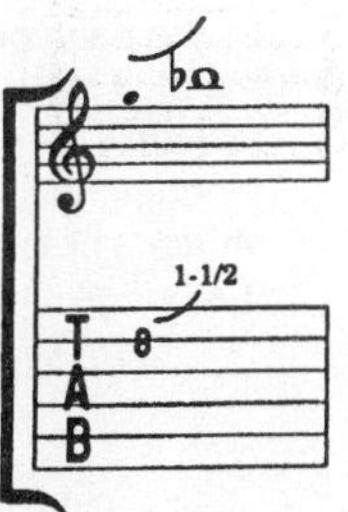

WHOLE STEP AND A HALF: Play the note and bend string a whole step and a half.

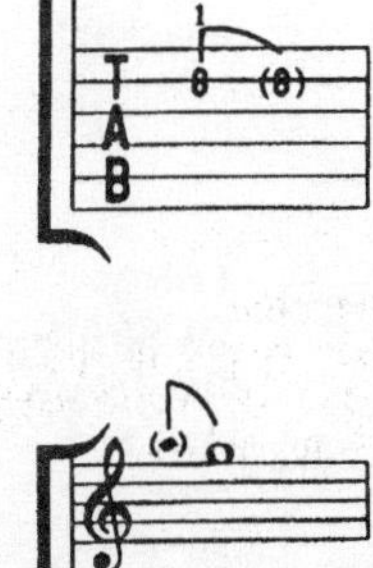

PREBEND AND RELEASE: Bend the string, play it, then release to the original note.

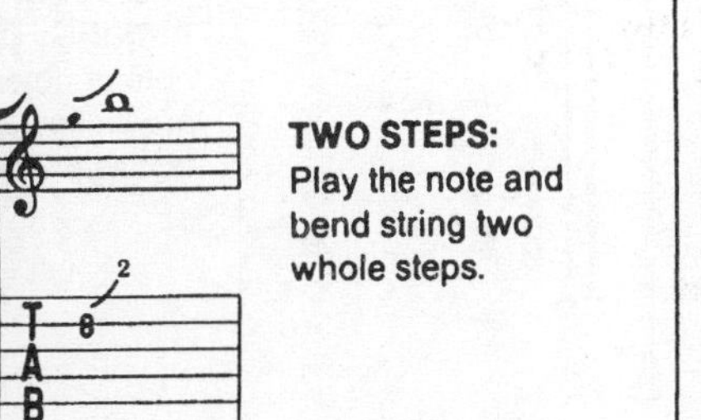

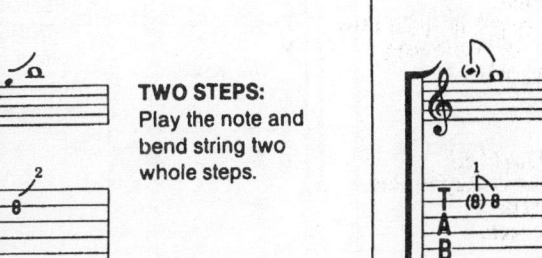

TWO STEPS: Play the note and bend string two whole steps.

REVERSE BEND: Play the already-bent string, then immediately drop it down to the fretted note.

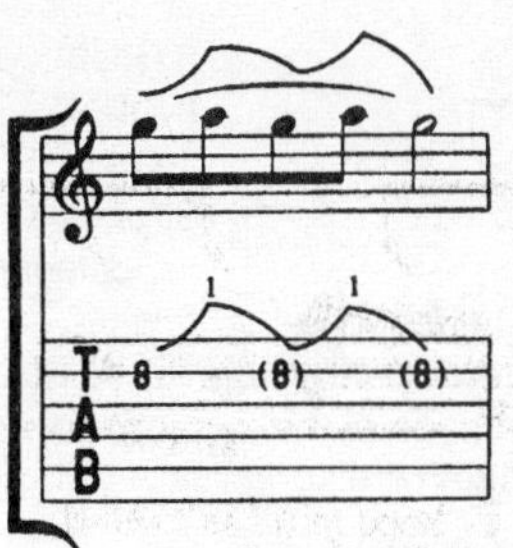

BEND AND RELEASE: Play the note and gradually bend to the next pitch, then release to the original note. Only the first note is attacked.

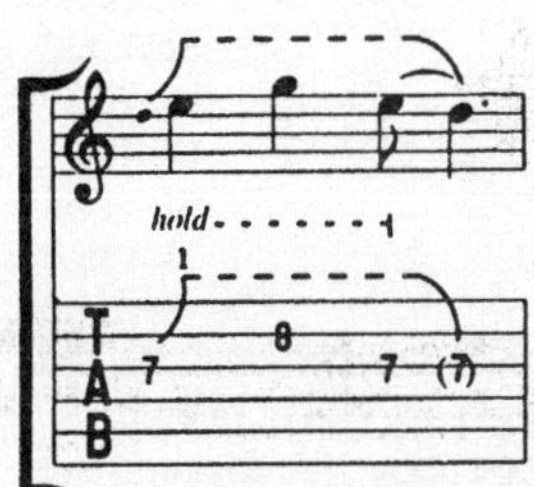

BENDS INVOLVING MORE THAN ONE STRING: Play the note and bend string while playing an additional note (or notes) on another string(s). Upon release, relieve pressure from additional note(s), causing original note to sound alone.

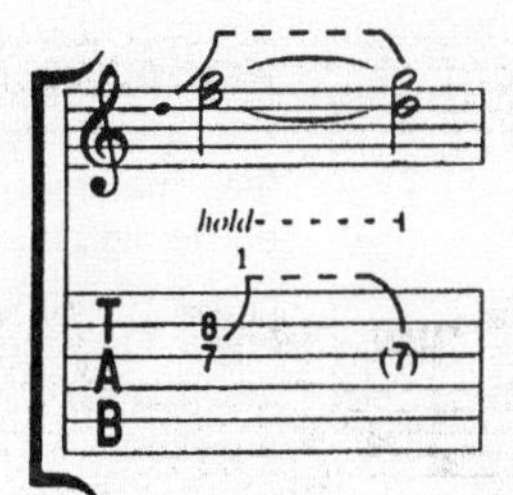

BENDS INVOLVING STATIONARY NOTES: Play notes and bend lower pitch, then hold until release begins (indicated at the point where line becomes solid).

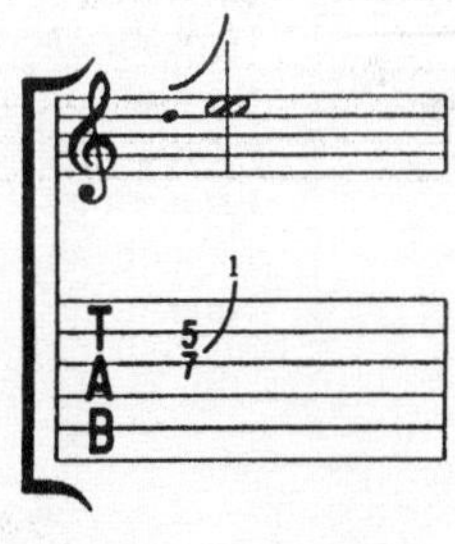

UNISON BEND: Play both notes and immediately bend the lower note to the same pitch as the higher note.

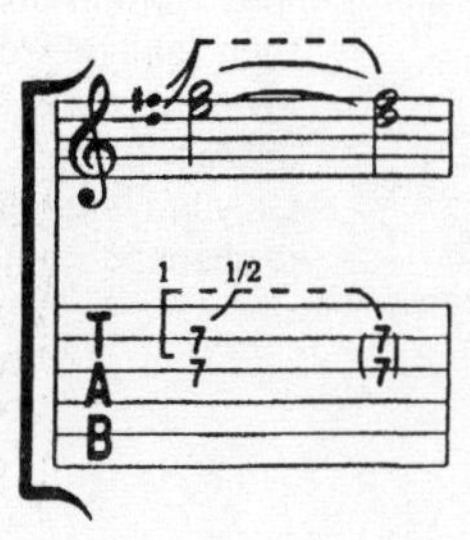

DOUBLE NOTE BEND: Play both notes and immediately bend both strings simultaneously.

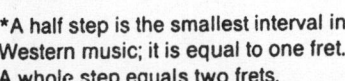

*A half step is the smallest interval in Western music; it is equal to one fret. A whole step equals two frets.

**By Kenn Chipkin and Aaron Stang

RHYTHM SLASHES

STRUM INDICATIONS: Strum with indicated rhythm.

The chord voicings are found on the first page of the transcription underneath the song title.

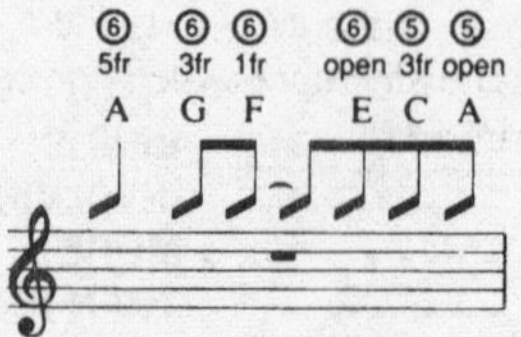

INDICATING SINGLE NOTES USING RHYTHM SLASHES: Very often single notes are incorporated into a rhythm part. The note name is indicated above the rhythm slash with a fret number and a string indication.

ARTICULATIONS

HAMMER ON: Play lower note, then "hammer on" to higher note with another finger. Only the first note is attacked.

LEFT HAND HAMMER: Hammer on the first note played on each string with the left hand.

PULL OFF: Play higher note, then "pull off" to lower note with another finger. Only the first note is attacked.

FRETBOARD TAPPING: "Tap" onto the note indicated by + with a finger of the pick hand, then pull off to the following note held by the fret hand.

TAP SLIDE: Same as fretboard tapping, but the tapped note is slid randomly up the fretboard, then pulled off to the following note.

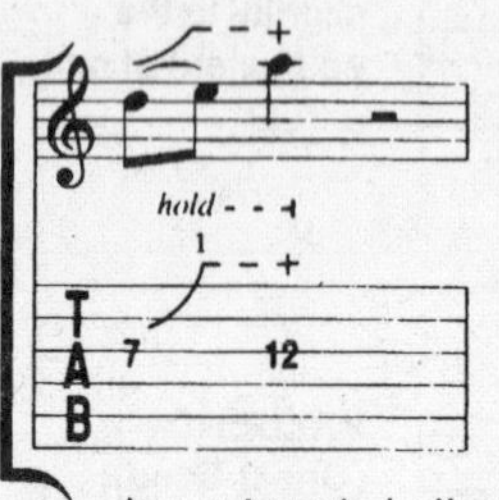

BEND AND TAP TECHNIQUE: Play note and bend to specified interval. While holding bend, tap onto note indicated.

LEGATO SLIDE: Play note and slide to the following note. (Only first note is attacked).

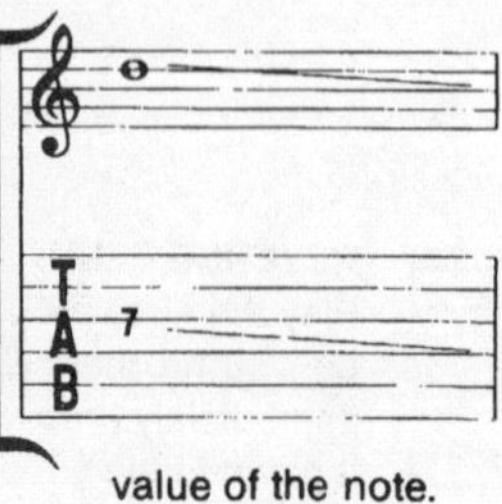

LONG GLISSANDO: Play note and slide in specified direction for the full value of the note.

SHORT GLISSANDO: Play note for its full value and slide in specified direction at the last possible moment.

PICK SLIDE: Slide the edge of the pick in specified direction across the length of the string(s).

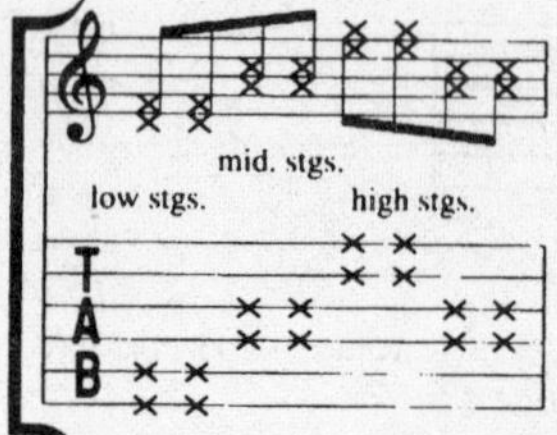

MUTED STRINGS: A percussive sound is made by laying the fret hand across all six strings while pick hand strikes specified area (low, mid, high strings).

PALM MUTE: The note or notes are muted by the palm of the pick hand by lightly touching the string(s) near the bridge.

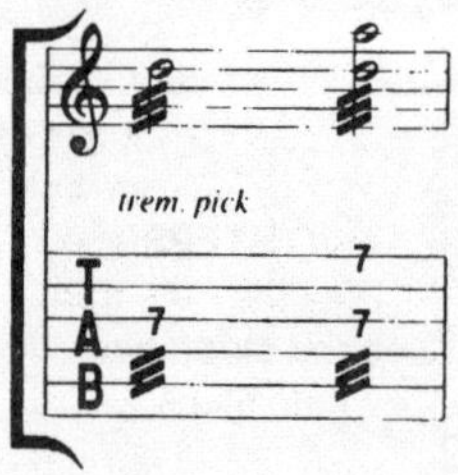

TREMOLO PICKING: The note or notes are picked as fast as possible.

TRILL: Hammer on and pull off consecutively and as fast as possible between the original note and the grace note.

ACCENT: Notes or chords are to be played with added emphasis.

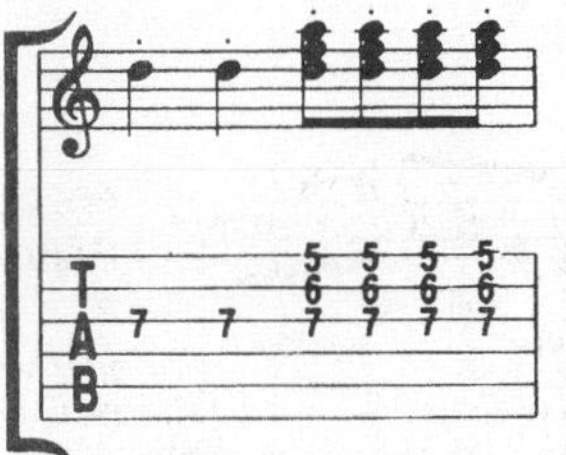

STACCATO (Detached Notes): Notes or chords are to be played roughly half their actual value and with separation.

DOWN STROKES AND UPSTROKES: Notes or chords are to be played with either a downstroke (⊓) or upstroke (V) of the pick.

VIBRATO: The pitch of a note is varied by a rapid shaking of the fret hand finger, wrist, and forearm.

HARMONICS

NATURAL HARMONIC: A finger of the fret hand lightly touches the note or notes indicated in the tab and is played by the pick hand.

ARTIFICIAL HARMONIC: The first tab number is fretted, then the pick hand produces the harmonic by using a finger to lightly touch the same string at the second tab number (in parenthesis) and is then picked by another finger.

ARTIFICIAL "PINCH" HARMONIC: A note is fretted as indicated by the tab, then the pick hand produces the harmonic by squeezing the pick firmly while using the tip of the index finger in the pick attack. If parenthesis are found around the fretted note, it does not sound. No parenthesis means both the fretted note and A.H. are heard simultaneously.

TREMOLO BAR

SPECIFIED INTERVAL: The pitch of a note or chord is lowered to a specified interval and then may or may not return to the original pitch. The activity of the tremolo bar is graphically represented by peaks and valleys.

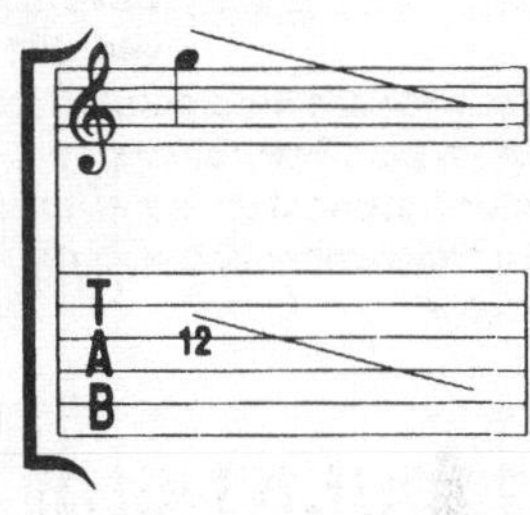

UN-SPECIFIED INTERVAL: The pitch of a note or a chord is lowered to an unspecified interval.

GUITAR TAB GLOSSARY **

TABLATURE EXPLANATION

READING TABLATURE: Tablature illustrates the six strings of the guitar. Notes and chords are indicated by the placement of fret numbers on a given string(s).

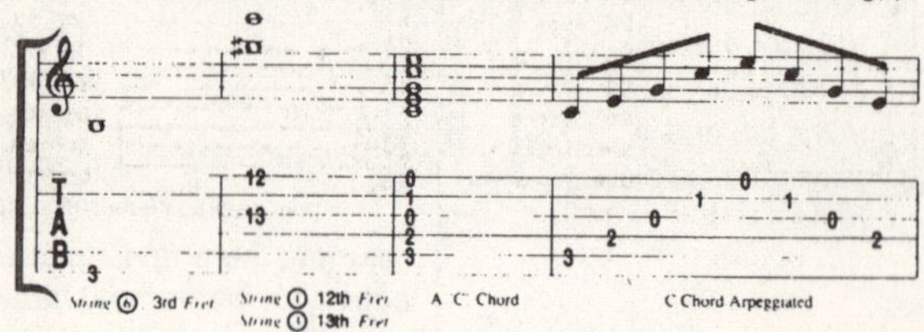

BENDING NOTES

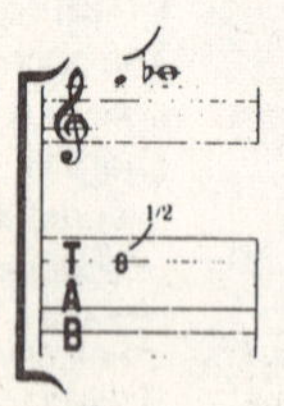

HALF STEP: Play the note and bend string one half step.*

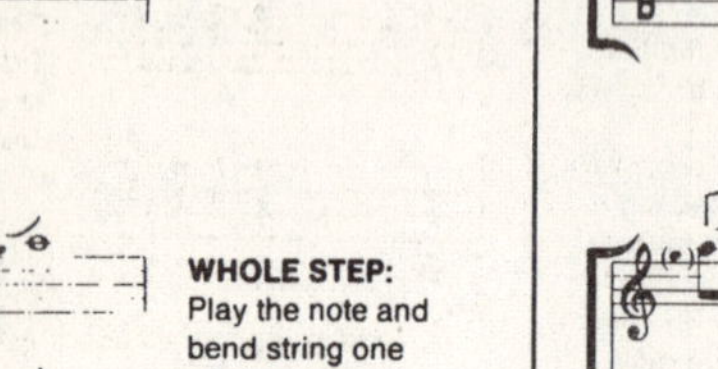

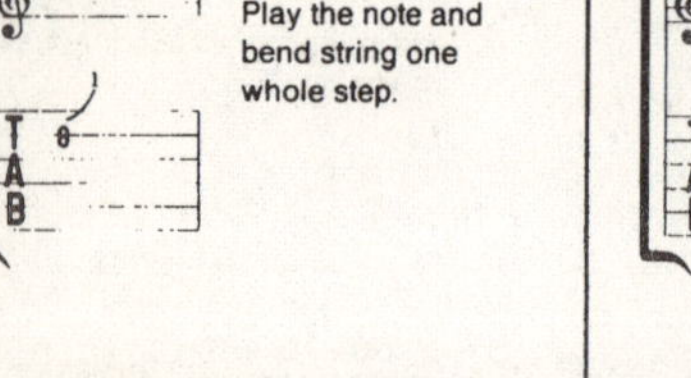

WHOLE STEP: Play the note and bend string one whole step.

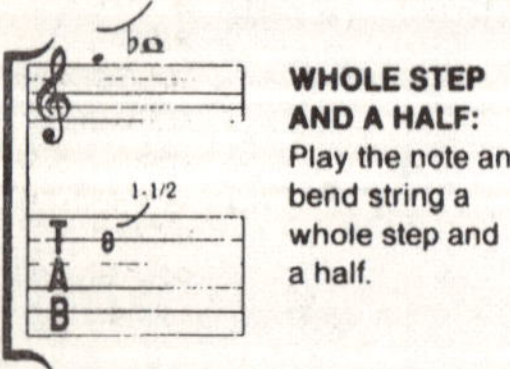

WHOLE STEP AND A HALF: Play the note and bend string a whole step and a half.

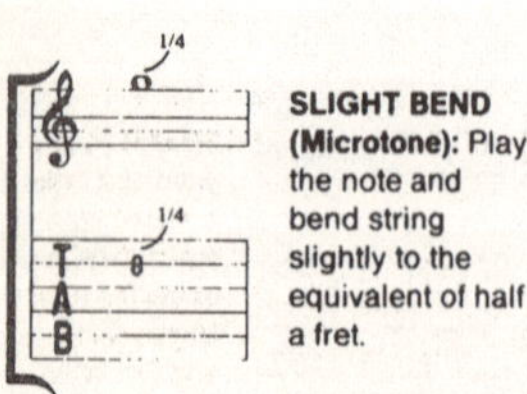

SLIGHT BEND (Microtone): Play the note and bend string slightly to the equivalent of half a fret.

*A half step is the smallest interval in Western music; it is equal to one fret. A whole step equals two frets.

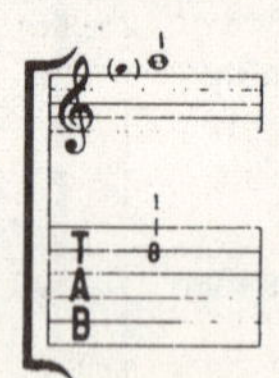

PREBEND (Ghost Bend): Bend to the specified note, before the string is picked.

PREBEND AND RELEASE: Bend the string, play it, then release to the original note.

REVERSE BEND: Play the already-bent string, then immediately drop it down to the fretted note.

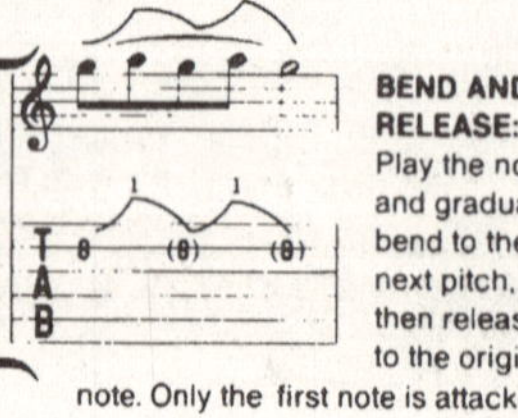

BEND AND RELEASE: Play the note and gradually bend to the next pitch, then release to the original note. Only the first note is attacked.

UNISON BEND: Play both notes and immediately bend the lower note to the same pitch as the higher note.

DOUBLE NOTE BEND: Play both notes and immediately bend both strings simultaneously.

BENDS INVOLVING MORE THAN ONE STRING: Play the note and bend string while playing an additional note (or notes) on another string(s). Upon release, relieve pressure from additional note(s), causing original note to sound alone.

BENDS INVOLVING STATIONARY NOTES: Play notes and bend lower pitch, then hold until release begins (indicated at the point where line becomes solid).

TREMOLO BAR

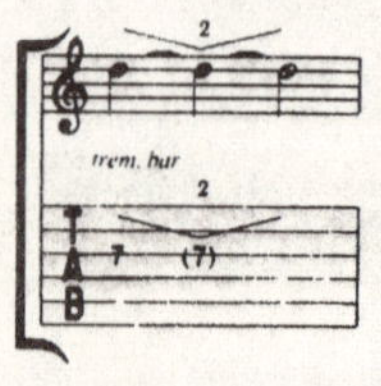

SPECIFIED INTERVAL: The pitch of a note or chord is lowered to a specified interval and then may or may not return to the original pitch. The activity of the tremolo bar is graphically represented by peaks and valleys.

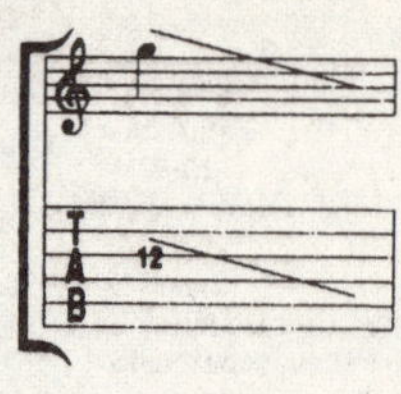

UN-SPECIFIED INTERVAL: The pitch of a note or a chord is lowered to an unspecified interval.

HARMONICS

NATURAL HARMONIC: A finger of the fret hand lightly touches the note or notes indicated in the tab and is played by the pick hand.

ARTIFICIAL HARMONIC: The first tab number is fretted, then the pick hand produces the harmonic by using a finger to lightly touch the same string at the second tab number (in parenthesis) and is then picked by another finger.

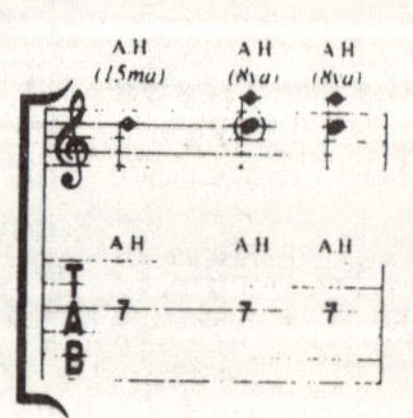

ARTIFICIAL "PINCH" HARMONIC: A note is fretted as indicated by the tab, then the pick hand produces the harmonic by squeezing the pick firmly while using the tip of the index finger in the pick attack. If parenthesis are found around the fretted note, it does not sound. No parenthesis means both the fretted note and A.H. are heard simultaneously.

**By Kenn Chipkin and Aaron Stang

RHYTHM SLASHES

STRUM INDICATIONS: Strum with indicated rhythm.

The chord voicings are found on the first page of the transcription underneath the song title.

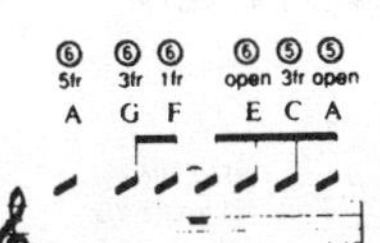

INDICATING SINGLE NOTES USING RHYTHM SLASHES: Very often single notes are incorporated into a rhythm part. The note name is indicated above the rhythm slash with a fret number and a string indication.

ARTICULATIONS

HAMMER ON: Play lower note, then "hammer on" to higher note with another finger. Only the first note is attacked.

LEFT HAND HAMMER: Hammer on the first note played on each string with the left hand.

PULL OFF: Play higher note, then "pull off" to lower note with another finger. Only the first note is attacked.

FRETBOARD TAPPING: "Tap" onto the note indicated by + with a finger of the pick hand, then pull off to the following note held by the fret hand.

TAP SLIDE: Same as fretboard tapping, but the tapped note is slid randomly up the fretboard, then pulled off to the following note.

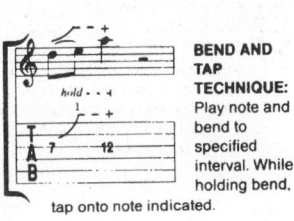

BEND AND TAP TECHNIQUE: Play note and bend to specified interval. While holding bend, tap onto note indicated.

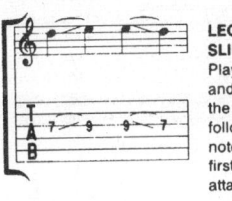

LEGATO SLIDE: Play note and slide to the following note. (Only first note is attacked).

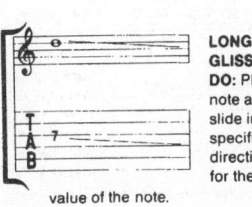

LONG GLISSANDO: Play note and slide in specified direction for the full value of the note.

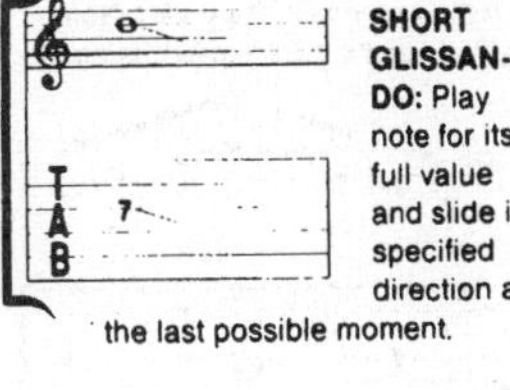
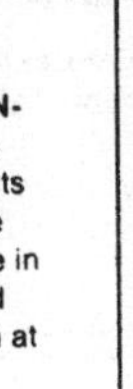

SHORT GLISSANDO: Play note for its full value and slide in specified direction at the last possible moment.

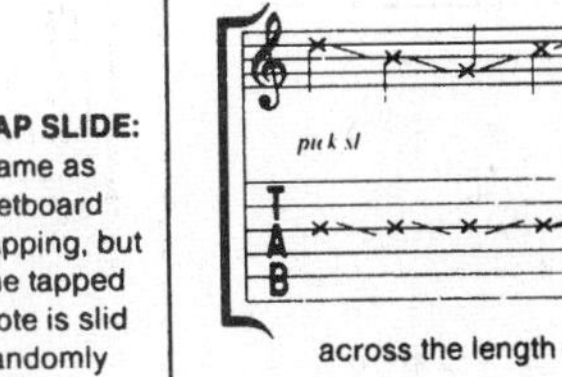
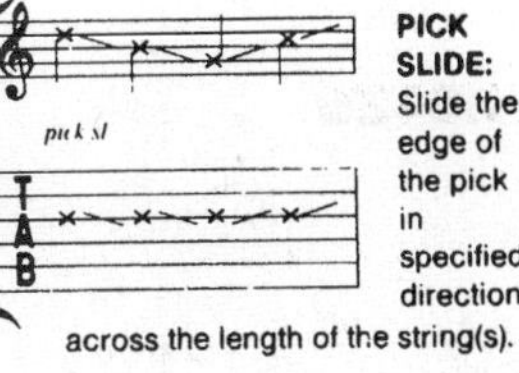

PICK SLIDE: Slide the edge of the pick in specified direction across the length of the string(s).

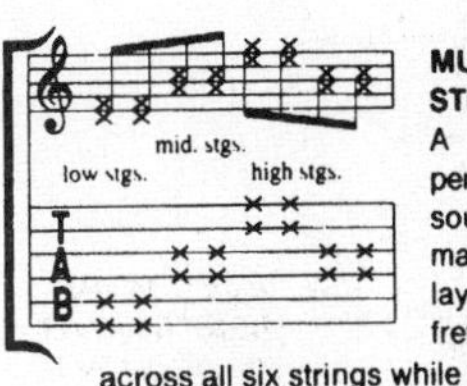

MUTED STRINGS: A percussive sound is made by laying the fret hand across all six strings while pick hand strikes specified area (low, mid, high strings).

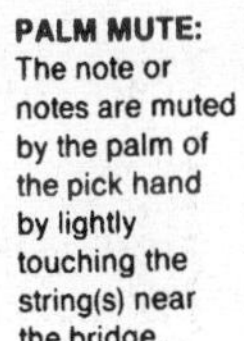

PALM MUTE: The note or notes are muted by the palm of the pick hand by lightly touching the string(s) near the bridge.

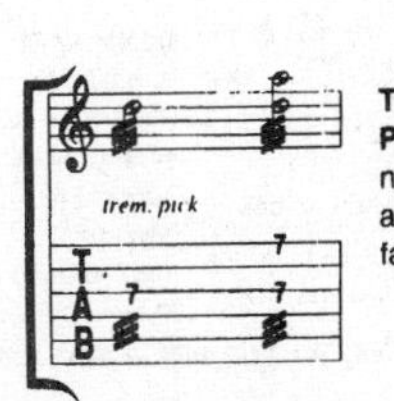
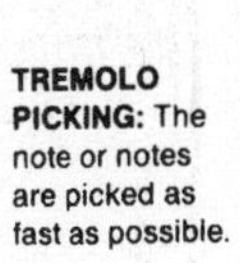

TREMOLO PICKING: The note or notes are picked as fast as possible.

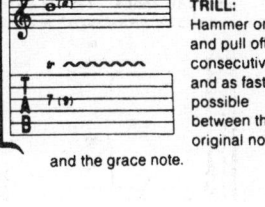

TRILL: Hammer on and pull off consecutively and as fast as possible between the original note and the grace note.

ACCENT: Notes or chords are to be played with added emphasis.

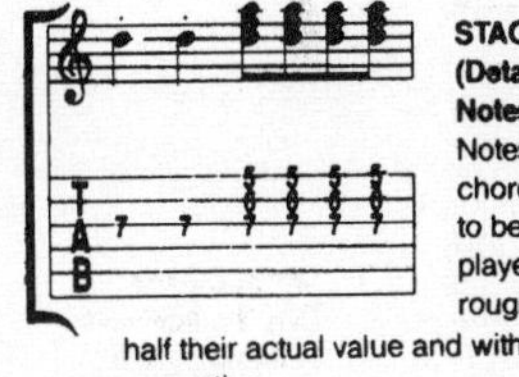

STACCATO (Detached Notes): Notes or chords are to be played roughly half their actual value and with separation.

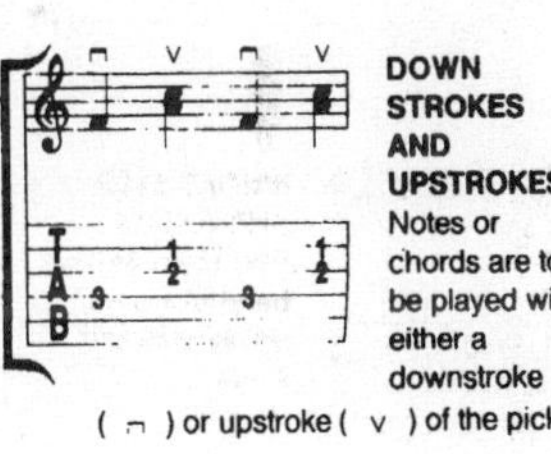

DOWN STROKES AND UPSTROKES: Notes or chords are to be played with either a downstroke (⊓) or upstroke (v) of the pick.

VIBRATO: The pitch of a note is varied by a rapid shaking of the fret hand finger, wrist, and forearm.

Alfred